PETER STEWART

ESSENTIAL
RADIOSKILLS

HOW TO PRESENT A RADIO SHOW

2nd EDITION

METHUEN

For my parents Margaret and John
for their love and support through school, university and life

For Bob and Marjorie Alexander
for their great friendship and support especially as I started my broadcasting career

For Mike Eaton and Brinley Page
Communications BA, University of Central England, 1986–9
who both died soon after

Methuen Drama

1 3 5 7 9 10 8 6 4 2

First published 2006 by A & C Black Publishers Ltd
This second edition published 2010 by Methuen Drama

Methuen Drama
A & C Black Publishers Limited
36 Soho Square
London W1D 3QY
www.methuendrama.com

Copyright © Peter Stewart 2010

Illustrations by Jannis Labelle,
Painter Sculptor BA, RAPD

ISBN: 978 1 408 12179 5

Typeset by Palimpsest Book Production Ltd, Falkirk, Stirlingshire

Printed and bound in Great Britain by Martins the Printers, Berwick-upon-Tweed

Contents

Part One OFF AIR

Part Two PRE-PRODUCTION

Part Three INSIDE THE STUDIO

Part Four GOING LIVE!

Part Five GETTING IN

Foreword

It was dark.

That's chiefly what I remember – the darkness, the bumping into furniture, and seeing a figure in the far corner. The man was sitting with his back to me, head bobbing left and right. Above him a single bulb threw light into his wavy hair.

I don't know what I had been expecting, but my first visit to a radio studio was not exactly a walk on the wild side. It was 1977. Aged 12, I was the young DJ on that week's Kenny Everett show on Capital – 'Don't be nervous! Don't be rocky! You're our teenage disc-jockey!' – but Kenny wasn't there and I was pre-recording with Maggie Norden.

Disgracefully, I chose a James Galway record in the middle of the punk explosion; I blame a sheltered upbringing for that. After we had taped a few halting links in my squeaky voice, Maggie said: 'Hey, I'll show you round.' And so, a floor later, I ended up in the darkness, knocking against the 1970s sofa and watching Roger Scott in the other corner of the room.

The visual experience only captured about 15 kilobytes of my memory, so I may never understand why it had such an extraordinary impact on my young life. I got back home and announced I was going to be a DJ. Then I fired off a letter to every single radio station in Britain asking for work (why did none reply?) while my mum and dad kindly encouraged me in the craziness, perhaps sensing that impossible dreams were not always a waste of time.

As time went by they added the sensible rider: 'You'll probably want to do something else when you're older, Jeremy. Playing records for a living is, well . . .' Like I say, good advice.

Life moved on and seemed to prove them right. At school I did hospital radio, but by Durham University I was in the middle of what the army call 'mission creep'. Editing the student newspaper was a different career – journalism. Surrounded by serious people who remain friends 20 years later, I decided my Roger Scott phase must be over. The *Coventry Evening Telegraph* trained me; moving to the BBC, I reported everywhere from Westminster to Timbuktu. As baffled as anyone by the timing of tides in the corporation, I then found myself dropped into the *Newsnight* chair by a surfer's wave.

But if life springs surprises, a media career is an endless string of them. Suddenly a lateral thinker at Radio 2 was asking if I would consider taking over Jimmy Young's show when he left. 'You realise,' they said, 'this'll be music too? I mean, you're a serious journalist and all that, are you sure you can be enthusiastic about *records*?'

I won't even try to write down what I said and thought by way of reply. A quarter of a century after walking into that dark room with one of the great music presenters aglow in the other corner, I had finally found my way back to it. The bug that bit that day at Capital had never left the system – when I tease my parents about their 'playing records for a living' stuff, we all end up laughing in astonishment and delight that a job could be such a perfect fit and so much fun.

A friend of mine in TV said the other day, 'We're being massacred by the technology. Of course,' she added, 'radio's fine.' While the old analogue TV channels now fight for attention with 250 digital ones, not to mention iPlayer, YouTube and the clipfest that is the internet, somehow Radio 2's audience has been driven up as the market fragmented. What is that – reverse centrifuge? A flight from the unknown?

If you are considering a life's work in radio at this moment, I literally have no idea what to tell you. Five years ago I might have given advice based on the existence of the BBC.

Now I can't even advise based on the existence of radio. FM may soon be history. The word 'wireless' has been stolen and used to mean something else. What's to stop Google launching an international network of stations, audible only through their website? (Hang on, have they done that already?) My iPod contains 9,335 songs. If I press 'shuffle', isn't that a better radio station for me than anything anyone else can broadcast?

If I had the answer to all of that, there would not be any questions. The joy of this technological lurch is the unknown. But surely the connection that radio makes – intimate and personal – is what will keep the medium alive. If you're reading this book it's because you want to learn. It's a great place to start. You'll see what makes radio the uplifting, enthralling, exasperating profession it is. Take Peter Stewart's advice would be my advice: push and push and don't give up, be sure of yourself, and don't be afraid to have quite inappropriate amounts of fun.

Radio may be changing, but it won't ever die. That's my feeling. My iPod can't compete with the friend who plays me a record I hadn't yet heard. My iPod never gave me John Peel or Kenny Everett.

So my guess? In 20 years, radio will still be here. And you'll probably be on it.

Jeremy Vine
Presenter, BBC Radio 2
January 2010

Preface

Welcome to the second edition of *Essential Radio Skills*!

From behind the scenes to behind the mic, in your hands right now is more information on how to present and produce a radio show than has ever been gathered in one place before.

All this at a time when radio, and radio staff, need all the help they can get.

Since the previous edition was published, radio around the world, and specifically in the UK, has gone through huge changes. New technology has squeezed audiences who are lured away by iPods, Facebook and Twitter. The *You and Yours*[1] generation has become the YouTube generation.

Years ago we owned the airwaves: there was no other medium that could touch us.

We didn't have to bother to be attractive or distinctive: owning a radio station was a licence to print money.

We cut investment: played more music and got rid of 'expensive' journalists who produced all that 'clutter' that got in the way of another music sweep. We gave presenters bland liner cards to read, made shifts longer and automated overnight shows . . .

Lowest common denominator radio was easy, cheap and convenient. Listeners had no other choice.

Until now.

It's been like radio's very own Global Warming Syndrome: we should have seen it coming and got ready for these other multi-platforms.

We didn't. But it's not too late.

As I said in the Preface to the first edition, one of the ways radio will win is with its great content.

Put simply, content is going to separate the winners from the losers.

I *don't* mean 'another six in a row': I can get a tailormade choice on my iPod, Pandora or Spotify (which really *is* the 'best music mix', because it's mine), and without adverts.

I *do* mean great content that *I can't get anywhere else.* That's more than giving the local news, weather, traffic and sport, which can be got from almost any mobile phone (right now! Because that's when I want it . . .). It's personality presentation that's yours alone. Material that's relatable, interesting and compelling, and exclusively yours. Content that's great and distinctively different.

Do you have a good EAR for radio? What is your *Exclusive Aural Reason* for existing . . . what do you do on your radio station or your show that no one else does?

Presenters who are mostly the best for the station, attracting most listeners most of the time, will tend to disappear. The ones who'll survive are those who may have fewer listeners, but are absolutely *loved* by them.

It's what you put between the records that should hit them between the eyes and make them think between the ears.

And this book will help you provide that.

Peter Stewart
Surrey
Spring 2010

[1] *You and Yours,* BBC Radio 4: http://tinyurl.com/qsvu.

Notes on using
Essential Radio Skills

Since *Essential Radio Skills* was first published, technology has changed rapidly and so have practices and the marketplace. Scandals such as the fairness of competitions (Ofcom fined the BBC £400,000 and commercial stations £1.1m for deceit and cheating), and the balance between comedy and compliance (the sordid Jonathan Ross/Russell Brand disaster at Radio 2 cost the BBC a further £150,000 and the job of its controller) have caused a tightening of rules and increased vigilance by the public.

Those changes are among hundreds reflected in the second edition.

Some chapters have been expanded slightly to give more prominence to recent developments including new sections on radio stations' use of Facebook, Twitter and apps. Other parts have been added to extensively, such as those regarding links, humour and team shows. There is also a brand new section on surviving redundancy . . .

Plus, in this second edition, there is the unique inclusion of my research into using psychological techniques to better connect with your listeners. Look out for the sidebars which include information on (for example) using NLP, understanding the Aha Experience and the Scarcity Principle, harnessing the Power of the Constructed Image, an explanation of the Gap Theory of Situational Interest, research into the power of musically instilled memories and so on . . .

I have included new quotes and pictures as well as including more content in footnotes,[1] which should make the main text easier to follow. There are links to sources and examples, further reading and recordings.

Space has to come from somewhere, so it seemed sensible to move 'pre-show production' material (such as getting guests) to the next edition of the companion volume *Essential Radio Journalism*. (On-air production remains in this book.)

Reference is also made throughout to the official Occupational Standards for Radio Content Creation,[2] published by Skillset, the UK industry body for creative media, which I helped to update in 2009.

As I mentioned in the first edition, ways of working are different not only between the BBC and commercial sectors, but also within the BBC and commercial groups, and between stations and between programmes. I outline the general tried-and-tested way of doing certain things, and explain why they're done that way, but do check with your programme controller (or in your station's house style book) whether they're appropriate for your station.

Occasionally, I write something like, 'Never do this . . .' or 'You shouldn't do that . . .' and a few days later you'll hear someone successful doing just what I warned against. Yes, there are many people who break the rules, but I think you've got to know what the *accepted* ways of working are, and why they're there, before you can change them for dramatic or creative effect.

---

[1] Like this! The positions and stations of those quoted are those which were relevant at the time the quote was made, and neither I nor the publishers accept responsibility for the content of linked internet sites, which were active when this book went to press.

[2] They are listed here in full: http://tinyurl.com/qh28t5. My cross-references are to the main Skillset units which cover much of the material in those chapters (not all criteria – for example production and journalism material – are included in this book).

Although much of what follows comes from my experience in and around radio, some of my suggestions have been adapted from other sources. That's because over the years I've taken notes from different books, style guides, handouts and presentations. I have given full credit where possible and linked to those author's sites or books. Some sources are not credited though, I simply have no way of finding out where my notes started life. It may be, for example, that a handout I've been given by one person, may have been 'borrowed' from another publication. However, if you recognise something here that you originally wrote, I apologise. Please let me know and I'll happily credit you in the future.

If you're starting out in radio I think most of this handbook will be invaluable. If you've been in the business a few years you'll know some of what's here, but may also be able to take on some ideas and adapt others. But, I'm not saying this is the *only* way. I'm just showing you *one* way.

It'd be great to get your feedback and suggestions for future editions. Perhaps you've got a great tip, or do something differently, or have a great example. E-mail me and I'll try to include as much as I can next time around: EssentialRadioSkills@hotmail.com.

The author

Peter Stewart is an award-winning broadcaster, radio consultant and author with 20 years' experience in speech and music radio, and TV.

He started on hospital radio and RSLs, then student radio before getting his first professional role presenting news and magazine programmes. He has hosted music shows, celebrity interview programmes and chart countdowns, and handled phone-ins, competitions and election coverage.

Peter's been heard on national and local radio, commercial stations, the BBC and BFBS, and in almost every time slot.

In radio management he has been group head of news and head of presentation, and in TV has hosted programmes, written scripts and recorded voiceovers.

He received an award for Best Personality Newsreader at the New York International Radio Awards in 1997, and was UK Chairman of Judges 2000–2007. He's also judged the Sony Radio Academy Awards (2007, 2008) and the Radio 1 Student Radio Awards.

As well as training hundreds of presenters, producers and managers for the BBC's national and local radio and television stations, Peter's also coached commercial radio staff in Britain and around the world.

He's written a weekly column in *The Radio Magazine* since 2001 and is co-author of the companion volume to *Essential Radio Skills*, *Essential Radio Journalism*, as well as *Broadcast Journalism*. He has also written for the BBC in-house newspaper *Ariel* and *The Stage* magazine. In 2009 he advised Skillset on their Occupational Standards for Radio Content Creation and has lectured on several of their courses.

Away from radio, Peter has a BA in communications and a Diploma in marketing and advertising, and has studied psychology.

Peter runs his own website at www.PeteStewart.co.uk, through which he offers several e-books and the Jock Doc Programme Checkup service.

Acknowledgements

First edition

Thanks to John Ryan, Managing Editor at BBC Manchester, who reviewed the final draft version and gave incomparable and invaluable insight and advice. Thanks also to the following who also came up with additional feedback: Ray Clark at BBC Essex; Will Jackson; Danny Pike at Southern FM; Richard Waghorn at the BBC.

Each chapter was reviewed by those working in the appropriate area, and who offered suggestions and corrections: Nick Alliker at BBC Essex; Paul Atkinson at the BBC; Martyn Blunt at Goose Communications; Shelley Bradley at the BBC; Mark Chapman at the BBC; John Cushing at LBC 97.3; Mark Hall at Heart 106.2; Faye Hatcher at BBC Radio Gloucestershire; Claire Jaggard at journojobs.com; Will Kinder at Radio 1; Sarah Knight at BBC South East Today; Neil Pringle at BBC Southern Counties Radio; Bob Symons at the BBC; Kevin Steele at BBC Training; Jo Walker at suzylamplugh.org; Jane Wickens; Jonathan Witchell at BBC Radio Kent.

More information and assistance was provided by Paul Chantler at paulchantler.com; Simon Furber at BBC Radio Devon; Margaret Hyde at BBC Essex; Lucy Mackay at The Radio Academy; Louise Hall at the BBC; Mike Skinner at the Hospital Broadcasters' Association; Kirsten Smith at Broadcast Bionics; the University of Central England, Birmingham.

For the pictures, thanks to Shona Harvey at GCap Media; Brian Cantwell at Radio St Helier, Carshalton; Fiona Clarke and Dawn Baxter at BBC Radio Scotland; Claire Martin at Essex FM; David Robey and Nikki O'Donnell at BBC London 94.9.

Many hours were spent by Ruth Evans typing handwritten notes and by John Stewart copy editing – my thanks to them both.

I am grateful to Jeremy Vine at BBC Radio 2 for his excellent Foreword and to the great and good of British radio who were kind enough to provide some terrific (and humbling) testimonial quotes for the cover. Many of the quotes in the book are courtesy of Paul Boon and my other colleagues at *The Radio Magazine*.

Jenny Ridout, Katie Taylor and Suzi Nicolaou at A&C Black steered me in the right direction from pitch to publication – I hope to work with all again soon.

Finally, to all those who over the last 20 years have given me the knowledge to be able to write this book . . .

Thank you!

Second edition

Thanks to all those who have been quoted in this edition, especially those who have given me permission to use longer quotes, such as Jay Trachman and Alan Burns.

Also to Paul Kennedy and Christel Lacaze at Rajar for the use of the Rajar diary photo, and for their explanation on the Rajar process and terminology.

To Dominic King, Robin Blamires, Jack Dearlove, Pete Sipple, Paul Millington, Bob Chadwick, Howard Ritchie and Toby Dolier for feedback and examples.

And to Jenny McConnell and Paul Marcus at Eagle Radio, David Robey and his staff at BBC London 94.9, and staff and colleagues at BBC Radio Kent for the photographs.

Let's hope you never leave old friend
Like all good things on you we depend
So stick around cos we might miss you
When we grow tired of all this visual
You've had your time, you've had the power
You've yet to have your finest hour
Radio

Radio Ga Ga – Queen
Roger Taylor
EMI/Capitol
1983

Part One
OFF AIR

1   The radio presenter[1]

SKILLSET – NATIONAL OCCUPATIONAL STANDARDS
RADIO CONTENT CREATION

Unit content included in this chapter:
RC1 Work effectively in radio
RC2 Research the structure of the radio industry
RC8 Pitch ideas for radio content
RC13 Operate a radio studio
RC16 Select and direct radio presenters, performers and voiceover artists

The key thing about great presenters is that they often possess a simple skill that evolves around an ability to engage you in a unique or stylish way. They are often the same off air as they are on it (although not always). The ones that catch my attention are those that often have a unique turn of phrase or view of life that makes you want to hear a little more of them. Great presenters can become brilliant. Poor presenters rarely become great because they simply do not understand that they need to give the audience something compelling. It's a skill but you also need talent.[2]

Presenters are the public face of the station, with a job to entertain and inform, but crucially to keep people listening for as long as possible through the day and to come back the next. As a presenter you're the glue that holds the other elements together. Your specific job will be different from station to station and from show to show, depending on the size of station, the style that's needed, the time slot that you're on and the help that's available.

Before a show you might research topics (perhaps for an interview or for your own short links), write scripts (either for longer features or short anecdotes) and select music (although not necessarily *choose* it).

During a show you'll most likely operate the studio desk, play music and jingles, interview guests, and read or introduce items such as the weather and travel news and interact with listeners.

Afterwards there'll be a programme review to discuss how it went and to come up with ideas for the next show, and that may be followed by a public appearance.

---

[1] The 'occupational profile' of a broadcast presenter: http://tinyurl.com/nxvzgu.
[2] John Myers, *The Radio Magazine*, April 2008.

The presenter's role:
Defining and delivering our brand personality and values.
Providing the 'packaging' – the variety, humour and passion that
listeners crave. Making a connection and building a relationship
with our listeners – presentation plays a vital role in building
listener loyalty.[3]

The on-air studio.
Courtesy: 96.4
The Eagle, Surrey

What are the plus points?

In short: fun, freebies and fame.

It's not really hard work is it, being on the radio? Not like being a farmer or a fire-fighter? A few hours on air playing some music and talking to interesting people, then off to do some lucrative voiceover work before swanning off to a showbiz party to get free drinks and have beautiful people fall at your feet. Instant friends!

And then there's the money! If you're good (or perhaps I should say, if you're popular) the financial rewards can be great. If your ratings go up, so too might your salary.

You may have the whole country as your stage, perform in front of millions, be sent free gifts, get to meet people you would otherwise never have had the chance to meet and go to places you would previously never have had the chance to go.

What are the realities?

Well, actually it *is* hard work. At least it is if you do it properly. You're always trying to come up with things to say in a relevant, interesting and compelling way because you know you're only as good as your last show, and if your audience figures slip you may be out of a job.

Other work? Unlikely. There's usually no time. Stations, BBC as well as commercial, are increasingly run by money-men rather than programme-makers. The commercial

[3] *GWR Brand Handbook 2000.*

stations have to report to their owners or shareholders about how much profit they're making, and the BBC has to report to its shareholders too – the licence-fee payers – on whether its services are value for money. That means that a four-hour air-shift is only the start of your work at the radio station. There's pre- and post-production and a programme to do six days a week, and possibly voice-tracking a show for another station in the group.

Showbiz parties? Not for most presenters. And those 'friends' probably want to know you for what you do and how much they reckon (vastly inaccurately) you earn, rather than because they genuinely like you. Or maybe they're after a celebrity notch on their bedpost.

Consider all these other potential drawbacks:

- Unusual, unsocial or unpredictable hours and a disrupted personal life.
- Intense competition to get work and then stay in work.
- A low starting salary until you hit the big time. In commercial radio especially, but not exclusively, there's no job for life. And there's 'multi-skilling', the definition of which seems to be 'more work, no more money'. If your ratings go down, so too might your salary.
- Meeting people who recognise your talents and stab you in the back to get the job that you were after, or being taken advantage of by the boss who knows that you're keen to impress ahead of your big break.
- Few training schemes – isn't that why you've bought this book?!

And here are some more points to ponder:

Do you like your bed? A breakfast presenter will have to be at work at 5 am. Think of the logistics for a midnight to 4 am shift. What about working on Friday and Saturday nights, or weekends? How will these hours suit your metabolism and family life?

Can you force yourself to be happy? Your role on the radio is usually to be entertaining, but if you've just split up with your partner and your car's been stolen, how will you feel about doing the act then?

Worried about your old age? It's precarious being a presenter. If your act gets stale or listeners aren't listening, you may be shown the studio door. Do you fancy hawking yourself around to find another gig? You may still be at the station if trends change, but not on air. How will you feel about that?

Fancy living as a goldfish? You'll be encouraged to reveal a bit of yourself on air to connect better with your audience. You may have your picture in the local papers, appear on stage at a roadshow and be asked to sign photos of yourself, and be stopped in the supermarket. Some people love all that, but what about being asked for your autograph while you're waiting in the doctor's surgery, or being stopped for a chat while you're in a toilet, or being stared at as you try and discipline your toddler in the high street?

Are you interested in presenting because you've been told you've a good radio voice? What *is* one of those? If it's 'dark and chocolatey' you may be pigeonholed presenting love songs for your whole career. Is that what you want? You'll certainly need more qualities to back it up.

If you've considered all of those points and you still think you've got what it takes, are willing to learn more and want to go for it – great!

Your qualifications

All sorts of people become radio presenters. You may be the fun guy who presents the outside broadcasts and the Saturday phone-in competition show, or 'the Intellectual' who's the anchor for the all-speech breakfast programme or who fronts the budget and election programmes. You may be neither of these and have other talents. You may have been to university and completed a postgraduate course in radio journalism, or you may have worked your way from work experience to producer, with your sights set on being a presenter and then programme controller.[4] Skills from further education can be useful: working to deadlines, having an appreciation of the wider world, knowing how to question and how to cut through complex ideas, having a life and interests outside radio.

A presenter might be a 'celebrity', either because they've been at the station so long, or because they are (or have been) a famous television presenter, sportsman, actor or years ago had their own show on Radio 1. You'll be more likely to get through the door of the station if you can show that you have some background in radio. That may be practical experience in RSL, community, hospital or university radio. Although qualifications may be useful, skills, interests and passion probably count for more.

Your qualities

Whatever makes good radio, no one has been able to pin it down exactly. Listeners don't buy it, and you can't smell or taste it, but you can *feel* it. That is, the station and all its integral parts have an overall attitude, and your attitude is part of it.

There's no identikit for the making of leading local presenters. They're often as different as the local landscape and as characterful. But they're invariably well-rounded, well-informed broadcasters with a commitment to the locality, some verve, a 'good listen', thought provoking, quirky even, but with that unmistakable knack of being in tune with the lives of listeners and the temper of the locality. Research shows that listeners can't abide presenters who are jokey with no wit; glib with no weight; trivial with no insight; or just plain dull.
They warm to presenters who have intelligence, zest and who lighten their day.[5]

Here, in alphabetical order, are the top ten qualities it'd be good to have:

Adaptability

Put yourself out, help where it's needed and you may well be rewarded with a show, or another one in a better time slot, with more potential listeners. You also need to be adaptable

---

[4] A 'programme controller' in commercial radio is the equivalent of a 'senior broadcast journalist for programmes' (SBJ programmes) in BBC local radio.
[5] *Connecting England*, BBC, 2001.

in case of any change to your programme while you're on air: maybe an emergency news flash which has the potential to throw the rest of the programme running order out of the window.

Confidence and friendliness

You'll certainly have to speak in front of an audience of hundreds, or thousands or maybe hundreds of thousands, but they'll most often be unseen. On other occasions you'll have to speak to a group where you can see 'the whites of their eyes' – half a dozen co-workers at an ideas meeting, a few dozen people at a Rotary group, or an auditorium-full when introducing a band on stage or in the station's local panto! Confidence is also needed to keep calm in a crisis.[6]

Courtesy

On air and off air you are representing the radio station as well as yourself. Unless you decide to become a 'shock jock', whose persona is one of being rude and arrogant to callers to gain more listeners (a format that works in the States, but less well in the UK), you'll lose an audience and maybe your job if you're plain rude to the people who pay your salary either directly (the radio station) or indirectly (the listeners).[7]

Good personality

You want to be someone who your audience can trust and relate to, and that needs to be reflected in the office as well. It's highly likely that you'll be earning more than those who are working in the background of the radio station (although their jobs are no less important than yours). They'll resent that salary if you're abrupt, unprofessional, late or rude, or simply refuse to make the tea. There are plenty of stories in the industry about household names who are one person on air and another off air – don't let your name be added to the list.

Humour

'There is,' as the saying goes, 'a time and a place for everything.' And that's especially true with humour. Part of being funny is being sensitive to the mood and expectation of the audience, but when you're on the radio the instant feedback that a club comic might get isn't there. This is why it's important to picture a typical listener in your mind as you broadcast. By doing this, and meeting your listeners as often as possible, you'll get an idea of what they like. Even if you're not a presenter who's cracking gags every link (and most aren't) you must still be able to laugh at the idiocies of life, and at yourself, especially if things go wrong.[8]

Lots of interests

If you spend so much time at the radio station that all you can talk about is the radio station, you are, frankly, going to be a dull broadcaster. You need to have a life away from radio,

---

[6] See Chapter 24, 'When it all goes wrong'.
[7] See Chapter 8 which has more information on compliance.
[8] See Chapter 15, 'Humour on the radio'.

doing things that your listeners do so you will have something to talk about on your next programme. You'll read lots, live life and love life, have anecdotes to tell and a yardstick by which to measure other experiences.

The more things you can do outside work; be it seeing family and friends, keeping fit, reading, cooking, going to the cinema or theatre – whatever – the more your life will feed your work, and the more interesting your work will be. If you live, eat and breathe radio then you're probably doing it wrong. All you have to do is love it and work hard at it.[9]

Sociable

Being a presenter is not the job for a wallflower. You may find yourself at a school prize-giving ceremony, or meeting prospective advertising clients. Develop your skills of making small talk and making people laugh. You must love meeting and working with people.

Get to know those in other departments. Your job will be easier if you make friends at an early stage with key staff such as the receptionist and the engineer, but don't forget those in the promotions or sales team, the staff who schedule the ads and so on. Treat others how you want to be treated. UK radio is a small industry and the chances are you'll keep coming across the same faces. Some of them, like you, will be on the way up and others will be on the way down. Some will make your heart leap when you bump into them again and others will make your heart sink. Some will be able to help you, others to hurt you. If you've hurt them before, what do you think they might do the next time they meet you?

Able to talk

You should be able to articulate sometimes complex ideas in an interesting and compelling way, as well as being able to talk to listeners on air or at an OB, and to everyone from poets, to priests and politicians;[10] you should also be able to adlib if it all goes wrong!

Well organised

Presenting a three-hour show, six days a week, seems straightforward enough, doesn't it? You just wander in with the tabloids and a list of friends to call on the studio phone while the songs are playing. There's more to presenting than that as we'll see, and that's off air as well as on air. You need to prepare your show, research your guests, devise and produce competitions, find the prizes for those competitions and send them off, conduct studio tours and appear at roadshows or outside events.

Each week you'll have to be able to pick up information on dozens of subjects, assimilate it and be able to interview someone about it intelligently on air. You may have to read books if you're interviewing authors and certainly read the newspapers each day to know what's going on in the world. If you're freelance, multiply all that by the number of different

[9] Francis Currie, programme director, Heart 106.2, *The Radio Magazine*, July 2004.
[10] With apologies to Sting: http://tinyurl.com/n9jlyd.

jobs you have and then add cold-calling prospective employers and sorting out your tax and national insurance paperwork; you can see that you have to be organised to be able to survive.

Above all . . .

. . . Be yourself.

What is there in common between the presenting styles of Wogan, Evans and Moyles? Nothing. They are all unique.

> If you are the exclusive distributor of you, then you're harder to replace and more valuable to the station.[11]

AUTHENTICITY OF INDIVIDUALITY

It's better to be a good version of you than a poor version of someone else.

As we grow up listening to the radio we start to assimilate the modus operandi[12] of presenters we admire. We assume they are doing it 'right'.

By the time we are on air, we're usually a copy, good or bad, of the (several) presenters we grew up admiring. But they were talking to us in *their styles*, which may or may not be appropriate at your station, and are not authentically you.

You will discover a better chance of success when you find and uncover your own individuality.

Although you may benefit from listening closely to what other presenters do and working out why they're successful, don't simply copy them.

The goal is to stand out. You don't get to the top by being like everyone else.

Possible earnings

It used to be said that you wouldn't get rich working in radio. As radio becomes more cut-throat, stations are willing to pay some large sums to attract and then retain the best talent, but that comes at the expense (literally) of other talent who may be let go.

Here's a very rough guide, bearing in mind that most people's salaries are confidential and those reported by the papers are usually over-inflated, paid over several years or include the cost of the presenter hiring their own production team or studio time.

---

[11] Graham Mack, presenter, TFM, *The Radio Magazine*, April 2009.
[12] Definition of this phrase: http://tinyurl.com/lgdlye.

In the BBC, presenters may be BAs (broadcast assistants) who will anchor a show as part of their job. Their basic salary may be (according to length of service and experience), around £20,000. They may be a broadcast journalist (BJ) whose salary grade can be between £20,000 and £35,000, but again the higher level will depend on your experience and popularity as a presenter. A senior broadcast journalist will be on anything from £35,000.

A local BBC presenter may be a freelance (with a fee decided between them and the station management for each show they present), who may get less than £100 a programme. There will be a contract between each party over the duration of the show, any preparation they have to do for it (either at the station or at home) and any notice the presenter has to give for holiday. They may, though, get paid much more than this.

Triple Sony winner Jon Gaunt has . . . criticised BBC bosses for sacking him from his job as breakfast presenter of . . . BBC Coventry & Warwickshire (after he started writing a column in *The Sun*) . . . Gaunt was replaced on his £3,000 a week breakfast show . . .[13]

At national level BBC presenters will be freelancers and will negotiate their salaries on an individual and confidential level. In 2006 it was reported that Radio 1's Chris Moyles was given £630,000 a year, and Radio 2's Terry Wogan, £800,000, but remember they're big audience-builders for the station and as soon as their popularity wanes they may be forced to accept a lower fee or have their contract terminated.[14] In the US talk show host Rush Limbaugh is reputed to get £200m over five years, but consider that he actually makes money for employer ClearChannel, by bringing in more money in advertising than is paid in his salary.

In local commercial radio, the salaries tend to start lower but end higher than at a local BBC station. (On a community station the presenters won't get paid at all as it's a not-for-profit set-up, run by local people for local people.) At a small local station a presenter may be on little more than the minimum wage[15] (little more than £20 for a four-hour programme). Others who get slightly more may also be expected to work six days a week and do other jobs at the station as well (such as selling advertising time, writing commercials or inputting data into the music scheduling system). The breakfast presenter, whose show invariably attracts the biggest audience, will get more than the other hosts, but even that may be as little at £15,000–20,000. At some stations, presenters aren't paid at all because the managers have so many people wanting to be on air. If you have this opportunity and you can afford the time and travel expenses, don't turn it down. Working at any station, even for a few months, is worth the experience, and you'll have some on-air material that you can use in your next demo for a paid gig.[16]

Local presenters at GCap's 28 Classic Hits stations will be taken off the air . . . and have instead been offered a voicetracking shift paying just £30 a week.[17]

[13] *The Radio Magazine*, 26 October 2005.
[14] http://tinyurl.com/qcn9nf.
[15] What is the national minimum wage? http://tinyurl.com/m87zuy.
[16] See Chapter 26 for more on work placements.
[17] *The Radio Magazine*, July 2007.

At a larger station, perhaps a countywide, city or regional one, the salaries will be based on the audience figures. Pay may start at around £25,000 and rise to two or three times that. At the country's biggest commercial stations, either those in major cities or national ones, the sky is virtually the limit.

Remember: many commercial stations (and increasingly, BBC stations too) don't have staff presenters. The company's income is so much governed by the numbers of those listening that it's better for them to be able to end a short-term contract with a freelancer and replace them with another potentially more popular (or cheaper) presenter, if necessary, without warning.

Your name

Should you change your name to be on the radio? It's one of the big questions that aspiring presenters consider, especially those who set out to hit the big time. Why may you want to?

- Because your real one is boring, easily forgettable and/or awkward to say.
- To make it more 'radio friendly'. Apparently, a good 'radio name' is when the first and surnames are interchangeable ('Peter Stewart', 'Stewart Peters'), or start with strong consonants ('Dominic King').
- Maybe you consider your name tricky to say (although Mariella Frostrup hasn't been held back).
- Possibly because you think that what you are called doesn't fit with what you do. (Perhaps Agatha Clutterbuck presenting the sexy late night love songs show may sound a surprising juxtaposition, but then it would be instantly memorable, and getting people to remember your name is half the battle as you forge ahead with your career.)
- Perhaps your name is awkward for other people to get right. You may have a fantastically long Asian or Eastern European name, full of heritage but a tongue twister for most English speakers. (I'm not saying you should change a name like this, just that it may be easier than having to explain it to every caller to your show, or spell it out every time you give out your e-mail address).
- You may want to be anonymous when you're off the air,[18] to protect you if you present a controversial show or to add mystery.
- Perhaps you consider your name sounds funny (and people crack the same joke every time you say it), you share it with someone else already in the radio business or with someone famous. (I once worked with a Paul McCartney, not a bad name to have if it's got to be someone else's but imagine if it was Gordon Brown or Peter Sutcliffe, someone who was disliked by some or all of your listeners.)

A changed name can cause confusion in the office (on salary slips, for example), and also on air if you say your real name instead of your stage one. If you're worried about this, perhaps you need to change your name by deed poll[19] and only have one, but remember, once you've changed your name there's little chance of you changing it back without great confusion.

A few final thoughts – some people think that making up another name can sound rather pretentious; what will your parents think? Will they be offended that you've denounced part of your heritage and history? Your name is part of what makes you, you.

Some people call themselves by a nickname – BamBam, The Fridge and so on – but this is rare. However, it's more likely to get you noticed and your show (and station) recalled

---

[18] See Appendix 3, 'Your personal safety'.
[19] How to change your name: http://tinyurl.com/5s64z

('It's the station with Fash the Fish at breakfast . . .'); so is a one-name name. If you're simply known as 'JoJo' you may want to ask whether the image that you have on-air is really the one that you want: a single name (usually given to female presenters) can sound childlike and be a touch demeaning.

Career prospects

It's quite conceivable that when you start in radio you may be the producer, technical operator and performer all at the same time. This kind of experience is why starting off at a low level is so useful. You get the opportunities and get to understand the whole process of radio much more than if you suddenly find yourself involved with a programme at a national level.

If you're good you can make a good living. There's often the opportunity to boost your income at the station (depending on what your contract allows) by taking part in roadshows, making personal appearances, writing a newspaper column and even performing pantomime. As you progress you'll be able to use the skills you have learnt in radio in other areas and make more money: maybe TV presenting, continuity, voiceovers, endorsing products and writing. But for all radio presenters, especially freelancers (and there'll be more and more of them over the next few years), job security is certainly precarious.

Competition for jobs in radio can be stiff, but the following pages will not only help you get in to radio, but also get on in radio.

This industry is fantastic and personally I wouldn't want to be doing anything else. It has given me the opportunity to do some awesome things. I've had tea and biscuits with Lionel Richie, beat-boxed with Justin Timberlake and even been to Number Ten to have dinner with the prime minister.[20]

Women in radio

I do think it's easier than ever for women to break through, because programmers . . . say 'a woman would be good there'. That tokenism annoys me, but it's also served me well over the years.[21]

A 2007 Ofcom report of radio-only broadcasters (that is, not including the BBC) found that women made up 45.7 per cent of the workforce in radio, with the highest representation in sales, marketing and admin. Only a third of radio programmers and producers are women, and just 12 per cent of technical and engineering staff. Despite the overall fall in the number of women employed in radio, their representation in senior management and boardroom level rose slightly in 2007 to 28.4 per cent. Disabled workers made up 0.4 per cent of the radio industry and representation of minority ethnic groups rose from 3.9 per cent to 4.2 per cent, but dropped at boardroom level from 16.9 per cent to 11.1 per cent.

[20] Adam Catterall, presenter, Rock FM, *The Radio Magazine*, March 2009.
[21] Fiona Faulkner, presenter, TLRC, *The Radio Magazine*, April 2007.

Women generally have a life. Often several lives, juggling careers, family and social life, rather than spending most of their spare time engaging in 'anorak chat' with other (male) colleagues. As a result women often tend to be better communicators because they have more life experience upon which to draw and are therefore able to engage more easily with their audience.[22]

THE TOP TEN PREFERRED PRESENTER TRAITS[23]

I have to feel as though I can trust the person.

Integrity and openness are important to me.

I have to know the person is a real person.

I need to know they care about what they tell me.

They are friendly and accessible, my friend.

I have to feel as though they are talking to me and have my interests at heart.

They're not Hollywood, they're real like me.

They show lots of sides to themselves.

They have a knack of putting my feelings in to words.

They sound really interested in what they talk about.

---

[22] Paul Easton, radio consultant.
[23] NBC TV, USA: quoted in *Certificate IV in Broadcasting Radio*, Australian Broadcasting Corporation.

2 The studio producer

The role of the radio producer is two-fold: the pre-preparation activities required before and after a programme goes live to air and those activities during transmission. One person may take on both roles, or they may be split between two different people.

How will you get the best out of one of the industry's most talented presenters?
How will you create compelling radio that really connects with its audience?
How will your previous industry experience elevate a breakfast team that's already flying high, to even greater heights?[1]

The radio producer is the person who helps a presenter put a programme together, and who directs them while they're on air. The job is different depending on whether the role is at a BBC or commercial local radio station. In fact, the job can vary widely between stations and between programmes partly depending on the role of each individual presenter.

Many large commercial stations will have a producer for each main show, for example, Radio Aire in the job ad quoted above; although at smaller stations, the breakfast show is often the only one with a producer because it is the most important one of the day. In general, other programmes are more music-driven.

The more speech-heavy BBC local stations have a producer for each programme because of sheer practicalities: there are more items and stories to arrange, and because a presenter

---

[1] Advert for breakfast show producer, 96.3 Radio Aire, Leeds, *The Radio Magazine*, September 2005.

can't talk on air and take calls or answer the door to a guest at the same time. The producer may be called a 'broadcast assistant' or the higher-graded 'broadcast journalist'. But for the sake of clarity, I'll refer to a 'producer'. (In the US the producer works for the presenter, and may even be paid by them: the presenter is the star. In Europe it's usually the presenter who is the boss. This can differ, so negotiate your own roles, responsibilities and chains of 'authority'.)

Studio production is an art, combining a series of complex behaviours involving tricky technicalities and potentially problematic personalities.

Before the programme you will be:

- Attending programme planning meetings, originating programme ideas that are creative and relevant to the show and station (such as links, competitions, phone-in elements, guests etc.) and which conform to editorial guidelines.
- Completing the paperwork – getting money or authorisation for projects, setting up technical facilities, PRS returns, arranging fees; booking guests, facilities and studios, researching and writing scripts and running orders and so on.
- Briefing the presenter and keeping them organised (co-ordinating their personal appearances with venues and/or the station's promotion/marketing department), producing them as they do pre-recorded interviews before the show.
- Editing, timing, checking and logging pre-recorded programmes or features.
- Setting up the studio with regard to levels, equipment, live feeds and patches.

During the programme you will be:[2]

- Keeping the programme and presenter on track and on time, keeping an eye and an ear on the balance of the programme, its direction, technical quality and legality. A producer should only let one item overrun if it is worth it and they know they will be able to shorten another item, or drop it completely, to make up the time. Some items such as travel, news and weather cannot be moved, so you should be very aware of the knock-on effect if something overruns.
- Directing the presenter in matters such as timings and content (including format compliance, keeping to music and commercial schedules, levels and sound quality) with prompts on closure of interviews and keeping them informed regarding what's going on, and what's next. A producer hears the show in a different way to the presenter, indeed much more like a listener does.
- Advising and reminding them on topics and questions for interviews and suggestions for a variety of 'light and shade' within the broadcast. Communicating your plans regarding the next feature, and preparing/informing them of emergency strategies (in the case of a guest 'no show', their phone being engaged or a bad connection . . .).
- Giving positive feedback, reacting and responding during the show, using eye contact and body language. Many presenters like to direct their comments to someone they can actually see rather than the invisible listener. That is why they may look at you as they talk or as they pose a question. By reacting normally, as a listener would if they were part of a conversation, you will help the host sound, well, conversational. On a bad day, the producer helps change the mood of the presenter by concentrating them on the programme in hand. They shield the host from the station politics, making their job easy and enjoyable, so they shine on air.

[2] This new section for the second edition of *Essential Radio Skills* looks at this second role: how to produce an on-air show, what you need to get the best from your presenter while they are broadcasting and the technical experience you will need to help ensure that their performance is faultless. As mentioned in the notes at the start of this book, the more 'journalistic' roles listed in this bullet point will be described in greater detail in second edition of *Essential Radio Journalism*.

- Liasing with guests. Greeting, briefing and giving them somewhere to wait. Providing refreshments and getting them in to the studio at the appropriate time . . . collecting them afterwards and thanking them.
- If it's a news programme, responding to breaking stories: thinking of whom to contact for comment and reaction, writing a cue and questions for the presenter, and moving around other features and guests to accommodate the new items.
- Collating and possibly presenting programme elements such as weather or traffic details, requests and so on. Working as a foil for the presenter for links and bits such as skits and sketches and becoming a roving reporter out on the streets in a branded vehicle to do live call-ins and stunts.
- 'Driving' studio desks to record, mix and play out programmes.
- Answering phones to the show as it is broadcast and deciding which callers go to air and in which order. Editing phone conversations recorded by the presenter while they're on air, for later broadcast.

After the programme you may be:

- Editing the show (if it's recorded), logging and storing it.
- Having to arrange payment for contributors (although this is rare in local radio) and corresponding with listeners.
- Maintaining a personal (or contributing to a station's) contacts file of regular contributors and callers.
- Getting the show talked about.
- Identifying clips from on-air items for programme trails, which you also write.
- Identifying longer items for 'best of' compilation shows.
- Producing drop-ins and beds[3] for the show.
- Contributing to presenter feedback and the programme debrief. The producer and the presenter, together with the programme controller, should review the show and discuss what worked well, what didn't, and why.

All of these considerations will help the show and help the host to be much more interesting and entertaining to the listener, giving a forward momentum that benefits the whole show team and the station.

If the show goes well it will be because of the presenter. If it goes badly it will be seen as the producer's fault. Read the rest of this chapter to help you be assertive in explaining why it's not.

The presenter/producer relationship

As a producer you will have to lose your ego, as listeners will give a lot of the credit for the show to the presenter (the 'name' or 'voice'). You'll have to cope with the personality of the presenter, most of whom didn't get to where they are by being shrinking violets, and others who have ideas above their (radio) station. Then you have to cope with the programme controller. They're in charge of everything that goes out on the station as their title suggests. *They* want one thing, but the presenter wants to do something else and you're caught in the middle!

---

[3] See 'Jingle jargon' in Chapter 10.

Remember, if you're a producer, you're a producer; not the presenter! One thing that rattles some presenters more than anything is producers who want to be on air themselves. So, if that's your aspiration watch and learn, but it may be wise to keep your planned career path to yourself. It's not going to make for a good working relationship if the presenter's always wondering if you really *are* working as hard as possible to make them as sound as good as possible.

No one gets on with everyone all of the time and that is as true in radio as in other walks of life. In a live and fast-paced environment such as broadcasting, where things can change just before transmission or a deadline, things can become fraught. An understanding of other people's problems will help oil the wheels of radio. That is why producers *and* presenters should learn and understand each other's role.

A radio producer is like a psychologist. You may have to deal with childish behaviour, work with someone's ego, give praise, sometimes give marriage guidance and work within bounds of confidentiality. Some presenters are particularly demanding and have special requests: they only work in one particular studio, only have a certain set of headphones and like their chair at a certain height, their coffee made in a certain way and delivered at a certain time in the show. Work with them! They will perform better if you do and they will love you more (although they may not show it).

You will certainly need to be confident when you are working with your presenter on a live show. They may be older, more famous and paid more money than you, but you still have to get the best out of them. Make sure they know this: that you are working as a team for the benefit of you both and the station.

How a presenter can help a producer:

- *Understand their problems.* Presenters get cash and kudos; producers get the complaints and the crap. Appreciate that a good producer is trying to make you sound your best. Do not put additional problems in their way, or if you really have to, make sure you do it in good time and in the best way.
- *Look after them.* It is unlikely a presenter will be able to arrange more money for their producer, but perhaps there is something you can do: perhaps you can buy them a coffee every so often.
- *Praise them.* Thank them as often as you can, especially when they go the extra mile or have to do a load of drudge work such as logging or dealing with complaints. And praising them in public is worth much more than praising them in private.

> I feel as though I'm swimming in treacle when my producer is off, so he would be first pick in any dream team. I don't want to give him too much ammunition for his next round of pay negotiations but he's helped me learn things about myself, let alone just radio.[4]

- *Bounce ideas.* Use your producer as a source of story ideas or thoughts for links or topical comedy. If you are a middle-aged female presenter and they are a twenty-something male, they will undoubtedly have different experiences and see things from different perspectives to you. Tap into this resource to give your listeners a more rounded picture of life in the area.

[4] James O'Brien, presenter, LBC 97.3, *The Radio Magazine*, September 2005.

- *Give them a try out.* Get to know your producer, try them out before they are given the full-time role and ask to have a say on whether they get the job of working with you (note: 'with you' not 'for you').
- *When you've got a good 'un.* When you find an ace producer, whether by chance, hard work or nurturing, make sure you do everything you can to keep them. Perhaps you can build their contract into the negotiations for *yours!* Some presenters take their producers with them from station to station. They obviously have a close working relationship and know what the other is thinking, which can be invaluable.

The C-word

We're in the communications business, but in general we're very poor at communicating with each other! Maybe productive on-air conflict in a programme spills over to off air and becomes destructive. One is friction, the other is fighting.

It is essential that you negotiate in advance how you are going to communicate when a programme is going to air. Producers need to remember that presenters are under a very peculiar type of pressure; every mistake they make is very public. These are some things that you may want to discuss between each other, bearing in mind that a wise producer will defer to the needs of the presenter in these matters as they are at the 'sharp end' of the broadcast:

- specific attention cues
- eliminating any distracting modes of communication
- when to communicate via the talkback and headphones
- prearranged hand cues
- organising signals for on-screen comments
- agreeing when to bring the guests into the studio
- agreeing how much eye contact is necessary to make the presenter feel secure.

Healthy conflict can be good. It can be a time-saver: in a live show things sometimes go wrong or become confused, and often the quickest way to resolve it at the time is a direct question or order: 'I've got ten seconds', 'I need it now', 'Shut up!'. Make sure that each part of the partnership knows that such communication isn't rudeness, it is simply necessary in a fraught, intense and live situation. Remember, volume has limited effect and shows that you are not in control. People look to producers for leadership and if you shout, that is not what you are showing.

Conflict can lead to creativity, but make sure you apologise as soon after the outburst as possible and see whether there was a reason for the situation developing so you can try to avoid it another time.

Alternatively, maybe there is more of a long-term problem. Maybe you are a presenter who hates the kind of interviews you are getting, or maybe you are a producer who is getting angry at the way the presenter blames you on air for technical mistakes they make. You've driven home gnashing teeth and complained to your partner more times than you can remember. And yet you know the only way to sort out the problem is to talk.

The broadcasting industry is sometimes notorious for the way people behave towards each other before, during and after the high pressure task of putting a show on air. There are stories of typewriters being thrown across a room, obscenities being used and sexual bullying.

Egos are often fragile in the broadcasting industry. There is also a high prevalence of perfectionism and more than a modicum of extreme narcissism pervades the industry: a potentially explosive cocktail, particularly in enclosed spaces! However there is no excuse for shoddy, disrespectful, infantile or inappropriate behaviour in the modern radio environment. In fact there are various rules, regulations, industrial agreements, and now, laws, that protect people against vilification, bullying, harassment and intimidating behaviour.[5]

Non-verbal communication

A producer can speak to the presenter while they're on air via the talkback system, but it's impossible for the presenter to reply! That's why hand signals have developed instead. Often they concern getting a programme started or stopped; some of these are in general use, others are different from station to station.

Message	When it's used	Description	Signal
Stand by	Given just before a programme goes live.	Hold one hand above the head with the palm forward.	
Cue	'You're on!' Used immediately after the above signal.	Pointing the index finger of this hand at the person who's to go to air.	
Cut	In other words, 'stop!' or 'kill' this item.	Drawing the index finger across the throat.	
Increase/ decrease the level	When a mic or music is too quiet/too loud	Raise your hand up and down in front of you, palm up/palm down.	
Start talking	To cue the presenter for broadcast or to request levels to set the mic.	Hold the hand in front of you with the palm down and thumb under the first finger, opening and closing the fingers in a 'chattering' motion.	

[5] *Certificate IV in Broadcasting Radio*, Australian Broadcasting Corporation.

Message	When it's used	Description	Signal
1 minute left	To indicate how long an item has left to run.	Hold up one (or two etc. as appropriate) fingers in front of you, palm front.	
30 seconds left	As above.	Using both index fingers, form a cross in front of you.	
Hold on, I am aware you're waiting, I'm nearly ready	When a producer is setting up an item that is almost ready (such as connecting a caller) and doesn't want the presenter to go to something new.	As '1 minute left' above: Hold up one, (or two etc. as appropriate) fingers in front of you, palm front . . . but without making eye contact with the presenter (who should see that you are on a call, writing a message on screen etc.).	
Time for a commercial break	Don't forget the adverts.	Holding two clenched fists side by side hori-zontally in front of you, and then moving them vertically (as though snapping a stick).	
Slow down	Carry on talking, extend this item.	A similar action to above but instead, pulling the fists apart horizontally.	
Speed up	End this item soon please.	Flat palms in front of you with hands facing each other as though about to clap, and moving them together and apart. Alternatively holding up an index finger and making a wide circular motion with your arm (wind this up!).	

What are the plus points?

The work is fun to do, partly because it is so varied. You may be talking to famous guests, getting comment on a breaking news story or arranging an outside broadcast. There's nothing like the feeling you get just before a live show whose agenda can change while you are on air. Or the feeling when you're involved with making a programme whose content you love. Of coming up with new ideas or developing old ideas so they still sound fresh. It may be a long-form programme, perhaps a documentary or maybe a consumer affairs phone in, or maybe a show whose music you're passionate about.

As well as those 'buzzes' there's also relief: relief when you get the guest you've been chasing for hours or weeks and when a fraught show is over without any mistakes. There's also a feeling of power! Often producers have more say about the content and direction of a programme than a presenter, both as it's produced and as it goes out.

Finally, for some people the biggest comfort of being a producer is that they're not the person whose name is on the credits. They don't want to be a star but they do want to be in radio and contribute to a successful show without the hassle of being famous.

What are the negatives?

The hours can be long, unpredictable and unsocial. If a programme needs to be edited and its transmission time ('tx' for short) is Saturday morning, you'll have to stay late on Friday to get it done. As presenters rarely want to work on Christmas Day and New Year's Day it is often producers who have to go in to work to play out pre-recs (pre-recorded items or programmes).

Being a producer can be highly pressured both before the show goes on air and especially while it's on. When that red light is lit all hell can break loose – equipment failure; a no-show from a guest; a phone-in with no one phoning in; a presenter with a tantrum. It's up to you to hold it all together.

Your qualifications

As with many entry-level jobs in the media, qualifications are not always as important as practical experience. An understanding of radio – perhaps through student, hospital, community or RSL stations, or work placement – will stand you in great stead. Some producers may have completed a postgraduate course in journalism or communications, or a basic media course. These will help you identify stories, be able to research them and know what to do with them, as well as being able to spot possible legal pitfalls.[6] A year-long postgrad course will go into these skills, and more, in greater depth to equip you well for your first producer position.

Possible earnings

Typical salaries in local radio range from about £15,000–£25,000 although the roles vary between stations, and so too do salaries. A more experienced producer at a city station, on a high-profile breakfast show, may get a salary more like £30,000–£40,000+.

[6] More on the law in Chapter 8.

Career prospects

Producers work their way up the radio ladder in a similar way as a presenter – producing a variety of programmes which are more demanding (for technical or creative reasons) or more high profile, and in a variety of larger and larger markets (station areas). Jump at any chance to develop your skills: perhaps sit in and watch another producer work on a phone-in or outside broadcast, then stand in for them when they go on holiday.

It's quite common for a producer to stay at a station for two or three years and then move on after building a bridge from local to national radio, or from radio to TV. Some producers work so well with their presenter, that they follow them from job to job. If the hotshot presenter goes to a big station with big bucks and wants you to produce them, you could be in line for big bucks too.

The rule of thumb will come as no surprise: the bigger the show/the bigger the market/the more experience you have, the more money you'll get.

Down the line you could be a presenter yourself. After all, you know what makes a good one. Or you may decide to jump in to the world of marketing or PR: with your experience of dealing with those kinds of people while producing, and after selling the show on and off air to listeners and clients, it'll be a doddle. A really competent producer could wind up as a programme controller.

3 The audience[1]

A radio station is nothing without its listeners.

There are so many newer technologies available for people to listen to their favourite music, why do people still use one of the oldest? With record players, cassettes, CD players, MP3 devices and the internet, people can choose exactly what they want to listen to and when – but perhaps that gives us a clue to radio's biggest selling points.

Radio is easy to use: you just turn it on and there's a service. OK, it may need retuning occasionally (and that's even easier on a digital radio, which displays the names of stations rather than their frequency). It doesn't need to power up or download. There are no moving parts to go wrong or licences or subscriptions to buy. It runs on mains power, batteries or in the case of wind-up radios, elbow grease. It's portable, personal (speaking to you on a one-to-one basis) and, with headphones, non-intrusive.

Radio is interactive. You can call a phone-in and tell thousands of others your opinion, take part in a competition and, bizarrely, phone a radio presenter and ask them to play a song on the radio that would be just as easy for you to select on your MP3 player.

The target audience

Commercial radio stations want the biggest and most easily identifiable audience that they can deliver to potential advertisers. That usually means that most of them target the 'masses', the 18–34-year-olds, with a mix of current chart hits and favourite older songs.

[1] The number of people listening to a radio station can affect both its output and the careers of those employed. If listening figures are down, stations will make on-air changes to boost the station's popularity. Commercial stations do this so they can charge more money for delivering a larger audience to the advertisers, and BBC stations so they can justify the licence fee.

Another consideration may be to target a section of the potential audience that's not already catered for. That may be people in a geographical area (like the community stations), or those interested in a specific kind of music or information (Classic FM or the Christian station Premier Radio), or it might be a certain demographic (the breakdown of a group of people by their age and income), such as Fun Kids radio.[2] However, in general, a niche output may have to broadcast to a large area to get a large enough audience to be viable.

Once a station has chosen its demographic, it may further sub-divide that group into the different kinds of people according to their interests, which helps the station programmers ensure that everyone's being catered for.

Their personality – unpretentious, young-at-heart, fun, gregarious and impetuous. Their demographic profile – they are best thought of as: 25–34 years old, more likely to be female than male.

This definition is important for two reasons:

▫ Commercially, it's vital that our profile is strong across a much broader target of adults 15–44. By targeting 25–34s we stand the strongest chance of appealing to this broad profile.

▫ A female skew again is used as a means of attracting the largest possible brand franchise. Whilst men will willingly listen to a station directed towards women, the converse is definitely not the case.

We are not, though, a female brand. It's crucial to understand that men remain a vital half of our audience whose perceptions of our station are just as important as those of females. Nothing we do should alienate them.[3]

The BBC targets an audience in a similar way.

The Sparkler research found there are three groups of listeners among the 15–24-year-old audience. The majority according to Parfitt (Andy Parfitt, Controller Radio 1), are the 'contended grouping' who might go to a Robbie Williams show but don't buy music magazines. The second group, 'Radio 1 heartland', are active gig goers and downloaders, and then there are the 'scenesters' who are making music themselves or are DJs.[4]

BBC local radio has similarly identified three distinct groups of people who it wants to target. There's the over 55s, the 'heartland' audience which is currently its biggest and most

[2] More details on this station here: http://tinyurl.com/kqd3h8.
[3] GWR Brand Handbook 2000.
[4] The Independent, 16 May 2005.

loyal listeners. The next group is the 45–54-year-old age group, the 'replenishers' who gradually come into the above age range and start tuning to BBC local stations more as they become older. Then the under 45s, the 'cherry pickers', who come to the stations occasionally for specific information or programmes such as news, sport, travel and weather.

Student radio is funded by the college or student union, so it stands to reason that their music and speech content should reflect their target audience, that is, young men and women between 18 and 23. An 'oldies' station is likely to target those aged 45+; an 'adult contemporary' station on 25–54s; a sports station on men aged 18+.

Non-target listeners

As a programmer you aren't going to actively discourage people from listening if they don't fit into your model of an audience member. After all, those people are just as likely to get a Rajar[5] survey diary as anyone, but you mustn't be diverted into thinking that you should pander to their desires – if a 50-year-old woman contacts your Top 40 station and says she listens all the time but wants more 1960s music played, you shouldn't do as she asks. That would water down the programming for those who you are actively targeting.

People tend to listen to stations that are not actively targeted at them for one of two reasons. They might wish they were in that targeted audience, or they can't get what they want from a single station and prefer to dip in and out of several (a chart hits fan who additionally tunes to Radio 4 for the comedy and Radio Five Live for the news, for example).

DEMOGRAPHICS AND PSYCHOGRAPHICS[6]

The station is programmed for a demographic, but the presenter should be performing while considering psychographics: a state of mind.

If your station is trying to attract 25–54-year-old women, you have to get into the mindset of that kind of person. What are the activities, interests, opinions, attitudes and values of people in that age group? What is their likely name, employment, family set-up and holiday destination? What are their views on house-husbands, health, the environment . . . ?

State of mind, not age, is what determines who will be interested in what we put on the radio and who will not. Psychographics are *similar* to demographics, but they're not the same.

Ratings and Rajar

Without an idea of who is in your area and who you are targeting, you will never know how successful you are or who you are up against.

---

[5] Rajar is explained in the next section of this chapter.
[6] Market segmentation explained: http://tinyurl.com/nkgae3.

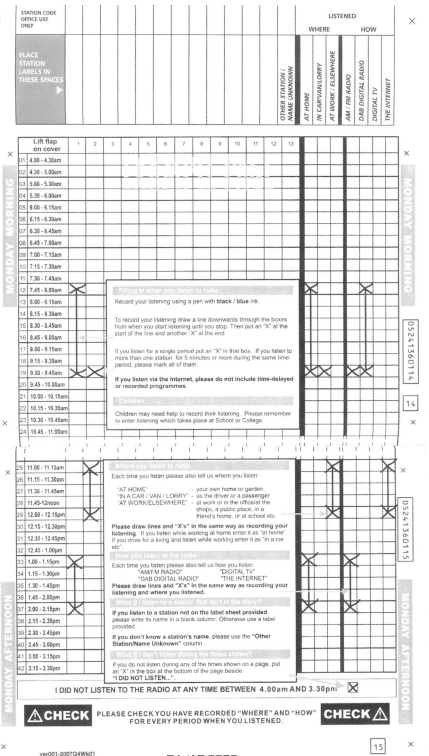

Ratings surveys show you sheer numbers of listeners, and also give a guide to how well the station is doing in attracting the demographic it sets out to. That can mean the difference between 'profit and loss' to a commercial station, or 'relevance and irrelevance' to a publicly funded station, which of course then affects its income and right to exist.

In 1992, BBC and commercial stations joined forces to create Rajar[7] (Radio Joint Audience Research) which contracts a research agency – currently IPSOS[8] and RSMB[9] – to calculate how many people listen to radio, when they listen and for how long. People are surveyed across the UK on an ongoing basis (a survey 'sweep') and reports are published every three months. Each of these is known as a 'quarter': Quarter 1 is the survey for January, February and March, Quarter 2 is for April, May and June, and so on. Some stations ask for reports every *six* months (over two quarters) because it effectively doubles the sample and so increases the accuracy, and allows smaller stations to gather their reporting sample over a longer period, which of course is cheaper for them.

The audience is counted by choosing a typical cross-section of people in a certain area. The National Annual Sample is around 130,000 people. In London, which has a 'listening' population (the population of adults aged 15 and over) of 10.5 million, the sample size per quarter is around 4,200: about 0.04 per cent. (For comparison, 'Newcastle' samples around 1,100 adults and 'Bristol' around 2,300.)[10] Those people are initially asked in a face-to-face, individual briefing what stations they're likely to listen to, and stickers of those stations (mentioning the name, logo, strapline and description of the station) are put on a fold-over cover-page of a special diary. Following a briefing by a Rajar representative, the person is then asked to keep the diary for one week, noting what station they listen to[11] in each 15-minute segment of each day.

Because stations have to pay Rajar (on a sliding scale according to their size) to survey their TSA (total survey area), many small stations decide not to be included, but this means that they don't have 'industry standard' audience figures to show prospective advertisers.

Note that Rajar provides *quantitative* research as it quotes actual figures (or quantities). *Qualitative* research is the type of information that comes from focus groups and deals with thoughts and feelings about a station ('I like the choice of music', 'It's best for travel news', and so on).

Radio's weekly reach hit an all time high of 45.8 million in the first quarter of this year, according to the latest figures from Rajar. The BBC still commanded the lion's share of listening, with 56.3 per cent, but commercial radio is showing some signs of recovery . . . Digital radio listening as a total of all listening breaking the 20 per cent mark for the first time.[12]

[7] The Rajar website: http://tinyurl.com/mwday9.

[8] IPSOS: http://tinyurl.com/59kaz5.

[9] RSMB: http://tinyurl.com/y9a4we6.

[10] Only 'London' is a Rajar-defined area where all stations are measured on the same agreed area. All other areas are defined by the stations themselves, so there is no such thing as the Newcastle sample or the Bristol sample. However there are different survey areas within, say, the geographical Newcastle area, as requested individually by BBC Newcastle, Magic Newcastle, Metro, etc. So, the sample numbers quoted here are an approximate guide to how many people *may* be surveyed in a city of that size.

[11] It's likely that many people will complete their diary at the end of each day, rather than during it, which is why Rajar statistics are often said to be a reflection of what people *remember* listening to, rather than what they *actually did* listen to. And that's why programmers are keen to have the name of the station said (or sung) as often as possible on air.

[12] *The Radio Magazine*, May 2009.

Reading the stats is the job of the managers of the station, so you won't have to know that much about it at this stage. Having said that, it's good if you understand the basics and the terminology so you know what they're talking about.

- *Weekly reach* is the number of people over 15 who listen to the station for at least 15 minutes over the course of the average week and is shown either in thousands of listeners, or as a percentage of the total population. (The three-month total is averaged out to give a weekly figure.) Note that in any area this will add up to more than 100 per cent as people listen to more than one station.
- *Total weekly hours* is the total of all the quarter-hours noted by each individual in the survey. Divide this by the reach and you get the *average hours:* how long a typical listener listens. This is often called *time spent listening,* or 'TSL'. (Trailing other features on the station should encourage existing listeners to listen again later, which will increase your TSL.) Note: if your average hours are 12 hours a week, that means that people are only listening for less than two hours a day.
- *Market share* is the percentage of radio-listening your station has, compared to others in the area (so it measures your *relative* success). This always adds up to 100 per cent as it's a division of all radio listening between all the stations in the area. So if you have a '5 share' it means that 5 per cent of the available audience that *could* listen, is. (If a manager says 'Our share was down, but then so was everyone's' it doesn't make sense! If your share goes down, someone else's has got to go up!)[13]
- The *total survey area* is the area that is surveyed for the listening figures and different to the *transmission* area (which is the main area in which your station is legally entitled to broadcast to). The TSA can be reduced by the station to capitalise on the likelihood of having more listeners in the core area rather than on the fringes. This has the effect of boosting the percentage reach of the station, although not the actual number of listeners.

A station might have quite a small *share* but a large *reach,* and that's what's usually most important in terms of radio listening: get lots of listeners first, then tempt them to listen longer. As people can only listen to one station at a time, the more your figures go up, the more your rivals' go down.

Headline figures come under these headings published by Rajar for everyone to see. Fuller figures, available only to individual stations (and anyone who subscribes to Rajar, for example advertising agencies), show the demographic breakdown of every half-hour segment through the day at that station.

Rajar statistics have a caveat attached to them: their accuracy (like most polls) are accurate only to +/– three percentage points.[14] That means that if your station is shown to have a reach of 26 per cent, it may in fact be 23 per cent or 29 per cent. So small rises or falls in quarterly figures should be treated with caution.

You can compare the Rajars from one three-month sweep to the next (*quarter on quarter*), but this may not be very accurate because of the small number of people with diaries. Although it may show if you've done spectacularly well or badly, unless you can pinpoint a specific reason for that (for example, your coverage of severe storms or a huge cash giveaway caused more people to tune in), these stats must be treated as more of a guide than as

---

[13] Another thing managers do is praise Rajar for its accuracy if the station does well, but blame it if figures are down!
[14] As with most surveys, its accuracy also depends on the number of people questioned and how high that figure is as a percentage of the 'universe' (the total number who could be surveyed). In other words, the more people who are asked, the more accurate the result will be; but one would have to ask *many more* people in a large TSA for that accuracy to increase at the same rate as in a smaller TSA.

the 'holy grail'.[15] Also bear in mind that people's listening habits change during a calendar year: with more people on holiday in the summer, there are fewer people available to listen (that's why most programmers put more emphasis on spring and autumn returns, when some stations forbid their main presenters from taking holiday).

It is probably better to compare the figures with what you had *this time last year* (*year on year*). Then you get a much clearer picture, although it also means there's a long time before any change that is made to the sound of the station (a new feature or presenter) is reflected in the figures.

HABITUAL BEHAVIOUR

It's suggested that it takes at least 18 months for a show to 'bed' in and become truly accepted by an audience.

Listeners have to discover the show, give it enough listens to hear something that hooks them, create a memory of that experience and deliberately sample another listen.

They gradually create a cognitive link between the act and the resulting experience through a conscious or sub-conscious weighting of preference. This assumes a real or imagined 'choice' between alternatives and their possibile 'rank order-ing' based on real or imagined attributes such as happiness, satisfaction, gratification (the positive emotional reaction of happiness in response to a fulfilment of a desire), enjoyment and usefulness they provide. Preference then leads to conscious motivation, in this case, to listen to the station or programme repeatedly.

So, only after 18 months should data be used as an accurate indication of the station's, or a programme's, popularity.

Critics of the diary system say:
- It's old fashioned to ask people to tick boxes on pieces of paper.
- The shortest time between results is three months, which makes the results of changes difficult to measure.
- People simply forget, or never know or realise, what stations they listen to (with digital stations and analogue ones, there are hundreds of stations that someone could be exposed to during a day).
- 'Heritage stations' (those which have been around for a long time) often do better than newer ones simply because people remember their name more readily.
- People's measurement of the length of time they listened for is not always reliable.
- The 'sample size' is too small to be accurate.
- The stats produced are only quantative and not qualitative.
- Why should those asked to fill in a diary be bothered? They don't pay to hear the radio, so it doesn't matter to them what they tick, if anything.

[15] Even then, as the reported figures are gathered over 3, 6 or 12 months, it is unlikely that short-term events such as one-off promotions will have much of an impact when averaged over those 3, 6 or 12 months.

In May 2008 Rajar ditched its multimillion-pound trial into electronic measurement (which would have been similar to the Portable People Meter[16] used by its equivalent company in the US, Arbitron,[17] and which can potentially give 'real time' ratings),[18] and launched an industry-wide consultation on how best to measure audiences. At the time of writing it is said to be trialing a new online diary system.

More detailed data[19]

It's often worth getting more detailed analysis of the Rajar results than purely the headline figures. By digging deeper you can work out listening patterns: for example, what kind of person turns off which programmes on your station, and what do they listen to instead? This 'switching analysis' may show that people are turning on specifically for a mid-morning presenter, and a controller may consider that if that person is such a draw maybe they should be on at, say, drivetime instead.

Tracking[20]

Specialist companies can provide stations with additional weekly information over several months. It's collected in a different way to Rajar figures, by phone or online, so it's not directly comparable, but it can give a useful trend of the audience's perception of the station. Answers to questions such as 'Which station's got the best music?' or 'Which station runs the best competitions?' are tracked over a set period and compared with the programme controller's strategy for the station. The stats are then used as an ongoing reality check on how the station's performing, and perhaps provide evidence for the need for change.

Focus groups

These groups are used to find out qualitative information (not *what* station people listen to but *why* they listen to it). A small group of people (usually six to ten) are asked their opinions about a certain topic to do with the station. An expert who remains objective throughout moderates over the course of a couple of hours and then produces a report on the key themes and trends that came to light.

Local audience panels

Another quite different way of monitoring the audience's reaction to programming is through these groups of listeners to BBC stations, which replaced Local Advisory Councils in 2007.

The panels[21] give their feelings about the programmes and presenters, and are more informal than the LACs and 'engage with a wider cross section of the population and particularly those whom the BBC finds hard to reach . . . and with the flexibility to consider a wide range of broadcasting matters affecting local licence payers'. There are also fewer members (six to eight rather than the 12 under the LACs) who meet around six times a year.

[16] More on the PPM here: http://tinyurl.com/dgch2z.
[17] The Arbitron website: http://tinyurl.com/5wjyv9.
[18] Read more on real-time ratings: http://tinyurl.com/kvkwno.
[19] This site from the US equivalent of Rajar, Arbitron, sets out the different analysis of figures they provide for stations: http://tinyurl.com/l4lex9.
[20] *The Listener Survey Toolkit*: http://tinyurl.com/l5ylbr.
[21] More information on audience panels: http://tinyurl.com/meznav.

Remove the reasons to listen less
– which is a lot easier than adding reasons to listen more.[22]

THE EXCHANGE THEORY FOR LOVE RELATIONSHIPS[23] (or 'listener loyalty')

Have you ever have found yourself desiring someone who was already in an existing relationship?

They appear committed to someone else because an investment of time and effort has created a strong emotional connection between them.

Their current relationship may have started for some of the following reasons:

- their physical appearance
- the excitement of something new
- instant gratification
- attractiveness of a sense of humour
- the two people have similar emotions, backgrounds, education
- the partner was generous with gifts or time
- self-confidence
- they are easy to talk with and a good listener
- the support they give
- their reliability, openness and trustworthiness
- they are challenging
- they are clean and well groomed
- they are unique.

Loyalty in a relationship is built when something is offered consistently to someone who consistently desires it.

But a relationship may start to break down and move into the 'emotional disengagement phase' when

- the reason for desire is altered or removed
- another emergent relationship tempts with an offer which is more convergent with a person's desires.

To persuade a listener to flirt, have an affair and then a long-term relationship with your radio station, you first have to prove your 'pair identity': that you can give them more of what they want.

---

[22] Mark Ramsey, President, RadioIntelligence.com.

[23] *The Diversity of Human Relationships* by Ann Elisabeth Auhagen, Maria von Salisch, Ann Robertson (Cambridge University Press, 1996).

Over time, it's possible that the loyalty dynamics of their current interpersonal relationship will be eroded as they assess, decide and commit to a new emergent relationship with you.

Like any relationship, it takes an investment of time and effort to steal and secure a new partner, who may be attracted for a number of reason which may include:

o Physical appearance – 'The station sounds different, ballsy . . . and big!'
o The excitement of something new – 'This new guy's much more attractive than that other one who's been around a long time and is getting boring.'
o Instant gratification – 'I feel great every time I turn on and hear one of my favourites.'
o Sense of humour – 'They're so funny in the morning . . .'
o Because you have similar emotions, backgrounds, education – 'They talk about things in the programmes and news that I'm interested in and can understand.'
o They are generous with gifts or time – 'Great prizes!'
o Self-confidence – 'The presenters know what they are doing and what they are talking about.'
o Easy to talk with and a good listener – 'She really gets on well with callers to the phone-in, she's like their friend.'
o They support you and others – 'They do loads of stuff to help the community.'
o Trust – 'I know the news is accurate and they won't mislead me with fake competitions . . .'
o Challenging and surprising – 'He can really make me angry with some of what he says, and then he explains it and I find myself agreeing', 'They did this stunt this morning where . . .'
o They are clean and well-groomed – 'I don't like smut, at least not in front of the children, and they sound polished and professional.'

In 'radio relationships' as in 'real relationships', everyone is always looking for something better, something that will offer them even more happiness.

To win them over you need to start understanding the strengths of your love rival (the other station), so you can build a relationship that does all of what your target desires, and then do it better . . . consistently.
Then find the holes. What is your love rival letting slip? What did they start off promising but now forget to do or do it half-heartedly? Do they forget the gifts? Do they not bother to love the listener? Is their personal grooming poor, do they have poor production values? What is the listener you have

got your eye on not getting from this relationship? A lot of people stay in a relationship because it's easy, because that's what they know and though they don't go looking for an affair, their passions are aroused when someone targets them.

Now make yourself more attractive to get the object of your desire.

Although they may be tempted by your flirting, human nature will make them reluctant to leave their current relationship that they have invested in and start an affair with you. Psychologists (Bloemer and Kasper et al.)[23] call this the engagement of *Decision/Commitment Theory*: an action taken after reasoning is likely to be more loyal and long-lasting than one taken on an impulse.

Audience interactivity and social media

Remember we're in the communications business with a radio station, not vice versa. Think how you can utilise burgeoning technology (texts and tweets, Facebook and blogs) to more clearly ally yourself with and help your audience or potential audience.

Does society need radio? The answer, quite clearly, is 'no'.
Society doesn't need radio, society needs what radio provides.
Society needs the comfort of our favorite songs.
We need the real-time connection to our community (however we define 'community').
We need to know what to wear today and whether or not school is cancelled.
We need to stay up to date or to revel in our past.
We need to be outraged and informed and soothed and amused.
We need to be told what to do in a crisis.
We need to know what's on sale and where.
And we need these things wherever we are – at home, at work, in the car, and on our hip.
These are all radio specialties, but did you notice that nowhere in that paragraph did I use the term 'radio'?
As an industry, radio needs to recognize that its social currency is in what it provides, not in the manner it provides it.[24]

Nowadays, everybody is used to getting what they want when they want it. Forcing people to wait until half past the hour for the weather, or quarter to for the travel news,

---

[23] *Journal of Economic Psychology*, Volume 16, Issue 2, July 1995.
[24] Mark Ramsey, president, RadioIntelligence.com.

is telling them that you're in charge; that they'll get what they're given when it's convenient for you, the broadcaster. That's not 'a service', and it's certainly not a great way to start a relationship.

Think of your audience: at this very moment there are some who want travel news, some who want the weather, others who want to know who's in the *X-Factor* final, others who want to know when their favourite band is playing (and so on). And for each of them there is only knowing 'now' and 'not now'. And if those services aren't being provided by you, 'now', they'll go where they are.

3 out of 4 Americans use social media. 2/3 of the global Internet population visit social networks. Visiting social sites is now the 4th most popular online activity . . . ahead of personal email. 57 per cent of the people on Facebook & Twitter are women; 64 per cent of the people on . . . MySpace are women.[25]

A station's 'benefits of listening' need to be produced in different ways, because even though the station is still the provider, the content is being consumed via a number of platforms.

These are those platforms.

Websites and messageboards

A website allow your listeners to get 'added value' from your station, by enabling them to:

- Listen live online (perhaps to a different service, for example station output in a one-hour delay, or a different football match commentary to the one on air).
- Get audio on-demand, for listeners to hear or download items they have missed or want to hear again (such as the successful BBC iPlayer service).
- Get more information on what has been broadcast (or which have not been broadcast because of time constraints): longer versions of the broadcast interviews, background interviews, advertiser links or what's ons.
- Have access on-demand, such as news, sport, weather and travel (most BBC stations have a link to the latest broadcast news bulletin).
- Contribute to the programme output via e-mail links on the site.
- Communicate with guests in the studio by e-mailing comments and questions, or off air in a web chat.
- See what's happening in the studio via the webcam.
- Find out more about programmes and presenters.
- Debate with other listeners through the forums and messageboards. (Be aware that it is against the law to have a message on your station bulletin board/messageboard which is defamatory, or if a libellous statement sent by text or e-mail is read on air. BBC stations have staff to check postings either before they appear on a site or soon afterwards, and who take down those which are illegal. As a presenter or producer, you should always be aware that not every message can be broadcast.)
- Keep in touch with home when they're away.

---

[25] Fran Lytle, consumer behaviourist, author of *Connection Moments* (with Bill Lytle, Trafford Publishing, 2006).

Trail the website heavily throughout the day. Try to refer to it as much as possible and give out the address every time. Some stations do this as often as once every 15 minutes so it becomes part of the listener's consciousness.

Some stations also have a policy that no other URLs should be given out on air, to reduce the number of complex addresses. Simply put other addresses on yours: '. . . and there's loads of information about this year's nominations on the website, go to relevantradio.com and click on the picture of the Oscar statue'. (Note to drop the 'www dot' at the start, and call the 'forward slash' simply 'slash', for brevity and simplicity.)

That mention of the Oscar statue is a good one, as the more specific the reason you give people to go to the site, the more likely they are to do so. A general 'Take a look at our website' reference is pretty much a waste of time.

Station sites are your shop window and carry a great deal of information for the listener, which could include:

- Items that back up or support on-air programmes (more information on a topic, websites of interest, full sports scores, contest rules, links to advertisers, a webcam or pictures from a station stunt/concert/celebrity visit).
- Items that feed into on-air programmes: anything that sparks a discussion on air or encourages interactivity with the station, and reinforces a listener's relationship. E-mails are a direct way for them to react almost instantly to what you do. Encourage listeners to e-mail via the website rather than to your own personal address: it reduces the number of complex addresses that are read on air and if yours is a commercial station it drives traffic to your site and increases the number of people who see the adverts.
- Items which appeal to your target audience, such as what's ons, or an online version of a game you're running on air to give listeners the chance to see it before they call in.
- Items that differentiate your station from others (a web-stream or podcasts).
- Items that generate income, e.g. adverts, downloadable tracks, a shop to buy albums or more information about an advertiser or sponsor.

Additionally websites can help in the production of an on-air programme or feature. Producers can use the website to:

- *Advertise* – booked guests, special programmes, talking topics and competitions.
- *Trail* – to promote, via links to other pages, their programmes, features and presenters.
- *Poll* – interactivity with listeners such as straw polls or voting.
- *Research* – asking for comments, ideas, personal stories or contacts for future programmes. 'Tomorrow we're talking about remodelling Bristol city centre. See the plans at relevantradio.com and then message me from the site to have your views included . . .'. Get listeners to send their phone number so you can chase interesting callers, rather than waiting for them to call you.
- *Reduce on-air clutter* – with information such as competition details, addresses, Snowline school closures or what's ons. The presenter can mention the exciting angle of an event, and point the listener to the website for the 'boring' information.
- *E-mail* – direct advertising of the programme to the people who ask for it (the next show's guests, topics, features, competitions). This could be through a VIP club and give away extra prizes and perks: 'Go on the website for extra clues to the competition . . .' or 'Listen to the Mystery Sound as often as you like . . .'.
- *Be one-to-one rather than one-to-many* – you can only have a few callers on air, but hundreds can send you their views/ideas and feel they have been included through e-mail. Really keen presenters can reply to as many as they like on an individual basis.

Many people would be hesitant to pick up the phone to a radio station, but most are happy using e-mail.

Facebook[26] and blogs[27]

Consider what you want to do with such sites before you launch them:

- What commitment are you willing to make to the site?
- Do you have the resources you need to keep it refreshed and relevant?
- For how long? (Facebook and similar sites have to do with relationships, and relationships take time and attention.)
- How will you measure success? Try to set a target and a review point before you launch.
- Is your overall investment in time and/or money likely to be worth the benefit the presence is likely to deliver?

Presenters can use sites such as these to:

- Increase awareness, build loyalty and be a research tool to learn about their listeners.
- Keep listeners engaged by letting them participate in a big discussion about them, their show, the competitions, what they say about the artists and songs . . .
- Have information and links from the station's favourite artists (that is, the ones that station research has told you your listeners also care about), their concert dates, music news, downloads and so on, plus a link to the station website and to other things you're doing.
- Give 'added value' to their listening experience. Updates should reach out to the listeners with thought-through comments, inside information, photos and links, which reflect the station sound and philosophy.
- E-mail their 'friends' with details of future guests or promotions.

WHO ARE YOUR 'FRIENDS'?

Check all 'friends' carefully before you approve them. Look at their profiles first, and if you do agree to them joining you, review their comments regularly and remove (or do not post) any that exceed your threshold. Once accepted, some 'friends' have changed from an innocuous group into porn or gambling spammers. Be careful if teens or children join . . .

If you want to update your list of 'friends' with a regular e-mail newsletter, make sure they're happy to get it. Only use the list for activities they have agreed to on that site, or you may be breaking the Data Protection Act.

Be careful if you want to make 'friends' with someone else or an organisation (e.g. a company or charity) through your page

---

[26] Forty-nine per cent of British people updated or created a social network account in 2009. (Source: the Oxford Internet Institute.)

[27] BBC guidelines for producers on the use of social networking sites: http://tinyurl.com/2otcvd.

and what that may show (or appear to show) about you and the station (for example some kind of endorsement).

Colleagues should be discouraged from becoming your 'friend' on your 'professional' Facebook page; otherwise cliquey in-jokes and office banter may alienate public readers, and the brand profile of the station become distorted.

Make your use of your site a two-way conversation between you and the listeners/readers, not be all about you. Any comments should be focused on the listener in the same way as what you say on air. Indeed never write something on the web that you wouldn't be happy saying on air. (That goes for the name of your page or site, too: the BBC says that a presenter's personal profile should not have a URL which contains a BBC brand or programme name.)

Text and e-mail[28]

The immediacy of e-mails can greatly enhance the debate within your programme. They also allow our listeners at work or abroad to contact us with ease.[29]

It is important to remember that just because someone has sent in a contribution to a programme, it doesn't mean that it has to be used. No one has an automatic right to airtime if what they submit isn't relevant, interesting or compelling. So, for example, if someone sends a joke that doesn't work or an inappropriate comment – simply don't use it. Keep the masses entertained, not the individuals. No one else will know what they missed, but they will notice if they have to endure it.

ACTUAL AUDIO

PRESENTER: 'It's good to have lots of reaction, but not too much please or we won't have time to read it out.'

BBC local station, January 2006

Texts will appear in the studio on a screen, in a similar way to e-mail. Texts to some stations are free (apart from network charges), or at reduced rate, while many commercial stations charge listeners for texting in. This charge doesn't have to be mentioned every time texts are asked-for, but does have to be said regularly. This is usually done in a produced trail in an ad break.

Given a choice of phoning or texting, people will often want to text: it's easier, cheaper and anonymous, but *calls* are more interesting. Save texts for competitions, votes and one-line comments, not for human interaction. For that, ask listeners to phone. (Some larger phone

---

[28] See Chapter 21 for information on the phone-in.
[29] BBC Five Live style guide.

systems allow for a text vote. This is generally a way of sorting the incoming texts into sepa-rate folders according to content. It can then produce graphs and statistics from the incoming texts. This is a great way to do a quick straw poll and get the audience involved.)

Anonymous comments on a text are less relevant, interesting and compelling than those with names, so think twice about the value of using them on air. And because they're anony-mous, you will suffer from 'textual abuse': 'Crap record', 'Shut up', 'You're boring' (and worse). The advice is just ignore it and don't react to it on air.

If you get a cracking text but don't want to just read it out, try calling the texter back (don't do this live on air as you'll lose the trust of the audience). Ask them if they'd like to make their comment in person. You never need mention the text on air at all.

Don't send a written reply to an e-mail during the show: it gives the impression that you have time, and even though that may be the case, it's not what we want to give to listeners. You could *write* the responses, just wait until after you have finished to send them all together. That indicates that you are busy, yet considerate and organised.

Twitter

Twitter should be one part of your station's overall 'multi-channel strategy', which should also include blogging, Facebook and MySpace pages.[30]

As with these other tools, decide what you want your Twitter page to accomplish, and then never, ever tweet anything that doesn't further that goal. Many stations have them 'Because everyone else has' and 'So I can tell the listeners what we're doing', which translates as 'It's all about me'. They think they're moving forward, when they're simply wasting their and other people's time. (Do your listeners really care what you had for breakfast?)

Used effectively this tool is a way to 'push' information:

- Show the listener something about you, your life, or the station they can't find elsewhere.
- Give added value. Perhaps a link to a text/audio download of morning show 'best bits', or useful feature (how to cut costs on your fuel bills or how ask for a rise at work) or real-time commentaries on sporting events.
- Create a compelling connection, for example by sending a message of each listener's travel hot spots to them individually each morning or asking contest winners if they are on Twitter and tweet a 'Congratulations for winning' message.
- Convey curiosity with a tease on a forthcoming guest or topic.
- Use it for urgency such as a news or travel flash or winter school closures.
- Use it to trail what's happening in the next few minutes.

And it's a great way to 'pull' information:

- Find out what people are saying about your output. Go to the Twitter homepage, put your programme or station name in to the search box and find out in real time. (You could even create a Twitter account under an alias and a fictitious bio, then 'follow' competing stations to see how they communicate with their fans . . .).
- Search for experts and follow them[31] ('crowdsourcing'); they might flag up links and stories that you might have missed. ('I'm looking for an expert on planting trees,

---

[30] A survey by News Generation Inc. (http://tinyurl.com/mlsqom_) in the US in 2009 found that nearly half of the newsrooms (45 per cent) use Twitter and Facebook, to offer their technologically savvy audiences an extension to conventional radio to provide another broadcast platform. Thirty per cent believe that keeping pace with technology and using social media builds listener loyalty and keeps listeners tuned in throughout the day.

[31] Anecdotally, 30 per cent of people on Twitter follow everyone who follows them.

know anyone?' or 'We're talking about the local floods tomorrow and would love to hear your story.')

- Find out who your important people on Twitter are following, and follow them your-self.
- More and more people are sending out their exact location as they tweet. This means you can use a tool like Twitterlocal to discover what people are talking about near you – or to track down users near a major news event.
- Got a question? Throw it out to your followers for unexpected and often illumi-nating answers

Produce your tweets: have tactics, create a storyline and build the drama. For example:

- First tweet: 'My boss has just called a meeting for later. Something's up.'
- Then, later: 'Rumour has it, my meeting with the boss later is about the 'Win A Holiday A Day' competition.'
- Then: 'Just came out of a meeting with the boss. It turns out, every Friday this month we have TWO holidays to give away!'

Note there's a bit of intrigue, a tease and a reveal, and how the 'story-so-far' is repeated in each message. Here's another example, of how you could create a conversation with your followers:

- First tweet: 'Should we be playing the new Leona Lewis song?'
- Then, later: 'Lots of people want to hear more of Leona Lewis. What do you think?'
- Then: 'The boss doesn't think the new Leona Lewis song is strong enough to play, but I'm not so sure. It's growing on me.'

Again, note the repetition of the topic in each message, so it's easy for followers to track the conversation, and also how to encourage replies by asking a question that gives the impres-sion that the listener's input is wanted and appreciated.

To 'reveal a secret', you could have the character of a work placement/junior producer/new staff member share some 'inside knowledge' with followers:

- 'Don't tell anyone, but the Secret Song will be on just after half past.'

If you give the time, rather than the 'time until' (for example, 'in fifteen minutes') then you'll help those who may not get the message immediately. Finally, create the mood of excite-ment rather than one of promotion in everything that you tweet:

- 'We get back at a guy who dumped his girlfriend in front of all her mates in moment.'
- 'The council leader's on in five minutes, what should I ask them?'
- 'Thought you'd love to know: we've just confirmed Lily Allen for tomorrow's show!'

Other Twitter tips:

- As in broadcasting, the best way to twitter is to engage, rather than shout. But regardless of the topic, all tweets should convey excitement and contribute to the sense of community that the station strives to build.
- Everything you post helps share your personal and station brand, good or bad. But that doesn't mean you use Twitter for generic station imaging: 'J and J in the morning with the greatest music and latest news from 5 on K-RAP 101.1'.
- Use proper words without abbreviations (apart from the obvious). The format, although evolving to a certain extent, is different from text speak, especially when you are representing the station.

- Make sure you have a house style for tweeting. Exclamation marks make you look immature. Don't have one person use capital letters, the next write all in lower case for example. And check your spelling: Twitter is your showcase.
- You only have 140 characters but don't try and cram too much in. And don't create a page design that distracts from information in your tweets.
- If you send pictures in a tweet, use the type of URL shrinking-and-redirect[32] service that lets you customise part of the address. By having a link that ends in 'ConcertPictures' rather than a random series of letters and numbers, your fans are significantly more likely to click through.
- Include your station name in your tweet, so when someone tweets back, they promote your station to friends.
- Be careful if you retweet (pass on someone else's tweet) in case it implies endorsement. Who are they, what's their agenda, is it political, are you somehow inadvertently promoting or advertising a product or cause?
- If you have a celebrity in, ask them to tweet to their followers that they are going to be on the radio station. And, if they tweet you a thank you afterwards, that message will go on their twitter page. (Entertainment figures are more likely to follow you as they want a big fan base.)
- Finally remember, a tweet (the same as a blog and a Facebook page) is for life. Even if you delete a message you've sent, other people will have received and stored it. So be careful what you say. Don't say anything on Twitter that you wouldn't say on air! And don't get into a fight on Twitter. If you respond to a tweet that someone sends in anger, you give them access to your database of followers.

Twitter is not just about twitter.com. There are dozens of other sites and applications that let you access Twitter more effectively such as:

- Twitterfall – which shows the topics that are currently most popular and most discussed.
- Tweetdeck – which connects you with your contacts across Twitter, Facebook, MySpace, etc.
- Tweetmic – which lets you upload audio (including that recorded on your phone), and posts links to it on your Twitter page (great for posting audio from an OB, or concert . . .).
- Twellow – the Twitter *Yellow Pages*.
- TwitSeeker – which finds groups of users defined by a set of parameters.

Apps

A lot of radio companies are creating applications for mobile phones so people can listen to their stations. But in reality there are very few people who actually need such a device. It's the solution for a problem that doesn't exist.

Your app may very well play the station, but it needs to add to the station brand and give people another way to experience it . . . with extra content. Not just give them another way to get the same thing.

So, it may be that your station app 'front page' links through to another app (also branded with the station logo) that gives music news about artists that your station plays, or one that lists and locates local events, or allows listeners to read and comment on local issues. Perhaps you could link from each song that's playing to artist biogs, and their iTunes website . . .

---

[32] Some URL-shortening services only give a temporary redirect to a site. Search engines will find a permanently shortened URL (such as Tiny, or Budurl).

You have to give a rich experience of using the station, and ideally that is not about replaying what's on the radio . . . it's about creating something extra, that the radio can't provide.

In conclusion

Perhaps it's time to rid our on-air service of 'clutter' (and it *is* clutter, if it's getting in the way of something else that the listener wants instead, right now).

In the future, maybe news, weather and traffic will all but disappear from the 'broadcast' bit of a radio station. It'll still be collated and produced by the radio staff, but will be delivered to other platforms. And while that happens, the live personality and interactivity will continue on air.

Part Two
PRE-PRODUCTION

4 The programmes

**SKILLSET – NATIONAL OCCUPATIONAL STANDARDS
RADIO CONTENT CREATION**

Unit content included in this chapter:
RC1 Work effectively in radio
RC3 Research audiences for radio
RC4 Contribute to the creative process in radio
RC5 Originate and develop ideas for radio content
RC6 Undertake research for radio
RC8 Pitch ideas for radio content
RC22 Produce music radio
RC24 Produce live radio broadcasts
RC29 Present a radio programme

Radio stations divide each 24 hours of airtime into different slots: the programmes. These may be four hours long, some are up to six, and they may contain different elements such as songs, news, competitions, guests and phone-ins; or they may be as short as half an hour and be based around just one of those elements (such as those on Radio 4).

Station managers use the target audience as the starting point for deciding not only the overall style of the station, but also the specific items that go to air.

Let's take the style first. Each station has as part of its licence a 'format',[1] which outlines the essential nature of the service and details any specific expectations.

Any changes to a format can only be made by following the correct procedure and with the appropriate permission from Ofcom. Some programmers deploy their format very rigidly, saying that whenever someone tunes in to the station they should know the kind of output they'll get. Some call this the 'hot tap policy' (when you turn on a hot tap you know what's going to come out. In the same way when they turn on a particular station a listener should know what they're going to hear: this is called *instant gratification*).

Programmes through the day on any station are constructed to mirror the lives of the majority of those who are tuning in. It's one of the basic ways that a programmer can connect with the listener and make the station seem more relevant to them.

The style of these shows remains the same from day to day, although the actual content will change as new presenters and programmers take over and as there's a reaction to listening figures, and to what other stations in the market are doing.

---

[1] More on Ofcom formats: http://tinyurl.com/meksfk.

At a time when the same songs are being played from station to station, it's the personality of the presenters who help make each station unique.

It's not unlike making new friends. If you meet two similar people at the same time and spend more time listening and talking to one than the other, then after three months you will be closer to the one that you know more about – the talk presenter with personality, rather than the five-in-a-row music jock.

Different times of the day require differing styles, which means hiring presenters accordingly. There seems little point in putting people somewhere in the schedule that isn't right for them . . . perhaps giving the breakfast show to their longest serving presenter as a means of persuading them to stay.[2]

The breakfast show – c. 06:00–10:00

This is the linchpin of the station's output and sets the tone and personality for the station as a whole. Indeed the mantra of many programmers is that the three most important elements of a radio station are 'music, mornings and marketing'.

It's a dynamic and entertaining start to the day that gets you out of bed and out to work – brimming with great music, stacks of listener interaction, entertainment and all the local and national information you need. Valuable social ammunition.[3]

This programme is the flagship, attracting the biggest audiences of the day in most localities and reaching the widest spectrum of age and social class. The most successful of our breakfast programmes combine journalistic impact with wit, warmth and unmistakable local characteristics. The output should be a showcase for our best journalism and led by high-profile, popular and respected presenters.[4]

In the morning, ten times as many people listen to the radio than watch TV (36 million versus 3.6 million). In fact, more people listen at breakfast than at any other time of the day

[2] Paul Easton, radio consultant, *The Radio Magazine*, August 2008.
[3] *GWR Brand Handbook*, 2000.
[4] *Connecting England*, BBC, 2001.

with the peak audience usually between 7:30 and 8:30; one of the reasons that a station's breakfast show is often referred to by programmers as a 'relationship programme' is because it strives to build a specific link with listeners.

As more people are listening, commercial stations charge more for their airtime during the breakfast show. Local BBC stations are committed to 100 per cent speech output during the peak morning period.

By 7:00, there are more people awake than asleep. It's a busy and highly structured time for families as they get the kids up, washed, dressed and breakfasted and out of the house for school and themselves to work. The morning commute peaks at around 8:30, and the radio is with most people as they rush around in the bedroom, bathroom, kitchen and car. TV just doesn't fit with our lifestyle at this time of day, as it needs to be watched.

> It's hard-wired into the DNA of the British. People don't have time for a primary medium in the morning. Radio is a secondary medium. It fits into people's lives while they are performing ablutions, picking up their toolbox and making toast.[5]

It stands to reason, then, that radio schedulers should put their best and most popular presenters on at this time, to take full advantage of the large potential audience.

> Your breakfast show is your flagship; it defines the entire tone of your station.[6]

A typical breakfast show will have the three Fs – fun, familiarity and format.

Fun, because people want their mood lifted by what the presenter says and the music that's played. The programme might:

- o   be dynamic and fast-paced to get the listeners 'up and out'
- o   be fun to listen to
- o   play the most instantly liked, recognisable and upbeat music
- o   have lots of listener interaction such as texts, e-mails and calls
- o   have high-profile, big-prize competitions
- o   have 'talked-about' or 'water-cooler' factors such as stunts or big name guests
- o   include entertainment news.

Familiarity, because at this time of day people are creatures of habit and want comforting consistency on the radio as much as they do in their get-to-work routine. Knowing which programme element comes next (though not the actual content) gives structure to this busy time. The show should include lots of 'the basics', often called 'the need-to-know' information.

- o   The news, so listeners know that, after eight hours out of touch with the world, everything's still OK. Also, so they don't feel left out of the loop, are 'social-proofed' and know what everyone else is talking about.
- o   The right content at the right time. Think of who's listening when. Your bulletin may

---

[5] Paul Brown, CRCA chief executive, *The Radio Magazine*, June 2005.
[6] Paul Jackson, programme director, Virgin Radio, *The Radio Magazine*, June 2005.

include more finance-type news at 6 and 7 (for early-rising commuters), a news angle on a road closure at 7, 8 and 9 (as the roads become busier with those driving to work and school) and so on.

- The travel, so listeners get the kids to school and themselves to work on time (or so they can leave earlier or make other arrangements if it looks as though they'll be late).
- The time, so they aren't late. People *need* to know what time it is.
- The weather, so they know what to wear.
- Other regular features at regular times.

Format, because the show to the biggest audience should:

- set the tone of the station. Make every 15 minutes representative of the station as a whole. So, a music station will play two or three songs, have news, weather and travel, have several time checks, an ad break and a few entertaining links during this time
- reflect the station's personality to the biggest audience
- play trails promoting other programmes on the station to this big audience, to increase the likelihood of them sampling the rest of the output.

> Think of your breakfast show hours as four 15-minute shows, each containing several of the key programme elements.

Breakfast is the ultimate gig on any station and the pinnacle of
one's career.
To present the breakfast show is an honour bestowed upon the
chosen few.[7]

When presenting breakfast, don't mention how tired *you* are. Your job is to motivate, not moan!

Daytime shows – c. 10:00–16:00

The output should reflect the rhythm and flavours of the day, being bright, original and enjoyable, not grey and cramped. Although predominantly speech-based, music will play a significant role – music for pleasure, to provide punctuation and music for a purpose . . . Long-running strands, in particular, may need to be regularly refreshed before – rather than after – the audience start to lose interest.
Generally, the audience ask us to be bright and intelligent, not Radio

---

[7] Robin Galloway, presenter, Real Radio Scotland, *The Radio Magazine*, June 2009.

Glum; often providing background radio, accompanying other activities. Our tone will be conversational, engaging laced with good humour. We will avoid the banal, but at the same time understand that some of the output should be entertaining. The quiz format is still a popular audience attraction and a good vehicle for the creation of a phone dialogue with listeners.[8]

Few people watch TV during the day, so radio reigns! Only till around 4 pm though, when more people are watching than listening. Before that, over the course of a week, around two-thirds of adults tune in. The BBC's *Daily Life Survey*[9] says that 19 per cent of all British radio listening is done in the workplace, with another 20 per cent in cars. Forty-six per cent of commercial radio's female listeners tune in on the way to the shops, 65 per cent of its audience listens in the kitchen, with 53 per cent in the bedroom, 20 per cent in the garden and 14 per cent in the bathroom.

The weekday can be split into two broad groups of listeners: those at work and those at home. For those at work the morning and afternoon shifts are much the same. In an office there may be the opportunity to listen to a station online or catch up with the news at lunchtime. In the factory a radio may be on non-stop and workers will enjoy music to help them get through the workday. Speech radio is difficult to follow in this environment, and for these people radio is background.

At home people are usually busy with jobs in the mornings and then relax in the afternoon ahead of picking up children and preparing meals. Radio is a companion.

By 4:30 there are more people at home than out at work or travelling.

Whereas the big-name personalities are often on air at breakfast, their lesser-known colleagues are often on mid-morning or mid-afternoon. That's not to say that they're less important, just that their role is different and inevitably they have fewer listeners. It's also why stations which network shows usually do so between 10 am and 4 pm, saving the cost of several presenters broadcasting to small audiences.

The breakfast host plays less music because there's not much time between the other elements that listeners demand, but once 9 or 10 o'clock comes most people are either in their office or factory, working around home or out in their car. There's less need for time checks and travel news (although these are still provided, there are fewer of them) and news bulletins are short updates.

To help listeners get through the working day the amount of music played is increased (perhaps two or three songs in a row — unheard of at breakfast), there's less interruption from the presenter, and less interaction from the listener. More music, such as with the popular feature the 'no repeat workday' (where between 9 am and 5 pm no song is played twice), encourages people to listen longer. As one of the biggest complaints against music radio is the high rotation of songs, this can be a great lure for listeners.

Stations in the BBC local network now target the mid-morning show as the second most important of the day (rather than drive). They try to maintain the high listening figures of breakfast and lure an audience through the day with speech and music (where commercial radio becomes mainly music) and increased listener interaction.

---

[8] *Connecting England*, BBC, 2001.
[9] Quoted in the *Sunday Times*, 6 November 2005.

Drivetime shows — c. 16:00–19:00

A vital show linking daytime and evening output covering the key afternoon travelling period.[10]

This is the time when children leave school and adults leave work. At home, chores are finished and meals prepared. There are more TV fans than radio fans for the first time in the day.

Most people are in a good mood as the strains of the day ebb away and they look forward to their free time.

There are different sensibilities as people's moods are different. At breakfast people are more easily annoyed, but with drive, if they've had a shit day they're on their way home so things aren't as bad. And the audience is constantly changing at breakfast so you're constantly resetting subjects.[11]

These shows are often seen as a mirror of breakfast shows, although they have smaller audiences (TV viewing overtakes radio listening at about 4 pm) and so make less money for the commercial stations. However, the breakfast and drive shows are, if you like, the two 'tent poles' of the weekday schedule, holding up the programmes that precede and follow them.

These two day-parts have similar content and style, because getting people to work on time mirrors getting them home. A round-up of the day's news (rather than agenda-setting or a reprise of the overnight stories); lots of travel news and time checks (so they can get home and get out on time); weather (often looking forward to the following morning); what's on information (often clearly targeted to new films, new clubs to visit, and so on).

In the past, afternoon hosts have been used to deputise ('dep') for the breakfast show presenter when they're away, but this is becoming less common. Drive hosts would often aspire to present breakfast, for the larger audience and larger salary, but such depping has often been at the expense of their own show's audience figures, which would invariably go down in their absence. If you consider their absence from their own afternoon show while covering for breakfast, and their own holiday time, they could be away from their own listeners for two or more months a year. Then there was the question of who fills on drive? And who deps for *them*? A kind of musical chairs developed, and all that change caused havoc with so much of the day, and made Rajar figures difficult to interpret, so that nowadays it's common to simply call in a weekend presenter to dep for breakfast instead.

[10] *GWR Brand Handbook*, 2000.
[11] Geoff Lloyd, Virgin Radio, Radio Academy event, October 2005.

Evening shows — c. 19:00–22:00

There's little radio listening done in the evening, as most people are out socialising or watching TV (the 'soap zone' is between 7:00 and 8:30 pm), although there's a small rise in the early evening as meals are prepared and the washing up done, and another around 10 pm as people go to bed.

Those who are listening at this time are more likely to be men, because of the midweek sports coverage, and 15–24-year-olds tuning into commercial radio music shows, although one of the most popular programmes at this time is *The Archers* on Radio 4! People are more relaxed than at any other time of day, and are in an especially good mood on a Friday as the weekend kicks in.

From 7 pm most of the potential audience is out or watching TV. Because few people are listening you can experiment a little more with your style of presentation, the features you run or music you play. This is safe in the knowledge that those who are listening really do want to hear you or at least the music that you're playing.

BBC stations seek 'ratings by day and reputation by night', so their programmes tend to be more specialised in the evening, catering for smaller, niche audiences. Musically this might include jazz, country, big band, alternative new music and the like. These may be presented by musical aficionados who have no real desire to be full-time broadcasters.

> In relevant areas, output for specific ethnic minority groups will have an important and prominent place in the evening schedule. This will often be local in origin and attract specialist audiences.[12]

Speech programmes might be scheduled here, such as Asian programmes for a minority group in the station's TSA. These are 'appointment to listen' programmes for those who tune in, and are seen by BBC stations as part of their remit to extend listener choice.

There's less scheduled information in the evening shows: fewer time checks, news and weather and travel reports, again because programming tries to reflect people's lifestyle needs.

In the evenings and overnight, local stations often join together in 'clusters' or become a larger network, to share running costs.

Overnight shows — c. 22:00–06:00

By 10 pm TV viewing has peaked and many people are at least thinking of going to bed (a third of adults are in bed by 10:30). Commercial music stations are more popular than BBC stations through the evening, night and overnight.

From 11 pm until 4 the next afternoon, radio reigns over TV, listened to by those going to bed, those working night shifts, insomniacs, and those getting up for the start of a new day. These listeners tend to be very dedicated, and a club-like atmosphere often grows up around overnight shows and their presenters.

> I do like the extra dimension that the night time seems to add to a

---

12 *Connecting England*, BBC, 2001.

phone-based show. Things seem to happen at night that just couldn't happen in daytime. People seem to be more receptive to the idea of joining in and going with the flow.[13]

This slot, commonly called 'the graveyard shift' (or 'shit shift') because so few people are listening, is valuable in helping recycle listeners from one day to the next. The station that people fall asleep listening to will invariably be the one that they wake up to the next morning. So it's important that this shift is not seen as any less important to the station's figures than other day parts.

Overnights used to be the training ground for new presenters. Overnight audiences are relatively tiny, sometimes too small to measure, so there was room for innovation. However, new technology and the increased need for branding in a commercial environment have meant there's now often one presenter broadcasting to a number of stations at this time of day, which of course means that the programme may be live but not necessarily local. Other stations may have an automated show played off computer, which is local but not live.

The overnight show is traditionally somewhere to cut your teeth as a presenter. It's a place to nurture raw talent. I fear for the future of raw talent as they don't have a place to hone their craft.[14]

The advantage of working overnight is that you have, obviously, so much more time in the day. You can enjoy the sunshine, go shopping, banking and to the doctor, pick the kids up from school and so on: all things that 9–5ers can't do. At work, there's less interference from managers, fewer interruptions in the studio, and much more of a relaxed atmosphere on air.

The drawbacks are that you can't go out at night to concerts or meals with friends. And at work some of the advantages are also some of the disadvantages: you never see the boss for feedback and you miss your colleagues' banter and gossip.

I don't have any romantic misconceptions about the middle of the night. Unless you're making mad passionate love or solving the world's problems with a dear friend it's a bloody awful time to be awake. Ergo let's make it pass as quickly as possible.[15]

By the end of your overnight shift, your energy and enthusiasm may be waning, but many of the people who're tuning in will be those who are waking up early for the start of a new day and need to be invigorated. Similarly, the breakfast presenter will come on, all guns blazing for the first hour of their show. So to

---

[13] Clive Bull, presenter, LBC 97.3, *The Radio Magazine*, April 2005.
[14] Adam Catterall, presenter, Rock FM, *The Radio Magazine*, May 2009. (Of course this lack of a training ground in a live situation is potentially storing problems for the future as there'll be a generation of radio presenters who haven't built up their 'flying time' and learnt from their mistakes. Where will future talent come from?)
[15] Rhod Sharp, presenter, BBC Five Live, *The Radio Magazine*, October 2007.

> avoid a massive gear-change, you have to keep energised
> throughout your programme.

If you are on this shift, make sure that you occasionally stay late or arrive early and meet up with the other on-air presenters. That way you'll feel much more part of the team and they'll be more likely to mention your show during their show.

Saturdays

Morning output will be more relaxed than on a weekday, recognising a more leisure-based focus to the day. A younger audience is available, adding listeners in some areas, but it's counter-productive to try and attract the under 45s with programming that drives away our heartland and secondary audiences. However, potential heartland listeners, working during the week, will be available and efforts should be made to draw them in. Sport remains a big attraction on Saturday afternoons and whenever possible this should include live match coverage.[16]

Saturday mornings are the furthest point from work for most people and they wake up positive and with thoughts of what to do for themselves and their families. Like weekdays, morning radio is popular, but the number of people listening is lower and the breakfast peak lasts longer – often through till lunchtime – as people take longer to get going. Most listening is done at home and in the car as background.

During the afternoon the TV takes over, but radio listening is still strong, especially for sports coverage and sports round-up programmes, for example on Radio Five Live. Between 5 and 8, people wind down from their day and start getting ready for their night out and may have a music station on as they prepare.

Weekend radio shows reflect listeners' increased leisure time. Breakfast shows usually start an hour or so later and are less frenetically paced, with fewer travel bulletins and time checks, and more music. There are inevitably more suggestions on what listeners can do with their free time, extra what's on information and BBC local stations may also broadcast gardening or DIY advice.

During the day most stations will offer mainly music programmes, with 'feel good' tunes ahead of people's night out. But it's Saturday afternoons that are most distinctive.

Most stations will continue to produce major local sports output on Saturday afternoons where we achieve one of our highest audience shares of the week. Many stations have developed evening sports programmes (on weekdays) with football phone-ins proving particularly successful in some areas. We should build on

---

[16] *Connecting England*, BBC, 2001.

this 'fanzine factor' especially in areas where we have retained extensive high-profile match coverage.[17]

In the recent past, commercial stations were prepared to pay an increasing amount of money to have the rights to broadcast live match commentaries. They saw them as audience-builders and revenue-raisers. However, over time the high price was reviewed by most stations who decided not to renew contracts with their local clubs. Now it's BBC local stations that broadcast sports shows on Saturday afternoon. These are often three or four hours long, with reports and live commentaries at the big matches involving local teams whether home or away. If several local teams are playing, priority is given to ones who are away, and therefore will have fewer local fans travelling to see them. These stay-at-home supporters can follow the match action on the radio along with, increasingly, ex-pat fans from other parts of the country or the world and who listen via the internet. As most BBC local stations have several frequencies (plus DAB and internet streaming), stations can cover several matches at the same time.

Commercial radio coverage on a Saturday often amounts to lots of music with flashes of goal news and extra sports bulletins. It's cheaper and is a good halfway house: sports fans are kept up-to-date with the action while non-sporty types don't mind the odd interruption if they also get a good dose of music.

It's understood that real fans may migrate from the local commercial station to the local BBC for Saturday afternoon's full match action. Commercial radio stations hope that their weekday promotion pays off and that the listeners will return. For the BBC locals the opportunity's on a plate for them to 'sell' their station and programmes to a new audience, and tempt them to stay longer or to retune later in the week (perhaps for a midweek commentary, or longer weekday sports bulletins).

Sports journalism captures a crucial audience of younger listeners.[18]

Of course, given the big business of football in particular, sports output can travel across a station's schedule. Obviously there are the midweek matches, but also the kick-off times of matches (on whatever day) are dictated by TV schedulers rather than those in radio.

Stations are key supporters of their local teams and provide passionate coverage of their regular trials and tribulations. Sport-focused commercial radio shows often include a high amount of listener interaction, through phone-ins, guest interviews and competitions, allowing listeners to voice their opinions and engage with the pundits.[19]

---

[17] *Connecting England*, BBC, 2001.
[18] *Connecting England*, BBC, 2001.
[19] The RadioCentre.

> Sport is a great way for a station to connect with its audience. Presenters are talking about something that's happening locally, something that people know about, care about and are talking about themselves. Sport is about where people live and their emotional involvement. And these emotions help the station bond with its listeners.

It's important to see a match as more than just a 'game of two halves'. Even for those who aren't interested in sports, there's human drama, passion, battles, fitness and even fashion. All topics which can be linked to sport to make it more accessible.

Sundays

Breakfast will set the tone of the day and output will be dominated by religious and spiritual concerns, reflecting our local multi-faith communities . . . Religion is an audience winner on Sunday mornings, often achieving the second biggest share of the week . . . Mid-morning is a crucial showcase for our output. It provides a good platform for debating big issues and demonstrating the BBC's commitment to the local community at a time when listeners are available. It needs a high quality presenter able to combine both serious and light-hearted material in an attractive magazine format. At weekends we must be careful not to simply duplicate BBC output elsewhere, or produce specialist music programmes in single localities for small audiences.[20]

Sunday is more leisurely, with people sleeping in. Then there's the long breakfast and the Sunday papers to read, followed by shopping, errands, meeting friends and doing things with the family, so radio is the top media through till lunchtime when TV takes over. People don't want to think about the week ahead, but by early evening homework's being completed and bags packed. The feeling of freedom fades. Throughout all this, radio is the secondary activity: background to whatever else people are doing.

Sunday mornings on BBC local stations invariably sees an increase in their religious or ethical obligation. Often this is early, between 6 and 8 am, for example. Sunday afternoon is traditionally the time when BBC Radio 1 and most commercial stations have their chart show (such as *The Big Top 40 Show*) from 5 until 7 pm. Radio 1's biggest audience of the day is when listeners (mainly 15–34-year-olds) tune in to hear what's number one.

---

[20] *Connecting England*, BBC, 2001.

5 Music programming

In broad terms, music is used in BBC local radio in two ways:
Music for pleasure – as a break from speech, a breathing space; as an entertaining interlude, much appreciated by many listeners; as background harmony, acknowledging that many listeners use the service as an accompaniment to other activities.
Music for a purpose – as production punctuation in idents, quizzes, trails and other promotional material; as an illustrative device; as part of programme formats, such as a 'Down Your Way' device; as part of local identity, when the music or musicians have strong local connections.
Extensive audience feedback across the country tells us that while some music is appreciated by listeners, it will not in itself attract an audience to a speech-led service. Those who principally want music will find it elsewhere. However, inappropriate and badly scheduled music can repel even our most loyal listeners.[1]

Most stations in the UK are music-based, and music is perhaps the single most important factor when the choice of station is made.

For listeners:

- Instant gratification.

Gratification is the positive emotional reaction of happiness in response to a fulfillment of a desire.

Instant gratification is the feeling when the time interval between wanting something and getting it is as short as possible (the *satisfaction of immediacy*).

---

[1] *Connecting England*, BBC, 2001.

Deferred gratification is linked with patience and anticipation. It describes the stronger emotion (real or perceived) that comes from saving (e.g for consumer goods) or waiting (e.g for sex).

In radio, instant gratification is the pleasure that comes from turning on a station and always hearing a song that you know and like/love.

So, research the music and play people's favourite songs . . . frequently. No one will ever complain that you play their favourite song too often. Songs that people complain about, or become tired of, are the ones that they don't like.

For the station:

- It's relatively cheap to play: although stations do have to pay for each track they play.[2]
- The mix of songs instantly identifies the style of the station (its brand): music more than anything else determines the format of the station.
- Music gives a show time to 'breathe', and the presenter and producer time to 'regroup' and consider what's coming next.

Classic FM has brought classical music to the masses; stations such as Galaxy and Kiss cater to dance music fans; stations such as Planet Rock satisfy rock aficionados. DAB radio has also provided a new platform for dedicated music stations like The Hits, Chill and NME.

Presenters remain a trusted musical guide. Consequently, radio continues to be the most vital driver for both discovering new music and stimulating music purchase. Three times as many respondents cited radio as the most important source for discovering new music compared to the internet. 68 per cent of respondents said that hearing music on the radio influenced them to go out and purchase it.[3]

To work out which songs are the best ones to play (the 'most loved'), stations need to do some research. Many use 'phone-outs' in which hundreds of people in the target demographic are asked about their musical tastes and then to identify their current favourite track from a shortlist of musical 'clusters' played down the phone to them. They may also be asked their opinion on a list of current songs. All this information helps the station to work out what songs they should play and how often.

There's also auditorium research — it's a similar process but done en masse in a room full of people, rather than on the phone to individuals.

---

[2] See the section on PRS and royalties, later in this chapter.
[3] The RadioCentre.

Researchers for BBC local radio play 'the hook' (an instantly recognisable few seconds, usually featuring the song's title) from individual songs to volunteers, and ask them what they think: do they recognise the track? If they do, do they like it? If they don't, could they tolerate it or would it make them turn the radio off? Their responses assist programmers in deciding whether the song's scored well enough to be included on a station's core music list.

'Assist' because a good programmer works with a mixture of 'gut feeling', as well as careful use of research data, and doesn't follow the figures blindly. That 'gut feeling' is a combination of the instinct of what will work with the station's target audience, and the 'ears' to spot a 'radio-friendly' hit that's also a good 'listener record'.

Once, radio was the primary place to find new music and ones favourite music. It was a strategic point of attraction.

Now, when people can get music from so many sources (and create their own running order), playing the music the listeners want to hear has become *the most basic element* of programming you must provide.

However, if you're *not* playing what they want to hear, it is a dissatisfier, and will hurt you.

By continuing to treat it as a satisfier (as the only/most important element to attract and keep an audience), your station is in danger of becoming irrelevant.

When something becomes widely available it loses its ability to become a satisfier, and becomes a dissatisfier.

Breakfast shows have less music, but what they do play will still be representative of the station's core policy. As they plays fewer songs, the ones they do play must be A1 hits, so the 'harder' songs will appear instead, later in the day.

The core[4]

The songs that test best are made 'core tracks' of the station and are ones that will be played most often over a long period of time. They're the ones that most clearly reflect the sound of the station, the all-time classic songs that the station plays. The core may be added to and reviewed on an ongoing basis, but won't change much from month to month.

You may also hear people talk about 'core artists', which are the singers or groups that also 'embody' the brand. Core artists for most commercial music stations are likely to be singers like Kylie and Robbie.

---

[4] As an interesting diversion, this site http://tinyurl.com/2fycqh – Gracenote's music maps – shows the most-searched songs and artists in dozens of countries around the world. At the time of writing Michael Jackson was the most popular artist, although the third 'most-searched for' artist in Iran was Chris de Burgh . . .

The playlist

The playlist is the tracks that the station plays on a regular basis (its 'active categories'). Commercial stations have a typical core playlist of about 400–500 songs, although 'tight' stations may have as few as 200 (and in the States this can be as few as 100). BBC local stations have a core of around 900, considered rather large in commercial terms.[5]

> Presenters and producers have criticised the introduction of a 600-track core playlist across the BBC's local stations arguing that listeners will tire of familiar songs and be deprived access to new music.[6]

> I'd come from a Hot AC station with a playlist of just 280, to a station that has thousands, and they all tested well. Our rotation means you can stick us on and not think . . . 'not this song again'.[7]

In the mid 2000s a format known as 'Jack' became popular in the US and Canada. This format, often without presenters and with a much larger core of over 1000 songs, is known unofficially as 'random radio' or an 'iPod shuffle format' (even though it pre-dated that device) and often uses anarchic slogans such as 'playing what we want!' Pre-recorded links are updated regularly by the station voice and, like the slogan, also have an 'attitude' which reflects the station's brand values.

Although the Jack format is untested in the long term, critics say that without presenters the stations lose one of the main advantages over an iPod: the sense that a live person is programming the music. Indeed, *Newsday* described the format, with the lack of local programming and personalities, as 'another step towards the McDonaldisation of radio'.

Stations playing more specialist music are only likely to get a big enough audience to let them survive if they broadcast over a wide area (terrestrially in a city, or digitally across a region) so there are more potential listeners who have an interest in their output. Most commercial stations stick to a safe 'middle ground' of contemporary hits, which is what most people enjoy listening to, although this can mean that a large potential audience is split between several competing stations. Ownership regulations mean that one group can run several stations, when it's in their best interests to broadcast slightly/largely different playlists to maximise their potential audience. So, radio station programmers monitor their competing stations to determine how similar or different their playlists are. That is easily done because of real-time track listings on station websites and DAB screens, and because of a website which lets any listener compare stations' output.

Comparemyradio[8] shows the most-played artists and tracks on British radio from the last 30 days, information that's also tabbed by station. It shows how much variety (crossover) there is amongst the industry which at the time of writing was 9 per cent (the closer to 100 per cent the more variety); total tracks played by the whole radio industry over the last 30 days (139,109); total unique tracks played by the whole radio industry over the last 30 days (12,966). It also allows comparison of two stations' playlists, which includes a 'variety gauge' indicating how many different tracks are played by each one.

---

[5] The 'running order' is the list of music for an individual show amounting perhaps to ten or so tracks an hour.
[6] *The Radio Magazine*, May 2008.
[7] Nino Firetto, presenter, Exeter FM, *The Radio Magazine*, March 2008.
[8] CompareMyRadio: http://tinyurl.com/yjcfq6p.

So, Capital FM shares 22 per cent of its playlist with Heart, and 2 per cent with Xfm (all three have roughly the same TSA and are owned by Global Radio); whereas BBC 6 Music shares 36 per cent of its playlist with Xfm.

Scheduling music

Once the overall style of the station has been decided (by considering which tracks tested best with the audience the station wants to target), the songs have to be scheduled.

> Any music scheduling software is a tool that is only as good as the rules you set up and the music you have in your database . . . utilising the rules we have in PowerGold to guarantee variety and carefully controlled repetition.[9]

For each song on the playlist, the head of music will input various data into the computer software system (often Selector[10] or PowerGold[11], both trade names). The information is so the computer can shuffle the songs, and much of it is basic and obvious:

- The song's title, artist, duration.
- The year of release (so the computer doesn't suggest two or three similar-sounding 1970s disco songs in a row).
- Whether the artist is a mixed group, boy group, girl group, male solo or female solo (so you don't get James Blunt followed by Elton John followed by Will Young, for example).
- Additional artist information (so a song by Wings isn't played next to one by Paul McCartney, and one by Destiny's Child doesn't follow one by Beyoncé Knowles. If this happens it's called an 'artist clash').
- The speed of the song (beats per minute).
- Payment details such as who wrote the song, the publisher and distributor (so PRS royalty payments can be made).

Other information is more subjective (and so should be entered by the same person, to ensure better 'sound coding'):

- Its tempo, energy and mood. Although speed can be a good indicator of mood, it's not always. Some fast songs are 'sad', some slow ones are 'happy'.
- Its genre (rock, reggae or rap and so on – you've probably seen similar categories on your iPod).
- How often it should be played (its rotation). Some songs are on low rotation (played less often than ones on high rotation) either because they don't research as well, because they're brand new and are being introduced to the listener, or because they're falling down the charts (often, but not always, a good guide to a song's popularity). You want the most popular songs, both the current songs and those from the core, to be played most often. But if you play them *too* often people will get fed up with them, so once every three hours is usually a good rotation.

---

[9] George Ergatoudis, head of music, BBC Radio 1, *The Radio Magazine*, May 2007.
[10] The RCS website: http://tinyurl.com/ndjh42.
[11] The PowerGold website: http://tinyurl.com/mqdte6.

▫ When it should be played. Some stations separate their songs into different time zones. Stations programme their output to mirror the way their listeners lead their lives day-to-day, and in a similar way, more lively songs are usually played at breakfast time, slower songs at night and a broader mix during the day. (This isn't always the case: *Club Classics* on the Heart network of stations will play upbeat songs in the evening, notably Friday and Saturday nights when its listeners are preparing to go out.)

▫ Other reasons may be because of the length of the track, for example, playing a long song in breakfast when there are other elements to fit in would cause problems.

▫ It may be because the style or content of the song is more appropriate to play in the evenings rather than to a family audience at breakfast time, or may be because of the title: 'Wake Up Boo' might sound odd if it's played at 10 at night, or 'Nightshift' by The Commodores at 9:30 am!

A brighter, hot day requires a very different approach from a chilly winter's morn when you might hear Madonna's 'Frozen' or Elvis' 'In the Ghetto'.[12]

▫ Ideally, each song should play in a different part of the day over the course of a week before it's repeated. That means that it may play in breakfast on its first outing, then evening, then afternoon, then morning, before being played again in breakfast. That's so listeners in each day-part get to hear the songs evenly. The music scheduling system will ensure this is what happens.

The computer is also programmed with the details of the overall station sound that is required to ensure an even distribution of tracks' style and speed through the hour. The first choice of song will be determined by category (see below), after which the computer will consider the other 'rules' that it's been given. It will then provide a running order for each show that fits with that request.

Music and mood are closely linked psychologically.

A 2006 study[13] of the role of music in influencing audiences used music theory to analyse and investigate the effects of music's structural profiles on consumers. The experiment's results indicate that music may have significant impact on audience moods and purchase intentions, without necessarily affecting intervening cognitions.

In 2006 Delta Airlines started playing pop music as passengers boarded their flights. Attendants realised that it encouraged them to get into their seats faster, so more research was carried out. Now it's the norm on all Delta flights: welcome passengers on the plane with familiar tunes, get them to their

---

[12] Richard Park, radio programmer, *Independent*, June 2006.

[13] J.I. Alpert and M.I. Alpert, 'Music influences on mood and purchase intentions', *Psychology and Marketing* Vol 7, Issue 2 (2006). See also: http://tinyurl.com/5g5aq9.

seats quickly with upbeat tracks and help them settle in with more relaxing songs.

How does a programmer know that their presenters are following the playlist? One way is of course for them to have an ear to the radio and a hand on a playlist printout. Another is to employ the services of a company[14] which monitors their station, and provides information about what every station in the area is playing, when and how often. This lets programmers crosscheck the performance of songs, and, to all intents, view the programming logs of their competitors.

POSITIVE PRODUCT MEMORY

Whether listeners return to your station again is likely to depend on whether they remember it fondly or not.

Research[15] on consumers' memories for experiences (e.g., listening to music) shows that whether they remember an experience as good or bad is affected by three key aspects of that experience:

- what the final part of the experience was like
- what came before it
- how similar its parts were.

So if you play a mix of songs that are relatively similar (e.g., all love songs from the same artist), they remember their experience as more positive when the songs are ordered from least to most liked. In other words, a positive memory is affected by whether the trend became more positive or negative. In contrast, if they are listening to a mix of songs that are quite different from one another (say, different artists), their memory for whether the experience was good or bad is affected purely by how much they liked only *the last song played*.

What this means is that it's not just about the mix, it's also about the sequence. Try to ensure that the overall experience gets increasingly better, and peaks at the end, with the highest perceived value.

The playlist meeting

The choice of what will be added to that week's rotation of songs is usually made at a weekly playlist meeting. At small stations it may be the programme controller who decides what makes it to air, at larger stations a group will listen to the tracks and decide the policy, probably for several stations. Group-wide music policies exist so the sound is consistent across those stations.

[14] One such company is here: http://tinyurl.com/l7pzhm.
[15] Loraine Lau-Gesk, 'Understanding Consumer Evaluations of Mixed Affective Experiences', *Journal of Consumer Research* (2005). http://tinyurl.com/ldlezx.

Music categories

Programmers often talk about 'A-list', 'B-list' and 'C-list' songs. These are terms used to define certain groups of music and their rotation.

- A listers are playlist songs from the current chart (and so are likely to be on high rotation).
- B listers are new releases travelling up the chart, or one-time A-list songs going down (which are played less often).
- C listers are usually songs yet to be released and which are being introduced.

These are the most-used music rotation categories on a typical chart hits station. Some stations and programme controllers use different terms or have slightly different definitions and rotations, but this is a good basis:

'Introduction': when you first add a new song to the playlist.	**Introduction**	The initial period after a song has been added to the playlist.	May be here for two or three weeks before it's familiar to the audience.
'Adoption': the time during which a listener hears and becomes familiar with the song.			
	Current		
	Current light	Generally used to introduce new songs to the listener, so they become familiar before being moved to a higher rotation. These could be songs yet to be released. Often called the 'C list' and played in non-peak hours, perhaps in the evening to a younger audience.	Fewer plays than the A and B list, as they're still new to the listener.
'Decline': don't reduce the rotation of former hits too dramatically or, to light listeners, it will seem as though you have stopped playing them completely.	*Current medium*	New songs going up and hits on their way down. Also called the 'B list'. Probably around six songs.	One of these an hour.

	Current heavy	The 9–15 most important songs of the moment, which set the style and sound of the station. Often called the 'A-list' songs. (There's usually an odd number of these to give easy rotation in quarter hours.)	One per quarter hour, each played every three to four hours.
'Recurrents': songs which are too old to be current hits, but not yet oldies. These help build and maintain an audience. On a station playing 'younger music' playing songs on high rotation ('high rot'), the recurrents may be 6–12 months old. On an older targeted station recurrents could be 18–24 months old.	**Recurrent**	One-time A-list songs up to a year old. There may be around 30 in this category.	Two of these might be played each hour.
'Maturity': some all-time favourites spend many years here.	**Power oldies**	Older, 'classic' songs that are on the station's core from the 1990s and 2000s, possibly numbering around 250 songs.	A couple of these may be played each hour.
	Gold	The biggest hits from the 1980s numbering around 150.	Two of these might be played each hour.

Every station will have a different rotation policy which determines not only what songs are on what list (the A, B and C lists) but also what their rotation is, and how many from each list gets played each hour. That rotation is all-important: if you play too few from your A list it'll take you most of the day to play each one of them. By the same token, if you play too many an hour, and the time between each one of them (the 'turnover') is say three hours, the list will need to be longer.

If a station which plays a song every few hours has people listening for an average of seven hours a week, the majority of people will only hear it a handful of times in that seven-day period. So getting through that song's life cycle (introduction, adoption, maturity and decline) will take several months. For 'heavy' listeners (including presenters) they'll be sick to death of the song just as 'regular' listeners have heard it enough for it to move from introduction to adoption and maturity stages.

If there are too many songs overall on the station's playlist, people have to listen longer before they hear one of their favourite songs (which of course is one of your 'most effective' songs). That lowers the overall 'listenability' of the station.

So, a greater variety doesn't necessarily mean that people will listen longer.

The rotation

Some stations have a policy to play a certain number of songs in an hour or a certain 'minuteage' ('another 40-minute music sweep'). Others guarantee the *kind* of music they play ('Your no-repeat workday station – between 9 and 5 you won't hear the same song twice', 'Your hotter, fresher mix', 'The best of the '90s and today . . .').

The choice of music, determined by the criteria given to the music selection computer program, should give the general music show a good mix throughout each hour. The contrast may be between a solo male singer, followed by a female group, followed by a male/female group. Once the computer has also considered the tempo of songs, their genre, year of release and rotation, you can begin to see that there's an infinite combination of songs from hour to hour and day to day.

The role of the computer

It's often a surprise for listeners to discover that most of the music played on a station isn't chosen by the presenter themselves, but having said that, of course it's a human who inputs the details of each track into the computer in the first place.

The head of music will look over each hour's schedule to double check the selection that's been made. That's because the computer is only working to the rules it's been given, and it doesn't have ears! Two rules together may produce a quirk that hadn't been anticipated, and you could end up with two songs together which you *know* won't sound good. Indeed, a scheduler can give the computer so many rules about what songs can't go together, that it provides either a very stilted and limited running order, or can't produce one at all!

I choose every single record as I go along. One new song may spark an idea for something next that might be 50 years apart but sounds good. I might slap in say, Feist or The Songbirds with

something new and then next to it fire off one of the great so
called girl groups of the 60s.[16]

Some presenters, for example those on specialist music shows or experienced presenters, may be given a free choice, but this is the exception rather than the rule, and even then the choice would usually have to be within the station's format. The reason is to stop a music free-for-all, with each presenter playing their own favourites, not necessarily those of the audience. Some songs would be played too often, others not at all, and the whole station sound would be watered down.

Street-level scheduling strategies

- Remember the basic idea behind music programming is to have a balance of music that flows through each hour, with a variety of styles and artists, and tempos that rise and fall.
- Play more of what people know and love. Stations are rarely hurt by what they don't play, but can be by what they do.
- If listeners think there's too much repetition, it may be because there are too many 'borderline'-scoring songs on poor rotation. People don't complain when their favourites come around more often, only when they regularly hear songs they don't like.
- Playing the *best* songs is better than playing the *most* songs. Quality is better than quantity.
- Playing too many songs which have 'burned' (ones that people are tired of) is as bad as playing too many unfamiliar songs.
- Cut back on playing new and unfamiliar music at breakfast. At this time of day people want to hear their up-tempo favourites.
- Rotate music evenly. In other words, a song should not appear in the same hour from one day to the next because it'll be heard too often by some people and not enough by others.
- Every 20–30-minute period should have a mix of music that represents your station.
- To create a slower feel for the station, increase the rotation of the slower songs. To give the feeling of a 'hotter and fresher' station, you do the same with the up-tempo songs on the playlist.
- 'Music of your life' songs help listeners recall their teenage years and are often a big hit. This is because teenage years are our formative years, when, as one presenter put it, 'Having fun was our job . . . before our job was our job!'
- 'New gold' songs are ones which are about six months old, that is two seasons ago. They remind listeners of recent memories. For instance, if it's winter now, it reminds them of last summer.
- Similarly, 'anniversary songs' remind people what they were doing this time last year.
- 'Sunshine songs' or 'Friday feeling' songs are classic up-tempo songs that make people feel good.

---

[16] Randall Lee Rose, presenter, Big L, *The Radio Magazine*, February 2008.

People need to know that even if they don't like the song you're playing now, they'll like the next one and love the one after that.

If the figures go up we're playing the right music. If they go down, it's the wrong DJ.[17]

Hour-starters

Some programmers say the first song out of the news should be a classic, others that it should be a current hit. Most agree that this is the location for a 'showcase' song, one that represents the sound of the station, and that it should certainly be a strong and generally up-tempo song. Whenever you come out of a speech insert, such as commercials or an interview, play a huge hit. Talk that's long should be followed by a song that's strong.

Radio songs

A good 'radio song' is a powerful 'memory key' that is able to take the listener back to a time and place where they felt great. Radio songs don't necessarily work at home, only on the radio. That's because they have to have the element of surprise. At home you know the song is coming up on your CD or iPod and so it doesn't have the memory power. Being on the radio adds value to the song.

It's been shown[18] that music is an important influence on our memories as we associate songs with emotions, people, and places we've experienced in the past.

Researchers of music-evoked autobiographical memories probed the cognitive and affective properties of the evoked memories. On average, 30 per cent of the song presentations evoked autobiographical memories, and the majority of songs also evoked various emotions, primarily positive, that were felt strongly. The third most common emotion was nostalgia.

And researchers[19] at Kansas State University say merely thinking about a certain tune, even if it's not actually playing, can summon vivid memories of a time, place or emotion. They say that's why oldies stations are so popular because the music reminds us of specific times in our lives.

---

[17] Geoff Lloyd, presenter, Virgin Radio, Radio Academy event, October 2005.
[18] Petr Janata, Stefan Tomic and Sonja Rakowski, 'Characterisation of Music-evoked Autobiographical Memories' (2007): http://tinyurl.com/lbsrmy.
[19] More on this research here: http://tinyurl.com/lf325x.

In the study, the researchers asked teenage music listeners between the ages of 18 and 20 to pinpoint meaningful songs from five life stages: early childhood, grade school, middle school, high school and college. Then, they picked the most memory-evoking song from each category, indicating their predominant emotion: happiness, anger, sadness, love, hate, fear, surprise or disgust.

For the early childhood stage, the runaway winner, with one in four votes, was 'Sesame Street'. In the grade-school era the highest percentage of participants pointed to Vanilla Ice's 'Ice Ice Baby'. At middle school, 36 per cent reported strong memories associated with Coolio's 'Gangsta's Paradise'. High school is a real battleground, with Green Day's 'Good Riddance (Time of Your Life)' narrowly edging out, believe it or not, 'Eye of the Tiger' by Survivor. Even though the latter song was released in 1982, before many of the study participants were born, 24 per cent of them said it provoked a strong memory of high-school sporting events.

All the hits?

Remember, just because a song has been number one, doesn't mean that your station will play it. It has to research well with the target audience.

An easy listening station such as Smooth Radio in London will not play the Scissor Sisters just because it does well in the charts, but may play a track from that group if it's compatible with the station sound. An oldies station, of course, wouldn't even consider playing a new release. Others may refuse to play a novelty song.

If you listen to some stations you'd think Abba only made 'Dancing Queen'. The repetition on oldies stations just gets on your nerves a bit. I've never understood why we can't broaden it out.[20]

The playout computer

The playlist computer in the music scheduler's office 'talks' to the playout computer in the studio, so the music running order for each hour is seen on screen, and the tracks are loaded automatically to play from a hard disk.

The hard disk also contains all the station's jingles, adverts, news clips and so on, which saves you loading all those elements manually. That means that you have more time in which to think about your verbal links. You can take calls off air (and interact with your listeners), record calls that can be played later (making them tighter and more relevant), or talk to guests when they arrive (and help the image of the station).

On the studio screen the song title and name of the artist is displayed, together with the

[20] Tony Blackburn, presenter, *The Radio Magazine*, November 2008.

The music playout screen. Courtesy: 96.4 The Eagle, Surrey

duration of the track and whether it 'ends' (comes to a dead finish) or fades out. These are usually marked as E or F alongside the track listing. That's handy for a presenter to know, to make it easier to link from one song to the next. Other information that you might find useful to know may also be mentioned, such as the chart position of the track or when the artist is next in concert.

Selector and other similar music programming systems will also give presenters easy access to the station's database of songs, for requests and dedications on so-called 'jukebox' shows. As well as showing the song's availability (whether it's one that's suitable for the station and is therefore allowed to be played), it will also show the last time it was played. This ensures that such a 'free choice' by a presenter doesn't cause the same song to be played too regularly.

The presenter and the music

As mentioned before the music-scheduling computer doesn't have ears, so it's down to a human to check whether two songs go well together or not. That human may be the programme controller, or it may be you while you're on air. Always check that you're allowed to change the order of songs before you do it, even though it may make perfect sense to you at the time. Altering the music policy at a station is no small misdemeanour and may well be a sackable offence. Any discrepancies should be questioned before the programme or after it. The programme controller may see it as the top of a slippery slope when songs are dropped on the whim of individuals.

Sometimes there will be exceptional circumstances: you may want to play a song by an artist whose death has just been announced, or a song by a band that's appearing locally. In such cases your own experience of your programme controller will tell you whether altering the playlist is appropriate.

> You'll get fed up with songs faster than listeners ('music burn'), because you hear songs in concentrated periods of time. A current hit will almost certainly come around once in each of your four-hour shows, possibly twice. The typical listener will spend just eight or so hours a week listening to the station.
>
> So you might hear the song six times in a week on your show alone, whereas they may only hear it that many times in a month. That means that after a month or longer on the playlist, it's only just starting to become a strong favourite with many listeners.

One of the arts of music programming is to recognise how listeners perceive a song, and to have the strength of character to keep it on high rotation even though presenters are fed up with it. (A song's airplay and release date can be as much as six weeks apart, and some songs are very 'slow-burners'. The Verve's 'Bittersweet Symphony' peaked a year after release.) Indeed, some programmers say that you should never stop playing a hit record completely, just slow down its rotation. So currents are played several times a day, recurrents a couple of times a week, and golds a couple of times a month.

Arguably, the music played on a BBC local station has to have researched better than that on a commercial station: if you listen to a song on a commercial station and it's not your favourite then you know that there'll soon be one that will be. Listening to a BBC local station, you may have to wait 10, 15 or 20 minutes for a song (because of the station's increased speech quota). That means every song needs to be the very best.

> We rotate somewhere in the region of 5500 songs, covering the '60s, '70s, '80s, '90s and 2000s. One minute you can hear a classic Beatles' tune, the next it's Avril Lavigne's brand new hit single. People on the street seem to enjoy it, they tell us that if they don't like one song, they at least know that in a couple of minutes, they'll be hearing something completely different.[21]

Radio is also important in that, unlike MP3 players, listeners are introduced to new music through it. Despite the growth of the internet, a 2008 survey showed radio is still the number one place to discover new music. The presenter can be a 'trusted friend' who can recommend new tracks, a technique which some music sites have developed to sell more music.[22]

---

[21] Derek McIntyre, programme controller, Your Radio, Scotland, X-Trax magazine, July 2005.
[22] Message on the Last.fm website: 'Last.fm recommends music, videos and concerts based on what you listen to . . .'

Music features

Music features (such as a 'Golden Hour', or 'Classic Top Ten From When') should include tracks that the station plays all the time (in their core) or certainly still be in format. Songs that go on the radio have been carefully chosen and tested to appeal to a target audience. They're part of the station brand and to dilute that by playing your own personal favourites will undermine that hard work.

Inappropriate music

You may have to adjust your playlist when, usually because of news events, playing a song with a certain title or by a specific artist may not be appropriate. For instance, after the hurricane in the southern United States in 2005 many stations dropped, for obvious reasons, 'Walking On Sunshine' by Katrina and the Waves. Other songs are effectively banned at hospital radio stations, 'I Just Died In Your Arms Tonight' being an obvious example.

There had just been a news story about a fatal house fire in Leighton Buzzard. A producer or presenter didn't quite make the connection between the bulletin's headlines and what song they were about to play next: 'Disco Inferno'. Cue the inevitable email to all staff, warning about getting burned. But perhaps there's a rebel in the ranks. Immediately after a bulletin about Margaret Moran stepping down as Luton South MP last Friday, someone, intentionally or not, played The Moody Blues 'Go Now'.[23]

Occasionally it may not be obvious that a song needs to be dropped, as the offending words don't appear in the title. It may not occur to you that it may cause offence if you come out of a news bulletin which includes a story of a shooting, with 'Bohemian Rhapsody'.[24] However, you can take things too far and be over-sensitive. When you're head over heels in love, every song you hear seems to have been written just for you. In the same way, when a news story is uppermost in your mind, almost every lyric takes on a subtle second meaning.

Songs by individual artists may be banned if that singer's life takes a turn for the worse. Gary Glitter is rarely heard on British radio any more after he was found guilty of child abuse charges. A similar thing happened to Jonathan King. Even though both of them had successful and long-lasting pop careers, few of their songs are now played. In 2005 Michael Jackson appeared in court charged with various offences alleged to have been committed against a young boy who stayed at his Neverland ranch. Some radio stations were said to have dropped all songs from his back-catalogue including those of The Jacksons. Before the verdict was announced, a memo at Radio 2 said:

It depends if he is found guilty and on what grounds. It's possible it may end up as a charge of supplying alcohol to a minor, which is

---

[23] BBC *Ariel* newspaper, June 2008.
[24] See the lyrics here: http://tinyurl.com/wnb2c.

unlikely to attract a jail sentence given his past record. Under these circumstances there would be no real reason to stop playing his music, however, I would go easy on rotation because reputations will inevitably be harmed and feelings raw. However, if he's found guilty on the more serious charges of child molestation etc then we have a duty as public service broadcasters to take in to account the feelings of our listeners. There'll be an immediate backlash in the media so it would be best to rest the tracks for the time being. The difference between Jacko and King is the sheer volume of the music that Jacko has provided over the years. His status as one of the world's greatest pop artists is unquestionable. Michael's legacy to pop music radio has been immense while King's has been more novelty than substantial. Many of our listeners will always love Michael's music because it's so good, but the whole question of paedophilia is so sensitive and abhorrent that many would not deem it appropriate to listen to his music.

Appropriate music

You've got a local biker's club in to talk about their charity run – don't play 'Motorbiking'! A similar rule if you're talking to some lottery winners and are tempted to use 'Everyone's a Winner'. These are musical clichés and have been used many times before. Try to think of songs that are equally appropriate but used less often.

Obit songs

All stations have songs which have been highlighted as suitable to be played in the event of a royal death or that of any other VIP (such as the prime minister), or national tragedy. These need to be reviewed regularly with some tracks added and others taken away so, come the event, your appropriate songs are not from a time frame that stopped five years previously. Such a playlist was used for more than a week after the death of Diana, Princess of Wales, and included classical music as well as more modern instrumentals ('Song For Guy', 'Albatross') and even more recent songs with lyrics ('Everybody Hurts').

Not only should a list be available (in the Obit Book that is kept in every studio), but it's also wise to have the songs recorded onto a few CDs for immediate access.

Radio edits

Some songs contain lyrics which are likely to be offensive to listeners and may, if aired, break broadcasting codes. That's why some songs have what's called a 'radio edit', a version of the song with the offensive reference either edited out and replaced with a 'bleep', or by a slightly different lyric (such as James Blunt's 'You're Beautiful' with the replaced lyric of '*flying* high'). Be sure you play the right one: there are stories of the wrong versions of Smokey's re-release of 'Living Next Door to Alice', and The Beautiful South's 'Don't Marry Her . . .' both being played on air!

Another reason for a radio edit might be because of the length of the original song: 'American Pie' has a radio edit version which is about half the duration of the album track.

Power starts

Other songs have starts which simply don't sound good on radio. Perhaps they make it diffi-cult to cross-fade with other tracks or don't fit in with the style of station, even though the rest of the song does. One station edited off the start of Belinda Carlisle's 'We Want the Same Thing'[25] because of the shouts, another did the same with 'Happy Christmas War Is Over'[26] because of the whispers.

Christmas songs

There are stations in the States which play non-stop Christmas songs from just before Thanksgiving (at the end of November) well in to the new year. In the UK, festive tunes are usually played for about a fortnight before Christmas (with one an hour the week before) and tail off completely by a few days after. Each station is different in terms of the number, type and rotation of songs.

Christmas countdowns

Many stations fill the awkward week between Christmas and New Year with a countdown of listeners' Top 500 of All Time. They're handy because you can easily schedule 100 songs for each of the five daytime periods (the usual station playlist runs overnight) and it gives the impression that you're playing what listeners have chosen.

That's not strictly true for several reasons:

- Such countdowns attract very little listener response.
- The most-suggested songs are usually those that have been in the charts most recently.
- Stations are never going to play some of the songs requested because they simply don't fit with the station format.

These countdowns are difficult to administer accurately, not least because of the low number of votes cast. That means that dozens of songs in the lower reaches of the 500 may only be separated by one vote. Then you're forced to 'smooth out' the results – you can't have 30 songs all tying for the same place. In this circumstance, put the songs most repre-sentative of your station's core up as high as you can, while also bearing in mind the usual scheduling mix of singers, speed, years and genres.

PPL, PRS and MCPS

There is another great time-saving device that is built into music scheduling computers and that's the ability to sort out the paperwork for music payments. It was well into the 2000s that presenters had to time the duration of each song they played down to the last second, plus the duration of every jingle and music bed that was used. This was all while they were trying to present a show. Now much of this is done automatically.

Stations are allowed to broadcast music from CDs (and records, etc.) because of an agree-ment with the Phonographic Performance Limited, the main society that represents record companies and performers. Stations pay PPL a sum for the blanket use of their songs, and are obliged to tell them which songs were played and for how long. That's so the money is

[25] Hear it here: http://tinyurl.com/4sc2k3.
[26] Hear it here: http://tinyurl.com/2qrjzh.

fairly divided between all of their members, the music publishing company, the distributor, the composer, arranger, lyricist and performer of the song.

The Performing Rights Society collects money for its members (composers, lyricists and publishers), the amount being linked to the audience size of the station on which the song was broadcast. In 2008 this totalled £608m. The Mechanical Copyright Protection Society collects dues for its publisher and composer members.

There is an argument that by playing songs on the radio, stations are giving free publicity to the artists. The member groups say that playing music attracts listeners, and therefore advertisers, and so stations can well afford to pay the people who created the music in the first place. PPL, PRS and MCPS have won the argument, but at least send stations free copies of songs as their part of the deal.

The paperwork for the music that's played ('the returns') is down to trust to a large extent. Every piece of music is logged by individual stations and details sent to the copyright societies. The blanket licence money is then split between copyright society members entitled to royalties. Spot checks are made on stations to ensure that returns are accurate, with penalties charged if they're not.

> All rights of the manufacturer and the owners of the recorded work reserved – unauthorised copying, public performance and broadcasting of this record prohibited.[27]

> A PRS licence doesn't give you the blessing to use well-known songs in advertisements. PRS covers 'public performance and broadcast of musical works', it does not give you the right to use PRS members' music in anything you see fit.[28]

You can't just use music for whatever you want. In the run-up to the millennium celebrations, the band Pulp banned the use of their song 'Year 2000' for any use apart from as a straight track – it couldn't be used for adverts or beds or anything else.

Also be aware that all audible music has to be reported. That includes:

- Traditional or out-of-copyright music such as 'Auld Lang Syne' or 'Happy Birthday' (you may not have to pay for using it but it still has to be reported).
- Ice cream van bells or football chants (for example, in a feature you produce).
- Sound effects from a publisher's library recording.
- Even one second of a tune – all has to be logged and reported.

Some music can be used without additional payment but still needs to be logged so publishers can receive royalties from the PRS. This may be music that's been bought outright by the station and is of the type used for adverts, music beds or theme tunes and is called 'library music' or 'production music'. They are composed in a wide range of musical styles, everything from hard-core rock to slapstick and each piece has several versions (or 'cuts') timed to 15, 30 or 60 seconds to be used for different situations. But be warned, you have to listen to an awful lot of tracks to find the one that's right for your purpose.

---

[27] Label on CDs.
[28] John Calvert, MD, Airforce commercial production, *The Radio Magazine*, April 2005.

You can't get around paying for what you use by simply broadcasting plays, poetry or comedy instead of music. That's because the agreements stations have don't extend to the use of the spoken word. That means that a station would normally have to get individual permission from the copyright holder before they could use such items.

Some stations play clips of TV programmes or cartoons either as features or mixed with their sweepers. In the mid 1990s you were bombarded by Homer's 'Doh!' on almost any station you tuned to, nowadays it's more likely to be clips of the previous night's big reality TV show. Again, it's a risky procedure: the actors or producers are entitled to more money if their work is being used in places other than they agreed, and even though the TV channel may like the extra publicity that you playing clips from their show would bring, it's probably best to get their agreement in writing.

Taking music off the net (either new releases or theme tunes) is also not advisable, as you don't always know if the recordings are legal in the first place: a pirate copy of a live concert, or an unauthorised remix, for example. Although it's safe to buy from recognised sites (iTunes, for example), you can't be sure that other sites have the right to record, use or sell the track that you're after.

6 Speech programming

**SKILLSET – NATIONAL OCCUPATIONAL STANDARDS
RADIO CONTENT CREATION**

Unit content included in this chapter:
RC1 Work effectively in radio
RC3 Research audiences for radio
RC5 Originate and develop ideas for radio content
RC8 Pitch ideas for radio content
RC10 Write for radio
RC18 Select and brief radio contributors
RC19 Direct or commission others to create content for radio
RC21 Produce speech content for radio
RC24 Produce live radio broadcasts

The previous chapter dealt with what type of music to play, when to play it and in what order. Now the similar process for more speech-based programmes (such as the ones usually heard on BBC local stations).

Presenters don't just go on air with a list of topics to talk about, phone numbers of interviewees to call and songs to play. Each programme needs to be planned – you need to know when you'll run all those elements.

There has to be structure:

- So that the items go in the most appropriate place . . .
    - according to the size and make-up of the audience . . .
    - according to what other items are either side of it . . .
    - according to what's in the rest of the hour or programme.
- So you know what you're doing from one moment to the next.
- So you can schedule space for it.
- So you can prepare for it.
- So you can promote it.

A lot of the output of BBC local radio is music-and-speech programming, usually about 40:60 in favour of speech. Producers have to be careful how they balance their items: too much speech and it may sound odd to have a song suddenly appear, or it may sound like a music show with an ill-placed interview intruding.

A lot of the considerations about what to put in a show have to do with the time of day it's on (BBC local stations have a policy of no music at breakfast and little at drivetime, but more during the day), the style of presenter (whether they're more comfortable doing longer interviews or presenting their own short links) and the resources available (it's more time consuming to set up speech items than it is to programme another hour's-worth of tracks).

A balance is what's needed, so when putting together your music/speech programme, consider where in the hour you want to place your songs to balance, or complement, the speech items.

Planning the running order

It's exciting, but also a little daunting, to be given an hour (or two, or three) to fill with material. Here's how to make it much more manageable.

The programme clock (aka 'the programme pizza')

Regular features (the building blocks of the show, sometimes called 'furniture') are often depicted on an easy-to-follow 'programme clock', for each hour of the show. The clock (or 'pizza' as it looks as though it is divided into slices) shows the location and duration of each item, and makes it much easier to understand what goes where in your empty hour and how you can place other items in their optimum position.

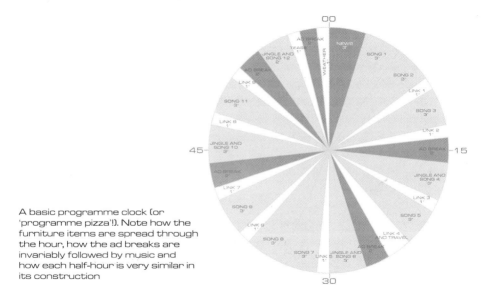

A basic programme clock (or 'programme pizza'). Note how the furniture items are spread through the hour, how the ad breaks are invariably followed by music and how each half-hour is very similar in its construction

The placing of furniture items usually follow a sequence, which helps listeners become familiar with the format and helps them navigate around it (for example, travel follows weather, or 'if it's the second song after the news, it must be about 10 past 8'). The placing of such items in regular places to ease programme junctions, and please listeners is an example of a 'uniquely consistent behaviour' which helps a station's on-air branding or 'station sound'.

The clock here is for a very basic music-heavy commercial radio station show, and could additionally give specific instructions for 'music sweeps' (or 'multi-plays', two or three songs in a row), where to play certain station IDs, and even when to give the time. You can see how it could be adapted for a programme with more speech, or a BBC station with no commercials. One or two of the links shown here could very well actually be a pre-recorded trail or a what's on event, or the adverts could be replaced with a guest interview, competition, newspaper review, financial report, TV review or job spot.

A clock is an easy way to picture the programme, although a list of features and their duration is more practical when you're entering information in a running order on a computer.

This is an alternative running order for the same programme shown above:

Start time	Content	Duration
:00	NEWS	3'
:03	SONG 1	3'
:06	SONG 2	3'
:09	Link 1	1'
:10	SONG 3	3'
:13	Link 2 and tease	1'
:14	AD BREAK	2'
:16	JINGLE	10"
:16	SONG 4	3'
:19	Link 3	1'
:20	SONG 5	3'
:23	Link 4 and TRAVEL and tease	2'
:25	AD BREAK	2'
:27	JINGLE	10"
:27	SONG 6	3'
:30	Link 5	1'
:31	SONG 7	3'
:34	SONG 8	3'
:37	Link 6	1'
:38	SONG 9	3'
:41	Link 7 and tease	1'
:42	AD BREAK (NB: start calculating back time)	2'
:44	JINGLE	10"
:44	SONG 10	3'
:47	Link 8	1'
:48	SONG 11	3'
:51	Link 9 and tease	1'
:52	AD BREAK	2'
:54	JINGLE	10"
:54	SONG 12	3'
	SONG 13 (in reserve)	3'
:57	Tease	10"
:57	AD BREAK	2'
:59	WEATHER into NEWS	1'

Fixed items – news, ad breaks   Jingles and songs   Links and speech

First, place the features that can't be moved, the fixed items or furniture, on your clock or list. These are usually speech items such as news, travel, weather, what's ons and commercials. They are in fixed positions in each hour decided by the programme controller, usually evenly spaced at the top and bottom of the hour and at quarter past and quarter to.

That 60-minute block is then broken up into four much more manageable quarter hours.

If the news is three minutes, headlines another one minute, two travel bulletins a minute each, weather a minute and another for what's ons (and they're conservative estimates) then that's already eight minutes of the hour gone. Then add the ads (sometimes up to ten minutes' worth) and you can start to see how the original 60 minutes are being eaten away.

You'll probably want to put music either side of the fixed items you've just put in. You may even be able to fit in some pairs of songs back-to-back (even if you only play four songs in the hour that's another 12 minutes and almost half the hour has gone).

Scatter your music as evenly as you can through the hour, don't cluster it all together. You can't 'bank' music with the listener before a speech item. If you play several songs in a row and then go to a slab of speech, the listener won't know what kind of programme they're listening to; better to spread out all the different elements as evenly as you can throughout the hour.

When you've placed the music you'll be able to see how much time you've got left, maybe for an interview or competition.

A typical BBC local radio running order on ENPS. Note the instructions and reminders to the presenter; the mix of music, furniture items and guests. Courtesy: Ray Clark at BBC Essex

Many producers still construct a programme as they'd write a news story. In other words, they start the hour with the best item and follow it with items that are progressively less important. The listener almost slides down the interest-scale as the programme continues. After they've done that a few times, listeners will realise that after the first ten minutes there's little of value in the remainder of the programme. So instead of a slide, we need to think of each hour of a programme (and the programme as a whole) as a roller coaster, with a series of peaks and troughs.

We've already seen that music schedulers place songs through the hour so there's a spread of different genres, tempo, male and female singers, groups and eras. You should think in the same way when placing speech items.

Let's take the example of a news-magazine programme, with interviews and music, that you're likely to hear on a BBC local station at drivetime.

First take your running order and fill in what you know you have to do at certain times:

```
00:00
00:15   TRAVEL
00:16
00:30   HEADLINES
00:31   WEATHER
00:32   TRAVEL
00:33   SPORT
00:38
00:45   TRAVEL
00:46
00:58   TRAVEL
```

You can see that there are four travel bulletins evenly spaced through the hour, and there's a news/weather/travel sequence at half past, followed by sport.

Now, put the songs in the running order, considering that it is best to have them
- evenly spaced through the hour
- either side of a speech block.

```
00:00
00:12   SONG
00:15   TRAVEL
00:16
00:27   SONG
00:30   HEADLINES
00:31   WEATHER
00:32   TRAVEL
00:33   SPORT
00:38   SONG
00:45   TRAVEL
00:46   SONG
00:58   TRAVEL
```

That's quite an even spread, songs every 12 minutes or so, and is a good skeleton for the rest of the programme.

After the programme theme and introductions at the top of the hour, it makes sense to have the lead story (the one that's most relevant and interesting to the audience) and probably follow that with the second lead. It's good to keep the speech items no longer than the duration of a song, about three minutes, but I've given these stories four minutes to include the time it'll take to read the cue (the introduction to the piece) and to wrap up the item (bring it to a conclusion) if it's an interview.

PSYCHOLOGICAL HOMEOSTASIS

Any organism will adapt itself to a 'continuing stimulus', so if there is no continued threat, it will eventually 'tune out' so it can return to complete rest in its environment.

This could be the noise of a fridge humming or train passing. A human reacts immediately it starts but after a few seconds of the steady (or predictable) sound your mind adjusts and cuts it out.

The same is true for radio. Anything that goes on for too long invites people to tune out.

Avoid having your listener lapse into homeostasis: don't do any one thing for too long.

Then it's important to play a song as a break from the speech content, so let's bring what we'd scheduled at :12 forward slightly. That will give us a couple of minutes just before the travel news to remind listeners what else is on the programme and read one or two what's on items.

After travel news, there's 11 minutes to fill before the song and the speech block. That gives us time for two more news stories (perhaps a live or pre-recorded interview, or feature), and a little time over. We could do the third lead here, but it's probably better to put *that* item after the half-past speech block to give some weight to the second part of the hour. But you can't have the two top stories followed by the two bottom stories – that would sound unbalanced. Consider taking leads 4 and 6 at quarter past the hour, and having 3 and 5 later. That gives a peak and trough.

We may need the extra time in case we're running late, so we'll keep it in hand but also prepare something to fill with just in case. At :12 we mentioned the rest of the show and the what's ons, so we can't do exactly the same again. Instead consider teasing ahead what's in the next half-hour, and also what's on the station later that day or the next day. It's best to do these mentions before SONG 2, so we don't add to the length of the, already consider-able, speech block.

00:00	INTRODUCTION
00:01	STORY 1
00:05	STORY 2
00:09	SONG 1
00:12	Tease and what's ons
00:15	TRAVEL
00:16	STORY 4
00:20	STORY 6

00:24	Tease and trail
00:27	SONG 2
00:30	HEADLINES
00:31	WEATHER
00:32	TRAVEL
00:33	SPORT
00:38	SONG
00:41	STORY 3
00:45	TRAVEL
00:46	SONG
00:49	STORY 5
00:53	And finally story . . .
00:58	TRAVEL

Above is what our running order looks like, together with the regular 'and finally' item at the end of the show.

Don't programme your show for efficient listening.

Listeners may tell you that they want to hear the funny horoscope at 8.22 every day and the 'dumb criminal' story at 8.40. They want to have the entertainment items they love at a time that's convenient to them, so they can listen efficiently. In other words, so they can turn on, get what they want and then turn off (either mentally or physically).

But what's 'efficient listening' for them is a drop in 'time spent listening' for the station.

Of course your service elements (news, weather, travel, sports, etc.) must be in the same place each day. But your entertainment elements (skits and sketches, joke of the day, dumb criminal spot etc.) can move.

Listeners want to be surprised.

The music/speech mix

There's certainly a balance to be made: after a long period of speech does the listener want a song to lighten the mix? If the answer is yes, then consider playing an up-tempo and well-known (core) song to maintain interest, rather than a relatively unknown track which may alienate the listener. On the other hand, too many songs and the listener may feel hungry for more information.

Other speech-scheduling techniques

o   Commercial broadcasters have an added consideration when they're running a music/speech mix because they may also have up to nine minutes of adverts an hour. If you put a song either side of an ad break, then you're fast running out of time to have meaningful speech. In such a situation, interview slots are usually placed just before a break, with music either side of that whole 'speech block'.

o   Put your best material where your best audience is – it makes sense, doesn't it? So, if your programme is on at breakfast, don't 'waste' your top story, best observation or most interesting guest in the 6–7 hour. Ask your programme controller to tell you when the audience peaks and consider putting the item there instead.

o   Sometimes producers are tempted to put an item in the running order even though they know that it's not really strong enough. In other words, they think that 'slot fill-ing' is more important than making an item relevant, interesting and compelling. Quality should always take precedent over quantity.

o   Position items to prolong listening. If you've an item on 'what to buy your wife for Christmas', consider putting it after the sports news, to keep one audience (possibly mostly men) listening for longer. If you continually chop and change different kinds of content, the show has no flow and listeners may go.

o   Make sure that you have various peaks during the programme and that you end on a high. Consider whether, once you start the show, it's a case of downhill all the way.

o   Even though slots are often best kept at around three minutes, it doesn't mean that you have to then get rid of your guest after that time. They may be worth longer, in which case give them longer, but not in one slot. Spread them over two slots instead.

o   In a news programme you may consider placing those slots at two different parts of the hour rather than consecutively. You may start with a 'pro' opinion at the top of the programme and then promote that you'll be hearing from the 'anti' view just after the headlines at the bottom. That way you have a balanced show (with both sides of the story) and a balanced hour (with the lead story starting each half-hour segment).

o   Also consider the kind of audio that you have in each slot. It is best to have a variety of different kinds during the course of a programme. There may be someone on the phone (a 'phono' or 'phoner'), perhaps a guest in the studio with you (what's called 'in quality'), several people recorded on location in a feature (or package). If you can, try to spread out these different kinds of sounds through the hour so it's not phone interview followed by phone interview.

o   Similarly, if you're able to, have a range of different kinds of voices. Try for a range of male and female, young and old, experts and those with experience. In short: light and shade.

o   Don't start a programme item too near to the top of the hour. The news is a fixed junction and can't be late, so starting an item here (or maybe continuing one) may mean that it's rushed, and that'll show that you hadn't planned your programme properly.

o   Other fixed junctions in the hour are also important, but you can use a live interview to build in flexibility: you can wrap up a 'liver' so you get to another item on time, but it's more difficult to stop (or 'pot') a pre-recorded item.

o   Things go wrong, of course they do. One guest may bomb but then another may be better than you'd anticipated. Feel free to alter a running order to take these situa-tions into account. Cut the crap and extend the friend.

FORMULA VS. STRUCTURE

A formula is a method that relies on an established approach. It's a by-numbers method that will get you off the ground while you are a new presenter.

A structure is the next step and uses a formula to create or recreate something different.

It will develop and always be a 'show in progress' as listeners will continue to change, develop, have new experiences . . . and the presenter and the show shift and grow and react to those changes.

7 Outside broadcasts

An 'outside broadcast' (usually called an 'OB' for short, although they're also called 'remotes') is a broadcast from a site other than the studio. This would usually consist of some kind of transmitter, on a radio car, a full rig or a backpack. The station may decide to present an OB from an open air concert, for example, and have presenters interviewing the bands back stage, and have a roving reporter interviewing the crowd.

A 'roadshow' is when a station is at an event and puts on special entertainment for that audience, usually on a stage attached to the side of a large rig or OB unit. A roadshow may involve games and competitions on stage with the presenters and the public, interviews with people at the event, singers or dancers performing, and lots of station giveaways thrown into the crowd. These elements of a roadshow are not usually broadcast because, as the presenters are playing to the crowd and not to the at-home audience, they don't make for very good radio. A roadshow may be the sole reason that the station is at, say, the county show (that is, there's no OB element), or there may be a roadshow before or after the station goes live on air. A client of a commercial station may pay for a roadshow, to draw crowds to an event, for example at the opening of a new car dealership.

Why an OB?

This is the second of the two strands of a radio station's link with its audience: output and outreach.

> Our presence in the community, whether it's at events, with sponsorship, holding stunts, whatever, is about so much more than being seen by x thousand people.

It's a vital part of establishing our brand positioning within the local area.[1]

Outside broadcasts:
- Help the station get involved in the local community. Some events are goodwill gestures for local charities.
- Help you meet people – listeners and *potential* listeners – face-to-face, help create new fans and solidify relationships with existing ones. (The smaller the station the more relevant OBs are: you stand a chance of meeting a greater percentage of your actual audience than with a larger station.)
- Help *them* meet *you*, so they can put a face to the voice.
- Create interest in the station's output.
- Create and strengthen brand awareness of the station.
- Could bring in some income if it's paid for by a client.

It is easy for someone to suggest doing an OB, but that usually comes from someone who doesn't have to put it together. Among the considerations before you start organising what is an expensive and time-consuming production are:
- *Does this event add to your portfolio?* A station needs to be at a variety of events, not only the big mainstream events (with a full OB unit and main presenter) but also the smaller and more unusual ones (maybe an exhibition, sporting event or public meeting), simply with a radio car and reporter doing inserts into the programme.
- *Is it appropriate to your brand?* All station promotions should project and protect the station's image as well as the actual station: an outside broadcast at the opening of a new model railway shop would not be appropriate for a Top 40 station, however much the sponsors are paying for your attendance.
- *Is there publicity or PR potential with this event?* If you can meet a variety of people, lots of them, and get your message in other media, then an OB looks more likely.
- *Can you maximise the visual presence?* What will the station look like? Consider the OB unit, publicity material and whether you can hire other elements to help you put on a show and create impact. Maybe a bigger rig, a stage, dancers, celebrities.
- *Will your presence exceed expectations?* Many listeners and potential listeners will be seeing you and meeting you for the first time. Will you live up to, or surpass, the picture they've got of you in their head? That's both on an individual presenter basis, and when they experience the overall station brand.

Before an OB

The first thing you need to do is get some more information about the event and what editorial justification there is for being there. In other words, is it going to sound good on the radio? Speak with the organiser, or anyone from the station who was at the event the previous year, or the sales person who wants you there this year:
- Will there be enough to talk about, people to talk to, and things to do, see and hear?
- Will the at-home audience be interested in it?
- Will your presenter be interested?

[1] *GWR Brand Handbook* 2000.

- Does the whole show have to be broadcast live, or could there simply be short inserts? If it's the latter, what happens on your stage for the rest of the time? Perhaps you need to arrange some giveaways or games for the visitors so your station stand looks exciting and inviting.

Then go and recce (make a 'reconnaissance visit') the site to visualise and anticipate where you'll be at the event and what you'll need to be able to perform there (either on or off air). Take the station engineer and someone from the sales team/promotions department with you. It always helps if those people are the same ones who'll be there on the day of the event, the conditions are realistic and you meet the right people on site (for example, the organiser).

Editorial questions might include:
- Does your position have a good vantage point?
- Will there be crowds? Some atmosphere is good, but you don't want to be right beside the toilets or the beer tent.

And technically:
- Will you be able to get access and permission to broadcast from the site or the event?
- Is the signal strong enough for an OB? Or will an ISDN line need to be booked? When by?
- What about signals for the radio car, backpack and mobile phones?
- Will there be a PA system at the event that the station can use, or should one be taken?
- What about other noise perhaps from generators, air conditioning or fluorescent lights, the event's PA system or the nearby warm-up area for the marching band?
- Are you able to use radio mics without causing or picking up interference?
- What's the layout of the building, grounds and the event itself?
- Consider the room needed for any or all of the following: a mobile studio, stage and equipment, commentary position, the crowd.
- Take your OB truck on the recce so you can check that it can get through the gate or under the barrier and that there's enough room for it to turn.
- Where's the car park? When can you have access to the site? Where is the refreshment tent and the toilets?
- How will you be able to get an electrical supply and how reliable will it be?
- Will anything be different on the actual day?

Now you need a meeting for anyone else who will have a part in the OB. That could be other producers and presenters, the engineer, marketing and promotions people and sales staff. Check with them:
- The date of the event.
- The location of and directions to the venue.
- The location of and directions to the pitch the station has been allocated.
- The arrival time for the OB staff.
- The start time of the event.
- Who will be there from the station (presenters, producers, sales staff, promotions staff).
- Their names and mobile numbers.
- Draw up a schedule and running order to outline everyone's responsibilities.
- Decide what the on-air commitment will be.
- Is there a signal for your phone or laptop, so you can download scripts, headlines, and weather reports etc. sent from the studio?

- What facilities will there be for pre-recording items and then editing them for later playout?

On that last point, organisers of large events (such as the Ideal Home Show, Boat Show and Chelsea Flower Show) often provide studio facilities for stations to broadcast their programmes, but because of the sheer size of such events (and because interviewees may not be available when you need them live) a presenter and producer arrive several hours early to pre-record interviews. These are self-contained so they sound live when they go to air. That means the interview may start with a back anno of the song that will have just ended. These are then played out from the event 'as live', giving listeners plenty of guests and lots of flavour of what's going on.[2]

By now you should be building up a good picture of what more needs to be done to make the OB a success, but there are more considerations:

- Get any necessary permission. This could be from the organiser of the event who gave their verbal agreement to you having an OB truck when you spoke on your recce, but didn't have the authority to do so. It may also be the police, council or traffic wardens. You may also need access passes, tickets or, for a royal visit, a COI Rota Pass. (The Central Office of Information distributes limited passes to local media on the understanding that audio and pictures are pooled, or shared, with those media who did not go.) Shopping centres, railway stations and so on are private property and you will need authorisation to be there (a programme at a railway station may need the agreement of the British Transport Police. To be able to use a radio mic from a hot air balloon you'll need permission from the CAA). Always get permissions in writing – never trust anyone.
- Start putting together a programme running order and briefs for each item/interview. What's going to happen, who the guests will be and so on. Make sure these people know what is expected of them.
- Prepare some background information on the event, so its history, organisers, timetable of events and so on are all to hand for the presenter.
- Consider what will be done in the event of wet weather. Could the event be changed or cancelled altogether? How will the event organiser contact you if it is?
- Security and/or crowd control. Is it necessary? Where will it come from? Is the station appropriately insured?

Whether you are broadcasting from an event or not, tell people about your presence: talk-ups and on-air trails before the day, banners and posters on site, together with giveaways and competition prizes. If yours is a commercial station you may be able to negotiate a deal with another company to supply the freebies. For example, a company with a new chocolate bar would love to organise its taste tests at your stand as you would both be attracting a similar audience. Work with them or, better still, get them to pay you for the publicity they will get at the event and on air!

Could you get extra coverage from your appearance at the event? Think of an imaginative way to draw the public, and the press, to your stand. Maybe you can get a local celebrity, or a national star to appear, perhaps the local majorettes, a school gym display or karaoke.

Make sure the station looks as good as it sounds. The stage should be well dressed with banners and posters. Make it look as though you own the event. Publicity material should be available (stickers, presenter photos, bugs and paper hats and so on; you may also consider

---

[2] Safeguarding trust issues mean that BBC presenters can no longer give the impression that an item is live when it isn't; they have to specifically use phrases such as 'earlier I spoke with . . .'.

some careers advice material, too), together with paid-for merchandise such as T-shirts and mugs. You will need people to staff the stand and to hand out the freebies (promotional CDs for example), and rota them so they don't work longer than they should and have rest breaks (staff shouldn't work for longer hours just because it's an OB).

If you don't have a large events stage you may be able to hire one through an event management company, which may also advise on the rest of the stand: such as providing you with an inflatable. Many stations own one of these, often in the shape of a radio. You can let children have a session for free and attract more people to the stand. Again you'll need to be able to staff the inflatable, and check your insurance company is aware. Make sure the blow-up remains clean and in a good state of repair.

All staff, on stage or off, should be dressed appropriately. It should go without saying that everyone should be neat and clean, be on good behaviour and not be seen lolling around the stand or smoking anywhere near it. Any station vehicles used should be washed and polished with the logos up-to-date and not fading or peeling.

Everyone involved in the OB should meet up again before the event. Everyone needs to be sure of their roles and responsibilities, and reassured that nothing's been forgotten. Consider a second recce, to reassure yourself that nothing has changed.

What to take on an OB

There are lots of items outlined above; these are some additional ones that you might need to have in your OB kit box and take with you. This standard kit should be checked out and in again for every event.

Essential kit:
- ☑ Gaffer tape, string, sticky tape and cable ties – to stick down cables or hold up banners.
- ☑ Station mobile phone – with emergency contact numbers for the programme controller, engineer, head of sales, promotions manager, etc.
- ☑ Laptop – so scripts and messages can be sent to you via a wifi connection.
- ☑ Pen and paper – for scripts, notes and requests.
- ☑ Money – for car parks, petrol, tickets and stalls.
- ☑ First-aid kit and accident book.
- ☑ Passes and permissions – so you can get in!

To help the programme:
- ☑ Radio-controlled clock – so the OB and studio are working to the same time.
- ☑ Clipboards – to hold together scripts, programme of events, questions.
- ☑ Plastic sheeting – to cover the clipboard and sales table in the event of rain.
- ☑ Paperwork – scripts, running orders, music and ad logs.
- ☑ Security/crowd control.

Promotions material:
- ☑ Banners – to publicise the station.
- ☑ Barriers – to keep the crowds back, or away from the transmission mast or generator.
- ☑ Freebies – stickers, programme schedules, presenter pictures.
- ☑ Business cards – to give to possible clients or contacts.
- ☑ Camera – to take pictures for the website.
- ☑ Audio recorder – to record vox pops or interviews for the OB or another show.
- ☑ Radio – so the visitors can sample the sound of the station.

For comfort:
- ☑ Tables, chairs – your staff can't stand up all day.
- ☑ Refreshments.

Technical items:
- ☑ Personal radios – so staff away from the stand can monitor output.
- ☑ Walkie talkies – so staff at the stand can keep in contact with reporters at the stalls.
- ☑ Mic flags – to help promote the station and look 'corporate'.
- ☑ Batteries – for the clock, the radio mics, walkie talkies, personal radios.
- ☑ ISDN kit/backpack (portable transmitter).
- ☑ Wet weather clothes.

On the day, check all the equipment again to make sure that you have got everything, and arrive at the site early. Meet your contact and go over your plans with them; do the same with the rest of the team when they arrive.

Do another signal check and risk assessment once your equipment is set up, and before the public arrives.

The broadcast bit of an OB

So far we've talked about the 'O' of the phrase, now here's what's involved in the 'B'!

Years ago mobile studios were all the rage. Songs, jingles and commercials were all duplic-ated so the entire programme could come live from an event. Then came a period when the presenter was on location with a mic and a mixing desk, and a technical operator played in all the other inserts from the studio back at base. Now we're moving back to square one – with a difference. Increased ISDN bandwidth means data and audio can use the same line, so a presenter on the road has remote access to the station's studio computer. This puts them back in control of the programme rather than relying on a TO (technical operator).

The next couple of paragraphs are for the many stations which still rely on a TO, on whom a lot of the success of the OB will depend. They will need to know:
- o The programme back to front.
- o All the junctions and regular features, and where the jingles and themes are.
- o Whether they need to play in any audio or pre-recorded interviews.
- o The in and out cues to all the links (or crosses, if you are contributing to someone else's programme, rather than presenting the entire show from the event).
- o What to do if it goes wrong, the line goes dead ('goes down') or the signal starts distorting.

When you are on an OB you need to make sure that you are able to talk to the studio TO down the OB mic while a song is playing, without your voice going to air. That way you can be in constant contact with them. See if the engineer can rig up a way for them to be able to talk back to you too. If not you will have to give the TO clear and specific instructions and hope that they understand and follow them. Alternatively, have the TO call you on your your mobile, every ten minutes or so, just so you are reassured that everything is running smoothly as the programme goes to air.

Your aim as a producer is to make the OB sound as seamless as a studio-based show. You will still have produced a running order and done your show prep, and balanced items of interest through the hour.

The trouble is that there are not always loads of people to talk to and things to describe at an event. That is why it will pay dividends to prepare material in advance if you can.

Pre-record some interviews and either play them out from the event or send them down the line (over the air, but not on air) back to the studio before the programme starts.

Another advantage of doing this is that in places like a county showground, where stalls are scattered over large areas, you need some material to fill time while you and your presenter race with a radio mic and back-pack, to another interviewee that you're going you talk to live.

When you are putting an OB programme together do not make it too tight or too loose: build in an item each hour that you can move or drop if you need to. It may take you longer than you had anticipated getting from the display of Shire horses to the majorettes' arena! Also, don't change the product: keep some regular programme elements (benchmark features), so the three-hour OB doesn't sound as though it is on a completely different station.

The live audience

Do not play just to the people gathered around the stage, remember those at home. It is a balancing act to keep the live audience involved and entertained but to also give a flavour of the sounds and sights to those who aren't at the location (by far your biggest audience).

Remember the listeners *and* the location:

◦ Don't let what's happening on location compromise what's on air.
◦ Don't let what's on air compromise what's happening on location.

Consider taking some pictures on a digital camera and posting them on your website or YouTube so those at home get to see what's going on.

After the event

◦ When you leave, help tidy up. The way you leave the site or event also reflects on the radio station.
◦ Thank the organiser. Personally on the day if you can, if not, then later by phone or letter.
◦ Consider a review meeting. What worked well in the lead up to the day and on the day itself? What could have worked better? Can it be fixed for next time? Who will make sure it is? Write this down so it is available for the next OB.

Risk assessment

As you can imagine there are lots of legal and Health and Safety (H&S) implications in running an OB. You may need to consider these points so you can complete a risk assessment form which helps you to realise your obligations to the safety of yourself, your colleagues and the public. You should really go on a proper H&S course, but in the meantime here are some main considerations for a radio OB.

◦ Be aware of cables that are lying on the ground around your stand that people could trip over, or other items that they could collide with. All leads should be taped down or secured over doorways.
◦ Gangways and fire exits should always be kept clear.
◦ You may need to consider the security of the public, especially if you have organised the event yourself.
◦ Consider the volume and height of speakers so deafness isn't caused.

◻ What about the effect of light or chemicals at the event? You may want to use strobes or dry ice and there are health implications for both.

◻ Make sure that any transmitting aerial and other live equipment is well guarded from the public.

◻ Ensure that you are not causing a nuisance. For example, drivers looking to see what you are doing, or staff at their place of work (say a factory) who may be distracted.

◻ Do not cause an obstruction to passengers or passers-by. For example, if a crowd forms on the pavement outside a shop, which causes other people to walk into the road.

◻ Are there any outside dangers? (It is forbidden to broadcast from a petrol station or near overhead wires.)

◻ Will you be near any machines, for example at a factory or on a farm, which could cause a danger to staff or the public?

◻ Does the station need extra insurance to be at the event or does the organiser have public liability insurance which covers you? (NB: if you sign an indemnity form to clear an event organiser from any blame should there be an accident, you may negate all the rights of your station's own insurance.)

◻ Does the OB crew need to wear any special clothing or need to hire particular equipment? On a boat you will need soft-soled shoes; in a factory you may need to wear masks, overalls, reflective jackets, ear defenders, hard hats or goggles.

◻ If you are thinking of travelling during the outside broadcast (perhaps a boat ride or pleasure train), is the operator trained and licensed? Do they have safety equipment?

◻ Is your own outside broadcast vehicle roadworthy and recently serviced? A reminder that the radio car or OB vehicle must not be driven with the mast up, or carry any passengers (other than station staff).

◻ Do you need weather protection for the staff or crew? Wet weather clothes, or wind or sun protection?

◻ Do you have emergency money and first aid equipment?

◻ Are animals involved? (Quite likely at a county show event or farm open day.) Will the animals have trainers or handlers with them? Do any of your crew have allergies or are any of them pregnant? Animals may resent intrusion into their territory and there is a risk of bites and scratches.

◻ If cooking is involved, consider whether the cook is experienced and using equipment which to safe.

◻ Does the weather forecast change any of the above? Are strong winds, driving rain, ice or fog forecast?

◻ Lifting equipment: is there any to help carry OB speakers and help put up the stage?

◻ Where will the radio car or OB unit be parked, and is there enough room to erect its mast?

◻ Are there barriers to protect the equipment from the audience – and vice versa!

Personal appearances

If you are the only person going to open a fair or fête you have a slightly different role than on an OB where you have the whole station behind you.

Call the organisers personally and check that what you have been told is what they are expecting. Check the time you are wanted, the location of the event, where you can park and (if appropriate) how much you will be paid, and who will give you the money.

Double-check what equipment you need from them and what you need to take. If you feel it necessary, ask for the brochure or programme of the event to be sent to you in advance, that way you can prepare notes for any speech, announcement or introduction that you have been asked for, and double-check the station logo and your name and spelling.

Speak to your promotions department. You will need a station sweatshirt or jacket to wear and some giveaway promotional items. Will you take them with you or will they be delivered to the event? What about a mileage fee for driving to the engagement and a few pounds from the kitty to spend on the stalls, so you don't end up out-of-pocket.

As a local personality you will often be asked to open or compere charity events *for free*. This puts you in an awkward position: it is difficult to say no to worthy causes which don't have much money, but you can't say yes to everyone and be out of pocket yourself. Going to these events is work as you are on display and meeting listeners and clients. It isn't really enjoyable because you can't relax. You are working and not getting paid, although other people, such as the catering staff, *are* working and getting paid. Choose a couple of charities that mean something to you, and agree to appear for free at two or three of their events each year. Then when others approach you, you can explain politely that you help these other causes and don't have time to take on any more.

The presenter's role

You are the station – the brand is reflected in you: how you look, dress and interact with the public. Everything.

Your behaviour at the event should be impeccable. It is fine having fun, that's what you are there for, but make sure it doesn't appear to be too juvenile. Be aware that some of the crowd won't be listeners and may try to disrupt the event with catcalling. Work out in advance how you will handle this. Some people have the ability to deal with hecklers but unless you are one of them it is probably best to avoid trying. A clever-dick put-down may backfire on you.

Image is also about not smoking. A group of staff wearing logo-ed jackets and smoking, in front of the stage, on it, or around the back of the rig, looks awful. If you need to smoke, remove your branding and walk some distance from your stand. It is unlikely there will ever be an occasion when it is OK to drink alcohol on your stand (indeed to do this while on duty may be breaking your contract).

When you are at the event, however bad it gets, keep smiling and keep up professional appearances. You don't want to let down yourself or the station. Back up the station and its policies on music or adverts even if you don't agree with them. Criticising your station or another one should not be done in public.

Always stay in character. If you are the 'grumpy old git' on the radio then that is what the general public is expecting, so don't disappoint by laughing and joking.

If you have to make an announcement, such as opening the event, start off by saying who you are, the name of the station and what show you present. You may have a couple of funny lines relating to life on the radio that you can tell both at this event and every other one. Thank the event organisers for their hard work and highlight some of the major attractions, and finally thank everyone for attending and ask that they listen to your station on the way home.

Then, meet and motivate. Shake hands, have a chat with stallholders and visitors and keep moving: don't wait for people to come to you. Smile and thank people for listening. Be polite. If you are assured without being cocky, courteous without being sycophantic and competent without being over-confident, you will form a strong bond with them. Because they will have met you, you will become *real* and they will have a greater loyalty to you.

Every interaction with a listener is important. If you meet them, there's a good chance they'll listen to you.

To the organisers, the event is the culmination of months of hard work and sleepless nights. To you, let's be fair, it is another couple of hours of gym displays, dodgy homemade cakes or dull conversation with the owner of a car showroom. You will be encouraged to stay beyond your booked time but be firm. The best way to do this is to drop into the conversation as early as possible, 'I wish I could stay but I have to rush off to another event after yours and I really can't be late . . .'.

PR and networking tips

- Leave internal jargon and politics alone. If you are asked a specific question then reply along the lines of 'We're Radio X, this is what we do and we think you'll like it because . . .'.
- You are the best ambassador for the station and programme you work on – sell it! Remember you are also a representative of other media too, perhaps TV, online media or the local newspaper which owns you. All these options may also appeal to the people you will talk to.
- Always wear your branded clothing for relevant events and take schedules or business cards to give out if relevant.

Be prepared:

- Do a little light research on the host and relevant organisation(s) before going to an event to learn more about their members, speakers, mission and focus. If you know something about the people you approach it's much easier to start a conversation – and to keep it going.
- Find out the format, timings, location, what to wear and if there are any event sponsors or special guests.
- Make a list of people you expect to be there and want to meet and if appropriate ask for a list of attendees in advance (or if only available on the day – take a few minutes to study it before you get going).
- Don't forget to prepare your 'personal pitch' – it shouldn't be a speech but you'll need it to introduce yourself to people at a networking event quickly and easily.
- Networking works best with a goal in mind: e.g. seeking out initial contact with someone, re-introducing yourself to a recently made contact, making yourself known to new officers/committee members or other representatives who could refer you on to their contacts.

Out and about:

- First impressions matter, the way you come across is very important – you are their first (or at least most recent) impression of the company.
- Always stay focused on the person you are talking to and maintain eye contact. Don't scan the room trying to decide who to talk to next (tempting though it can be – better to extract yourself and regroup!).
- Make a polite getaway if you need to move on (e.g. you need the toilet, you have to deliver something to a fellow guest or speaker or simply go for 'a close' by offering your card and saying how nice it was to meet them and you hope they enjoy the event).

- Show interest in the people you meet. You can make a great impression by asking a few thoughtful questions that arise from what they have told you about their work.
- Be confident, smile and make eye contact.
- If in doubt – listen first. An easy way to relax at a networking function is to take the focus off you by first listening to the other person. This technique also helps you gain insight as to how that contact can help you, making the connection that much stronger.
- Ensure you ask someone to repeat their name when you don't hear it. You need to know who they are so you can keep in touch!
- Use your business cards: always have plenty on hand and don't be shy about handing them out!
- If you talk too much, say too little or arrive unprepared, you can ruin your chances.
- Remember why you're here: to advance the business and to advance professionally. It's a social event – but a professional one. You want the people you meet to remember you as capable, competent and polished – so . . . never get drunk.

After the event:
- Thank-you notes and quick follow-ups to requests for information are little courtesies that mean a lot.
- Forward a link to an article of interest to a contact you met at a function.
- Send an e-mail with contact information for a referral to a contact.

Finally

PAs and OBs are great ways of reinforcing the station brand directly with the public. Never miss an opportunity to get involved in one: they are great ways of converting non-listeners into listeners, and listeners into loyal listeners. Be friendly, pose for photos and sign T-shirts. Ask people what they like about the station and your show and get instant feedback that will help you do a better job and increase your fan base even more.

8 The law, regulation and guidelines

**SKILLSET – NATIONAL OCCUPATIONAL STANDARDS
RADIO CONTENT CREATION**

<u>Unit content included in this chapter</u>:
RC1 Work effectively in radio
RC4 Contribute to the creative process in radio
RC5 Originate and develop ideas for radio content
RC6 Undertake research for radio
RC8 Pitch ideas for radio content
RC9 Evaluate ideas for radio content
RC10 Write for radio
RC11 Write for multi-platform use in radio
RC18 Select and brief radio contributors
RC19 Direct or commission others to create content for radio
RC21 Produce speech content for radio
RC24 Produce live radio broadcasts
RC27 Evaluate the success of radio programming and projects
RC29 Present a radio programme
RC31 Comply with the law when working in radio
RC32 Conduct yourself ethically when working in radio

This is just a guide to some of the main aspects of the law for broadcasters. Invest in proper legal training to save your skin, your career and a whole lot of money. There have been very high-profile cases where presenters have commented on ongoing trials (those of the mass murderer Dr Harold Shipman and childkiller Ian Huntley), and have lost their jobs as a result. Ask and cajole your manager for a media law session (perhaps in an e-mail so you have proof you requested the training . . .). Certainly get your hands on the newest edition of *Essential Law for Journalists*[1] and ask your head of news what sections you should read. You should also download Ofcom's Broadcast Code[2] and read the BBC's Editorial Guidelines[3] too, both of which give more information on what you can and can't say and why (and in the case of the BBC, what their complaints procedure is).

Remember, ignorance of the law is no excuse. Saying 'I didn't know I couldn't say that . . .' will not let you off the hook.

---

[1] Read more about *Essential Law for Journalists* here: http://tinyurl.com/n3cruf.
[2] The Ofcom Broadcasting Code can be read here: http://tinyurl.com/32td2j.
[3] The BBC Editorial Guidelines' site: http://tinyurl.com/32arvd.

Libel

Defamation is an umbrella term and covers libel (defamation in permanent form: what's 'published' in print or online or *what's broadcast*) and slander (what is said out loud, face to face).

Committing libel is a serious offence.

Libel is anything which:

▢ holds somebody up to hatred, ridicule or contempt
▢ causes them to be shunned or avoided
▢ lowers them in the eyes of right-thinking people
▢ damages them in their office, trade or profession.

So, are you liable to libel someone?

Libelling someone attacks their reputation. Think: 'Would I like it if someone said the same thing about me?' Calling someone a cheat, liar, homosexual, drug addict and so on could all be libellous . . . unless you can prove that what you said is true.

Watch out for these potential traps:

▢ Libel by innuendo – you don't have to say the libel specifically, the implication's enough. For example, dropping regular hints that someone is gay which, when added together, give the implication that they are.
▢ Nameless libel – not actually naming the person is no defence if it is quite clear whom you mean. If you described them or revealed where they worked and they could be identified from that information, you could be sued.
▢ Unintentional libel – ignorance is generally no excuse. If you made the comments about Mr A, and the clues you gave to his identity were too vague for him to be identified then you may still not be safe. What if the clues pointed to Mr B? He could then sue, even though you hadn't actually meant him at all.
▢ Libelling somebody just because everybody else is. Each repetition is a fresh libel, so stay clear of the more salacious stories you may read or hear.

There are a few defences that you may be able to rely on: one is if the comment is actually true, but you would have to prove that what you said was true, rather than the other person having to prove that what you said was not. And that could be pretty difficult, and expensive.

The station is responsible for any libel that is broadcast; it does not matter if the person who made it was a presenter, a guest or a caller. That is why it is important for you, or your producer, to take the phone number of callers you intend to put to air and to screen them; consider recording them or putting the programme into delay.

If you are discussing a contentious subject you should be listening out for guests libelling each other and be ready to take down their fader and distance you and the station from the comment. 'Well, that's your opinion and not the view of Radio X . . .'. *Do not* repeat what they just said: 'When you said that Charlie Farnsbarnes stole your song lyrics, you were giving your view not that of the station . . .', as that repeats the libel.

Then take a break or play a song and speak with the guest and explain what the problem was, and consider whether they should still be a part of the programme. If the libel happens with a listener on a phone-in show,[4] get rid of the caller immediately.

Libel can happen almost before you realise it, in the most innocuous of circumstances.

[4] See more on phone-ins in Chapter 21.

For example, the Radio X Roadshow at an OB. A presenter's on stage, running some fun and games and has asked for a contestant from the crowd which has gathered around the rig. A young boy is chosen from the audience and makes his way up the steps.

PRESENTER: Hi! Who are you?
JAMES: James.
PRESENTER: Hi James. How old are you?
JAMES: Thirteen.
PRESENTER: And what school do you go to, James?
JAMES: Blankstown Secondary.
PRESENTER: OK; and what's your favourite subject?
JAMES: English.

Up to this point all is going swimmingly (apart from the fact that the presenter keeps asking closed questions which are eliciting short answers) and there is no legal problem. You will probably agree this is just the kind of conversation that you have heard many times.

PRESENTER: And what's your worst subject?
JAMES: History, because Mr Cromwell smells of beer and fags and can't control the class.

You have just allowed James to potentially libel Mr Cromwell (if it is true, remember, there is no libel). Mr Cromwell has been identified by name, school and position, and what James has said will have held him up 'to hatred, ridicule or contempt', will 'cause them to be shunned or avoided' and will 'lower them in the eyes of right-thinking people' and 'damage them in their office, trade or profession'.

Do not insult people even as a joke, do not talk with heavy innuendo, cast doubt on whether someone can do their job, or suggest they are lying. Don't rubbish a product on air (there are some ways to get out of such a situation, such as 'fair comment', but a good rule of thumb is not to do it in the first place). Do not let any of your contributors do any of these things either.

Those who feel that they have been libelled have a year in which to bring a case against the radio station (three years in Scotland), so if the incident happens on your programme you have potentially a lot of sleepless nights ahead of you.

Just because they make these kind of comments on the TV show *Have I Got News For You* and follow them with the word 'allegedly' does not mean that you can. That show is recorded and heavily 'legalled' (checked by lawyers) before transmission. You probably don't have the benefit of either of those. Saying 'allegedly' after a libel does not cover you one tiny little bit.

Take particular care to avoid publishing defamatory material through your user-generated content such as material posted on message boards.

Contempt of court

The Contempt of Court Act 1981 states that a person is in contempt if they create a substantial risk of serious impediment or prejudice to active proceedings. As soon as an arrest has been made (or a warrant has been issued for an arrest), anything you say could influence the mind of potential jurors who may be listening to your programme. It is they who decide if someone is guilty or not, after hearing all the evidence put by both sides, not you.

You could be in contempt without realising it, but again, not knowing the law is no excuse. So, you can't say, 'I see they've arrested the man who attacked the woman in Blankstown', although you may be able to say, 'I see they've arrested *a* man over the attack on the woman in Blankstown' (note: '*a* man' rather than '*the* man'). The first comment presumes that the person arrested and the attacker are the same person, the second one (which is safer, but also ill advised) does not.

◀ **ACTUAL AUDIO**

NEWSREADER: A woman from [town] is due in court today accused of stabbing a 72-year-old man on Saturday evening. Twenty-seven-year-old [name] will appear at the town's magistrates this morning. Her victim was found in his home on [street].

BBC local station, June 2005

Here the use of the phrase 'her victim' implies that she (the woman named) *is* the culprit.

Never say anything about current court cases. Leave it to the journalists who should have had proper training (although that example above came from a news bulletin).

When the case is not current then you are able to say more. That is when:

▫ The arrested person is released without charge.
▫ No arrest has been made within a year of the issue of a warrant.
▫ The case is discontinued.
▫ The defendant (the person charged) is acquitted (found not guilty) or sentenced.
▫ The defendant is found unfit to be tried or unfit to plead, or the court orders the charge to remain on file.

But that does not mean you can say whatever you want, or allow others to, because you could still be found guilty of defaming them.

There have been serious and well-highlighted cases in the past of radio presenters passing comment on the serial-killer Manchester GP Harold Shipman and the Soham child-murderer Ian Huntley while those trials were actually going on.[5] In those and similar situations, the accused could have been released and the presenters jailed instead, for contempt.

No excuse

▫ *'It's not us saying it – we're just quoting him'* – One of the most common causes of libel actions is repeating statements made by people you interview and not being able to prove the truth of what they told you. If you quote something that is published elsewhere, say in a newspaper, and is libellous or defamatory, both the newspaper and your organisation can both be sued. You have repeated the libel.
▫ *'We're only denying a rumour'* – It is dangerous to repeat a defamatory rumour in any circumstances unless you're in a position to prove it is true. It is even dangerous to repeat the rumour for the bona fide purposes of contradicting it.
▫ *'We gave equal time to both sides'* – Not enough – you still broadcast a libellous statement

---

[5] The Soham case: http://tinyurl.com/mure4d and what happened to the two radio presenters: http://tinyurl.com/n7hfnp.

even if you let the person give their side of the story. The only safe way is not to broadcast the statement unless you can prove it is true.

o *'I said "alleged"'* – That word is used in court reports to show that the jury has yet to decide what information presented to them is correct. It has no legal protection.

o *'I only asked a question'* – 'Are you still beating your wife?' implies the person did so before, making it and questions like it highly defamatory.

o *'I didn't name anyone'* – But if you give enough information for someone to correctly identify them (perhaps how they look, where they work) then they could sue if what you say is incorrect (or at least if you can't prove that it's correct).

o *'I wasn't talking about them'* – Additionally if someone else (mistakenly or deviously) says the description fits them, then they could sue too.

o *'It was a joke!'* – Again, this is no defence.

> Veteran country singer Dolly Parton is considering legal action against US shock jock Howard Stern after he broadcast a fake recording which manipulated her voice to make it sound as though she was swearing and making racist remarks. In a statement, Parton said 'They have done editing or some sort of trickery to make this horrible, horrible thing. If there was ever going to be a lawsuit it's going to be over this'.[6]

Elections

There are also rules covering elections. If you break them you could cost the station thousands of pounds. Like the laws covering defamation and contempt, they exist to ensure fairness: in this case so each party has the same opportunities to persuade the public to vote for them.

Play safe as soon as any election is called. That could be:

o a general election

o a by-election

o a local government election

o mayoral elections

o Scottish Parliament election

o Welsh, Northern Ireland and London Assembly elections

o a European parliamentary election.

The law says that equal coverage must be given to each of the major parties during the election period (usually around five weeks), and that the smaller parties must be given coverage appropriate to their support. The start of the election period is always publicised: it may be the dissolution of parliament or the publication of the notice for the election.

If a candidate takes part in an item about their constituency (the area that they are trying to represent) then other candidates must also be given the chance to take part. Although the item can still go ahead without them, they must have been invited to participate in the programme. You can see how tricky things could become if a caller to a phone-in show

---

[6] *The Radio Magazine*, May 2008.

starts giving their views on the council tax during an election period, only for a producer to discover subsequently that they are one of the candidates. So do not mention elections. Leave it to the news people.

Here's a reminder why: in 2000, Virgin Radio was fined £75,000 for Chris Evans' on-air support of Ken Livingstone in the run-up to the London mayoral elections during his breakfast show.[7] Here's another: James Whale's contract with talkSPORT was terminated (and the station fined £20,000) in 2009 after he urged listeners to vote for Boris Johnson in the London Mayoral elections.[8] The station said he was 'guilty of a gross error of judgement which we found to be totally unacceptable'.

Incidentally in 2008 talkSPORT announced they were to stop using a freelance presenter, not because of anything they'd said on air, but because his name appeared on a leaked membership list of the far-right political party the BNP.[9] So, it's not just what you do at work that can affect your job, but what happens in your private life too.

Other legal issues

Children and young people

Briefly, children in court cases (those aged under 18) must not (except in very rare situations) be identified, that means by their name (or that of their parents) or school or even cub pack. It also means that if you inadvertently gave some information about the child (so small that they *could not* be identified) and another presenter, station or newspaper gave some more (also, by itself, not identifying them), the child may be able to be identified *when both 'clues' are put together*. This is called the 'jigsaw effect'. Do not talk about children involved in court cases.

Sexual offences

The jigsaw effect can also work with victims of sex crimes. You cannot identify anyone who claims they have been raped (either a man or a woman), even if a court throws out the case as unproven. You can, though, name the person *accused*, whether they are found guilty or not. The victim can agree to waive their anonymity but, to cover yourself, you must ensure that they put this agreement in writing.

Rehabilitation of offenders

The Rehabilitation of Offenders Act 1974 was passed so anyone who has been convicted of a relatively minor offence can live it down and get on with their life, without the incident being dragged up in the years to come. The length of time which has to pass before a conviction is spent depends on how long the sentence was in the first place. Generally speaking, do not comment on spent convictions.

The nations

Note that laws vary in different parts of the UK (that is, Scotland and to a lesser extent in Northern Ireland), and abroad. So if you are on holiday in the States and watch the TV news

---

[7] When Chris supported Ken, the full story: http://tinyurl.com/layf6p.
[8] What James said: http://tinyurl.com/kwzt38 and Ofcom's judgement: http://tinyurl.com/ltojc5.
[9] The story here: http://tinyurl.com/nhnr5f.

or hear a radio presenter commenting on an ongoing trial, remember: their laws allow them to, ours do not.

Regulation and Ofcom[10]

Codes of practice

Broadcasting networks operate under both voluntary and compulsory codes of conduct and practice. Ofcom's Broadcasting Code[11] relates to the principles your station adopts to guide its activities and relationships with the audience, and covers issues such as independence, programme content[12] and language, accuracy, fairness and balance; advertising and so on.

Ofcom has ruled that the heated on-air exchange that cost veteran speech radio presenter Jon Gaunt his job at talkSPORT was in breach of the broadcasting code. The regulator received 53 complaints about Gaunt's interview with . . . a councillor in the east London borough of Redbridge . . . In its ruling, Ofcom said it was concerned that 'the overall tone of Jon Gaunt's interviewing style . . . was extremely aggressive. Ofcom considered that the language used by Jon Gaunt and the manner in which he treated Michael Stark, had the potential to cause offence to many listeners'.[13]

As well as Ofcom, the BBC is governed by its own Editorial Guidelines,[14] and commercial radio by the Advertising Standards Authority.[15]

The incidents which came to light in 2008 (concerning the use of language, and misleading listeners in areas such as competitions[16] and over live/recorded programmes), moved broadcasting into the world of 'fraudcasting', and cost radio companies thousands of pounds and cost some presenters and producers their jobs. Such incidents certainly had the potential to damage the public's trust.

I found my boss being a lot more careful and he was saying: 'it's less to do with thinking Ofcom are on our backs and more to do with the fact that the public now know what Ofcom does.[17]

[10] Figures show that talkSPORT was the most complained-about radio station of 2007 with nearly 140 listener complaints, of which five were upheld. The most contentious BBC radio station was Radio 4, which attracted 75 complaints to Ofcom, none of which were upheld (source: Ofcom).

[11] The Code and how listeners can complain: http://tinyurl.com/amnarm.

[12] Radio presenters have been criticised for promoting heavy drinking so as to be seen as 'cool' by their listeners: http://tinyurl.com/l7q5dm.

[13] *The Radio Magazine*, May 2009 and this article: http://tinyurl.com/mpqbwq.

[14] BBC Editorial Guidelines can be downloaded here: http://tinyurl.com/32arvd.

[15] The ASA website: http://tinyurl.com/2g2y7a.

[16] Also see the chapter on 'competitions'.

[17] Anon, *The Radio Magazine*, February 2009.

Safeguarding trust[18]

◊ Are you planning or commissioning factual output that will give the audience the impression it is listening to something that it is not?

◊ If you are using creative artifice, does it have to be acknowledged? Is it demonstrably fair to contributors and listeners?

◊ When inviting participation, including competitions and phone ins, are you doing everything you can to ensure that everyone has a fair chance to take part or win?

◊ Don't say or imply something is live when it is not.

Everything now needs to be signed, sealed and approved 18 times. We're not trying to change the world but because radio is so dull and boring and so formulaic, anyone different – me or Jonathan Ross – stands out.[19]

We think that lively, distinctive and risk-taking radio is alive and well in the BBC. We have a duty to ensure all our programmes are editorially compliant, but that doesn't mean that our producers and presenters can't take creative risks if that means better programmes for listeners.[20]

ROTs

This stands for Recording Of (or Off) Transmission, in other words, a copy of what was broadcast. There are various different kinds of recordings, each with its own name.

Every station has to keep an audio copy (usually on hard drive) of everything that's transmitted for 42 days. It is the law. Called 'the logger' it allows the regulator (either the BBC and/or Ofcom) to listen in case there's a claim by a listener that something was wrong. It may be that they feel they were misrepresented in an interview or that they were libelled. An advertiser might want to check that the ads they paid for actually went out (there's often a paper ad-log that each presenter has to sign to verify that the commercials were played, but some advertisers may want to hear for themselves).

Failure to supply this recording is a serious and significant breach of the broadcaster's licence.[21]

Some stations also have an 'autorot' which is the same as the logger, but which staff can edit. It's usually on a hard drive and accessible from your desk. You may want to use this to take a clip of an interview for a news bulletin, take a clip of a guest for a 'drop-in' (short voice

---

[18] More on the BBC's 'Safeguarding Trust' policy: http://tinyurl.com/npxt2v.

[19] Chris Moyles *The Radio Magazine*, July 2009 . . .

[20] . . . and the BBC's reply, in the same edition of *The Radio Magazine*.

[21] Ofcom. This is a sobering tale: http://tinyurl.com/l7pqfg.

clip that you drop in over music), for the archives of great guests or for your review of the week/year show.

The 'snoop tape' is the recording (usually via the cassette deck in the studio) that starts every time the mic is on and pauses when it's turned off. It's used when a programme controller wants to review a show with the presenter. The snooped show stops and starts (it is 'telescoped') so only the links are heard, not the music. This means that one cassette can last for around four hours and that, during the review session, the programme controller doesn't have to continually fast forward through music and ads.

A 'dub' is a recording of a recording. If the programme controller asks for a dub of the programme, they want the whole programme rather than the snoop tape mentioned above. Ofcom may want a dub so they can hear a programme in its entirety, too. A guest might ask for a dub of their interview, and a company that's provided prizes may ask for one to hear how the competition was won and to check that their product got the number of agreed mentions. Dubs can be recorded onto CDR or sent as an e-mail attachment.[22]

A guest may ask for a transcript of a show, but they're unlikely to get it. That's because of the huge amount of time it takes to listen through a show and provide a written version of every word uttered. There are, though, several independent transcription companies[23] that provide this service for a fee.

Occasionally you may get a call from a solicitor asking for a transcript or a recording of an item that was broadcast, perhaps because they believe their client was libelled on the station. These calls should be passed to the programme controller. They will ask the solicitor to put their request, and the reason for it, in writing.

Finally

Remember, ignorance is no excuse and the purpose of training is not necessarily to find out how far you can push a comment or discussion, but to realise when you're heading for dodgy ground. Many radio groups have access to lawyers 24 hours a day, as well as senior managers or compliance officers, so check any problem or potential problem with them before it becomes larger. Do not try to handle it yourself or put a correction or apology on air without speaking to them, or at the very least to a senior producer or manager.

[22] This is a great free site to use for this: http://tinyurl.com/4or5v.

[23] Two media-monitoring companies: http://tinyurl.com/lsyfvn and http://tinyurl.com/kk79ou.

Part Three
INSIDE THE STUDIO

9 Knobs, buttons and switches

**SKILLSET – NATIONAL OCCUPATIONAL STANDARDS
RADIO CONTENT CREATION**

Unit content included in this chapter:
RC1 Work effectively in radio
RC12 Manage audio material
RC13 Operate a radio studio
RC14 Record audio on location & in studio
RC20 Assist with radio productions
RC28 Use and develop the voice for radio
RC29 Present a radio programme

The signal path

Before looking at the different equipment in the studio, it is useful to understand a small amount about how the signal gets from your studio to the listener's radio.

Here's a simple 'signal path' and the different sound sources being mixed through the studio desk, processed and then travelling to a transmitter site where the signal is broadcast . . . before being received.

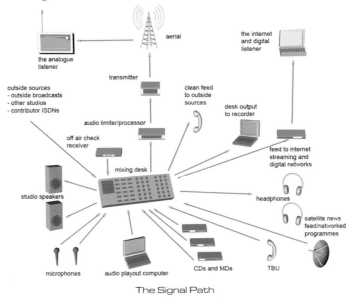

The Signal Path

Sometimes that transmitter is in the same building, which certainly cuts costs. If the signal has to travel to another location it's often via a landline (or landlines for a stereo signal), ISDN (with a coder or decoder at each end), or studio-to-transmitter link (STL) which sends the programme to the main transmitter over the airwaves.

Stations broadcast on AM, FM and DAB (internet simulcasting is not truly 'broadcasting' or 'transmitting').

AM	FM	DAB[1]
Amplitude modulation (Also referred to as 'medium wave')	Frequency modulation (Previously known as VHF – 'very high frequency')	Digital audio broadcasting
AM and FM radio transmissions are known as 'analogue' or 'terrestrial' broadcasts. The technology is well established, easily available and cheap to manufacture.		An upgraded version of DAB was released in 2007, called DAB+, but DAB-only receivers will not be able to receive DAB+ broadcasts. DAB+ is approximately twice as efficient as DAB due to a new audio codec, and can provide high-quality audio with as low as 64kbit/s rather than DAB's 128 kbit/s. DAB+ stations are to to launch in the UK between 2010 and 2013.
Lowest broadcast quality	Better broadcast quality	Claims of best broadcast quality[2]
Cannot broadcast higher and lower frequencies as well as FM can.	The most widely used transmitting/receiving system.	The digital information is decoded by a compatible radio receiver into sound, but this takes more power than analogue radio and leads to a signal delay.
Greater coverage area than FM.	Stereo capability.	Needs more transmitters to have the same 'footprint' as an AM or FM station.
Transmitters are more expensive to run than FMs. (As the music gets louder, for example, an AM wave increases in power, while an FM wave moves to a higher frequency).	Cheaper transmitters and receivers and cheap to run (up to 1/12 the power used to run a DAB radio).	Can use the same frequency for transmitting the same programme, even from different transmitters.

[1] More about DAB radio: http://tinyurl.com/lru7m3.

[2] DAB broadcast quality depends on the 'bit rate' of the processed audio. If too many stations are on the same multiplex, the rate can drop, and broadcast quality can suffer from drop-outs. And, although when a perfect signal is received it can be 'CD quality' (by reducing the bit-rate of audio on the other channels sharing the same multiplex, broadcasting in mono rather than stereo, or removing those channels completely), some experts claim the signal can sound a little flat.

AM	FM	DAB
Amplitude modulation (Also referred to as 'medium wave')	Frequency modulation (Previously known as VHF – 'very high frequency')	Digital audio broadcasting
Signals can be affected by electrical interference and the weather, buildings and night time.	·	Can also transmit pictures and text alongside an audio signal. Offers services such as pause, record, and tune-by-name.
Very crowded waveband.		Less pirate interference.

The studio

A studio can be the self-operated room in which the main desk is based and where the presenter is (a 'self-op' studio). However, it may also be the room with the studio desk, from where the programme is operated (by a tech-op or panellist) with the presenter speaking in another room (which may itself be called a studio or a cubicle), separated by soundproofed glass and linked by a talkback system. NPA is always the BBC term for the news studio from where bulletins are read (news production area) and the NCA is where contributors speak to other stations in the BBC network, from your station (network contribution area), although both of these may be referred to by the generic term 'studio'!

The area where a producer may sit (setting up guests, answering phones and so on) and from where they may also go on air, is rarely called a studio (unless it also happens to be one), although it may be called a booth, a production area or more usually an MCA (master control area – known colloquially as a mission control area). Or gallery . . .

Areas where audio production is done may additionally be called a workshop or an edit suite although this latter term is usually used in TV rather than radio. (And of course nowadays a 'production studio' might merely be a PC running an editing program on a desk in the corner of the room.)

Having said all that, for the purposes of clarity and brevity, let's call the place where the self-op presenter works from, 'the studio'!

Below is virtually everything you need to know about all the bits of kit in a radio studio. They are in the most logical order, but because a studio is a sum of its parts you will probably need to read everything through a few times so you can see how it all works together.

A studio is a room from which a sound is sent from a source, then monitored, balanced, and effected via a mixing desk to a destination (a transmitter, recorder, another studio or simply speakers). Studios can look complicated and daunting, but, like driving a car, with practice and training operating the controls should all become second nature (in fact, it's often referred to as 'driving a desk'). It doesn't matter how witty or incisive your comments or how creative your competitions are, if you can't press the right button at the right time, it's all going to sound very messy. You will get better at operating a studio the more 'flying hours' you put in: increase the hours and you will increase your skill and confidence.

Most stations have more than one studio: one for the live, on-air programme and another for pre-recording, voice-tracking or production work.

A typical BBC local radio studio.
(Courtesy: BBC London 94.9)

1 Anglepoise microphone.
2 The RadioMan audio playout screen used by BBC local stations and its operating keyboard used to cue and play songs, jingles and interview clips.
3 The screen used to assign sources to specific faders.
4 The faders. There's no big panel of knobs here – just little more than basic fader, cue and gain controls.
5 The visual talkback screen is used by production staff to tell the presenter information such as the name of the travel presenter and which caller is on which line.
6 This phone can be used by the presenter to patch or route phone-in calls through the studio desk, or to dial out on a line which can then be put to air via the TBU.
7 Studio headphones.
8 TV monitor and analogue and digital clock. The smaller screen next to the clock shows the scene from the NPA news studio so a presenter can be reassured a newsreader is ready for their bulletin. The lights under this screen will illuminate when (MIC) the studio mic is live, (RATS – Radio Alert Transmission System) the station alarm (for a major breaking story such as a royal death) has been operated, (RDS) the tone for travel news has been activated, (TEL) the studio phone is 'ringing'.
9 The talkback system. Note the microphone and the keys for the location of talkback receivers.
10 Professional MD and CD machines.
11 Level control meters.

Ergonomics, acoustics and aesthetics

Ergonomics

'Ergonomics' is how design can help reduce tiredness and discomfort.

The design[3] and layout of the studio are important, as the area will be used by a series of people, working by themselves, perhaps over night, for several hours at a time. Studio equipment is usually laid out in a U- or L-shape around a presenter so everything is within arm's reach (or is accessible through remote controls). Inevitably the layout differs from studio to studio as does the height of the desk. Some are of the 'sit-down' design, others are built so the presenter can broadcast while standing up, others have hydraulics built into them so their height can be changed according to the needs of each presenter.

Any computer screens should be about arms' length from the presenter (not only as they may be 'touch screen' technology, but also to reduce eye strain), and the top of the screen should be just under eye level. Monitors which are too high can cause neck strain.

[3] Various studio designers: http://tinyurl.com/kmuzh3, http://tinyurl.com/nmzopu, http://tinyurl.com/yzyettx, http://tinyurl.com/nsnkqm. See inside BBC network studios here: http://tinyurl.com/bohu9g.

Keyboards linked to a monitor should preferably be just in front of it rather to one side, so the user doesn't have to keep turning to see what they have written. The mouse should be usable without having to stretch.

There should preferably be a line of sight to your studio guest (obviously) and the producer (if you have one), as well as to any other studio, including the one where the news comes from. The latter issue is sometimes overcome with a CCTV camera set up in the news booth and a screen in the main on-air studio so the presenter can see that the newsreader is in position and ready to read. (As well as studio webcams, some stations also set up a camera in the studio with the pictures sent to a screen in reception so guests can see what is going on. Be sure to be on your best behaviour: rowing with your co-host or picking your nose will all be seen.)

Acoustics

'Acoustics' is the term to describe how sound behaves in a space.

When a noise hits any surface, some of it is 'absorbed' and some 'reflected' back. The harder the surface, the more is reflected. If the surface is irregular the sound wave will be 'diffused', if sound goes through the surface to the other side it has 'penetrated'. When building a studio, designers have to manipulate these characteristics to create a pleasing balance of echo and diffusion.

Some reflected sound can be absorbed in carpets, curtains and coverings on the walls. This will create a 'dead studio', with no reverb and a softer sound. Studio acoustics should not be completely 'dead'; a small amount of reflection makes the sound more natural. The opposite is a studio which uses irregular surfaces to break up sound reflections (rather than absorb them), which makes the reflections less noticeable and produces a harder sound. (This can partly be achieved by not having parallel walls.) Such a space would be referred to as (perhaps confusingly) a 'live studio'. (Additionally some studios have a live end and a dead end, called a LEDE studio!)

Recording and broadcast studio staff are having to report sick and being forced to take time off because the combination of their loudspeakers and their working environment is driving them mad. TV and radio professionals who balance, mix or dub music and speech programmes know that listening to harsh treble sounds or aggressive middle frequencies leads to fatigue. The symptoms include headaches, nausea, and tiredness. Hard-sounding speakers, in hard rooms are hard work on the ears. In today's bit-reduced, MP3 culture, convenience is put above audio quality.[4]

Soundproofing stops unwanted outside noise from leaking into the studio, and inside sound of the programme leaking out.

- o If the station is on a busy street the studio may be in the centre of the building so that noise or vibration from the traffic won't be heard on air.
- o If there is a window, it will be double-glazed with an air gap in between the panes to stop the intrusion of exterior noise, and the internal pane sloping down to reduce reflected sound.

---

[4] Harbeth Audio, speaker manufacturer, at http://tinyurl.com/lyqukc.

- Heavy soundproofed doors, tightly sealed and often in sets of two, with an 'air-lock' in between, are usually fitted.
- Walls, ceiling and floor will be covered with material to either reflect or absorb sound: the floor will be carpeted, the ceiling covered in sound-absorbent tiles and the walls covered in wadding and material. (Stations on a budget simply hang curtains on the walls – the use of cardboard egg cartons, as was the case in the past, is discouraged for fire safety reasons.) Some of the desk surfaces will also be covered in material, to stop sound reflecting from them. The colour scheme is often pale green or pale blue which are considered restful.[5]

You can test the acoustics of a radio studio, or any other room in which you are going to do some recording work, with nothing more technical than your two hands. Simply clap and listen for the sound that is made. If it sounds flat and dead then it is a well-treated room with little sound reflection. If there is an echo effect when you clap then it is not such a good room for recording in or broadcasting from: microphones pick up sound slightly differently from the way our ears do, and that reflected sound will be exaggerated.

Aesthetics

There are also other considerations that help make the studio a pleasant place to work for several hours at a time, perhaps alone.

Fluorescent lights should be avoided as their hum may be picked up on air, and they produce a harsh, glaring light. It is very important that the lighting is right for the programme and the presenter. They have to be able to read their scripts and screens, but also use lighting to create an appropriate mood for their show, so a dimmer switch is a good idea. Lights full on might be appropriate to give an intensity to a chart show, low lights will help create a 'love songs' environment. Spotlights on tracks can be repositioned for each presenter and made to point away from the screens and so a shadow isn't cast on the desk or keyboard. Anti-glare shields can be fitted to monitors.

The chair is an important part of the studio. Although some presenters do their show standing up (so they can be more animated in their vocal delivery to give the show more energy, and also because it's the best posture to use when speaking), most present sitting down, so it is probably going to be the most-used chair in the station! That makes it essential that everyone is going to find it comfortable. Not so that they fall asleep, but so they can sit upright and not get a bad back after a four-hour show. The height and tilt of the chair should be adjustable, as should the back. The chair may be armless so it can be pulled in close to the desk. It should have wheels so the presenter can turn easily from one piece of equipment to another.

Static build-up can be a problem in radio studios. Greater use of air conditioning, plastics and synthetic materials, combined with modern synthetic fabrics, can generate high voltages of static electricity that can result in a small shock, and trigger remote controls turning studio equipment on or off. The wheels of studio chairs often have rubber mats under them, and engineers also use anti-static spray on controls, or fix an anti-static touch pad that harmlessly grounds any build up.

The key to good working conditions for the staff and equipment is good ventilation. In a studio it's the playout machine that is most at risk, especially as it is often placed on the floor. That's where a lot of dust and fluff is floating about and being sucked into air vent holes, leading to the machine starting to malfunction: computer chips rely on cooling to stay operational.

[5] http://tinyurl.com/mfekfo.

The other studios

There are usually at least two studios at a station. As well as the main on-air studio, another may be a production studio for making commercials or trails, or for recording interviews or links (voice tracking) for an automated show. It may also be used for reading news bulletins from, and that means that other production staff may be asked to leave for a few minutes either side of the top and bottom of the hour, to allow that to happen.

If there is only one main studio, presenters have to perform a hot-seat changeover, when one presenter is tidying up at the end of their show and the next one is setting up theirs in the same studio.

The producer will probably be sitting in the control room (or ops room – operations room) separated from the main studio by a heavy door and thick double-paned glass, which keeps out extraneous sound. The visual contact with the producer allows the use of gestures and hand signals and for the presenter to use them as an 'audience' while they're talking to the unseen audience.

The studio is the place that everything goes through before it goes to air. All the station's work is channelled through this small room: the work of the sales and advertising copywriting teams, the promotions staff and the news, production, and music scheduling departments. Without a studio from which to broadcast, all the other departments are pointless. It is (arguably) the single most important part of the building.

That is not to say that a presenter should feel self-important and full of ego. Far from it. The presenter's job is to link together all the material provided by their colleagues in a relevant, interesting and compelling way – to make *their* work worthwhile.

Green Room

This is the room or area where guests wait before they go into the studio for an interview. It is close to the studio and should be clean and tidy and have a few comfortable chairs, a water cooler and some reading material (including station literature) . . . and with the station output on! Some interviewees may bring other people with them (friends, family, PR person . . . minder) and they usually wait in the Green Room while the interview goes ahead.

New technology

There are pros and cons of the increasing amount of computers in a radio studio.

- *An easier life* – presenters don't have to spend time cueing up records and then putting them back in their sleeves and filing them away.
- *Timesaving* – any piece of audio is played instantly at a touch of a button. That should mean that the presenter has more time to spend preparing what they are going to say, which makes for a more relevant, interesting and compelling show.
- *Digital audio* – the quality of the audio sounds better on air.
- *Accessible audio* – an item edited in one place can be played out in a studio, perhaps miles away, without physically taking it there.
- *Archiving* – saving audio is easy, cheap and takes up a small amount of room.

On the other hand:

- *Different makes and models* – there is more kit to learn, each with a slightly different way of editing, saving or playing audio.

- *Increased speed* – technology has made more things possible, but increased the pressure on getting things done.

In practice, each system is based on similar concepts and it does not usually take long to learn a new system. Indeed, any presenter makes themselves much more employable the more expert they become in the different makes and models.

The basics

Microphones – mics

A microphone is an acoustic-to-electric sensor that converts sound into an electrical signal: a thin membrane vibrates in response to sound pressure and that movement is subsequently translated into an electrical signal. The mic helps create the main live element of your output (rather than CDs and computer systems which play out pre-recorded items).

There are various types of microphone[6] for different situations, usually used when recording drama, concerts or when you are outside.

'Omni-directional' mics pick up sound from a wide area around the mic head and so are good when you have several interviewees around a table all sharing the same mic. A 'cardioid' mic is a type of directional mic, which picks up the sound that is right in front of it, a little to the sides and none from behind and so are the usual ones used in a studio where the presenter's voice can be picked up, but paper rustling and button pressing cannot.

The main presenter microphone is one of the single most expensive pieces of equipment in the studio: a good one can cost many hundred pounds. It gets a lot of use, though! Whereas guest mics tend to be quite basic and are placed on a stand on the table, the main desk mic may be held in place on a 'boom arm' (similar to that on an 'Anglepoise' lamp) that can be positioned wherever is comfortable for each presenter. Alternatively, it may hang from the ceiling with a complicated-looking system of wires and weights (simply called a 'hanger').

[6] A brief history of microphones: http://tinyurl.com/kva629.

Looking like the children's string game 'cat's cradle', an arrangement of 'elastic suspension shock mounts' keep the mic in place and protect it from knocks which would be heard clearly on air.

Although it is best to sit about 15–20 centimetres away from a microphone when you are speaking into it, presenters vary in the height and distance that they sit away from the desk and of course they all have a different volume of voice, so it is essential that the position of the mic can be altered. Another tip is not to talk directly into a mic, but position it so you talk across its head.

Position the mic so it is comfortable for you to work with, do not necessarily use it in the same position that the previous presenter had it. You can often position the mic so it hangs down to your mouth, point it up to it, or point it to your mouth from the side.

If you talk too closely into a microphone you will get a strange popping sound when you say words beginning with letters such as P and B. Put your hand in front of your mouth and say, 'Polly baked a piece of brown pitta bread' and you will notice the rush of air that comes from your mouth as you say the Ps and Bs. These are called 'plosives', as they explode from your mouth. (Say 'Tony toasted a wholemeal loaf' to notice the difference.) If you are too close to the mic when you say plosive sounds, the rush of air will be picked up and momentarily distort what you are saying.

On-air mics will, therefore, have a pop-filter attached to them. This is the foam-covering which helps disperse the air before it reaches the sensitive mic head. If your plosives can still be heard, alter the angle of the mic so you are not speaking directly into it, but at more of a 45-degree angle. That way the airbursts pass over and not into the mic. Additionally, some mics have close-talking shields built into them, made of fine mesh.

Another way to reduce plosives, especially in close-mic work, is using a pop-screen (different from a filter). Typically they comprise one or more layers of acoustically semi-transparent material such as woven nylon stretched over a circular frame and a clamp and a flexible mounting bracket to attach to the microphone stand. The pop shield is placed between the presenter and the microphone.

Check your mic, and set your levels off air before you start your show, and not by tapping it or blowing into it. Doing this can seriously damage expensive studio microphones. The best way to set level is to read a few sentences into it: just saying 'check' or '1 . . . 2 . . . 3' won't give you enough sound to set a good level. Also most of us will say a *sentence* at a different level to repetitively saying the same *word*.

With some mics it is not easy to see if they have been turned around the wrong way, and if you talk in to the wrong side then your voice will sound distant. There is usually a logo on the correct side to talk in to!

Some presenters use headsets with a mic and headphones in a single unit. These are also called FM microphones, RF (as in radio frequency) mics, wireless mics and radio mics, and are powered by a pocket-pack, the kind singers wear on stage. A lack of wires means they have the freedom to move around the studio or the station and use their hands. These mics are really mini-radio stations themselves: mic, transmitter (from the power-pack) and receiver (on the studio desk, which converts the signal back into audio). Remember that a problem with wireless mics is that they can pick up interference from other radio frequency users such as cordless phones. Another is that the presenter can have the mic too close to their mouth and end up 'popping'.

Sports commentators use 'lip-mics',[7] which are designed to be used close to the mouth to help cut out background noise. The 'roof' over the mic also protects against extraneous sound

---

[7] Lip-mics put to the test: http://tinyurl.com/lyvpfh.

and acts as a guide for the reporter on how close they should hold it (just above their upper lip). There's a fine mesh on that roof to stop breaths from the nose being picked up by the mic, and another inside the mic to help filter the breaths from the voice. As the manufacturer Coles Electrical Acoustics[8] says, lip-mics are 'perfect for cutting out the roar of racing cars at Brands Hatch or the screams of the little old ladies in the ringside seats at wrestling contests'.

When you go into a studio you should be aware of anything on you that could make a noise that may put off or confuse listeners. That means that mobile phones are turned off, not just put on silent, as the signal will still be picked up by studio equipment (another reason is that you need to concentrate on your show and not be sending or receiving personal texts). Also, take off bangles, bracelets or pendulous earrings that may make a noise. Bear this in mind if you are presenting an outside broadcast: the continued rustling of a nylon-textured raincoat every few seconds will drive your listeners mad!

Similarly advise any guests about phones, jewellery and coats. It is also an idea to warn them against touching the microphone itself, knocking the stand, banging the table or drumming their fingers on it. All these sounds will be picked up and magnified by the mic.

Some guests move away from their mic during the course of an interview. If you turn up the level on their mic, it will also pick up some of what you say too, as well as the hum of the computers and studio air-conditioning system. Before you start an interview, always ask a guest to stay about 20 centimetres away from the microphone.

The mics are controlled by a fader on the main desk (details later), but some older studios also have an additional button for the presenters or guests to use: the cough button simply lets you turn off the mic momentarily so you can clear your throat.

Feedback and other curious mic effects[9]

'Feedback' (or 'howl round') is a sudden, loud and high-pitched tone generated as sound from a speaker is picked up by a mic and amplified. That sound is then played out through the speakers, which is picked up by the mic and amplified again, and so on into infinity. In effect, the mic 'hears' itself.[10] Similarly, as your headphones are like mini speakers, feedback will also happen if you put your cans too close to a mic, or have them too loud and allow 'bleed-through' (excess noise 'leaking' from the earmuffs). It can also occur when the fader on a record channel is left open as you start recording (the 'source' sound is recorded and then played out by the recorder, only to be picked up as another source). Feedback is very serious, and even one exposure to it can do long-term damage to your ears. Stop feedback by reducing the volume of the speakers, or turning off the mic or the channel that you're recording to.

'Proximity effect' is an exaggerated bass boost that can happen when a sound source, such as your voice, gets closer to a microphone. If you move away from a mic, the bass diminishes. Some presenters use the proximity effect to their advantage: if you naturally have a thin voice, you can get closer to the mic to add bass. If you already have a bassy voice, close mic work will create a muddy sound. Of course if you get too far away, the more ambient or room noise will be recorded, so it's important to find a happy medium. If you need to get really close to the mic in order to defeat room noise, you might want to invest in a mic that has a bass roll-off switch. This allows you to cut out the extremely

---

[8] Coles Electrical Acoustics' website: http://tinyurl.com/mphy58.

[9] There's also the effect an open telephone channel can have on a mic, which is explained later in Chapter 21 on phone-ins.

[10] In radio, feedback is generally minimised by having the speakers cut-out (muted) when the mic is switched on.

low bass frequencies that would be enhanced by the proximity effect while still working close to the mic.

'Multiple microphone interference' is the 'hollow' sound when you have too many mics open at the same time, too close to one another. The audio is coloured and feedback is more likely to happen.[11]

Station logo and mic flags[12]

It always looks good when you see a presenter interviewed for the TV sitting in their radio studio, with a huge station logo as a backdrop. That may cost a lot of money, but at least have a poster or two showing the logo and frequency, or the logo on a mic flag (the box that is attached to the mic). It reminds guests where they are and makes the station look corporate.

Headphones – cans

Headphones are usually of two main types. Closed-cushion headphones (also known as 'circumaural') have a muff that surrounds the ear, providing more bass, cutting out more outside noise and reducing headphone leak. But they're usually heavier, larger and more expensive than other designs. Open-air headphones (or hear-through cushion headphones, or 'supra-aural') have a muff that sits directly *on* the ear which deliberately leaks noise (and are more common in studios these days because of Health and Safety requirements). They are lighter and cheaper but the sound which leaks from them may be picked up on air. Earbud-type headphones are rarely used in professional radio studios.

Circum-aural and
supra-aural
headphones.
Courtesy: BBC
London 94.9

---

[11] This effect is explained here and lots of information on how best to position a microphone is also given: http://tinyurl.com/nmzdw2.

[12] One of several companies that produce such mic flags: http://tinyurl.com/n5u992.

When a song is being played, the presenter can hear it in the studio through the speakers, but when the mic is turned on, the sound from the speakers is cut, to avoid feedback (see earlier). So, one reason why presenters need headphones is so they can monitor the programme and its levels when the microphone is open.

There are other reasons too:

- When a song is playing on air, the presenter needs to be able to hear how the next song starts. By flicking a pre-fade button (see later) they can listen to this other source in their headphones, without it being broadcast.
- It is similar when a guest comes in to the studio and their microphone level needs to be set. You cannot turn their mic on as it would go to air, so you listen on pre-fade through your headphones instead.
- The enclosed nature of headphones makes it much easier and clearer to hear what is actually going to air than listening via the studio speakers.
- Your producer can speak to you when you have the microphone open, by using the talkback system. Their voice will be heard in your headphones, but not go to air.

Always wear your headphones when the mic is on.

Most presenters like to sound big and butch as they present their show and perhaps move the various settings on the mic channel on the desk until they think they sound just right in their headphones. The truth is, though, that by the time their voice has gone through various bits of kit in the desk, racks room compressor and transmitter and into someone's stereo it probably won't sound anything like they intended; your headphones can give you a false impression of what you actually sound like. That is why many presenters like to work with one side of the headphones on an ear and the other side off. That way they can hear themselves as they *actually* sound, as well as what the studio desk is making them sound *like*.

But there are problems using this technique:

- There is an increased chance of feedback, as the sound from the off-the-ear half of the headphones may be picked up by the mic. The same problem can be caused by open-backed headphones that don't fully encase the ear, which is why many presenters prefer models such as the Beyer DT-100.[13]
- You can't properly assess the mix of sound that is being broadcast.

When you are on air, don't get too hung up on your voice. Concentrate on *communicating*. When you are doing a show the most important thing is what you say, not what you sound like.

> I've got to use my own headphones. Since the Health and Safety thing went mental, the engineering staff have put limiters on the headphones so you can't turn them up too loud, and if you do they distort. I like to use my own headphones because I like it nice and loud.[14]

---

[13] Beyer's headphone range: http://tinyurl.com/nqg733.
[14] Gareth Brooks, presenter, Xfm, *X-Trax* magazine, September 2005.

Limiters on cans are set to 93dBA as listening to loud volumes for a long period of time can permanently damage your hearing.[15] Many presenters like to use their own headphones. Whether they are fitted with limiters or not, it is much more pleasant to know whose ears have been up against that piece of foam!

Proper working headphones in a radio station are like gold dust. Cans are not always as robust as they were years ago and the electrical connections crack and break very easily. That causes sound to cut out in one ear either totally or intermittently, which is annoying when you are presenting a programme.

The main volume controls for the presenter and guest headphones are usually on the mixing desk, but an additional personal control may also be found next to where the cans plug into the desk or table. They are set independently to the speakers and the desk output that goes to air.

Incidentally, guests rarely need to wear headphones. They often don't need to hear other sources being prepared or to hear what the producer is telling the presenter (especially if it is 'They're boring, get them off!'), and may be put off by hearing the sound of their own voice. They will, of course, need headphones if they are asked to take calls from listeners in a phone-in.

Some studios have 'foldback' which means you don't have to use headphones. Foldback allows the studio speakers to be kept on, even when the mic is on, but you have to be careful to set the level so that foldback does not cause feedback!

Twenty per cent of Britons are hard of hearing, according to German researchers[16] who found that one in five 16–20-year-olds have inner ear damage from having headphones at too high a level.

Additionally, Colorado University found listening at 100dB leads to damage[17] after just five minutes.

There are no current European standards on volume controls for MP3 players, though under French law personal music players must be limited to an output of 100dB. The Apple iPod, which can reach 130dB, was briefly withdrawn from sale in France in 2002 until Apple updated the software to reduce the maximum volume. All iPods sold in Europe are now limited to an output of 100dB. In October 2009, the European Commission proposed the default setting on all personal music players to be 80dB.[18]

And shared earphones[19] collect 68 per cent more bacteria than having your own headphones would do, such as otitis externa[20] – which causes a painful inflammation inside your ear.

---

[15] Headphone-use advice sites: http://tinyurl.com/lqa5xg and http://tinyurl.com/npvqgm.
[16] Source: *Men's Health* magazine, July 2009.
[17] Go to http://tinyurl.com/2r4bhv to give yourself an online hearing test.
[18] Source: http://tinyurl.com/yaf9eye.
[19] Disposable headphone covers: http://tinyurl.com/827gkb and http://tinyurl.com/lg2y9u.
[20] More on this condition at: http://tinyurl.com/lemhkh.

Monitoring

You are wearing headphones to hear what is going out on the radio, but there are slightly different mixes of that signal that you can listen to.

◻ *Desk output* – you will hear what you are *sending to* the transmitter *from that studio*, but this isn't necessarily what is being heard by the listener at home. Another studio may be live (either inadvertently or on purpose) and also sending audio to the transmitter, or the transmitter may be broken and not transmitting anything. If you are only hearing what only *you are sending*, you wouldn't be aware of either of these scenarios. So, if you are in an off-air studio, to record a trail or a pre-recorded interview, *monitor desk output so you can hear what you are doing* (and not what is going to air).

◻ *On-air output* (or 'on-air feed/send', or 'programme feed') – selecting this will let you listen to what is actually being sent from the studio or the station to the transmitter, probably after it has been processed.

◻ *Off-air output* (or 'programme') – monitor the (perhaps confusingly named) off-air output (usually fed direct from a radio receiver tuned to the station) to hear exactly what the listener is hearing. The quality of your voice will be slightly different as it will have been through a processor to make it sound more resonant, and there may be some slight static, but you will be aware of any problems that develop.[21] It may not be possible to listen to off-air output on an AM station because of distracting interference. Digital stations have their signals coded before transmission, so monitoring this off-air output would be impossible (you'd hear yourself a second in delay). In such circumstances, the presenter is usually fed the on-air output (above) instead.

◻ *Delay* – this is similar to 'desk output' and used when a programme has a short delay into it for legal or profanity reasons.[22]

◻ *Cue* – so you can preview audio before/without it going to air. [23]

Monitor speakers (aka studio speakers)

A loudspeaker converts an electrical signal to sound, and so is the inverse of a microphone. In a studio, speakers are used to hear the output of the mixing desk, but cut-out when a microphone is opened, to avoid feedback. They may also cut out (if desired) when a PFL is used.

Speakers should be placed acoustically symmetrically to each other so you get a clear balance of sound, and if they are wall mounted they should be isolated with rubber shock mounts (if away from the wall, they should be a couple of feet away to prevent excessive bass boost). Some people claim the best sound is heard from speakers which are positioned at, or just above, ear level ('near field' or 'close proximity monitoring'), and to have them 'toed in' (angled towards the listener). Ideally the listener is based in front of and equidistant between the two speakers so, especially in a stereo environment, the sound is properly balanced. Have speakers either magnetically shielded or far enough away from monitors that they don't distort the picture.

You can of course change the volume of the monitor speakers for your own comfort either directly on each speaker or via a knob on the desk. But it is important to realise that their level does not affect the volume of sound going to air. So check the input and output levels on the desk independently of those on the speakers (or indeed, the headphones).

Near the speakers' control on the desk there is usually a 'dim button' to reduce their

---

[21] See elsewhere for which occasions you have to listen to the desk output.
[22] See 'delay' in the section on phone-ins.
[23] See the section on PFL a little later in this chapter.

volume instantly by a set amount. This allows you to more easily cue, prepare or talk to your producer. Restore the speakers to their usual volume when you can so you become used to that 'reference level' for all your on-air work.

Mixing desk

This is the piece of equipment that, as its name suggests, mixes the different sounds (or sources) as they go to a destination (the transmitter to be broadcast, or a recorder for editing or playout). A source could be a piece of equipment in the studio (the mic, a CD machine) or an outside source (or 'OS') from an OB, another studio, a phone call and so on. Even for the simplest mix, you need at least two sources which are controlled by the various knobs, faders and switches on the desk. For example, one to control the CD player and another to operate the microphone.

The mixing desk has three main functions:

o   It allows you to select and mix various audio input signals – such as microphone or music player.

o   It allows you to process those signals – most simply, to alter ('amplify') the volume level.

o   It allows you to choose one or more audio output destinations – such as the studio speaker (for monitoring), a recorder, or transmitter (for broadcast).

There is a series of faders along the bottom of the desk and above each of them is a row of buttons. Desks can look very daunting but are really quite straightforward: when you know what one 'channel' does (one vertical line of knobs) then you will realise the same principle is replicated across all the other channels. There are many makes on the market, but just like a car dashboard, they all operate in much the same way – they just look a little different.

On some older analogue desks each channel will only do what it is wired-up to do: one channel for the main mic, another for the CD machine, and so on. On others you can switch between different input sources for each channel – perhaps a CD at position A, turntable at B, and recorder at C. Doing this though, means you have to be very careful what source you have where, and when you want to use it: that's because, obviously, no two pieces of equipment can be used at the same time on the same channel.

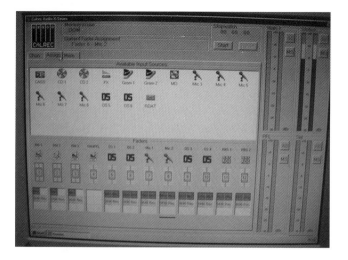

By clicking the icons at the top of the screen and dragging and dropping them onto the virtual faders below, a presenter can easily personalise their on-air desk

Now, digital desks have assignable channels (which makes them smaller and neater). Each presenter can decide which sources they will be using for their show and which fader they would like to control that source, by simply dragging and dropping icons on a screen, which re-sets the desk. So, if you have got a discussion programme with no music, you can easily change the CD channel to a mic channel instead; you can change the most-used main-mic channel to be where is comfortable and convenient. And that means you make fewer mistakes.

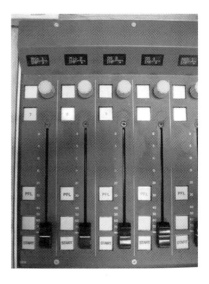

Finally, separating the different sets of channels is a space for your scripts – the script space.

Faders

On the desk, each vertical row comprising a fader and series of buttons or knobs is known as a 'channel' and each channel controls one particular source at a time.

It is called a fader because you use it to fade the sound up or down, by moving the button along a vertical track. Faders' slider-controls are different colours to make it easy for the presenter to see at a glance what each one controls. Although different stations assign different coloured controls (white, blue, green, etc.) to different sources, red buttons are often used for the main mic channels.

Think of a fader as a volume control: the further away from you it is, the louder the source on that particular channel (and the closer, the quieter). There was a time when all BBC desks worked the other way around (you brought a fader towards you to make it louder and pushed it away to get quieter). That meant that if you were asked to put the mic up, you moved the fader down, and vice versa!

Let's take an example of a simple mix using two channels, say one for a CD and another for a mic, and you will see how varying the position of each fader gives a different effect. To talk over the start of a track you would start the song with its appropriate fader at a low position and start speaking through the mic channel, the fader for which would be at the top. Assuming that you had pre-set your levels correctly, the listener would hear you talking at a normal volume with the music quietly playing in the background.

The effect can be altered by moving each fader – you may want the music louder than at half-level so move that channel's fader further from you. There will come a moment when the mix of voice and music will be optimum, beyond which the song drowns out what is being said. Those two levels are reached from experience, what sounds good on other stations you have heard, and what sounds good with the combination of your voice and that particular song on that particular occasion.

There are three ways to put a source, such as a CD, to air:

- You can put the correct fader up to the desired level, and then reach to the piece of equipment and press 'go' or 'start'. The disadvantage of this is that the machine may be some distance from you and you may have to turn away from the mic to be able to reach it. If the song is played off a touch screen in front of you though, it is quite straightforward.
- You can put the correct fader up to the desired level and then press the 'on' button below that fader on the desk. This is called a 'remote start' and saves you stretching across, or looking away to a machine and going off-mic, but it may be a split second between you using the remote and the source actually starting. Always gently press, or preferably squeeze, a remote start. Some presenters punch them, and the resulting click (or sometimes thump), can be heard on air.
- Or, you can use a 'fader start'. Activate the fader start for that channel on the desk (by pressing a small button alongside the fader). Then when you raise the fader by even the slightest amount from its 'home' position (the 'end-stop') the track will start playing. This can be convenient but it means the item will start quietly for a split second and you can't set the channel's level in advance.

All of these starts are quite acceptable; different presenters use whichever method they feel happiest with.

Be aware that on some desks, as well as putting the fader up to allow sound from that source to go to air, you may also have to make sure that the channel is on. You can do this at the start of the show and then it should stay on throughout.

Some larger studios have a 'master fader' that controls the level of final mixed signal going to the transmitter. If that's not up, then no matter what other faders are up, the signal won't go anywhere.

Often, when you raise a fader or press a remote start button, a clock will start running on that channel. This can be set to count up or down to show you time elapsed or time left to run.

Note that when you are about to talk, you do not fade yourself in, but you should open the fader fully before speaking and then close it smartly when the link has ended.

PFL (aka 'cue', 'cue switch', 'pre-hear', 'audition')

This is the 'pre-fade listen' switch, usually called the 'pre-fade', which does as its name suggests. It allows you to listen to the source of that channel before you put the fader up. The signal does not go to the transmitter or recorder, only to your headphones or studio speakers. Using it means you can preview the track, check it is the correct one, how it starts, set the level and so on without going to it blind on air. In other words, you have 'cued it up'. Cueing is important on a music programme so you can listen off air to the style and mood of the song and adapt your delivery accordingly.

You can also use PFL to talk to other people; for example, to check that a travel news presenter is at the end of an ISDN line before you introduce them on air. You do that by using the PFL together with the talkback system.[24] By pressing the talkback button on that

---

[24] See later in this chapter for a discussion of the talkback system.

channel you'll be able to speak to them (off air) down the mic (either the main studio mic or one connected to the talkback unit). Your voice will cut across their feed of what's going out on air (it won't be heard on air, unless you've inadvertently opened your mic channel) and you'll hear their response in your headphones or on the studio speakers.

Using PFL and the mic channel is often how presenters record phone calls with listeners off air, while a song is playing on air through the same studio desk.

When you use the cue button, the rest of the output of the desk will be muted (you won't want to hear the PFL track on top of the on-air track). Some desks have a switch for the headphones and studio speakers, so you can alternate between listening to the output in both ears, listening to the PFL in both ears, or having output in one ear and PFL in the other. This latter combination is useful so you can pre-fade a track at the same time as you are broadcasting. Make sure you know how to turn the PFL on and off, as it is easy to be distracted when one is left on or accidentally turned on – causing unexpected sounds, or the listeners to hear something while you hear no sound! Many beginners forget to cancel the cue, which means that the signal from that channel won't go to air.

If you are recording a programme, occasionally monitor its progress by switching to the PFL of the equipment it is being recorded on (do not put up the fader on that channel or you will get feedback and ruin the recording). You should hear what is going onto that channel a split second after it leaves the source . . . then switch back to monitor the 'broadcast'.

Levels

The best signal received by the listener depends on the best signal being sent to them, and to ensure that you need to be able to read your sound level meters. These show you what level of sound is being sent to the transmitter (or recorder) and may be at the top of each channel (so you can monitor each source) or, more commonly, may comprise just one meter which monitors the overall mixed output.

There are many types of meters; some comprise a row of green-to-red LED lights, others are more traditional in style with a moving needle on a graduated scale. The top of this is usually calibrated in decibels (dB) and the lower position in percentages (a bit like the mph and kph on a car's speedometer). 0 dB is 100 per cent volume – the loudest you want the signal to go.

A programme will have many peaks and troughs of levels every minute, most of which will go unnoticed by the ears of the presenter and listener. But it is important to monitor the overall output and keep a steady average programme level. Peak programme meters (PPMs) capture the high and low levels and then hold the information for a second, to give you some idea of the overall peak volume, so they may miss occasional sound bursts.

The level of your voice should peak at 6 on the PPM (which goes from 0–7), and music at around 5.5 (generally 80–100 per cent). Obviously, the meter will quite often show a level below this and occasionally above, but these are the average peak readings that you should aim for.

Sometimes the meters will show you that the level is too high (more than 100 per cent): on an LED system the lights change to red, on a needle display a separate red light will flash. This is a warning to lower the level of the appropriate source. It is acceptable to dip 'into the red' but if the signal is there for anything more than a few seconds it will be over-modulated and start to distort. (Often there is a metal peg at the far end of the meter. Letting the needle touch this because of a high volume, is called 'pegging the meter' or 'pinning the needle'.)

In practice, and with experience (and especially if you have your pre-recorded items, or headphones and speakers at a set level), your ears will tell you when levels are too loud (or 'getting too hot').

If the signal is too low (say around 20 per cent) then it is 'under-modulated' or 'in the mud'. If the presenter or producer has to consistently monitor and alter the volume of an item as it goes to air then they are 'riding the levels' or 'riding the gain'.

Levels are important for several reasons.

If you've got a channel that is peaking too high for more than a few seconds, the sound will start to distort (sound 'mushy' and 'squashed') which will be unpleasant to listen to. If you have a song that's too quiet the listener will struggle to hear it and may turn up their radio, only to have another source, at the correct level, boom out and surprise them. So, having standard levels at the studio end of the process means that only one person (you) has to alter levels of everything that's being heard rather than lots of people having to do it at home.[25]

Some music can sound loud even though it's not peaking very high. This may be because bass notes make visual level meters respond more readily than treble frequencies as they have more energy, because there is a 'full' sound such as an orchestra playing, or when you are mixing several sources.

Indeed the perception of loudness varies from one human auditory system to another, as it is affected by parameters other than sound pressure, including frequency and duration.

Some studies[26] show that the desired loudness balance between speech and music in audio broadcasts is influenced by the type of programme, the age and sex of the listener, and various other factors, and that the requirements of various groups of listeners are often contradictory.

Certainly, complaints of poorly mixed music and dialogue are often received by broadcasters, which in 2009 prompted the BBC to investigate further.[27]

Other factors to consider when mixing music with other music or with speech:

- In general, older listeners find it difficult to distinguish what is being said if the music level is too high.
- A music programme will be mixed differently from a news programme where the speech is more important than other sounds.
- It's also down to experience – make sure you use your ears! If it sounds wrong, it probably is.
- VU meters can overreact to bass frequencies from a source, so the total sound signal at that moment may not be read accurately.
- AM radio, also called medium wave, processes the mix of sound differently, so if you're broadcasting on one of these wavelengths make sure that the music is dropped significantly before you start introducing another input.

---

[25] Message board containing complaints about background music in natural history programmes http://tinyurl.com/nqkg7z.

[26] Research into 'The Loudness Balance of Audio Broadcast Programs': http://tinyurl.com/mxrjph.

[27] 'BBC launches probe to find out why so many of us can't hear actors on TV': http://tinyurl.com/nus6lw.

Remember Five Live is on AM and the sound is therefore heavily processed at the transmitters. Music has to be carefully balanced to avoid swamping speech or it disappearing completely . . . As a rough guide, if you're working on Sadie, Cooledit, or in the studio – balance the track under the speech so it sounds punchy and well-mixed, then reduce the music level by about 3dB for broadcast.[28]

When using a PFL or cue button, not only will sound be cut from the speakers and head-phones (so you can hear what is being rehearsed) but also the main meter will 'die', and respond only to the level of what is being cued. That way you can set the volume from this new source before you put it to air.

Signal-processing equipment

'Compressors' are based in the racks room (where the main computer and transmission equip-ment is based). These act like a super-expensive graphic equaliser on your home stereo, changing the bass and treble on everything. In other words, they 'process' the sound. In a complicated process, they can be set to give the impression of a louder volume without actu-ally altering the volume of the output at all. (Ever wondered why TV adverts sound louder than the programmes around them? It's often because the sound on them has been compressed to *appear* louder, not because it actually is.) To a certain extent, a compressor will be able to boost the quiet parts of a song and 'damp down' the louder parts – but it can only work with what it's given. By sending it the best possible mix of levels it will work hard to make them sound even better, but by sending levels all over the place it will struggle to cope.

Some radio aficionados hate compressors and say they make all the output sound the same with quieter parts boosted and louder parts quietened to fit into a small volume range. It is down to each station how theirs is set, but it is certainly true that to hear everything with so little variety in level can be quite tiring to listen to for any length of time.

Some stations have their own house rules on levels and require you to, for example, peak music at one level, speech at another and commercials at another. It is worth checking at your station what the guidelines are.

In general, it can be said that as processing is increased the total number of people listening to the station at least once within a given time period (typically one week) tends to rise, while average time spent listening falls due to long-term listing fatigue. On average, males are less likely to be irritated by certain types of processing-induced distortion than females. And the level of irritation also changes with the age of the listener: adolescents tend to be much less irritated by distortion than 40-year-olds. A canny programmer will use all of this information to adjust a station's processing to complement the target demographic of the station. The correct processing is the processing that maximises the station's share of its target audience, not the

---

[28] BBC Radio Five Live Style Guide; BBC Guidelines on mixing music: http://tinyurl.com/lxfj3k.

processing that satisfies purists. For several decades, all Optimod instruction manuals have contained the following text: 'Never lose sight of the fact that, while the listener can easily control the loudness, he or she cannot make a distorted signal clean again. If such excessive processing is permitted to audibly degrade the sound of the original program material, the signal is irrevocably contaminated and the original quality can never be recovered'.[29]

Processors can cost a few thousand pounds to many times that, and inevitably you get what you pay for. Some give the station engineer, in negotiation with the programme management team, a wide range of set-up controls to alter the 'sound' of the station. Considerable trial and error may be needed to achieve the desired effect – and even then what one person likes another may not. Some units are 'set-and-forget' types, while others can be re-set remotely and in real-time, depending on the content of the music show being transmitted.

Compression[30] can be set so the signal appears louder, but in the wrong hands can simply make it distorted. Another example might be to have the processor set so it boosts quieter moments of a transmission, but at the same time 'grabs' every breath of the presenter. (Engineers refer to 'attack time' as how quickly the volume is reduced once it exceeds a threshold, and 'release time' as how quickly a compressed signal is allowed to return to its original volume.)

'Limiters' are devices which stop too loud a volume signal being sent to the transmitter and can help reduce the impact of poor monitoring of levels through the desk by the presenter. However, the best thing is to record (and subsequently play back) everything at the correct level, to reduce the need for the limiter to do its job.

'De-essers' are particular equalisers which reduce the sibilant sounds by acting on the frequencies in which sibilance occurs.

'Special effects' processors can digitally create dozens of effects for example a chorus of your voice, change its pitch to make it sound like a chipmunk or the creature from the black lagoon, or give it echo and the impression you are in a bathroom or concert hall.

'Speed controls' can quicken the pace of an item without increasing the pitch (as would usually be the case) and can be used to shave a few seconds from an advert that's slightly too long.

Gains

Gain controls are usually at the top of each fader channel. The faders control the overall volume of the source; the gain control adds extra volume. The reason for using them is when you 'set your levels', you are ensuring that when each source is broadcast and its fader fully opened, the PPM is 5.5 (see above). However, on some quiet tracks you may have your fader right at the top and yet the level is still not peaking at 5.5. So, you turn up the gain slightly until it does.

Similarly, if you are playing a loud track, or have someone on a mic with a booming voice, put the fader all the way up, and then fine-adjust the volume by turning down the gain.

The rule of thumb is, when the fader is fully open the channel's audio has to peak at 5.5 and you should adjust the gain until it is. Use the fader to do just that: to fade something in and out; do not use it for setting your 'standard' volume, for example, by playing a song all the way through with the fader only half open because the song is peaking too high.

---

[29] Robert Orban, vice president and chief engineer, Orban/CRL, *The Radio Magazine*, June 2005.

[30] Compression in this sense is not the same as the process by which an audio file is made smaller to save on disk space.

EQ – equalisation controls

These buttons control different sound ranges for each source, through each fader. Acting like the graphic equaliser on your home stereo, by turning each one you can boost or cut the bass, midrange and treble sound to alter the tonal quality of what's broadcast. Turning the button say, clockwise, will increase the volume of that frequency range. An overriding 'EQ' button will turn the resulting effect on and off, so you can compare the audio with and without EQ.

EQ can also help remove unwanted sound for a recording: traffic rumble or electrical hum can be reduced by turning down the low frequencies, scratches on a vinyl record or a background hiss can be less obvious by turning down the high frequencies. Or you can make a voice sound 'thin' and more trebly, as though someone is speaking on the phone.

It's usually easier to eliminate/significantly reduce an individual noise (such as a scratch) or a constant noise (such as background traffic rumble), than it is to cut out noise from closer and occasional traffic where each engine has a different frequency. Use EQ with care or the audio may sound much worse: less is more. That's because the controls affect all of the sound, even the parts of the audio that you want *un*changed.

So using EQ is usually a compromise between reducing one problem and creating another, and of course is subjective. It is rare to need to use EQ in an on-air studio, though they are widely used in production. In these cases it's often better to EQ the final mix when different sounds can be heard in relation to each other, rather than to EQ each sound as it is input.

Pan controls – (aka 'panoramic controls')

These can alter the perception of the location of the sound to the listener at home, by changing the balance of the programme between the left and right output channels. The rotary control's 'home' position is at the equivalent of 12 on a clock face. The further it is turned to the left the more the sound of that particular source will appear from a stereo's left speaker. The further to the right, the more it will come from the right speaker.

Consider a situation where you are interviewing two guests. Ordinarily, you would all appear to come equally from both left and right speakers of a stereo, but if you turn the pan of Guest 1's mic slightly to the left of the home position, and that of Guest 2 slightly to the right, they could appear to be separated in the listener's room – just as they would sound if the listener were sitting in the room with you. (Indeed this is called 'separation'.) In drama the effect can be used to give the impression of someone moving across a room.

Care must be taken when using pans. A subtle use is invariably best. Someone listening at home will become confused or annoyed if different sounds appear to come from widely different parts of the room.

Sources

Potentially there are a number of sources that are needed on even a basic studio desk. Two mic sources and another two or three for the audio playout system. Other sources might include a CD player, news studio and various ISDNs and phone lines.

You make different sources appear on different faders by re-patching the desk (plugging wires from equipment to different sockets on the mixer) or doing it electronically via a screen.

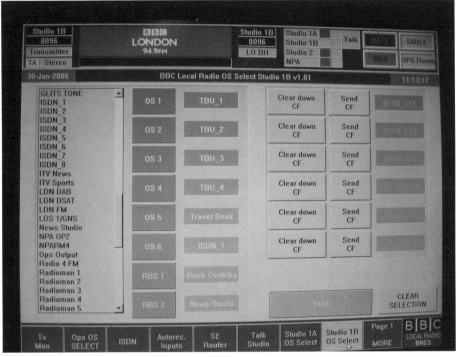

A BBC radio touch screen BNCS system. Through this, the producer can assign any source (some of which you can see on the left) to any of the outside source channels (OS1—6), send clean feeds, put different studios to air on different transmitters and dial up ISDN numbers. (Courtesy: BBC London 94.9)

ISDNs

This is short for Integrated Services Digital Network. It's a high-quality phone line used for carrying audio to and from radio stations, for example, from a remote studio such as a travel centre or satellite studio. It's got a similar connection to a phone line and is usually routed through the desk and comes up on a fader.

If you're dialling a contributor you will need their ISDN number (just like a phone number), which you usually key in on a phone-like pad. Be aware that there are several systems available and they're not all compatible with each other, so check before you rely on the link working.

Tones and feeds

The 'tone generator' is a bit like the audio equivalent of TV's test card. To help set the desk levels to a standard 'norm', these generators emit a tone (either 700 Hz or 1 kHz) that you can use as a reference point. They are most usually found in production studios to make sure that the playback level of a pre-recorded item is at the optimum (that is, best *not loudest*) level.

You may have a guest in another studio, maybe one owned by a PR company, and be dialling them on the ISDN. The 'line-up tone' is the signal sent back down the ISDN line to you, to show two things: that a connection has been made and (because the single tone is of a set frequency) what level has been set for the microphone in the other studio. You will then have to send the remote studio the sound of your programme (the feed — the actual output), so the guest can hear your introduction and questions.

There's a difference between a 'cue feed' and a 'clean feed' that you may send down the line. A cue feed is the actual programme as it goes to air: the music and presenter mixed with the contribution from the guest in the remote studio. In other words, the guest will hear themselves in their headphones as they talk (albeit with a slight delay after their voice has travelled to the main studio and then been fed back to them). Contrast that with a clean feed, in which the remote contributor hears the programme *without* their own voice. This may be to avoid feedback, for example if the guest is hearing the presenter on a loudspeaker rather than through headphones.

Patch rack

These are increasingly rare now that digital desks allow you to assign different sources to different channels with the click, drag and drop of a mouse. The racks, or 'patch panels' or 'patch bays', look like old telephone exchanges and allow you to easily change sources by plugging leads between input and output channels without getting into the internal wiring of the desk. Using them means that equipment which is rarely used can be moved from one studio to another and can be connected to the desk through the rack and male and female connectors (known as 'plugs' and 'jacks'). The top row of sockets is usually where the audio is coming from, and the bottom row where it is going to – connect and configure the audio signals as necessary, remembering to use two cords (or a single, double cord) for a stereo signal.

The lights

These lights are usually seen outside the studio or production room as well as replicated inside for the presenter and guest to see.

Red light

A red light is usually wired so that whenever the microphone is turned on this 'on air' light is triggered. It can mean that the studio is on air (of course, a studio may be live without a mic being live; a mic might be live but not the studio!). A flashing red light (which is rarely used) usually means 'stand by', that the studio is *about* to go to air.

Never enter a studio with a red mic-live light unless you are beckoned in by the presenter on air, or if your need is urgent. Then, open the door quietly and close it manually behind you (don't let it 'click' shut with the closer).

If waiting in a studio to collect or give something to the presenter, wait patiently until the red light has gone off (not just until they have stopped speaking, they may be playing a jingle and talk again when it has finished), and until they have taken off their headphones. This is not just so they can hear what you say but also as this signifies the end of their current link.

When you are in a studio with a presenter, they may say 'stand by' to alert you that they are about to turn the mic on.

Green light

Well, if a red light means 'stop . . . mic live', green means 'go!'.

In a situation where a presenter is being driven by somebody else, a producer may make the decision when they want them to read the next link. (When a programme is 'self-opped', that choice is of course solely down to the presenter.) So, a red light would show that their mic was live, but a green light (which would follow a few seconds later) means 'start talking now'. For this reason a green light only stays on for a few seconds. It is usually based on a console on the presenter's table.

An alternative to a green light is for the producer to physically point at a presenter through the glass from the production studio to the talks studio: this is a 'manual cue' or 'visual cue'.

Blue light

This light, not in common use, signifies that that studio is being used, possibly for rehearsal. The rules of entry are similar to those for a red light, wait for permission to enter the studio. To barge in or creep in quietly may disrupt the proceedings; for example, a dry run of a complicated link or timing of a programme insert.

White light

This may be on the desk or may be on the wall of the studio alongside other lights. When it flashes, it signifies to the presenter when a phone is 'ringing', probably the studio XD line which should be answered as soon as is practically possible.

Orange light

This is usually the fire alarm light, which flashes. An alarm in a small, enclosed studio may cause considerable problems if it rang while the mic was on. If the presenter was speaking on air at the time and wearing headphones, it could cause considerable damage to their ears. If this light is activated, put on a pre-recorded emergency CD or put the playout computer into automatic mode and leave the studio.

Obit light – obituary light

There is no set colour for these but they are usually labelled as 'obit alarm' or similar. They're activated by the station's national news provider and signify that a VIP (such as a major royal or the prime minister) has died.[31]

Talkback unit

This is the internal communication system through which you can talk to people in different parts of the radio station and to outside sources. The unit has different buttons for different locations. Simply press and hold the button for the location you want to speak to (for example, another studio or the newsroom) and talk about 10 or 12 centimetres away from the mic. The mic you use may be one connected to the talkback unit (sometimes called the 'squawk box' as it can suddenly squawk at you like a parrot without warning) or a small condenser mic built into the desk, or may be routed through the main on-air mic. After speaking you need to release the button to be able to hear the reply, through a speaker in the talkback

---

[31] There's a section on obit procedure later in this chapter.

box, the main studio speakers and/or your headphones. Your conversation will not be heard on air (unless you have the mic channel open at the same time).

There is certain etiquette in using talkbacks:

▫ There's the problem that you can't always actually see the person you are talking to. Many times, people at radio stations have wanted to criticise, say, an engineer to a colleague in another studio and pressed the button labelled 'Engineers' by mistake! Check you are about to press the correct location button.

▫ There is no warning that the talkback box is about to burst into life. As the unit is often on someone's desk (or, going to a presenter, directly in their ear), to suddenly speak in a loud voice can make them jump. Press the button and keep it held for a second before you speak so they hear the background sound of your location and are ready to hear what you have to say.

▫ Start your message with the courtesy of saying who you are and where you are: 'Hi, it's John in the newsroom . . .'. It's basic: that way the person you have contacted knows which button to press to be able to reply.

▫ Of course, you don't know whether someone has heard your message until you hear a response. Is there anyone actually in the area that you've called? Have you pressed the right button? There may be no one there, in which case, try your message a minute later. On the other hand the person may be on the phone and unable to reply, so don't just keep repeating the message.

▫ It's protocol to always answer a talkback message, especially one from an on-air presenter who may need assistance urgently (a piece of equipment may have failed or they may need someone to play in the next song while they go to the toilet). Therefore never turn the volume down on a talkback unit and never ever turn it off. To do either of these is almost a sackable offence: the needs of the on-air presenter always come first.

▫ Remember that your message is being heard loud and clear to whichever area in the station you've selected on the unit. So be careful what you say. You don't know (because you can't see) that the managing director or editor is showing a local dignitry around the newsroom just as you launch into a tirade about another presenter.

So much for using a talkback to another area of the station. What if you are using it to talk to someone during their on-air shift? The talkback audio comes into the studio, either through the talkback speakers, the main studio speakers and/or the headphones, but when the microphone channel is open (as it would be if the presenter is speaking or about to speak) the speakers (main and talkback) are automatically shut off. So, when the mic is open, talkback can only be heard through the presenter's headphones, not even the guest's. This is great because a presenter can be given direction by their producer without anyone else hearing: 'Mary is on line 4 with the correct answer', 'You've forgotten to go to the travel news' or 'Your guest is starting to get boring, can you wind up the interview, please?'

However, if someone on the talkback speaks too suddenly, it may make the presenter jump and possibly let out an oath on air. If they speak too loudly the same thing might happen plus, the message may 'bleed out' (or leak) from the presenter's headphones and be heard on air through the mic. Last, but not least, it can be very confusing for someone to be talking on air and suddenly have another voice telling them something at the same time. It's not too bad if you are doing a straightforward link, but much more annoying if you are in the middle of a penetrating and serious question and suddenly, without warning, you can't hear yourself but instead hear a (possibly irrelevant) comment from a colleague.

If you need to use talkback to speak to a presenter while they are on air, first check they are not actually speaking at that moment. If they are and the comment can wait, hold fire until they play a song. If they're in an interview and it's urgent, wait until the *guest* is speaking. Then, double check you're about to press the correct location button, squeeze it and hold it for a second to give the presenter time to register that someone is about to speak to them. Then, without shouting, give a succinct message and clear the line. Remember, they may not be able to reply to you on the talkback if they are actually live at that moment, so don't keep repeating the message thinking that they didn't hear you.

A presenter's temper can go from placid to furious if, while conducting an in-depth interview in the studio, they suddenly have someone shout, 'How many sugars in your tea, Sue?' several times by someone wondering why Sue (in the newsroom) isn't replying to their message being sent to the studio.

On occasion it *is* necessary to talk to a presenter while they are talking themselves, for example to help them with a question for a guest if they are floundering or to correct an important inaccuracy. At these times, hold the button for a second, then speak slowly and succinctly in a normal voice and release the button.

Other equipment

CD machines

Professional stations, and many hospital and university stations, nowadays use a computerised playout system, with songs played off a hard disk, rather than having the presenters cue up CDs individually. However, CD machines (the first piece of digital equipment used at stations) are often kept in studios for back-up in case the playout computer crashes and also for music features when certain non-core songs aren't on the system. A studio would usually have two CD machines, so while one is playing, another can be cued (although some professional CD machines allow you to select one track while another is playing from the same CD, the two cannot be neatly segued). Most CD players cue to the start of a track, though you can set some to cue to an index point within a track.

Always set the timer on the CD player to count *down* rather than *up* – you need to know how many seconds are left on the track, not how many there have been. And it is always wise to PFL 'end play' on each track (not every CD machine has this facility): first, to familiarise yourself with it for the forthcoming segue, as once the track starts there won't be another chance, and second, to check the timing on the track. Some CDs have poor duration information and you could have several seconds left on the track even once the display shows 00:00. Alternatively, it may end 15 seconds 'early' or, after a period of silence, there may be extra noise recorded on the end of the song or the song may restart, which is what happens with the Beach Boy's song 'Barbara Ann', of course.

Other features on a professional CD player may let you stop the machine after each track or continue to the next, or play the tracks non-stop in a specific order.

Turntables, carts, DATs, MDs and cassettes

The use of turntables was dying out towards the late 1990s as more and more recordings came out on CD. However, they are making a reappearance for a few reasons. First, because not every song has been released on CD, so if a request programme wants to play an obscure track then it may be that the only recording available in the station library or from the BBC's central gram (gramophone) library, is on disc. That is just as true for specialist music shows of the type heard on many BBC local stations, such as a big band programme or a show-tunes programme. In these instances the discs are usually copied onto minidisk or CD before being played out on air. And of course other specialist programmes may only have their material released on vinyl. Finally, some presenters just prefer playing songs from a record rather than a CD, especially if they are doing a dance mix show, as a turntable allows them to mix beats and to scratch the songs much more easily (although such facilities are available on some CD and computer systems).

Remember, if you're using a turntable, it will take a second or two for it to pick up speed. So find the start of the track with the needle on the record, and then manually move the turntable back a quarter to half a rotation. Then when you start the record playing (about half a second before you need it to start on air), the music will not 'wow' in. At the end of playing a record, take down the fader so you don't broadcast the next track or the repetitive scratches at the end of a single.

Cartridge machines,[32] or 'carts', have probably died out from studios completely but in their day they were incredibly useful. Inside a plastic box (about the size of two packets of playing cards side by side) was an endless loop of tape, of various durations between 20 seconds and five minutes. Jingles, sound effects, signature tunes, commercials and sometimes songs were recorded on the tape.[33] Once a cart was played in a special machine, it automatically re-cued to the start by detecting an electronic pulse that was put on as it was originally recorded. Carts were bulky and despite being re-recordable they had to be wiped clean with a demagnetiser before each use. The main reason for their decline though is that computerised playout systems now hold all the audio one needs at the touch of a screen.

DAT, or digital audio tape,[34] was hailed as a huge step forward in technology in the 1990s. The small cassette-sized tape worked like a video recorder with slowly rotating heads. The sound quality, being digital, was very clear, but DAT had its drawbacks. The tapes were very difficult to cue accurately and they were very prone to being chewed up by the machines. They therefore fell out of favour and are now mainly used to archive long recordings although not always with good results.[35]

Minidiscs[36] (MDs) are good because they are robust, reliable and high quality; they can record in mono or stereo and are re-recordable, are editable, you can move tracks around on them and they're cheap. However, some audio aficionados say the compression on an MD can be too overbearing.

Cassette[37] players, remarkably, still have a place in even the most advanced studios. It's because they are cheap, rarely go wrong, are easy to use and because most people have a cassette player at home.[38] That means that if a guest comes for an interview and wants a recording of their contribution, it takes little effort or expense to run off a cassette copy as the programme is being broadcast. Cassettes are also used for presenter snoop sessions,[39] where a telescoped recording of the programme is made without the songs or adverts. The cassette player is linked to the mic channel; it starts recording every time the mic is opened, and goes into pause when it's closed.

---

[32] More on the historic cart machine: http://tinyurl.com/ljr8ap.
[33] The Retro Radio 1 Cart Machine Simulator: http://tinyurl.com/2hgdpo.
[34] The history of digital audio tape: http://tinyurl.com/2obrj6.
[35] 'Archivists Warn: Don't Depend on Digital Tape': http://tinyurl.com/nbswd3.
[36] Minidisc frequently asked questions: http://tinyurl.com/mskcee.
[37] More on the history of cassettes: http://tinyurl.com/kvgzcd.
[38] Make your own 'virtual cassette': http://tinyurl.com/yv22ph.
[39] Radio 1 jock twitters about a snoop: http://tinyurl.com/lljczj.

The screens

Playout systems

Virtually all of the audio that is played on the radio comes from a single playout system.[40] That's the songs, the jingles, the pre-recorded interviews or news stories, the competition sound effects and the ad breaks. Once recorded onto the system, items such as songs and ads are loaded on to the studio playout system automatically, taking direction from the music scheduling computer and the ad log computer.

Other audio, such as jingles that the presenter has a free choice in using, can usually be accessed through another screen on the same system. Some pages of these may be open to all presenters, others may require a log-in so each host can have their own personal bank of effects or personalised jingles to which only they have access, via 'hot keys'.

Audio is usually played out either by using a keyboard or touching the screen.

Such automation has several advantages:

- It takes the drudgery of repetitive tasks (such as cueing CDs or putting records back into their sleeves) away from the presenter so they can concentrate on more important things such as devising a compelling link.
- A presenter has the time and technology to record items through the desk or edit other pre-recorded items, while a song or ad break is playing.
- Information can be tagged to what's being played out, so the presenter instantly knows an artist's concert dates, album release date or chart position.
- Music that goes to air can be more easily controlled by managers who set an automated playlist to be loaded and can retrospectively check whether any unauthorised free-choice (or 'pirate play') songs have been added by presenters, which may break format.
- There is automatic logging of songs (for PRS) and commercials (for clients' billing). A printout of the latter can certify that an ad booked for a certain daypart or to run alongside a certain feature was played at the correct time.
- The playout system is integrated with others at the station to save on time and personnel.
- Songs, news clips, adverts are all instantly accessible by more than one person, and can be edited non-destructively, and archived easily.
- By putting the system into 'live assist',[41] songs, jingles and ad breaks can be played seamlessly to air, perhaps on overnight or weekend shifts or to allow a presenter to prepare material. Links and drop-ins are automatically backtimed and played out in professional segues. At smaller stations, 'live assist' may be used when a host has a different live show on two stations at the same time (presenting a live link on one service while songs segue on another and vice versa).

Although songs are cued automatically (they are loaded onto the playout system by the computer and their title showed on screen), pre-fading how an item starts can be tricky. The more expensive systems have two or three soundcards so you can listen to a song off air while something is playing on air. More basic systems with only one card won't let you do this as the song you are checking will be heard on top of the item you have chosen to broadcast.

---

[40] DRS radio automation software: http://tinyurl.com/kp95jw; Jutel's RadioMan: http://tinyurl.com/m3futb; Google's RadioAutomation software: http://tinyurl.com/asujqr; radioBoss software: http://tinyurl.com/mx3dul.
[41] See 'automation' and 'voicetracking' later.

Also be aware of the configuration of the desk faders in relation to the playout screen's sources. In analogue studios the record player to your left would be controlled by a fader on the left, and similarly with a deck on the right of the presenter. Similarly a presenter could have chosen to always have say, the travel jingle (recorded on tape and housed in a plastic cartridge) in the same 'cart slot'. But as a screen plays items sequentially, each is controlled by one of two (or possibly three) faders whose use simply alternate. That means that the same pre-recorded programme items appear on different faders throughout a programme.

Text screens

As well as a talkback system described earlier, messages can also be sent from the production area to the presenter onscreen, for example, saying who has won a competition or who the next caller is to a phone-in. This system may be as basic as two screens linked together or may be part of an ENPS-type system, and is usually called a 'visual talkback'. (ENPS is the Electronic News Production System used throughout BBC news as well as in many programme production departments. The sophisticated network allows the easy sharing of news stories and messages between staff.) There may also be a screen showing text messages and e-mails that have been received.

TV monitor

It is quite usual for a radio studio to have a TV in it, so you can keep abreast of the news, so keep the channel tuned to the BBC News Channel, Sky News or a text page.

Be careful how you refer to the use of the TV screen. Certainly never say that you are watching it. Even if it's a news item just make an oblique reference, 'I understand that the prime minister has just left Downing Street . . .' or at the very least use the term 'monitor', rather than TV. 'I can see from our studio monitors that another plane has just crashed into . . .'.

The reason? Why tell your listeners that you are watching TV when you are supposed to be working? It gives them the signal that something is more interesting to you than keeping them entertained. Additionally, they may pick up on what you say and turn on the TV and turn off your programme.

◀ **ACTUAL AUDIO**

PRESENTER: 'We're not supposed to watch TV in the studio, but on GMTV this morning . . .'

Commercial station, January 2006

The phones

Phone lines and TBU ('telephone hybrid')

Stations usually have half a dozen lines from which they can put callers to air. This is usually done through a computerised switchboard and a TBU, the call then appearing on one of the channels on the desk. The TBU is the 'telephone balancing unit', which increases the quality of the phone signal through automatic gain control and noise filtering.

Presenters can talk to a caller off air once they have been put through to the studio. This is usually done by pressing the PFL for the phone line channel (to hear them) and then the PFL for your mic.

By pressing just the PFL on the phone channel you will be able to eavesdrop on the caller as they wait on the line (so you can hear as they rehearse what they are going to say to you).

You can often record a telephone conversation with a caller off air, while your programme is on air. Doing this gives you the opportunity to edit and tighten up the conversation for later playout. Make sure the correct channels are selected to be sent to the record channel otherwise you'll also record the output. Similarly ensure those channels are not going through the desk and being heard over the song that's going to air!

Callers should be reminded to turn their radio down or preferably off when they are about to go on air, or there'll be feedback (as their voice from the radio is picked up by the telephone microphone). In a 'delay' system they'll be battling to be understandable as they hear their voice from the radio several seconds after they've said it.

When a caller is on air, the TBU will usually 'duck' their voice under that of the presenter, so the host is able to take precedence and to prevent feedback in the telephone. The ducker must not be set so it is too sensitive though, otherwise every word of encouragement ('Yes', 'I see', 'Go on') will throw their level down for a second making their argument incomprehensible.

On occasion the presenter's voice can sound distorted (hollow or tinny) when talking to a caller. This is because the telephone line can change the phase of the audio at different frequencies as it's mixed at the desk. To counteract this, dip the phone fader slightly when you are talking and dip yours slightly when the guest is talking.

The 'mute to call' button allows you to say something on air over the top of a caller, without them hearing what you are saying.

Phone delay

Delay equipment is used so if a caller makes an obscene or legally dubious comment while through to the studio it never actually goes to air – even though they think it has. In delay, the caller and presenter talk 'live' but the rest of the audience hears the conversation around seven seconds later.

Years ago, when a station went 'into delay', the station output was rerouted through a machine which had a replay head seven seconds back from a record head. Nowadays, a digital machine is likely to stretch out what is being broadcast (by cutting out fractional moments of the broadcast) until the desired delay (or 'buffer') is reached over the course of a few minutes. Only then can a presenter safely take calls as the programme is stored electronically and then released in a continuous flow to the transmitter.

In order not to confuse everybody taking part in a delayed programme, the presenter must listen to the *desk output* rather than the *off-air output* which would normally be moni-tored. If they don't, they too will hear themselves seven seconds after they have started speaking! And it must be stressed to callers that they must turn off their radio and only listen for the presenter to introduce them down the phone, for the same reason.

Here's what happens in a delay situation:

PRESENTER: And now here's Sue on the line from Northport. Hi Sue, what are your thoughts on the rise in local bus fares?
SUE: The people who run the buses should f★★★ off!

As soon as you, the presenter, hear the obscenity:

- Push the 'dump' button connected to the delay machine to immediately switch the station output back from the delay (seven seconds ago) to the *desk* (what you're putting out right now). The seven seconds leading up to the comment have been erased from the delay's memory and are never put to air, and the caller is automatically disconnected.
- You carry on talking making no reference to what has happened: 'Sue, Sue? We seem to have lost Sue but if you want to call us then our number is . . .'.
- Start the procedure for going back into delay before you take another call, and then return to listening to off-air output.

Sue is left thinking she's shocked the world with her comments but in fact the only person to hear it was you! The rest of the listeners are none the wiser that anything's gone wrong.

Although talk radio stations such as LBC 97.3 and talkSPORT have output delay systems, they're rarely fitted, or used, at BBC local or small commercial stations.

Taking calls to air was never quite as risky as we made it sound . . . we were protected by the seven second delay, so when people did call up and try and scupper us with libel or swears we were pretty protected. It didn't always work though. One night a guy called up and said 'Iain Lee you are a c***'. I dumped it but the system didn't quite work. So it was dumped on FM but was still broadcast on DAB and Sky.[42]

The studio XD – batphone or boss line

This is the XD phone line in the studio which may be used (but shouldn't be) by a colleague who doesn't want to call on the usual number, but is more likely to be the police asking you to put out an appeal for a missing person or your programme controller congratulating you on your last link.

You may find that your PC may also use the 'hotline' to call you in the middle of your programme to criticise or complain. Unless you've made a basic error or said something that needs to be rectified immediately (perhaps you allowed a caller to defame someone), most managers' feedback (especially negative) should be given face to face after the show, not on the phone during it. Otherwise your concentration is thrown while you deal with the call and the conversation could affect the rest of your performance. Not everyone agrees with me: I know of one station manager who, fond of strong drinks, once called a presenter more than a dozen times in an hour while under the influence. This affected the presenter's performance; they stopped thinking creatively and understandably felt intimidated. It may also have stopped a real emergency call getting through to the studio.

---

[42] Iain Lee, presenter, Absolute Radio, *The Radio Magazine*, July 2008.

Don't forget!

Clocks

Some studios have digital clocks but most have ones with traditional faces and hands, and that all-important second hand for accurate timings. That second hand may either move second-by-second or 'sweep' around the face.

The clocks are radio-controlled[43] so all of them in the building, and indeed the country, tell the same time. They are fallible though, if the signal cannot get through from Cumbria, which may mean you introduce a feature early, or late. Many studio desks have built in clocks or stopwatches, so you can easily monitor the duration of an item or programme whether it is live or pre recorded. Playout systems have on screen countdown clocks to show time left to play, with the digits often flashing about ten seconds before the end of the item.

Whiteboard

This includes basic reminders such as the phone-in number, as well as updated information such as the current rollover total for the Mystery Voice competition, which presenter is filling in for who, reminders for shows or features to promote and so on.

Webcam

These are increasingly common in radio studios so listeners can *see* what is happening as well as hearing it. Such cameras should be visible to you as a presenter, rather than hidden, and there should be a notice near the camera warning guests that the camera is operating.

There may be another CCTV camera which shows what is happening in the studio on a screen in reception so guests can see what is going on. These two cameras are likely to be live all the time, so be careful how you behave!

Studio protocol and etiquette

As the presenter it's down to you to make sure that that product accurately reflects everything that everyone else has worked towards. Most non on-air staff don't realise that you design links and plan what you are going to say before switching on the mic, so if someone suddenly bursts into the studio it risks causing a distraction. Presenters also often have little idiosyncrasies about putting things in certain places and follow strict routines. If someone walks into that space and inadvertently upsets it, they risk disrupting the host's whole presentation . . . and affecting the whole station's product.

There are few places where this is more important than in *studio protocol* (i.e. *who* goes into the studio, *when* they're allowed to and *what* they may or may not do).

There are occasions when someone from, say, sales needs to enter the studio to check up on something. The problem arises when they barge in, grab the ad schedule, have a moan, cross something off the schedule and walk out again.

Friends and guests will rarely be allowed to sit in the studio with you as you present your programme. This rule helps protect the presenter who doesn't like to say no to friends who are always asking. The studio is not a place to 'hang out'.

---

[43] The radio-controlled clock: http://tinyurl.com/jwu7w.

If you let this rule slip then before you know it you will be joined by the head of news who wants to borrow a newspaper and stays for a chat, the silent work experience person who hovers over your shoulder, a sales exec wanting to book you for a personal appearance at the weekend, your producer asking about tomorrow's guest and the 3rd Great Blankstown Cubs on a station tour. When you slip up and play the wrong song, who'll look stupid? You. The station is only as good as the sound coming out of the speakers.

If a tour is hovering just outside the studio door, and you think that it is going to come in, look busy. Put your headphones on to give the impression you are about to speak on air. Some presenters will also nudge the mic fader open slightly so the 'mic live' light goes on outside the studio, and that deters visitors further. Alternatively, or additionally, look busy on the computer or go searching for a CD in the racks, or fill out an important looking form. Or turn the speakers up really loud.

If the tour still ventures in, keep your answers polite but short and then explain that you will gladly do the tour or explain the workings of the desk *after* the show, but not right now.

It is very likely that at a small station the manager will also have an on-air shift and colleagues may be tempted to treat the studio as an extension of that person's office. The way to get rid of them? 'Sorry, I'm the DJ. The station manager is back at 12.'

If you find you've got five minutes for a chat, you're not working hard enough. Your studio is your stage.

Although the hosts may be commanders of the space, that position is temporary. This is where the concept of studio etiquette comes in. When you finish a radio show, you hand over control to someone else and *they* become the 'captain of the ship', and *you* the deck-hand. Clear out anything that shows you've been there: CDs, magazines, scrap paper etc. Set all the necessary controls to off ('zero the desk') and pull down all the faders – except of course the one which is sending audio to air.

Food and drink shouldn't be in the studio at all. You may like a can of Coke or a hot milky coffee, but the desk won't. The water and sugar will gradually rust and corrode the elements inside, resulting in expensive and time-consuming repairs. Some stations ban all food and drinks in studios; others say that only water is allowed and that either cups are placed well away from the desk, or spill-proof sports bottles are used and placed on the floor.

Most presenters need a minute or two when they take over to focus and arrange the studio around them. It doesn't help if they have to spend the first five minutes cleaning up after someone else. If you're really good, you will watch how the next presenter arranges the studio, then next time set it up that way before you leave.

During your own shift be as clean and tidy as possible: the more organised you are, the faster you will be able to find what you want, when you want it.

Turn up at least an hour before your on-air shift. It shows professionalism and also gives you time (although arguably not enough) to ensure all of the elements of your show are prepared. You can read your e-mails, post and memos, and acquaint yourself with any changes. Arriving on time regularly also means that if you fail to appear, the programme controller (or at a weekend, the presenter of the show before yours) can call your mobile to check what's happened and if necessary arrange cover.

Turn up in the *studio* at least ten minutes before your programme starts. This gives you time to log in to the computer, set the mic level, assign sources to the faders and cue your first few songs. At some stations you are obliged to talk to the current presenter about what is in your show (a 'handover'), as well as taking control of the output ('putting your desk to air') and playing in the news bed. All that means that you can't bumble in to the studio while the news is on.

Additionally, it means that you should listen to the presenter who is on before you so you can comment on a song, feature or a comment they have made. That way the station sounds more 'joined up' and fluid, giving listeners fewer opportunities to tune out.

Walk, don't run,[44] to the studio as you may arrive out of breath.

Studio fault log

Studio faults, such as a piece of equipment not working, should be logged here, together with your name and the date. This is so the equipment can be repaired and other presenters be made aware of the problem. The station engineers will date the entry when they read it, add the progress of the repair, and then the date once the item's been mended.

This fault log is also the place where you will write non-urgent messages to other members of the station team. This may be a song clash, wrong song or intro duration on the playout screen, an ad break featuring two car showrooms, and so on. The programme controller will look at the log daily and bring any problems to the attention of the appropriate department.

You should refer to the log before you start your programme to note, for example, if the CD player is skipping, the studio chair has lost a wheel or one of the phone lines is faulty.

Obviously if there is an urgent problem, such as a complete transmission failure or an ad for a sale today that still says 'starts tomorrow' then you should call the relevant manager immediately to alert them.

Competition[45] log

This is the place to log all the winners to every competition run on air. It is what the promotions team will go to before they can send out the prizes from a competition. It's what you should look at before you run any competition to double check the 'mechanic' and to make sure that the same person isn't winning again and again.

Studio bible

Every station should have one of these, but like the logs mentioned above, not every one does.

It is the place where all the important memos and procedures are kept for every eventuality on the station such as:

- *Staff office, mobile and home numbers* – personal numbers should never be given out on air, but you may need to contact the head of sales one weekend if a disgruntled advertiser calls you, or the head of music if a major artist dies[46], and you want to know if you can schedule some of their songs.
- *Other emergency numbers* – local police stations, your national news provider, the on-call lawyer, the local councils'/electricity/gas/water press officers, Floodwatch and so on. One station added the number of the Samaritans: a good idea. Callers in the middle of the night may contact the station because they're desperate and you can pass the number on.

---

[44] 'The Ventures': http://tinyurl.com/5u4vpj.
[45] More on competitions in Chapter 19.
[46] How radio failed to respond to the death of Michael Jackson: http://tinyurl.com/mvgo6b.

- *Snowline and Stormline procedures* – this will outline what to do when winter weather strikes: who to call, the changes to the programmes and so on.
- *Bomb threat forms*[47] – are used if a caller to the station makes a threat (either against the station or anywhere else). Yes, it may be a hoax, but that's for the police to decide. Your job will be to complete the form while the caller is on the line, or soon after, with details such as their likely age, accent, location and what they actually said.
- *Complaints*[48] *forms* – most people who call to complain just want to let off steam and, if you deal with them correctly there and then, don't want to take it any further. Some want blood, and this is where you note down the details so you can pass it all on to the programme controller: the complaint, the complainant's name, address and phone number.
- *Pronunciation*[49] *guide* – how do you pronounce those small villages in the back of beyond in your area? Or foreign or difficult names? People expect you to know, and you will do by looking them up here.

Obit procedure[50]

There's more on the procedure later, but here it's important to note that a copy of what to do should be in the studio at all times. The obit procedure ('obit' is short for 'obituary') will tell you what to do when a VIP (for example a royal or top politician) dies. It may be that the death is announced during the day, in which case there will be plenty of staff at the station who will help out and advise, but it may happen overnight (such as that of Diana, Princess of Wales) or at a weekend when you'll be on your own.

The procedure will tell you how you will be likely to hear officially about the death, who on the station staff to call, the songs to play and the changes to the schedule. Included in this file will be a few CDs of appropriate music.

You should read this procedure regularly. Being on air and coping with a royal death is not when you should be going through the plan for the first time. In the past, stations, presenters and newsproviders who have broadcast inappropriate material at a sensitive time like this, or none at all,[51] have been criticised by the newspapers and their listeners. Don't let it happen to you.

House style guide

Everything that goes out on air reflects the ethos of the station and a lot of branding and imaging techniques will be laid out in the house style guide. Some stations are very disciplined and have very tight styles, even down to what presenters say out of songs, or what jingles are played and when.

A brand-enforcing style is necessary, especially in such competitive markets as today's. When was the last time you went into McDonald's and were greeted with the phrase 'Welcome to Mickey D's, would you like a large burger?'? Never! It's always referred to as 'McDonald's' and a 'Big Mac'.

---

[47] 'Actions To Be Taken On Receipt Of A Bomb Threat': http://tinyurl.com/mlmufw.
[48] More on handling complaints in Chapter 24.
[49] 'The Oxford BBC Guide To Pronunciation'; http://tinyurl.com/mb3nxj.
[50] More on obit procedure: http://tinyurl.com/kt9q9h.
[51] 'Blunder Sparks Radio Silence over Queen Mother': http://tinyurl.com/ngnymp.

The house style guide may list how to say the time (some stations specify whether it's 'ten twenty' or 'twenty past ten'), the date ('February the fourteenth' or 'the fourteenth of February'), the name of the station ('Radio X, across Blankshire' or 'This is X the sound of Blankshire'), the frequency, the station strapline, the temperature, what you call the what's ons and so on. It may also give presenters information such as the target audience, TSA and programmes' pace and style.

Be sure to ask for a copy at each station you work at so you're not caught out when someone says 'I thought I mentioned that . . .'. Such guides may be only a few sheets of a Word document, or they may be professionally printed and bound. The layout isn't the issue as much as the content, and its very existence.

You have to ensure that what you do is distinctive and consistent, and that your product is always sold in the same way.

10 Audio imaging and production elements

**SKILLSET – NATIONAL OCCUPATIONAL STANDARDS
RADIO CONTENT CREATION**

Unit content included in this chapter:
RC4 Contribute to the creative process in radio
RC12 Manage audio material
RC13 Operate a radio studio
RC20 Assist with radio productions
RC26 Produce station branding, radio trails and commercials

Radio, of course, is sound[1] and as presenters and producers we use different elements to stimulate interest in our broadcast.

- *Music* – the most-used element in radio as it's easily available, professionally produced, sets a mood and tone to the programme, and is the main draw for listeners. 'Music' includes commercially produced songs as well as jingles and beds produced for the station or used on commercials.[2] Not all adverts need music; indeed many of the most powerful ones comprise simply a voice. But music can be used to great effect to instantly transport a listener to a place, thereby saving time and words: think of the image in your mind as soon as you hear the sound of a didgeridoo, 'deep south' banjo playing, or a 'Parisian' accordion.

- *Voice*[3] – whether it's the presenter on a music programme from whom you only hear every 15 minutes, an interview guest or phone-in listener, the different voices also help create the 'brand' of the station. A station manager may well choose a presenter because of their vocal talents (because the timbre of their voice fits with the overall station sound) before their presentation talents, as the latter skills can more easily be taught. As you will see later, producers to phone-in programmes may well put to air the callers who represent the kind of listener they want to attract.

- *Natural sound*[4] (or sound effects)[5] – this can set the tone of a commercial or link. If you're giving away a holiday, think how much more effect your 'sell' will have if you describe the prize over the sound of waves gently breaking on a sandy shoreline . . . If you're doing a link about your child's birthday party at the weekend, how much

---

[1] Great presentations on the value of sound: http://tinyurl.com/yf56rex and http://tinyurl.com/ygkvbqv.
[2] 'Lament for the Radio Ad Jingle': http://tinyurl.com/d55wl6.
[3] 'Recording Jingles for BBC Radio': http://tinyurl.com/nvxwow.
[4] The BBC's 'Save Our Sounds' campaign: http://tinyurl.com/nwbckx. Also see this on sound artists: http://tinyurl.com/nwbckx.
[5] Various sound-effects websites: http://tinyurl.com/q4czq, http://tinyurl.com/m68lwl, etc.

more effective will the story be if you include audio from the event? The happy cries of laughter, the singing of 'happy birthday' and so on. Sound effects set the scene and help the listener visualise what's happening. Sound effects are also sometimes called 'atmospheres' (for longer pieces, such as 'an English country garden') or 'stingers' (for short effects like a gunshot or smashing glass). Like music beds and jingles, sound effects can be bought on CD, downloaded online or made yourself. Remember though, that the sound has to be realistic and must add to, not take away from your item. Realise that on occasion, the right effect may simply sound wrong: that of a tractor may sound like a taxi and confuse a listener. And don't underestimate the expertise of the public: many is the time an 'eagle-eared' listener has called a station to point out that the effect used was that of a Hurricane plane not a Spitfire, for example!

▢ *Silence* – don't underestimate the value of silence. And note the difference between 'silence' and 'dead air', which is explained later.

'Jingle'[6] is the generic term for a short piece of music, maybe with a sung strapline, station name or frequency. As well as (or, instead of) jingles, some stations have other audio brand imaging such as 'sweepers' (spoken announcements over a 'whoosh' bed).

Such on-air branding:

▢ helps the flow of the station – launching music sweeps out of speech breaks, and bridging tempo changes

▢ helps the sound of the station – creating a unique identity and personality and letting listeners know what they can expect

▢ can help punctuate or provide a bridge between items – such as in promos and adding excitement to features

▢ lets listeners know when a certain item is going to appear such as news and traffic reports

▢ exists because a musical message may be more memorable than a spoken one.

Scientists have discovered[7] that a song is probably the best all-around mnemonic device for facilitating recall of facts, definitions and concepts. It is most useful when students are faced with a lot of novel material to remember. A song is a mnemonic because its melody, rhythm, rhyme, imagery and other poetic devices provide a structure for the acquisition of new knowledge, an organisation of this knowledge in long-term memory, and cues for retrieval of this knowledge.

Studies, predominantly by Wanda Wallace and David Rubin from the late 1970s through to the early 1990s, have demonstrated that several variables enhance the recall of a song's lyric. A simple repetitive melody and a consistent rhythmic structure across the verses are the most important musical considerations. Lyrically, the use of strong end-rhymes, imagery, internal rhymes and poetic devices (such as alliteration and assonance) are the important factors.

---

[6] The 'world's biggest jingle community': http://tinyurl.com/nda5qy.
[7] Source: http://tinyurl.com/l63aje.

The choice of jingle or imaging package, like the choice of music, adds to the overall style of the station – the tune and tempo should reflect its image.

The imaging is the character, attitude and identity of your radio station.[8]

Many stations don't have music jingles at all and rely on verbal announcements, either by the presenters or pre-recorded, to get the station's name, frequency and strapline across. These are said in a way that reflects the format of the station they're on: soft, slow and smooth, or fast, urban and cool, for example.

Many stations make on-air brand imaging (such as spoken sweepers or liners) in-house, and have sung jingles produced by a specialist company. The jingle package will contain cuts of various type and duration around a common theme. That's usually based on a series of notes which reflect the number of syllables in the station name or strapline.

Heard every few minutes on air, jingles/sweepers are vital to reinforce the station name and its values, by what is said or sung and how. They're the station's audio trademark or audio logo and reinforce the station's name and frequency through constant repetition.

Other generic jingles are available on 'library music'.[9]

A few rules

- Use jingles/sweepers that are appropriate for what you're doing. Don't play one that sings or says 'fun at the weekend' on a Wednesday, don't play one that refers to 'much more music' before an ad break or an interview.
- Never play musical jingles over a song. They'll be in different keys and will clash horribly.
- Don't just play your favourite cuts, get to know others in the package and experiment with them. Ones that you don't like will be liked by many listeners.
- If you create your own, check with your programme controller before you use them on air as they may 'water down' the brand or message.

All station imaging should reflect the station brand. So, your programme controller should be 'signing off' every single item that's made by the image producer before it goes to air. Every week they should be asking three basic questions:

- Should it have gone to air?
- Should it still be on air?
- What is its 'best before date'?

Although there's a huge glossary of new radio words and terms at the back, all the ones about jingles and sweepers are collected right here.

---

[8] Steve Pigott, Pure Tonic Media, *The Radio Magazine*, July 2008.
[9] See more on this in Chapter 5.

Jingle[10] jargon

Acappellas are jingles that are sung 'dry', that is, without music. It's rare that you'd use one of these over the top of another piece of music, whether it was a bed or a song, as they would both be in different keys. As well as giving variety to your jingle package, acappellas are particularly effective if played into a song which starts with a vocal, but only if the tone fits. For example, to play a soft acappella into The Beatles 'Help' would grate, as would a hard acappella into Celine Dion's 'Because You Loved Me'.

Beatmixes[11] (or 'power intros')[12] mix the station jingle or logo into the intro of a song creating a seamless transition and branding the music with the station.

> The challenge of radio imaging has become much more subtle and specialised with the result that new categories of imaging tools such as logo tones, beatmixes and music segues will equal or surpass pure jingles in importance.[13]

Beds A bed may be a small music-only section of an individual jingle. Some jingles have singing at the beginning followed by music: that music part is the bed. The most common occurrence of this is what you hear going into the travel news: there may be a sung or spoken announcement, followed by a couple of minutes of music, over which the travel news is read. Or a bed may be a complete music track, with no sung or spoken part at all.

By their very nature, beds are usually 'backing tracks' rather than the full 'orchestral' theme, as the less instrumentation there is the easier it is for a voice to be heard and understood. A listener could be distracted by a full 'theme' playing underneath a voice, for example. (A full orchestral version is more likely to be a signature tune, see below.)

Don't play a music bed too loud: many people find them intensely annoying.

Custom packages are jingles that are written and performed to the radio station's requirements. The music may reflect the format of the station and so the strapline fits when it's sung. If there's nothing suitable on the jingle company's demo, then go for a custom package: the music tracks and vocals will be created from scratch to suit your specific specifications. The station will brief the creative team, who will then write lyrics, compose and arrange the music, record and mix the package. A custom package takes more time and is considerably more expensive[14] than a generic package, but you are guaranteed to get exactly what you want.

Alternatively, some stations use a cheaper 'off the peg'[15] (or 'syndicated', or 're-sings') package. It is still a collection of beds, transitions, acappellas and so on, but written in a generic style. Choose a package that closely resembles the sound attitude you want to project. Keep in mind that your own lyrics could change the complexion of the entire package of the demo that you hear. For instance, the demo might sing 'Today's Best Country', but if the tracks are very contemporary they may suit your sound with a simple lyric change. (If your

[10] Collection of radio station jingles and information: http://tinyurl.com/kuffwu.

[11] Examples of beatmixes: http://tinyurl.com/n5rggn.

[12] These are not the same as 'power starts': songs that have a slow or quiet start edited off, so they can start more 'cleanly' or 'powerfully'.

[13] Erik Huber, ReelWorld, *The Radio Magazine*, May 2008.

[14] Free radio jingles website: http://tinyurl.com/mjcns6.

[15] iJingles website: http://tinyurl.com/kksyub.

station name doesn't perfectly match the original package syllable for syllable, there are many ways, within reason, to alter the vocal arrangements for a good fit.)

Demos[16] can be downloaded from jingle production companies' websites, which demonstrate what kind of packages they provide.

Donut is the term used for a jingle that has a sung section each end and a music-only 'hole' in the middle (hence 'donut'). Presenters can talk over this middle bed, or play a dry drop-in.

Drone. Think of the questions asked in the later stages of *Who Wants To Be A Millionaire* on TV. The long, low single note that you can hear in the background is a 'drone'. In the same way, a drone is used during radio competitions to add tension to what's going on. Today a voiceover with bleeps, swooshes and drones is the preference over sung jingles for many stations.

Dry drop-in is a spoken phrase (it may be the station name, frequency, phone number or the presenter's name), with no music underneath. You can, as the name suggests, drop one of these into a donut, or onto the start of a song, or use one 'solus' (by itself), perhaps between two songs.

Drop-ins come in a variety of styles, 'soft', 'medium' and 'hard', and read by a male or female voiceover. These are the 'station voices', artists who will appear on all of your spoken 'on-air station imaging' (the trails, announcements, drop-ins and so on). The 'voice' will also help embody the format and brand of the station, in their perceived age, accent and attitude. Some stations use one of their own presenters to record the drop-ins, which sound really cheap. At the very least get a presenter from another station in the group to record them, and then return the favour.

You can use drop-ins in a variety of ways. Use a 'hard drop' going into (or over the intro to) a loud and lively song, a 'soft drop' over a slower song. Try to drop the drop over music to fit with the musical phrasing: perhaps mid-way in a short musical break, or backtimed just before the vocals or a key change.

Instrumental jingles are usually quite short (like most jingles, up to about ten seconds) and so a little different from longer beds. Where they are similar is in the fact that neither of them contains either sung or spoken messages.

Jingles are otherwise known as on-air brand imaging, sonic branding, audio logos or brand triggers.

jx is the abbreviation for jingle.

Liner is what some stations tell their presenters to say at certain points of the programme. It's not a jingle as such, as it's said live by the presenter and certainly not sung. However, it does include elements such as the station's name, frequency, area, slogan and so on, and is often used in place of a jingle.

Loop is what you can do to a short musical phrase or instrumental break from a song when you want to increase its duration to use as a bed. Take the short section and edit it together

---

[16] Various jingle companies' demo pages: http://tinyurl.com/nlzj5o, http://tinyurl.com/m73p4h, http://tinyurl.com/nwge9g.

several times. But be warned, editing music is easier said than done, and if done badly can sound horrific.

Music demonstrator is the name given to the sequence of clips from songs that are representative of the ones played on a station. There's a short 'hook' from three or four hits, together with a voiceover saying, 'We play songs like this . . . and this . . . and this . . . that's why we're Blankshire's number one hit music station . . . Radio X'.

News beds and jingles[17] are also called TOTHs or 'top of the hour' jingles. They usually reflect the drama and urgency of the news and invariably include the station name, frequency and coverage area, read by the 'station voice'. 'Across north and south Blankshire, on 99.9 FM, this . . . is Radio X.'

Stations often re-record this jingle to include important station information, because it is probably the most-heard ident (identification) on the station. 'With more listeners than ever before/the home of the Martin Knight breakfast show/the place where you can win a grand-a-day, this . . . is Radio X'.

Jingles can be of any duration, but they are usually (beds excepting) around ten seconds. News jingles are different. They can be short ten-seconders played at ten seconds to the hour, or have that ten-second start and then continue as a bed. But they can also start with a bed, say of 50 seconds, and then *end* with the announcement. If this news jingle is started at :59 minutes past the hour then it gives the presenter 50 seconds to tease what's happening later in the show, before the station name and frequency kicks in. This kind of jingle can help with backtiming.

Some news jingles have time signal 'pips' on the end, the last one of which signifies the exact top of the hour. These pips are either recorded onto the jingle or, at BBC stations, are played in live. Only BBC stations are allowed to use the traditional tone and sequence of pips (five short ones, followed by a sixth long one): commercial stations have to make their own variation.

Niklas Ravaja and Kari Kallinen studied the emotional effects of music played during news reports.[18]

The results showed that news stories with startling background music may have beneficial effects (e.g. a positive emotional state with more facial and respiratory changes in the listener, together with a stronger positive engagement, that is the story is considered more 'interesting'), or adverse effects (e.g. negative arousal) depending on the dispositional sensitivity of an individual.

Out of news jingles and hour openers are as important as the 'in to news' jingles. That is because so many people listen to the radio at the top of the hour to hear a bulletin and then what comes after it. The first song out of the news is important to re-set the format of the station, and the same goes for the jingle. An up-tempo, loud-and-proud jingle with the station name included, is a great way to start the next hour of songs on a typical chart music station.

---

[17] This essay considers the history and traditions of the underscoring of news with music http://tinyurl.com/lyx5qk; remixes of the BBC *News Channel* theme: http://tinyurl.com/q4hpy; archive of US TV stations' news themes: http://tinyurl.com/28b8wj; TV news themes website: http://tinyurl.com/mh23ja.

[18] Niklas Ravaja and Kari Kallinen, 'Emotional Effects of Startling Background Music during Reading News Reports', *Scandinavian Journal of Psychology*, Volume 45, Issue 3: published online 4 June 2004.

Ramp is the musical part of the jingle over which you can talk before the vocals come in. (Compare with donut above.)

Shotgun is the term used for a short, fast-paced instrumental.

Shout is a sung fast-paced, short acappella.

Signature tune ('theme tune'). The best ones are those that reflect the content of the programme and the tone of the station as a whole. Usually the brighter, catchier ones are the best. Also consider those which are easy to fade and that have a strong ending so you can backtime their start. Sig tunes can be a barrier between you and the audience. Some themes have become memorable for all the wrong reasons – because they're disliked with a passion. Indeed, many Radio 4 programmes don't have a theme tune at all and its news programme PM was forced to drop its short theme tune because of listener complaints.

Slogan refers to your radio station's 'positioning phrase', which may be used in your jingles either spoken or sung. An early example is 'Radio One is wonderful' or 'It's just for you – Radio Two'.

Stabs are, like 'shotguns', short, fast-paced jingles. A stab is used in conjunction with a bed. The travel jingle may start with a said or sung announcement, 'Travel news on Radio X', followed by the bed which is dipped for the presenter to read their bulletin over. When the bulletin is finished, the separate stab is played at 'standard' volume. The effect is one of completeness for the listener.

Station theme is a long and orchestrated theme tune for the station[19] (heard less and less on stations nowadays). As well as reflecting the format of the station, it has at its core the main musical phrase that is repeated in all the jingles in the package.

Sting is a short jingle, maybe as short as two seconds, used as a punctuation or exclamation mark between two items.

Sweeper A spoken announcement over a sound effect 'whoosh' to help transitions between songs. These are increasingly common, especially on commercial music stations.

Transitional jingles are really handy as they help you move from one tempo of music to another. Transitionals are sung, instrumental, dry or sweeper jingles which start off slow and finish faster or vice versa. So if you are going from a slow song to a faster one, you can fade song A, play the slow-to-fast jingle/sweeper, and when it's finished, play song B. They can also be used between music and speech (or vice versa).

Verbal idents (also see 'liner') are when the presenter says the elements of a jingle themselves. They don't sing but may include all or some of the following:
- the name of the station
- the frequency
- the strapline
- the area it broadcasts to

[19] Similar to 001 on this page: http://tinyurl.com/lxuzwz.

o   the name of the presenter
o   the programme title.

Vox IDs (or 'testimonials') are the sweepers which contain clips of listeners commenting on the station or its mix of music, in the style of a vox pop.

Whisper is exactly that: a whispered voice-only drop-in, which is useful to play into a soft love song for example.

We're all about increasing station recall and thus Rajar ticks. The art of creative imaging will become the science of successful radio. Strong jingles, the right voices, compelling trails, effective sweepers . . . great content. In a networked mid-morning show, the news is local but serious, the ads are local but selling stuff, which only leaves the stuff you're making as the local content selling the station name. Imaging is back and now it really matters.[20]

[20] Chris Stevens, vice-president, Jones TM, Dallas, *The Radio Magazine*, May 2008.

Part Four
GOING LIVE!

11 Stand by studio

The level of creativity in radio in this country is unique in the world and we can look forward to understanding our audiences more deeply and using different distribution platforms to build stronger relationships with our listeners. The future is bright for talented presenters and programme management talent – there's never been a better time for great programmers![1]

Checking the studio

Just as a pilot won't take off without first checking all the plane's controls, you shouldn't embark on your trip without giving the studio the once-over.

- Check the equipment – that the headphones are there and that they work, the same for the mics. Adjust the height of the chair and the level of the air-con. Check the mic levels and put the faders on or off fader/remote start. Set up the channels so they are assigned in the way that you'll need them.
- Read the fault log, competition log and whiteboard to check for any broken equipment, a new competition or changes to the programme schedule.
- Tidy up – chuck the rubbish away, pile up the papers, put away CDs and put guest chairs under the desk. Use a disinfectant wipe on the faders, keyboard and mice.
- Set yourself up – make sure that you've got your scripts, spare paper, pens and show prep. Check that your scripts are in the same order as the running order, and that both of those tally with the playout screen. Cue up as much as you can before the show starts.
- Go to the toilet and get a drink – you don't know when you'll get another chance, but walk, don't run, back to the studio.
- Listen to the output, so you can comment if necessary on something said by the previous presenter. Get ready to take control. Prepare for take-off.

Your mental mindset

Before you start broadcasting you need to give yourself confidence and remind yourself of your 'attitudes'. Only then can you perform to the best of your ability. Think through these[2] mantras as you prepare:

[1] Dirk Anthony, GCap Media content director, *The Radio Magazine*, September 2005.
[2] Adapted, with permission, from work by Jay Trachman, US radio presenter and author.

- 'I am performing to just one person, whose face I can picture before I open the mic. They like what I do and who I am' – This sets up one half of the one-to-one illusion that the listener wants to feel as though you are speaking to them directly as an individual and friend. It also provides a safety zone, liberating you to show some emotion such as vulnerability, sadness, and frustration – things that you would never show to a group of strangers but which lend reality to your personality, since they're things that friends show each other.

- 'The more I show of myself, the more people will like me' – Especially when it comes to emotions. Never miss a chance to break out of the 'up and bright' mode if you want to be seen as a real person rather than just 'an act'.

- 'Good announcers are two-a-penny. What makes me worth my pay is my ability to share my personality with a listener' – Employees who are interchangeable never get far. You want to be the exclusive distributor of what it is you do.

- 'My friend will listen if I have something to say – but just because I say something doesn't mean anyone will hear it' – A lot of what we offer are wasted words, repetition of slogans, promos without commitment. We train people to ignore us. But if occasionally we commit entertainment we train the listener to pay attention because there may well be pay-off in it for them.

- 'Perfection is not the standard – communication is' – Nobody expects their friends to be perfect. They expect them to be *real*, to say what they are thinking, to refrain from lying, to be authentic.

- 'I want to convey the illusion that I was listening to the music' – After all that's what you expect your listener to be doing. The choice here is 'two good friends, sharing a part of their day together, enjoying some music along the way' versus 'the slogan reader who comes on between the songs'.

- 'I am the one thing that the station has to offer as an exclusive benefit at this hour' – If we fail to entertain, to keep the listener company, then their only reason for staying is the music. There's a one in three chance they will leave when a song comes on that they don't like.

- 'I'm here because I enjoy being here' – People are drawn to others who seem to be having a good time. You can't fake it. If this isn't one of the things you enjoy doing most in the world, you probably shouldn't be doing it at all. If you are enjoying yourself, you'll usually smile before you open the mic. Everyone hears it.

- 'Emotion beats information' – Listeners with a heavy appetite for information are probably listening to the news/talk station. The entertainment our listeners crave is having their heartstrings plucked. That's what the music does. That's what we should make sure we do too. Smart advertisers already know this: that's why they limit their pitches to a single item or two and try to heavily play on the listener's emotions. When giving information we should know it too: a little goes a long way.

- 'The most offensive thing I can do is lie about who I am. Right behind that is not being anybody in particular' – So many of us are preoccupied with offending the listener, we use it as an excuse not to share our lives, responses, opinions – oblivious to the intuitive knowledge that friends don't just turn on you just because they disagree with you. What really offends is when someone is pretending to be something they are not – happy all the time, hiding their true feelings, feigning excitement over things they are not really excited about. You can't succeed in this business with 'baloney and white bread'.

Operating the desk

Most presenters, certainly those in local radio, drive their own desks (self-operate/self-op). Those in national radio (or those presenters who are 'celebrities' and have not come up through the ranks of radio) often have a producer to operate the equipment: they are 'driven' by a tech op/technical operator. Being driven means you can concentrate on your links, self-opping means you have flexibility and control of what's going out.

Driving yourself can seem quite daunting at first as there's so much that has to be done at the same time. It all looks really complex, but if you can drive a car and hold a conversation at the same time then there's no reason why you can't drive a studio desk. It's all down to practice. Grab every opportunity you can to sit in a studio and watch other people present their programmes. When you do, wear headphones to hear how what they do in the studio changes the sound on air. When it's convenient, ask questions: why they chose a particular jingle at a certain time, why they cued a song past its start, or why they talked over the end of one song and not another.

Then ask if you can sit in a studio after the show and see how it all feels: what happens when you alter faders, what it's like to hear your own voice in your headphones and how to talk out loud and PFL a song at the same time.

One of the tricks is to think one or more steps in advance. Know what you are going to do next, and after that and, in case something goes wrong, the step after that as well! Bear in mind that, even though it's easy to set up the next item while a song is playing, it is rather trickier to do it as you are talking to a live guest.

12 Your voice[1]

It's the presenter's job to keep people listening between songs, using three main tools:

- the voice – using the one-to-oneness of pitch, projection, pace and pause
- the words – the language and style to engage and persuade
- the content – what you say and how you say it.

Talking and communicating are two different things. 'Talking' is how you verbalise thoughts through the sound of your voice and the use of techniques such as pitch, projection, pace and pause. 'Communicating' is 'connecting' with people through the words you choose and the topics you talk about, and are the subject of the following two chapters.

Good radio speech should be:
Warm but not smarmy
Friendly but not intrusive or too cosy
Clear, but not over-elocuted or precise
Natural but not undisciplined, authoritative but not aggressive
Fluent but not unbelievable
Sympathetic but not patronising
Understandable but without obvious or unpleasant speech
impediments.[2]

One of the unique things you can bring to the role of presenter is your voice. What you say will only cut through to the listener if they like your voice, its quality and your style, and if they feel you are warm, friendly, sympathetic, easy to understand, positive, enthusiastic and believable. They won't listen if you sound boring, lack interest, are too complicated, too fast or sound confused.

Spoken information remains in the sensory memory up to eight
times longer than visual data . . . humans are wired to respond to
speech far more than any other sound.[3]

---

[1] Anne Karpf, *The Human Voice: The Story of a Remarkable Talent*: http://tinyurl.com/nbu5lf.
[2] *BBC Local Radio Training Manual*, 1987.
[3] Dr Aric Sigmund, *Campaign Magazine*, February 2000.

Remember, radio is a single-sense medium. The entire concentration of the listener is focussed on the voice[4] and the Four Ps, so it's important to know what we can get out of it, and how we can look after it.

> Acoustical analysis[5] of the 'best' voices has shown that the preference is melodious, relatively low-pitched voices with little high-frequency noise. The 'worst' voices are high-pitched relative to the norm for the speaker's gender. Those voices also demonstrated high-frequency noise, a 'screechy' voice quality.
>
> The average speaking pitch for the best male voice is 126 Hz. Normal pitch range for males is 110–130 Hz. In analysis Sean Connery's pitch reached 158 Hz and Mel Gibson's 108 Hz.
>
> The average pitch for the best voices among females was 201 Hz, while the female norm is 200–230 Hz. Barbra Streisand's was at 228 Hz and Julia Roberts' 171 Hz. The average pitch among the 'worst' of the female voices was 262 Hz. Roseanne Barr had a pitch of 377 Hz.

Pitch

Whether a voice is high or low in tone is determined by the rate of vibration of the vocal cords as air passes over them. The more vibrations per second, the higher the pitch. (The rate of vibration is to do with the length and thickness, and the tightening or relaxation of these cords. Generally, women have a higher pitch than men because their vocal cords are shorter.)

Do not rely on changing the EQ controls on the microphone channel or altering the compressor to make you sound more 'butch'. If you're not careful, such changes can have the effect of making you sound muffled. Far better to change your voice in your body instead.

Like much of the work of the voice, pitch is affected by your breathing. You've seen those diagrams showing you how to sit at a computer?[6] Well, it is a similar posture for presenting a radio show. Feet flat on the floor, upper legs in contact with the chair, a straight back (but not so straight that you are tense) carefully supported by the chair, shoulders back (again, not so you are strained) and head up. You can afford to relax a little, but not too much: I call it 'informal formality' and here's why. The more you sit up, the more air you can get into your lungs. This will reduce tension, keep you alert, increase the resonance and lower the pitch of your voice. (A lower pitch can be used to signal calmness, control and authority.)

Once you are sitting correctly, your breathing should be done from the stomach — if your shoulders rise when you breathe you're doing it wrong. Stomach breathing is deeper breathing and when you have more air getting into your lungs it will also steady your nerves.

---

[4] In the 1960s Professor Albert Mehrabian and colleagues at the University of California, Los Angeles (UCLA), conducted studies into human communication patterns. He supposedly found that 7 per cent of the information conveyed by a voice consists of words and their meaning, while the rest of the communication comes from vocal and facial expression. Read why that's not the full story here: http://tinyurl.com/la26mc.

[5] Source: the Center for Voice Disorders of Wake Forest University http://tinyurl.com/lwhuf4.

[6] How to sit at your workstation: http://tinyurl.com/5ufz6n.

Breathe *from* your stomach, but *through* your nose gradually while you are talking. Filters in your nostrils clean the air, warm it and help add moisture. If you breathe through your mouth you are letting bugs and cold air in, which will make your vocal cords dry and you will start to lose your voice. So, in through the nose and out through the mouth.

If you breathe properly, you will relax, make the most of your natural pitch and trip over fewer words. Then, because you are making fewer mistakes and sound good, you will build up more confidence and so be more relaxed and sound better, and so on.

Inflection is a *change of pitch*. Naturally we do not speak on one pitch level alone. The voice (usually naturally) slides up and down the scale as we express various shades of thought and feeling.

Usually an upward slide or inflection expresses a question or an uncompleted thought, and a downward inflection expresses a completed thought. It is such intonation that we have to identify and mirror when we are reading the written word, to make us sound naturally conversational.

Listen to how you and others talk in every day conversations: 'He did what??!!', 'Yeah, su-u-u-u-u-re you do . . . !'. Then try and reproduce these techniques on air to make your intonational sound increasingly natural and ear-catching way.

Those who have a 'sing-songy' voice which goes unnecessarily up and down in tone (the 'seasick syndrome'), can come over as patronising. It may sound 'up and bright' to them but to the listener it sounds cheesy and as though the presenter is on 'auto-pilot' without a care for the content of the message. Other presenters go up at the end of every sentence? Like this? Whether it's necessary or not? Are they really asking a question? Or have they got into the habit . . . *of really annoying their audience*?

Conversely, those whose voice never rises or falls, who drone on and on in the same monotone, lose the interest of those they are talking to.

It is often effective to use a voice that is unexpected for a certain situation: think how threatening a whisper in a horror film is.

If your inflection patterns are too consistent, then you're sounding bored rather than interesting. Depending on the material, sometimes your delivery should be fast, sometimes slower. Sometimes you should be excited, sometimes calm. Sometimes your voice should carry a smile, sometimes you should sound dead serious. By constantly varying your pattern (without sounding like a pastiche) you increase the possibility of being perceived as human rather than automaton . . . and therefore someone that the listener can connect with.

Remember, the voice that holds attention is one that conveys emotion and interest by change of pitch or inflection. The owner of that voice is communicating.

To increase your pitch range, try the following exercises with a piano accompaniment:

Starting with the middle C count aloud from one to eight on the pitch of middle C.

Drop down one note and repeat, continuing until you have gone as low as you can without straining your throat muscles.

Then, starting again at middle C go up the scale, counting from one to eight on eight pitches.

Projection

HUMAN SPACING

Anthropologist Edward T. Hall[7] posited the ideas of *human spacing*, from which we understand the projection needed to speak conversationally on the radio.

There are very specific social rules about this social distance (in the developed Western world):

THE PUBLIC ZONE

This is generally over 3 metres. That is, when we are walking around town, we will try to keep at least this distance between us and other people. The closer others get, the more we become aware and ready ourselves for appropriate action.

THE SOCIAL ZONE

Between 1.5 and 3 metres we start to feel a connection with other people: we can talk with them without having to shout, and is a comfortable distance for people who are standing in a group but maybe not talking directly with one another.

THE PERSONAL ZONE

In the personal zone of 0.5 to 1.5 metres the conversation gets more direct, and this is a good distance for two people who are talking in earnest about something.

THE INTIMATE ZONE

When a person is within arms reach or closer (under 0.5 metres), then we can touch them in intimate ways. We can also see more detail of their body language and look them in they eyes. When they are closer, they also blot out other people so all we can see is them (and vice versa). Romance of all kinds happens in this space.

Associated with human spacing are our *vocal proxemics*: the kind of voice we use in each zone. The further away someone is, the louder and less personal your voice becomes. You have a different voice when you are with your lover in the intimate zone, than you use to a room of people in a public zone.

Translate that into the studio situation. You give the impression you are sharing your thoughts with one single person in the room with you. Imagine them sitting the other side

[7] Irwin Altman and Martin M. Chemers, *Culture and Environment* (Wadsworth Inc., 1980): http://tinyurl.com/kvcd6n.

of the desk in your personal zone, and talk to them in *that* voice. Don't talk to the micro-phone or to the other side of the room, talk to the empty chair opposite you, and you should get the projection of your voice about right.

> He talks to me as though I were a public meeting.[8]

Speaking loudly alters your pitch and puts a strain on your voice, and it also signals domi-nance in a 'conversation'. Shouting does not necessarily mean excitement. It does, though, usually mean simply more noise.

> I hear a lot of presenters screaming.
> It's perceived that yelling at the top of your voice is energy.
> It isn't.[9]

Pace

However resonant your voice may be, it won't matter if you speak too quickly to be under-stood, or if your diction isn't clear, or if you run words or sentences into each other.[10] TV presenters usually have an easier time as viewers can subconsciously lip-read, watch facial expressions or even put on the subtitles. There is no such help for your listeners, so you have to help them as much as you can. This means speaking clearly and being careful technically.

A slow pace may indicate you are being thoughtful and considering your next phrase. But to a listener you may come over as patronising or bored.

Are you speaking too fast? If you are, your words will be unclear, you may stumble and your message will be lost. The average talking speed is three words a second.[11] Slowing your pace to this will add clarity, lower the tone of your voice and make you sound more authoritative.

Many presenters like to talk with a music bed running underneath them. It makes them feel safe and less exposed as they can pause for a moment and know that there's no 'dead air'. But music beds can encourage presenters to talk too fast as they confuse pace for 'momen-tum' or 'excitement'. Although your delivery should mirror the bed, do not let it force you into speeding up so much that you garble. Do not let the music bed 'chase you'. Increasing the pace won't necessarily increase momentum or excitement at all. Doing something that's not interesting faster, does not make it more interesting.

Pause

The human voice adds additional dimensions to speech and can be used to send particular signals. In particular, any variation in the way anything is said can act as a signal.

---

[8] Queen Victoria on her prime minister Benjamin Disraeli.

[9] Tony Blackburn, presenter, *The Radio Magazine*, November 2008.

[10] A South African study researched understanding levels of an audience when exposed to different presenters' person-alities, speed of delivery and questioning styles: http://tinyurl.com/nvuxqr.

[11] In 2008 the Advertising Standards Authority ruled that legal terms and conditions at the end of an advert for a mobile phone company were not clear, because the 28-word disclaimer and web address were read in just eight seconds. See http://tinyurl.com/lehqxr.

There is more to variety in the spoken word than just pitch, projection and pace. A change of pace can be a reduction to complete standstill: the pause. This could come before or after significant words or phrases to add emphasis; a pause for dramatic effect before a punch line; to show respect or comprehension after a guest has made a poignant remark or many other situations ('The funniest bit on last night's *Britain's Got Talent* was the bit where the farmers did synchronised dancing . . . [pause] . . . with wheelbarrows!').

The strategic pause adds tension and anticipation, but only if it is not followed by an 'errrm' or 'ummm' which will merely show you are ill prepared. It's a great skill to have in your repertoire but should be used sporadically for best effect.

Your vocal health

Warm up by singing something silly. Play with your voice. Don't push it and hurt it, but do see where it can go. Play Elvis's 'Way Down'[12] in the car on the way to work and see if you can reach his tone (but don't *force* your voice down). Do something similar with Bronski Beat's 'Tell Me Why'.[13] Make silly sounds and do imitations. Swoop your voice high and low. Do not do any of these if they hurt or if you feel dizzy but use them as a way of finding what else you can do with your instrument. Some presenters warm up by chewing gum before they go on air to relax their jaw muscles.

It is very easy to stay still in a studio and only at the end of a programme realise that you have been in the same seat for three or four hours. Sitting still will make you sound dull and lifeless. Get re-invigorated by walking around the studio whenever you have a chance. It will get some air into your lungs and help you sound more alert the next time you open the mic.

Many presenters stand up to present their programmes saying that it gives them a more energetic performance. That would certainly make sense. Standing up gives you better control of your breathing, helps you stay alert and means you can move around much more freely as you gesture. Stations which have presenters who 'stand to deliver', have studio desks which are raised slightly so they don't have to slouch to operate the faders and some even have microphone head-sets so their presenters can walk around the studio as they talk.

Nerves and tension

These affect the muscles across your jaw, throat and chest making your voice sound a little thin, strained, irritated or bored. There are lots of relaxation methods you can try both before you go into the studio and while you are on air. The easiest and most effective one is to take three deep breaths to steady your nerves. Releasing tension opens the diaphragm, which gives deeper breathing which in turn helps the voice sound more open and confident.

During times of dramatic or significant news, it is even more important for radio presenters to manage their personal tension. Feeling anxious, angry, sad or depressed can make it difficult to sound sane, comforting or calm. But that is what radio presenters need to do for the sake of their listeners.

---

[12] That song here: http://tinyurl.com/cym8ly.
[13] That song here: http://tinyurl.com/djlv9q.

Health tips

The first thing to be considered is what sort of voice we have and next, how we use it. The natural power of the voice is judged by its quantity and quality. The good qualities of the voice are improved by attention and deteriorated by neglect.[14]

Drink loads of water! The best way to keep your vocal cords in shape is to down a couple of litres a day through constant sipping. But do not think that the water you drink will immediately relieve any tension in your throat by lubricating it, it won't. You need to have enough water in your whole body, so that the blood stream is healthier and lubricates the cords from the 'inside'. There is an old maxim that says 'If your pee's all white, you'll sound all right', which does make a certain amount of sense.

Drink the right kind of water – drinks from the machine (cold and fizzy or hot and caffeinated) do not count towards your two litres a day. You need plain, ordinary H_2O at room temperature – cold water can give your throat a bit of a shock. Hot drinks make your vocal cords swell; caffeine speeds up the production of extra-thick phlegm and that will mean you spend more time swallowing hard or coughing.

How to cough – if you have a tickle, don't 'hack' as that will inflame your vocal cords even more. Simply swallow hard, preferably with some warm water.

Don't whisper – whispering when you have a sore throat only makes it more red and angry. Try it right now and feel the strain your vocal cords are under. What you are doing is pushing them into an unusual shape and then passing extra air over them that only adds to their dryness. Instead, if you are going hoarse, just speak really softly.

Accents[15] and impediments

It's probably fair to say that to reach the top of the broadcasting ladder you need to have an accent that's understandable and middle-of-the-road. That's not to say that an accent is a bad thing: having a brummy accent on a Birmingham station would probably be an advantage, though *perhaps* less so on a national station where people from across the country would have to 'retune' their ears. (Though the Irish accent of Colin Murray on Radio 1 is well accepted.) *If you want to*, you get rid of an accent by listening and learning the different speech patterns of those you want to sound more like.

When I was on air I tried to change my accent, because I felt working at the BBC you needed to be posh. At the time every DJ modelled themselves on Dr Fox and tried to sound southern. Trying to change your style doesn't work because you just sound ridiculous.[16]

---

[14] Quintilian, first century AD, was a leading instructor in eloquence at the school of oratory in Rome.

[15] 'What's in a Voice?': http://tinyurl.com/mnnbbf.

[16] JK and Joel, presenters, Virgin Radio, *The Radio Magazine*, March 2008.

Your accent may not matter as long as it is not too broad — in fact, a local and relatable accent may be a positive advantage. What matters most of all is that your voice is clear, well rounded and easily understood.

Winston Churchill, actors James Stewart, Julia Roberts, Bruce Willis and James Earl Jones, and singer Carly Simon all had speech impediments which they overcame.[17] Whether it's rhotacism (unusual pronunciation of the letter r, or too much emphasis on this sound), a lisp (the sound produced when s and z are pronounced like a soft 'th' sound), a stutter (repeating sounds frequently when attempting to pronounce them) or cluttering (running words together rapidly), you can usually overcome it and reach your goals with the help of a good therapist, time and concentration. Or use it to your advantage (Jonathan Ross, anybody?).

Your 'personal listener'

Always keep in mind the first eight letters of the word 'personality'.

Each listener should feel as though you're having a personal conversation with them.

Include them, don't exclude them.

Radio people often talk in terms of 'the listener' rather than 'the listeners', because we speak to them on an individual basis. So it's never 'all our listeners', it's 'you'; it's never 'all of you', it's 'you'; it's never 'some of you', it's 'you'; it's never 'everybody', it's 'you', etc. Don't talk about 'our listeners', or ask if 'anybody heard what happened . . .' (especially not, 'anybody out there . . .') or refer to 'you all'. Like a confirmed bachelor, keep yourself single.

ACTUAL AUDIO

NEWSREADER (to another presenter): 'What we want the listeners to do is to call us with their experiences of . . .'

BBC local station, June 2005

To sound credibly intimate, and less like an 'announcer', you need to convince yourself that you are talking to one single person. That way each listener will fantasise that that person is them.

To help remind them, some new presenters create a personal listener whom they can picture in their mind (and may even have a picture of them in the studio). Your fantasy personal listener should be a 'perfect you'. You, without any insecurities or negativities and someone who accepts the real 'you' for being 'you'. A perfect friend if you like. Direct your comments to this person, and in doing so you'll become more 'real'; communicating on a

---

[17] Famous people and speech differences: http://tinyurl.com/msfw53.

one-to-one basis with someone that you know and with whom you feel at ease. You will feel more free to express real emotions, and so become more relatable and believable.

Conversationality

Radio presenters talk to millions of listeners, one at a time and yet the best ones still sound natural. But some new (and young) presenters hide behind an artificial 'radio persona' of what they think a presenter 'should' sound like. They sound 'micro-*phoney*'.

> Be yourself. Keep your style natural, conversational, lively and engaging. Try to help the listener feel they're part of the discussion. Address the listener in the first person – this is more intimate and encourages a sense of belonging. Use the present tense wherever possible – it gives a sense of immediacy. Five Live vocabulary should be accessible, jargon-free, simple, clear and intelligent. Be careful not to overcomplicate things and don't be unnecessarily formal in your delivery. Try to avoid becoming too predictable or repetitive, particularly at regular junctions. It's easy to get into habits such as repeating the same expressions e.g.: 'to be fair', 'you know', 'I have to say', 'I mean' or starting your programme, strand or bulletin with exactly the same phrase every day.[18]

Radio is intimate and personal in a way that television is not. People often listen to the radio alone – in the bathroom, bedroom, kitchen or in the car – and it is the skill of talking to people singly while actually speaking to an audience of thousands that the presenter has to master.

> TV at its best is an amazing medium of pizzazz and excitement. But radio is fantastically intimate: one person, a microphone and a relationship.[19]

Talking to everyone, one at a time, is something that many newcomers to radio have trouble grasping – especially those who have previously been television presenters where the style is different. You're still *broad*casting, so you would think it natural to refer to listeners as a group, a crowd. But where most TV viewers tend to watch in a group, most radio listening is done alone.

> In broadcasting your audience is conjectural, but it is an audience of one. Millions may be listening, but each is listening alone, or as a member of a small group, and each has (or ought to have) the feeling that you are speaking to him individually.[20]

---

[18] BBC Radio Five Live style guide.
[19] Roger Mosey, head of BBC Sport, ex-controller BBC Radio Five Live, Radio Academy event, November 2005.
[20] George Orwell 'Poetry and the Microphone', *The New Saxon Pamphlet*, March 1945: http://tinyurl/yge9q82.

Your listeners are your friends so talk to them in the same way that you do with your 'real' friends: conversationally. That's not only what you say, but also how you say it. The easiest way to sound conversational is with good writing, excellent adlibbing and preparation.

Be aware of a repetitive pattern of inflections: in real conversation, inflections vary widely from sentence to sentence. In announcing, people will tend to say everything the same way.

Maybe your tone is too repetitive. If this is the case, it may be because you have give the same information (such as introducing the weather, or reading about travel delays) over and over again. In which case, once you've identified this speech pattern, work to change it: come up with different phrases to help communicate the information; say the words with thought and feeling; ensure you're not using cliché rather than conversation.

Listen back to your aircheck: does your tone sound like you could be talking on the phone with a friend? If so, fine. But even so, most people will begin to sound tired after a four-hour conversation with one person (which is in effect what you are doing), so work hard to maintain freshness. Sounding conversationally casual is good, sounding bored isn't – make sure you stay alert.

Emotional authenticity

People have to feel like they know you, before they can begin bonding with you. And that means that you have to show a variety of real emotions.[21]

Think about what you are saying and the listener's likely reaction to it, just as you would if you were speaking with a friend who was right in front of you.

AUDITORY DISCONNECTIONS

Avoid an auditory disconnect between the words and your tone of voice, which will make you sound fake and confuse the listener. Talk in a tone that is appropriate to the message. You may, for example, use an inappropriate upward inflection when you are talking? Like that! The tone will contradict the words and listeners will subconsciously work to make sense of the conflict. Their mind is not on what you are saying, and you are not communicating.

You need to show that you have a variety of emotions, but realise that does not mean that you have to be 'emotional'. It may be that you read something with sincerity or authority. Or you pass on a story with humour or excitement. Or you give details of a personal experience with anger or frustration . . .

Understand the need to exaggerate your natural emotions. Actors are taught that if they acted totally naturally when they performed to an audience some intensity is lost. The emotions seem flat. They have to overplay to seem normal. The same is true for radio. Your highs and lows need to be pushed just a little further, to give a sense of naturalness when they come out of the speaker the other end.

[21] I once trained a TV newsreader who had a story in her bulletin about a missing girl who was thought to have been murdered. She almost sang the story, with no feeling for the story or the victim's family who may have been watching. The reader and I worked out that because she had read the story so many times, she had forgotten its significance.

Understand the difference between 'authoritative' (confident, comfortable and factual), and 'arrogant' (which is the phoney attempt at being authoritative). Be yourself without affectation. You'll sound much more credible.

Reading out loud

Increasingly, presenters are reading their scripts straight from a computer screen and that causes several problems. It means that it's difficult to sight read a few lines ahead of what you are currently reading. It also means that you can't mark your script with which words to lift or drop in emphasis.

If you are reading from paper, take a pen into the studio so you can scribble on your cue (mark the words to lift, rewrite sections if necessary, add extra notes) and of course separate any pages that are stapled or held together with paperclips. Just as pages on a screen can freeze or go missing, so can their paper alternatives. Check before you start reading an item that you have all the pages you need.

If you're reading something on air and you want the listener to think that you're adlibbing, you have to sound as if you're processing what you're talking about and sound conversational.

To do this you have to:

- Make sure you understand the sense of the story, why it is relevant and interesting, and then you stand a better chance of making it compelling when you read it.
- Consider what is really happening. It is often a case of 'while this is happening over here, that's happening over there . . .'. In your head you probably just read that sentence, slightly lifting the words 'this', 'here', 'that', and 'there'. That is because they are the 'balancing words'. Look for balancing words in your scripts and lift[22] them too.
- Also lift people's names, places and titles.
- Also lift new information, and subdue old information. So, in the sentences 'Mary had a lamb. The lamb's name was Larry', you lift 'Mary', 'lamb' and 'Larry' because they are names or new information, but subdue the second reference to the lamb, because that's old information.
- Throw in the occasional pause, as if you're just checking the facts in your head or otherwise searching for a word.
- If it sounds as though you are reading an item, you are doing it wrong. You should sound as though you are telling a friend something of interest.

Here's an example:[23] Read the following aloud as if you are reading it to someone:

The future behaviour of America as the current lone superpower is terribly important to China not only because America can disrupt China's vision of a harmonising world by doing its own thing in the Middle East and elsewhere, but also because a recession in the American economy (caused by debt, deficits etc.) would immediately have a knock-on effect on the Chinese economy.

---

[22] Lift gently, rather than 'stress' or 'emphasise', which we rarely do in normal conversation.
[23] Source: http://tinyurl.com/ksdfbz.

Now read it as it is written below but
- ☐ pause for a breath at '. . .'
- ☐ lift a word when it's in italics
- ☐ speak more quickly where words-are-run-together
- ☐ slow down where a phrase has underlining.

> The future behaviour of America as the current lone super-power is . . . terribly important to China . . . not only because America can disrupt China's vision of a . . . harmonising world by . . . doing pretty-much its own thing in the-Middle-East-and-elsewhere . . . but also because a recession in the *American economy* would of course immediately have a <u>knock-on effect on the Chinese economy.</u>

Just by pausing and emphasising certain words and changing the pace you now sound as if you're thinking about what you're saying; as if you're drawing on your vast general knowledge of China's macroeconomic policies. You've also been bit sneaky and thrown in a word or two: 'pretty-much' and 'of course', suggesting you're familiar with the economic relationship between the US and China.

Sometimes it's obvious you're reading something because it contains too much information that you couldn't possibly know or remember. As an example, here is something that if read as written will definitely sound as if it is being read:

On Thursday July 7th 2005, three bomb explosions hit London Underground trains . . .

The reason it sounds as if it's being read is because few people would remember what day of the week it was, so clearly the information is in front of you. If you want to come across powerfully, you have to engage in a little play-acting and say something like this:

July the 7th 2005 . . . I remember it was a Thursday . . .

There's only one occasion when you should sound as if you're clearly reading something; and that's when you are quoting someone, in which case you should say exactly that: '. . . and I quote . . .'

Ironically, reading something flawlessly doesn't sound impressive when you're trying to make out you're adlibbing. It sounds cold and matter-of-fact. If you throw in the occasional hesitation, gentle emphasis and change the pace of your presentation, it'll sound like you're thinking about it, as if it's something honestly important to you. This will have more intellectual and emotional impact, which is what you want, if you want your listener to think you're smart.

Rehearsing reading out loud makes you a better communicator; it's a skill that must be learnt and practised so it sounds as though you are speaking off the top of your head.

Script reading tips:

- Unless there's a real emergency, never read anything on air that hasn't been practised aloud. Tongue-twisters, double-meanings and inaccuracies are not always apparent until they are spoken aloud.

- Never read anything that could be confusing to your listener. Your voice will reflect it. Take the time to rewrite the script before reading. Never think 'I don't understand, it must be me . . . I'm sure it's OK'. If you don't get it, not only could it be wrong, but how will you communicate its meaning to your listeners? Keep the message, but change the style: use your words and your speech pattern. Usually, the thought is the important thing, not the exact words that someone else has chosen, and the message will be much more effective if you are communicating it in your language, not theirs. We rarely trip over ourselves when we adlib – we're more likely to do it if we're reading a script that someone else has written and that we're not familiar with.

- Mark the script. Underline key words, mark pauses and the words to lift. Write phonetic pronunciations for foreign or difficult words. Identify strange pronunciations or unusual words, such as people's names – for local place names refer to the studio bible, which should have a list of them. If you do not know how to say something, ask. It is better to be thought a fool in front of one person in the office, than thousands of people on air.

- Choose the appropriate tone of voice. How much emotion/feeling should be conveyed? Should the tone be light-hearted or serious?

- Look ahead. Don't look at the script word by word. Train yourself to take in phrases at a time.

- Learn to sight read by reading out loud from a newspaper or the credits on TV as they scroll up.

- Learn to talk while processing other information – by repeating, word for word, news stories a second or two after a bulletin reader presents them (useful for when you are presenting and someone uses talkback to you at the same time).

- Learn what your variety is – by reading different kinds of items: news reports, commercials, what's ons.

- Learn about your 'on-air' voice – talk to yourself out loud using a variety of tones and inflections as though you were on air.

> Your presentation is about what you say and how you say it: entice, engage, inform and be warm.

You may be fortunate enough to work at a station that values its staff enough to employ a voice coach on an occasional basis to work with all on-air staff. This does happen at some BBC and commercial stations, but isn't done nearly often enough. Students on radio journalism courses sometimes have as little as half an hour's tuition on how to use their voice in their entire year. Unfortunately, it shows on air. Surely this is a false economy. You will know yourself which radio voices you love and which ones you immediately turn off. Surely a station manager wants the best possible sound coming from the radio – the best possible voices, communicating in the most effective way?

Is it worth paying for voice coaching yourself? It may be, but there are several companies that promise you the earth and only give you mud. Poor advice about your voice can literally do more harm than good. Certainly go to a voice coach who is used to working with broadcasters. It is difficult to communicate voice techniques in the written word, especially when every person has different needs, so if you really want to develop a strong voice with a wide range drop me a line at my e-mail address and I'll pass on some recommendations.

One secret is to be yourself. Do not try to copy someone else because you will sound obviously false. Another is not to force your voice into something that it cannot be. Instead, learn to enhance the voice that nature gave you, to enhance the message that you want to give to others.

Be your own critic

You will improve your voice when you start to listen to it. Record and listen to your programme on a regular basis and be aware of any vocal mannerisms you may have. It could be that you hesitate too much, or that you use verbal crutches such as 'kind of', 'sort of thing', 'good old', 'the hour of' or 'to be fair'. Or perhaps you introduce songs or items in the same way time and time again: 'Here's a classic from The Beach Boys . . .', 'Here's Alex with the travel'.

To break a bad habit you need to replace it with a different action. Once you've realised what it is that you want to stop doing, identify what happens immediately before you do it: 'the trigger'. It may be that you are hesitating and saying this word between two actions, because you're trying to come up with the correct word, or because you've been distracted. Then, realise what you need to do to break that chain of events (trigger > habit). This may be to practise more, to write yourself a few notes of what to say, or to say nothing at all (half a second of nothing is better than half a second of 'ummmmm').

Don't listen to each show too soon after you do it, leave it a week or more. You need to have a certain distance so you can hear the content with a fresh pair of ears and be more objective — almost as though you're listening to someone else rather than yourself. A good way of doing this is to listen in the same way as other people listen to you, perhaps in the car or in the kitchen preparing a meal rather than sitting down with a notebook and pen ready to dissect each link. Remember it may take a while to like the sound of your own voice.

13 The words

Are you using the language, words and metaphors that the listener understands? How can you choose the most appropriate words and terms to better communicate and build a relationship with them?

The most basic advice for talking on the radio is to use simple and straightforward language that relates to an audience by painting a picture.

But as the latter part of this chapter shows, there are several other ways to persuade and engage the audience, to get them more emotionally involved in your programme and to get them to stay with you for longer.

RULES FOR EFFECTIVE COMMUNICATION[1]

1. *Simplicity* – Use short and sharp words: the average radio listener has not graduated from university (just one in five people in the UK are educated to degree level).
2. *Brevity* – Use short sentences because it's an increasingly fast world and there's no time for a second-thought to work out what you've just said.
3. *Credibility* – Because your listener must relate to you and to do that she must trust you. (You may need to regain her trust since the 2008 'fraudcasting' competition scandals.)
4. *Consistency* – Because your listener won't hear you the first, second or third time, you have to be true to your on-air character.
5. *Novelty* – Offer some new content, stand out. If you're not different, you're lost.
6. *Sound* – Think how you talk, the exact words you use and the phraseology. Think of a clever turn of phrase, rhyme or alliteration. Capture interest, attention and break through the clutter.[2]

[1] Based on: Frank Luntz, *Words That Work*: http://tinyurl.com/kk6yy7.
[2] Loads of ideas on phrases here: http://tinyurl.com/lphlz3.

7. *Speak aspirationally* – Because we all dream of a better life.
8. *Ask a question* – Because it involves, engages and is conversational.
9. *Provide context and explain relevance* – The greater the impact you have in the listener's daily life the more likely she is to pay attention to you.
10. *Visual imagery matters* – see 'The power of the constructed image' in Chapter 19.

The basics

One-to-oneness

'You orientation' is a marketing concept which works on the principle that there is no more powerful word than the word 'you' when trying to communicate with someone. (Go in to the street and shout 'Hey you!' and see how many people think you're talking to them!) When you put the word 'you' in your set-ups you trigger that same reaction with your listeners. To stay on a one-on-one level with the listener, avoid using plural terms like 'the audience' or 'everyone'. It's not 'some of you might have seen her last night on *Strictly Come Dancing*', it's 'you might have seen her . . .'. Not 'we'll take your phone calls', it's 'you can call now'.

Stay in the singular and talk to all of your listeners individually.

Use contractions

When you are talking with a friend you will automatically shorten words. Ahem. When you're talking with a friend you'll automatically shorten words. Won't you? So make sure you talk the same way on the radio. And, if you are writing something to be read on air, use the same style to make it friendly on the ear. That means instead of 'it is' you write 'it's' and 'you have' becomes 'you've' and so on.

The presenters that work are the ones who talk to you exactly as you imagine they would in real life.[3]

Linguistic appropriateness

Don't get caught up with using phrases that are trendy, police-speak or radio jargon: 'The hot, top sporting stories', 'Up and coming between now and the top of the hour', 'There's been an RTA on the bypass', 'I can't find my weather stab', and so on. Although some programme controllers may say using some technical terms helps break down barriers between the station and the audience and demystifies broadcasting, using radio jargon on air is mostly confusing for people outside the business.

[3] James O'Brien, presenter LBC 97.3, *Guardian*, March 2005.

The tinsel of Lexiphanic[4] language in many places involves his argument in almost inextricable mystery, and pains whom it was intended to please, by making them toil for instruction, when an easy, natural communication was practicable.[5]

ELIZABETH: Captain Barbossa, I am here to negotiate the cessation of hostilities against Port Royal.

BARBOSSA: There are a lot of long words in there, Miss; we're naught but humble pirates. What is it that you want?

ELIZABETH: I want you to leave and never come back.

BARBOSSA: I'm disinclined to acquiesce to your request. Means 'no'.[6]

Clichés, crutches and clutter

Speak naturally and straightforwardly without using a DJ cliché.

The first edition of this book had a long list of them, among them:

'That's the sound of . . .'

'We'll be back after the break.'

'It's 8 minutes past the hour of . . .'

'Keep it here.'

'I'll just put my teeth back in.'

'The phone lines are lit up like a Christmas tree.'

DJ clichés (and crutches and clutter) are what some radio presenters say because they think they're the first to think of them, because they once heard someone else say the same thing, because they think that's what radio presenters do, or because they don't know any better. They're phrases you use while stalling until you think of what you really want to say; it's taking five seconds to say something that should take one. Clutter makes listeners say things like, 'I like their music, but the DJs talk too much' (they never say that when what the presenter says is informative and entertaining). They are crutches because you use them to support the natural you!

Replace a cliché with the real you. Your unique thoughts and humour. Your words and experiences.

Using clichés means that even though you may be *talking* you won't necessarily be *communicating*.

TOP TEN POWER WORDS YOU SHOULD USE IN YOUR ADVERTISING[7]

According to the psychology department at Yale University, some words in the English language are more powerful than others. Here is their top ten most powerful:

---

[4] Lexiphanic: people who use bombastic or pretentious language.

[5] US statesman William Pinkney, 1764–1822.

[6] *Pirates of The Caribbean*: http://tinyurl.com/nhlkv9.

[7] Source: http://tinyurl.com/lnv54l. A similar study from the University of Vermont is detailed here: http://tinyurl.com/nogmjb and shows that the top ten 'happiest' words are *affection, win, comedy, fun, free, rainbow, sex, rollercoaster, beauty, pillow*.

1. '*You* – Listed as the most powerful word in every study reviewed. Because of the personal nature of advertising copywriting, you should use 'you' in your headline, opening line and as often as possible. In fact, many copywriters will throw out a headline if 'you' is not in it.
2. *Results* – Works in rationalising a purchase.
3. *Health* – Especially powerful when it applies to a product.
4. *Guarantee* – Provides a sense of safety at the time of purchase.
5. *Discover* – Presents a sense of excitement and adventure.
6. *Love* – Continues to be an all-time favourite.
7. *Proven* – Helps remove fear from trying something new.
8. *Safety* – This could refer to health or long-lasting quality.
9. *Save* – We all want to save something.
10. *New* – It's part of basic human makeup to seek novelty.

Advanced techniques

If *effective communication* helps the listener understand what you're saying, *persuasive communication* helps them feel what you're feeling, and motivates them.[8]

Emotional word pictures

An emotional word picture uses either a story or an object to help people to understand and feel what the other person is feeling. EWPs stimulate both the left brain (analytical) and the right brain (emotional) of men and women, so can simultaneously communicate with a person's heart and mind, to convey understanding and emotional feelings. For example, the Union Flag is an emotional word picture. It represents democracy and freedom and stirs up emotions of patriotism. Biblical parables and Aesop's fables are also EWPs, as are figures of speech: 'You're a diamond', 'He's one sandwich short of a picnic': they make their point instantly, more powerfully and memorably by using another frame of reference which is more easily illustrated.

EWPs tend to get someone's attention, bring the thought communicated to light, motivate someone to respond and lock the point into their memory . . . and are an effective communication tool.

The more people know about you from your stories, the more you have a reason for them to care about you. These aren't full-blown stories of course, but anecdotes that the audience can identify with, that help create common ground between you.

The primary purpose of personal storytelling is not to entertain listeners or educate them, but to engage them with your own experiences and to prompt them to recall their own.

Big stories are the ones we remember first as they have the greatest personal significance and so they can be recalled more vividly.

---

[8] See also Chapter 16 'Teasing and trailing', which persuades people to continue listening by tempting them with intriguing and incomplete information about a forthcoming feature.

Little stories tend to be less personal and so have broader appeal to the audience. They tend to be less intensely personal and unique as individual experiences, but illustrate more common aspects of shared experiences (the first day of a new job, getting lost on holiday and so on)

You may feel that you cannot remember stories. Actually you probably could if you were prompted. So get in touch with what might inspire those situations to be recalled by you. One good way is to trawl through photos, talk with friends or draw a timeline of significant situations in your life and then fill in the blanks.

Techniques used by psychologists and counsellors are:

- *Think* backwards – mentally pursue a chosen *subject* step by step into your past: dating experiences, cars, hiding places.
- *Feel* backwards – entails digging down layer by layer into *emotional experiences* being an emotional archaeologist: peak experiences, jealousy, feelings for my mother; times when I was torn by conflict, physical pain.

When telling a story on air, don't worry about the full truth: the story has to fit with your on-air character, so you can enliven them while still keeping to the essential facts. You're not under oath!

THE THREE Es OF STORYTELLING

Use these principles to enliven your stories and excite your audience.

ENERGY

It's your energy that brings the story alive. Some stories work well told quietly, for example tragedies and horror stories, others (adventures and comedies) may benefit from more animation. You can animate yourself (moving in and out of the mic) and your voice (not cartoon voices per se, but use a little vocal dexterity) as you tell the story.

EXPRESSION

As with energy, your voice should be used to tell the story in a way that engages the audience. Vary the pitch, volume, timbre, etc. of your voice to keep the story alive.

Do not do this randomly. Talk quietly about secret things. Talk loudly and quickly in battle. Speak excitedly in a car chase. And so on.

ENGAGEMENT

If you can engage your audience in the story, then they will be drawn in all the more.

Ask them questions that engage them (even though they can't directly respond): 'Now what do you think happened next?', 'So how do you think that made me feel?'

Kinaesthetic language (touch and movement) To help listeners feel connected to experiences and emotions		Auditory language To help people connect with what they have heard		Visual language To create word pictures	
Feel	Throw out	Hear	Silence	See	Dawn
Touch	Turn around	Listen	Be heard	Look	Reveal
Grasp	Hard	Sound	Resonate	View	Envision
Get hold of	Hang in there	Make music	Deaf	Appear	Light
Slip through	Concrete	Harmonise	Question	Show	Imagine
Catch on	Scrape	Tune in/out	Unhearing	Clear	Hazy
Tap into	Get a handle	Be all ears	Clear as a bell	Foggy	Crystal clear
Make	Solid	Rings a bell	Tell	Focused	Up front
contact	Get to grips	Loud and	Blabbermouth	Paint a	In view of
Hang on	with	clear		picture	Image

'I've got hold of your argument now.'	'Listen up . . .'	'I see what you're saying.'
'Get in touch with us.'	'Can I sound you out?'	'Can you illuminate me on that point?'
'I think that song's going to catch on.'	'I hear what you're saying.'	'Your argument is crystal clear.'
'She feels as though she's coming to grips with . . .'	'It sounds to me as though you are working in a well-orchestrated team.'	'I'm a bit hazy on that.'

'*Imagine* what you could spend £10,000 on when you win this competition. You could be lying on a beach, *listening* to the waves lapping on the shore and *feeling* the *warm* sand between your toes . . .'

People better understand language that helps them *picture* what it is that's being explained, even if you are not telling a story. That way they are using another sense (the words *and* the image), and the situation becomes more real and relatable. The language of the senses uses visual language:

We experience the world through our senses, which in turn relate to how we process language. Each person has a preference in how they prefer to hear language in terms of sensory expression; for most people speech is related to one of three main sensory groups, so for mass broadcasting it's best to use a combination of these kinds of phrases to engage as many people as possible.[9]

Some people respond best to language which is *kinaesthetic* (they need to 'feel' the prize you're tempting them with, and have information), some to *auditory* language (who need to 'hear' it, through your tone of voice and enthusiasm) and some to *visual* language (the listener who understands pictures better and who will respond best to a great description). So how do you communicate with all of them in one link?

- For the kinaesthetic listener: 'Wake up with The Judge tomorrow and at 7.07 you could win a week at the carnival in Rio . . .'
- For the visual listener: 'Imagine leaving the concrete and grey behind and partying on the white sands Copacabana beach from sunset to golden sunrise . . . dipping your toes in the cool crisp waves and then relaxing in the shade of a palm tree. Then experience the exuberant energy, the colours, the floats . . .'
- For the auditory listener: . . . 'the glamourous dancers moving to the infectious samba beats of the biggest street carnival in the party capital of the world . . . Boy, does that sound great, or what?!'
- For them all: 'So make sure you hear The Judge tomorrow at 7.07, to find out how you can turn that dream into a reality . . . only here on Triple Z.'

Maximise your connection to your listeners by communicating in ways they relate to.

Using NLP

The Milton Model

Milton Model language patterns are sets of sentences that, because they are deliberately unclear, distract the listener. While this is happening, you are able to increase your ability to influence. These are well-used techniques in everyday conversation, as well as being used by advertisers and counsellors. For the first time the information has been adapted to work specifically for radio presenters. By using similar sentence structure in presentation, we can better communicate with and relate to, our audience.

Mind reading

Stating that you know what another person is thinking without stating how you know.
Example: '*I know that* you'll want to know the update on that heathland fire . . .'

Lost performative

Making a value judgement without stating who or what is making the judgement.
Example: '*It* is a good thing to consider what you may do with that prize money . . .'

Cause and effect

Implying that one thing causes another either explicitly (A makes you B) or implicitly (If A . . . then B). Statements usually use words such as *because*, *and*, *as*, *when*, *causes* and *makes*.
Example: 'You'll know what's going on first *because* we've got reporters across the county', 'Text in *and* you could be our big winner', 'The station that *makes* you smile in the morning'.

Complex equivalence

Attributing the same meaning to different things as if they were directly equivalent. Words used include *means*, *so* and *therefore*.
Example: 'It's Friday afternoon at 5.30, *so* you'll want the travel news.'

Presupposition

Assuming something is true, using phrases such as *Did you know . . . ?*, *Are you aware that . . . ?*, *Have you heard . . . ?*, *Did you see that . . . ?*, *Lots of people . . .*, *You realise that . . .*

Example: '*Are you aware that* this is the only station with commentary of . . .', '*Now you know* why so many people are listening to . . .', '*Have you heard* how easy it is to win . . .', '*Did you know* that more and more people are listening to . . .'

Universal quantifiers

Words that are universal generalisations and do not refer to a specific person or thing. Use words such as *none, all, everyone, every, each, everything, never, always.*

Example: '*Everyone's* saying Kylie's new song's her best yet . . .'

Modal operators

Words that form rules (implying necessity: *must, mustn't, will, won't, have to, should, shouldn't*) or set out options (implying possibilities: *can, can't, will, won't, would, could, might*).

Example: 'You *must* be able to imagine going to the concert on Friday . . .' 'Just suppose you *could* take part in . . .'

Tag question

A question added after a statement in a way that is likely to get a positive answer, by hinting at it in the previous phrase.

Example: 'You know we have the most up-to-date travel news, *don't you* . . . ?'

Lack of referential index

A phrase that does not make it clear who or what is being referred to.

Example: '*Everyone's* listening to us now.'

Comparative deletions

Comparing something without saying what you are comparing it to (using words such as: *good, better, best, worst, more, less, most, least*).

Example: 'The *better* music mix . . .', 'The *most* music . . .'

Double binds

Giving an illusion of choice, but in effect giving no choice at all, in this first example you presume that the listener will be going to the event.

Example: 'Will you buy tickets for the Big Beach Bash before, *or* on the day?', 'Where will you be listening tomorrow morning when we read out the hotline number, in bed *or* in the car?'

Conversational postulate

These require a simple yes or no answer, and invite the listener to do something straightforward and almost immediately.

Example: '*Can you* just give me ten seconds while I explain this?'

Quotes and extended quotes

Putting words in someone's mouth so 'It's not me saying this'. An extended quote is where the words you put in someone's mouth are themselves quotes from another person. This induces confusion about who is saying what.

Example: 'When I was talking to John last week *he said* that on one of his outside broadcasts last week, *a woman said* she really loved my show . . .'

Selectional restriction violation

Attributing human or animal characteristics to inanimate objects.

Example: 'Give your *wallet a relaxing break* too, because if you win, we pay for everything . . .'

Adjective presuppositions

Whenever the following words are used, what follows them is presupposed, because to make sense of the sentence, the listener must accept the rest of the sentence as being true: *Obviously, naturally, easily, some, clearly, already, repeatedly, exceedingly, truly, many, undeniably, most.*

Example: '*Obviously* you'll want to stay with us for that', '*Clearly* the best choice for the county's travel news', '*Most* people prefer waking up with . . .', '*Easily* the most comprehensive weather forecast . . .'

Spatial presuppositions

These influence understanding by creating imagined physical relationships between things by creating powerful imagery in the mind of the listener by using words such as *beyond, among, above, contain, further, another, behind.*

Example: 'Be *among* our special winners if you can guess the answer to . . .', 'Leaves the other stations *behind*', '*Another* great song from Keane', 'We go *further* to bring you the biggest and most exciting prizes', 'Get *on top* of what's happening that'll affect your family . . .'

Temporal presuppositions

You can influence understanding by embedding the suggestion that you want the listener to carry out, in the sentence, to create an unconscious influence. Use words such as: *whilst, during, before, finally, after, still, first, when.*

Example: 'The station that's *still* number one for . . .', '*After* you've listened to our breakfast show you won't want to go anywhere else', '*Before* I explain how you can win, here's what you can win', '*Finally*, a station that all the family can listen to'.

Influencing commands

These help prompt listeners to change their thinking by using words such as *now, stop, listen, look, hang on.*

Example: '*Stop* what you're doing and listen to this incredibly emotional interview', '*Now*, listen to this amazing new release from . . .'

Embedded commands

With these you can make suggestions that bypass the listener's conscious filtering system and influence at a deep level, a bit like hidden instructions. To use embedded commands first decide what habit you want to instil in the listener, then place that emphasised command within a sentence:

Example: '*Keep* your radio tuned to us, you're *listening* to the best place for new music', 'It's your *call*. *Now* the new one from Snow Patrol', 'I'd love to know how you *feel* about that. *Good* morning! I'm Johnny Jock.'

Emphasise the embedded words by saying them slightly more loudly, using a different tone or pausing slightly before each one. It's a tricky technique to use in adlibbed speech but you could script some 'off-the-shelf' phrases to use on a semi-regular basis.

Yes sets

Get someone to subconsciously accept a second or third statement, because they have already accepted that previous ones are true.

Example: 'It's summer. The sun is shining. Picnic In The Park is the only place to be', 'It's 7 o'clock. You've gotta get up. Johnny Jock is the only person to be doing it with.'

Numerical anticipation

This technique harnesses your audience's natural craving for 'closure' on a list that's already been started.

Example: 'Coming next . . . the three biggest songs of the year', 'And I've got a second "dumb criminal" story after the news.'

These sentence structures, based on NLP but for the first time explained specifically for radio presenters, can entice the listener to feel comfortable with you, agree with you and to listen longer.

Because of the words used and where you use them, the listener subconsciously feels as though you are both on the same 'wavelength', and they warm to you and relate to you.

Instead of talking to them, you are communicating.

Finally, some other linguistic tips[10] for radio presenters:

- ◻ Don't use the word 'try' as it implies that work has to be done on the part of the listener ('Try and give us a call . . .')
- ◻ Replace 'but' with 'and' or 'so' which are more affective logical persuaders ('Johnny's not on tomorrow and/so Richard's going to be here after 10').
- ◻ Don't use negatives, as these are often subconsciously filtered out, and the listener ends up with the exact opposite message ('Don't turn your radio off' is better phrased as 'Keep your radio on'). Negatives are processed differently by neurology than they are in language (if you say don't do something, you have to imagine it to understand what not to do).
- ◻ Be specific in your links. So instead of saying 'Over the holidays I took the kids to the

---

[10] More on NLP at http://tinyurl.com/kqgd86, http://tinyurl.com/m2ehs6 and http://tinyurl.com/cswvay.

park to play and have something to eat' say 'I was determined to spend time with Jake and Carrie, so we went down to Nonsuch Park and flew this huge yellow stunt kite and then feasted on muffins and hot chocolate'. It paints a better picture and makes a better connection. And, when you give characters names your audience gives them faces. (You may want to change the names of your kids for privacy issues but you get the idea . . .)

□ Use active verbs not passive, clunky and uninvolving ones. So 'We'll give out more information nearer the time' becomes 'If *you'd* like to go and find out what's on and when, keep listening as you'll catch all *you* need to know'.

How to talk to a woman, or a man[11]

A woman's highest personal value is developing and nurturing relationships. They use indirect speech as it helps them avoid conflict. If a woman says 'I think the kids are growing out of their shoes' the man hears an observation on how the children are growing up fast. What she has meant is 'We need to go shoe shopping this afternoon'.

Men's sentences are short, direct, solution-oriented, and peppered with facts. Men use quantifiers such as 'none', 'never' and 'absolutely' to help them close deals quickly and efficiently and assert authority. But when men use direct speech in their relationships with women, it often makes them appear abrupt and rude.

Now you can use this behavioural insight when speaking to better connect with you audience. If you are directing a comment to mostly men in the audience ('win tickets to the big match and we'll throw in a case of beer'), speak in short sentences, be direct and use bullet points. If you are talking to women, engage them in a conversation. Develop and nurture a relationship and tell them a story.

Talking without words

Use body language to help you explain things and get a message across – it is only natural! After all, in evolution, gestures came well before speech. A presenter who gestures naturally as they talk will communicate more clearly. Listeners will notice the difference even if they can't see the gestures.

Think about how you give directions to someone: you don't stand with your hands in your pockets, you use them as you explain about traffic lights, bridges, roundabouts and turnings. Use the same techniques on air to help you communicate. As well as making your sentiments stronger, gestures such as a clenched fist or a smile will also help you change your voice to fit the mood.

When you present, be interesting and interested. 'Interesting' – so if you say you are angry about something make your voice sound angry! If you are excited make sure that is how you sound. 'Interested' – so you sound as though you are enjoying your programme and are interested in your own material. On radio a smile is the equivalent of making eye contact. A smile, even if no one sees it, makes a person sound more inviting, confident and fresh. Of course, a smile is not always appropriate. For example, news reports on serious subjects are seldom delivered with a smile, unless a lighter story is included at the end. Also, think about the fact that there are many different kinds of smiles. In addition to smiles of happiness, there are smiles that indicate understanding, sympathy or comfort.

---

[11] Adapted from work by Fran Lytle, consumer behaviourist and author of *Connection Moments* (Trafford Publishing, 2006).

14 Your content

Create unique and compelling content

There will always be good ambitious people wanting to do it, because it is the most exciting thing in the world to do, but radio at its pure best is a long way from segueing The Lighthouse Family into Mariah Carey and then doing a seven-second ident and if you're lucky a competition that wouldn't stretch a guinea pig.[1]

Listeners tune in to a radio station for items such as good music, an entertaining and informed presenter, news and travel, weather and so on. They tune out when they hear an incompetent or bumbling presenter, long and boring interviews, content which has no relevance to them, too many adverts and uninspiring music.

It is one of the jobs of a presenter and producer to increase the 'tune in' factors and reduce the 'tune out' ones.

You have to play listeners' favourite songs and talk about things that interest them – hardly rocket science, is it?

Most commercial radio is so lacking in decent content right now and listeners are crying out for more than a constant jukebox. They need an appointment to listen and if they can't get it from the radio they will get it from the Internet or their phone. Radio and

---

[1] Nicky Campbell, presenter, BBC Radio Five Live, *The Radio Magazine*, June 2009.

programmers beware you don't lose the ability to connect with your listeners in the unique way only radio can.[2]

A link is a short, spoken comment between two programme items, usually songs. A 'bit' is a longer link, perhaps a few minutes long and is more likely to be a conversation between co-hosts, a competition, a pre-recorded windup phone call or a spoof song. Together, they are the glue that holds the rest of the structure of the programme together, so it's important that they're not 'tune outs'.

The similarity with both of these is that preparation is the key to making them work. Know what message you want to get across and work out how you are going to do it. Don't become an 'emergent theorist', believing that if you talk enough rubbish something amazing will emerge. Don't simply talk until you've got something to say.[3]

Ask yourself these questions before you start a link

- Is it relevant? Have I localised it? (See below for what I mean by local.)
- Is it interesting? Will everybody understand it?
- Is it compelling? Will this add excitement or enhance the station?

Relevance alone is not enough: you could do a half-hour feature on prostate cancer, but even though it affects men, few will listen. The presentation has to be interesting or compelling too: the more immediately relevant the information, the less important the presentation.

Being interesting and compelling provokes reaction. And one of the most effective ways of getting your listener to react is to challenge them, subtly. That's not a dramatic, angry re-action, but something to cause them to think or feel some kind of emotion.

- So they stop what they're doing to concentrate on what you're going to do or say.
- So they turn up the radio to listen to what you're going to do or say.
- So they phone/text/e-mail in.
- So they react verbally to what you've just said ('I can't believe that!').
- So they react non-verbally to what you've said (nodding or shaking their head).
- So they actively listen to you, not just hear you.

TRIPLE-FILTERED CONTENT

Like a brewer, triple-filter your output.

Filter 1 – The 'So What?' Filter. This removes cloudy slot-filling material that is boring, dull and largely irrelevant to the audience.

Filter 2 – The 'Target Audience' Filter. This filter ensures the output is tailored to the target demographic (socio and psychodemographic).

Filter 3 – The 'Unique' Filter. This guarantees that you're offering listeners something unique.

---

[2] Graham Torrington, BBC Radio Bristol, *The Radio Magazine*, May 2009.
[3] Galimatias: gibberish, meaningless talk, or nonsense.

Basic advice

Most radio seems spontaneous and conversational – a lot of that is down to the skill of the presenter who has done their show prep. They know the features and the topics that they want to talk about, as well as having a lot of background knowledge about local and national events to 'fall back on' if it's needed.

Apart from the cues and introductions to interviews or rules for competitions, scripting links is unusual. (Having said that scripted 'liner cards' were used on some stations in the 1990s to concentrate the presenters into broadcasting in the station's style.) What is more likely is a presenter referring to some notes they made earlier and mentally rehearsing the flow and duration of the link while a previous feature is going to air. However, the exact words will be adlibbed live.

When you go into the studio you will have prepared the show inasmuch as you know where the different planned elements will be, but you should also be prepared for other events (breaking news or breaking inspiration). Always have a pad and pen so when you have an idea for a link you can jot down ideas, phrases and words to use in the link.

Remember, an effective link should have a dramatic opening that captures the listener's attention, a well-structured middle that holds and develops their interest and, more importantly, a powerful climax. By taking the time to take notes and structure the link in your mind, you can keep your link concentrated and punchy. You also reduce the risk of forgetting the name of someone or some place that is integral to the link; and that happens to everyone.

Adlibbing takes experience and those who have been on radio for a while may tell you that they don't know what they are going to say even as they open the mic. This may well be true for them after years of broadcasting, but do not let their comments fool you into thinking that you can get away without planning at an early stage of your career.

How often should you do a link? Every station and circumstance is different. However, as a guideline, if it's a mainly music programme then talk after every other song, or do four voice links for every six songs (link, song, song; link song; link, song, song; link, song, etc.), not after every single one. Some stations demand that you segue three songs before you open the mic, but the main rule of thumb on music radio is to let the music flow.

How long should a link be? As long as it needs to be to create and keep interest and/or evoke emotion. That emotion could be humour, interest, empathy and so on, but as soon as it's boredom or offence then you've failed.

A link could be two minutes long, if that is what it takes to grab the audience, tell the story, stir passions, and build up to a climax. A link could be five seconds if all you need to do is ID the station and trail the next song.

> A radio link is twenty seconds in a lift to tell an acquaintance
> something important.[4]

Some stations will have rules about how often you should talk, and for how long, and this will change depending not only on the station but also the kind of programme. For example, a breakfast presenter will talk more than a mid-morning show host.

Bear in mind the phrase 'bin it after a minute', or 'shrink your link': however long it is,

---

[4] Charlie Wolf, presenter.

it could probably have been shorter. If removing any element of a link doesn't weaken the link, that element shouldn't be there.

Criticism that you talk too much often means the talk is irrelevant and not connecting on any emotional level: 'talking too much' is not the problem; saying too little of relevance is. But don't just talk faster to get more in the time allowed. Instead use more economical speech: get to the heart of the link quickly and use your tone of voice as well as shorter, more specific words. Fast talk does not = good content. If you are on a time limit, remember 'Maximum impact, minimum time'.

Momentum

This is not how fast you go or how much energy you have, it's how economically you can get from A to B. A link can be three minutes long and still have great momentum, because that's as long as the item needs to be to move forward and develop an organic flow of ideas and information. Another link could be 20 seconds but have no momentum, because it was repetitive and robotic.

Similarly, having a music bed underneath you can be comfortable in case you fall over, but it's not the best way to get forward momentum. You'll sound more intimate without a bed; don't use one in links where you're trying to make an emotional connection, because your message and mood will be buried. At first you may feel naked and vulnerable, but over time you will sound more natural, adult and real.

Momentum should be in your links and your overall programme and your *programmes* over the weeks and months. It is structure that builds the next item on the previous item to a climax or finale of the show, not speed.[5]

What you need to get over in a basic link are three firm facts:

- ▫ the name/frequency of the station
- ▫ what you have just played
- ▫ a tease to something coming up.

Radio X 99.9 FM playing Supergrass and Charlotte Church . . . where there's your chance to win our weekend in west Wales in the next hour . . .

Supergrass and Charlotte Church on Radio X 99.9 FM . . . where there's your chance to win our weekend in west Wales in the next hour . . .

That was Supergrass and Charlotte Church . . . on the station where in the next hour, there's your chance to win our weekend in west Wales . . . that's here on Radio X 99.9FM . . .

This is also known as the 'that was, this is' link as, essentially that is what you do: just giving the briefest of details of what song was just played, what is coming up and the station ID.

---

[5] *Magic and Showmanship* by Henning Nelms. This book deals with the psychology and performance of magic, and performing in front of an audience: http://tinyurl.com/kodm7t.

Format jocks

> There has to be light and shade. Yes, you have to have big
> personalities on your station and allow them to express
> themselves, but you also have to have great music jocks on the air
> to complement. Too much either way can be damaging.[6]

A presenter (usually during the daytime), whose main job is to keep the music flowing, is called a format jock. They stick to format (or 'the formatics') and links may consist of little more than what's called the basics:

- the time and temperature
- the name and the numbers (station name and frequency)
- the slogan and the song.

These presenters (called time and temp jocks in the States) usually have a low profile on the station, but they are confident and competent in what they do, and are hired specifically because they are a safe pair of hands. Although perhaps not Mr Personality in the same way as their drivetime colleagues, they are not going to do long links and they are not going to say anything offensive. Their very job is to be unobtrusive.

Radio is free and therefore usually taken for granted. So to get the credit you deserve, say the station name often.

This is so listeners:

- know what station to find in the future, especially if they're listening online
- can tell their friends their station of choice
- know what box to mark in the Rajar diary – regular mentions should help increase listening figures
- for commercial stations: so listeners can tell advertisers they subsequently shop with, where they heard about them
- for BBC stations: to remind listeners where the licence fee is being spent.

Most stations have a policy of mentioning the name of the station (sometimes together with some other piece of information such as a frequency or strapline) *every single link*. You may think that this gets to be rather repetitive and formulaic, but it is down to you as a presenter to ensure that it doesn't. If people listen to your station for an average of an hour a day, and you only mention the station name every 20 minutes they may only hear it two or three times.

The programme controller may tell you that you have to say the station name as the *first element* in every link but this doesn't sound very conversational and also means there is a chance that the station name (perhaps the most important part of the link) may be subconsciously 'thrown away' and garbled by a presenter wanting to get to the 'meat' of their link.

Others maintain the station name has to be the *last element* in every link: that way it is reinforced as the last thing the listener hears you say.

Most say that it can be anywhere in the link, as long as it is in there somewhere.

You can, of course, vary the way you identify the station, either by simple verbal mentions: 'You're listening to Radio X' or weave the mentions into a script or conversation.

---

[6] Steve Penk, presenter, Key 103, *The Radio Magazine,* March 2005.

- '*Radio X* playing Coldplay's new single, where we're giving away £1,000 in our Secret Sound Competition . . .'
- 'That's Coldplay's latest on the station which is giving away £1,000 in the *Radio X* Secret Sound Competition . . . [details] . . . so make sure you're listening at 4.30 this afternoon and you could be a winner on the Secret Sound, only here on *Radio X*.'
- 'That's Coldplay's latest on the station which is giving away £1,000 in the *Radio X* Secret Sound Competition . . .'
- 'Simon's on the line now to *Radio X* . . .'
- 'Tara, thanks for joining us on *Radio X*.'
- 'Later here on *Radio X* . . .'
- 'Peter Porter reports for *Radio X*.'

There is more to identifying your station than simply saying its name. Keep saying *where* you are as well as *who* you are: '. . . here in Leeds . . .' or '. . . here in West Sussex . . .'. These informal mentions remind people they are listening to their own local service not one from miles away. This is especially important when many stations have 'generic' names that are not linked to their location.

Mention your name[7] often, about every second or third link, although some stations may like you to do this every time you open the mic. Remember, not everyone will know your name or recognise your voice. If the listener doesn't know who you are, they can't build a relationship with you. Mentioning your name humanises the show and reminds people that you are the only purveyor of 'you' and what you do.

When you tell them your name, tell them in a conversational way: '*I'm* Peter Stewart' is much more friendly, natural and relatable than '*This is* Peter Stewart', and certainly avoid 'My name is . . .' or 'Peter Stewart here' (if you're here, the listener is 'there' and you've created distance between you both). Remember, you're saying 'hello', not announcing who you are.

You should also identify and re-identify your guests, and always back-anno interviews – listeners often find it difficult to recognise a voice if they start listening in mid-conversation.

One to one-ness

Speak directly to someone, one on one, person to person. Refer to 'you' not 'you all' or 'everybody'. It's more natural and conversational. Radio is an intimate and immediate communication between one person and another. If you use 'you', you engage.

Isolation of thought

A rule of radio is 'one thought, one link'; in other words do not cram in too much information. If you do, your message will be lost. That doesn't mean that you can only give the name of the station or only give the title and artist of the song you have just played, it means you do those and then one on an item of substance. Act like the SAS: do what you need to do and then get out.

Consider what your single core message is that you want the audience to hear, understand and remember, and say it clearly, powerfully and memorably. Apart from the formatic elements (station name and so on), any two things done in one break are only 50 per cent as effective as they could be if they were done in two separate breaks, because they *compete* with each other in the listener's mind.

---

[7] Also read about 'zoo programmes' in Chapter 22, 'Double-headed and team shows', to see how to identify your on-air colleagues.

So no 'laundry lists' of songs in the next hour or of next week's guests. Sound focused and help the audience understand the message.

Always know what you want to accomplish before you open the mic: what you are going to say and where you are going with it. In other words: know the point and the pay-off.

Let's take an example of a link about poor driving — you were cut up on the way into work. That's a good angle (or 'peg to hang it on') and will be a good way to get in to the link — 'I was driving into work this morning and had just passed the Red Lion on East Street [note the relatable reference] when a blue Fiesta [don't mention the registration] cut me up . . .'.

In the office earlier you and some colleagues came up with a few more examples of what annoys you about people's driving habits and you intend to do a 'mock rant' on these and ask listeners to call in with their stories of motoring mayhem. You've decided to call the bit 'Drivers From Hell' and have produced a bed with a voiceover and a clap of thunder going into 'The Ride of the Valkyries' music. It's going to be the main topic of the show. But even though you know what you are going to say to get in to the piece (you were cut up), what you will say when you are in it (other examples of bad driving) and what you want next (more examples from listeners), do you know how you are going to get out of that introduction?

You have got the beginning and the middle but what about your end? What is your denoue-ment, your 'out', your punchline going to be? It might be something like, 'So many people ignore the Highway Code, it might as well be called the My-Way Code!' Straight into a song.

Many presenters don't know when to get out of a link, whether it is a conversation with a caller or even when they are talking by themselves! They just do not have the confi-dence or speed to realise that what's just been said is the funniest, most poignant or ironic point.

The climax is sometimes tricky to see, especially when there are several presenters all vying for 'the last word' and it's someone else rather than you who comes up with the best line! Get ready to seize the moment at the optimum point and go straight to the jingle or the song. Identify the impact point to leave listeners on a high with something strong and memor-able. Don't leave the bit to lose momentum, wither and die . . . and fade away . . . like this . . .

When planning a link know what you want out of it *and* how you'll get out of it. Prep your 'out'.

Many new presenters can plan one step at a time, but not what happens after that. So, they might know what they are going to say, and how to wrap it up, but won't have consid-ered what follows it, leaving a moment of dead air.

Know the next thing you must do when you have finished your link so you don't just stop. Are you going into an ad break, another song, introduce a guest? Think it through, and get it ready.

Hellos and menus

Many presenters have a standard programme sheet that they complete before each show, giving changeable information such as their guests, who's presenting travel news, the current total on the roll-over competition and so on. Also on the sheet is static information such as the XD phone number for the travel news service, often-used web-addresses or backtimes. This sheet gives all the basics they need for each show all in one place. Some presenters who use a 'stage name' even put that the top of the sheet so they don't forget it.

At the start of your show, either straight after the news or after the first song, it is customary to 'set out your stall' and tell listeners what they can hear over the next few hours.

This is called a 'programme menu' or a 'programme run-down', but it has to be used with care. Very few people will tune in to the start of your show with the intention of following it for three or four hours, all the way through – however much we wish they would! So at the start of the show give people an *idea* of what is ahead, your strongest two or three features, but don't mention everything in a laundry list style. The more things you promote, the less someone will care about any of them And certainly don't promote items giving specific times that they will go to air. If you do, you are giving listeners the opportunity to turn off and only come back to hear that specific feature at that specific time. This will not, of course, dramatically increase your listening hours.

Also avoid giving a list of songs or artists:

- It's boring.
- People will know what they don't want to listen to.
- You may not be able to fit in the last scheduled song in the hour, disappointing the listener who's waited 55 minutes to hear it.

Instead keep promoting all the way through the programme, teasing[8] with specific benefits or advantages of listening.

A start-of-show plea to 'stay with us for the next three hours' is pretty pointless – people have busy lives. But you may just get them to listen for another 15 or 20 minutes, and that's the key.

'*We've got a busy/full/packed programme*': it may be busy for you but saying this sounds as though you are desperate for the sympathy vote. It also sounds that the other shows aren't busy – does that mean they're not as good as yours?

'*We've got a lot to get through*' gives the signal to the listener that they are going to have to concentrate and work hard to follow everything that is happening. How many do you think will be bothered? From the listener's point of view the programme has 'lots of great things' in it, which you will then promote (although not all at once). If it truly is packed, then perhaps you have got too much in it, or it has been poorly produced with too much speech or too many songs.

Show prep

No entertainer would ever think they could take to their stage without preparing and rehearsing material. Apart from the radio presenter.

It is in your own selfish interest to prepare material for your show ('show prep'). That's how you learn more, perform better, and get a bigger audience . . . and more money.

> Preparation is king. I'm constantly on the lookout for ammunition for links for the show, and always insuring that what I'm doing is relatable radio. The old saying is true – if you fail to prepare, you prepare to fail. If anyone tells me I'm lucky, I always tell them it's funny that the harder I work the luckier I get.[9]

One of the biggest concerns among new presenters is knowing what to say between the songs. Presenters of magazine shows have a lot of their links written in the form of cues (or

[8] See Chapter 16, 'Teasing and trailing'.
[9] Simon Ross, presenter, Radio City, *The Radio Magazine*, May 2009.

introductions) to their stories and interviews. But presenters of music shows have to talk off the top of their head. Where do their ideas come from?

Some of your colleagues will say that they don't prep, and scoff at you with your notebook of ideas. These people say they're experienced enough to wing it, and that preparing material means they can't be reactive and spontaneous. They're also usually the people who do poor shows.

> I was listening to Gold and I heard three records in a row and I was bored. The guy came on afterwards 'Hi this is Gold, it's now 10 minutes past 10' and that was it. I'd waited ten minutes for that.[10]

Every professional prepares for their working day: pilots check weather conditions, doctors check a patient's records and barristers check their briefs. What do you do?

> The future of radio is determined by the people we have on the mic. They are the shop window of everything we do and it does wind me up to hear poor preparation or presenters who umm and err because they have forgotten what they were about to say.[11]

Material for bits and links are all around us, but that is only good if you can remember it all. Always have a notebook and pen with you, or record a memo on your mobile or Dictaphone. Some presenters always take a portable MP3 recorder with them wherever they go, so they can record a comment, interview, scene set, or effects for a link. Broadcast quality recorders such as these are only £20 or so.

Make a note of:

- what's annoying you right now
- what you've noticed that's new, unusual, changing . . .
- what you feel about the situations and people you come across
- what you are musing about right now
- reminiscences about your childhood and youth
- what you've spotted that's made you laugh or smile
- what you've overheard at the shop/pub/gym.

Links come from everywhere.

You get material from what you've observed and what you've overheard. It is what you would actually talk about even if you weren't on the radio. Your own show prep should be going on all the time. Everything you read, watch, see, hear and do is a potential source of material for your show.

> Unlike some DJs, Christian O'Connell has always worked hard at his banter, trawling magazines and websites for ideas, including *Rolling Stone, GQ, Esquire, The Week,* the *New Yorker* and even *Marie Claire.* 'I tear through them like a vampire, sucking life out of them.'[12]

[10] Tony Blackburn, presenter, *The Radio Magazine*, November 2008.
[11] John Myers, *The Radio Magazine*, April 2008.
[12] *Independent*, May 2006.

Life content

What are your own responses to your own life experiences?

How do you react and interact with the people around you, your family, friends and colleagues? What it's like to be you?

Life content includes all those little ironies and universals you notice and share with those close to you.[13]

You gather life content by watching for things that you respond to emotionally. Train yourself to notice when you have a thought of surprise, shock or amusement. Realise when you laugh at something, get cross at an idiosyncrasy, success or failure.

Develop an interest in another area and become passionate about it. Meet people with other experiences, or read about issues that help you make different connections and discover more about yourself, your personality and reactions.

Work like this as a matter of routine. After a while it will get to the point where you'll get really frustrated when you're on holiday and not doing the show. You'll be conditioned to look out for stories and material during your everyday life and get really frustrated that you can't use it on air, especially if it's topical material that won't last until you're home. It's a good sign that you're moving in the right direction as a presenter.

Tell your life content stories from your personal[14] perspective and the more your comments will resonate with the audience. That's because a personal connection humanises a story – people connect with people.

> When you think about the best presenters working today in music radio – Wogan, Ross, O'Connell, Moyles – then you have to concede that what endears them to listeners is not the music they play but the conversation they engage in between the records.[15]

You need to be intensely personal, but also universal.

Some presenters are personal inasmuch as they talk about their lives, experiences, and opinions. But if the subject only means something to them, it's not universal enough for listeners to feel a common bond. We want them to have a 'Yeah, I know what you mean!' moment. An emotional connection.

> If you are interested you are interesting.[16]

Some presenters are universal inasmuch as they talk about subjects that everyone goes through . . . but they don't bring a personal angle to it. And that means, again, there's no emotional connection made with the listener.

So much radio is boring and generic. Presenters play it too safe; they're not personally revealing enough. No passion = no interest level from the listener.

Life content is the most personal, most individual material you can offer; no one else will have quite the same experiences you do, or see them in exactly the same way. More

---

[13] Such as these: http://tinyurl.com/nv55bq.

[14] Note: there is a difference between something that's personal and something that's private.

[15] James O'Brien, presenter, LBC 97.3, *The Radio Magazine*, July 2007.

[16] Loretta Young, US actress.

than anything else you do, life content makes you un-copy-able. It gives you qualitative difference.

The only real long-term sustainable points of difference are people. Music, production, benchmarks and features are all copyable, but people are not: they are the points of difference. But they are poachable![17]

Observation and conversation[18]

Observe life unfolding around you — what you see and hear other people do.

Eavesdropping may not be the most honourable of pastimes but it can be very effective. Train yourself to do it in every situation, in the supermarket queue or the dentists, bend an ear to take away talking topics. (But try not to be too obvious. There are those stalking laws!) Eavesdropping is not asking family and friends what they're talking about, or what they think about news stories. They're not representative of the general public: because they know you and what you do, they'll tell you (subconsciously or not) what they think you'll want to hear. The chatter at the station is likewise suspect: you'll find a lot more news awareness there than at the shopping centre, supermarket or gym. Hear what's really on people's minds. Ask people what they think. You're not going to know that if you stay at home and watch the news channels and read political blogs and the papers.

Go outside and watch *people*. Drive a different route to or from work every day, even if you just take a turn earlier. You'll see something you hadn't noticed before, a new building going up or a shop that used to be one thing becoming something else.

Look around you. We are all used to filtering out vast amounts of external stimuli, but effective presenters pay greater attention when out driving or walking, and pick up on changes to the surroundings and incorporate them in their shows. Build your powers of observation.[19] You can't talk about life unless you *have* one.

THE AHA EXPERIENCE[20]

Wolfgang Köhler (1887–1967) researched how humans and animals learn and solve problems, including the moment of 'sudden understanding' or 'epiphany', the moment when elements of a task or problem 'click'.

This moment of insight is what psychologists call the Aha Experience.

An example might be the story of Archimedes who discovered the principle of buoyancy while taking a bath ('Eureka!').

---

[17] Mark Browning, programmer, Heart 106.2, *The Radio Magazine*, April 2006.
[18] *1001 Top Talking Topics*, ideas and inspiration for radio presenters: http://tinyurl.com/nurj2w.
[19] Observation Skills Test: http://tinyurl.com/mo4vp4.
[20] More on the Aha Experience: http://tinyurl.com/m242o3.

Another might be when someone is talking to us and we know exactly what they're talking about and we nod enthusiastically ('Yeah, that's so right! That does happen!). The speaker has created a link with you. They have communicated clearly.

It also happens when talented presenters give insight into what is already in the listener's subconscious mind.

It has to do with relevance and a deep understanding of what the core target of the station is most interested in.

Content can be what's overheard and what's observed, and then you having a conversation with the listener about it on the air. Like friends do when they're talking to each other.

A story has to lead to an opinion.

It's great to read and experience lots, and then talk on the radio about it, as long as you avoid the straightforward process of:

reading → regurgitation

which amounts to little more than the bland recitation of facts.

Instead, make the process:

reading → assimilation → *reaction*

in other words, discover what's happening, then discover your own feeling towards it and put that reaction on the radio to more powerfully connect with your audience.

Self-revelation

Reveal something of yourself: that could be a response to a song, a personal comment about the weather . . . it makes you human rather than a jukebox, or a bland, any-format Jock-in-a-box.

That's not enough for the listener who came for some companionship, or enough to set you apart from other stations playing similar music. It's not enough to keep your job.

OK, it's not easy being yourself. An actor has lines, and a 'character' to hide behind. We have to take risks and let our own feelings show through to strangers.

I stay true to myself. I don't let anything go out that wouldn't happen in real life. I hear so many programmes that sound so contrived. It's like people reading off a script. My show is real, designed for real people. I relate to my audience because I am my audience. I do the same things that they do, so when I talk about it they relate.[21]

You become more conversational when you drop the façade of being Mr Personality who is trying to impress with stories of your DJ lifestyle, and instead talk from the heart about issues that matter to you and to your listeners — the stories that are relatable, interesting and compelling. Make 'eye contact' with your listener.

I can honestly say that I am true to myself on air . . .
If I had to maintain some kind of act it would be impossible.[22]

The more you reveal just a little glimpse of your personal life, the more you will connect with the audience and get them to trust you. Personal stories — not personality stories. And not (necessarily) 'private stories' either (about your pregnancy, money worries or child's bad school report).

Revealing something of yourself means saying something that no other presenter could possibly say. It makes you unique and memorable. Your personal journey of how you came to have those feelings can bring you and your listener closer together. It makes you real and someone the audience can relate to, and that helps build a powerful connection.

But this is revealing something of your *true* self. Fake passion is as bad as no passion, and listeners can sense it. Even if you don't care about what's in the news, there will be something you *do* care about: Maybe you're worried about the car payments this month, your son's driving you crazy over wanting something you don't want him to have, perhaps it's a litter problem where you live. Maybe the weather is depressing, or you're several weeks into the year and you haven't made a start on that resolution. Maybe you wish you had a better car, maybe you're debating growing a beard, maybe you're putting off going to the dentist. Share your life on air.

That's your show. Talk about the stuff you might not think is important. It's not the Queen's Speech, the NHS or insurgents in Iraq . . . but if it matters to you, it'll make for a better show than if you try to fake something.

The emotion quotient

Emotions stimulate the mind 3,000 times faster than regular thought. They move a person to act long before the rational mind has the chance to catch up.[23] That's why using them in a story makes the telling so much stronger.

Remember that 'emotions' are anything that cause a reaction with the listener — that's not necessarily anger or sorrow, it could be pity, frustration, humour, concern, envy, wonder, recognition, thanks, joy.

Listener reactions are caused when something is relevant to them, so it's good to know

---

[21] Adam Catterall, presenter, Rock FM, *The Radio Magazine*, May 2009.
[22] Stephen Nolan, BBC Radio Five Live, *The Radio Magazine*, November 2005.
[23] *Marketing To The Mind* by R.C. Maddock and R.L. Fulton (Quorum Books, 1996).

what those relevant subjects are. They can be easily divided into four general groups, shown in the box which follows.[24]

WHAT'S PERSONAL

For example, stories to do with the family, education, careers, love and relationships,[25] differences between men and women, learning and self-discovery. Stories which are geographically local. (The psychologist Sigmund Freud said that people are only interested in two things: work, out of necessity, and love, for comfort: both of them are contained in this group.)

WHAT'S IN THEIR PURSE

Our hard-earned cash and what it's spent on: savings, mortgages, pensions, bargains, private health and private education, the price of petrol, cigarettes, taxes.

SKIN AND BONES

Sex, babies, general health, vitamins, diets, cancer, old age, health of parents, cures and treatments, popular psychology, looking good and feeling good.

FUNNY BONES

Funny stories and anecdotes, overheard conversations, quirks and contradictions, wry personal perspectives, the unexpected, the rare or unusual. The weird and wonderful, the first, last, biggest, smallest, most expensive. Plus gossip about celebrities in sport, entertainment and politics.

Some of these topics merge: for example, choosing private over state education for your children to give them the best start in life is 'personal' and 'purse'.

So, consider using stories, anecdotes or comments about these kinds of subjects so you can relate more to your audience and their lives.

AWAKENING EMOTIONAL BEHAVIOUR

Aim to evoke desire (for the concert tickets), happiness (when they win those tickets), anger (when you talk about MPs' expenses), sadness (when you remember the career and music of Michael Jackson) and so on.

---

[24] Note also that the examples given in each group may not be appropriate for your station's specific target demographic; they're merely illustrative.
[25] Audio: *The War of The Roses*: http://tinyurl.com/zz2d8.

But you can heighten those feelings to become more emotional by making them *personal*.

So instead simply throwing out to your audience a comment on, say, bad cyclists ('They're a law unto themselves'), you use a question that draws in your listener on a personal level ('Don't you sometimes fear for the safety of your children whenever a cyclist is around?'). This comment plays on the emotion of *fear* and although it possibly wouldn't actually instil fear, it would certainly generate a *feeling of concern*, which is a far more effective form of radio than simply being *informed*.

The secret is to think of which of the primal emotions you hope to tap into (see below), and then how you can try and generate feelings within your listener.

Remember, listeners remember how you make them feel more than they remember what you say.

I've never dealt with whodunnits. They're simply clever puzzles, aren't they? They're intellectual rather than emotional, and emotion is the only thing that keeps my audience interested. I prefer suspense rather than surprise; something the average man can identify with. The audience can't identify with detectives; they're not part of his everyday life.[26]

Affection	Anger	Annoyance	Angst	Apathy
Anxiety	Awe	Boredom	Compassion	Contempt
Curiosity	Depression	Desire	Despair	Disappointment
Disgust	Ecstasy	Empathy	Envy	Embarrassment
Euphoria	Fear	Frustration	Gratitude	Grief
Guilt	Happiness	Hatred	Hope	Horror
Hostility	Hysteria	Joy	Jealousy	Loathing
Love	Pity	Pride	Rage	Regret
Remorse	Sadness	Shame	Suffering	Surprise
		Wonder	Worry	

Relevance

Listeners don't. Which is why you have the make them by getting information through to them. Effectively.

They may *hear* the music and you talking, but very rarely do they actually *listen*. If you don't make the listener *listen* to you, you are wasting your time and the station's valuable airtime.

[26] Constantine Sandis, 'Hitchcock's Conscious Use of Freud's Unconscious', *European Journal of Psychology*, August 2009.

RETICULAR RETENTION

Because radio is free, listeners don't ask for a refund if they don't like what you do.

If they don't like what they hear, you stay irrelevant to their life and they switch over or switch off.

In fact, listeners aren't really listeners at all. They are *hearers*: they hear until there's something on that relates to their life, and then they *listen*.

The reticular area of your brain filters incoming stimuli to discriminate against irrelevant background stimuli. So, inconsequential background chatter is ignored, until there is something which interests or excites.

When we talk about something on the air, we have to provoke and awaken that reticular area. We have to talk about what's going to relate to them, interest them, and make them want to listen.

We have to create a connection between 'useful stuff' and the radio station name.

We simply have to find out what they want to listen to, and them tell them.

For it to be *information*, a stream of data has to have meaning (otherwise someone will turn off mentally or, even worse, physically). That goes not only for the words that are used, as we have already seen, but also *how* that information is presented.

The key word is *relevance* and, more importantly, relevance to as many people as possible. So before you talk about anything you think is information, you must first consider who it is directed at. Then ask yourself if they represent the core of your target audience. Then you must think about the language (words and terms) you're going to use. Will your core audience understand it? Will they be able to relate to it? Will it have relevance to them? If so, it could be considered 'information'. If not, your audience might hear it, but they won't listen to it.

Effective communication is dependant upon mutual understanding. Finding the commonality in your idea and the listeners' experiences builds an emotional bridge between you and them.

Always ask:

- What are our listeners thinking about and what will they be talking about today? On some days this process is easy. On average days it isn't. So, don't overlook the obvious because the little, obvious things in listeners' lives are much more relevant than most wacky internet stories. Obvious concepts such as the weather, things that happen to kids in school, things that happen to people at work, things that happen to people while shopping, etc., provide the foundation for content that is much more relevant to listeners. In order to be relevant you've got to start with something that's already on the mind of the listener. You've got to understand the target well enough to be able to understand what they are already thinking about.

▫ What in this story or idea have the greatest number of listeners experienced?

▫ What can they most relate to?

Get the answer to those questions in the first sentence. For example, if your link is about who's going to the Cup Final this year, the common experiences might be losing a bet, having your home team finally win the big one, being a huge sports fan, and so on. Set-ups like this help turn *listening* into *hearing* because they tap into listeners' emotions and emotion is the key to memory. You merely wanting to talk about something is not nearly as important as the listener's wanting to hear about it.

A woman listens with both sides of her brain simultaneously. So radio is an excellent medium to reach her with your message. She has the ability to listen to the radio and have a conversation and incorporate what she's hearing with what she's saying. Men on the other hand can only listen with one side of the brain at a time. This distinct gender difference is the driving force in retaining and growing your female audience. How many of your shows engage women through conversations that are relevant to her? Any shows that use loud conversations and attempts to solve problems or establish or defend rank will not resonate with her. Building a relationship with women is all about conversations that engage us . . . Since a woman's Highest Personal Value is establishing and nurturing relationships, she's more likely to engage your brand if you attempt to develop and nurture a relationship with her.[27]

Show inclusivity with the audience by seeing stories from their point of view: make what you do listener-centred rather than self-centred.

Film director John Ford[28] once asked John Wayne[29] to do a picture with him.

The actor asked 'Well, what's it about?', to which Ford replied 'It's about *people!*'

To the director, the storyline was virtually insignificant. The point of the film was to learn about people and their behaviour.

The same goes for radio. It's not about you doing something for them, it's how they will benefit from interacting with you.

[27] Fran Lytle, consumer behaviourist, author of *Connection Moments* (Trafford Publishing, 2006).

[28] More on John Ford here: http://tinyurl.com/l6ansd.

[29] More on John Wayne here: http://tinyurl.com/ll9ukw.

It's not the local school closing down, it's the dozens of youngsters who have to travel further, make new friends and learn a new way of life at a new school.

Every single thing on your station should be reflecting people.

So, instead of 'I've got lots of things to give away on the OB tomorrow', it's 'Come along and see what *you* can win . . .'. From telling the time, reading the weather and relaying the travel news, it all has to be done in an everyday way: is your listener going to get wet on the way to work, will they arrive on time? Tell them that information, not about the 'chance of precipitation', or about 'a driver shortage on the Blankshire branch line'. Talking from a listener's perspective makes the information you are trying to get over more relatable and easy to use.

In a world where the control belongs to the consumer – the listener – the rules are different.
Now relevance will mean what's relevant to me.
Broadcasters must recognise that this challenge requires seeing the world from the perspective of the individual, not the perspective of the station or, God knows, the group.[30]

The bits between the songs, the presentation, is more important than ever, because as more people have iPods and music-filled mobiles, the songs you play aren't exclusive to you and the market any more.

If people do not understand what you are trying to tell them, why should they work hard to listen? They won't. It's what is called the 'Shit/Click Factor'. The listener thinks, 'That's shit!' and clicks off the radio. If you turn them off, they'll turn you off.

People don't listen to radio programmes. They listen to what interests them and sometimes it's your programme.[31]

What if the specific experiences of your story don't match those of your listener?

How will they be able to relate?

Human experience is largely universal, so even when the specifics are unique to you, the emotions won't be. When you talk about something that's stirred up strong emotions and you express those well, the listener will experience their own similar emotions in empathy (because they are connecting

---

[30] Mark Ramsey, president, RadioIntelligence.com.
[31] Dick Orkin, Radio Ranch (US advertising company), *The Radio Magazine*, March 2008.

> with you as a person they like) and in memory (of similar situations they have been in, or dissimilar situations which have stirred up similar emotions).

Just because something has happened geographically locally, does not make it interesting. For example, if yours is a chart station in the Midlands, you could still talk about Britney Spears getting married, a new jet that can fly to Australia in record time or an unusual delicacy in Japan. None of them is *geographically local* to the Midlands, but each is local to your listeners' 'sphere of interest'. The 2004 tsunami wasn't geographically local to UK listeners, neither was Hurricane Katrina the following year, but people were talking about them. The 2005 hurricane that destroyed oil terminals in the Gulf of Mexico wasn't local but it was relevant (because it affected how much we had to pay for petrol) and because it was an interesting story (happening now), and told in a compelling way (with stories of human emotion).

In radio you need to use both these definitions to try to keep your audience. So talking about Britney or Beyoncé is OK, as long as you also consider more personally relatable themes as well.

You will notice that there is a crossover between the two types of local. What's ons could be local in both senses, for example, a station targeting over-55s may mention flower shows happening in the area, a chart station may mention a club event happening in the area. These are events happening locally, and also local (of relevance) to their audience.

'Local' could include news, information, comment, observation, what's ons, travel news, interviews, charity involvement, weather, local artists, local arts and culture, sport, phone-ins and so on.

Content that is drawn from and/or relevant to the area . . . output specific to their area . . . the feel for an area a listener should get by tuning in . . . confidence that matters of importance, relevance or interest to the target audience will be accessible by air . . . programming likely to give listeners a feeling of ownership and/or kinship particularly at the time of a crisis (snow, floods etc.).[32]

Connecting with your target audience emotionally is crucial. It's also about broadcasting 'inclusive content' that makes listeners feel part of the station. Gone are the days of providing 'so what?' radio. Every link matters – audiences have so much entertainment choice now that if you don't include them they'll quickly leave you. You have to make your brand compelling so the listener wants more, day in and day out.[33]

Site specificity

What is local to the station and its listeners: the places they live, go to and are familiar with. (One station group used to have a '4–1 Rule' which required the presenters to mention four

[32] Source: Ofcom, 'Localness on Local Commercial Radio Stations' http://tinyurl.com/n62hbu.
[33] Lisa Higgins, brand marketing director, Century Network, *The Radio Magazine*, August 2005.

local place names in the first hour of their show, three in the second, two in the third and one in the fourth.)

Know what is in the news, especially in the bulletins on your own station. Obviously, you will not want to comment on every story (especially the political ones) but you may be able to give a comment about a new local shopping development, or a local celeb. Remember: newspapers contain 'yesterday's news'. You can be ahead of the game if you comment on stories in your bulletins in your show, not when they appear in print the next day.

If soon after a news bulletin which mentioned that a missing girl had been found, you say, 'I wonder whether that toddler's been found yet', you're showing your audience that you haven't been listening to your own output. If you don't care enough about your own output in your own show, why should they? There is really no excuse not to listen to your own station and catch at least one news bulletin as you drive into work.

Syndicated national programmes are there for a reason: they're good (oh, OK and they're comparatively cheap). So if you're a local host and you're looking at fewer and fewer opportunities, you have to step up your game. You have to be better than anything else a station could put on the air instead of you. You have to play the local card.

Seize every local issue and own it. Is the local MP proposing something stupid? Is the county council poised to raise taxes again? Don't just talk about it for an hour. Seize it. Own it. Launch campaigns, get in the papers and on TV news. Make it an issue with your name, face and station name all over it.

Relate everything to the local listener. For every topic, ask yourself: does this really matter to the local people? Why should they care? Why should local people, in particular, care more than anyone else? If you can't answer those questions, maybe you need another topic.

If it's something the national shows will or can talk about, don't. The goal is to be the only person on the dial talking about a particular on-target topic, and that's easiest if it's a compelling local issue. If it's a typical national radio topic, ask yourself why someone would choose to hear you talking about it rather than a national presenter.

I'm worried about localness. I know it saves a ton of money and it means that we can hire a much more competitive presenter. It doesn't hold together as well as the local hero, blending in local conversation and local events and local issues for local people. It's handing over one of our best assets to reduce costs.[34]

According to the *British Attitudes Survey*, nine out of ten people take part in voluntary activities or belong to local clubs, societies or churches. And in the report *Britain 2010* there is a suggestion that, in an increasingly uncertain world with less job security and more unpredictability affecting issues as diverse as the weather and terrorism, the local community is becoming increasingly important to people . . .

I think that it's a great advantage for a presenter to be able to talk to a caller and know their patch, know the places they're talking about. Most of the time they're places I've been to, places that I've

---

[34] Richard Eyre, ex-GCap Media chairman, *The Radio Magazine*, June 2008.

had nights out at. I find it so irritating when presenters move into an area they know nothing about and try and hijack the local football team, pretending they're supporters.[35]

I firmly believe that the 'localness' of local radio will continue to be the key to its success. If local radio were to 'de-localise' its broadcast content, it would simply fade into a sea of similar radio stations that offer no particular USP to their audiences.[36]

Localness is:

- The issues that interest, annoy or concern local people and businesses.
- Having your finger on the pulse, being 'one of us'.
- Adding to as well as reflecting local life.
- What happens on air — the news, competitions, phone-ins and even adverts . . .
- . . . and off air — event sponsorship and charity activities.

Talking about the area (people, places and activities) in a modern, outward-looking, rather than an insular, parochial way, reinforces your connection with the community. Just adding a local place-name into a story, localises it. Even though the place has no direct relevance to the event, you have made more of a connection with your listener. 'I was driving through Blanksville yesterday and my little girl said to me . . .' Similarly, don't just say, 'When I was shopping . . .' mention the name of the town, or the shopping centre.

Know the local area — be the expert, understand who's who and what's what. When telling anecdotes about somewhere local, make it even more relatable and memorable by mentioning a landmark. This automatically makes listeners picture the scene and you've made a stronger and clearer connection with them. 'Have you noticed the new paving stones in Blankstown High Street? They're just near the clock tower . . .'.

Of course not everything that happens to you, happens in your TSA, so presenters bend the truth a little. If something happens to you in another part of the country (or even if a friend tells you something that happened to them), when you tell it, change the location to your area, or touch the local base in some way. 'A-12-year-old girl in Kentucky took her pet pig to school yesterday . . .' becomes 'Imagine you're a teacher at Blanksville Secondary, and in comes one of the pupils with a pet pig! Well that's what happened in Kentucky yesterday . . .' Now it's visual, and something your listener can identify with. Instead of just being an item about a city I don't live in, you've *made* it local by referencing something here.

When you have a caller on the air, don't just say which town they are in, ask them to tell you the *part* of town they are in. So it's 'the St John's area of Tunbridge Wells' rather than simply 'Tunbridge Wells'. Or ask them, off air, what is near where they live, such as a landmark, a major shop, pub or park. Then when they get on air include the information they gave you in *your* comments:

PRESENTER: Next up it's Andy in Blankstown. Hi Andy, where in Blankstown are you?
ANDY: Westcliff Road . . .

---

[35] Paul Gough, presenter, Metro FM, *The Radio Magazine*, 25 May 2005.
[36] John Myers, author of *Independent Review of Local Radio 2009*, discussed at: http://tinyurl.com/cm8c5q.

PRESENTER: Oh right, that's near the rec, isn't it? I remember playing football there with the kids last summer . . .

Using this technique sparingly, adds to the feel of connection to the area. (Localising something makes it more relatable. Specifics make it more memorable.)

Of course actually *being* local is a distinct advantage: that means having a local accent, understanding the significance of local events, knowing how to pronounce local place names, being able to refer to local landmarks. But newcomers can also talk about what strikes them as unique about the area. The things that only happen there: 'That fantastic view from the top of the Blankshire Tower . . .', 'The feeling of the sand between your toes as you walk down the beach from Northend Pier to Golden Bay, with a bag of chips . . .', 'The sound of the church bells on the Little Blanks village green as you sip a pint of Blanks' Bitter . . .'. Help people feel good about their local area – celebrate and be proud of local success. These types of link give what the GWR radio group called a 'love of life round here' factor. This was particularly clever as it had a double meaning: 'love of life' (listeners who were 'up for it') and 'life round here' (in other words, local).

Represent the whole of your area, not just the part where your studios are based. Be careful of using phrases such as, 'Up there in Chelmsford' or 'Over in Vange'. Similarly, avoid, for example, 'Traffic's heavy coming into Southend' and say instead 'Going into Southend', if that's the town in which you're sitting. Reinforce where you are broadcasting to but not where you are based.

You will of course have in your studio bible a list of how to pronounce all those awkward local place names. A quick way for any presenter to slide down the credibility scale (taking the station with them) is if they don't know how to say a town in their patch. Remember, there are many local quirks! Tonbridge and Tunbridge Wells (both in Kent) are both pronounced 'tunbridge' despite the different spelling. Leigh can be pronounced as 'lee' or 'lie' depending on whether you are talking about the place in Essex or the one in Surrey. Then there are the really awkward ones such as Towcester (toaster), or the ones that may get you lynched in the streets (pronouncing Edinburgh as 'edin-burra', for example).

To get a local place name wrong is insulting; being new to the area is no excuse, so make yourself aware of the name traps. Don't ever say on air something like, 'I've had a text from Simon in the Vale of Belvoir . . . I think that's how you pronounce it . . .'. If you haven't taken the trouble to find out how the local place names are pronounced, why should locals listen to you?

Target your demographic

Be one of your own listeners: do what they do and go where they go. It makes sense to find out as much as we can about the people we want to build a relationship with.

Women are said to be interested in:[37]

- *Relationships* – that's not just sex, it's establishing and nurturing family and friendship-relationships.
- *Conversations* – for women, conversations are to share information (telling stories) and create connections. For men, conversations are to transmit information (state facts) and solve problems.

[37] Adapted from work by Fran Lytle, consumer behaviourist and co-author of *Connection Moments* (Trafford Publishing, 2006).

    ◦ *Inward competitiveness* – A woman is inwardly competitive and wants to do a task better today than she did yesterday, while a man is outwardly competitive and aggressive. So, to be attractive to a woman, don't appear to be loud, fast and demanding.

Read lots, especially what your listeners read (and watch what they watch, and go where they go) so you can reflect their concerns and interests. Speak with your programme controller and ask for a demographic breakdown of who is listening and how they live their lives (all but the very smallest stations will have this kind of information).

    ◦ What to read – national and local newspapers, the trade magazines, pop culture magazines, anything on psychology or advertising (to give you insight into how people think and react).

    ◦ What to watch – go to the cinema, watch TV, know which celebrities are doing the rounds and why.

All sounds a bit expensive? You can probably get a freebie to the local cinema if you do a review on air, and stations are often sent free press copies of magazines before they hit the newsstands. That means you can be talking about the features and the fashions before they do.

What do they *want* to know and *need* to know?

What are the bullets of 'social ammunition'[38] that you are passing on in your link? Is it new information? Are listeners learning something new that they can use? Is it information that they're going to want to share, so they look clever or well-informed in front of their family, friends and work colleagues?

> Hold my interest, tell me something new, entertain me,
> inform me or educate me.[39]

Information that affects the target listener indirectly and that they want to know about could include:

    ◦ Information about a song, the memories hearing it evokes, the band's next concert.

    ◦ Or your considered, maybe humorous, thoughts on a TV programme or film.

Information that affects the target listener directly, and is 'need to know' could include:

    ◦ the time, travel and weather information

    ◦ suggestions on how to spend their well-earned free time (what's ons).

---

[38] This is what psychologists call 'social reciprocity': something of value has been given back to the listener in return for the time they have invested in the show.

[39] Dan McCurdy, writer and producer, *The Radio Magazine*, July 2008.

Topical material

News items tend to make some of the most powerful radio content because it is much easier to get listeners to pay attention to material involving something they are already thinking about in their own lives.

Of course you should make sure that you vary the content of your links. It's great to hear a presenter talk about preparing for their wedding, or problems with their car. But if that's all you do, you're going to get boring. So rotate that topic with others (news comment, artist info, humour, showbiz). Even though the strongest topics should continue throughout a show, or over a period of time (to build up rapport) the story must develop, like in a soap opera. But if you beat a topic to death, it's probably because you haven't prepared enough for other listeners who aren't interested.

Every link should be the continuation of a conversation you're having with the listener. Each individual link should add to that conversation, whether they are a 'new-joiner' to the show or have been with you from its start. Welcome them, explain what's happening, make them comfortable and make the conversation as easy to join as possible. If they feel excluded, they'll make an exit.

The structure of the link

How you treat your content also plays a major role in whether your audience just *listens* to it or *hears* it. Whether it is just *on the air* or gets *into their heads* depends greatly on the content set up.

Every link should be prepared in advance – even the 'that was, this is' link – and possibly even as much as scripting them word for word. At a minimum you should be working from notes. To this end always have a pad in the studio with you so before you open the mic you can jot down a few bullet points on what you are about to say. That way you will be fluent, will only say what you need to, and will know when you've said it.

Avoid waffle by planning your links so they have a beginning (what occurred to you, the 'headline' of your link), a middle (the main content, the facts, story or observation) and an end (the phone number, pay-off line, station ID). Otherwise you will meander on the way toward making your point.

Say you want to talk about a great concert you went to at the weekend. Think what you remember of it: maybe the crowd, the music, the scale, the showmanship, the emotion (yes, how you *felt*, not just what you saw and heard!), and put your own spin on it . . . something only you can add. Something that will make you relatable. Bullet point your thoughts to give it structure, and then feel it as you say it. Don't read it, tell it. Just like real people might talk to each at work or at a party. (What a concept: actual natural-sounding conversation!)

If you are opening the mic just because you haven't said anything for four songs and feel as though you should, you are probably in the wrong job! You don't get paid to talk; you get paid to say something.

The audience's attention to the radio is highest at the end of a song — in anticipation of what is next. We pay greater attention at the end of one idea and the beginning of the next. If you want the greatest number of listeners to pay attention to a new idea, start each one with a strong, listener-focused headline, question or comment. 'All parents who allow their children to skip school should be jailed . . .', 'Aren't you fed up driving around the area in the day and seeing kids who should be in school, wandering the streets, or even out shopping with their parents . . . ?', 'Let me tell you about something that's been bugging me for a while now, and I reckon many of you will share my concern when I say that . . .'

You are on the radio, in part, to give your opinion and your position. But how do you do that without coming over as overbearing, as a 'know it all', or as someone who's abusing their on-air position? If you appear to be doing any of these things you risk alienating some of your audience, but at the same time you can't be a fence-sitter and need to encourage reaction.

You could go on air and say something like:

> The England manager should be fired. Another bashing last night . . . He hasn't got a clue. He should be replaced with someone who knows what they're doing!

Shooting your mouth of like this will not endear you to many people. You'll come across as arrogant . . . as though you could manage the team better.

The trick is to be a little self-deprecating, suggesting your point of view without arrogance:

> Now I don't know much about football, and even less about managing a team, I'm just an average guy but isn't there something wrong with the squad at the moment?

Now you've aligned yourself with most of your listeners, you've come over as a little humble, yet still *used your on-air authority* to ask the question. Here's another example:

> Personally, I always make sure my children don't watch TV until they've done their homework and brushed their teeth.

Reaction: You appear cocky and laying down the law.

> Personally, I always make sure my children don't watch TV until they've done their homework and brushed their teeth . . . but y'know, I wonder if I'm being too harsh and a bit out of step . . .

In a strange reversal of logic, now people will come to your defence. You have shown humility, suggested doubt . . . yet still given an opinion, just as you would if you used phrases such as

'Surely it would be better to . . .', 'Correct me if I'm wrong but . . .', 'I *think* it was . . .', 'I'm open to correction here, but . . .' Convey confidence without being cocky.

How the topics are aired is also very important. Bring your experiences to the audience in a manner that varies and doesn't always start 'I noticed on my way to work . . .' or 'I was talking with friends about . . .'. There's a fine line between it seeming like you only brought something up so you could talk about yourself and give your take on it, or having it seem like what you're talking about came up logically, in the course of a conversation, and then you add what you think about it.

The cart and horse

You're probably thinking, 'Strange, surely it's horse and cart?' Well, horse and cart is how most presenters deliver their information: they give the facts and then a comment. With the cart and horse set-up you make your comment first, then give the information.

A quick example:

- Horse and cart – 'It's raining later, so take your umbrella' (information → comment).
- Cart and horse – 'Better get your umbrella, it's going to rain later' (comment → information).
- Horse and cart – 'Tickets for the Lemonheads concert in Blankstown are going fast. If you want to be there on 15 July, you'd better book now' (information → comment).
- Cart and horse – 'You'd better be quick if you want to be at the Lemonheads concert in Blankstown in the summer. Tickets for this 15th of July gig are selling fast' (comment → information).

By putting the cart before the horse, you use a comment to hook people into listening to the rest of the link. Listeners ask themselves, 'Why?'. By putting the horse before the cart, the listener knows all the information in the first sentence and they can mentally switch off. You've failed to make the link compelling.

Ask a question

Another way of involving the listener when you do a link is to ask them a question. They cannot help but respond in their own mind to what you are saying, and in doing that they have continued their interaction with you. For example: instead of saying, 'Now let's see what's happening in the area this weekend . . .' it's, 'Are you just hanging around this weekend with nothing to do? If so, let's see what's on . . .' Instead of saying, 'The news is next . . .' it's, 'Have you been wondering what's happened to those people caught up in the floodwaters in New Orleans? We've got the latest on that horrendous situation for you next.' Instead of saying, 'Now the weather with Anne Enometer . . .' it's, 'Doesn't it make you feel so much better towards everything and everyone when the sun is shining? Let's see if it's going to last . . . here's Anne Enometer . . .'.

I'm not suggesting you start every link with a question. Like all these techniques, it's another blade in your Swiss Army knife of ideas. Asking questions is a great way to hook and engage the listener. It draws them in and they find themselves subconsciously answering it, but be careful not to overuse it as a device.

Talk about your own station

Many times presenters do not even have the most basic knowledge of other programmes on their own station. They sound ill informed and the station, which tries to foster an on-air family feel, suffers as a result. You must have a thorough knowledge of your station's output at all times. Check your pigeonhole and e-mail for the latest memos on station promotions or changes to the schedule. This information may be repeated on the studio whiteboard, so check all of these places to cover yourself.

Actually *listen* to your own station! That way you can comment on the rest of the output to create more of a bond with your audience. Notice the difference between a link that runs '. . . and Dave Matthews is back tomorrow from ten' and one that goes, 'I was listening to Dave Matthews on the way in this morning and heard the Secret Sound. It's been running for, what, six weeks now and is so infuriating! Dave's told me that the guesses are getting closer now, but he won't tell me what it is. So, I'm just going to listen tomorrow from ten to find out . . .'. The second one is *longer*, but it works *better*. Spending five seconds saying something that *doesn't work* is not saving time over a 20-second link that *does*. It's wasting five seconds.

Sell other parts of the station by offering benefits for listening (mentioning that someone is turning up for their shift, is not giving a reason to tune in). If you want other presenters to promote you, then set a good example.

- Promote benchmark features or contest opportunities.
- Quote something that the other presenter did on the air, and remind the listener when they are on.
- Play a clip from someone else's show – a great winner, part of an interview they did . . .

If your station is trying to get people to listen for, say, ten hours a week, then that's at least as long as you should be listening too (on top of your actual show). Know your schedules and features back to front. Listeners should not know more about the station than you do.

If you're *talking about* another presenter, use their full name, 'Simon Jones is on after the news, with another chance to win . . .'. The image and recall of the station (the brand) is down to a number of factors, the station name, logo, strapline and (although admittedly down the list) the names of the presenters.

If you are actually *talking to* another presenter, by all means use their first name (to use both in this situation would sound ridiculous). But do use a name.

If you are introducing yourself, use your full name, 'Radio X, I'm Barnaby Rudd', rather than, 'I'm Barnaby'. The exception to this is if you're only known by one name.

Incestuous links

These are links about the family at the radio station. Apart from the fact that they are usually not funny and may invade the privacy of your colleague, these links exclude the listener, are discourteous and bad mannered. So, in-jokes and references to things only you can see, problems at the station or a broken piece of machinery in the studio are all incestuous.

◀ ACTUAL AUDIO

PRESENTER: 'Well, it's been a pretty bad day here at the radio station. Several of our friends and colleagues have lost their jobs, so forgive me if the show has sounded a little different today, it's just that we're all really shocked with what's been going on.'

Commercial radio station, October 2005

Don't continually comment on the physical appearances, attributes or lack of attributes of fellow presenters, as it usually sounds insulting.

◀ ACTUAL AUDIO

PRESENTER 1: Where's [fellow presenter] today?
PRESENTER 2: Dunno. Probably off doing something, like getting his hair cut.
PRESENTER 1: Or transplanted . . . or re-glued.
PRESENTER 2: He does look odd doesn't he?
PRESENTER 1: Do you think he has different hair for each season?
PRESENTER 2: Seriously, is that a wig?

Commercial radio station, December 2005

Asking your producer on air to get you a coffee is pointless. Making a joke about the food in the BBC canteen is old and tired. And comments such as, 'Tina's cracking up at a joke I've just told her, but I can't repeat it on air' are one of the things that some presenters still do, and then wonder why listeners who feel left out, tune out.

Another problem with an on-air conversation that should be off air is that one comment, 'See you've had a haircut, Dave!' encourages a reply. 'Yes, I had a fight with a lawnmower!' and then another, 'I know – you have a haircut once a year whether you need it or not!' and so on . . . 'At least I've got hair to cut . . . err . . . baldy!' Excruciating.

Don't put yourself down on air. It may be self-deprecating in a Jack Dee style but makes it sound as though you lack authority. Avoid saying your age. If your audience is much older than you, they may question your credibility. Let them keep the picture they have in their mind – the age you are in that, is always 'real'.

Also crass is mention of technical words and phrases that mean nothing to listeners (see also Chapter 24, 'When it all goes wrong'). 'Argh, I can't find my bed', 'Sorry, I couldn't give you the pips', 'I remember the days when we had carts in the studio' and 'Tina Travel has gone down on me' will have completely different connotations to your listeners.

◀ ACTUAL AUDIO

PRESENTER: Sorry for the bleed through on that ISDN line . . .

Commercial radio station, August 2005

Remember the listener's life is outside the studio. Their life is going to work, running late, and then finding out that half the car park is closed so new white lines can be painted. Or going to the dry cleaners, dropping the kids off at school, queuing at the bank and waiting for the 97-year-old woman to take 15 minutes to write a cheque for a 70 pence tin of cat food at the supermarket. They do not want to hear you messing about in an air-conditioned studio, playing your favourite songs, making easy money that you work at for a few hours a day. Remember to relate.

Happy Radio

This title of an Edwin Starr hit could be the philosophy of those who say it should always be a sunny day on their station.

In other words, almost everything can be given a positive spin:

- Only ever take people to air whom you know have the correct competition answer.
- Peter Presenter isn't ill, he's 'off on an exciting holiday'.
- It may be windy – but 'what a great day to put the washing out' and so on.

> Doing a breakfast show from war-torn Kosovo was quite a challenge. When you go away with BFBS, you live with the troops so it's nothing glamorous. You might regularly wake up to find your bed's soaked because the snow has got through the air-conditioning unit, and then there'll be no hot water for a shower. But you have to be chirpy on the radio, so the troops have something to take their minds off the fact that there's no hot water! That was a bit of an eye opener and having to keep your spirits up because you're out there to entertain the troops was quite a challenge.[40]

You may sound false if you always accentuate the positives and are bitter about the negatives. The trick is to turn the situation around: 'What a rubbish day – rain again. It's totally ruined my plans for a kick-about in the park with the kids . . . so we'll have to stay in and play that new Wii game I got for Christmas. Boy, I really didn't want to do that!' Or, if there has been unseasonably hot weather, don't just moan about the studio air-conditioning but laugh about bathing with a friend and offer practical advice on how to keep cool.

Putting yourself on the same emotional level as your listeners may mean you communicate with them better. The trick is to realise what gets you down, without sounding negative yourself. See humour in the situation, or a positive side, do not just carp and complain.

Some people call this the 'glass is half full' philosophy, or 'Looking up and looking forward: today and the future, not yesterday and the past'.

Sell the station and sell the music. If you do not like the song you have just played, and you feel as though you can't lie and say it was great, then just do a straight outro (mentioning the title and artist). The song *must* be great, otherwise why would you be playing it?

If you feel as though the same song is on too high a rotation then have a word with the music scheduler. There may be a reason, there may have been a mistake when the song was entered on the database, or it may be your perception of repetition. After all, you listen to the station far more than an 'ordinary' listener so you will notice it more (especially if it is a track that you are not very fond of).

---

[40] Gareth Brooks, presenter, Xfm, *X-Trax* magazine, September 2005.

If a competition 'mechanic' (the way a contest is run) seems too complicated, do not make a meal of it on air. Work out a way to make it simpler and speak to the promotions department. They may not realise that what looked good on paper is in fact complicated to explain, making it difficult to attract contestants.

Problems with music and management, commercials and colleagues, promotions and prizes are all dealt with in the office and not the studio. Why criticise your employer on air? It shows the utmost unprofessionalism, not to mention possible suicidal tendencies for your career. It also gives the message to listeners that, if the presenter doesn't enjoy the station, why should they?

Sexual innuendo and crudity are unlikely to be part of your station's output at any time (unless it is as part of your late night sex and relationship show). Yours is likely to be a family station with a family audience, especially at breakfast, so keep comments clean.

◀ **ACTUAL AUDIO**

BREAKFAST PRESENTER: I don't smoke after sex, I smoke during sex. At least I tried to but the ashtray kept falling off my girlfriend's back.

Commercial station, October 2005

Do not lose the common touch. If your listeners are those who holiday in Spain and you talk about taking your yacht out to the Maldives, then figuratively you are going to become rather more distant to them. If they are struggling single parents, do not talk about how difficult it is to find a nanny. In other words, do not make it hard for them to relate to you, do not alienate yourself. Do not build a wall between you and the listener that they have got to climb over. Some won't even bother.

If you really feel strongly about an issue there may be certain occasions when you should *not* speak your mind. It is like the old dinner party convention: don't talk about politics or religion. Now, politics in the general sense is allowed if you have a point to make about, say, car park charges or how often the bins are emptied. Much more than that – 'There are yet more asylum seekers in the town, they should all be kicked out . . .' – is going too far, unless you are a talk show host who is experienced, both in terms of years' service and also in the laws of libel.

THE THIRD PARTY TECHNIQUE[41]

This strategy used by advertisers to great effect, puts a message in the mouth of someone else.

If you want to say something, or comment on something that your on-air character wouldn't, have someone else make the comment to which you can react.

That could be another person on the on-air team, or someone you know off-air that you can paraphrase:

---

[41] More on this technique here: http://tinyurl.com/mwstqe.

> My neighbour gets so angry about [issue]: this morning he stopped me and said that . . .
>
> So, it's not you making the comment (a scenario about which your listeners may object), but someone else whom they don't care about.

You should not usually have an editorial standpoint. To do so could land you in trouble with the radio regulator Ofcom and also with a large proportion of listeners who may say that you are politically biased, something radio in the UK is not allowed to be. Make sure that you read the section on the law around election time, and speak to someone in the newsroom if you want it explained further.

Content from other media

Do not read these out word for word; in fact do not read them out at all. Instead, read the story, note what is funny, sad and unusual or whatever about it, then put the paper to one side and *tell the story* to your listeners. That way the best bits (the facts and emotions that resonated with you) will come to the top of the tale and the boring, unimportant bits (the man's name, age, job that kind of thing) will be self-edited out. Of course, you will have prepared all this in advance, so you can add your own comment, observation or punchline off the back of it. When you simply read a story out from the paper you are not interpreting the story or adding anything to it. In other words, you are not communicating as you would in real life. You need to process information, not merely regurgitate it. Yes, there may be the odd pause but that will make it sound as though you know what you're talking about.

Certainly do not say, 'It says in the paper that . . .'. If you say that, they might as well stop listening to you and just pick up the paper themselves. Just talk about papers in general or say, 'Have you *heard* that . . . ?'.

> Newsworthy stories about rival broadcasters should definitely be reported, but try not to mention the actual brand more than once. Remember that Five Live is part of a competitive world and every mention of a competitor is a free plug for their brand. Find other ways of describing the station – e.g.: Sky = the satellite broadcaster, talkSPORT = the sports station.[42]

Some stations do a run-down of what is on TV each evening, but surely there is enough competition for your radio station without promoting it and encouraging people to go elsewhere. Added to that, what does it say about your own station if you are suggesting people try another media? How does your evening show presenter feel about it? Instead, why not tease and trail what is on your station at the same time as the latest soap or reality show is on TV?

Television shows create 'water cooler moments' – subjects about which office colleagues can chat. A link about *X Factor* (if that is appropriate to your demographic) will have an

---

[42] BBC Radio Five Live style guide.

instant recognition with your audience who will understand the format, the key players and know the latest events. But instead of *promoting* TV programmes, talk about them *after they've happened*. After all, doing this will actually give you something to talk *about*! Instead of saying, 'This *may be* interesting', you can say, 'That *was* interesting *because* . . .'.

> We never worry about the competition, we worry more about getting it right.[43]

It is not so bad talking about the other stations if you are the underdog, perhaps you have got nothing to lose, but why raise their profile or alert your listeners to their existence and prompt your audience to sample them?

There are occasions when BBC local stations are asked to trail a show on Radio 4 or Radio Five Live; in which case those trails and talk-ups must be run. But there are few reasons why you would otherwise want to talk about another station, even to criticise it, especially if it is in your area.

Handovers

Of course, if your station allows, talk to the next presenter and ask them what is in their show and so on, but remember there is a fine line between fun conversations that listeners enjoy and annoying banter that excludes them and encourages them to turn off. The point of such a conversation is to have a seamless transition from your show to theirs, without an obvious 'exit point'. That encourages people to listen longer and makes the show and station 'stickier'.

Don't make the end of your programme sound as though it is the end of the day's broadcasting, but promote positively the next presenter. Indeed, on some stations the next presenter takes over just before the 'watershed' news bulletin to ease this transition.

Don't let your colleagues down by putting them on the spot during a handover. If it makes them appear to lack knowledge or authority on air, you're not only being incestuous but also you're also letting down yourself, your colleague and the station. Do not have incestuous jokes that exclude the listener. Leave 'inside humour' outside.

Playing the piano badly

It may be frustrating to read the advice in this section and realise that it goes against what many radio presenters do on their shows, particularly some of the famous names who may inspire you.

Sometimes you see comic-musicians who play their instruments badly. However, in order for that to be funny and not just a noise, the musician has to be able to play the instrument very well. The same is true of radio presenting. You have to know how to do it properly before you can start doing it 'wrong'.

> I was producing a very high-profile DJ at the time of 9/11. The

---

[43] John Myers, chief executive, Guardian Media Group, *The Radio Magazine*, March 2005.

planes hit minutes before we went on air. There was no way we could have done our normal show. However, despite his normal irreverent style he was able to fall back on the 'right' way to do it and presented a sensitive and informative show that received praise from listeners and the media.[44]

So, what do you do at times of tragedy or disaster? Will talking about the event 'bring the audience down'? Remember that 'bad news' can give you a great 'topical emotional connection' with your audience. Read the mood of your listeners. Think about what they will want and expect from you and how they want you to handle it. Get it right and you will win big. Get it wrong and the bad feeling will linger. So learn the rules, use them, be professional and then as your personal style develops you might feel you can begin to bend or even break some!

What to say, what not to say and why:[45]

What was said	Possible listener reaction	Why you should avoid this type of phrase
'Hello to all of you out there in listener land!'	I don't live in 'listener land', and I am by myself.	Makes listener feel part of a crowd rather than an individual.
'Thanks to our lovely newsreader Angela — she's looking drop-dead gorgeous today.'	Angela is a professional, just as you should be.	Such comments are incestuous, patronising and sexist.
'Whoops! Finger trouble again, we've just got a new computer in the studio so bear with me.'	Why should I? I expect you to be able to do your job, and practise until you can. I've got problems of my own.	Unprofessional and amateurish.
'Well I seem to have run out of time again. Join me again tomorrow. Goodbye.'	Why have you run out of time? It sounds as though the show was poorly planned. In which case I probably won't bother again tomorrow. Yeah, goodbye to you too.	Amateurish.
'And here's a special song to my boyfriend Zenon. He'll know why it's so special.'	Why should I have to listen to you sending a private message over the airwaves?	Feeling of exclusion rather than inclusion.
'Well let's pay the rent with a few messages from our sponsors.'	Oh, adverts. I wonder whether another station's playing music . . . ?	Exit point.

[44] Will Kinder, producer, Radio 1, in conversation with the author.
[45] Adapted from material produced by the International Women: Media Foundation (their website is at: http://tinyurl.com/mqr9hd).

Breakfast show prep

Of course the great thing about producing and presenting breakfast is that a lot of what's in the papers is new to your audience. The bad thing is that that means a lot of work for you first thing to scan them and identify the key listener-grabbers. You'll realise that most of the stories are the same from one paper to another (so you can skim past them when you see them a second time). You'll also notice which papers are best for which features (funnies, quirkies, letters, features. Hint: it's not always the 'red tops') and you'll soon be able to spot stories and angles which are appropriate or different.

If you're working on breakfast as a producer, you may want to talk to the presenter about what's set up, the evening before. That way they can mentally prepare for the topics that you have in mind, or be able to suggest a better idea or angle.

It's good for presenters to talk about TV shows that will interest their audience, and it's often best to talk about the programmes after they've been on rather than before. But if you do breakfast, it's tricky to watch a night-time show, as you have to be up so early the next morning. Here's a trick. Always try to see the first episode of a new show that is likely to appeal to your target audience and read the TV critics' reaction to it. These are the shows which introduce the characters, settings and themes. After that you may only need to watch the first few minutes of each episode (the story so far) together with a quick flick through the TV guide to get an idea about what's happening. Come up with a comment from the first few minutes and it gives the impression you saw the whole thing.

Show prep services

Script-writing companies advertise in the trade press, offering to send subscribers daily information to use on their radio programmes. Most show prep services are filled with useless diary and birthday information, weak one-line jokes and embarrassing, simplistic parody songs. There may also be horoscopes, fascinating facts, a web page of the day, celebrity birthdays and 'this day in history' items, too. Others may additionally send you audio pieces: interview clips, custom-made jingles and so on.

Such material can certainly help you prepare for your programme, but notice the words 'can' and 'help'. In other words, buying these pages doesn't mean that you don't need to do any other work yourself.

> Working with colleagues whether presenters or producers to make better radio than yesterday's programme is still the key driver for me.
> The best bit is sitting down with a blank piece of paper and coming up with ideas.[46]

Not everyone *needs* to buy show prep. If you're happy writing your own material that's great. It'll be original and totally personal to you and your station. Bought-in prep isn't. Remember, nothing they list is any good without it having some thread of connection to your listener's life and interests, *and your particular spin on it*.

---

[46] John Collins, presenter, Forth 2, Edinburgh, *The Radio Magazine*, January 2005.

How to choose a prep service

Enquire about several services and ask what they provide, how often, at what cost and about market exclusivity. Ask which other stations or presenters use them (they may not tell you) and whether you can see some examples of their work. Beware those who send you what seems to be a sheet or two of their 'best bits', rather than an actual sheet from a recent day. Also be wary of the quotes from other 'satisfied customers'. Whether or not these testimonials are credited, don't use your hard-earned cash on a service just because a hotshot DJ uses it. If it doesn't work for you it will be a waste of money.

Even when you are happy with your provider, keep an eye on what else is available. It may be worth changing service if someone else is writing material that is more appropriate for your audience or show. You may want to look at buying more than one service. If several fit with your criteria and offer you more material (or different material for different parts of your show) then don't limit yourself to just a single source.

Some show prep services are free but the better ones usually charge a fee, and may offer you some market exclusivity with your subscription. This may be an agreement that no other presenter at your station will be accepted as a subscriber, or that no other presenter in your station's TSA will be accepted. Exclusivity may go further so no one else from neighbouring (rather than overlapping) stations will be sent the same material, or it may be written solely for you (in which case it will cost really big bucks!).

In general, the more money you pay the better the material and the greater the exclusivity. If your station won't finance the service then you may want to consider buying it yourself. If you're freelance then it will be tax deductible, but either way it's an investment in you, your programme, and your career. (In 2008 a survey by research agency Hallett Arendt showed more than 60 per cent of presenters said they lacked the resources they needed to make their show better.)

How to use one

If you simply go into a studio and read the prep service's lines on air and expect to be an overnight success you're probably fooling yourself. It's similar to buying a Jamie Oliver cookbook and thinking they're going to be a master chef. You have to make the material your own, not change yourself to fit the material. That may mean rewriting the item completely. You may think that as you have paid for the items then they should all be radio-ready, but as you'll share the same writer with dozens of other presenters around the country, not every item can be personalised to all of you. If you want a tailormade script, then you will have to pay a great deal of money!

One of the easiest ways of making the material your own is by making it real to you and your situation. So, instead of saying, 'A woman went to the doctors and . . .' transplant the comment on to yourself, your spouse or partner. Each item has to be something that your on-air character would be comfortable saying. If you think an item is great (be it funny, sarcastic, outrageous, topical or whatever) but your radio persona would not say it, then you can't use it. Consider giving it to another character on your show.[47]

Another way to personalise it is to change the location of the anecdote and use local places, streets and landmarks that your audience will recognise and connect with. So, if the comment is about someone stuck on the elevator on the New York subway, make it about how you were stuck in the lift on the London Underground. If it's about a boys' football team in Anytown, put them on the Red Rec around the corner. Certainly rewrite anything

---

[47] See more on on-air characters, later in this chapter.

to fit your own speech pattern and using the words that you would use. Put it into your own language and that of your audience.

You have to practise reading the items and ensure that you really understand them. Do you know the significance of the item, why it's funny or what the underlying tone is? Have you got the pronunciation correct? Be comfortable with the material and deliver it with confidence.[48]

The vol-au-vent advantage

Always over-prep your show, then if there is an unexpected problem you've still got enough material. Having plenty ready-to-run means you've got a safety net and that you can self-edit as you go along. You will find that some items that seem great at home, don't seem quite as good when you are preparing to read them on air. If you have plenty of material spare that's not a problem. You can't do that if the amount of material and the amount of links are the same. It's like holding a party and having the last person there eat the last vol-au-vent and drink the last glass of wine, and you thinking, 'I planned that well!'. You always over-cater for a party, and on the radio too, you should always be left with a figurative plate of vol-au-vents.

Never come out of the studio having just used your last piece of material. That's not good timing, it's good luck – and bad preparation.

To continue the food analogy: look at some content like it's perishable. Use it quickly, or else it'll go bad. If you have something that is time sensitive, find a place for it on the air now, or today. Otherwise, you'll put it into the fridge for another day, and when you come to use it it will have gone off. Other material is like a tin of beans. It can be used any time. So, use the perishables first. If last night was the last episode of the big TV series you'd better be talking about it today. By tomorrow it's old news.

Remember to make your last hour as focused and passionate as the first. Great waiters sell their menu as enthusiastically to a diner at 10.30 pm as the one at 6.30 pm. The third performance of a stage play on a Saturday is just as energetic as the lunchtime and matinée.

One rule of thumb is to prepare an hour off air, for every hour on the air. If you have ten links an hour, and each one is a minute long and the show is four hours, that's 40 minutes of material that needs to be prepared for each programme. If you present six shows a week (not unheard of) that is four hours of material you need to find. So, together with prep for a guest and putting together competitions and so on, you need to put aside around a day each week to prepare your week's shows.

Prepare but don't *practise* – over-rehearsing loses spontaneity.

Other tips and hints

As well as writing links relating to something in the news or something that happened to you on the way to work, show prep also consists of preparing basic liners for your regular features. Otherwise there's a likelihood that you'll always introduce them the same way. Spend several minutes a week devising new ways of saying old things. A different way to introduce the travel, for example or how to describe your regular competition.

Put these new phrases in a Conversation Book, and over time you'll have a stock of

---

[48] See more in the section on celebrity birthdays in Chapter 17.

devising different ways of delivering repetitive information,[49] an ever-evolving repertoire of sentences, phrases and comments to add a spark of freshness into your presentation. Thinking hard about such lines and saving them for future use saves you from relying on clapped-out clichés that anyone else could come up with.

Always strive to deliver your idea, link or comment differently from how everyone else would do it. Think 'What's the audience expecting me to do?' and then give it a twist.

Share ideas that work for you with other presenters and producers in the group, ideally a market or two away from you. Compare guests, contacts, programme suggestions and angles. Steal the idea and then develop them for your own station and with your own spin – you could set up a web-based forum, or have a conference call once a week.

Don't guard your best ideas, sharing makes them even better. You could swap suggestions for upcoming programmes: a colleague could have an insight that'll improve it. If several of you are keen, you could share the workload for writing the script or producing the audio. The more you give the more you will have.

As you will come up with more ideas than you can use each day, keep track of them in a book or ideas file. If you see an article that could make a feature or a follow-on, put it in the file. An interesting observation which you couldn't use because the planned event didn't happen? Write it in the book. Also make a note of what you, and other media, did on major anniversaries. If the local paper did a feature on the residents of Christmas Road in December, you can do it yourself a couple of years later. What you did at another station one Halloween you can do again at your new station.

Inevitably, there are slow days, perhaps when you've just got back from being unwell, or have to battle through while moving house or soon after the death of a relative, when you simply haven't had the time or attitude to do show prep. Over-prepping by having lots of items in your file or notebook means that this won't be a problem and you'll always be using the very best material.

On a day-to-day basis, recycle your best content. Advertisers know that they need to run a commercial 13 times before the audience has heard it three times. Don't run your best stuff 13 times, but do run it more than once! Can you use a morning bit in hour one and then again in hour three? Or in the afternoon show? Or make a weekend breakfast show from the best bits of the week?

A 2008 survey by Hallett Arendt[50] revealed that 23 per cent of presenters spent less than an hour preparing for their show and 54 per cent arrived at the studio less than an hour before it started. Forty per cent said their show was their only job. This prompted radio consultant Francis Currie to warn programmers to watch out for presenters who 'treat a radio show like a hobby'.[51]

Remember that preparation is the difference between a presenter who is at the top of the hill and another one who is run of the mill.

In 2009 Ryan Seacrest[52] (a radio and TV host in the US, whose KIIS FM show from LA is syndicated across the country) was told to talk less between the songs as ratings allegedly declined when he did so. Ryan was rather miffed:

---

[49] Ready-made phrases: http://tinyurl.com/mhbgmm.
[50] Survey presented at the 2007 Radio Festival run by the Radio Academy: http://tinyurl.com/6e42mt.
[51] At the NAB Europe conference http://tinyurl.com/mh8su5.
[52] Ryan Seacrest biog: http://tinyurl.com/mk2svc and his site at: http://tinyurl.com/c4drq8.

They said the ratings were great . . . and then they believed we could hang on to this position if we . . . actually play more music and do less of what you're doing. It's not like this was the only place to hear Lady Gaga. I come in and actually put time and effort into it and try to do the best I can and then they say we kinda don't want you to do so much of it.[53]

Whenever a mic opens it is *bound* to please fewer people than the song which preceded it. That's because (unless it's an all-talk station) nothing the presenter says is likely to be more familiar and more appealing to as many people, as the song they just played.

But people increasingly listen to personality music shows for the personality that they can't get from their music-players. Some of your links may not be classics, but you need to create enough 'can't-miss moments' (and the anticipation of those moments) to bring people back, again and again. You can certainly 'trim the fat' from the links and make them sharper and crisper; but the real trick is to add more muscle.

That's not to add more songs (which anybody can do). But to add more content that's you.

When you have nothing to say, shut up and play the music!' is a phrase some programmers tell their presenters. Surely this misses the point: make sure you have something to say on your show that's relevant, interesting and compelling. Something that's said effectively, engagingly and entertainingly.

Your on-air character

You need to be honest, sincere and warm when you are a radio presenter. Indeed you need to be you, 2.0 – with some of the negative corners smoothed off and some of your better attributes emphasised. You need to come over as a likeable friend, not someone who's putting on an act. But how does one balance 'exaggerating the good parts of one's personality' with 'not being a fake'?

POSITIONING THEORY

You have to position yourself as the only person who can do what you can do.

There is little point being a 'jock-in-a-box', an off-the-shelf presenter whose brand is bland.

[53] Quoted in http://tinyurl.com/m64nsx.

And your niche position comes down to two things: uniqueness and substance.

How can you achieve this?

By being yourself.

Sharing feelings. Being honest.

Before you go on air, take some time to be a little introspective: ask yourself what makes you tick, what are your feelings, thoughts emotions and reactions to different things.[54]

What makes you, *you*?

This isn't some big counselling session stirring up unpleasant thoughts about your childhood but a way of realising and reconnecting with your personality, so it's front-of-mind when you go on air.

And you come over as natural.

And if, on occasion you do a topic that listeners don't like, but they like you, they'll stay.

Here are a few tips to bring out your natural warmth:

- Life is not one big joke. Don't focus on humour exclusively to the detriment of other equally important emotions. It's good to show a whole range of emotions (sad, frustrated, angry, tender) because that's what shows you as human.
- Be a good guy. Say positive things about other people on air: another presenter, the cub scout in the local paper who's got an armful of badges.
- Step out of character occasionally. We all say surprising or unexpected things occasionally (note: not necessarily 'shocking') so doing this on air lends you authenticity as a well-rounded, real person.[55] When something unusual happens, allow yourself to respond to it spontaneously.
- Listeners are friends not fodder. Don't simply use those who phone as a resource: thank them for their call and show a genuine interest in them. That'll make them feel good and the rest of the audience feel good, and show you care about other people's feelings. For the same reason, occasionally thank people for listening 'Glad you could be with me today', 'Good to have you along' and so on. Say it with sincerity and focus on a single person as you say it.
- Loosen up occasionally. Talk about a bad decision, a mistake, a lost opportunity ('I was so embarrassed', 'What was I thinking?'). Acknowledging a bad move, as long as

---

[54] Free personality assessment: http://tinyurl.com/nl8ua.
[55] Radio 1's Chris Moyles gets emotional on *Who Do You Think You Are?* http://tinyurl.com/n3x7t7.

you laugh about it and not beat yourself up about it, shows you are confident and comfortable with yourself and don't need to impress.

STATIONALITY

The branding of the station is enforced with everything the station does on air and off: that's the state of the rig on the OB, the sign on the front window, the driving of the sales cars, the smartness of the news reporters out in the field . . . and of course what happens on air itself.

Maybe the presenters sound 'together', like a family, and genuinely enjoy work (rather than having a false 'up and bright' persona).

Or maybe they sound dull, mechanical, uninspiring or simply silly (rather than funny, or better still 'fun').

Both of those scenarios contribute to your station sound . . . your 'stationality'.

Refer back to the 'hot tap policy' mentioned earlier (it's where the listener should know what they're going to get from your station when they turn it on, in the same way you will always get hot water from the hot tap). If 'hot water' is your brand, every presenter should still sound unique within it (different degrees of 'hot water' from the tap if you like, but never different liquids completely!).

Stationality is a consistency, a feeling that each individual presenter and their 'attitude', is part of a unique overall whole that people will remember the station by.

15 Humour on the radio

**SKILLSET – NATIONAL OCCUPATIONAL STANDARDS
RADIO CONTENT CREATION**

Unit content included in this chapter:
RC4 Contribute to the creative process in radio
RC10 Write for radio
RC21 Produce speech content for radio

A quick browse of lonely hearts ads will confirm that women look for a good sense of humour in a potential partner. And, according to psychologists,[1] men in the humorous adverts are rated as more intelligent, more honest and better material for a relationship or a friendship. We seek out people who make us laugh and feel good.[2]

Gelatologists, scientists who study humour, say laughter has beneficial affects on our bodies. The midbrain and hypothalamus[3] – regions where dopamine[4] is released in response to pleasurable stimuli – are activated by laughter. Dopamine is the major component of 'reward' pathways; it reinforces pleasure-seeking behaviour and influences our happiness.

Laughter also stimulates the release of other feel-good substances, including endorphins,[5] which are capable of relieving pain, decreasing blood pressure and bolstering immune function.

---

[1] More on this research: http://tinyurl.com/lln7ja.

[2] Men who make fun of themselves are seen as sexy, according to a University of New Mexico study. 'It makes you more approachable to women when you use humour to show a little weakness' says study co-author Gil Greengross, a PhD candidate in anthropology. But self-deprecating humour can highlight your faults, so deliver the punchline with confidence. http://tinyurl.com/mlh2j2. Women are said to enjoy laughing at themselves and stories that mirror their situations and their relationships. However, they feel uncomfortable when listening to banter that could be perceived as offending others. This is because a woman's highest personal value is establishing and nurturing relationships. She's also more inwardly competitive than outwardly competitive (which is a hereditary male trait). So, you can engage her by sharing funny stories. Just make sure the stories are relevant to her life and aren't outwardly competitive. (Adapted from work by Fran Lytle, consumer behaviourist and author of *Connection Moments*; Trafford Publishing, 2009.)

[3] 'Hypothalamus' definition: http://tinyurl.com/mmyq6o.

[4] 'Dopamine' definition: http://tinyurl.com/mh9vnv.

[5] 'Endorphins' definition: http://tinyurl.com/nsxf3x.

Unexpected associations and surprise generate a laughter reflex in our brains, which in turn produces a cognitive reward by stimulating the release of substances like dopamine. The surprise factor of humour is exemplified in the punch line of a joke.[6]

Humour helps bring people together, helps communication and highlights similarities (when other people all laugh and you don't 'get it' you feel left out). So, if you make someone feel good, by starting a positive chemical reaction in their brain, they will associate you with that feeling and you start a relationship.

Humour also reflects on the tone of the station: that it's a fun one to listen to. Some listeners may use your line with their friends, and when their friends laugh they will return to your show to get another one: laughter increases loyalty.

Remember 'funny' can often come from being 'fun' – is Dermot O'Leary[7] funny? Perhaps not, but he's certainly fun and entertaining. Many listeners will remember how you make them *feel* not exactly what you *say*. So, relax and your humour will come through naturally.

The situation must be right before someone will laugh at what you are saying, or find it FUN.

- **F**reedom to laugh. Someone has got to have permission to find it funny, according to the time and place and who they are with. A rude joke may be funny but not if it is told on the breakfast show.
- **U**ninvolved feeling. Most events are funnier if you are not personally involved: someone falling over, for example.
- **N**onsensical atmosphere. The tone of the show has got to be set up. Black humour occurs in unusual situations, but people will laugh more readily if they are already relaxed and expectant.

The laws of laughter

Comedy is often in response to a situation:

- *Abruptness* – The best humour comes from something that's unexpected. Say something original and say it well, so the audience can't guess the punchline before you give it to them. The humour of surprise is also when something happens at the wrong time, or the wrong place, or to the wrong person. Most people kill humour by putting too much information in the set-up. Too much story detail confuses listeners and risks allowing them to guess the ending.
- *Recognition* – Laughter often comes when people recognise what is being described. Being social creatures, we love to bond through common experiences, and laughter reinforces our sameness. There is also humour from the recognition (of a character or situation) that comes with using a catchphrase, although bear in mind that the best catchphrases are usually ones that develop naturally or spontaneously rather than ones which are created deliberately.

---

[6] More research: Robert A. Johnston, 'Humor: A Preventative Health Strategy', *International Journal for the Advancement of Counselling*, Vol. 13 (1990): http://tinyurl.com/n8vpyd.
[7] Dermot O'Leary: http://tinyurl.com/ntzdc6.

- ◦ *Superiority* – We naturally laugh at those worse off than ourselves: a social icon or institution, someone in power, someone with bad luck. But sometimes people feel uncomfortable laughing at others, so make yourself the target of the joke and allow listeners to laugh at you. If there's no target, it's just conversation.
- ◦ *Enjoyment* – This happens when a climax has been resolved and people laugh out of sheer delight for themselves or someone else. Think of the resolution of a station competition when, after speculation and tension, someone laughs when they win a huge prize.

Considering these elements will help you develop your own more-humorous take on the world. Once you've got the concept, write it down and turn it around. Does the idea work better another way (perhaps the funny observation and *then* the explanation?). Can you push the idea even further (if this is what's funny in an everyday situation, how would the Queen cope with it, or a spaceman? Did the same thing happen in Stone Age times?). Change the words – some are intrinsically more amusing than others ('negligee' is potentially funnier than 'underwear'. A banana is a funnier fruit than an apple. A guava or a paw-paw may be funnier still . . . or not).

Fifty-seven years in this business, you learn a few things. You know what words are funny and which words are not funny. Alka Seltzer is funny. You say 'Alka Seltzer' you get a laugh . . . Words with 'k' in them are funny. Casey Stengel, that's a funny name. Robert Taylor is not funny. Cupcake is funny. Tomato is not funny. Cookie is funny. Cucumber is funny. Car keys. Cleveland . . . Cleveland is funny. Maryland is not funny. Then, there's chicken. Chicken is funny. Pickle is funny.[8]

According to psychologists words containing the letter K are funniest because they force you to smile: 'facial feedback', also hard consonant sounds are funnier . . . softer vowel sounds are more emotional.[9]

In *The Simpsons'* episode 'Homie the Clown', Krusty the Clown tells Homer during a lesson at his clown college:

Memorize these funny place names: Walla Walla, Keokuk, Cucamonga, Seattle.

Upon hearing the word 'Seattle', Homer bursts into laughter.

There are also 'funny numbers': according to Douglas Adams, the idea that the answer to 'life, the universe, and everything' in *The Hitchhiker's Guide to the Galaxy* is 42 is funny because it is an 'ordinary, smallish' number.[10] On the DVD commentary for the British sitcom *I'm Alan Partridge*, its writers put forward their own theory of funny numbers, going

[8] Neil Simon, *The Sunshine Boys: A Play in Two Acts* (Samuel French, 1976).
[9] Richard Wiseman, 'The Truth about Lying and Laughing': http://tinyurl.com/n6shgv.
[10] Read the comment here: http://tinyurl.com/llews3.

against the more common view that smaller, specific numbers are funny and instead employing large, round numbers.

> Like the number 37. Everyone uses that as a funny number. It's used quite a lot as a random comedy number, like 'that's the 37th time this has happened.' People should use random numbers more. Like 'fifty.' Alan Partridge's assistant is fifty. That was her age. And it sounded funny; I would say, 'this is my assistant Lynn, fifty'.[11]

Play with the form until it's as funny and fast as possible.

> One way of interpreting it constitutes the target assumption; the second way of interpreting it reveals the reinterpretation.[12]

Comedy connections

Connecting subsets

Explore themes under a topic. For example: the first day of the new school term, for which the connection process might look something like this:

First day of term → kids starting a new school → kids going back to school → what celebrity needs to go back to school? The *reinterpretation* or *surprise* is: 'Simon Cowell needs to go back to school. I mean have you seen those trousers? He hasn't even learnt how to dress yet . . .'

Parallel connections

This involves comparing things that have some commonality, but not everything in common.

A parallel connection could link:

  ○ the number of stories about youth knife-crime stories and . . .
  ○ dealing with insurgents in (latest war zone).

The target assumption or expectation is the traditional sentencing for these criminals. The *reinterpretation* or *surprise* is the idea of sending them to (latest war zone) to deal with the current 'enemy'.

Dissonant connections

This is linking things that have nothing in common. In some ways, these make the most compelling content because the distance between the expectation and surprise is the farthest.

A dissonant connection could link the story of a misbehaving MP and *The X Factor* TV show. The target assumption or expectation would be a comment on the ethics of the MP.

---

[11] Steve Coogan, creator and star of the sitcom quoted at http://tinyurl.com/55v7eg.
[12] Greg Dean, author of *Step by Step to Stand-Up Comedy* (Heinemann Drama, 2000): http://tinyurl.com/l6zey9.

The *reinterpretation* or *surprise* would be having MPs forced to perform in front of a real audience where they could be voted off immediately.

> (expectation + surprise) + (information + exaggeration) =
> amusement and entertainment

Note that this process is not about writing jokes. It is about creating humour and 'streams of entertainment'.

> The most direct path to disaster in improvisation is trying to make
> jokes. Jokes are not necessary; they are a complete waste of time
> and energy that is better spent developing the scene. Chances are
> if you're concentrating on telling a joke, you're not looking for
> connections in a scene. And the connections will draw much bigger
> laughs than any joke.[13]

Do not try to be something that you're not. There is nothing more embarrassing than someone who just can't be funny, but never gives up trying. If you feel the need to be funny all the time, it will sound forced and unnatural. Avoid pressing for 'jokes' or artificially set up (and easily predictable) 'punch lines'. Being relevant and compelling trumps failed attempts at humour every time.

Most of us aren't capable of 'stand-up' type comedy, but we can do observational humour from time to time: comments about the little ironies and absurdities we've lived through personally.

The set-up

It's called this because you're setting up the audience's expectation. So the punchline can be a surprise, the audience has to be thinking in one direction so you can hit them with a line from the left field at the end. If your set-up wanders, there is no clear train of thought. If a detail doesn't have a direct connection to the punchline, leave it out. The longer the set-up, the bigger the punchline must be to justify the listener's investment in your story. So make sure you include all the information needed to follow the story, and not one word more.

The funniest part

This comes at the end of a joke, yet some people wonder why their material isn't funny when they move the payoff so it's two or three words earlier!

For example, 'Last Christmas I ordered a turkey and when I got home and opened up

---

[13] Del Close, *Truth in Comedy* (Meriwether Publishing, 1994): http://tinyurl.com/n2wes2 and http://tinyurl.com/3h95zg.

the packaging, it was two legs and a breast all in pieces in the box. I had to put it together myself. I'm telling you, that's that last time I get my turkey at Ikea.' That's funny(ish) but it'd be less funny if the punchline 'Ikea' (the joke simply doesn't work without it) appeared elsewhere: 'I ordered a turkey from Ikea . . .', 'the last time I go to Ikea for . . .'. No. The funniest bit has to be the last bit.

A punch after the punchline

You may want to use a 'boing' effect, or a crowd applauding after a punchline, but may think these draw too much attention to it and sounds rather 'music hall'. Also, the listener can feel treated like an idiot: that was the punchline, and I'm going to draw attention to it by using a silly sound. It also makes it sound as though the gag was set up and scripted rather than amusingly adlibbed.

Instead, play a 'musical exclamation mark' such as a jingle stab (not a slow lead-up one, which will spoil the effect of your pay-off) or go straight into an ad break or song. They will all have the same effect.

Don't laugh at your own joke, it sounds even worse than having a sound effect of other people doing it. Paul Merton, Jack Dee and Jimmy Carr – a deadpan delivery is common to all three of them, and they're funnier to watch because they give the impression that they don't know what they said was amusing. Instead, move on to say something else but be careful that you don't go into something that really jolts. Also, make sure that the next thing you say isn't really important as the listener may still be musing or chuckling at the pay-off and miss it.

The comedy clauses

Only use the material if:
- You understand it.
- You find it funny.
- It fits with your on-air personality.
- It's not illegal (for example, defamatory).
- It's not offensive.

Is it funny?

If you're going to use a line or humorous story written by someone else, first consider whether you understand it and if *you* think it funny or fun. You may have been a best man at a wedding and bought a book of one-liners, and ploughed through it trying to find what you consider to be a funny line for your speech. It's tough! Only use a line that someone else says is funny if you personally agree with them. If you don't, try and work out *why* it doesn't appeal to you. Can you at least see why it is *supposed* to be funny? In which case, consider whether you can rewrite it so it's better. There's no harm in that, in fact it's the best thing to do. You've paid for the material, so you can do what you want with it to make it work for you. Maybe the characters in the scene are unbelievable, or they have names that are ridiculous – or maybe not ridiculous enough. Perhaps the pay-off is great, but the situation has to be changed to fit better with your target audience. Maybe move it from a hairdressers to a rock concert, for example. Perhaps you've missed the punchline completely. If so, look again to see what the writer was trying to do. Can you develop the idea further or use the set-up for a gag of your own? Perhaps the line just doesn't fit with your own speech pattern; in which case rewrite it so that it does.

When you rewrite, don't do it word for word. Humorous comments always work better if they're adlibbed to a certain extent. Jot down bullet points on what to say in the set-up but write down the punchline in full in case your mind goes blank. Reading someone else's lines word for word sounds stilted and false.

Remember, if you don't find it funny, then neither will anyone else. Or they may be laughing *at* you, rather than *with* you, and for all the wrong reasons.

Avoid 'bad' words that children could hear and their parents could complain about, by alluding to them rather than saying them. Use a clever *play on words* that will go over the heads of the children, but adults understand.

> The search for the man who terrorises nudist camps with a bacon slicer goes on. Inspector Jones had a tip-off this morning, but hopes to be back on duty tomorrow.[14]

The comment works on two levels, one for children and one for adults: it's only 'rude' if you understand the meaning. If you understand the meaning, surely you can't be offended because you drew your own conclusion.

Another way of doing this is to upend expectation: lead a listener in a direction that it seems will be smutty, but turns out to be innocuous:

> I have no trouble getting women. They love it that I look like a model, I'm really funny, and I've got a huge . . . bank balance.

It's funny because you upended expectation and yet it's also 'naughty' because you led the listener towards what seemed to be a smutty destination, but then stepped back before you got there. You took them to the edge, but it was they who stepped off it.

MORE COMEDY RULES

In the example above (about the bank balance) note that the punchline is the third comment of three, which has what is considered to be the best rhythm for comedic timing.

In the example about the chicken and Ikea, note that part of the comedy is in the use of the specific word 'Ikea', rather than a more generic 'self-assembly furniture store'. In general specifics are funnier than generalisations.

---

[14] Ronnie Barker, comedian: http://tinyurl.com/5djhdf and http://tinyurl.com/leb74c.

I'm not a fan of the modern railway system. I strongly object to paying twenty-seven pounds fifty to walk the length and breadth of the train with a sausage in a plastic box.[15]

In general, don't talk about sex or bodily fluids and secretions: if it leaves the body, leave it alone.

Also remember the audience, format of the station and time of day: the files of Ofcom and the BBC are full of complaints made against presenters who said something that was (arguably) funny, but said it at the wrong time of day. That could be an 'adult-themed' joke, said in the breakfast show and heard by kids being driven to school. If you present yourself on the radio as a funny person, always ready with a quick quip with lines from a prep service, but in real life when you meet your listeners you're not actually that funny, your credibility takes a knock.

How good is your sense of humour? If it can come over as sarcastic rather than dry you may lose more listeners than you gain. When you put others down regularly (unless it's a regular part of your on-air character), you come across as an egotist. It's OK once in a while but when it becomes a pattern, and the material isn't that good, then it reveals something about you that the listener may not like. And there are some things you never put down: your music, the commercials, your newsperson and listeners who phone in.

If you are setting up a punchline about a story in the news, make sure the listener knows enough about the event so they can understand the gag. It may just need to be as quick as, 'So, we're using credit cards more than ever before . . .' or 'I'll never forget the first time I saw . . .'.

The listener has to have a framework, before they can find a joke funny.

Humour in team shows

Also consider whether the on air 'you' would make such a comment. If it's a humorous dig at a reality show celebrity, but your persona is one that loves watching such shows, then probably not. If it's a clever comment about a politician but you're portrayed as the 'dumbo' on air, again, probably not. If it's something you wouldn't say, but the line is still funny, give it to someone else whose personality does fit with the content. You can either say another on-air team mate, or quote that it's from your brother, a friend, a girl down at the pub. That way the material works, but you are disassociated from it. Don't break the on-air spell.

The first rule of any team show member is to make your partner look good. Be willing to take a back seat. Don't try to top them or outsmart them. Give them the perfect pass so all they have to do is score the goal.

April Fool jokes

Most stations will do an April Fool joke, but these are notoriously difficult to do successfully. Perhaps it is because most of the really good ones have already been done, perhaps it is because people aren't as gullible any more. More likely it is because they take an awful lot of time and hard work to sound convincing. Bad ones are embarrassing.

---

[15] Victoria Wood: http://tinyurl.com/jb9y2. *As Seen On TV*: http://tinyurl.com/cyv23z.

If you do have a fantastic idea, make sure that it is cleared with the programme controller before it goes to air, and do this well in advance. Many bosses have a serious humour by-pass if they come across a Fool that they didn't know about, especially if listeners are complaining about it. And people *will* complain if they have been seriously misled, if the joke has caused them to be late for work or if it has cost them money. Sometimes they can seriously disappoint children who believe them to be true. Those who complain may be your listeners who will find it hard to trust you again (especially if the spoof ran in the news bulletins — how will they perceive your news output from then on?) or non-listeners who won't want to even sample your station. You could get a lot of positive publicity if it all goes well, but a lot of negative publicity if it goes badly.

Then you have to make sure *you're* not duped. There are groups of students and even professionals who try to dupe the media as often as they can. At one station the news editor ran a story about two teenagers who had been locked in their loft over a weekend, when the hatch slammed shut. They couldn't get out so spent two days playing *Monopoly*. The story turned out to be a hoax.

Perhaps the best trick is to pretend you have done an April Fool joke but actually not to have done one at all!

Wind-up calls[16]

These can be hugely entertaining, but following a series of complaints in the 1990s, regulators decided that the permission of the 'victim' has to be given before the item can be broadcast. It is a quirk that it is within guidelines to record the call, but not to then transmit it without that permission. So make sure you get permission either on tape or, preferably, in writing.[17]

---

[16] Some great wind-up calls http://tinyurl.com/kpv62h.

[17] The final line on punchlines: recommended reading: http://tinyurl.com/ng5d84, http://tinyurl.com/nlpggw, http://tinyurl.com/nhvlv7, http://tinyurl.com/kuqkgl. And the 'world's funniest joke': http://tinyurl.com/6z26zg.

16 Teasing and trailing

SKILLSET – NATIONAL OCCUPATIONAL STANDARDS RADIO CONTENT CREATION

Unit content included in this chapter:
RC1 Work effectively in radio
RC4 Contribute to the creative process in radio
RC10 Write for radio
RC26 Produce station branding, radio trails and commercials

As a radio presenter or producer your main job is as a maintenance person. By that I mean you are a 'quarter-hour maintenance person'.[1] It is a skilled job and involves you giving listeners a reason to listen longer and listen again.

When someone indicates on a Rajar diary how long they have heard a station for, they tick boxes which are divided into quarter-hour segments. It is your job to get them to tick as many boxes as possible. That is done by teasing and trailing (T&T). Teasing and trailing both promote what's still to come. Trails simply explain what's happening and when, whereas teasers tempt by revealing only some of that information.

> If something's worth doing on the radio, then surely it's worth letting people know you're going to do it. Why plan to do something that is relevant, interesting or compelling without giving people a chance to anticipate it and keep listening for it? Throw ahead, don't throw it away.

Teasing and trailing may:

- get someone to hear your show for longer, ideally for 16 consecutive 15-minute segments = your four-hour show
- persuade them to tune in at a different time and sample more of the output (recycling listeners)[2]
- improves continuity by giving the presenter something focused to say to bridge between one item and another
- give forward momentum to the station by providing anticipation ('delayed gratification') of programmes or features yet to be broadcast

[1] The longer someone spends listening to a commercial station, the more chance there is of them hearing, and acting upon, one of the advertisers' messages.
[2] Getting people to listen for another 15 minutes is relatively easy; it's getting them back once they've gone that's hard. Satisfy your audience so they return the next day. What is it about you and your show that makes listening to you an essential experience tomorrow? Because without 'tomorrow', a longer 'today' does not matter.

- reduce 'exit points' which give a subconscious message that it's OK for a listener to turn off; instead back announcements are fused with forward announcements, for example, so the link becomes a junction point where a listener decides to stay travelling with you
- create the impression of 'timelessness', that the station is not merely living 'in the moment'
- reinforce the central station slogan or message helping to strengthen your brand, even if the listener doesn't actually listen to the item that's being promoted
- reflect the station style.

People hearing more of one show, or turning on at another time for another, can affect your Rajar results in two ways.

- It increases the time spent listening to the station, which is reflected in the 'average hours' and 'total hours' stats. This can only be a good thing. Put another way, the easiest way to increase these figures is to talk-up other shows to people who're already listening.
- By not teasing and trailing, listeners don't know that there's something of interest coming up, so may turn off early. Over time it's likely they'll conclude that there's nothing on the station of relevance to them, and go to another station and that will cause a reduction in your reach as well as your hours.

Remember, you don't actually want people to listen efficiently; you want them to listen longer. It's easier to get an existing listener to spend more time with you than it is to get a new listener.

FISH WHERE THE FISH ARE

Long-time US radio researcher and consultant Kurt Hanson[3] and others have distilled radio listening research into two basic categories, core listeners and non-core listeners, and have determined that most people use radio about three hours per day (roughly 21 hours a week).

They say that the vast majority (75–90 per cent) of that listening goes to a single ('core' or 'P1')[4] station,[5] with the remaining (c. four) hours split, unevenly between the two stations.

The concept of heavy users applies across many different consumer categories: much of the 50 per cent increase in Coca-Cola sales in just five years was driven by their strategy to gain and maintain heavy users:

---

[3] Kurt Hanson biog: http://tinyurl.com/n2zmme.

[4] People who listen to one radio station more than any other are P1 preference listeners. Next groups of people who listen a lot to a single station but less frequently than P1s, are P2 preference and P3 preference.

[5] It is more valuable to have fewer people listening for longer (because they *love* the station and have more exposure to the commercials), than to have a lot of people listening for less time (as 'samplers' who only like listening for a short while).

'Heavy' users are obviously more profitable than light users. So once you recognize them as a specific segment, you can tailor your marketing to maintain and increase the usage of your heavy consumers and to win your competitors' heavy consumers . . . develop programs that address heavy users.[6]

It's easy to see that you need more light (P2) users to equal the listening hours of a P1 user, and even more P3 users. So, it makes economic sense to focus on the P2s.

WHY P2S AND NOT P1S?

The P1s are already heavy listeners, and probably cannot physically listen (or 'love' you) any more. To persuade the P3s to listen longer, you'd need to run a lot of trails to stand a chance of them catching one of them – although if you can work out which part of the output they are coming to you for (say, Saturday afternoon sports), it's easier to drag them over to another similar part (say, weekday sports bulletins or Tuesday night football).[7]

If a P3 listens for an hour a week to your station, that's equivalent to listening less than 1 per cent of the time (1/126 of their available 'hours-awake'). That means you'll have to run over 500 promos for them to hear just five of them (1 per cent of 500 is 5).

But the bonus is that when you convert a P3 or a P2 to a P1, you *massively* increase your total TSL because each conversion effectively brings 1416 hours of increased TSL (and of course, cuts your competitors').

Converting P2s and P3s to P1s is by far the most efficient and effective strategy for increasing TSL and therefore AQH. In the main, you can get P2s to listen longer by on-air teases and trails, and P3s by using *outside marketing*.

A few definitions

Teasing

The teaser (or tease) is like foreplay. Just as kisses and caresses arouse, excite and create interest in what is to follow, so too should your verbal teasers for your programme content.

---

[6] Sergio Zyrnan, Coca-Cola chief marketing officer, 'The End of Marketing As We Know It': http://tinyurl.com/yec23ee.
[7] Incidentally, you know exactly where your P3 listeners are; they're your competitors' P1s!

> Teases should arouse curiosity and anticipation.
> Successful teases will hint at information that the [listener]
> will find useful.[8]

You'll give just enough information to the listener to let them have an idea of the kind of thing that will happen, but not exactly how, when, what way or in what order. Teasers tempt them, create interest and whet the appetite.

> Just imagine lying back, dangling your arm over the edge of the
> sun-lounger, letting your fingers playfully caress the white sand,
> and, oh!, that'll be the long, cool drink that the waiter just
> brought over from the beachside bar . . . that dream could be a
> reality if you play and win our new holiday competition, Life's A
> Beach later this hour . . .

Trailing

A trail (either verbal or pre-recorded) on the other hand is, to continue the sex analogy, more like talking dirty: 'This is what I'm going to give you, when and how.' You are promoting your item with a short-term specific selling point. You are saying what is going to happen so they can look forward to it.

> 'In ten minutes I'll give you the qualifying question for the Holiday of
> a Lifetime Competition here on Radio X. If you think you know the
> answer, call me on 01234 567 999, and if you're first through on
> the phone you can play for a two-week stay on the Florida coast.'

It promotes, but doesn't tease.

Telling

Saying that something is going to be happening later is simply passing on information. It is not *promoting* it: 'and at quarter past, information on our new holiday competition'.

Promoting is giving a relevant, interesting and compelling reason why someone should keep listening.

Headlines

Many stations ask news presenters to give two or three story teasers to the main presenter, which can be read at about ten minutes to each hour. Note that I'm saying 'teasers' not 'headlines'. Headlines are a shortened version of the whole story, whereas teasers merely hint at the topic. A teaser might be, 'We have the result in the Jackson Michael trial . . .' whereas a headline will be, 'Jackson Michael has been found not guilty on all ten counts at his trial . . .'. One cajoles the listener to listen longer (makes the show and the station 'stickier'), the other, because it has told the story already, gives them a reason *not* to.

[8] BBC Nations and Regions document, 2000.

Teasing and trailing basics

Listening to some stations' presentation is like watching the prize conveyor belt on TV's *The Generation Game*.[9] There's a song, then a link, then a feature, then some travel, then a song . . . it's all sequential. That does not build anticipation or surprise. It builds boredom.

TV on the other hand has perfected the art of the tease, creating anticipation for upcoming content. You feel as though you'll miss something if you don't stay with the programme after the break (think of the teases inside *Britain's Got Talent* and *I'm A Celebrity* . . ., or at the end of an episode of *The Bill* for the next episode). There's suspense whenever the audience is wondering what's going to happen next.

It is best to talk about what is planned for the opposite quarter-hour segment. Note: that's not the *next* 15-minute segment, but on a clock-face the one which is diagonally opposite the quarter in which you are in currently.

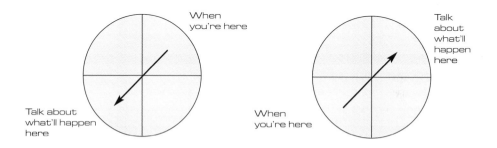

That is because a promotion any further ahead than that is 'out of reach' of the average listener, whereas they are much more likely to stay for another 20–30 minutes, and that could see another two ticks in your Rajar column.

The exception is when it's a big announcement or feature, then T&T further ahead and work with the maxim 'The bigger the explosion, the longer the fuse . . .'

Construct your show around highly promotable content in each quarter hour, whether it's music, contactable-content, a feature, an interview or an event, so that it'll mystify, intrigue, excite and enthrall and so someone feels compelled to stay listening.

Teasing or trailing too much or too often, can cause the presenter to be a 'plate spinner' with too much to handle all at the same time. It can also cause the listener to become confused and unable to identify the key messages. Identify *one* item which needs to be T&T'd in the opposite quarter, not everything.

As much as we strive to broadcast relevant, interesting and compelling items all of the time, we have to face facts that for some people, some of those items will not hit home. An 'exit point' is just such an occasion – when the listener is being given an opportunity to leave the programme. That could be an ad break, a song they don't like, an interview they are not interested in, the news at the top of the hour and so on.

The trick is to hide that exit point: to act like a museum tour guide to the rest of the show, and usher them past that exit door by promoting 'something you'll really like just down this corridor'. We promote (a generic term for teasing and trailing), so people do not notice that there is an opportunity to leave.

---

[9] *The Generation Game*: http://tinyurl.com/l8btfh.

'What's for pudding?' That is what children say when they are faced with a main course they don't much fancy and want the anticipation of dessert. In a similar way you have to tempt the audience. So, before you say what you're doing *now*, say what you're going to do *the other side*.

Before the commercials sell sofas and double-glazing, make sure *you* sell the song that you will be playing on your station in three minutes' time. 'In a moment A, but first B . . .', 'Music on the way from X, after this from Y . . .'. Do this, and you hide an exit point.

Remember that fairy tale about the pot that wouldn't stop producing porridge?[10] Consider that in terms of radio, because programmes never end either. (A programme that ends is another 'exit point' – that change of gear gives the opportunity for someone to tune out.)

So, when promoting other shows, say what time they start but not what time they end: '. . . that's the breakfast show, back tomorrow morning from 6 . . .'. If you continue '. . .' til 10 . . .' it shows up the exit sign in big green letters.[11]

Some programmers also suggest that you 'back-promote' or 'back-sell' items, and tell those who have just tuned in what they have missed. If you say what you are going to do, do it, then say what you have done, you multiply the experience.

The idea is that if a newcomer is intrigued by the back-sell they may well tune in earlier the next day to hear the actual feature. So, extending listening time is not just about getting people to keep listening longer, it is also about getting them to turn on earlier. Therefore, when you back-sell don't give the specific time of an item:

At 10 past 9 we had a great interview with Simon Showman and he revealed the most intimate details of his holiday . . . that's all part of 'A Celeb A Day, Every Day' just after 9 every weekday . . .

To someone who isn't able to listen just after 9, that link is wasted. However, if you say, 'Earlier we had . . .' then that same person may subsequently tune in as early as they can in an attempt to hear the feature.

Having said that, generally, forward-sell (saying what is coming up) rather than back-sell (saying what you have done). Back-selling may help set the tone of the station or help people tune in earlier the next day and as such is an effective blade to have in your Swiss Army knife of ideas, but it is teasing that is more effective at helping people listen longer.

You never 'do' anything on the radio. Many times you hear someone say something like, 'Later Jenny will be doing the sport' or 'Later it'll be time for the school's news . . .'.

Just saying that you will be 'doing' something sounds mechanical, and as though you have to do it because there's a slot for it (it's time to do it), or that is what you have been told to do. It doesn't persuade people to keep listening. Give people a *reason* to stay tuned, say what is in it for them. Make the relevance obvious.

So, 'Is your school mentioned in the schools' news this morning? If it is, you could win a Radio Super goody bag for everyone in your class . . . find out if you're a winner in ten minutes.' Or, 'There's an amazing comeback from one of England's greatest football legends. Kevin Keegan's been called up to play for the national side in Tuesday's match against France . . . details with Jenny Wren at half past.'

---

[10] Remind yourself: http://tinyurl.com/c86dxu.
[11] Like this: http://tinyurl.com/n2c4df!

You slog your hardest to put together a three-hour show, and then no one sits through it all. How rude! That's because listeners are selfish, they want to know what they are going to get out of the experience. They want to know how their investment of time is going to be rewarded, by asking themselves:

- How will I be entertained?
- How will I be informed?
- How will you surprise me?
- What will you give me that I can use?

So, make it really easy for them to answer those questions. Instead of saying, 'The latest report from the government says that . . .' say, 'I'll tell you how you can save money . . .'.

Pre-empt their 'What's in it for me?' question.

Breakfast is the most listened-to and therefore the most important programme of the day so talk about it often and sell its strong features. But don't do this to the detriment of other programmes: breakfast is important, but so too are other shows.

Remember, the station is more than a series of presenters and certainly more important than just one. Work with your colleagues to promote each other. Always talk about other shows in your show. You will all benefit.

It is simple and quick to say, 'Toby's here with Drivetime after the news', but it is also pretty pointless. Instead say something such as, 'On Toby's Drivetime after 4, your chance to get in the "Life's a Beach" draw for a holiday of a lifetime' or even, 'Toby's first song on Drivetime after 4 is the only one I can think of where the title is not actually included in the lyrics . . .'.

If you never usually listen to Toby, once in a while do, and decide what his strong points are that you can mention. Alternatively speak to him and ask him about his show, and how he'd like it to be promoted – get an idea of what he does that makes him or his show unique, and sell him that way.

Yes, it takes more time to think up and to say, but it is also more creative and has more impact.

Teasing

The rules of teasing:

- *A teaser doesn't tell: a tease intrigues* – so don't tell the whole story in one of them.
- *Involve the listener* – make it sound as though they will miss out if they don't listen longer. Hint at a reason to stay.
- *Create minor suspense* – 'In a moment I'm going to play you a hit song that mentions the man's name Ian . . .'. Say that a few minutes before you play Paul McCartney and 'Let 'em In' and you have created listener involvement and suspense, as people will actually want to hear the answer.
- *Hook them with an angle* – then make them d-a-n-g-l-e.

DARWIN'S SUSPENSE FORMULA

You add suspense by getting the audience to wonder what is going to happen next. But they have to be in that state to think through the 'wonder process'; they have to want to wonder!

They won't wonder what song you will play in ten minutes, but you can get them to if you say 'In a moment, we're going to hear the Bond theme that Roger Moore says is his favourite because it encapsulates everything about the persona of 007'. When you say that before you play 'Nobody Does It Better' you prompt the listener to wonder; you get them involved and create suspense that they want to have satisfied.

Think about the typical trivia question feature: 'What are the three most-spoken languages?' The audience will be compelled to find out the answer. But if you simply said: 'Did you know that Mandarin Chinese, English and Hindustani are the three most-spoken languages?' people would look at you like you were out of your mind. The information is the same, only the delivery system is different.

Make them care, then make them wait.[12]

Teases work because of the tension and release principle: you hook them with a question or comment and they stay listening in order to get 'closure' on what you've suggested. Human beings have a natural desire for completion, whether it's jokes or stories (have you ever had the TV recorder cut off before the end of the film?).

THE GAP THEORY OF SITUATIONAL INTEREST

Curiosity is the driving force behind all successful entertainment.

George Lowenstein,[13] a behavioural economist at Carnegie Mellon University, says curiosity happens when we feel a gap in our knowledge. That gap causes pain. To get rid of that pain, we feel compelled to fill that knowledge gap. We watch to the end of bad films, even though they are painful to watch, because it's too painful to not know how they end.

Films cause us to ask: 'What will happen?' Mystery novels cause us to ask: 'Who did it?' Sporting contests cause us to ask: 'Who will win?' Human beings are wired to be interested in just about anything if it is posed in the form of a mystery. Therefore the formula for compelling content, it seems, is:

mystery + resolution = memorable content

What we're doing on the radio is the continuation of a normal human trait that happens every day: 'Guess what happened to me at work . . .', a child saying 'I know something you don't . . .' or the boss saying 'Can I have a quiet word . . . ?'

---

[12] Close-up magician Darwin Ortiz: http://tinyurl.com/lpm6w9.

[13] More on George Lowenstein: http://tinyurl.com/nf5m7d.

Teasing vocab

Useful words and phrases to use:

- soon[14]
- next[15]
- later[16]
- in a bit[17]
- after this
- coming up
- in a moment
- in a short while
- before X o'clock
- just around the corner[18]
- remind me to tell you about . . .
- don't let me forget to tell you . . .

Try and give a clear time frame ('in the next 20 minutes' or 'this hour') using 'rounded up' minutes (that is, not 'within nine minutes'; that's too exact. No one's listening with a stopwatch). That way, if you overshoot to the next five-minute increment, the listener won't miss it.

> Listeners want to listen 'efficiently': they want to know exactly when each feature is on.
>
> But:
>
> efficient listening = less time spent listening.
>
> Although you should have your 'service elements' such as news, travel and weather at the same time, 'entertainment' elements can move within a few minutes to persuade listeners to listen longer.

When not to tease

If you have got important or breaking news that will affect a lot of people, then you should not play with their emotions and annoy them by only hinting at what is to come. To do that will lose you listeners.

> ◄ **ACTUAL AUDIO**
>
> PRESENTER: '. . . and big problems on the M25 this morning, which has been closed in both directions. I'll tell you where in ten minutes . . .'
>
> *Commercial radio station, November 2005*

[14] 'Coming soon' means, I would suggest, in the next ten minutes.

[15] 'Next' means that it will follow what's happening now/about to happen.

[16] 'Later this hour' would refer to the clock hour, not something within the next 60 minutes.

[17] 'In the next few minutes' would give the impression of the next five.

[18] Don't suggest that an item, say a competition, is 'just around the corner' when in fact it's an hour or so away. That is deceiving the listener who will be wary of placing their trust in you again. If an item is happening in the next 30 minutes then it is OK to use the general terms outlined above, but if it is in the next 60, say so.

In a situation like this, when you have got important or time-sensitive information, don't play games.

You should also not lie in a tease and worry listeners unnecessarily or tempt them to listen by giving them an out-and-out untruth. They will find out what you have done and may not trust you again. For example, if you said that an *EastEnders'* actor has been found taking drugs on set and booted off the show '. . . I'll tell you who, next . . .' and it turns out to be a bit-part actor on one of the market stalls whom no one has ever heard of, then listeners will feel cheated of their investment of time in your programme.

Look after your listeners — don't abuse their trust or waste their time. Tease, don't deceive.

✗	'Join me again after the news.'	Arrogance that the listener will want to stay purely because it's you, rather than for any content they will be able to use, coupled with the inference that the listener and/or the presenter are going to miss an important programme element.
✗	'Coming up it's news time.'	Not only a cliché but one which signifies that you are doing a programme item (the news) because it's time to do it, rather than because it's got any value to the listener.
✗	'The travel news is here in five minutes.'	Does nothing to illustrate why that's an attractive proposition.
✓	'You want to stay on top of those terror threats, don't you? Fiona's got the very latest in the news at 5.'	This appeals to the listener's 'social proofing' instinct, they need to know what's going on.
✓	'Sylvie's got the latest travel news in five minutes to help you get where you're going on time, and after that you won't want to miss Karli Rogers who's got some fascinating ways to get more sleep and better sleep, even if you work long hours and have small kids . . .'	There's a specific 'listening benefit' followed by the offer of something special using the 'scarcity principle.'

Trails and promos

These are either:

- o straightforward, live, presenter-read mentions of future programmes or features, which tell (rather than tease)
- o or pre-produced (built) short 'adverts' for these items.

Both kinds of trails may be scheduled to run at a certain time (although that is most likely to happen with the produced trail) and are used to tempt listeners to listen longer.

These are usually produced by the presenter or by a specialist producer at the station. They are not usually made by independent companies because they have got a short shelf life and so many are needed.

The style of these trails, the music used, the presentation, the content, all have to be carefully considered to reflect the station brand.

Scheduling trails

It is most effective to schedule trails to play at a time when the person listening is likely to be interested in what you are trailing. For example, in a Saturday afternoon sports show it would be obvious to promote weekday breakfast-time sports bulletins and the midweek evening match coverage. The kind of caller to a gardening phone-in might enjoy the big band programme later that night – so tell them about it!

It is also a good idea to think of promoting other programmes horizontally and vertically. A *vertical* schedule would place a trail in the breakfast show that told listeners what was happening later that day (think of the vertical programme listings in the newspapers). The thinking is that someone listening now may be available to listen during the day perhaps because of a day off work. (If you are specifically targeting workers then you will want to tell them about your station's drivetime show, of course.) So, vertical is down the hour, show or day.

Horizontal promotion is again best thought of in relation to newspaper listings. Each day the programme details go down the page, and each day is presented the same way on a page-by-page (that is horizontal) basis. In radio terms, someone who is listening to the breakfast show *today* will probably be interested in what is happening at the same time *tomorrow*. So, horizontal is across the week at this time.

SELF-INTEREST

The number one rule for writing effective headlines[19] is to appeal to your audience's self-interest. In radio terms, that means having the most compelling listener benefit in the first sentence of everything you say on the air.

> I'm Johnny Jock, join me this Saturday afternoon at the Whitewater shopping centre from 2, as we broadcast live in association with Andy's Autos – the place to go for the best deals on wheels. There'll be free pizza and your chance to win a trip to the town of Cortina in Italy . . .

Move the most compelling listener benefit (free food and potential prize), from the end of the item to the start. Where it is currently, by the time the listener hears what's in it for them, the location details have already been given.

> Then add emotion, perhaps along the lines of:
> 'Here's a great way to kick back on a Saturday afternoon . . .'

---

[19] Gary Blake and Robert Bly, *Elements of Copywriting* (Longman, 1999): http://tinyurl.com/klsmo2.

> 'Free food! Yeah, I thought that would get your attention!'
> 'Do you sometimes get fed up when you're out shopping on a Saturday afternoon? Well here's a way that you can get free food, and stand a chance to win a free holiday to Italy!'
> 'I hope you don't mind me saying, but you're looking a little tired . . . you could do with a holiday. How does Italy grab you?'
>
> Despite what some people think, just *repeating* something over and over will not make a listener care about it. You have to make it matter.

Think of trailing in terms of looking ahead to:

- the next hour
- the next show
- later today
- the next day
- the weekend.

Promoting the weekend is all-important as weekday shows are essentially the same format day to day and because people's availability to listen (and to listen for longer) increases at weekends. TV stations start promoting their weekend coverage from the previous Tuesday as it gives the viewer something to anticipate.

> People blogged on Sunday what they did on Saturday night and their sentiments on Monday might still reflect good memories of the weekend. By the middle of the week, people were at their lowest point.[20]

You should certainly be talking about the weekend shows, the what's on events, the weather and what you are going to be doing from Thursday onwards. Then, over the weekend, certainly on Sunday, talk about reasons to stay listening for Monday's programmes.

In constructing a music bed for a trail make sure that it is the correct length for the speech. In other words do not have a promo that lasts musically for 30 seconds if the speech ends after 25, or indeed have the music end before the speech. They should both end at the same time – faded music should do so under the speech content. The exception might be if you have a music stab or crescendo at the end of the promo. The item should be accurately timed. Not only is this professional, but also will also help your colleagues with their back-times and help an automated computer playout system that may be scheduling trails.

To explain, some stations have split ad breaks (different sets of commercials that play on different transmitters on the same station, or on different stations in the same group). The computer will schedule the ads for each break depending on the 'rules' which have been set for each ad (how often it's to be played, and what time of day, as well as avoiding clashes with similar products in the same break), so each break is the same duration. 'Fillers' such as trails may be used by the computer to balance a break on one transmitter, but if yours has

[20] 'Tweeters and Bloggers Show we do like Mondays After All': http://tinyurl.com/nogmjb.

an 'awkward' duration such as 27, 33 or 41 seconds then it is less likely to be used than if it is 30, 35 or 40.

Your own promos can be as basic as taking a 'magic moment' from today's show and wrapping it with a top and tail announcement to promote tomorrow's show:

> On Wednesday's Chris P. Bacon Breakfast Show we called film sensation Holly Wood and asked her about her new movie [clip]. On Thursday's show Mr Nasty from TV's *The Z Factor* is with us. With news, travel and weather every 15 minutes, that's Breakfast, from 6 on Radio X.

Note that the promo can be played for the rest of Wednesday and Thursday, because of the use of those day names – it doesn't say 'today' and 'tomorrow' which would have dated it and made it unusable in the early hours of Thursday.

An alternative way to promote your own show is to record a short, dry trail and leave it on the playout system for other presenters to use. Then, when they have a ten-second intro to a song, they can play your dry drop-in over the top, which idents the station and promotes your programme:

> Hi Sammy here, from 'Sammy and Vicki in the Morning' – y'know I've got a thousand pounds burning a hole in my pocket for the winner of our Trivia Challenge . . . and that could be you! Listen from 7 am on Tuesday for more clues, here on Radio X.

Cross-promote, highlight and talk up other parts of the station's output. Support your colleagues and encourage your listener to sample other dayparts. Personal recommendation is very effective. An adlibbed line after a trail such as, 'Did you hear Chris with Holly this morning? It was great, especially when she sang him "Happy Birthday" . . . don't miss tomorrow, it's gonna be fantastic . . .', adds to the impact of the pre-produced bit. That's because it is you who said it rather than an unknown voiceover on a trail. Your listeners like you, that is why they are listening to your programme, so what you recommend to them will carry more weight.

You don't bully friends or people you're trying to build a relationship with: 'Stay right here', 'don't move', 'don't you dare turn off', 'make sure . . .' Give people a reason to listen, invite them to take part, appeal to their self-interest and reasons for closure. Sell, don't bully.

Three promo pitfalls

- *Promoting something that is 'coming up next'* – This promo example[21] was nicely written and delivered but fell short in terms of maximising listener loyalty. Why? It's much more likely that a listener will stay tuned for the next 60–90 seconds anyway, than for a report airing in 15 or 20 minutes. That's why your goal should always be to aim for that next quarter hour – not the next minute.

[21] Clips from NPR's Local News Initiative: http://tinyurl.com/makzql: http://tinyurl.com/nu62g8.

- *Revealing too much* – give listeners a compelling reason to continue listening. But don't steal the punchline.[22]
- *Writing crutches like 'coming up'* – Overuse[23] equals reduced impact.

Promos that work

- Place promos to build listening for the best/most important stories airing in the next 15 or 20 minutes.[24]
- Use audio in promos[25]
- Include names of 'star' names when possible.[26]

---

[22] The six links in this and the following notes take you to audio examples: http://tinyurl.com/nclwef.
[23] http://tinyurl.com/kt453o.
[24] http://tinyurl.com/nuptvb; http://tinyurl.com/ljxjm4.
[25] http://tinyurl.com/l6hewr.
[26] http://tinyurl.com/neojne.

17 Presenting programme items

The basics

Furniture features

You will know where in the programme your 'permanently formatted junctions' or 'furniture' is: the regularly scheduled features which cannot be moved. These may be items which are the same on most programmes on the station, each hour, each day, such as news at the top of each hour for three minutes, with travel news for two minutes at :15 and :45 past each hour, and what's on information every hour at :45. There may also be set times for commercial breaks.

Additionally there may also be furniture specific to your programme: set items at set times in your show. These may be things like a 'Top Ten at Ten' chart rundown feature at, unsurprisingly 10:00 each day or a shorter item like a 'Secret Sound' competition each morning at 11:30. It is important to keep these features in the same place each day so listeners know where to find them, although smaller regular items ('Today's Stupid Criminal' or topical gag) can be moved.

> I like radio where almost anything can happen. I hate it when shows are so structured that you know that at 8.27 you're going to get such and such and at 9.38 is when they do this little segment . . . it's so dull.[1]

Having said that, you may promote and schedule an item for, say, 11:30, even though it is not on air until 11:33. That's often OK – the listener will stay tuned for a few more minutes (indeed it is one of the main jobs of a presenter to get them to do just that), but never go to a feature *early*. The listener will, quite rightly, feel cheated if they keep listening for an item that you did before you said you would.

---

[1] Iain Lee, presenter, Absolute Radio, *The Radio Magazine*, July 2008.

Benchmark features

These are the regular items such as a particular competition or music feature, which are specific to your show or station, and are what you are known for.

Your station might be known as the one that has the daily 'Mystery Voice' competition, the 'Birthday Bong' game (a benchmark for Capital FM), 'PopMaster' or 'Factoids' (Ken Bruce and Steve Wright on Radio 2). Alternatively your benchmarks may be how you schedule your music (the 'No Repeat Work Day' on Absolute Radio), or even something as straightforward as 'double gold' (two classic songs) out of every news bulletin, or a 'then and now' artists feature.

Benchmarks are at the same time each day to help give a foundation and familiarity to the format.

> There is a terribly thin line between benchmark features that your show owns, and aspects that were once fresh but have turned stale. We are constantly evolving and reinventing. Breakfast shows must be habit-forming for the listener but should never become predictable. Familiarity is comfortable but must not become unsurprising.[2]

> Just because something happens at a specific time, and you promote it, does not mean that it's a 'benchmark'. It can only be a benchmark if the listener cares enough about it to make an appointment to listen to it. Otherwise, it's just a 'regularly scheduled nothing' that may or may not have any real value.
>
> A successful station may create three benchmark features that it is known for, and continually recycle listeners to these points of difference in their programming.

News

Listeners to a music station do not tune in primarily for the news; they mainly want music, entertainment and companionship. But they *do* want to be kept in touch with what is important to them.

If news is done well it can help make a music station sound local, immediate and in touch with listeners' lives. If it is done badly then not only can it be a waste of time, but also a potential exit point.[3] Many listeners may not turn on for the news, but may turn off because of it if it's not relevant, interesting or compelling.[4]

---

[2] Robin Galloway, presenter, Real Radio Scotland, *The Radio Magazine*, June 2009.

[3] As noted earlier, every time there is a change in programming between songs or features, it highlights the opportunity for a listener to leave. Teasing or trailing across junctions which some people may not find engaging (news, travel news, ad breaks) helps make such exit points less obvious.

[4] More advice on making your news relevant, interesting and compelling in Paul Chantler and Peter Stewart's, *Essential Radio Journalism* (Methuen Drama, 2009): http://tinyurl.com/mrodkb.

Your station's news journalists have a difficult job. They have to provide enough information of the right type to satisfy listeners' demands, without getting too much in the way of the music that the listener has tuned in for in the first place.

News should be informing and, on the right occasion, entertaining. It is not supposed to be boring, and just a little thought and training will help your station's news team learn how to make it relatable and accessible.

The news studio
(NPA).
Courtesy: BBC
London 94.9

Timings into the news

During the day most of your news bulletins will be 'in-house', provided by your station's own team of journalists. At other times, usually evenings, overnights and weekend afternoons, they may come from an external provider.

Those 'networked' news bulletins will be 'clock start' and 'clock end'; that is, they will start and stop exactly at a pre-set time.[5] Usually that will be a clock-start of :00 (on the top of the hour exactly) and a clock end of :03 (exactly three minutes past). This is so all stations can 'opt in' (take the feed from the outside source) safe in the knowledge that it'll be there and how long it'll last. This is especially important for automated shows: the playout system will automatically opt in to that networked news channel between :00 and :03 each hour. The presenter of a pre-recorded show needs to know the duration of a bulletin so they can work out the running order and timings for the rest of their hour.

With in-house bulletins, timings are less important. Many BBC stations play the time-signal 'pips' going into the top-of-the-hour news, so the jingle and the reader have to be ready. There is usually no reason (apart from professionalism) for a live bulletin into a live show to *finish* at an exact time, unless stations are joining up for a networked programme after local bulletins. Commercial stations are no less professional than BBC ones, but their attitude is often more relaxed when it comes to getting into the news bulletins.

As we saw earlier, listeners depend on the radio to schedule their routine, especially in the morning rush. They do this by not only listening to the actual time-checks, but also by knowing when furniture features are on. So if you broadcast an 8 o'clock news bulletin at 8:04, you mislead the audience, upset the newsreader and look unprofessional. It also makes the

[5] This can cause awkwardness: http://tinyurl.com/ngny2z.

station sound amateurish: if the news jingle says, 'News on the hour . . . this is Super FM . . .', does the reader come on and say 'It's 8 o'clock . . .' or 'It's 8:04 . . .'? Getting into the news on time is important for the listener and a courtesy to the reader.

> Bulletins on the hour should always be on time; the only
> exceptions are during live sport, or important breaking news. If in
> doubt, refer upwards.
> You can be slightly more relaxed about timings on the half
> hour but the bulletin should be no more than 2 minutes late –
> otherwise we're not providing a dependable service for
> the listener.[6]

News jingles

News jingles may be a few seconds long or they may consist of a bed of up to a minute. Either way, they often incorporate a list of towns in the station's transmission area, the name of the station and its frequency.

Longer beds can be tricky as you have to remember to start them, off air, at the correct time. There is little room for manoeuvre with these long news lead-ins, although some stations have a 'get out of jail' jingle – a shorter one to use in emergencies when you forget to start your usual jingle on time.

Longer jingles, usually with a music bed for 30 seconds followed by ten seconds of 'station ID' and pips (coming in from a separate source) will give you the opportunity to promote the next hour of your show.

What not to say

Don't say, 'I'll be back after the news . . .', 'Let's cross over/hand you over to the newsroom', 'Join us when we return . . .', 'Come back after . . .' for three reasons.

First, you're not going anywhere, so you can't come back (you won't be on air, but then you don't say, 'I'll be back after this song from Madonna', do you?). As far as the listener is concerned, the news and music is all from the same studio and certainly from the same station. (Obviously, the same goes for 'Welcome back', 'Hello again . . . .', after the news). The programme team may feel they are having a break, but the output is continuous – the bulletin should be perceived as a part of the programme, as it is by the audience.

Second, you should be promoting what is after the bulletin. So: 'I've got the Number One from this day, exactly a year ago, right after we've heard the latest on the hunt for the missing Blankshire businessman . . .' does two promotions in one.

Third, saying 'I'll be back after the news . . .' suggests to the audience that if you are going away then the news is of no importance, and gives them an exit point.

Everything the station does has value and the bulletin should be an integral part of your programme and the station's output.

---

[6] BBC Radio Five Live style guide.

Credibility

Radio news people are a skilled group of people, the best of whom straddle 'hard' news and 'entertaining' radio. They may not share the flashy profile of the presenter, but they are deadly serious about what they do and very protective towards their role as journalists. So don't interrupt a bulletin, don't ask them to take sides in a story or ask them their take on it, don't pick them up (on air) about a mispronunciation or misfired audio clip.

Never ask a news presenter a question *on air* that you haven't asked them *off air* and that *you know they know the answer to*. The news person's role is to know everything, and if they do not it damages their credibility and authority and those of the station.

ACTUAL AUDIO

(After the sports bulletin presenter had run a story about Chelsea being fined £300,000 by the Premier League for 'tapping-up' Arsenal defender Ashley Cole.)

PRESENTER: Where does that money go? What's it spent on?
SPORTS READER: Err . . . I don't know. I can try and find out if you like . . .

BBC station, June 2005

Get credibility to work positively: when there is a big or complicated news story a presenter can quiz the prepared journalist, who has researched the subject and given the host the questions to ask. The reporter then 'miraculously' knows everything about everything! Doing this will mean:

- *you* sound clever
- the *broadcast journalist* sounds clever
- it will help develop a powerful partnership between the two of you
- it will add value to your show . . .
- and it will increase your value to the station.

Comedian Sean Hughes startled listeners to the BBC's London radio station GLR yesterday morning when he interrupted newscaster Jason Kay to argue over the nationality of Formula One driver Eddie Irvine. Rounding off the 10 am bulletin, Kay described Irvine – second in the Japanese Grand Prix – as a 'British driver'. 'No, he's not,' interjected Dublin-born Hughes who was preparing for his regular Sunday morning show on the station. 'Eddie is Irish.' With remarkable aplomb, Kay retorted: 'He is Northern Irish.' Sean and Jason are technically both correct. Irvine was born in Newtownards but lives in Dublin.[7]

The news person is the voice of authority on the station. That is why some stations shy away from having a 'zoo' of characters, where the news person is encouraged to be silly or the butt of jokes. Their credibility suffers if they then have to talk about '200 dead in an air crash' moments later. Of course the news reader can be funny, react to something in the

---

[7] *Daily Express*, November 1998.

show or be a 'personality' reader (we are a long way past the days of a boring guy in a bow tie), but presenters should think twice before making them the subject of a jibe or asking them a question that they may not know the answer to.

News teasers

Presenters often fail to realise that by promoting the news in their show, they're dragging their listeners through another quarter-hour, and keeping up the figures for themselves (news isn't surveyed separately in a Rajar diary, as bulletins are too short).

- News teasers have got to be strong. Never promote a soft story – it's pointless. Indeed, it could have a detrimental affect on your attempt to pull listeners through.
- It's not teasing the news to give a minute by minute rundown of when the next bulletin will be: 'It's 20 to 12, so the latest news is just 20 minutes away . . .', '. . . and Jerry Journalist will be here in 14 minutes with the news . . .', 'Don't forget, all the latest news with Jerry just eight minutes away . . .'.

Back teasers

These are also important. Most stations will insist that the presenter comes out of the news with a sweeper and then two songs back to back. Fine, but later you could say something that relates to the previous bulletin. It is part of your show after all. What about a straightforward line such as, 'Sounds like the police have got some interesting clues into where that missing man might be . . . it must be awful when a relative just disappears like that . . .'. This will mean you have got to listen to the bulletin, or talk to the news reader, but a personal thought creates a link between you and your audience.

Tip-offs

Any information that is called into you in the studio that may be a news story should be checked with the duty reporter. They are better placed to confirm its accuracy before it goes to air. Indeed, they may have had the same information and already found it to be untrue or been asked by the police not to broadcast it for operational reasons.

One such possibility is details of a bomb warning. It may be that you are called on the phone-in number with this information. Imagine the scare and panic that you could cause by using the phrase 'bomb warning' on air – that would be part of the aim of the caller who could be a real terrorist, disgruntled office worker or bored teenager.

Your station should have a form to be completed for these types of calls in the studio bible (see p. 138). Remember as much as you can about the accent of the caller, their likely age, what exactly they said and so on. Then pass the information to the newsroom. Bomb scares will not usually be mentioned on air as they only encourage copycat calls and cause distress. However, mention would be made about the knock-on effect of such incidents such as railway station closures or shopping centre evacuations.

Mention of road accidents and fires, if reported irresponsibly ('. . . so don't go shopping in the High Street today . . .') could cause a loss of business for local traders, losing your station money, as these businesses may be advertisers. Better to report the '. . . accident that has closed the High Street . . .' (a fact) and not give further comment.

And finally . . .

Ask your news reader to always tell you if they are going to include a funny 'kicker' story at the end of the bulletin. Ask them what it is about so that you can prepare a comment or reaction, or maybe play an appropriate song. Also ask them to always tell you if there is a breaking serious story that they are going to include (especially if they intend to repeat it at the end of the bulletin) so you can avoid a music clash (playing a song with a title that might be seen as a comment on the story).

Travel news

'Traffic' is the name given to the department at a commercial station which schedules the advertisements: they 'traffic' the ads. Understandably this can cause some confusion with those people who collate and present the traffic and travel news. 'Traffic' may also be used to describe the department at the BBC which books studios and lines to other remote studios! It's always safer then, to refer to 'travel news'. Some stations refer to 'traffic and travel news' in reference to their coverage of public transport information and possibly flight delays or ferry cancellations as well as road news.

Travel news is more than reading lists of road works and locations of accidents. It's another important link you have with the local community and should be relevant, informative and accurate.

- The information is immediately relevant to them (it will take them longer to get to work or to get the children to school). Together with the weather, travel news is one of the key reasons why people listen to the radio. In the morning and afternoon drivetime around 50 per cent of your listeners could be in cars.
- The information is about places that your listeners know, so news of a crash that has closed the high street is of interest to people even if they are not intending to use that road.
- Bulletins often complement the rest of the output. For example, sports fixtures can be affected by delays and traffic can be affected by weather, security scares, etc.
- You become a trusted source of local information which reflects your brand.

Many stations will have bulletins every 15 minutes at peak drive times and every half or one hour during the rest of the day. They are often 'balanced' in the hour, for example at quarter to and quarter past the hour. Bulletins should not be longer than necessary and rarely longer than a minute or so. If there is little or nothing to report, then the travel presenter should say so.

Travel presenters from remote sites may have a quick turnaround between you and another station (as explained below), so it is a courtesy to them to hit the travel junction on time. You shouldn't drop the travel if it is scheduled in your programme: 'reliability' refers to the scheduling as well as the content of bulletins.

Information sources

The information is often collated and presented not at the station, but by a national company such as Trafficlink[8] or GTN.[9] These suppliers get the information from sources such as the police (who can tell of accidents, or severe weather), councils and utility companies (who pass on details of long-term road works for resurfacing or pipe-laying). Additionally they

---

[8] More on Trafficlink: http://tinyurl.com/bwuxbx.
[9] More on Global Traffic Network: http://tinyurl.com/nrkdr7.

may have access to motorbike or car-based reporters (the AA used its network of staff in emergency call out vehicles to pass on news of delays for its travel news service), access to CCTV cameras, and traffic-speed road-sensors. Because so many stations now overlap, the information gathered from a few calls can be broadcast on several stations. This saves a duplication of effort by the travel news collators and those providing the information, for example those at police motorway control. Travel information from sources such as rail, air and ferry news may be collated and presented by the same provider, or the radio station may set up individual arrangements with staff at those separate companies. All this information is usually accessible at the stations themselves via a secure login to the provider's website, so presenters always have access to the very latest information.

Commercial stations often barter[10] air time with travel providers (the companies are allowed to air commercials within their reports, and keep the revenue), although obviously BBC stations pay a flat fee for the service provided.

Your message is carried beside premium content, heard by a huge captive audience, who are actively listening, at peak times. We reach more people more often with more effectiveness than any other medium. People want to get where they're going. So they turn up our travel reports and listen. You want to reach people with your advert. We bring the two together, with your brand message right next to the travel news. Our traffic reports and adverts feature when radio audiences are biggest, at breakfast and drivetime.[11]

Another valuable source of road news is the listeners. A phone number (often called something like a 'Jambuster hotline') is given in each bulletin for listeners to call on their mobile phone, often together with the phrase 'as long as it's safe and legal to do so' (in other words, using a hands-free), and pass on details of tailbacks or the exact location of an accident. That information can then be double-checked with the authorities. Doing this encourages a high level of interactivity and provides a valuable source of information.

The problem with using a caller's contribution is that you don't know how accurate they are. Some information may be from people who deliberately want to mislead. Others may report a 'serious crash', which *looks* bad but is soon cleared up, or 'long tailbacks' (how long is 'long'?), or refer to 'heavy traffic' on a route that they don't usually use and so have nothing to compare it with.

Often the callers use a nickname, which can add colour to your bulletin, but beware of double-meanings.

Use callers' names regularly to:
o add credibility to the report
o help personalise the bulletin
o encourage a sense of belonging.

Some stations have access to a plane or helicopter to give travel reports from the best vantage

---

[10] An arrangement between a station and service provider where *goods* are exchanged in return for air time is called a 'contra deal'. For example, a hotel might provide a venue for a commercial station's Christmas party for free. That cost is 'contra'd' against a number of 'free' adverts for the hotel on the station. Remember, the only thing a commercial station can bargain with is its air time.

[11] From GTN: http://tinyurl.com/lvzmyo.

point possible. The trouble is that even though queues can be spotted, the airborne reporter is unlikely to be able to know what caused it. That is why information is often collated on the ground and then relayed to a 'spy in the sky' reporter to read on air, together with their up-to-date view of the congestion that's been caused.

> Airborne reports are a great option for three reasons: they sound great, enhance information gathered on the ground and are a way of the radio station being seen by its listeners.[12]

Getting the news on air

As far as listeners are concerned, the traffic news broadcast by the station was collated *at* the station. So, Trafficlink or GTN reporters present their bulletins via an ISDN line which makes it sound as though they are in the station rather than in a regional centre. Reporters present bulletins on several stations around the region during each hour and care is taken not to have one presenter on two which overlap, so the image of individuality isn't broken. Additionally, the hotline numbers for neighbouring stations are different, to further the effect.

Do not play a travel jingle that says 'Travel News on Radio X' and then say, 'That's right, it's time for the travel news . . .'. Try to be a bit more creative. Listen to the previous bulletin and make a note of what is going on or ask the travel presenter off air what they are going to lead with on air. Then you can say something like, 'Well half an hour ago, Tina, we heard that the M99 was down to 40 miles an hour northbound at Blankstown's exit . . . has that eased at all?', which provides a much smoother flow into the bulletin.

Similarly, relate to the news after the bulletin. If a major route is closed, sympathise with your listeners: live their life vicariously. Acknowledge that the information affects people (essentially you're showing empathy with words and tone that says 'I heard it too and I care about you and we're going to help you out by keeping you updated . . .').

Saying 'up next, travel' is not a tease. Telling listeners that they'll find out *where* something has happened or *why* it has happened is. Give them a *reason* to listen.

Travel jingles

Travel jingles are distinctive so that they can cut through the mayhem that is the morning or afternoon rush, and 'signpost' the travel news to the listener. If you use a music bed remember to keep it low under the voice so you don't distract the listener.

RDS[13] (Radio Data Service) tones are either an audible three bleeps, or inaudible, and are broadcast as part of the travel jingle or played in manually by the presenter. Either way, the RDS can automatically retune a car radio to the nearest station that is playing a traffic bulletin if this function is enabled on that car's set.

You can use the time between the end of your report and the 'out tone' of the RDS to promote:

[12] Paul Hutton, European managing director, Global Traffic Network, *The Radio Magazine*, June 2008.
[13] RDS is also the device which displays the station name and a short scrolling message, and retunes to a stronger frequency for that station. More on RDS: http://tinyurl.com/yjj8ct and http://tinyurl.com/m3hzoy.

> your station name and frequency — as new listeners may not otherwise be aware of you
>
> your next song or competition — in the hope that some new arrivals may stay listening to you.

You should not deliberately leave the RDS on for any longer than this, say for several minutes at a time.

The order of the info

It is important to prioritise the order of the information presented. The general rule is: motorways first, followed by A roads, then public transport. Usually public transport should always get a mention even if it is just 'no reported problems', to reassure people. In exceptional circumstances, this order may be changed, for example, if your local airport is closed because of fog or the rail network is disrupted because of a crash. Then, work through the roads in a logical order — do not keep jumping back and forth across the area, or up and down the motorway in different directions.

Picture a funnel to remember how to present the information most effectively, with the more general information given first, and the more focused detail given last. This funnels the attention of the listener to where the problem is.

> . . . and here's an important traffic update of special interest to you if you're travelling southbound on the M23, from Crawley to Brighton: just at Pease Pottage there's a queue, especially in the left lane. This is after a lorry overturned, so if you can move over to the right hand lane if you're approaching Pease Pottage just south of Crawley.

Within that framework, always mention the location before the situation. We best retain traffic reports when the information is presented in that order, from the general to the more specific, so say *where* the problem is — then *what* the problem is.

The result and the reason

Adding colour to a travel bulletin occasionally can help its 'interest factor'. Try to explain what is causing the tailbacks — people get less annoyed if they have the reason rather than just the result. So if a lorry has shed its load, try to find out what it is that's all over the road. Painting a picture makes the situation more vividly relatable.

◀ ACTUAL AUDIO

TRAVEL PRESENTER: . . . because an escalator's fallen off the back of a lorry.
PRESENTER: And we've had an e-mail, apparently police are taking steps to find out how it happened . . .

BBC Radio Five Live, June 2005

Travel language

Say 'road' rather than 'carriageway' and avoided using 'incident'. These are boring technical words which make your bulletin less relatable. Use ordinary terms that your listener uses. Another to strike from your word list is 'RTA' (road traffic accident) which you should call merely an 'accident'.

Be careful about apportioning blame in the travel news. If you say, for example, '. . . delays on the A99 where a car has hit a lorry . . .' you've suggested that the car driver was at fault. Instead, say 'have hit each other', 'have collided', 'a collision between . . .'

You only need to use 'collide' when both objects were moving or could have moved (for example two cars or a car and a pedestrian). But it's ridiculous and unnecessary to say, 'a car collided with a tree'. Say simply: 'the car hit a tree'. And certainly never use 'the cars collided into each other' as 'collided' means just that!

Other useful tips:

- *Your travel news area* – The vast majority of the travel information you broadcast will be within your TSA, however, you'll sometimes stray outside it. For example, if there is a large accident 'over the border' which causes the closure of a major road that runs through your 'patch'. The tip is to think logically where are your listeners are travelling to.

- *Say it once, say it twice* – Just use the word 'shut' or 'closed', you don't need to say, for example that the train services are 'shut *down*' or a road is 'closed *off*'. If the story is affecting a lot of people then give the information again. 'Traffic is slow between Anyville and Anytown on the A999. An accident at Blanksville is making things slow in both directions . . . that's the A999, an accident at Blanksville, slowing things to a crawl both ways.' This makes it easier for those affected to register the details.

- *Routes and directions* – If referring to the main road between, say Anytown and Blankstown, the 'Anytown road' is certainly appropriate to those listening in Blankstown, but to those in Anytown it's the 'Blankstown road'. It is probably better to talk about 'the road between Anytown and Blankstown', or 'between Blankstown and Anytown'.

- *North and south* – You can't 'head northbound' so don't say it! Drivers are either 'heading north' or 'northbound' – not a combination of the two. In fact, it is probably better to say specifically, 'If you're heading for Charlottesville . . .' as more drivers will know that, rather than the actual compass direction. Alternatively, you may consider it clearer to say, 'Heading for Anytown on the A999 at Blanksville', for example, rather than 'westbound on the A999 at Blanksville'.

- *Motorways* – When talking about motorways, make sure you use 'northbound' and 'southbound' (or 'east' and 'west', whatever is appropriate), together with the junction number and name. First because most people know junctions by their name or number, and secondly because it helps reinforce what you are saying. The exception is where the road is commonly known by another name. For example, 'Where the M111 meets the M222' is probably preferable to 'the Redbury Interchange' if most people have never heard of it.

- *Road numbers* – These are traditionally read as splits of two numbers, i.e., the A-twelve, or the A-twenty-two. However, roads of three digits are usually read separately: A one-two-seven, for example. You will, of course, find situations where this is not the case!

- *Report good news* – It can be just as useful to know that an accident is cleared and the situation's back to normal. This is so someone who heard about the initial problem and who's planning a diversion can be reassured that it's OK to stick to their original route.

o   *Don't cause upset* – When presenting a news story about town centre delays, or problems on the way to a major shopping centre, avoid putting listeners off travelling to those places. For example, it is fine to say, 'Avoid the A99 London-bound at Adamstown because of a crash', but not to say, 'Avoid Lakewater shopping centre because it's grid-locked.' Obviously, report the congestion, but stick to the facts and do not take an angle that will concern shopkeepers who could be advertisers, listeners or both! Similarly, avoid overtly publicising an event. 'The [competitor station] Roadshow is on at the Blankstown Showground, so there's lots of traffic going there . . .'.

o   *Local quirks* – Every area will have these. For example, drivers from Essex into Kent cross the River Thames on the Dartford Bridge, but those going the other way use the Dartford *Tunnel*. It is all part of your local knowledge, on a local station, to be aware of these.

o   *Local landmarks* – Make your bulletin easy to follow and easy to picture by talking about local landmarks. For example, 'An accident on London Road near the Cross In Hand pub . . .' or '. . . opposite the superstore . . .'. It is another way you can make the information relatable, even to those listeners who aren't drivers.

o   *Rewriting* – If you are presenting the travel news, try to rewrite your script to avoid the same phrases every single bulletin. It is inevitable that some lines will come round day after day, so think up some new ones to use. Instead of using the word 'queue', for example, you could use 'jam', 'nose to tail', 'congestion', 'tailbacks', 'bumper to bumper', 'stationary', 'chock-a-block', 'like a car park', 'crowded', 'struggling', 'slow-moving', 'stacked up', 'inching forward', 'driving in first gear', 'stop-start', 'trickling' and so on.[14]

o   *Mispronunciation* – If the bulletin is being read by someone outside the area they may get the name of a town wrong, which is almost unforgivable. Make sure they only do it once. Tell them off air what the correct way to say it is, do not draw attention to it on air. In their defence, the travel presenter may be broadcasting on different stations every few minutes so may not have had a chance to read their script beforehand. Even though they should have a list of town and village pronunciations for your area in front of them, they may be forgiven for being thrown by some unusual road names!

o   *One to one* – Remember that radio is one to one. Never say, 'Motorists are advised' or 'If you're all going to the county show then . . .'. Use language that is simple and relatable.

o   *Weather and travel* – Include bad weather in a travel bulletin if the problems are severe, because the two are so closely linked. But be careful not to patronise the listener and talk about shovels, blankets and flasks of tea as soon as the first flakes of winter start falling.

o   *Cross-promotion* – Most stations have travel details on their website too, so mention this so those without a radio later in the day (perhaps in an office) can check information online before they head for home. Point people to other bulletins on your station, for example the evening travel news if they are going to the big local match (and if they are not, this acts as a reminder to listen to your station's commentary).

---

[14] The book *Find-A-Line* (Lulu, 2008) lists dozens more alternative phrases for everyday travel news expressions: http://tinyurl.com/kpz9ol

- *Banter* – From time to time, there will be opportunities to banter with the travel presenter, but only do this at the end of a bulletin, and then only if both of you have something worth saying! Drivers get understandably annoyed when they miss their last possible exit to avoid a jam, because of studio wittering. If you have a comment to make after the bulletin, then prepare the travel reader off air beforehand: 'Tina, I've been talking about last night's *EastEnders*, did you see it? Good. Can I ask you what you thought about Dirty Den's ghost haunting the Queen Vic?'
- *Sign-offs* – Bulletins usually end with the Hotline number and an SOC.[15] This is necessary so if the bulletin is coming from a remote studio, the presenter knows when the reporter's finished.
- *Tip-offs* – If a listener calls the studio with news of an accident make sure you get as much information as possible, and if appropriate pass it on to those who collate and present the travel news. When your bulletin comes around, listen to it carefully; do not use it as an opportunity for a daydream. There may be a story in there that you can pass on to the news room (for example about a major accident that has closed the local motorway). Journalists can be pretty unforgiving, quite rightly, if an obvious story was broadcast on your programme and you did not tell them about it.

The audio playout keyboard

It used to be said that radio would always be the main provider of traffic news. How else could you get information on your route beamed directly into your car? Not through a CD, iPod, phone or sat nav. But then someone thought of putting a lot of that different technology together. This[16] arguably provides better in-car solutions to the traffic problem than any 'travel news every 15 minutes' or 'the eye in the sky' can. Especially as it's as-near-as 'live' information and tailor-made for your journey.

---

[15] SOC: standard out cue (such as 'This is Ken Berrigan, back with an update in 15 minutes. Meantime, if you know of a travel problem, call us on 01234 567 890').

[16] Aha Mobile: http://tinyurl.com/lw35vn.

The weather

[Commercial] stations broadcast, on average, over 17 weather bulletins and 12 travel bulletins each day. The average weather bulletin lasts just under one minute, an increase of 29 per cent on the 2004 audit. On average, stations broadcast over an hour of weather updates per week. The average travel bulletin lasts just over one minute, representing a 10 per cent increase on 2004. On average, stations broadcast nearly an hour and a half of travel bulletins per week.[17]

As with the travel, the forecasts you broadcast are a vital service which listeners should be able to rely on. Indeed, it is perhaps the single most useful item that you give, as it affects every single listener. For those with pre-school children especially, the weather is an important part of their decision-making process.

One of the most important elements on a radio programme is the weather, especially in local radio as the forecasts are more specific. That is why forecasts are scheduled so regularly.

Just because you read it so often, does not mean you can go into auto-pilot and throw it away. It needs to be presented clearly and read with significance. Do not race through the details because you are running late going up to the news, or so you can get to the next song — most people are genuinely interested in it.

Information is usually from PA or the Met Office via the stations' news suppliers, and BBC stations often use weather presenters linked with their local TV news output, or via ISDN from a regional weather centre.

The majority of stations have the weather either going up to or following the news bulletin at the top and bottom of the hour. Some may also have a more detailed forecast at other times of the hour.

Some stations do things a little differently, to be distinctive. One presents the bulletin at ten-past each hour (a benchmark feature), and names it the 'Ten-Past Forecast', which helps the station sound distinctively different.

In principle:

- At breakfast — say what it's going to be like today.
- In the morning — say what's going to happen this afternoon and tonight.
- In the afternoon — say what's going to happen tonight and tomorrow.
- On Thursdays — start looking ahead to the weekend.
- On Fridays — do the forecast for Friday, Saturday and Sunday to help people plan their weekend.

When the weather is making the news, you need to check that your script corresponds with what your colleagues have got. Sometimes weather stories are exaggerated to make good news reports, but you need to ensure the station's facts are consistent. It sounds unprofessional if the newsreader is saying 'the coldest winter in history', but the out-of-news forecast contradicts that.

Present the forecast so it has relevance to how your listeners live their lives.

---

[17] The RadioCentre's 'Action Stations' document: http://tinyurl.com/5pwdfh.

Ask yourself the following questions:

- On any given day, are you able to say with any degree of accuracy, what the temperature is?
- When was the last time you said the word 'precipitation'?
- Given that there's a big local outside concert tonight and you are on air now, how are you going to talk about the wet weather that is forecast?

Here are your probable answers.

- No. You'll probably say that it's 'pretty hot' or 'quite cold' or 'a bit warmer than yesterday'. So surely it makes sense to give a temperature in relation to something that Larry Listener already knows: yesterday's temperature! '16 Celsius, 61 Fahrenheit today . . . so that's a bit colder than the past couple of days . . .' is relatable and conversational.
- You probably never have. So why do some presenters say it? 'There's a chance of rain . . .' is better than, 'There is a probability of precipitation . . .'.
- 'So, if you're going to see Ray Dio and The Transistors tonight, better take a coat . . .' Again, this is more relatable and connects with the audience more than, 'It's going to rain . . .'. It takes a fraction of a second to make a great difference to basic and potentially boring content. (Just be careful you don't come across as patronising!)

People don't want to know about isobars, they want to know about the wind and the rain. They want to know whether it is going to be frosty and whether or not to put the heating on. They want to know whether to take an umbrella or a coat, leave early for work, or plan a weekend barbecue. So, do not just make the weather a list of facts, make it relatable. Make it friendly, conversational and one to one (like your other links). Like everything you read on air, read it through off air first and make the item your own.

Think what events your listeners could be doing that will be affected by the weather and use those to prompt the angle for your forecast. These events could be washing the car, having a barbecue or mowing the lawn. Or, more relatably and specifically: walking down the beach (at Blankshire Bay), flying a kite with the kids (on Blankshire Downs) and walking the dog (in the Blankshire Country Park).

Other useful tips:

- Consider the effect of changing your weather language to be more positive. So 'mostly cloudy' becomes 'partly sunny', 'increasing cloudiness' becomes 'becoming cloudy'.
- Forget percentages. It is not necessary to throw more numbers at listeners, so if the chance of rain is 30 per cent say 'a slight chance', or if it is greater 'a good chance'.
- Similarly, drop wind speeds. How many people know what a 15–20 mph wind feels like? Instead use the descriptions from the Beaufort Scale,[18] so you are told that the wind will be around 15 mph, describe it as 'a moderate wind' and so on.
- Do not say something like, 'Rain's expected in the towns in the north of our area . . .'. Listeners don't necessarily know where your area is! Make it relatable by naming towns or landmarks ('north of the M99').
- Do not push people away. Do not say, 'It's going to be sunny, over in Petersfield . . .' just simply say 'in Petersfield'. Reinforce where you are broadcasting to but not where you're based.

---

[18] Beaufort Scale: http://tinyurl.com/6qlruv.

- Consider that the word 'mild' means two different things depending on the time of year. In summer, a 'mild night' means it is chilly, and in winter a 'mild night' means it is relatively warm, so use this term with care. It sounds strange to say in autumn, winter or spring that it is 'warm' when it's say, 6 degrees. That's not warm, it's 'mild'.
- Remember it is incorrect to say that the temperature is 'colder' or 'hotter'. The temperature is a number on a scale so it can only be higher or lower — it is the weather that's colder or hotter.
- Some presenters will also make light of the phrase 'top temperature' when it is say 6 degrees in winter. 'If you can call that a top temperature!' they'll say. Well, yes, you can. If that is the most you can expect, it is the 'top'.
- Confusion happens in March when the clocks go forward. It is the first day of British Summer Time, not the first day of summer. It can't be the first day of summer; spring only starts a few days before! Yet every year presenters get confused.[19]
- 'It's 16 degrees outside . . .'. The outside temperature is what you usually give! Drop the word 'outside'.
- 'The rain's coming down . . .'. What direction were you expecting?
- Finally, if the forecast's wrong, don't draw attention to it, as you will lose credibility and listeners. Most weather bulletins outside breakfast are only once an hour, that means that you have 59 minutes in which to keep an eye out for what is happening and update your script accordingly. That way you will avoid saying, 'Well, my forecast says it is sunny and dry but it's teeming down outside . . . what a load of rubbish . . . !'

Refresh your weather bulletin often and look out of the window to see if it makes sense 'in the real world'. Mark Twain once said 'if you don't like the weather in England, just wait a minute'!

Drop mention of the day's 'high' or 'low' as soon as it has been reached. At the very least put it into the past tense: 'Today's high was . . .' is perhaps of some interest, but saying 'Today's high is . . .' at four in the afternoon is pointless.

Try not to use the same terminology all the time. There are other ways of saying 'hot and sunny'! You may want to consider 'Sunday roast', 'a thirsty Thursday', 'hot and humid', 'things can only get wetter', 'scorcher torture', 'complete heat', 'like toast on the coast' and so on. Be creative,[20] but only if the information is still clear.

If you can, promote that you are going to be telling people what the weather is going to be like. Notice that's not 'that you are going to be doing the weather forecast' — see all information strands from the point of view of what value the item is to the listener, not what you are going to give them. Even a basic throw-ahead such as, 'It's umbrella weather this weekend, I'll tell you when you're going to need it after this from Arctic Monkeys . . .' or 'What's the best day of the weekend to have a barbecue? I'll let you know after this . . .' or 'My grass needs its first cut of the year, but I keep putting it off. I may have the perfect excuse this weekend . . . the forecast follows this from . . .' are all better than suddenly reading the weather. Or saying that 'the weather's next', or worse, 'It's *time* for the weather . . .'. That phrase tells the listener that the only reason you are doing the forecast is because it's the next item on the running order, not because it has interest or value.

---

[19] When is the first day of spring, summer, autumn and winter? http://tinyurl.com/oww5b.
[20] The book *Find-A-Line* lists dozens more alternative phrases for everyday weather news expressions: http://tinyurl.com/kpz9ol.

Snowlines

At times of severe weather, stations often set up a Snowline service. Regular music and guests are replaced with rolling news, travel and weather information, details of school closures and cancelled events. Your job is to keep your listeners in touch with the information as it comes in and the problems they face.

Websites can play a huge role when it snows: get the details online in an easy-to-read format, to reduce the deluge of phone calls and the on air clutter. Presenters can then point listeners to the website rather than reading out long lists of cancellations.

Details of school closures are now often put on a school's individual website, or texted/Twittered to pupils direct, so there's increasingly less point in reading such information out, but still possibly worth having a record on the web.

Don't waste time reading out information that people can get elsewhere. Instead, do something that other services can't provide, such as accurate and updated weather and travel and snow-related journalism.

Snowlines (or similar services set up in the event of flood, hurricane, power failure, fire, major accident and so on) are:

- A great public service in the truest form.
- A way for the community to focus on the situation.
- A local morale-booster.
- A way to increase the listening hours.
- A way to add new listeners (through unexpected sampling).
- A way to make money (commercial stations may get their Snowlines sponsored).

All programme staff are expected to be available to broadcast. Backroom staff such as managers, sales and promotions executives are called upon to help collate information. If you live a long way from the studio and will have problems getting in, then arrange, with plenty of time, to stay locally. Leave may be cancelled and shifts altered as the situation develops.

If severe weather is forecast you owe it to your listener and employer to be ready to implement the plan of action, whatever the inconvenience to you (although avoiding putting yourself in danger).

Do not forget it is important to tell your listeners what you are doing as you do it. Reinforce the message of when the information will be given and why yours is the best station to hear it on. Do not be thrown by the excitement of the moment – remember to keep mentioning the name of the station. There will be lots of people who will be tuning to their local station for the first time.

During severe weather or disaster, simulcasting with your sister-station makes perfect sense. It saves duplicating your effort and maximises your audience. For example, during the terrrorist attacks in London in July 2005, Capital Radio joined with other London stations in their group, Xfm and Choice FM, to give Londoners the full coverage of what was unfolding.

Telling the time

There are few things that people want on a radio station more than time checks. This is especially true at time-critical parts of the day such as weekday breakfast and afternoon drive times when a time check, or even two, each link may not be too much. But for other shows in the daytime, for whose listeners the time is less likely to be an issue, a time check about every 20 minutes is probably a good suggested average.

Some programmers like their breakfast presenters to say the time in two different ways immediately after each other in each link. Their point of this so-called 'double-trucking' is that because the information is so crucial for people getting the kids to school or them-selves to work, once is not enough. They say listeners may hear that you have given a time check but have not registered exactly what it was so do it twice and they can't fail to get it! For example: 'Gwen Stefani's latest on Radio X breakfast . . . 8:20 . . . twenty past eight . . . and your chance to win a Porsche for the weekend in 'Porsche Or Pull' in five minutes . . .'.

Give the time to the listener as you would give it to a friend. So:

- Out go DJ clichés such as 'Coming up on 8:20', 'It's 20 after 8', 'It's 11 past 8', 'It's 40 before 9', and so on.
- Drop other time-related DJ clichés: 'Here's a time check', 'The top of the hour', 'The bottom of the hour', 'Minutes past the hour of', 'It's 4:35 right now'.
- In the second half of an hour, it's more relatable to say '20 to 9' than '8:40' as people work in relation to what's still to come, not what's been and gone.
- Super-precise time checks are also unnecessary ('It's 5¾ minutes past 10'). Instead make use of words such as 'nearly', 'just after' and so on.
- Drop the phrase 'It's time for . . .'. 'It's time for the news', 'It's competition time' – just say, 'Here's the news' or simply ask the competition question.
- Avoid tautology: 'The doors open tomorrow morning at 9:30 am'. AM means in the morning so either say 'tomorrow morning at 9.30' or 'tomorrow at 9.30 am', not both.

Be careful when saying 'good afternoon' or 'good evening'. In the summer, 5 o'clock is prob-ably still regarded by many as the afternoon. In the winter, when it is cold and dark, it is certainly perceived as the evening.

The verbal crutch

Here is another example: a presenter on a Sunday show gave a time-check in three of her four links: 'It's 6 and a half minutes past 1', 'It's 12 minutes past 1', 'it's 22 minutes past 1'. Regular and super-accurate time checks such as these are simply not necessary on a Sunday afternoon, when time isn't critical for your listeners, and give the impression that you haven't prepped properly.

Ad breaks

Going in to a break

Never draw attention to your ads. Do not say, 'I'll be back after the break': you aren't going anywhere and you hope your audience isn't either! Saying this gives an exit point, an opportunity to leave the station. Similarly, 'welcome back' after a break should also be a banned phrase!

ACTUAL AUDIO

PRESENTER: We're going off on a commercial break – back in a sec.

National commercial station, January 2006

Also consigned to the DJ dustbin are 'after these messages', 'after the commercial break' or the cliché 'after we've paid the rent'. Instead, promote what's happening the other side of the ads by saying 'soon', 'next', 'in two minutes' and so on.

Perhaps the one time when you can refer to the ad break is when its short duration is a selling point. Most station's breaks are around three minutes, but if you have one that's only *one* minute, it may be something to occasionally mention to stop the listener reaching for the dial. 'Lady Gaga is just 60 seconds away . . .', 'The Foo Fighters in two ads' time . . .'.

Some stations say that a link into an ad break should be limited to 20 seconds, so the duration of a presenter's talking doesn't significantly add to the speech block that follows.

In the middle of a break

Some programmers have a policy of stopping an ad break halfway through to tease the next song. Check if you are allowed to do this. If you are, interrupt the break between commercials, and about two-thirds through a break, to make a short comment such as 'Radio X, where The Prodigy are next . . .' and then resume the break. Doing this re-establishes the station name and is an opportunity to throw ahead.

Coming out of a break

Most commercial stations have a policy of always playing a jingle and then a song out of an ad break. This is to re-establish the identity of the station and get back to the music. As listeners will have just heard two or three minutes of talking they will not want another minute or so from the presenter.

Be careful playing a jingle out of a break though: most stations' trails are scheduled at the end of breaks and often end with a station ID, so it may not be necessary for you to play another one straight afterwards.

Come out of breaks the same way as you come out of the news, with an upbeat, strong song that's representative of your station.

The what's on diary

Stations broadcast regular What's On bulletins. The average stations broadcasts at least five of these information segments every day and over 37 bulletins every week . . . The average station promotes nearly 28 different community events and organisations per week.[21]

---

[21] Action Stations! The RadioCentre, 2008: http://tinyurl.com/lcghe5.

These are variously called Community Events, the Information Exchange, Public Service Announcements (PSAs) and so on, but the point of them is the same:

- you mention charity events on the station to stay connected to the area you broadcast to;
- by saying the names of local people and places you continue to have relevance to your listeners and the way they lead their lives, by giving them ideas of what to do with their hard-earned free-time;
- you give the impression of doing good work by publicising charity events for free;
- it is information listeners can't get from a national station.

So you think that reading information about another village fair is boring? Perhaps you had better get a different job. First, such announcements are the life-blood of local radio stations as the events relate your station to the area you serve (note the use of the word 'serve'). Second, it is up to you to present the information so it's *not* boring!

Presenters have traditionally seen reading what's ons as fillers — something to do when they are waiting for the travel presenter or to pad with up to the news. This should not be the case. Every moment on air should count.

It is true that each item is only important to a very limited number of people, that is why you have to work to make it of interest to many more. And if you do that, and speak to those who are interested personally and help make the event a success, you've strengthened the station's bond with that person and their organisation.

Choose your items to reflect your target listener. The events you mention say as much about the station as the music you play, so even though the local flower group has sent in event details to a rock station, does not mean it has to go on air.

How to read an item

There is a skill in presenting the sometimes tedious information: add something of yourself to them to make them relevant and interesting to your target audience.

Often each pre-written what's on script will be in the same format, such as the date and time of the event, then what it is, where it is and a contact number, all on a pro-forma sheet. And that is where the main problem lies. It makes it very tempting for the presenter to read out each item by simply working their way down each sheet, so you get 'On the 22nd of June at 2:30 in the afternoon, there's a jumble sale at St Peter's Church Hall, on London Road, Blankstown. There'll be refreshments and a bouncy castle and admission is 50 pence . . . On the 19th of June at 7:30 pm there's a meeting of the Blankstown Neighbourhood Watch at the secondary school on Freemantle Lane. Tea and biscuits will be available . . . On the 23rd of June . . .'.

So Rule One for reading what's ons is to make them relatable to your audience (so details of a tea dance aren't given out on a chart station, for example). Rule Two is to vary your order of delivery within a certain format. In the example above, anyone who was interested in the jumble sale would have missed when it was on because that information was given first. So if the date comes first, repeat it after you've given the other information.

The next point is to approach the items with a bit more creativity and relatability. This does not have to be convoluted, but will help draw people in to what you are telling them, rather than merely broadcasting a list of facts: 'I was clearing up the other day and realised that I just couldn't fit any more clobber into the cupboard under the stairs. What started off as a clear up turned into a clear out and I've now got a boot-full of jumble that I really must take down to St Peter's on Saturday for their jumble sale . . .'.

Alternatively: 'I always love a good bargain, and if you do too . . .', 'Here's a chance for you to help St Anthony's Hospital – just in case one day they have to help you . . .', 'If you've been spring cleaning but are loathe to just throw things in the bin . . .'. Just four ways of introducing a straightforward jumble sale notice in a slightly more creative way, by starting with the listener and not the event. Each one will take about ten seconds to think of: and you *are* in the creative business.

If you want to make your what's on more creative but are lacking a piece of information to give it that extra 'something', then call the organiser and ask them for some more details about the event, the cause or the stalls. An easy two-minute task.

Read items conversationally and sincerely. Never make fun of them because if you do that, you risk losing the organisers of the event and other listeners too.

Never refer to 'the public' ('. . . and it's open to the public' and so on). People don't see themselves as the 'public', instead say '*you* can get in for two pounds fifty . . .' or whatever. Despite adding the relatable angle at the top of the listing, try to keep the rest of the what's on short and clear. Occasionally repeat the time and place of an event for those who are only half awake, but don't do this for every item or it will get very tedious.

Remember the what's on is a headline, not a report. Give the 5Ws (who, what, where, when and why) and then move on.

Plugs are usually for charity and non-profitmaking events, so be careful if you are sent information for moneymaking businesses (such as tours around the local stately home) or commercial ventures (an open day at the local car showroom). This would be against BBC policy and a commercial station's sales team would understandably be cross with you for giving a free mention to a company that should have paid!

How to read dates

Do not give the listener extra work!

If you simply give a date, say for the Neighbourhood Watch meeting mentioned above, this is the thought process that everyone listening has to go through:

- What's today's date, I think it's the 13th, let's have a look at my watch, yes, the 13th.
- So the neighbourhood watch meeting is on the, what did they say, the 19th?
- OK, so if today's the 13th and it's Thursday that means that the 19th is . . .
- Hold on . . .
- OK that makes it next Wednesday.

Why don't you, the presenter, just say 'It's next Wednesday'?

◄ ACTUAL AUDIO

TRAVEL PRESENTER: And that line will be closed on the 14th and 15th of January for engineering works . . .

BBC local station – Saturday night 8 January

Community information

BBC local stations run Action Desks in partnership with the Community Service Volunteers (CSV) and help local charities and organisations by getting them featured on the radio promoting them to an audience of thousands.

Action Desks can be used to:

- produce an on-air appeal – perhaps for volunteers to drive a community minibus or to give a make-over to a hospice garden
- run on-air features to publicise things as crime prevention or adult education.
- provide a confidential off-air helpline service for listeners, giving contact numbers for charities and agencies who can help them
- run events in support of local campaigns.

Again, such work by stations' Action Desks provides strong links with the community and enhances its reputation.

Other programme items

Fascinating facts

In these days of the internet, most 'fascinating facts' aren't fascinating. Your listeners are likely to have been sent them from friends already, so you will have to do something pretty special with them before using the same material on air.

Again the trick is to make the feature your own by adding something of your personality to the list of information. Steve Wright's 'Factoids'[22] on Radio 2 are presented in a tongue-in-cheek way, and the presenters add their own spin on each item as they try and outdo each other with increasingly bizarre facts. Often an item leads one of the presenters off on another direction completely, before being brought back to the feature.

So you could:

- make the feature a challenge to find X facts in X minutes.
- link the facts with a current news story.
- play on-air true/false competition with the facts.
- have listeners give marks out of ten for how fascinating each fact is.
- check out the facts with an expert who can explain or disprove them.

With some time and creativity you can make such a feature your own.

Celebrity birthdays

> ◀ **ACTUAL AUDIO**
>
> PRESENTER: The Russian author Dostoevsky [pronounced: dos, dostovskee], who wrote The Brothers Karamazov [said falteringly], was born today in 1821.
> *Commercial radio station, November 2005*

First ask yourself if you have heard of the 'famous' person whose birthday it is. If not, then it is pretty certain that your audience hasn't heard of them either, and therefore won't care.

---

[22] More on Steve Wright http://tinyurl.com/dbvb5m and his Factoids: *Steve Wright's Book of Factoids* (HarperCollins, 2006), http://tinyurl.com/ljduw2.

Second, does the person whose birthday it is have any kind of link with your target audience? To tell an audience of teenagers that it is the birthday of the first BBC television newsreader, will mean nothing to them. Indeed it may alienate them. The above Actual Audio was on a breakfast show to a station targeting 15–34-year-olds. The presenter obviously hadn't heard of the writer (he couldn't pronounce his name) but still read it out. That was probably simply because it was the next item on the show prep sheet he'd bought.

The first two rules then: *do they know them?* and *do they care?*

Third, do not say when someone famous was born. If you tell me they were 'born today in 1969 . . .'. I have to stop and work out how old that makes them today. If you ask someone in the office how old they are, they will give you their age, not their year of birth! Do the maths for the audience, make it easy for them. Say how old they are now.

Fourth, linking with the point above, if someone is dead (as well as thinking about the relevance of mentioning them at all), say what age they would have been had they still been alive, not the year of their birth.

Too many birthdays on such a list gets boring. Limit yourself to three or four of the most interesting and relevant people, about whom you have got something personal to say.

This day in history

These features are very popular with presenters because they can simply read out a list of dates and events from a prep sheet. They can get away with doing as little work as possible. Like every item you do though, it has to be interesting to your audience. Preferably that means that it is local, but remember, being local does not automatically make an item interesting! 'Today in 1981, the mayor of Blankstown died at the age of 75.' That is completely local and completely boring! 'Today in 1981, the mayor of Blankstown, Indiana, USA, died when his ceremonial chain got caught in his kitchen's waste disposal unit . . .'. That is *not* local, but *is* interesting.

Look for what is local to people's sphere of interest: if that is geographically local, fantastic! If it's not, it's still great. Just make sure it *is* interesting!

Does the event have to have been in *recent* history, to make it interesting? No. Some of the biggest selling genres of books are westerns and historical novels. Some of the largest grossing box office films are *Star Wars, Star Trek, Alien* . . . Just because something did not happen in our lifetime, it does not mean it is not of interest.

So, are 'This Day in History' features popular with listeners? Yes, if they are interesting, they can be. The item may:

- Be amusing (like the mayoral story above).
- Be ironic, considering what we know now in retrospect: ('This day in history was the day the EMI record executive turned down the Beatles, because he said that guitar-based groups were on the way out').
- Make listeners think a little about where they were when they heard the story the first time around . . .
- . . . or the changes that have happened since.

But only if the item is interesting.

Once you have mentioned the event, you can make it more relevant still by adding a comment of your own, either for listeners or for your co-host to react to. For example, you could make a humorous comment: 'It was today 35 years ago that the London Marathon was first run. I've never entered: it's not the 26 miles that bother me, it's the lap of honour if I won . . .'. By adding something of your own, a comment that's related to you and that is personal and relatable, you make a stronger connection and make the item unique to you.

Or set up a phone-in topic: 'It's this time of year that thousands of birds fly back to Britain after spending the summer in Spain. Why do you reckon they go back there every year? Is it because they have no imagination for better holiday locations, or they want to hook up with young Spanish waiter-birds? Call me with your suggestions . . .'.

Or use the item as a springboard to a trivia question: '. . . the anniversary of the first airing of the TV prison sitcom *Porridge*. But can you tell me, what linked that show with *Only Fools and Horses*? Call me on . . .'.

So, add something of your own to the information: something that no one else can give. What is your own take on the story? What makes you laugh about it? Why? Share that with your audience.

One more thing: it is usually best not to use items that are too serious, or about death: 'Today in 1975 an airliner crashed in the Himalayas, killing all 330 people on board'. Not much fun is it?

Lists

Items such as the 'Top 10 DVD Rentals This Week' or 'Last Week's Most Watched TV Shows' are, frankly pointless, unless you can add something of your own to the list.

Do your listeners really care about such lists? Have you ever heard anyone talking about them? No. However, they may be interested in a good DVD to hire this weekend, the plot and who is in it . . . not simply what place it is in the charts. So give the listener that kind of information, or add something of your own. What film have *you* seen recently? Was it any good? Why? What were the best bits? What should people look out for? What mistakes were made, or what were the holes in the storyline that didn't add up?

And if you do do a Top Ten list, present the items from 10 (the least popular) up to 1 (the most popular) not the other way around.

Entertainment news

Judging by the popularity of magazines such as *heat* there's certainly a call for this type of information and your programme controller will tell you whether it's appropriate for your station's demographic. Remember though, that if your station doesn't play Slipknot then there is no point telling listeners about the band's latest exploits. Similarly, if yours is a rock station, those tuning in probably do not want to hear about what Britney Spears has been up to. If you don't play 'em, why talk about 'em?

The only exception to this would be if the item is of general interest and appropriate to your audience for a different reason. For example, rock music fans may have been interested in the death of Michael Jackson because of his name and status and his influence on music over 40 years.

Other unique features

Finally there are a few features that are particular to certain individual stations for specific reasons:

- *Visitors' List* – The Falkland Islands,[23] the self-governing overseas territory of the UK in the South Atlantic, is 8,000 miles from the UK and 300 miles off the coast of Argentina. One of the most popular features on the radio station[24] is who's visiting

[23] More on the Falkland Islands: http://tinyurl.com/kkcf3f.
[24] Falklands Radio: http://tinyurl.com/mxy4yp.

each week. This was a hangover from the days before the British Army was based there, but was still of great interest to the Islanders. So, station staff regularly read out a passenger list of those on board the plane that was landing or ship that was docking.

- *The Lamb Bank* – There's an annual problem for sheep farmers in Cumbria as many ewes reject their lambs after birth and won't allow them to feed. Running from Christmas until May every year since 1973, the Lamb Bank[25] on BBC Radio Cumbria gives out the number and breed of lambs, along with details of ewes in milk who may be able to feed them – a unique information exchange!
- *Obituary notices*[26] – Several local radio stations in Ireland read out news of those who've died, details of where the 'remains are in repose', when the funeral is and where donations can be made.

Obituary notices are one of the most listened-to strands on local radio and they're quite specific to Ireland. There's a tradition here to provide community support for bereaved families, through attendance at funeral homes and churches. So in these days of urban sprawl, the obituary service is vital for people to pick up that information easily and quickly.[27]

---

[25] The Lamb Bank: http://tinyurl.com/ceumbb.
[26] An example of Obituary Notices on the web: http://tinyurl.com/n69qun.
[27] Clem Ryan, KFM (County Kildare) station manager, *X-Trax* magazine, September 2005.

18 Presenting music

SKILLSET – NATIONAL OCCUPATIONAL STANDARDS
RADIO CONTENT CREATION

Unit content included in this chapter:
RC4 Contribute to the creative process in radio
RC13 Operate a radio studio
RC15 Edit, process and mix audio
RC17 Select and direct performing musicians for audio

Music is the largest part of most stations' output.

> The music is the star; the presenters are there to entertain in an informative way.
> The bulk of our speech content is material that helps a listener enjoy the music more, so it's information about the artists, the song and what's going on in country music – it's not making jokes about what we read in the paper that morning.[1]

In this chapter there are some pointers for presenting music: introducing songs and outro-ducing them (what you say when you have played them), and some ideas on basic mixing.

> Lots of research has gone into the importance of music to human beings, most recently:
>
> Researchers investigated memory and the 'feeling of knowing' (FOK) for titles, lyrics and melodies of songs as well as the effectiveness of these three components as cues for each other.[2] Among their findings: music and titles are recalled more easily than actual lyrics; people who are given lyrics of a song more easily recall the title or the tune (than those similarly tested with being given, say, a melody, and asked to recall lyrics); but giving actual titles of songs elicited stronger FOKs for lyrics, melodies elicited stronger FOKs for lyrics, and titles elicited stronger FOKs for melodies than vice versa.

[1] Pat Geary, station manager, 3C Continuous Cool Country, X-Trax magazine, August 2005.
[2] Zehra F. Peynircioğlu, Brian E. Rabinovitz and Jennifer L.W. Thompson, 'Memory and Metamemory for Songs: the Relative Effectiveness of Titles, Lyrics, and Melodies as Cues for Each Other', *Psychology of Music*, Vol. 36, 47–61 (2008).

Before 2008, little research had examined the link between popular music and autobiographical memory. Then there was a study[3] in which college-age participants recalled a memory associated with a song from each of five lifetime eras and then described and rated the memories. Participants heard part of the song, read the lyrics, saw a picture of the artist or began describing their memory immediately. These findings showed that music is a valuable cue to evoke autobiographical memory.

A crucial issue in research on music and emotion is whether music evokes genuine emotional responses in listeners (the emotivist position) or whether listeners merely perceive emotions expressed by the music (the cognitivist position). To investigate this issue, researchers[4] measured self-reported emotion, facial muscle activity and autonomic activity in 32 participants while they listened to popular music. Results revealed happy music generated more zygomatic facial muscle activity, greater skin conductance, lower finger temperature, more happiness and less sadness than sad music. The researchers concluded that: 'The finding that the emotion induced in the listener was the same as the emotion expressed in the music is consistent with the notion that music may induce emotions through a process of emotional contagion'.

Four experiments[5] examined whether it was possible to quickly and easily increase the appeal of unfamiliar rock songs presented to American college students. In Experiment 1, reading an essay about an artist increased the appeal of the artist's songs, but repeated exposure to the songs did not. In Experiments 2a and 2b, repeatedly following an affectively neutral song with a liked song increased the appeal of the first song. In Experiment 3, listening to a music critic praise a song increased the song's appeal. 'These results show that intramusical and intrapersonal strategies, evaluative conditioning, and persuasion by authority can be used to increase a song's appeal. It should be possible for radio stations to use these cost-effective techniques to expand their playlists without a net loss of listeners.'

Love the music

As that final study suggested, listeners will enjoy the music more if the presenter enthuses about it. Indeed, at a time when people get a lot of music from a non–interactive MP3 player,

[3] Elizabeth T. Cady, Richard Jackson Harris and J. Bret Knappenberger, 'Using Music to Cue Autobiographical Memories of Different Lifetime Periods', *Psychology of Music*, Vol. 36, No. 2, 157-77 (2008).

[4] Lars-Olov Lundqvist, Fredrik Carlsson, Per Hilmersson and Patrik N. Juslin, 'Emotional Responses to Music: Experience, Expression, and Physiology', *Psychology of Music*, Vol. 37, No. 1, 61–90 (2009).

[5] Kathleen M. Silva and Francisco J. Silva, 'What Radio Can Do to Increase a Song's Appeal: a Study of Canadian Music Presented to American College Students', *Psychology of Music*, Vol. 37, No. 2, 181–94 (2009).

this can be one of radio's points of difference. Both on music and music-and-speech stations, presenters often fail to engage with the music, either because there's so much of it, or because it is often seen as a 'filler' between speech items.

There is an exact science behind the physical and psychological effect of sounds and music; it has been proven to have an influence on what you buy, on your health and, it's claimed, makes you smarter.[6] Why would you simply 'throw it away' in a show? Music is one of the most powerful positive emotional experiences that humans have, partly through the strong emotions and memories which are evoked. Think of national anthems as well as the first dance at your wedding, the song your mother loved to hum around the house, your favourite band when you were balancing revising for exams and meeting your girlfriend or boyfriend . . . Put simply, music triggers responses in the 'primal' areas of the human brain.

A 2009 review by US radio consultant Alan Burns[7] (below) revealed that listeners to a typical CHR or AC station in America are 15 times more likely to hear the station plug its web site, text number or competition, than to hear a comment about the music it plays. Alan concludes:

> Why should the audience be passionate about a station's music if the station itself doesn't reflect any excitement or interest?

The research also shows that 72 per cent of all links contained station positioning messages, while less than 7 per cent were 'non-station-based addresses to listeners or their interests'. In other words, those stations were much more likely to talk about themselves than their audiences.

On radio, the most intimate of all media, what would the most common topic be? Wouldn't you think it would be the listener, or something important to the listener?

And on music radio, would you think perhaps the #1 or #2 most common topic would be music?

The answer in both cases is a resounding 'No.' Instead, radio stations dominantly talk to their audiences about the radio station.

On a typical music station, a song (or multiple songs) is identified four times an hour. Other than that, on average there are *no* comments about music.

Even when combined, listener-focused and music-based comments (total 9.5 per cent) are so far down the priority ranks, that web/text liners (21 per cent) or contest liners (20 per cent) are much more common topics.

---

[6] *The Power of Music* in a BBC programme which explores this: http://tinyurl.com/mvvbqs.
[7] Alan Burns and Associates: http://tinyurl.com/nczozk.

The table below shows the average, and the numbers for the highest and lowest stations in each content area. Note how far from the average those extremes can be:

	Percentage of breaks		
	Total	Low	High
Recorded positioning and other station attributes and benefits	46.0 %	7 %	86 %
Live positioning and other station attributes and benefits	25.8	0	50
Title/artist (both/or)	24.8	0	79
Website or text program	20.7	0	71
Contest/promotion	19.6	0	46
Station name (only)	15.8	0	39
Listener	6.8	0	23
Client/sponsorship	6.2	0	29
Hollywood	4.8	0	33
Weather	3.0	0	15
Music	2.7	0	14
Self	1.0	0	7
Public service announcement	0.4	0	8

Courtesy: Alan Burns & Associates.[8] (In the US, a 'break' is a presenter link.)

Music radio does need to find ways to make what we do more about the listener and the music, and less about the station. It's a lot like trying to interest a newly-met girl when you were single: the more you bragged about yourself, the less interested she became; but the more you talked about her interests, the more interesting you became.[9]

Talk radio presenters are usually hired for their journalism background rather than their understanding of the music. They can often step all over the music, sound awkward and ill-informed, bored, disconnected, fade music early, throw away the significance, mispronounce the artist, use it as a filler or treat it as trivia. This can alienate the listener who may resent what those actions represent to them while they are in an emotional zone.

- Treat the music:
  - with respect.
  - with importance.
  - Sound like you value it.
  - Find a reason to make it count.

[8] Alan Burns, 'What Does Music Radio Communicate When it's Not Playing Music?': http://tinyurl.com/mqeex7.
[9] Alan Burns.

> The feeling of playing a record you really love, on this almighty record player, and sharing it with millions is hard to describe.[10]

Music is not just 'padding' between the important bits. Work at embracing it: it's desirable, new, intriguing, memory-evoking, cool, exciting, soothing, provocative, uplifting. Music makes one want to jump and shout, get tender or romantic or sarcastic, or be silly. Get with the beat yourself in the studio. Move to the music, tap the table, listen to the lyrics . . . then when you open the mic enunciate your feelings as you respond to what you and the listener have both just experienced. Don't miss an easy chance to have some feelings that the listener will very likely share.

'That's a great new one from the Black Eyed Peas' is not getting enthusiastic about music.

On the other hand:
  'That just turns my inside to jelly, it's so coool . . .'
  'Every time I hear this, I just want to kick and shout, it makes me feel so good'
  'This one always reminds me of a certain beach holiday in Ibiza . . .'

When you respond to the music, you're entertaining. You're offering the listener something beyond hype. You're inviting them to respond to you, and in the process, to bond with you as a friend.

You obviously can't enthuse over every song (it's tricky, with a limited playlist, when you hear the song half a dozen times a week), and of course very often, you're simply too busy to have the luxury of listening. And, nobody responds to everything. But once in a while, when the time is there, and the feelings are real, you should say to your best friend what that song did to you.

Music is entertainment. Entertainment works by affecting the emotions. If you don't show, at least occasionally, that a song affected you too, the impression created is that you're not paying attention.

Presenters follow a music playlist, but the listener thinks you walk into the studio and 'play your favourite songs' . . . at least that's the image we want them to have. When you comment on a song it gives the impression that you had a purpose for playing it.

You don't have to do this for every song, just every now and then. The secret is to imply that you selected that show's music for a reason; that you thought-through the choice and have been itching to get on air and share the amazing music you've selected. Not that you simply follow a computer-created playlist.

---

[10] Nicky Campbell, presenter, BBC Radio Five Live, *The Radio Magazine,* June 2009.

'I heard this recently on (TV show, film, iPod, advert) and wanted to share it with you.'

'I played it the other week and got a great response.'

'This is just the song for this kind of day.'

'This song reminds me of . . .'.

'One of my all-time favourites.'

'This gets me thinking of . . .'

'I've got a song from XX in a few minutes that always raises a lump in my throat – see if it does the same for you, too.'

'I thought to myself the other day that it's ages since I played some XX.'

'Did you hear the news about XX? That reminded me of this song . . .'

Using phrases like these creates the impression that you are in control of the music and therefore you have compiled a show. It illustrates that you have taken ownership of the programme and that you are passionate about putting everything into it for the listener.

This image is destroyed if you:

o mispronounce the name of the song or artist
o have no feeling for the music (use an inappropriate voice as you introduce it, have a 'happy' song after a serious news item . . .)
o give the impression the music rotation is as much as a surprise to you as it is to the listener by using lines such as 'good to hear that again . . .' without mentioning that that is the reason why you decided to pick it out to play today.

THE LANGUAGE OF LOVE

'You'll love this!' (What if I hate it?).
'This song just makes you feel good.' (What if this song makes me smash the room up?)
'Here's one you'll really like.' (How do you know?)

No one wants to be told what their reaction should be. Indeed almost everyone's subconscious reaction to being told what to think or feel is, 'Not *me*! You can tell me what *you* think, but don't tell me what I should!'

Instead, personalise it.

> 'I think that's a great song from a fantastic film' says some-
> thing about you. Whether the listener agrees with you or
> not, they've learned a little about you. You're a little more
> familiar and you've built up more of a connection with them.

Introducing music

It is the start of your hour and you have got a whole playlist of songs,[11] but do not be tempted to tell everyone what they are. Don't promo a whole hour of music, because if the listener doesn't like anything you are promising, they may switch off. Remember: 'programme run-downs are for run-down programmes'.

Instead mention two or three examples to whet the listener's appetite, and make those songs representative of the music you play. So, if you have a 'one hit wonder' (someone who only had one hit song) then it is probably not worth promoting, as it will be obvious to the listener what you are going to play. Instead choose two others that are different in tempo and tone from each other. Maybe a current and a 1990s' track (if that example fits with your format), or a female artist and a boy band, or a pop hit and a classic ballad. But not more than three songs at a time.

Only mention artists, not songs. The reason is that it gives a greater chance that a listener will stay tuned to hear if their favourite is the one you've chosen. If you say that next you'll play 'Material Girl', and someone doesn't like that song, they won't want to hear it. But if you simply say that Madonna's next, they will stay listening in the hope that it is going to be, for example, 'Celebration'.

It is usually better to announce the name of the song *before* you play it, and the name of the artist *after* you play it. That's because after someone's heard a song and enjoyed it, they are more intrigued to know who was singing it. This is especially important for new songs. If someone hates Kasabian then announcing that this is their new song may turn that listener off. If, on the other hand, they hear the song and like it, they may be intrigued to hear who sang it. Adding a small amount of suspense may make them stay for another three minutes!

Be careful about promoting songs scheduled for later in the hour – there may be a chance that time restraints mean you won't get to one of them. That is going to make the listener angry that they trusted you and invested time in the station that they got no return on.

Of course, you don't always have to give the details exactly as they appear on your screen if you are being creative/compelling and easily relatable.

Say you have just played 'Summer Drive Home' by The Dollar Bills:

o   'The Greenbacks on Radio X . . .' you could occasionally use a shorthand for the group, if it's a recognised nickname (although you won't be the first to call Madonna the Material Girl, you could occasionally refer to Lily Allen as 'Keith's daughter' and so on).

o   'Ahh, open-topped cars and girls in T-shirts . . . The Dollar Bills on . . .' a comment about the title of the song is another way of back announcing what you have just played, without actually giving the title. (Be aware of DJ clichés: 'The Beatles' 'Ticket To Ride' . . . and I never knew they visited the Isle of Wight . . .' and so on.)

Of course, if the song is an all-time classic it may not need a name check. This will depend on your station house style, but to back-anno Rod Stewart's 'Sailing' or The Rolling Stone's 'Brown Sugar' may insult the intelligence of your audience. Also, if the name of the song is

---

[11] Although the terms are interchangeable, you do not play 'records' (as the music comes from CDs or hard disk), 'tracks' (as they are essentially not album tracks) and they are not 'tunes' (too cheesy). You play 'songs'.

the first or last words in the lyrics, be careful how you phrase your link, or it will sound as though you haven't been listening to the output: 'Now here's The Beatles and "Help" . . .'.

◀ ACTUAL AUDIO

PRESENTER: Here's Duran Duran and 'Wild Boys'
SONG: 'Wild boys, wild boys, wild boys, wild boys . . .'

Commercial station, November 2005

A standard intro

Most people listening to most shows on most stations neither know nor care to know too much about the music they are listening to. They just know they like it. Giving too much information would be a turn-off for them. Most stations will not want you to say much more about the music than the name of the song and who sings it.

Having said that you may want to occasionally mention information such as:

o the song's performance in the current charts[12]
o its chart position in an older chart or year[13]
o a tour[14] or an album[15]
o the artist's birthday[16] if it's *today* (see links with the music below).
o a *new* news story[17] about them.
o trivia about the song or band[18] (see the discussion of trivia below and the section on clichéd links later in this chapter).

'Occasionally' means that this kind of information may be mentioned on one song an hour, maybe two. No more, or you start to alienate most of your listeners.

Build up your personal collection of information on core artists in an indexed notebook[19] so you can mention it the next time the song comes around, and date each item when it is read, so you don't use it again too soon.

Using trivia is another great way to occasionally talk about what you're playing: 'The Dollar Bills from a time when songs came out on vinyl. And the flip side to that song later became a huge hit for . . . who? I'll tell you after the travel news with Emma Leven . . .'.

Here we go with the Top 40 hits of the nation this week on American Top 40, the best-selling and most-played songs from the Atlantic to the Pacific, from Canada to Mexico. This is Casey Kasem in Hollywood, and in the next three hours, we'll count down the 40 most popular hits in the United States this week, hot off the record charts of Billboard magazine for the week ending July 11,

[12] This information can come from newspapers and gossip columns; internet prep services; artist's websites; TV shows, as well as UK charts: http://tinyurl.com/4m86v.
[13] Online list of hits and positions: http://tinyurl.com/konmqa. (Remember most listeners won't want to hear how old a song is: it reminds them how old they are and a good song is a good song, despite its age. If a younger person hears when it came out they may be put off it as it's 'old'.)
[14] Concert dates: http://tinyurl.com/llnxee.
[15] Album release dates: http://tinyurl.com/lszad3.
[16] Recording stars' birthdays: http://tinyurl.com/yq5fbg.
[17] Music news: http://tinyurl.com/8y7r8.
[18] Song and artist research at Wikipedia: http://tinyurl.com/2unsh.
[19] Indexed notebook: http://tinyurl.com/nk8ayv.

1970. In this hour at number 32 in the countdown, a song that's been a hit four different times in 19 years![20] And we're just one tune away from the singer with the $10,000 gold hubcaps on his car![21] Now, on with the countdown![22]

Similarly:

- 'Next, the British band that had 13 hits in the US charts . . . at the same time.'[23]
- 'The first time female singers took the top three places in the charts in the US was in 1986. The songs were "When I Think of You" by Janet Jackson, "Typical Male" from Tina Turner . . . and the song I'm going to play next . . .'[24]
- 'The next song was written for a horror film, and was sent to the producers of a hit film about a girl who wants to be a ballerina, by mistake. And that's how it got to be famous.'[25]

Note that these are not *trivial* facts such as chart positions or year of release which are both easy to come by and easy to forget. These are *trivia* (there is a difference) that perhaps set the song in a little more context and give the listener something of interest. They stay tuned till after the break to hear the answer and then they've learnt something of interest. They've been rewarded for the time they've invested.[26] (Background information such as this, which give the music context, has a more powerful impact when it is used to tease than as a back-sell and it can make people listen for longer.)

Personal connections

Sometimes mention the memories the song brings back to you, or how you feel when you hear it. When you share your memory you'll trigger someone else's. And if you reveal something about yourself, the listener gets to know you better.

It could be the year that the song played all summer long. The one that came out when your daughter was born. The one that your dad always did a daft impression of. You get the idea.

- 'I remember when that was first out . . . August 2003 . . . odd because it was one of the wettest summers on record . . . The Dollar Bill's summer offering on Radio X . . .'
- 'I was 16 when I downloaded that song on my first iPod. We'd only just got broadband and I was at home in Worcester Terrace in Blankstown when . . .'
- '"Summer Drive Home" . . . it's great isn't it, when you come back late at night from the day at the coast and can cruise along the deserted Blankstown Bypass without being forced to slow for other cars on the slip roads and roundabouts . . .'

More intimate stories and connections can be provided by listeners. Casey Kasem read out long distance dedications on his American Top 40 show and Simon Bates had 'Our Tune,'[27] a listener's tale often starting with a happy courtship but followed by a disaster such as illness or death, with the story concluding with a record chosen by the correspondent. Both tapped into human curiosity and helped give the songs a personal connection with the whole audience, not just those who had written in.

---

[20] What that song is: http://tinyurl.com/kq4naa.

[21] Who that singer is: http://tinyurl.com/kvx64w.

[22] Casey Kasem on the first American Top 40 show, 1970. More info on the programme and features within it: http://tinyurl.com/37toc9. Hear historic archive recording of AT40: http://tinyurl.com/ne9j4o.

[23] The Beatles in 1964.

[24] 'True Colours' by Cyndi Lauper.

[25] 'Maniac' by Michael Sembello. The film was *Flashdance*.

[26] See facts about songs here: http://tinyurl.com/m6btql.

[27] 'Our Tune': http://tinyurl.com/mnshqv.

🔊 **ACTUAL AUDIO**

PRESENTER: That's Rick Astley. I was in a record shop the other day and he's got a new CD out. Dunno what it's called or if it's any good. So there you are.
Commercial radio station, August 2005

Other possible links:

- Memorable or notable events linked to the music.
- Comment on the voice or the music itself.
- Give a story or news[28] about the artist.
- Talk about the artist's impact on musical trends.
- Reveal information about the recording, when and how.
- Mention the film it features in.
- Use humour, perhaps with a link to an event or programme item.
- Pick out a curious, interesting, moving line in the lyrics.[29]
- Discuss the genre: a protest song, a heartbreaker, etc.
- Make it a feature – birthday file, today's number ones, cover versions, one hit wonders.
- Talk about the memories or emotions it stirs for you.
- Link it to someone famous 'the song Stevie Wonder calls his favourite . . . and it's not one of his!'
- Artist biography or tour dates.[30]

You will, of course have done your research and programme prep to know that it's Beyoncé's birthday today[31] . . . so why not play a Beyoncé song? Then perhaps mention her age and what she's up to now? Similarly, if an artist is touring locally, has a song that is being used on a TV ad, or won an award the previous night, play the song and mention the fact. That's not overloading the listener, it's putting the music and the knowledge in context. A good programmer will add information like this to the music playout screen so you can see it when the scheduled song appears.

If you're on an oldies station, only the tracks should be old (there's a limit to the number of times you can intro the same song in a different way, or give some trivia about a band that people first heard decades ago!). So stick to current events and topicality that transcends the music. The content should be anything but old. It's 'yesterday's music in today's world'.

SPECIALIST MUSIC SHOWS

Presenters on this kind of programme will give a lot of background information to the aficionados listening. If that is you, you will certainly have to know and care about the music. That means a lot of research: surfing the net, subscribing to

---

[28] Music news site: http://tinyurl.com/cx4xgq.
[29] Great lyrics site: http://tinyurl.com/rkeuq.
[30] Tour dates: http://tinyurl.com/n8248.
[31] See birthdays at http://tinyurl.com/mf3y82. Beyoncé's is 4 September 1981.

relevant publications, talking to producers and record companies and so on.

The new release by Pure Tempest from the album *Days of Thunder* which is out on March the 27th on the Xylophone label, their first album with them, of course, since they ended their contract with Triangle, and that means it was recorded at the world-famous Cathedral Road studios in Norwich, and produced by Norma Collier. And I think you'll agree that you can certainly hear her influence coming through on the bass riff there . . .

This kind of link can give added value to the listener, and shows that the station is employing someone who knows and cares about the music they're playing. And that gives credibility to the presenter and the station. On this kind of show, you may be able to use the 'expert listener' to help you with research. Ask them for feedback on new releases or to remind you of key dates or changes in band line-ups. Such listeners are very loyal and will probably listen for the entire show. This will boost your hours listening column in the Rajar diary, although there'll be fewer listening compared to a more general programme.

Listeners to specialist shows will pick up on the slightest inaccuracy. If you set yourself up as an expert your credibility has a long way to fall if you get something wrong and may take a long time to recover.

Info or advert?

Make sure your enthusiasm for the new song, or details of its release information, doesn't turn into a blatant plug for the artist. As you develop strong links with specialist record companies they may lure you with interviews, pre-release songs and so on. That is OK but you could be in deep trouble if you accept personal gifts to encourage you to play or thank you for playing a certain song.[32] (Some stations do not even accept the train fare for going to meet a celebrity to interview, as they feel that the integrity of the programme could be jeopardised if the interviewer wants to ask an awkward question.)

Screen information

Songs will be marked on your computer screen with the name of the song, artist, intro duration, full duration and whether it ends or fades. However it is wise to double-check any of the information if you are not sure about it.

---

[32] This is called 'payola': the illegal practice of payment or other inducement by record companies for the broadcast of recordings on music radio, in which the song is presented as being part of the normal day's broadcast. In 2007 four US broadcasters paid a $12.5 million fine and agreed that their 1,653 stations wouldn't engage in payola practices: http://tinyurl.com/lryx4u. (But why should payola be illegal? http://tinyurl.com/mqgcta.)

> ◀ **ACTUAL AUDIO**
>
> PRESENTER: That's the a song from a new band called 'Everything But The Gi.'[33]
>
> *Commercial radio station*

Intro times can be wrong, which will lead you to crash the vocals, and the E or F which signifies whether the song ends or fades may also have been entered incorrectly, so you may still want to double check each one by pre-fading the song first.

Clichéd and tortuous links

You're not the first to say 'Chicory Tip and "Son of my Father"[34] – did you know that that sound is one of Rolf Harris's Stylophones?', call Errol Brown the 'Singing Malteser', or say after Shania Twain's 'I Feel Like A Woman', 'Yeah, so do I!' and so on and so on . . . so please don't!

> ◀ **ACTUAL AUDIO**
>
> PRESENTER: That's Sting and 'I'm an Englishman in New York'. Well, I'm not, he is . . . I'm a radio presenter in [town]!
>
> *Commercial radio station, November 2005*

Tortuous links are when the presenter tries to tie one song into the next – at all costs! 'The Beatles there and "Ticket to Ride". Well, you've got a ticket for the love train with me Silky Smooth Steve Sanders, through till midnight, so hop aboard! Where do you want to go? France? OK – how about Brittany? Here's Britney Spears . . .'

In fact, writing that makes me think of the spoof local radio DJ Alan Partridge! [35]

Bad songs

Never criticise the product. If you don't like the song that you're playing then make no comment at all, certainly do not say on air that you don't like it. It's bound to be a favourite of some of those listening and you'll have just spoiled their moment. You'll also have got them wondering: 'If he doesn't like it, why's he playing it?' as most listeners don't realise that the presenter doesn't pick all their own songs.

> ◀ **ACTUAL AUDIO**
>
> PRESENTER: Simply Red and 'Stars' – never thought I'd be playing that!
>
> *Commercial radio station, January 2006 (after recent format change)*

---

[33] . . . which is in fact: http://tinyurl.com/kook7k.

[34] Song details here: http://tinyurl.com/mfre5x.

[35] Alan Partridge: http://tinyurl.com/4njful. 'ROTs' here http://tinyurl.com/665eos and http://tinyurl.com/myjzda and http://tinyurl.com/lbul2u.

You may have heard a song dozens or hundreds of times, but your audience hasn't. You work at the station and hear it in the office, as well as driving there and on the way back. Plus there is your three- or four-hour shift (during which you could play a chart song twice). So as the burnout starts for you, listeners are only just getting used to hearing it.

Levels and speed

The level of your voice should also be similar to that of the lead vocal on the song slightly dominant yet clear and audible. The speed of your voice should be similar to the speed of the song – a slower delivery for a slower song, for example. In general, be quick but don't hurry. There is a difference between being succinct and rushing, which may cause you to trip over your words. So, your intro to Daniel Merriweather's 'Red'[36] will be at a different volume and speed than the one to ELO's 'Mr Blue Sky'.[37]

The order of the words

Over the intro of a song do other information first (maybe a tease, competition phone number, what's on) and *then* the song information. Do the fillers then the facts, not the other way around. When outroducing do the facts (the artist and title) and *then* the filler stuff (the tease, the travel or the time, for example).

Most programme controllers agree that the last thing you say in any link should be the name of the radio station. They say that way it will be more easily remembered. There are others who say this should be the *first* thing you say – just make sure you know what your PC wants you to do!

Do you have to talk up to the vocals on every song? No.

- If you talk right up to the vocals (or 'jock the vocals') every time, it becomes tedious and repetitive.
- If the singer starts at 15 seconds and you stop talking after 15 seconds, there is going to be a split second when both of you are on air at the same time. It sounds messy, and is known as 'crashing the vocals'. If you lose your train of thought mid-link and you take several seconds longer to end your sentence, you could end up trampling over the first few lines of the song. 'Vocal over vocal' is bad.
- An intro is an integral part of the song. So, if you have a classic track that is a well-known crowd-pleaser (you will have to decide what this may be for your station's format) you will annoy a large percentage of your audience by talking over it. It may be Abba's 'Dancing Queen' or Robbie Williams's 'Angels', such intros are distinctive and the first few chords are instantly recognisable, unless your comments spoil the experience for the audience.
- Within each introduction there is often another 'music post' at which you can stop talking, as well as the start of the vocal itself. (A 'music post' or 'music marker' is when a song has a key change or other instruments appear midway though the intro-duction. Listen to Hot Chocolate 'Everyone's a Winner' [38] and you'll hear what I mean, about ten seconds in). Working up to one of these posts can arguably be more effective and creative than going 'up to the vocals'.

---

[36] Hear it here: http://tinyurl.com/d2aea4.

[37] Hear it here: http://tinyurl.com/ystrvd.

[38] Hear it here: http://tinyurl.com/my9dlh.

- Do not talk all over the start of *every* song, no matter its duration. What about 'Together in Electric Dreams'?[39] This is a song that has one or two other possible 'music posts' for you. Just because it has a 45-second intro, it doesn't mean that you have to talk for 45 seconds. Even experienced presenters don't talk right up to the vocals on every song. Remember the golden rule: say what you want to say and then stop. Fellow presenters (usually of the 'deejay' school of broadcasting) might think it is super-slick, but listeners will just think that your show is filled with 'pop and prattle'.
- Other tracks you might play are instrumental, so when do you stop if there are no vocals to hit? Either head for a music post, or don't do it at all. Otherwise you'll be tempted to wander and waffle.

Time after time, listeners say one of the things that most annoys them about DJs is that they talk over the introductions. Indeed some stations say their presenters should never talk over any music – that once the song starts, it belongs to the listener.

What to do

If you have got an introduction of 15 seconds and you have got material which will take up to 14 seconds to read, then you can start the song (at a low level on the fader, of course) at the same time as you start talking. You may want to try practising this with pre-written material first so you know exactly how long it will take to read (the guide is three words take one second to say).

If the script is only ten seconds, then you can stop talking at that point, bring up the level of the music to play for five seconds until the vocals start. Alternatively you can fill that five seconds with an adlib, 'And this is Lady Gaga, on 99.9 Triple X', which at three words a second will take you to the vocals.

After a while you will learn how to self-edit your link as you speak so you can add extra information, or take some out, depending on whether you're over- or under-running. If it is the latter situation, you will find yourself using one of a series of off-the-shelf stock phrases, such as:

- The station name – 'This is Radio X' – 1 second.
- The time – 'and it's 8 minutes to 8' – 1.5 seconds.
- The station name and frequency – 'This is Radio X . . . 99.9 FM' – 2 seconds.
- The station name, frequency and strapline – 'This is Radio X . . . 99.9 FM . . . the county's best mix of music' – 3 seconds.
- A trail – 'This is Radio X . . . where we've got the new song from James Morrison after this 1980s' classic from Black Box . . .' – 5 seconds.
- . . . And so on!

If you have 20 seconds of script and the introduction is just 15 seconds, just start talking and after five seconds *then* you start the song playing, again at low level. This technique may be used in conjunction with another song: talk for five seconds over the back of Song A, then start Song B and stop playing (or fade down, or take out) Song A at the same time. It is tricky to start with but sounds slick if you are in control. The potential problem the first few times you do this is that with so much to think about (stopping and starting different tracks at the same time) your delivery may slow down or falter, leading you to crash the vocals. Quick tip: pick a station which plays a lot of music and, as soon as each song starts playing, start talking. Identify the song and artist and then fill with other comments (trail, ident, your name, time, weather and so on), up to the vocals. Don't use the same content in every link though!

[39] Hear it here: http://tinyurl.com/5pcjn8.

You can of course play a recorded announcement over the whole of the introduction or just over part of it. The potential problem is that when you speak 'live' you can self-edit your comment to finish on time, but once you start the drop-in, you are committed to letting it play to the end. And if you can sense that you started playing it too late and it will crash the vocals, there is not much you can do about it.

It all takes practice, a 'feel' for the music and confidence.

Know when to shut up

It is a DJ cliché to fill, or pad, with inanities, just for the sake of talking up to the vocals: 'And this is the Black Eyed Peas, right here on 99.9 Radio Active, the sound of the city, on Tuesday the fifth of May, with the temperature at 14 degrees and the wind direction south to south west . . . err . . . err . . .'.

Something some presenters do (which personally I find most annoying) when they have more time than they have things to say, is spread out their comments throughout the whole introduction. They don't add any extra information, they just leave lots of gaps in between the comments and raise the level of the music in between. This ducking in and out of intros is called 'riding the fader'. (See Fig. 1 on p. 283.)

If you have opened the mic to speak don't bring back the music. In the same way, if you're talking over the *end* of a song don't stop and bring back the music. It sounds jerky, and you sound like a jerk.

Once you have learned the basics of presentation then you can try some of the more advanced techniques such as fitting your voice *and* a drop-in over the introduction to a song. The thing is not to run before you can walk.

Master the basics by going into the studio whenever you can, watch what others do and ask them why they did something a certain way, then practise that technique yourself when the studio is free. When you listen to the radio at home, listen out for what the presenter does and try to work out how the sound was achieved. It won't be long before you become more confident in your presentation style as you master different ways of helping the programme flow.

Getting from one song to another

The basics

Getting from one song to another is called a 'segue' (pronounced *seg-way*).

There are different ways a song can start:

- With a musical introduction (most of them start this way, with the intro being anything from one second to over a minute).
- A vocal in — called a 'hard start' (such as Owen Paul's 'Favourite Waste of Time', or The Beatles' 'Help!').[40]
- A fade in (Limahl's 'Never Ending Story',[41] 'Telstar' by The Tornadoes).

---

[40] Hear it here: http://tinyurl.com/66fetf.
[41] Hear it here: http://tinyurl.com/6eh2hv.

Fader channels

The lower part . . .

1   The source option for each fader is shown here. So, either the first fader can play tape machine 1 (list default setting) or output from the cassette. All of these faders are currently closed, apart from the one for Tape 3 which is very slightly open.

2   The On/Off light. A presenter can raise the fader and then press this 'remote start' to play the source linked to it. The light will come on and stay on until the item is stopped.

3   As well as the fader control there's also the PFL button. Press this to hear the channel's source without putting it to air. Press it again to cancel the prefade (the little light on the button will then go out), then stop the source from playing and only then raise the fader!

4   Simply press this button to enable the fader start: the source will then start playing when the fader is moved from its home position. The light will come on to show that fader start is activated.

5   Press these buttons to alternate between the main source and the alternative on each channel.

6   When a fader is up, the audio that it controls goes to the transmitter. But on this desk by pressing Send B or C, audio from that channel can *also* be sent somewhere else. So, if your podcast is a best bits of the programme compilation without the music, send the audio from your mic channels not only to the transmitter but also to a separate recorder which has been routed (or patched) through to the Send B (or C) switch. The programme sounds the same on air, but your recording contains only the audio that's been sent specifically to that machine.

The upper part of those same fader channels . . .

1   The balance control. Turn this to send more of the audio from that channel to the left or right of the listener's speakers.

2   The auxiliary control is used when that channel is linked with an effects machine to change the sound of that source, for example to give it more echo. By turning the aux knob further to the right, the amount of echo on that channel can be increased to make it sound as though you're in an empty room, or a large cave.

3   Press this EQ button to activate the knobs above it

4   The sound of each source can be altered by using these EQ buttons, which can change the low, medium and high frequency of the audio.

5   Pressing either of these button will send all of the audio from that channel to either the left or right speaker. If you have a stereo recording, you can make it mono by pressing both of these buttons.

6   Boost or lower the level that you are sending to the transmitter by rotating the Gain knob, but only after you've put the fader up completely. The home position for this control is at 12 o'clock.

There are three different ways a song could continue:

- ☐ An intro followed by the vocals (most songs are like this).
- ☐ ★An intro, followed by a vocal, followed by some more music, then the song getting underway (such as the line 'My life is brilliant' at the start of James Blunt's 'You're Beautiful').
- ☐ A vocal start and then a musical break before the verse starts properly (Simply Red's 'Fairground'[42]).

★ When songs start like this they may be edited to provide a power start (see earlier).

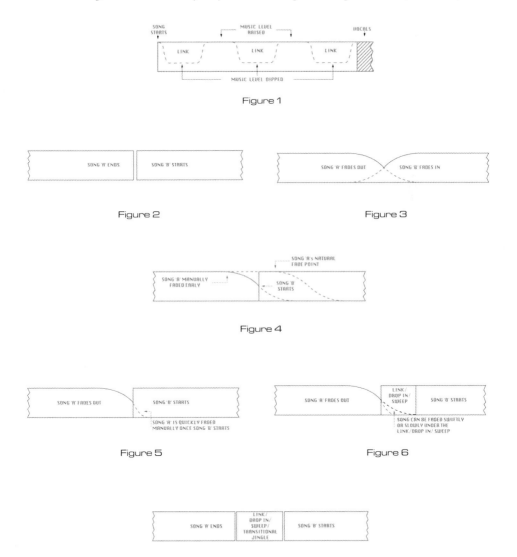

Figure 1

Figure 2

Figure 3

Figure 4

Figure 5

Figure 6

Figure 7

[42] Hear it here: http://tinyurl.com/lf9hsp.

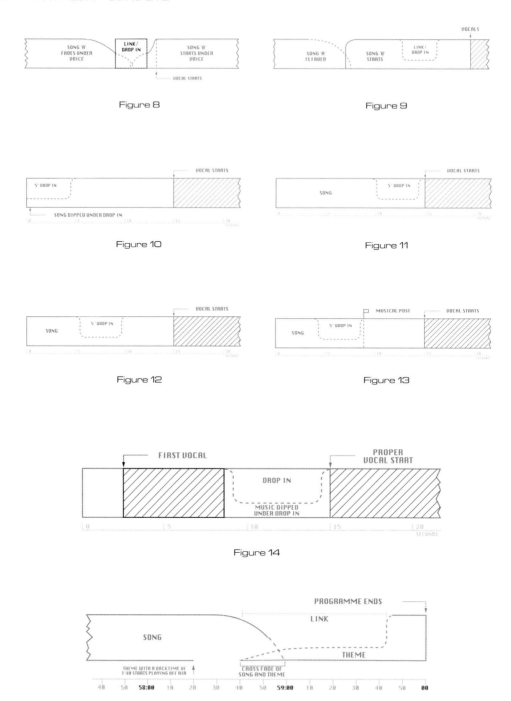

Figure 8

Figure 9

Figure 10

Figure 11

Figure 12

Figure 13

Figure 14

Figure 15

Various ways to mix songs with speech, drop-ins or sweepers

There are basically three ways a song can end:

- A fade or soft out – marked on your screen as F (most songs are like this).
- A hard out – meaning that it ends or stops and marked as E or S (a large minority of songs end this way, such as Robbie Williams's 'Angels'.[43] 'Penny Lane'[44] by The Beatles is unusual in that it has a hard start *and* it ends).
- Sometimes there's an end/fade (also called a 'sustain end')! This is unusual and is perhaps better described as a 'quiet end' or a 'soft end', such as Whitney Houston's 'I Will Always Love You'.[45]

SONGS THAT FADE

You shouldn't talk over the vocals at the start of any song, but you can at the *end* of a song that fades. Don't talk over more than the last 20–30 seconds, even if it is instrumental at that point, or is merely repeating itself. The song will be someone's favourite. To promote your station contest over the sax ending to 'Baker Street'[46] or 'Layla'[47] should be (and may well be at some stations) a sackable offence.

To keep the music flowing use the last 15 seconds of a song to talk over and then as it runs out, start the next song underneath your voice and talk over that introduction up to the vocals.

SONGS THAT END

A good rule of thumb is: don't talk over the ends of songs which end. On some classic tracks you should neither talk over the beginning nor the end. You'd be held in great disdain by your listeners if you told them about a funny thing that happened to you at Tesco's at the weekend as they were listening to the final notes of 'Candle in the Wind'.[48] If the song ends, let it do just that.

To stop early a song that ends, especially within 30 seconds of the end, is a heinous crime. Backtime properly.

There are several ways that you can get from one song to another (do a segue):

- Song A ends naturally, you start Song B (Fig. 2). This is perhaps the easiest segue. The temptation many presenters fall into is to start B just as A ends. It's actually better to feel the music, and leave a beat's pause between the two.

---

[43] Hear it here: http://tinyurl.com/2qxbpv.
[44] Hear it here: http://tinyurl.com/nm9q4v.
[45] Hear it here: http://tinyurl.com/649gth.
[46] Hear it here: http://tinyurl.com/mzf5z5.
[47] Hear it here: http://tinyurl.com/depkzw.
[48] Hear it here: http://tinyurl.com/3xus4s.

◦   Song A fades naturally, Song B is faded in (a 'cross-fade') (Fig. 3).
◦   Song A is yet to end but is faded manually, Song B is started (Fig. 4).
  ◦   Fade A at a natural point, for example, at the end of a chorus (best), or as the singer *starts* the repeats to fade at the end of the song (that is, while the song is still 'hot') or (and this is least preferable) at the end of a line in a verse. Don't fade midway through a verse as it sounds very poor. Talking or fading in the middle of a music or vocal line shows a basic lack of understanding of musical phrasing.
  ◦   Don't fade a song too early (less than two-thirds of the way through) as listeners will wonder why you have bothered to play their favourite song at all if you don't actually play all of it. In reality what has probably happened is that you have miscalculated your backtime.
  ◦   Don't fade a song which ends, as this makes the audience feel cheated much more than if you do an early fade on a song which fades naturally. Avoid letting songs fade too long by themselves.
  ◦   Take control and fade it out manually when the track itself starts to fade.

The problem with a cross-fade is that the two songs may jar musically when mixed together, even momentarily.

◀ **ACTUAL AUDIO**

'All Night Long'[49] by The Mary Jane Girls segued into 'Domino Dancing'[50] by The Pet Shop Boys without a drop-in or speech link.

Commercial station, November 2005

◦   Song A is faded naturally, Song B starts (Fig. 5).

In reality, of course, you would put a station ID in between the two songs[51] (Fig. 6); this could be a sung jingle:
  ◦   Use a transitional jingle to go from a loud or fast song, to a quiet or slow one or vice versa.
  ◦   Playing a jingle as you fade a song can sound rather bad, as for a moment you will have two pieces of music playing at the same time, and it is unlikely that the tones will match.
  ◦   You would have three different tones of music within just a few seconds (the end of one song, a jingle, then the start of another).

Or it could be a dry drop-in, sweeper or your own voice link:
  ◦   If you have got a song which ends and another that starts, you can play the drop-in between the two, very neatly (Fig. 7).
  ◦   You can use a drop to help hide the transition from one song to another: fade A,

---

[49] Hear it here: http://tinyurl.com/5dd2ap.
[50] Hear it here: http://tinyurl.com/cueo75.
[51] Even if you aren't voicing a link yourself, it is still good practice to ident the station between every song with a jingle, drop-in or sweeper.

play the drop and midway through it start B underneath. Bring up the level of B when the drop has finished (Fig. 8). (This is called 'bridging'.)

- Or play the drop over the last seconds of the fade, then as soon as the drop ends, start the next song (Fig. 6 again).
- Or you could fade A, start B, and play a drop over B's introduction (Fig. 9).

There are variations on that last technique. For example, if you have an intro of 15 seconds, and a five-second drop-in you could:

- Play the drop-in over the first five seconds, then fade up the song for the remaining ten seconds (Fig. 10).
- Start the song and, nine and a half seconds from the start of the vocals, play the drop in (the extra half second gives that space of a 'beat' mentioned earlier). You'll have 'backtimed the drop-in to the vocals'. Be aware that this technique can sound ridiculous if a three-second drop-in is played at the end of, say, a 30-second introduction, and certainly if *you* suddenly appear and say something at this point (Fig. 11).
- Play the drop-in midway through the intro (for example five seconds after the intro has started, giving intro/drop/intro/vocal all evenly spaced) (Fig. 12).
- Back-time the drop-in to a music post within the introduction (if there is one) (Fig. 13).
- Play the drop-in after a 'false vocal' and before the song starts properly (for example, after James Blunt sings 'My life is brilliant' at the start of 'You're Beautiful', or after the vocal start to Bon Jovi's 'You Give Love a Bad Name'.[52] (Fig. 14).

If the drop-in is longer than the intro you simply start the drop first, either dry (that is, without music) or over the end of the previous song. So, if the drop is ten seconds long and the intro is five then play the first six seconds of the drop over the end of Song A, then start Song B when there are four seconds left to run.

It has to be said that in reality, many of these techniques sound rather ridiculous and are rarely heard on air. In the main, play a drop-in as you fade a song underneath it; to cover the join of two songs; or as a song starts.

Remember, don't use the same techniques relentlessly time and time again. Presenting segues requires practice and confidence. And as there really isn't time to rehearse all of your segues before you go on air (in fact doing that would make your actual broadcast sound dull and flat), you need to get lots of flying time under your belt first. When you are on air, you may be able to rehearse to a certain extent (for example talking over the introduction to a song on pre-fade) but you won't be able to practise all your segues because, very often, the song you need to practise will already be playing on air. It takes plenty of off-air work to be good on air.

What to do when a song's playing

Work out what you are going to do next, and *how* you are going to do it. Structure your link, note down bullet-points bearing particular attention to these questions:

- What's the point of this item?
- What's the top line to grab attention?

---

[52] Hear it here: http://tinyurl.com/l9defb.

- How can I flesh it out and add detail, interest and colour?
- What's the punchline or conclusion? How will I know if I've got there?
- What will I do *next*, once I've finished the link? (Are you going to go to another song or a break or a pre-recorded interview, or someone on the phone? Is that item ready? What will be the transition between the two items? If that item is live, for example, a guest, how will you get from *that* to the *next* item? There may not be an opportunity to think about it or set it up while you are conducting an interview.)

Outroducing music

This is known as back-announcing or back-annoing. It is especially important to outroduce *new* songs: people aren't that interested beforehand. It is once they have heard it that they are intrigued and want to know who it is by. Doing this also keeps them listening longer too!

It's not really necessary to intro *and* outro every song. If you do that you sound patronising, and also give the impression that you don't have anything else more worthwhile to say. Although there may be an excuse for in-and-outing *current* songs, there's not one for *classics*. Indeed, one radio group's policy was to 'not mention the artists and title at all [unless] . . . playing a brand new record or . . . a more unfamiliar oldie'.

As with not introing songs which have their title in the first line, a similar thing goes for outros too:

▶ **ACTUAL AUDIO**

('New Sensation'[53] by INXS repeats to fade)
PRESENTER: That's 'New Sensation' . . .

Commercial station, May 2005

Beware of songs with awkward ends/false ends such as:

'Mr Blue Sky'[54] by ELO which has a climax, then silence, before music fades in again to a second crescendo

'Too Funky'[55] by George Michael, which has a clip of a woman talking on the end after the singing itself has finished!

'Barbara Ann'[56] by The Beach Boys, 'Hello Goodbye'[57] by The Beatles, 'Calling All The Heroes' by It Bites, all of which have false ends.

---

[53] Hear it here: http://tinyurl.com/lvkwsf.
[54] Hear it here: http://tinyurl.com/dhzvef (in fact this song has an awkward start too!).
[55] Hear it here: http://tinyurl.com/336dqs.
[56] Hear it here: http://tinyurl.com/mj5lc4.
[57] Hear it here: http://tinyurl.com/2veyrg.

'Summer The First Time'[58] by Bobby Goldsboro is an example of a 'story song', which tells of a young man's first sexual experience. It would obviously be wrong to cut this kind of song short.

Backtimes, dead rolls and overruns

This is the art of preparing so you don't run out of time at the end of the hour or the end of the programme. Finishing late sounds messy. You can't join a bulletin half way through, or have the newsreader introduce the news with: 'It's a minute past ten . . .'. Indeed it may be that your show has a 'clock end' and you're cut off in midstream if you don't finish your programme on time. Or perhaps you have to take another live source at a certain time. (This is called an 'opt-in' and if it's at a specific time it has a 'clock in'.)

Finishing early is downright embarrassing. Most presenters have at some time misread the studio clock or miscalculated a back time and been left with a minute or so to fill – rather more difficult than it sounds! So, backtiming determines what time you have to start a sequence of events, in order to finish when you want to (that is, on time).

You have to add together the durations of each item between where you are now and where you have to be at a certain time. It's tricky because you are dealing with units of 60 rather than 100, and because no song is a uniform length. But it gets easier with practice!

As you should do a mental back time in your head from the last 20 minutes of each hour, here is an example.

It is around 20 minutes to 2 and between now and the news (which you pride yourself on hitting on time) you have a travel bulletin at :50 and three songs following that:

- X of 2:56 which fades.
- Y which lasts 3:19 which also fades.
- Z the final song of the hour which ends after 3:42. (It's handy that Z ends, it just sounds neater than fading a song to the news. Indeed, some presenters swap their order around to specifically place an end-song as the last one of the hour.)

There is also a nine-second news jingle.

Working backwards:

- the news starts at :00 so the news jingle has to start at 59:51;
- therefore Z has to start at 56:09.

The most important calculations are now done. Y and X fade anyway so to fade them early would be acceptable, as long as you have given them a decent play (see earlier).

Letting each of these go right to the very end would sound odd. The timings are based on the complete duration of each song, not where the best opt-out points are. So if you based a backtime calculation on the *full* duration you would have to let each track play to its bitter end with the song getting progressively quieter, which would sound pretty poor, but as we've seen, you can fade a song early.

So, back to our sums!

---

[58] Hear it here: http://tinyurl.com/2u4w27.

We have to start Z at 56:09, with Y starting no earlier than 3:19 before that (or we'll be left with a gap). That makes the new backtime 52:50 – the time we have to start Y by. Using the same calculation, X has to start no earlier than 2:56 earlier, giving us 50:04.

Make a note of when each item has got to start by and then count *forward* from your start-point to check that the backtime's accurate.

Of course, while all this number crunching is going on, the song on air is counting down and getting closer and closer to its end; so as you can see, backtiming is rather like chasing your tail. If you leave it too late, you realise that you should have started the last song ten seconds ago, and the moment has been lost: that song that you wanted to let end will have to be messily faded after all.

The above calculations do give us, remember, the times at which both those faded songs have to start by, which as I say, will cause us to have to play them to their bitter end. If we listened through to each of them we could work out the best opt-out points on each one and then build those timings into our equation instead, but that would be too long and tedious and would not be done in practice.

Instead, take a guess that we can fade X and Y about 30 seconds from time, giving us a start-time for this sequence of three songs and a news jingle of one minute later at 51:04. And to mask any clashes of musical tone or tempo, be ready to talk over or play a drop-in over the segues. So, if you can go to the travel presenter slightly early, which would usually be possible and ask them to 'be out (to have finished talking by a certain time) by :51, please' you should be on track to hit your back time. Easy!

As the 20 minutes reduces to 15 and certainly ten, recalculate your timings.

Timing is of the essence if you are to present a professional programme. There must be no half-played songs, ad breaks must be broadcast on time and in full, the travel presenter must have all the time they need to tell of delays and diversions, and the show must begin and end when it is scheduled to.

Dead rolling is a technique similar to backtiming, but easier.

With this, you still start the final piece of music at the 'backtimed' time so it ends when you want it to, but it begins by playing off air (with the volume down). Note 'music' rather than 'song': it would sound very odd if a vocal track started half way through so this technique is best used with an instrumental theme. So if you have two and a half minutes to fill at the end of the show and your bed (see earlier) is four minutes long, start playing it off air at 56 minutes past the hour. Then when the final vocal track ends, fade up your bed safe in the knowledge that it will end at exactly 00. This is the dead roll.

(See Fig. 15 of the diagram on p. 284 for a representation of starting a backtimed programme theme 1:40 from the end of a show.)

Filling for time

This may happen when:

- You've not calculated your backtime properly.
- Someone else isn't ready for you to cross (or 'cross over') to them.
- A piece of equipment fails unexpectedly.

Look back at the section on stock phrases and also those about knowing about the station, the features, programmes and presenters. If all that's in your head, and with the knowledge you have about teasing and trailing, you should be able to adlib for a minute or more without any trouble.

19 Competitions

When broadcasting became fraudcasting

In 2007/8[1] a scandal engulfed British radio and how stations ran competitions. A string of 'editorial lapses' dating back to 2005 were uncovered. Here's a selection:

August 2007 – GCap Media is fined £17,500 by phone regulator Icstis for a premium rate competition on the One Network.

May 2008 – Two breakfast show presenters were dismissed because of alleged competition fixing. It was alleged that, when text entries could not be received by the studio, the presenters found someone else to pose as the winner.

June 2008 – GCap is hit with a further £1.11m fine by Ofcom for the 'Secret Sound' competition where callers with the wrong answer were put to air in a bid to deliberately prolong the competition and raise more money through a premium rate entry phone number; in what the regulator called a 'deliberate and premeditated' attempt to fix the outcome.[2] Each of the 30 stations on which the competition was broadcast was fined £37,000, bringing the total fine to £1.11m, the biggest radio fine in Ofcom's history. GCap was also fined £17,500 by phone regulator Icstis.

---

[1] Despite the huge publicity surrounding these incidents, the practice continued into 2009: http://tinyurl.com/mexaqc.
[2] Is the incident described here: http://tinyurl.com/3dtp7b fakery, or a legitimate production technique to increase tension and interest?

July 2008 – The BBC is fined[3] £225,000 for unfair competitions on four shows. In one case listeners were invited to enter a competition that had already been recorded and the winner was a listener to the previous day's show and the name of a second participant was made up. In another, on a pre-recorded show, a member of BBC staff posed as a competition winner, and listeners called or sent texts when they had no chance of winning.

December 2008 – The BBC was fined a further £95,000 for pre-recorded competitions (Ofcom: 'repeated instances of premeditated, deliberate deception . . . in the full knowledge that the audience stood no chance of either entering or winning'). On another show which had no competition entrants, producers made up the name of a 'winner'.

Generally immediate interaction in pre-recorded programmes is not possible. Broadcasters must consider carefully whether information they choose to include in pre-recorded programmes broadcast 'as live' has the potential to materially mislead their audiences.[4]

Following these incidents, in November 2007 the BBC announced its first Code of Conduct for competitions:

Competitions and voting will be handled with rigorous care and integrity . . . to ensure that winners of competitions and votes are genuine and never invented, pre-chosen or planted by the production team.[5]

It goes on to say that prizes must be described accurately, and there must be clear rules in place that are readily available to the public.

Whatever pressures there may be to keep the show on the air, the BBC must never compromise its editorial integrity. If things go wrong with running a competition or vote, the BBC will not cover up or falsify the outcome.

---

[3] The fines imposed on the BBC do of course have to be paid from its licence fee income.
[4] Ofcom, *The Radio Magazine*, February 2009. The latest incidents of broadcasting deception are catalogued here: http://tinyurl.com/4pxthk.
[5] The full guidelines: http://tinyurl.com/m8t4z2 and http://tinyurl.com/kmt363.

WHEN COMPETITIONS GO VERY WRONG

In January 2007 a radio station competition in California led to the death of a contestant. The victim, a 28-year-old mother of three, was participating in a contest called 'Hold Your Wee for a Wii', in which she competed to see who could drink large amounts of water without going to the toilet, to win a game console. The woman died of what a coroner ruled were symptoms consistent with water intoxication.[6] In October 2009, a California court found Sacremento radio station KDND and its owner liable for the death, and the family of Jennifer Strange were awarded $16m (£9.7m) compensation.[7]

A Birmingham radio station was fined £15,000 after four people were left with severe frostbite after a competition stunt went wrong in August 2001. The station challenged contestants to sit on blocks of dry ice – carbon dioxide frozen at temperatures of – 78°C – to win tickets and back stage passes for a music festival in the city. The incident resulted in four people being treated in hospital for severe frostbite, with three of them requiring prolonged stays.[8]

Why radio stations run competitions

The most effective competitions have a genuine editorial purpose and clear marketing objective. Perhaps to:

- Boost figures by attracting new people to the station.
- Keep existing listeners listening longer and increasing TSL (such as announcing a 'cue to call' song in breakfast and playing it later in the day).
- Add fun, interest, excitement and suspense to the output, increasing the listeners' perception of the station as a place to go for a good time. (If the competition's confusing or dull then it's not worth running.)
- Provide awareness (a 'talkability' factor) in the community and on air.
- Make the station look generous when it gives away a huge prize . . .
- . . . or fun when it gives away a unique, smaller prize.
- Link with the station's core brand values (the competition and prize should link with the core personality and highlight the attributes of the presenters and the station).
- Drive on-air content and give something for the station to promote (or talk up) at other points in the day: either by repeating a recording of the contestant who won, playing the qualifying question or providing 'talkability' for other presenters. (Five desperate brides-to-be, each appealing to the audience for their votes to award them a dream wedding and dissuade votes from going to the others, that's dramatic and compelling content!)

[6] The full story: http://tinyurl.com/mx7gsa.
[7] The court case: http://tinyurl.com/yje3bb9.
[8] The full story: http://tinyurl.com/ydkvlu.

○ Earn money for the station (a company might pay a commercial station to run a competition with its product as a prize as part of an awareness campaign, or might sponsor an existing contest).

Competitions can be basic (the 'Mystery Voice') or more complicated (perhaps with a qualifying question, followed by several rounds against another contestant). They may be one-offs ('Win a pair of tickets for tonight's performance of . . .') or more long term ('Our jackpot is now at £3,000 . . .'). The prizes may be basic (The Breeze in Essex gave away 'gold plated' bath plugs) or expensive (holidays or cars) or exclusive (film premier tickets). They may take place on air (as most do) or off air (at an outside broadcast), or a mix of the two (an endurance contest such as 'Touch the Truck', with regular on-air updates from the event).

Although small competitions can occur at any time of the day (giving away CDs or concert tickets) the biggest ones are invariably scheduled at breakfast. That is because there's already a large number of people listening at that time, so there is a greater chance of some of them being Rajar diary-holders. Other contests are usually run at regular times each day, so listeners can be 'trained' to listen and call.

There are fewer competitions on UK radio since the scandals mentioned above. BBC local stations for example have to have every one they run 'signed off' by a senior manager which means that stations which used to have a competition per show, may now have none at all.

Once upon a time there was a Top 40 station in a very large market – a very, very large market. And they were doing an on-air call-in giveaway of concert tickets. I don't know how many calls they took, but it doesn't matter to my tale. This station was doing this, obviously, to engage the audience and activate them. To create an opportunity to interact with the audience, one on one. Now when the phone lines are jammed and the jock is punching one call after another you might consider this tactic a success, right?

Well guess what?

This station called the phone company after the contest ended, and they asked a simple question: How many different (i.e., unduplicated) people attempted to dial in to win that prize in that time window? The answer was 200.

Yes, for one of the biggest stations with hundreds of thousands of active Top 40 listeners in one of America's biggest markets there were a mere 200 people playing their game. But the phone lines were jammed! With the same 200 people calling over and over!

What is the point of wasting your time on something which motivates only 200 people to participate when your audience numbers in the hundreds of thousands? What do you think that does for the rest of your listeners, and how do you think it will affect you at ratings time?

This is not engagement, it's delusion. It's random motion.

It's clutter.[9]

Even though competitions have their place, they do take time away from other things that the presenter could be talking about. As many people don't play them you might be better spending more time pushing increased listening with strong content to more people, and less time promoting increased listening to competitions that 95 per cent don't care about. It's interesting to note that the removal of them from many stations has not caused an outcry from listeners . . .

Competitions vs. lotteries[10]

Simply put, one is something you can legally run, and the other is not. A *competition* is lawful if success depends to a substantial degree on the exercise of skill. You will risk prosecution if the authorities believe there is insufficient skill, although the exact definition of 'skill' is hard to determine. If there's not enough skill involved, it's more likely to be an (illegal) lottery. But that 'element of skill' only applies when there is a 'payment to enter', that is, anything more than the 'normal rate'. Therefore any competition that does not involve 'payment to enter' does not require an element of skill. A competition can also be unlawful if it asks entrants to predict the outcome of future events, for example, who will win the cup final.

A *lottery* is a scheme for distributing prizes purely on the basis of chance where participants have paid to enter. Small charity lotteries such as raffles are exempt (subject in some cases to registration with a local authority) as, of course, is the National Lottery. Just to complicate matters a 'free prize draw' where no skill is required (a winner is drawn at random by chance alone and no payment has been made to enter – and note that payment can mean a premium rate phone call cost) is lawful.

So, to sum up, you need to ensure that any competition you run involves sufficient skill and doesn't ask entrants to predict future events, to keep your station out of trouble.

The mechanic[11]

How the contest works, how it's run and won, is called 'the mechanic'. Competition experts say there are only 11 basic contest formats in the world, which are listed below.

Examples are from TV as they are more likely to be recognisable, but bear in mind that these contests or games, like the ones on the radio, may borrow from several formats, not just the one listed alongside:

---

[9] Mark Ramsey, president, RadioIntelligence.com.
[10] More advice: http://tinyurl.com/ktfurs, http://tinyurl.com/kjkvk5.
[11] Download this part-work on devising TV games shows, for free: http://tinyurl.com/np4evz and get the full book here: http://tinyurl.com/mqvxbp.
An interview on devising reality gameshows: http://tinyurl.com/m2l3kf.

1 Fill the Blank — *Blankety Blank*[12]
2 Crack the Clue — *321*[13]
3 Cryptic Clue — *Treasure Hunt*[14]
4 Show Your Skill — *Hard Spell,*[15] *X Factor*[16]
5 Ordeal — *Mastermind,*[17] *Gladiators*[18]
6 Every Second Counts — *Beat the Clock*[19]
7 One to One (against another contestant) — *Ready Steady Cook*[20]
8 Play or Walk Away — *Who Wants To Be A Millionaire,*[21]
9 Total Chance — *Strike It Lucky,*[22] *Deal or No Deal*[23]
10 Multiple Choice — *Who Wants To Be A Millionaire?*
11 50–50
   ◦ higher or lower — *Play Your Cards Right*[24]
   ◦ true or false — *Win The Ads*[25]

So clash a few of these ideas, but don't steal them outright (many game show formats are legally protected, although in principle it's difficult to prove that someone's stolen an idea).

A competition can only progress in one of two ways: fast, finish slow (with a build up of tension, like in *Millionaire*), or slow, finish fast (with an against-the-clock round, like in *Win the Ads*).[26]

TRIVIA QUESTIONS

These *may* have their place, but only in short and sharp bursts and with a creative twist. As mentioned earlier, BBC Radio Two's Steve Wright has made Factoids one of his furniture features, but there are other presenters who set an 'impossible question' and then devote lots of airtime telling listeners they are wrong . . . before revealing a fact that doesn't add anything to their day.

The key is to do trivia entertainingly: one Christian station does 'Bible or Babble'[27] in which you guess which one of three phrases that sound like scripture is the real thing. Other stations do 'Canadian or Dead' (which celebrities fall in to

---

[12] More on this show here http://tinyurl.com/27zef6 and here http://tinyurl.com/prgc88.
[13] More on this show here http://tinyurl.com/nk4zrn and here http://tinyurl.com/lp3cyl.
[14] More on this show here http://tinyurl.com/lsfkxv.
[15] More on this show here http://tinyurl.com/m4fdaj and here http://tinyurl.com/l6tuq3.
[16] More on this show here http://tinyurl.com/n3lm59 and here http://tinyurl.com/mn9bjv.
[17] More on this show here http://tinyurl.com/86qrsy and here http://tinyurl.com/lfbnqj.
[18] More on this show here http://tinyurl.com/nusj96 and here http://tinyurl.com/nxxwsx.
[19] More on this show here http://tinyurl.com/kl6dbc and here http://tinyurl.com/ksstbv.
[20] More on this show here http://tinyurl.com/l45ebs and here http://tinyurl.com/lcjws3.
[21] More on this show here http://tinyurl.com/u7xgb and here http://tinyurl.com/na9o98.
[22] More on this show here http://tinyurl.com/mgrcnf and here http://tinyurl.com/n3v67d.
[23] More on this show here http://tinyurl.com/kuldp6 and here http://tinyurl.com/nmyt7y.
[24] More on this show here http://tinyurl.com/mmj8vd and here http://tinyurl.com/mvqrx9.
[25] More on this show here http://tinyurl.com/n5a355 and here http://tinyurl.com/mowjpp.
[26] See the finale here http://tinyurl.com/ktkjrw.
[27] Details here http://tinyurl.com/nrznuq.

which of two categories), or 'The Good, The Bad and The Birthday' (a this day in history story which was lucky, another which is unfortunate and then the studio team guesses ages of birthday-ing celebrities). With all these, the fun of playing the game itself is the point.

Unless you have a POD (point of difference) in the way you present the item, running a trivia question is no advantage for you. So either steer clear and do only things you can do, or repackage it in a way that's unique.[28]

◀ **ACTUAL AUDIO**

PRESENTER: 40 per cent of Chinese people do what?

Local commercial radio station, November 2005

PRESENTER: The answer is 'red'. What's the question?
PRESENTER: The answer is 'button'. What's the question?

BBC local station, January 2006

The mechanic must fit with the station (the host brand), the prize or sponsor (the guest brand) and the listener, to be effective. It sounds odd to hear a question that has nothing to do with the prize, or a prize that has nothing to do with the format of the station, so make sure everything ties in. If the competition doesn't sound interesting and exciting, then it won't cut through the clutter to become compelling.

Create a mechanic that is interesting and intriguing to those playing on air as well as those playing at home. Often the best ones are where there's simplicity with some suspense. Radio should never be 'I've got some prizes to give away', it should be 'This will be fun or challenging for players . . . and listeners'.

Ask:

▫ Why are we doing this competition or promotion? What do we want to achieve?
▫ Does everyone understand the goal and how the competition works?

The name[29]

A good competition often has a catchy name that may tease, intrigue and is relevant to the mechanic.

You may want to consider one that:

▫ Is straightforwardly descriptive – *The Mystery Voice, Bullseye.*
▫ Adds tension or excitement – *Gladiators, University Challenge, Don't Try This At Home.*
▫ Is alliterative – *Going for Gold, Supermarket Sweep.*
▫ Uses an existing phrase – *Who Wants To Be A Millionaire?*
▫ Is a pun on the format – *Wheel of Fortune, Play Your Cards Right.*

---

[28] Here's a good example: http://tinyurl.com/nubrxo.
[29] Puzzle and games consultancy company: http://tinyurl.com/nre4ey.

Questions

Never refer to the question as 'easy' or 'simple' as you devalue the whole contest. If it's easy why should someone bother to enter? If you say it's easy and someone gets it wrong, how will they feel and how will you look? What happens to the station's credibility? That doesn't mean the question can't be easy or simple, just don't say so!

Make the question appropriate to the station, the audience and the competition prize.

◀ ACTUAL AUDIO

(In a competition for tickets to the local theatre to see a musical.)

PRESENTER: What kind of animal is a chameleon?

Local commercial radio station, September 2005

Suspense and surprise

Many of the great contests have a second level of excitement built-in: suspense. Think of *Millionaire* where the stakes get increasingly higher and of Chris Tarrant's teasing across the break.

Create suspense by giving the contestant an option:

▫ Walk away or stay and play.
▫ Take the money or open the box.

Consider that although too many wrong answers can have a negative effect on the competition as a whole, having some builds suspense and lets contestants show emotion.

Occasionally hold back part of the prize to give 'spontaneously' at the time of winning: 'You've just won tickets to the see The Sugababes live in concert in Vegas! And . . . can I do this? Heck, I'm going to . . . I'm going to throw in £500 so you've got some spending money too!'. It creates excitement and unpredictability. And the listeners will love you!

THE EMOTIONS

Contestant may undergo different sorts of emotions during competitions:[30]

Smugness – getting a question right[31]
Disappointment – losing the game
Greed – playing for a stated, valuable reward
Surprise – winning an unexpected reward
Shock – something frightening happening suddenly
Relief – avoiding a jeopardy
Anger – arguing with a team-mate
Disgust – at your own performance or that of a team-mate

---

[30] David J. Bodycombe, *How To Devise A Game Show*. http://tinyurl.com/np4evz.

[31] 'A curious phenomenon about quizzes is that, as a broad-brush observation, wealthier people have had a better education and therefore can get even richer by winning quizzes. It might be worth thinking of alternative testing systems that have a more equitable methodology in order to capture a "everyone has a chance to win" feel to your show' (*How To Devise A Game Show*).

Gross out – having to do something deeply unpleasant
Fear – having to do something seemingly dangerous
Laughter – laughing at themselves or the host's jokes
Anxiety – not knowing which tactical choice to make
Panic – when time's running out
Hate – when voting off a competitor you intensely dislike
Love and lust – as used in dating shows

PROSPECT THEORY

This was observed in the 1970s when psychologists discovered that if a decision was taken to avoid a loss, it would be a bolder decision than one taken merely to achieve a gain.

So in a 'competition' setting, if you have a mechanic where you give something (say £1,000) and then the player loses or wins money from that standing point, rather than merely adding to it, people will be more likely to gamble thereby creating more tension . . . than simply adding to an amount (especially if that amount is zero).

RISK

Economists[32] have a scale for assessing propensity to take risks. Zero on this scale means complete indifference to all risk; you'll take any gamble that's offered. Anything above one means you are risk averse. Above ten and you probably don't dare cross the road.

The average risk for the whole population is one and at that level, people are prepared to take fairly rational risks: they will risk £100 on a bet that gives them a 50–50 chance of getting £200. It's been found that *Millionaire* contestants came out at almost exactly one, behaving with a high degree of rationality.

Contest production

Not all competitions have to have lots of whizz-bang production elements, but they should certainly have some of the basic ones to make it more interesting – more of an event. That might be a music bed, a drop-in and a winner's fanfare, for example. Production must be thought of at the same time as the name of the competition, the mechanic and the prize as they all go hand in hand. As well as considering whether you need any production elements, is the question of how and when the pre-launch activity starts, to build interest and increase the talkability factor. In a busy world, this all helps cut through the listener's mental clutter.

[32] Professor Ian Walker, of Warwick University, studied *Who Wants to Be a Millionaire?* for his research: http://tinyurl.com/nq6rxy.

The prize

Remember the two main criteria for a competition are:

- What would they like to win?
- How easy is it for them to win?

Then consider that a great prize should be:

- fun
- expensive
- or 'something money can't buy'. Listeners want the chance to meet a celebrity, to go backstage, to be invited to something exclusive or the chance to be famous themselves. Cash gives the listeners freedom to buy exactly what they want. (See the 'Scarcity Principle' below.)

Give away something specific away, not just, 'Something nice from our prize cupboard . . . we'll see what we can find'. Say what it is, and why someone would like to win it.

- Is the prize appropriate for the station's brand . . .
- and listener's lifestyle?
- Would they want to win it?
- Have you actually got the prize? Now. In your hand? If not then it is probably best not to run the competition. It has been known for promises from PR companies not to translate into reality.
- If it is provided by a third party, are you absolutely certain what it is, any conditions or warranties, the value? Do you have it? Check 'extras' such as travel to the concert, spending money etc.

THE SCARCITY PRINCIPLE

If something is exclusive or difficult to get, then getting it demonstrates to ourselves and others that we are in control of our environment. We are in effect, a winner (in life and in the radio competition). Threats to take something away (perhaps by the host in a radio competition) shows the other person that you are in control.

> That is why what comes to us only at long intervals is pleasant, whether it be a person or a thing; for it is a change from what we had before, and, besides, what comes only at long intervals has the value of rarity.[33]

If something is not scarce, then it is not desired or valued that much. Praises from a boss whose praises are rare means more than from someone who hands them out liberally.

In short, if something is rare (such as meeting a celeb, front row tickets or behind the scenes tours) it seems we find it somehow more desirable.[34]

---

[33] Aristotle, *Rhetoric*, Book 1, Chapter 11.
[34] Further reading: Peter Lunt et al., *The Psychology of Consumer Detriment* (office of Fair Trading, 2006): http://tinyurl.com/nmgebt.

Remember though that big prizes can fail to make a personal connection with the listener. Often lots of small prizes work better than one large one, as there are more chances to win, more actual winners and therefore more people to spread the word about your station.

Some low-cost items are often perceived by listeners to be more 'winnable', as they determine that only one person will win the round the world trip and so the chances are slim of it being them. However, the chances of them getting a book or CD are much greater, as those types of contest are run more regularly. Listeners have their own perception of the value of a prize, and it is not necessarily in financial terms. They weigh up their chances of winning, consider the likely popularity of the contest and the difficulty of the questions.

Consider prizes that can't be bought. When he was the breakfast presenter on Breeze, in Essex, Peter Holmes gave his contest winners bathplugs. They cost a few pence each and every listener wanted one. They were personalised, gold-plated (or rather 'gold-painted') on a stand and had an obvious connection with the time of day of the programme. They were promoted as being 'exclusive and elusive' which increased their desirability. Peter once held a party just for bathplug winners. Over 150 people turned up, all with their bathplug as the entry ticket.

Such prizes may have three attributes:

- extremely limited practical value
- personalised
- inexplicably fun.

Cash handouts are fine, but unless they are really significant the perception of them is often lower than their actual value. In other words, sending a prize of £100 to a winner seems less exciting than a pair of concert tickets or a meal out which may actually cost less. A £500 prize is great, but the perception of a pamper weekend at a country hotel may seem better, and actually be cheaper.[35]

MONEY OR MEMORIES?

It's believed that material goods and money leave us flat, but experiences tend to be unique and the pleasure of a positive memory doesn't wear off.

> If you want to raise your happiness level . . . spend your money on experiences (a safari/Himalayan trekking/a concert) rather than a Rolex, a yacht or a Ferrari because they will bring you more joy in the long run.[36]

You can see how this might be used to determine a prize that a station gives away.

> Nowadays acquisition is very important. People believe that if they win the lottery they will become hugely happier, and for a while they do, but human beings have a surprising capacity to return to where they started. The problem is that once you're wealthy you become habituated to being

---

[35] Cheaper for whom, though? See the second item here: http://tinyurl.com/yk2do93.

[36] James Montier, *Behavioural Investing: a Practitioner's Guide to Applying Behavioural Finance* (John Wiley, 2007): http://tinyurl.com/n4ztfq.

> wealthy and you want to know what the next thing is. We're constantly striving, which stops us being happy.[37]
>
> Experiences, on the other hand, become more valuable to us as time goes on. Their charm does not wear off but increases as experience is central to our identity.
>
> Psychologists at the University of Colorado[38] in the US also claim the 'good life' may be better lived by doing things rather than by having things. So having experiences such as a meal out or a trip to the cinema or sports events makes you happier and gives a longer-lasting high than having a gadget.
>
> > We found that people receive more enduring pleasure and satisfaction from investing in life experiences rather than increasing their material possessions.[39]

Tangible prizes, that people can imagine themselves experiencing, are also easier to work into a mechanic and to talk up on air.

Are your winners getting prizes that represent the station brand or just ones that a keen marketing company has sent you and have been languishing in the back of the prize cupboard? I have heard a car alarm kit being given away on a school-run competition, bottles of wine as another prize and how many key-rings does one person need? (They seem to be the only things in many small stations' prize cupboard!) Think about what your listeners do and what they would like to win to fit in with their lives. One station called this 'made-to-measure treasure', with a prize chosen specifically for each individual winner.

All competitions must usually be cleared with a senior member of staff for several important reasons. If yours is a commercial station there may be an understandable grievance that the prize you are giving away has been given to the station for free. Your sales and promotions team have targets to reach on how much money they have to bring into the station each month and they won't be pleased at seeing a possible opportunity ('a lead') slipping through their fingers.

It is a little-known fact that the companies whose items are given away as prizes usually pay the commercial station to run the competition. The number of mentions and talk-ups (when presenters say how desirable the prize is) is carefully controlled by the promotions executive, so the company gets what they pay for, no more and no less.

Presenter mentions have more impact than an advert, as the listeners' favourite presenter is making what amounts to a personal endorsement of the product: added value is given to the company whose product is being given away. Promotions people argue that the company concerned should pay the station to run the competition as well as providing the prizes. You can see their point (their point, of course, also translates into your salary). So, don't be tempted to run a contest on air and give away any item that has been donated before checking it with the appropriate member of the team.

BBC stations have to tread very carefully in terms of competitions. They are not allowed to sell the competition in the same way that commercial stations do, of course, and even

---

[37] Dr Clive Wood, director of the Happiness, Personality and Health course at Cardiff University http://tinyurl.com/l9owdg.

[38] http://tinyurl.com/ntnhk3.

[39] Lead author Leaf Van Boven.

before the 'fraudcasting' fiasco there were more stringent regulations about the prizes themselves (they are not allowed to give away cash, for example), and what a presenter can say about the prize without veering into the area of advertising or endorsing the product. That is why many BBC stations buy the majority of their prizes and of course that is governed by budgets. More money being spent on a prize means less on programmes or staff: listeners and licence payers could justifiably ask questions about value for their money.

> Donations of substantial prizes cannot be accepted. Programmes should not broadcast brand names or any other details about a prize that might suggest endorsement of a product or service. In exceptional circumstances, for editorial reasons, some details may be given on the grounds that description of the prize would be inadequate without them. Brand names of household goods should not be given.[40]

Most stations have a policy that all freebies received (books, CDs, DVDs, tickets, etc.) are the property of the station and not the person they were addressed to.

> In 2001 a woman who was presented with a toy Renault Clio after winning a radio competition for a 'new car' won her courtroom fight to be given a real one. The station's managers and the disc jockey responsible for the hoax contest then had to decide who was going to pay the £8,000 price of a Clio. Cathy McGowan sued them after failing to see the funny side of what the Radio Buxton DJ said was just a joke to keep listeners happy.[41]
>
> In May 2007 a radio station's prize was described as a visit to Athens to watch the Champions League final – but Athens turned out to be a restaurant in Birmingham and not the Greek city. A winner who complained was offered the cost of her 25p text back by the station. Ofcom noted that the promotion for the competition was 'cryptic', but decided not to take the complaint further.[42]

The rules[43]

Contests must be very simple to explain and to understand. If the rules last more than 30 seconds or if there are too many rounds then it is probably too complicated and will take too long to run. Both are a turn-off for those taking part, those who would like to have taken part, and those listening at home who just want to get back to the music.

---

[40] BBC Radio Five Live style guide.
[41] The full story here: http://tinyurl.com/n3af9r.
[42] The full story here: http://tinyurl.com/magr84.
[43] How to write a game show format: http://tinyurl.com/n6gxkz.

Some stations run group-wide contests. This is when listeners from all the stations are invited to call a registration line, but only one contestant is chosen to play from all those entries. A recording of them winning the competition is played on each station. Such networked competitions have rules about how the contest is promoted on air, so listeners in each area aren't given the impression that they stand a better chance of winning than in fact they do.

Make sure rules are available on the website and include a line that under certain circumstances a prize of equal or greater value can be substituted. Then if tickets, CDs and so on get 'lost in the post' it's OK for you to give the winner something else.

As a presenter you should be aware that some competition mechanics are written in a script that you can't deviate from, so check before altering a single word. There is a great difference between '. . . and you *could* win . . .' and 'You *will* win . . .'. Also a sponsor may have agreed a certain tag line (such as the company's positioning statement) that you will have to read word-for-word, which will also take into account regulations on the phrasing of sponsorship credits set down by Ofcom.

COMPETITION CONSIDERATIONS

How are people eligible to take part? (Age might be a consideration.)
Is there a deadline?
The duration of the entry period and the competition.
How many winners you need or want.
How they'll win.
Is there an element that allows everyone to believe that they could be a winner?
Is the mechanic interesting and fun?
Is the prize weird or wonderful?
What happens if more than one person wins?
What happens if there's a tie? Is there another question or another round?
What if a contestant drops out midway?
What happens if a contestant claims an answer's wrong?
What if they enter a second time?
Insurance: in case someone actually does win the big prize . . .
Will the competition achieve your objectives?
Do the presenters know these objectives and the rules?
Has the contest been tested?
Are the idea, mechanic and prize new and different?
Is the execution of the competition appropriate for the station brand?
Are the rules easily explained, easily available and understandable?
Is it all legal?
Does everyone have an equal chance to play and win?
Have you guarded against contest fraud . . . or employee fraud?
What about judges or drawings? Are they beyond reproach, open and honest?
Much of this information should be made public on your website or in the reception.

Promoting the competition

Radio is a linear medium so first hook the listener, then say why you've told them, then what they've got to do.

If you say, 'Call me now on 01234 567890 and if you can answer the question "how long is a piece of string?" you could win a stack of CDs that weighs as much as you do . . .' you've put the reason for people to call (what they'll win) last! So, you told them how to enter, then what they have to do and then why, by which time they will have missed the number to call!

You have to first establish a context in which they want to hear, write or remember the number. So instead, say why they have got to enter (what they could win), what they have to do (the question) and then the way to do it (the phone number). 'Fancy winning a stack of CDs that weighs as much as you do? Then you may stand a chance if you can answer this question correctly: "How long is a piece of string?". If you think you know, call me on 01234 567890 . . .'.

Sell the sizzle!

Simply saying, 'Next, I'm giving away . . .' sees the situation from your view, that of the presenter. More effective is to talk from the viewpoint of your listener: tell them what they could win. Not, 'This is what we're giving away' or 'This is what we're doing', but rather, 'This is why what we're doing matters to you'.

Paint a picture! Explain the benefit of winning through positive visualisation.

- Tickets to the theatre becomes 'Have a night out on us', 'Spend some quality time together' or 'Take your mind off work for a couple of hours'.
- A new car is 'Think of the money you'll save on servicing and repairs', 'You'll be the king of the road', 'Nothing less than you deserve'.
- A holiday becomes 'Free fun in the sun', 'A week of pina coladas and pampering', '. . . and with a kids' club there as well, you've got all day to yourself'.

Radio listeners need help seeing your link and you can help them by placing pictures in their mind. Get them to picture the scene and themselves *in it*, *using* 'it' or *experiencing* 'it' and you've involved them.

THE POWER OF THE CONSTRUCTED IMAGE

There are two types of mental images:
- an *eidetic image* is one that you have seen
- a constructed image is one that you have created in your 'mind's eye'.

It is sometimes said that, whereas memory-images all reproduce or resemble something that we have experienced in the past, constructed images do not, and are novel. But although a constructed image on the whole is novel, its various elements all have their counterparts in our past experience. We have never seen 'gates of pearl' or 'streets of gold', but we have seen 'gates' and 'pearl' and 'streets' and 'gold', and the

> constructed image is a new creation only in the sense that it combines these elements.[44]
>
> So, once a vivid image has been created, whether it's an eidetic image or a constructed image, its power is very real. If you can get someone to *imagine* it, they're virtually *experiencing* it.

Don't use the word 'details' (it's so boring), just make it simple and straightforward. 'How you could win . . .', rather than, 'These are the details of what you've got to do . . .'. Then urge people to take part. Give the impression it is fun, exciting and challenging and 'You, yes you, could win'.

Call to action
How do people know to take part?

1 *The invitation* – This is the most straightforward call to play. 'If you'd like to play 'Beat The Intro' call now on . . .'. Take the calls as they come in and choose your contestant who'll be on air with you in a song or two's time.

2 *Registration* – Do potential participants have to register their entry in advance? Registration may be via a premium-rate phone number, the operators of which may send the station the name and number of a contestant that fits with pre-determined criteria (for example, a female from a certain town, although this is frowned on since the competition frauds mentioned above). Registration also captures the caller's information for future marketing, and helps make money for the station or helps finance the prize.

3 *Cue to call* – Players have to listen for a certain song to be played before they can phone and stand a chance of winning. This certainly helps increase your listening hours and that is why most 'cue-to-call songs' are played in the last 15 minutes of an hour (so the Rajar diary has as many ticks as possible). Obviously, the downside of playing the song too early in the programme or the hour is that listeners are then tempted to turn off.

There can be twists to this concept: you can choose a song that is on the album you are giving away; you can pick a song that has an appropriate title or fits in some other way to the prize ('Listen out for "Thriller" and call me when you hear it and you could spend Halloween at a haunted castle . . .'); a sound could be played rather than a song ('When you hear the alarm clock, call to win tickets to the New Year's Party', 'The thundering hooves could be your ticket to the races' and so on).

4 *Ring to win* – Some stations run contests where, say, the xxth caller will be the winner and that number is usually one that fits in with their station frequency (caller 104 for a station on 104.6 FM for example). In reality most stations won't get that many potential contestants, and as their lines aren't able to cope with more than half a dozen callers at the same time, they will never know exactly who is caller number 99. The presenter or producer simply waits a while, perhaps clears down the switchboard a couple of times then picks a call at random. Saying 'caller 99' on air sounds big, but the truth is that even if you get 99 callers, a lot of them will be the same listeners redialling.

---

[44] Rex Knight, *A Modern Introduction to Psychology* (University Tutorial Press, 1948); full text available at: http://tinyurl.com/ktamw2.

'Get through on lucky line 99' is merely showmanship. If you do use this technique, use a practical number: one that is low and is more realistic. You can still screen the callers as they don't know what line they are on unless you tell them! Answer the calls in turn and speak to them: who are they, where they're from and so on. In those few seconds judge if they are going to be a good contestant. If they aren't then, 'Sorry, you're on line four' and go to the next caller (who may also be told they are on line four if they are not going to be good on air). Think on your feet, as you have only a few seconds to judge each caller. If you are using this technique, don't ask for the answer to the question in the screening process: if the caller is right they will be even more cross they didn't get on air!

Alternatively, set up several potential winners on the phone and tell them which line they are on and then on air say '. . . and the winner's on line four!' at which time put up their fader to hear them whoop! Of course, you may only have that single contestant on the line, but it heightens the tension by giving the impression to them and the audience that you've got more.

Another technique is to line up several callers, the first two of whom have the wrong answer. Some people say this raises the excitement quotient for the listener and the caller, others that your station is known for having losers as well as winners and that that could harm your 'happy radio' image.

◀ ACTUAL AUDIO

CONTESTANT: I don't believe it. You've kept me on all this time to tell me 'no'? You're having a laugh!

BBC local station, February 2006

Good callers educate other listeners to be good callers. In other words, put on the callers that you want to be on air and then you will get more like them. Choose someone with the right personality and demographic (never put someone to air who's outside either) and from the right area (never put someone to air who is outside your TSA). You often only have the length of one song to get all this done and find your potential 'star'.

Two more points. Ask the contestant to sound excited and guess the answer if they don't know it, and to turn their radio off.

Some stations say that listeners should always be given at least two entry routes, to avoid discriminating against those without e-mail, for example. A typical competition would allow entry via the website (though unless it is a straightforward e-mail, a special page may need to be designed) and on the phone. Other options include entries by text or by post.

As well as the above, there may additionally be a qualifying question to get through to the main contest on air. This may be to weed out those who, for example, have no interest in a day at the races, but enter anyway. On such an occasion your qualifier may be 'Which horse won the Derby in 1985?' Think carefully about setting qualifiers, they add another tier of complexity to the mechanic and are often unnecessary as anecdotal research suggests that fewer than one in 800 people ever takes part in station contests.

Never admit there has been a poor response to a competition: you only usually need one contestant anyway. If calls are always slow it may be because the mechanic is too complicated, or the prize isn't interesting enough (and that doesn't necessarily mean that it's not expensive enough). Are you talking up the competition enough and in the most tantalising way? Consider changing some of these elements.

If you desperately need callers, recycle them from other occasions: when they do call, take their details and ask if you can call them the next day to take part. Ask the same question to those who call in for dedications and requests and so on.

Choosing a contestant

A radio competition is not all about giving away giving away prizes on air, it's about the *listeners* competing against themselves and, if possible, against each other.

There are two reasons why an on-air contestant is used in a radio competition:

- to be a foil
- to be an enabler.

The foil (or 'straight man') is used when the low-value prize is secondary to the banter with the presenter.[45]

More commonly the contestant is the 'enabler' of the competition and is the representative of the other listeners who are playing along at home, in the car or office. They may not all be playing for the prize, but they are playing for a *reward* of being entertained, and hear how 'their buddy' is going to do.

Work the switchboard to find the best listener to take part. You want them to sound fun, lively and interested, and to actually want to win the prize. Many times presenters have run a competition only to have the winner ask afterwards, 'What have I won?' or after having won tickets to an event say, 'Sorry, I can't go on that day'. You are then left with the problem of rerunning the competition to give away the prize that you've already given away!

You may want to get a caller from a specific area. If the tickets are for an event in a specific town, they are more likely to be used by someone who lives nearby than someone who is at the other end of the county. Alternatively, you may have a large item to give away that will cost a great deal to post, and want a winner who lives on your route home! (Some stations have a policy that station staff always deliver prizes, to give personal contact to their listeners.) Or you may simply want winners from across your area so you don't alienate those in certain towns. This may be a major problem if your phone-in number is 'geographic' as listeners in the town in which you are based will get through faster than those who have to dial the full code. (Note, these traditional 'production techniques' may now be banned at your station.)

If it fits with the competition mechanic, take the details of the caller before you put them to air. It avoids you saying on air, 'Stay on the line so we can take your details', or off air asking them to 'stay on the line if you win and I'll come back to take your address'. Or, take their phone number off air and call them back later. Or record and edit the whole conversation so it sounds quick and slick, and cuts the clutter.

PRIZE PIGS

Those contestants who have the competition line on their speed-dial are called 'prize pigs', because they're greedy for prizes – any prizes. They know that presenters want lively callers who will sound grateful, so they will put on that act to get chosen to play. They are not always loyal and may call any

---

[45] This a great example: http://tinyurl.com/nubrxo.

station for any competition. So, contests that encourage 'extended listening' (such as listening to wrong answers to work out the right one) will dissuade them from calling. Of course, as most listeners don't take part in competitions, the chances of the same person winning are, mathematically, much higher than if everyone entered.

You may have a book of recent winners or have a phone system which shows on a screen the last time each caller contacted you and why. Some stations have a rule that someone can't win twice within a certain period of time (ensure such a rule is published or there may be a complaint against you). But pigs call from other numbers or give you a false name or the address of a friend to get past this.

An obsessed woman with a knack for winning radio competitions has been fined and banned from phone-in contests after winning prizes worth more than £200,000 using fake names and false addresses. Bernadette Hurst was so successful at scooping the cash awards, holidays and electrical goods that she fell foul of competition rules forbidding more than one win per year. To avoid the loophole, she invented a series of aliases using forged documents. Hurst, 44, won £171,000 from Magic FM, the biggest prize in radio history, as well as further five-figure cash prizes, assorted holidays and at least one iPod. The grandmother operated from a specially equipped office at home, where she forged fake name change documents and offered countless unlikely excuses to suspicious radio executives. The court [was told] dubious station staff decided to carry out a voice recognition test and asked her to visit the studios and meet DJ Neil Fox . . . but because the defendant had met him before after a previous win and 'could not risk recognition', she sent her aunt to collect the prize instead, tried to explain away any voice difference on the basis of nerves, heavy smoking and difficulty reading. She then sent the station a forged deed of name change dated before the competition, showing she had the same name as her aunt, which purported to be signed by a firm of solicitors.[46]

This is an extreme example, but for most other 'pigs', consider why they are 'banned'. If they win lots because they listen lots, then they are among your most loyal listeners and will evangelise on your behalf. In other businesses, such as supermarkets or air travel, repeat sales (for radio, read 'calls') are rewarded and the best customers given special privileges, yet many stations don't

[46] The full article: http://tinyurl.com/yk554t2.

want them! Look after them well, even if you do stop taking their calls to air for a while, and consider letting them join your VIP club or sending them a prize pack out of the blue.

Running the competition

One of the most important things to remember about the competition is not what the prize is or that you have lots of entries; it's that you make it an exciting and enjoyable occasion for the contestants. There are many more people playing along at home, and you have to make the event interesting for them, too. Root for the caller to win. Be on their side. But don't give them the prize if they lose, as that devalues the whole competition.

MAXIMISING REWARD

Humans and other animals respond to the concept of reward for achievement from an early age. At its most basic level it's food, love or attention. Later in life it's money, praise or a bigger office. Sometimes it's internal, such as pride in a job well done. And that's the feeling you are aiming for a 'listener-contestant' to get as they hear one of their number succeed in an on-air competition.

As a 'listener contestant' they have the benefit of not being under pressure or putting anything at risk (their pride or their prize). They are in a better position to think more clearly, answer more quickly and have a slight feeling of superiority.

To be effective on radio a competition has to reward the 'listener contestant'. They have to be drawn in enough to play along, and their prize is one of fun and satisfaction or regret or sympathy with the on-air contestant. You are 'maximising reward'.

Every radio competition should be structured and executed in a way that the listener can take part off air. The on-air contestant is almost secondary. You want as many people as possible to be rewarded.

The caller on air

Never ask a caller a basic question on air that you (or your producer) haven't already asked them off air and know the answer to. Otherwise you get: 'How are you?' and the answer is, 'Well, not very well actually . . .' followed by a list of aches and pains. Or 'What've you been doing today?' answered with 'Not much . . .'. Ask them the boring stuff off air and identify some interesting thing about what they say, to ask them on air.

PRESENTER: What are you going to do with your £1,000?
CALLER: Go on holiday.
PRESENTER: OK, where, to?
CALLER: Dunno.
etc. etc.

PRESENTER: Well, what about a skiing holiday? Or a safari? Disneyland? Barbados?
CALLER: Yeah, Barbados.
PRESENTER: And who would you take?
CALLER: My boyfriend.
PRESENTER: And what's his name?
CALLER: Dean.
PRESENTER: OK, when I ask you what you're going to spend your money on, it'll be
             really great if you can tell me all about your fantasy holiday with Dean,
             the white sand, the cool water, the cocktails on the beach . . .

If all this fails, and the caller ends up on air and is poor, get rid of them as soon as is polite. No boring bits. No dead-end questions. No gaps. No awkward gear changes.

Another potential pitfall is echoing back what the caller has just said to you:

PRESENTER: Hello John.
CALLER: Hi, how are you?
PRESENTER: Fine, how are you?
CALLER: Good, thanks.
PRESENTER: Where are you calling from?
CALLER: Blank Village.
PRESENTER: Blank Village?
etc.

When they are on air, the caller becomes a surrogate for the listener. How you treat them will be how the listener feels treated. So use their first names frequently, and get involved with them as they play along. Express dismay when they fail a question, celebrate their winning. Help them have a good time and your listeners have a good time with them too.

When it's been run and won

Most listeners know what is expected of them: that they have to whoop and holler once they have won. Many stations also ask the winner, 'What's the name of your favourite radio station?' The presenter wants to end the call on a high by having the caller promote the station that's just given them a prize but this can backfire. Radio X's caller could often answer 'Radio Y' instead, possibly out of confusion, excitement, malice or because that's the truth. No other business does such a thing ('Tell me, who just sold you a fridge?'). It's a bit self-congratulatory, desperate and tacky isn't it? Shouldn't we just say 'Congratulations, that was great! Thanks for listening!'?

Don't let a listener reel of a list of hellos and that cliché 'and anyone else who knows me' at the end of the competition. Similarly, don't make a big fuss when a caller mentions the name of the place where they work. Ask anyone what they do and most will include in their answer the name of where they do it. A quick mention of 'Hi to everyone at Wellington's the Chemist in the High Street' cannot possibly be seen as an endorsement of the work of the store: no one is going to shop there simply because they heard a comment such as that on your station. However, if you draw attention to the comment by saying, 'You're not supposed to mention shops', it makes the listener look and feel bad. If they start launching into a commercial for the shop on the other hand, interrupt them politely and move on.

> Drawing attention to this phrase by saying 'you're not allowed to say that' not only prolongs the agony, it's also highly discourteous to the listener.[47]

Despatching prizes

Having winners pick up their own prize makes the station seem cheap and uncaring. They have to fit a visit to the station into their routine, and spend money on petrol and parking. The feeling the winner has, moves from excitement to regret. The competition climax turns to anti-climax. Winning a competition on the radio should be an exciting experience for the listener. That's the whole experience: from them calling on the phone, to the postman ringing on their doorbell.

If the winner does have to come in to the station to pick up their prize, make it worth-while. Ensure you are there to meet them and hand it over (not the 'anonymous' receptionist) and offer them a station tour and an explanation of how the studio works.

Never give away items that are going to be difficult or expensive to post (although some stations get their presenters to deliver prizes personally to the winners' homes). It is inevitable that the breakable items will get broken; recorded delivery is a good idea for expensive prizes. Perhaps do a contra-deal with a local courier company . . .

Think: can you deliver the prize so it gives added pleasure or value?

Promote the station at every opportunity. Every letter, and especially prizes, should include two car stickers and a personally signed presenter picture. The increased postage cost will be negligible when compared to the extra promotion and connection you are building between listener and presenter.

Food and alcohol are probably poor prizes. You don't know what state they will arrive in, whether they will be edible or who will open them (possibly someone who is under age).

◀ **ACTUAL AUDIO**

PRESENTER: So, congratulations on winning. Our reception's open from 9–5 weekdays so you can pop in and pick up your prize.

BBC local station, November 2005

---

[47] *County Sound Radio House Style*, January 1989.

Post-production

If a long-running competition is won in your show, you should be responsible for ensuring that the correct people are made aware. Alert the programme controller and the promotions team. They should arrange for a promo to be made of the 'winning moment' and alert other presenters so they don't still talk-up 'your chance to win'. You may also consider whether there is mileage in some press coverage. If it is a contest purely in your show, make a promo of the winning moment that other presenters can play.

With any long-running competition make sure the winning answer is repeated often for a day or so, to put listeners who missed the winning moment out of their misery!

Finally

Competition questions for you:[48]

- If you're going to ask for texts or e-mails for a show that's pre-recorded or voice-tracked, should you make it clear that they won't be used on that day's show but on a later date?
- Should you use premium rate numbers for listeners to call to register for a competition? Although this may pay for the prize, could listeners feel cheated? And could that feeling rebound on the station?
- If you run an on-air contest is it right to fake a winner if you discover all of the callers are regulars, in order to ensure that none of them gets the prize? Is it right to do so if you don't get any callers at all? Is it right to run a contest when the programme itself is pre-recorded and a 'winner' is announced later in that same show?
- If you don't get any callers, is it right to pretend you had a winner? Or should you admit you didn't get any response and say 'Thanks for your calls but as nobody got it right we'll roll the prize over to tomorrow', even though that is also not the real truth?
- Is knowingly putting three 'wrong' contestants to air before a 'right' caller a legitimate production technique to help build the tension and provide a touch of showbiz?
- Should the right answer be given as soon as someone gets it, or is it OK to save it until the end of the feature, while continuing to give out only the wrong guesses?
- Do the above only become a problem when you're making money off the calls/texts and therefore it's acceptable to do it as long as it's not profitable?

---

[48] Adapted from work by Paul Easton, radio consultant: http://tinyurl.com/ljw9sa.

20 Basic interviewing

**SKILLSET – NATIONAL OCCUPATIONAL STANDARDS
RADIO CONTENT CREATION**

Unit content included in this chapter:
RC6 Undertake research for radio
RC7 Work to a brief for radio content
RC18 Select and brief radio contributors
RC20 Assist with radio productions
RC21 Produce speech content for radio
RC30 Prepare for and conduct radio interviews

Preparation

This is the most important factor in getting a good interview.

> Sometimes you hear a radio interview with a celebrity and you
> hear more of the presenter than the star. I do a lot of big pop
> interviews and I prepare the same way as I would for TV . . . and
> keep it all in my head. An interview is a conversation with
> someone; so don't look down at your notes.
> Keep eye contact and you'll get a better interview.[1]

Get as much information as is appropriate, considering the time you have before the interview and its duration. You'll certainly want to write some questions to ask your guest. Some presenters say that doing this makes it more likely that they won't listen to the answers and simply work their way down the list. But although you should certainly not rely on a list of prepared questions, writing a list of key topics to be covered does several things:

- o   It forces you to think about the subject . . .
- o   and about the guest . . .
- o   and about the aim of the interview . . .
- o   and it gives you a safety net if the interview doesn't go according to plan, for example if either you or the guest clams up.

While you're drawing up the questions think about what you want to know the answer to, and what your listeners want to know the answers to. Don't be tempted to take the easy road by following the news release that the guest's publicity people sent you. Interviews are

[1] Katie Hill, presenter, Capital Radio, Radio Academy event, November 2005.

more interesting if they're inspired. Yes, you have to ask the obvious questions, but the successful presenter is the one who goes the extra mile, the one who asks the question no one else thought of and gets a terrific answer. Brainstorming is a helpful process for coming up with an initial list of questions. This is often done with your producer or other colleagues.

Questions should:

- Explore the story or topic. What is the purpose of the story? What does the audience need to know? What will listeners be interested in knowing?
- Add dimension to the obvious. 'Why?' questions are important. They open up room for exploration and can delve into what is not obvious.
- Provide different perspectives. Coming up with the list of interview questions may uncover a need to interview more than one person. For some interviews and stories, more than one perspective is needed.
- Paint the picture. Questions that ask the interview subject for description are important. They help listeners 'see' the story or message.
- Ensure the listeners are not left hanging. Wrap up questions, close loose ends and answer anything that is still unclear.
- Be short, simple and clear.

User-generated content is a great way of asking exactly the questions the audience wants to know the answers to. Opening an e-mail account to which listeners can post their questions, has several advantages:

- You can gauge the top talking topics in which most people are most interested.
- It's a great resource for some more 'left of centre' topics that you may not have considered.
- There's the opportunity for name checks for the listeners and the mention of local places.

What you're aiming for is the perception on air of a conversation, albeit one that you have prepared for. 'Structured spontaneity' if you will.

Before the interview

Chatting up or 'shampooing' your guest is a valuable thing to learn how to do. Don't give your guest a list of questions you'll ask, but do give them an idea of what *kind* of thing you want. They'll respond better if they're prepared but not rehearsed. You may though want to give them the first question in advance, one that you know they know the answer to, so they can get into their stride and 'warm up'. But don't make it too wide that they don't know where to start: 'You've just got back from your tour of America. Tell me about it.'

It's usually best not to have an in-depth discussion before you start your interview as it risks your guest saying, 'As I said before . . .'

The length of an interview

On a local music and speech station it's thought that each part of a conversation should last about the same length of a song, so about three minutes. You can then play a song and return to the guest for a second bite, but if you keep talking for more than a few minutes you stand the chance of driving away some of your listeners.

A BBC radio talks studio. Note the line of sight that a presenter would have with a producer in the control room; the small talkback unit on the presenter's desk and the green light which the producer will activate as a 'go' signal for the presenter to start talking

During the interview

5Ws and an H

The basic 'questioning words' are 'who', 'what', 'when', 'where', 'why' and 'how'. Each of them is used to get a different kind of fact about people, times and places and so on, but perhaps the most underused one is 'why'.

Starting a question with this word will often get your guest to explain themselves, and perhaps reveal a little about their motivation. Any question that gets a guest to open up in this way invariably makes good radio.

Clear questions

Under stress your guest may find it difficult to concentrate on what you're saying: they're in a strange environment and may never have heard or met you before, so make sure that your questions are straightforward. I don't mean that they should be short (although some of them may well be), but that they should be *clear*. Don't have long rambling questions: 'I wonder what you would say to some people who might think, or even say that, and in fact I think I've read that many people do in fact take this view, that this film, or indeed the last couple that you've made, haven't really been necessarily some of perhaps the best films of this type that, perhaps, could have been made with the budgets available at that time . . .'.

Don't ask more than one question at a time: 'Can you tell me how long it took you to swim the channel and how much money you raised . . . ?' Which one do you want them to answer first? And when they've done that, your guest may well have forgotten what the other question was!

Another problem for novice interviewers is that they ask questions that, although short and to the point, are simply too wide: 'This weekend's carnival, tell me about it.' OK, it's not really a question but most people would treat it as such and try to answer it. But where do they start? When it's on, what's going to be there, how long it took to plan, the problems they had getting the floats ready on time . . . ? Help your guest by giving them a little bit of focus.

Open and closed questions

Open questions are ones that encourage the guest to speak: 'How did you manage to stay up the flagpole for three days and nights?'

Open-ended questions are especially necessary when working with children, as closed questions will invariably illicit a simple 'yes' or 'no' response, although adults will give you a full answer, even if presented with a closed question.

Here are some question-starters to have up your sleeve the next time you speak with little Johnny or Josephine.

- Tell me about . . .
- Tell me how . . .
- What did you see . . .
- Describe it to me . . .
- What happened . . .
- How did that make you feel . . .

Closed questions are ones that may only get you a one-word answer – 'You were up the flagpole for three days?' – but can be used to pin down or focus the interviewee (if they can't stop talking, for example!). A good follow up for many one-answer questions is 'why?'.

Listen for your next question

Listen to what your guest is saying to give you a clue to your next question. This way the interview sounds more like a conversation.

> PRESENTER: So when did you become interested in music?
> GUEST: When I went to a Tibetan retreat for three years.
> PRESENTER: And why the oboe?

The presenter's completely missed a great follow-up question, which could have taken them in an exciting new direction. And that's probably the problem: the interviewer hasn't done enough homework to feel confident enough to leave their written list. They either feel as though they'll lose control of the interview or that they simply won't be able to get through all their prepared points.

Remember: it's not the quality of the questions you ask, it's the quality of the attention you give the answers.

QUESTIONS SHOULD FOLLOW A LOGICAL ORDER

Consider these guidelines:

The first question shouldn't be too deep, complex or broad because you run the risk of losing focus or control of the interview. Opening up questions might start with:

'Tell me more . . .'
'Take me back to the first time you . . .'

'What was going through your mind when . . .'

Core questions do not necessarily have to follow the chronology of events. You won't have time to cover everything, so focus your questions according to the key issues you want to address.

Follow-up questions are used when you want the guest to elaborate. The Magic Question is simply 'Why?'

Pinning-down questions might start with:
'What do you mean when you say . . . ?'
'Let's be more specific. Are you saying . . . ?'
'To recap . . . do you mean that . . . ?'

Closing questions wrap up the interview.

'What's your message to . . .' might work here.

You don't always need to ask your guest 'questions'.

Asking questions can sometime seem quite confrontational and can narrow conversations rather than open them up. Here are some other ways you can ask for information:

- Say what you want to know and why. 'Tell me how you came up with the idea in the first place: I still don't see how a grandmother could invent a revolutionary internet gizmo.'
- Ask them to elaborate on something they've already said. It shows you're interested in what they're talking about, and that alone should help them open up. 'Tell me more about your plans to tour south east Asia . . .'
- When they've only half said something, get them to tell you more: 'You say you're thinking of quitting your record label . . .'
- Ask open questions. Ask how they feel about something, their reaction to something, to comment on or talk about something else. We want someone who *reacts*, not just gives us *facts*.
- Focus on what effect the story will have on people's lives (remember *relatability*). Are there stories that can be told, or an example they can give rather than facts and figures? Is there a 'worst case scenario' that can be used to illustrate their point? Make the interviewee human. Invite the interview subject to give specific examples, experiences and stories. For example, 'Take us back to the first time you performed in public. What happened?'
- What's their opinion? How upset or cross are they? Or maybe they're pleased about a decision?

The more emotional the question, the more emotional the answer.

For example if you ask 'How did you meet your husband?' you will get information about the time and place.

If you ask 'When was it you knew you were in love?' the response will be a story.

Active listening

Effective listening will make interviewing easier, because it'll be more productive. You'll ask more incisive and pertinent questions, your interviewee will give better replies, and you'll end up with better audio. You need to listen with an open mind, not jumping to conclusions or anticipating what you think you're about to be told. Psychologists call this 'active listening'.

THE DIFFERENCE BETWEEN 'LISTENING' AND 'HEARING'[2]

Listening is active and emotional. You make a conscious effort to seek out the communication and understand what is being said. Listening means you know and care about the person and the message.

Hearing is passive and passionless. It happens without intention or interest. The communication has found you, and sound is merely background clutter. Hearing means you only care about your own interests at that moment.

Listen with genuine interest. There's also a difference between listening (and responding to what they've said) and 'waiting to talk' (thinking what you're going to say next).

We speak at around 150–200 wpm (words per minute), we can hear around 400 wpm and our brain can process upwards of 600 wpm.[3] So you'd think it would be easy to concentrate on what people are saying. Try to suspend your judgement until the person has stopped speaking, but while they are, reflect on what you're hearing and record it in your mind as a 'headline'. That way you'll end up with a mental list of bullet points.

Give the guest your attention. Don't start fiddling, cueing a song – pay attention and practise SOLER.

- **S**it up straight.
- **O**pen posture (arms and legs uncrossed).
- **L**ooking genuinely interested, listening attentively.
- **E**ffective eye contact.
- **R**emaining relatively relaxed.

Coach your guest

Inexperienced interviewees may need a little coaching to put them at their ease. They may forget what point they want to get across, be unsure where they're heading with a sentence, or talk for a long time but not actually say anything.

If someone's story is vague or dull, work hard for clarity and interest. If you want them to sound upbeat and lively, tell them (off air!). If you do it politely and diplomatically they'll invariably co-operate. They'll take it that you're as much an expert in your

---

[2] A *Sunday Times* article on the difference between listening ('means concentrating') and hearing ('just to catch it'): http://tinyurl.com/m93ce3.

[3] Carolyn B. Thompson, *Interviewing Techniques for Managers* (McGraw-Hill, 2002): http://tinyurl.com/nxgy74.

field as they are in theirs. (You're doing them a favour — they don't want to sound like a 'suit' do they?)

Ask them how they'd explain their story to the man or woman on the street. Remember, if *you* don't understand what they're talking about, with the benefit of your research and a distraction-free studio, what chance has someone listening at home with a crying baby, or someone trying to negotiate the rush hour traffic in the car?

You'll also get a better performance from a guest by getting them to, unwittingly, 'voice-match' you. So, if you speak to them in a bright and breezy way, with a lively attitude, and calling them by their first name, they in turn will give a much more lively interview. If you speak with a slow and quiet voice they will come down to match it.

Interview clips

If you're doing a news interview, the newsroom won't want your voice recorded at all. You'll have to keep quiet during the answers, so there's not a 'yep', 'uh huh', 'OK, I see' all the way through, which would be distracting to the listener when the clip is played in the bulletin. This is most unlike normal life where we're encouraged to keep giving signals to show we understand what's being said. Instead use non-verbal communication: keep eye contact with the interviewee, without staring them out; look in tune with what they're talking about — look serious when they're saying something serious, raise your eyebrows and start to smile when they're telling a humorous story; nod from time to time, to indicate that you're keeping up with what they're telling you.

Reflect their answers back to them

Your guest will be much more assured that the interview's going well and they're giving you what you want, if you pick up on what's said, and feed it back to them. 'So, what you're saying is that if everyone in the county donated a tea bag each, we'd be able to save the Hairy Mountain Gorilla from extinction?' It all helps to nudge the conversation along.

You can use phrases such as, 'That sounds important to you' or 'I'd like to know more about that' to show interest and encourage them.

Leave room

Don't feel obliged to jump in with the next question immediately after they've stopped talking. Staying quiet for a few seconds may just nudge them that little bit further to open up a little bit more. People hate silence, and the interviewee will feel as though it's 'their' silence and one that they should fill by talking a little more.

Signpost some of your questions

Your stream of questions should progress in a logical and ordered, albeit conversational, way. If they don't then you need to signpost the fact, both for the interviewee and the listener. 'On a different subject, how's the family . . . ?'

Handling the answers
- If the answer is too long . . . ask them to summarise it . . . interrupt and redirect them.
- If the answer is unclear . . . ask them it again in smaller parts.
- If the answer is going off track . . . interrupt and redirect them.

> o If the answer is evasive . . . come back to it later . . . or put it another way . . . or
> purposefully misunderstand it ('So what you're saying is . . .', 'No! I'm saying that . . .').

An interviewer should be responsive but does not steal the spotlight or use the interview to show how clever they are. If it is necessary to interrupt the interviewee, do it with a smile as they take a breath. Try not to raise the volume or pitch of your voice. Do not talk over what they are saying as it sounds aggressive.

Celebrity interviews

Most celebrities want a conversation. Start off by putting them at their ease and in the mood to have good time. Grab listeners' attention first off, with a question that's not too deep ('How did you get your first record produced . . . ?'). Avoid cliché questions, but instead ask quirky ones – perhaps ones suggested by listeners.

Interviewing politicians

Remember you represent the listeners. You're working for them. You have the opportunity to ask the questions that they want answered. Be polite but not deferential or too afraid to ask the tough questions or to follow up or challenge them.

Your job is to entertain, and to give your listeners what they want. They can't ask the tough questions, they want you to do it for them. And they want you to make sure the politician answers it, or for you to highlight it when they don't.

When you ask the guest a question, it raises an expectation in the listener for an answer. If the answer doesn't come they feel at best unsatisfied, at worst cheated. Listen, and if they don't answer the question, rephrase it and ask it again.

Two sugars

If you present your interview in short bursts with music in between you may be in a studio having an off-air conversation with your guest for the best part of 15 minutes before they're re-introduced to the listener. That's fine if the guest is interesting and you can easily make small talk, but you may feel your very life force being drained out of you if they're not.

You can busy yourself for a few of those minutes by explaining the desk and the equipment to them, then spend a while cueing the next song or checking the travel presenter is ready. Beyond that you may find that you have to ask them off air what you are later going to be asking them on air! To avoid this happening (and risking them saying later, 'As I said to you before . . .') you may want to set up a secret signal with your producer. A call on the talkback to ask for a coffee for the guest and one for me 'with two sugars' (when you usually don't take any) may be a signal for them to come in and either talk to you about an important programming issue or to join in the small-talk with the guest. One thing you can't do, of course, is to leave the guest alone in an on-air studio!

Remember to TALK

> o *Technical* – Don't get so engrossed in the conversation that you forget the technical
> aspects of your broadcast. For example, are the levels still OK? Has the guest moved
> away form the mic as they became more relaxed? (Never give them control of a
> hand-held mic, as you'll lose control of the conversation!) What about the pans? What
> about the timing of the sequence: are you on time for the travel news? How long

have you been speaking for in this segment of talk? Is there enough, or too much of interest to keep this guest for the allotted time? If not, how will you fill it?

▫ *Aims* – Also keep considering what you wanted to get out of the interview in the first place. Are you still heading in that direction and staying on course? There may be situations where a guest says something so interesting that you decide to veer away from your planned question areas to investigate another train of thought. Usually that's OK, but not necessarily always. If you do change course, think how you may want to get back on track to end the interview where you had intended.

▫ *Listener* – Don't forget them while all this is going on. What's actually coming out of the radio? Has the interview got a bit incestuous (you and the guest talking about 'in' subjects which exclude the audience)? Is the conversation flowing logically? Are there too many breaks and are they in sensible places? Is the listener getting from the conversation what they were promised, or what they expected, or is there a little bit more? (Maybe a surprise revelation or personal anecdote.) Don't forget to occasionally re-establish the name of the station and who the guest is, for new listeners who are joining all the time. This is particularly important if there are several guests. This is known as 'through-announcing', and is particularly important for 'late joiners' to the show to find out who is talking, their title or position (and so, what their specialist knowledge is) so they can make more of a personal connection . . . and listen longer.

▫ *Kill* – What are you going to do when the interview ends? Will you merely thank the guest, or do a summary of the conversation, or mention their book or song again? (This is 'back announcing'). Then what happens? Have you got the next item cued? And what about the item after that (you'll inevitably spend a minute or so thanking the guest off air and saying goodbye)? If you're going to go straight into another speech segment, how will this sound to the listener? If that item is travel, from a remote studio, how will you be able to dial them up and check the line and presenter's name if you're talking on air yourself?

At the end of the interview

Know when to start bringing the conversation to a close. Do it as naturally as possible. Don't say: 'Well, I'm afraid we have to stop there. We've run out of time.' The interviewee and the listeners will feel cheated, and you'll sound unprofessional. When you're nearing the end of the interview, don't say '. . . and finally'. The guest may give such a great answer that you *have* to follow it up! If you do say '. . . and finally' in a pre-recorded interview, perhaps to signify to a nervous interviewee that you are nearly done, make sure you leave a short pause at the end of those two words, for easy editing. Saying 'briefly . . .' or 'one last thing . . .' will also signify to the interviewee that you're nearly finished.

Finish the interview on a high note. Most people will remember how it started and how it ended, rather than the bit in the middle. Thank the person you interviewed simply; don't go overboard.

Copies of interviews

It's very unlikely that you'll ever provide these at your station. It's usually an awful lot of time and trouble to locate the ROT on the logger and dupe ('duplicate' or 'dub') it across and resave as an MP3 or put onto a CD, and usually it is only done if the request comes from a valued contact.

There are various ways you can get out of agreeing to dub off a copy:

- 'If you'd asked before I could've recorded it as it was broadcast.'
- 'Oh no. Didn't you ask a friend to record it for you at home?'
- 'I'm sorry, we don't keep copies of the interviews once they've gone out.'
- 'We're so high-tech here, you know we don't even use cassettes, so I can't dub off a copy for you.'
- 'You can listen again to the programme on our website/podcast.'
- Or even: 'I'm so sorry it's been broadcast now and we don't have any copies. Though there is a theory that all radio and TV waves go out into space and it's only a matter of time before they come back.'[4]

---

[4] This idea is one that scientists seem to agree on: that radio shows from the 1920s are coursing through space at around 186,000 miles per second. And if space is curved as is thought and one day we work out how to travel faster than light, we'll be able to hear them all over again!

21 The phone-in[1]

As the content of music radio becomes increasingly similar, it's what is said in between the songs (or instead of them) that will help keep people listening. When The Black Eyed Peas can be heard on any number of outlets (including your own personally scheduled iPod), it's the experiences and anecdotes of a phone-in presenter and their callers (other people like you) that are potentially more engaging.

Going round the LA Talk Radio stations a few years ago, they told me how the Talk format started up. About 15 years ago the big radio chains had bought up all the independent music stations, but were still looking for more acquisitions. They knew music was a winner on air, but the only stations still to buy were AM speech licences. So they bought a few to find out how they worked. They decided the stations had too many people working on each programme and that their main objective was to fill their running orders with items rather than to grab listeners and hold them. They felt the broadcasters were a smug bunch, positioning themselves above their listener, and the experts were even more remote. The output was authentic 'speech' programming: interviews, round table discussions about issues, an author explaining their book etc. It was expensive to do and not enough people listened. So they started to pull over some of their more experienced disc jockeys and put this to them: do a four-hour rock-and-roll show but without the music. Talk about the themes that make rock music popular: love, conflict, growing up and life in general. Sure talk about Bill Clinton, but not his fiscal policy, talk

[1] Phone-in programmes in some countries, notably Australia and New Zealand, are known as 'talkback shows'. There is a spoof radio phone-in on the BBC called *Down The Line*: http://tinyurl.com/ny3556 (hear examples at http://tinyurl.com/lrzbcz and http://tinyurl.com/q7orrh).

about whether he's a rat. Talk about things that people talk about amongst themselves and talk about them with your listeners, not 'experts'. And talk about them the way normal people talk about them. Audiences rose and overheads went down.[2]

Presenting a phone-in

Phone-ins are:

- *Cheap* – all you really need is a presenter and a producer (who are rather more than their colloquial title 'phone flicker' might suggest) to take the calls. In fact often the presenter takes their own calls while a song is playing.
- *Democratising* – the vast majority of listeners will have a phone at home, most will have a mobile as well and that means that any of them can get on air with their comment or issue.
- *Involving* – the station becomes a forum, a place where people can share their views in the community.
- *Flexible* – you can get instant reaction to the day's news from listeners, experts and those in power.
- *Informative* – with an expert in the studio callers can have access to information on everything from piles to postcards.
- *A way to get local people on air* – there's a chance for people to debate and be heard talking about local issues in local accents.
- *A place to challenge* – those in power such as politicians and councillors, the mayor or even the prime minister, can be put on the spot.
- *Not just for the callers* – the presenter and the producer should also consider those at home. What's the listener getting from this call, or this programme? You're there for those who call and those who don't.
- *Popular with listeners* – with a strong but even-handed host, phone-ins are some of the most popular shows on radio.
- *Difficult to do well.*

Commercial Radio pioneered the listener phone-in and today's stations broadcast, on average, over two hours of phone-ins per week. Adult Contemporary and Contemporary Hits Radio both exceed this total, hosting two and a half hours and over four hours of phone-ins on a weekly basis. This interaction with the listener is one of radio's key strengths, and enhances the community of listeners that radio stations naturally cultivate. [3]

Types of phone-in

These can be categorised as 'open' in various respects:

- *Open line* – these are the type often heard on BBC local stations' mid-morning shows where the presenter sets up three or four talking topics to be discussed and

[2] Tommy Boyd, presenter, BBC SCR, *The Radio Magazine*, 15 June 2005.
[3] In the RadioCentre's document *Action Stations*: http://tinyurl.com/lcghe5.

then opens the lines for callers' contributions. A completely open open line, where you take calls on all the subjects throughout the show, and in any order, may cause problems. Listeners could call with any comment on any issue at any time. That could either make for a lively and reactive discussion, or perhaps one that's confusing and disjointed. It would mean that you, the host, would have to be light-footed to jump from one issue to another. You'll have to continually explain the topic before each few calls as many listeners will have tuned in after the initial 'menu' has been presented.

o   *Open door* – an expert, (perhaps a doctor, a gardener, a job adviser or a collector of old records) is invited into the studio to take calls and questions from listeners. Although this type of show is a service for those who've called, it's particularly important to keep the programme relevant to those at home too. This is why many presenters introduce the expert and have a brief chat with them, but have listeners' questions taken off air. The show can then continue with its usual features and music, with the expert returning to the studio later in the programme to highlight any particularly interesting calls. Certain experts, for example a doctor or solicitor, should be wary of offering too much specific advice over the phone, as they won't have seen the patient's notes or read the background to their legal case. Other so-called experts should be warned about promoting their own private interests over those of the listener: '. . . well, I'd have to see it to give an accurate valuation. Why not pop into my shop at 35 The High Street . . .'.

o   *Open minded*[4] – many stations have programmes that are based around personal, emotional or sexual matters. Callers either phone with their own stories on a specific subject, or put a question to the host or to a panel of experts (perhaps a doctor and a relationship adviser) for their advice. Many of these shows are quite frank and are naturally scheduled in the evening. Unlike TV stations, radio doesn't have a specific 9 pm watershed after which more adult material can be broadcast, although most stations would take that time as a good guideline.

o   *Open ended* – these types of phone-in are increasingly popular, adding 'user-generated content' to the output. Although it's similar to the open line mentioned above, the topics thrown out to the audience to respond to are not hard news stories inviting opinion, but rather quirky subjects inviting personal anecdotes, and are much a part of music radio as speech radio. The subject may be running throughout a whole show, with calls taken between music, travel and news. And those subjects and the calls that arise from them are invariably diverse and creative. 'Have you ever been bitten by an animal?' 'Can you do an impression of someone that only you know?', 'When clothes attack their owners . . .'

All of the above formats are slightly different in their content, but they share common elements: the careful combination of time of day, presenter and topic. A lot of this will be determined by the overall station style (a gardening programme is unlikely to work on a station with a chart-based format because the target audiences are different). Other elements are much more subtle, but are for the same ends – maximising the audience.

---

[4] Judith Monaghan, Annette Shuh Wah, Ian Stewart and Leigh Smith, 'The Role of Talkback Radio: A study', *The Journal of Community Psychology* vol. 6, Issue 4 (2006): 357–6.

The phone-in presenter

If you want to get into radio but feel as though you don't know enough about music to be a music show presenter and anyway, you talk too much and have an opinion on everything, why not consider becoming a phone-in host?

> Good talk radio needs a host with gravitas, personality, intelligence and imagination. On top of that the extras amount to nothing more extravagant than a switchboard, a good tech/phone op, e-mail and text interaction, and maybe some newspapers. Good talk radio can be done economically in this country . . . our friends in the USA do it very successfully with nothing more than the resources I've outlined, and in some cases even less.[5]

Vanessa Feltz presenting her award-winning phone-in show. Courtesy: BBC London 94.9

You'll need:

- A good general knowledge.
- An opinion on virtually everything.
- To be able to talk knowledgably and entertainingly.
- Passion and an ability to argue any point with authority.
- An interest in what's going on and, especially for local radio, an interest in local news.
- Inquisitiveness, so you can see questions that need answers on a subject which is new to you.
- To be fast and sure of foot – so you can think, talk and act on your feet.
- A good working legal knowledge – the next caller could say something libellous and you need to know how to react.
- An ability to be abrupt, or even rude, if the occasion demands (such as a caller who won't get to the point or refuses to answer the question).

[5] Duncan Barkes, head of presentation, Spirit FM, *The Radio Magazine*, October 2004.

Some presenters of phone-ins are fence sitters, or 'conductors' of the various sides of the debate amongst listeners, and don't get involved with airing their own thoughts. Others know exactly where they stand:

I have never, ever been impartial because as a talk show host, you can't say 'on one hand there's this, on the other hand there's that' . . . I don't want to be anodyne like that.[6]

There's a place for both styles. Some stations want a host who can field calls from all comers and be a referee, while others prefer someone to be more confrontational and controversial – to say something that will stir up some emotion from listeners.

PERSONAL OPINIONS

They can get you in to trouble, but they're essential if you're going to come over as real.

Always make it clear, either at the time or over time, that you're not putting down someone with another view to you.

There are, after all, very few topics for which there aren't intelligent, right-minded, normal, caring, thinking people (just like you) on *both* sides.

Unless you're dealing with child-molesting or wife-beating, what you're offering is no more than an observation, a personal thought, a response . . . rather than The Truth.

You're not there to 'preach', but if all you do is utter pleasantries and platitudes, there's a machine that can do it better than you.

A good talker is not necessarily a good phone-in presenter. They have to listen and communicate too. And a good thoughtful and considerate listener is not necessarily a good phone-in presenter either, if they can't talk.

Great speech radio doesn't come from callers constantly agreeing with the host, the best moments are when there's conflict and tension. If you can't deal with that, or you try to resolve it by shouting and then cutting people off immediately, then you just haven't got what it takes.[7]

---

[6] Jon Gaunt, presenter, talkSPORT, *The Radio Magazine*, October 2005.
[7] Iain Lee, presenter Absolute Radio, *The Radio Magazine*, July 2008.

The phone number

Only give out the phone number, text number or e-mail address if there's a reason, not just as a verbal crutch to give you time to think of what to say next. It's pointless and makes you sound desperate. When presenting a phone in, there *is* a reason and you need to give it out regularly.

There will probably be a certain way you read the studio number. Often it's because the collection of digits has a certain ring to it, or because the number has been specifically chosen as it includes the radio station's frequency (LBC 97.3 is 0870 60 60 973). And it's always because the management team wants everyone to say the number in the same way for consistency, so the audience easily remembers it. For LBC the number is written up in the studio so everyone pronounces it the same way: oh-8-7-oh 6-oh 6-oh 9-7-3, rather than 'sixty sixty sixty-seven three' or 'six hundred and seventy-three'. Such detail should be written in the station's house style guide. (At the time of writing 0870 numbers cost around 6p a minute to call from a BT landline, and that allows stations to receive a share of the revenue generated from calls – providing extra revenue. BBC stations now use cheaper numbers starting 0370 which are included in mobile phones' free-minutes allowances.)

> We want our audience to be able to call us at the lowest cost. It's about being clear with the audience. It's saying we're on their side and we're not going to rip them off.[8]

You can easily confuse listeners by giving out too many phone numbers and web addresses. Try to stick to just your phone-in and travel line number, your text number and your own web address. Other information can be posted on this site, which saves you reading out details on air, saves the listener rushing for a pen, and drives listeners to your station site which will please the advertisers who are featured on it.

CHOICE PARALAYSIS

This marketing theory suggests that too many options can lead to information overload.

It seems logical that if you give listeners a choice of ways to get in touch with the station, they'll be more likely to contact you because it's more likely there'll be a method (e-mail, text, phone, carrier pigeon, semaphore) that they're most comfortable with. But that puts a decision in the way of their desire to contact you.

Choose one mode of response and push that only. If you suggest to listeners of a phone-in (the clue's in the name) that they can also text or e-mail, you limit the number of people who you can put on air (a certain number of potential 'callers' will choose to text instead) and the number of people you can put to air will drop as a result.

---

[8] Michael Stock, BBC head of business and partnerships, *The Radio Magazine*, July 2008.

> Don't use new technology to deliberately distance yourself from your listener.

Choosing topics

In a news and comment phone-in the topics have to be carefully considered. Setting up a discussion by the presenter may sound spontaneous but a lot of thought goes into each programme.

The ten steps to top topics:

1. What are today's hot topics?[9]
2. What are people talking about today?[10]
3. Which ones are relevant for our listeners?
4. More specifically, do our target listeners *care*?[11]
5. Do enough care enough to call and have a busy show?[12]
6. Is the topic easy to debate without getting bogged down in detail?
7. Is the presenter genuinely interested enough to encourage and engage callers?[13]
8. Will people talk from personal experience, not just have a knee-jerk reaction?[14]
9. What strong emotions does the topic deliver to engage and encourage listeners?[15]
10. Is there a good mix of topics? National and local, light and shade, serious and fluffy?

> Do you do a poor programme with the topic you think listeners want to hear, or do you do a good programme with a topic that you personally are interested in?
>
> Remember people are tuning in to hear you. And if you're not connected with a topic, that will come over and it won't make good radio.
>
> If you care, you'll communicate . . . making it interesting and entertaining.

---

[9] Obviously make sure you're listening to the news, but don't fall into the trap of merely opening the phone lines and letting people comment on the stories. Think whether there's an underlying trend or cause of what's happened, can you take the story on? For example, if there's been a road accident on a winter's morning you could ask why people don't clear their screens properly, all for the sake of saving five minutes.

[10] There are two subjects people will talk about forever: the weather and the best route to get somewhere. But those topics wouldn't make a good phone-in.

[11] You should consider not just those who are listening but also those who you want to listen longer. What topics will attract them to listen and call?

[12] The more callers you have to choose from, the higher you can raise the quality of those who get on air.

[13] If you, the presenter, are interested by the item, then you can make it interesting and listeners will be interested as a result.

[14] The people who have knee-jerk reactions are usually jerks themselves.

[15] Those emotions may be fury or frustration, but they may also be humour and happiness. Show the audience you care about the community by spending time explaining in a clear and compelling way the good stories as well as the bad.

Ask yourself how you would do an item different from anyone else. What is your personal take, your personal experience or viewpoint that no one else can attempt to replicate? Your 'point of difference'.

Don't put a boring story in as a phone-in topic, just because it's a big story. If everyone else is talking about it, consider whether you want to as well. You may want to – you don't want to be left out – but can you add any more to the discussion? Can your listeners? Do you have a unique view? Focus and keep it fresh.

Know your position and know your opinion.

> How dare you not be honest with them as they are with you? It would be fundamentally unfair. The great jocks aren't shock ones; they're the ones who give something of themselves. But all the same, you've got to have impact.[16]

It's a humbling experience to admit that you don't know and most talk show presenters are not humble. One of them is Jon Gaunt, BBC London, talkSPORT and new host on the *Sun*'s internet station. He's strong-minded and opinionated. But occasionally he'll admit that he doesn't know what to think about a subject. 'Call me and let me know what you think, because I really don't know' is a line that you (occasionally) heard on his phone-in show. As a presenter, don't be afraid to admit that you don't know something. Better ignorance than arrogance. It shows you're human and it shows that you're telling the truth – and the truth is easier to remember than an artificial and controversial standpoint the next time that same subject comes up.

Don't always take the predictable view. If you make listeners listen (rather than merely 'hear') and react, they'll remember. If you're always the same it'll be in one ear and out the other. Be predictably unpredictable, and yet consistent.[17]

Don't try to be something you're not when presenting a phone-in. Listeners and callers can spot a fraud a mile off, and don't like it when they do. (Although of course you can't say how you vote, or what you think about a wide range of highly controversial topics.) When there appears to be a wide consensus on one point of view, say so. If nearly all the text messages are on one side of an argument rather than the other, say so. And if you can express a point of view on matters which are far less controversial like football teams you support, then say so. In other words, appear rounded and interesting and provocative and the sort of person people might want to go for a drink with but don't let party politics show through.

It's a difficult balance to strike but getting that balance right produces something better to listen to and engage with than a shock-jock who rams his or her beliefs down the listener's throat every day.

Although you should always be true to your on-air character, occasionally surprise people with your angle or your view.

> The balance is always between the obvious and the inspiring – we can't miss out the biggest story of the day, but how can we

[16] Jon Gaunt, talkSPORT Radio Academy Speech Radio conference, 2005.

[17] You shouldn't regularly change your view on individual stories or situations for no apparent reason, although you could have unpredictable and differing views on, say, capital punishment and abortion.

surprise our listeners? Once they guess our choice of stories and approach we're dead.[18]

Make the talking topics and the way you present them, personal, and you become more relatable.

Opinions and experiences

Topics which ask people for opinions often produce less-good radio than if you ask for their *actual experiences*. Opinions are often poorly thought through, whereas experiences are (by definition) real, more emotional and compelling: people talk more convincingly and knowledgeably when they speak from the heart.

[Pat Loughrey, BBC director of nations and regions] wants to change the radio phone-in that he says too often presents ill-informed opinion instead of listeners' experiences.[19]

You'll encourage opinions by using phrases such as, 'What do you *think* about this?'; you'll get a better reaction if you ask listeners directly for their stories, how something has affected them or about how they *feel* about something. The more personal a story, the more universal and relatable it is.

I'm not a great fan of interviews in the traditional sense. Too often they just produce predictable answers and plugs for this book or that film. To me, real people with real stories and opinions make for interesting radio.[20]

THE THREE LEVELS OF COMMUNICATION

OBJECTS

We talk about tangible material things, many of which we can touch and pick up. The truth of an object is independent of people, it exists whether we are there or not.

CONCEPTS

We talk about ideas and thoughts we have had, which can be accepted or rejected. When people hear others' views, they are received as concepts, interpreted and evaluated: one reason why communication is so difficult.

---

[18] Jeremy Vine, presenter, BBC Radio 2, *The Radio Magazine*, 6 April 2005.
[19] *Ariel*, 13 December 2005.
[20] Clive Bull, presenter, LBC 97.3, *The Radio Magazine*, April 2005.

EXPERIENCES

At the this level, we talk about the experiences we have had. When two people talk about a common experience, they refer to the same objects, but may have different feelings about them. This is a common source of conversation, interest and maybe conflict. All of which makes good radio.

Consider how the listener will view the topic that you're discussing. That's *the listener*, not the caller. What are they likely to get out of the item? Will they get emotional, become angry, upset, frustrated? Is there 'social ammunition': information of value that they can use in conversations with other people? (Their 'show prep' for their *life*!)

Find the What's-In-It-For-Me Factor in every item to help focus and develop the item, and help keep callers calling *and* listeners listening.

As well as thinking of what stories to cover, also consider where they go in the programme and how much time they get. Balance your topics so you have a flow through the programme rather than a sudden gear change: people will stay with the station if one topic develops into another, but will turn off if it jars.

Most topics will start having equal time on your running order, but drop a topic if it's not hot, and stay with one that is. Plus, you may want to have a short ten-minute fun filler at the end of the show for people to react to: 'After the biggest jackpot win, what would you spend your millions on?'

Setting up the topics

At the start of the show (or even better, in the programme before) you need to tell people what topics are up for discussion and invite them to take part. This is sometimes called 'the churn'. There's certainly an argument for mentioning the topics together at the start of the show, but then having a running order in which you introduce them and the callers' comments on them, in depth. That gives the listener a feeling for the show at the start, and teases them with issues that'll be discussed later, and time to start considering their own thoughts and feelings before being discussed on air. You simply follow the initial churn with '. . . but first I'd love your thoughts on this . . .'.

- The laundry list – this is the most straightforward way of mentioning the items. A simple list of fact followed by invitation: 'Train fares are going up again. What do you think? Call me on . . .' . You could get through your whole list of four or five topics in less than a minute. The trouble is that saying, 'Here's something you may want to talk about' is weak and isn't making an attempt to engage or entice. You don't say in real life 'Here's a topic for us to talk about'!

◀ ACTUAL AUDIO

PRESENTER: Tonight we're going to talk about communication . . . have you ever had good or bad experiences . . . let me know.

BBC local station, December 2005

o   The flip flop – as above, but it takes a little more time as you'll be giving the pros and the cons of each side of the issue: 'Train fares are going up again. Companies say they need the extra revenue to improve services, but passengers' groups say there's been no obvious improvement since the last round of rises. Are you prepared to pay for a better service, and who do you think should be keeping an eye on the companies to make sure that passengers get what they pay for?'

ACQUIESCENCE EFFECT

When asked a question by another person, our answer is based not just on a rational consideration of what is being asked. What are called *identity needs* lead us to consider how we will appear to others. So, we tend to answer more in the positive than the negative, particularly when the questioner seems to be a superior in some way (perhaps in a radio presenter/listener relationship), or when answering the question fully seems like hard work.

So, people tend to agree with one-sided statements. They will also agree with two contradictory statements when they are framed for agreement. If you asked 'Do you think the government makes mistakes?', most people will say yes. If you asked whether the government generally gets it right, you may also get agreement.

These are *leading questions*, used to get people to think in a certain way and then agree with you.

Leading questions either include the answer, point the listener in a certain direction or include some form of carrot or stick to send them to the 'right' answer. This may be by using the *assumption principle*, by moving the subject of the sentence: 'How much do you think prices will go up next year?' forcing the other person to think first and possibly exclusively about prices going up.

Leading questions are great if you're selling double-glazing, less good if you're a radio presenter and want a more honest response.

o   The personal view – this stall-setting takes longer still but is usually most effective. Launch into a monologue, perhaps of a minute or two, on your own personal thoughts and experiences of the issue. It may not be immediately clear from the opening what topic you're talking about, but that'll help draw in the listener who'll become intrigued by the story. Tease them with the topic, dangle the angle, paint a picture and get them to think about it (without specifically *asking* them to think about it). Then pose a question and ask for calls. Give people a reason to call not simply because you thought it would be a good topic of the day – that just makes you sound desperate! This personal connection will either rile or enthral the audience who'll be encouraged to call to support the compelling views or shoot them down in flames. This technique isn't an excuse for you to spout your views without taking calls and hearing what other people have to say. The callers are the stars, and the presenter presents the callers. It's a dialogue not a monologue. Don't become a 'we talk, you listen' station. Raise arguments, either by posing specific questions or by getting listeners to react and respond naturally to what you believe.

Just before closing each issue, do a bit of 'plate-spinning' and start inviting people to call and contribute for the next one so you'll have someone to speak with a few minutes later. Finally close down each topic with a summary of the issues and say that it's '. . . time to move on . . .'.

This is usually best done using the news or ad break as a natural 'book end'.

As well as choosing items that are relevant, interesting and compelling, make that fact obvious to those who are listening. Tell them why the issue might matter to them, why they might be concerned about it.

Help people to create images of your subject material in their mind:

Globalisation is having the effect of removing the immunity that Australians enjoyed as citizens of the Lucky Country. It's transforming the globe into a singular market place where the microeconomic cultures of the world are being subsumed into one macroculture. This, combined with the trend of lower protectionism, widespread deregulation and a more fragmented laissez faire labour market, has placed significant pressures on the Australian workforce. Futurist Dianne Cohen is my next guest and she argues that developing self-reliance could be a key strategy in countering the impact of the changing world of work.[21]

That paragraph is not very interesting or compelling, the meaning is confused, the language is cold, formal and abstract.

I hate to tell you this but your financial security is truly on the line. The global economy is setting up every company, every town, every region, every country into open competition with other countries, towns, regions and companies around the world. Isn't this a bit like the theory of evolution where this frenzy of competition will leave only the fittest standing? And will yours be one of them? What happens if your division is downsized, re-engineered, or sold off because it can't compete with some distant town you've never heard of? What can you do to prevent the cold winds of globalisation from freezing you out of a decent lifestyle? I want you to meet futurist Dianne Cohen, because she has a number of solutions that will allow you to place your security where it belongs: on your skills, abilities and the qualities within yourself that no amount of globalisation can take away.

[21] *Certificate IV in Broadcasting Radio*, Australian Broadcasting Corporation http://tinyurl.com/ljt9ys.

You'll discover some simple answers that can immunise you from the heartbreak of redundancy and the anxiety that comes with job insecurity . . .

This example is longer, but more easily understood, more emotional, more conversational and pictorial.

Another way is to make comments and then suggestions that trigger emotional reactions: 'Maybe there's something I'm missing' or 'Perhaps you can see something here that I don't' and give the phone number. Really useful responses are driven by an emotional reaction to something that's said, not manufactured topics or 'tell us your story' pleadings.[22] What you want to elicit are responses that lead to stories from callers, examples of what the subject you're talking about means in their lives. If you put things on the air in a way that avoids simple 'black or white' responses, you'll get your listener revealing part of their own life and that's a lot more interesting to hear and strikes more of an emotional resonance with other listeners.[23]

Traditionally, radio gets two guests each with a different view and asks them to 'battle it out' on air. More creatively (and given that many topics have more than two conveniently opposite points of view), vary the guests through the phone-in. Have one for the first 20 minutes, then have them replaced by another, then maybe no one, then both together. The arrival of a new guest can help refocus the callers and there's a fair chance that an entirely new batch of people might appear on the phone. Which makes for more interesting and unpredictable radio.

You could say throughout the show 'you're always welcome to call', or 'you can get hold of me at any time' or 'any time you want to comment on anything'. Doing this:

o extends the invitation to call (as you would to a friend)
o gives the number when it may be easier for someone to note it down or put in their mobile
o lets people know they can call, because you're accessible, they want to and they want a conversation.

Finally, remember that putting an item on the air that leans towards a 'yes' or 'no' response is not a topic. It's a poll.

We all know how simple it can be to get phones ringing if you pick easy and trivial subjects. Making speech radio that produces surprises and creates appointments to listen is more of a challenge.[24]

Resetting the topics

During the programme present the topic again (but don't reread it word for word) and include a précis of some of the comments you've already received, perhaps even recorded and clipped:

---

[22] . . . and therefore avoid this: http://tinyurl.com/kjrorm.
[23] Another tip: Don't say 'call us' or 'call Triple X Radio', say 'call me'. Make it personal.
[24] Sandy Warr, broadcaster and trainer, *The Radio Magazine*, October 2007.

We're talking about school dinners and whether enough's being done to make them as healthy as they should be. Earlier we heard from Elizabeth in Southtown who said that her children's school has won a healthy eating award for its dinners, but Mark in Kingston Wells, you think that the meals are as bad as ever . . .

Putting their comments in context like this helps those at home (and especially those who've just joined the show) follow what's going on. It's like a story-so-far reminder that TV shows have at the start of each new episode.

You can't control when listeners are tuning in and out of the station, so re-establish the topics so that new joiners feel included. If they feel included they're more likely to stick around! If you don't reset, you are sending the message that unless the listener has some prior knowledge or experience of the show, they're not qualified to listen.

APPROACHING ASSUMPTION ALERT

I'm new to the area, or don't often listen to this programme. I'm in the car and just turned the radio on. The 'scan' has landed on your station. I don't know what station it is, what the format is, or who you are. You have 30 seconds to explain . . .

If someone's just tuned in for the first time, will they understand who you are and what you're doing? Will you welcome them and explain? If you are making references to things that they don't understand, they will feel left out.

The approaching assumption alert is when presenters assume everyone knows what's going on.

Reset the stage every few minutes: mid way through an interview, between callers on a topic and so on.

If, after several mentions of a topic, no one is taking the bait, ask yourself why. Perhaps you wanted to cover the topic because *you* were interested in it rather than thinking about the listeners?

- Have you phrased the set-up in the most relevant and captivating way?
- Consider changing focus.
- Use another anecdote to illustrate your point.
- Add something new; don't just rehash what didn't work the first time.

If no one's calling about the topic, quietly drop it. Don't announce that you're dropping it or that no one's called about it so, 'you're obviously not interested'. Doing that shows your failure and if listeners don't care enough to call about it, they don't care enough to know that you're not running it any more!

The pressure to articulate an opinion, engage listeners on a subject and then take them on a journey with the material is a constant challenge. If you haven't honed your topic or done your prep, it shows and a blank switchboard will stare back at you.[25]

THE EVIDENCE PRINCIPLE

In an experiment,[26] a home shopping channel changed six words in one of its pitch segments and that simple change caused sales to skyrocket.

They changed the words 'Operators are waiting, please call now' to 'If operators are busy, please call again'.

That is, they signalled that operators were busy, not waiting. And that gave the impression the show was popular, with other callers (just like 'you at home').

This is using the Evidence Principle, where the proof of other people's interest in something makes it more popular, and by not getting involved one may miss out.

The callers

Let's be brutally honest, most people listen to a radio phone-in show for the host — not for the callers! Anecdotally, only a very small percentage of listeners ever pick up the phone to make a call (perhaps 1 per cent). The show is actually for everyone else who listens. The callers are there to make the presenter look good because of what they've said or how they've said it. A boring person is not going to do that. A boring person is like a boring song — it gets turned off. Just because someone calls, it doesn't mean that they have the right to get on air. If they're dull, don't add anything to the debate or don't fit your target demographic, don't put them on.

Instead you want callers who are going to talk meaningfully about their own experiences. Why what has happened has changed them, moved them or made them what they are.

I'm not that interested in caller's opinions. To be honest, I couldn't care less what Doris in Ongar thinks about anti-social behaviour but if she can offer me a genuine insight into how it affects her life then I'll bite her arm off. I remember a lady who called in two hours after changing the locks on her flat because her 18-year-old had started stealing off her 12-year-old to buy drugs and she felt a failure. I was asking people about the best news they'd ever

[25] David Prever, presenter, TalkSPORT, The Radio Magazine, December 2008.
[26] Quoted in Noah Goldstein, Steve Martin and Robert Cialdini, *Yes! 50 Scientifically Proven Ways to be Persuasive* (Free Press, 2008): http://tinyurl.com/phmhxq.

received over the phone and a dad phoned in to tell us about the call he got to say that his daughter's leukaemia had gone. He said 'I'm six foot three and built like a brick outhouse but I can't think of this without wanting to cry.' He promptly burst into tears and I bet he wasn't the only one. Another example if you like, of stories being much more powerful than opinions.[27]

A good caller is relevant, interesting, funny, poignant or has a story to tell. They add to a show and make it better. Remember, not everyone who has *done* something interesting, *is* interesting.

Obviously the first thing is to answer the phone with an agreed phrase. It's very unlikely to be purely 'Hello?' but may be 'Hello . . .' together with the name of the station or the programme name. It's probably best to then get straight to the point and ask, without a beat, '. . . What's your point/question?'

Then go through this mental checklist of questions every screener should ask themselves:

1. Is their comment new or a rehash of what you've heard already? If it's new, and especially if they disagree with the presenter's view or most of the other callers, put them on. A strongly voiced and controversial view makes good radio.
2. Is their comment clear and valid? Most people aren't that interesting.
3. Do they add to the geographical mix of callers you've had so far in the programme? If they widen the net and especially if they're from part of the area you rarely hear from, they're more likely to get on, even with a weaker point. If they're from outside your area (even if they do listen on the internet) you probably don't want them on your local station unless their point is exceptional.
4. If your station covers a wide area, does this person add another accent to the mix? You may want to 'bump up' callers who fulfil these criteria.

The call screening area. Courtesy: BBC London 94.9

---

[27] James O'Brien, LBC 97.3, *The Radio Magazine*, September 2005.

5. Is it a woman? A senior phone-in producer at the BBC says fewer women call their show, so when they do, they stand a better chance of getting on.

6. Are they part of your target age bracket? Are they old enough to have knowledge of this subject?

7. Is the line quality clear? If they're on a walkabout home-phone, speakerphone or a crackly mobile they may not be any good.

8. Are they using the phone properly? Many people either have the mouthpiece too close to their mouth which causes distortion, or tucked under their chin which makes them sound distant and muffled.

9. Are they new? Some stations have specific 'first-time caller days' to encourage those who are usually put off from calling by hearing the same voices time and time again. First timers add new voices, new experiences and new perspectives and that helps keep the show fresh.

10. Are they legal? If they're driving they have to be on a hands-free.

11. Are they standing? During the period pending an election, check that they aren't a candidate, or if they are, that they aren't going to say anything political (see more in the chapter on the law).

Don't let the tail wag the dog. Too many calls go to air to satisfy the caller or to fill time on the show, rather than for the benefit of the show or the audience as a whole.

It's a self-fulfilling prophesy: each time you put a great call to air it teaches other listeners what they have to do if *they* want to get on. And vice versa.

The best way to get great on-air calls is to air great calls.

If you put a bad call up, it won't give you another caller.[28]

If the caller is vague, your producer should work for clarity. Ask exactly what point they want to make: it helps focus their mind and structure their thoughts and helps them both discover what their viewpoint is. That way they're better able to say it succinctly if you decide to put them through. If they give a great reply or use a sentence that's enthusiastic, funny or outrageous, then ask that they say that again when they're on air.

Too often on the radio we hear something like this:

PRESENTER: And on line 3 it's Larry in Lastownonearth. Hi Larry, how are you?
LARRY: Oh, not very well, it's my corns . . .

Or

PRESENTER: Here's Larry from Lastownonearth. Hi Larry, what are you up to this afternoon?
LARRY: I'm just rehearsing my lines for my first recording of *EastEnders* tomorrow . . .
PRESENTER: Great! So what do *you* think about rail fares?

---

[28] Jon Gaunt, presenter, Radio Academy Speech Radio conference, 2005.

The producer should chat up the caller and find out what's interesting about them before they're put on air. The presenter should listen to the answer when they ask a question! It is their job as ringmaster to make the audience (the 'performing animals') perform to the best of their ability, to provide an entertaining show for the rest of the audience.

If they sound good, you and your show does too. You can bask in the reflected glory. Other listeners will begin to understand what's expected from them should they ever phone in.

Don't just process them . . . prepare them for their 'star turn' in the hope that they'll perform better. Phone-in listeners do your show for you. But only if you explain how you want it done.

> Some people ring in 50 times to get through, wait 50 minutes to get on air, and then have absolutely nothing interesting to say.[29]

Now take their name, if necessary, phonetically. It may be unusual or foreign, or even one that can be misread. That way, the presenter will introduce Sean as 'shawn' rather than 'seen', and won't stumble when they suddenly see the caller is 'Gugulethu'. You're not embarrassed and neither is she. It's insulting to hear unusual names followed by 'I hope that's how you say it . . .'. If someone's texted in, you have their number, call them back and check how they say their name.

Additionally note, again if necessary, if the caller is a man or woman. It may be that it's a man with a high voice and you don't want them to be embarrassed on air. It may be that you can't remember whether Leslie is the man's or woman's spelling of that name, and want to make sure that the presenter doesn't cross to them with an unfortunate remark.

And take their number:

- You may want to call them back to check that they are who they say they are.
- You want them later in the show, rather than right now.
- Taking their number sieves out the cranks who're dissuaded from calling.
- If someone malicious does get through to the programme, you have their number in case any follow-up is needed.

Once you've decided the caller will make it on air, tell them:

- To speak up.
- To make their point succinctly.
- To call the presenter by their name.

Ask the caller to make sure their radio is off and to listen down the phone for them being introduced. This is because if a station was in delay, they'd be introduced in 'real time' several seconds before they heard their name on the radio. Even if the station's not in delay, there's still a split second between being spoken to on the phone and hearing it on the radio which causes confusion. Plus there's always the possibility of howl-round feedback.

> All radios must be turned off . . . nice and lively . . . straight to the point . . . we could come to you at any time.[30]

---

[29] Adrian Chiles, presenter, Five Live, *The Times*, May 2006.
[30] The phone producer's mantra.

Warn the caller they'll simply be cut off at the end of the conversation (in other words they won't be handed back to you), so thank them in advance for their call.

Pass the caller's name and town through to the presenter together with what line number they're on. Do this via the shared computer system (a 'visual talkback') that can be seen in the studio. It may be that the presenter takes the calls sequentially or maybe out of order, and they can do that if they know where each contributor is on the phone-in panel. Also let the presenter know if the caller has a particular point that needs to be drawn out (perhaps they're calling to comment about abuse, but don't mind mentioning that they were abused as a child), if there's something else the presenter should know (for example, if they have a quiet voice or a stutter), or how good the call is. But keep these comments (or your short-hand for them) consistent so the presenter knows what you're referring to.

There are many computer-based switchboard systems for radio stations but they all work in a similar way. The screen will show you when a line is ringing: touch it once to answer it and speak to the caller, press it again to put it through to the studio. The presenter will put it to air by selecting it and raising its appropriate fader. A further touch will disconnect the call. More sophisticated systems will also log each call giving you information such as how long the contributor was waiting on the line before it was answered and whether they've rung before. If they have (or at least if someone has rung from that same number) the computer system will show (if the information was put in by the previous producer), the caller's name and location, when they last called and what topic they called about. That kind of information is useful if you don't want to keep putting regular callers to air, although is not used any more by a number of radio stations because of data protection[31] compliance issues.

The more calls the better?

Lots of calls do not necessarily mean a popular show. Some topics attract lots of callers and few listeners, and others attract few callers and lots of listeners. Don't be fooled by 'fool's gold'.

You may have a psychic as a guest and lots of calls from people wanting their personal readings, but probably not many listening at home because the information is of little relevance to them. Or you may have a solicitor talking about how to get the best deal from your divorce, and no callers. That may be because, even though the subject is fascinating for most people listening, few of them will want to discuss their situation on air.

Flashing phone-in lights are not necessarily an indicator of a good show.

Producers should always make sure the presenter has enough information to cope if the quality or number of calls isn't high or if the phone system crashes. Can they carry part of the show by themselves? Has the presenter got enough back-up material to be able to talk about this issue, or enough other information to talk about others? Is there a guest that you can have on to talk about the topic (perhaps to help set it up)?

Scheduling callers[32]

Just as the music is scheduled, so too should callers be. You need a variety of content to help provide conflict, a variety of voices: young and old (which fit your target demo), male and female; 'pro' and 'anti' and so on. All these factors help provide balance and momentum,

---

[31] See more on data protection: http://tinyurl.com/kr638b.
[32] A texter can become a caller. Give them a ring and ask them to make their comment verbally.

The PhoneBox call
answering system
Courtesy: BBC
London 94.9

making the show more engaging to the listeners and provoking more callers. The music
presenter has a variety of songs in a programme – you need a variety of callers.

So with each call you take you should not only ask:

- *do* we get them on? but also
- *when* do we get them on?

The first calls should be ones that disagree with the presenter
to provide immediate conflict, which will fuel other listeners.

The last call into a break (ads, travel, news, song, end of show)
should be a short 'kicker' to end that part of the show on a high.

The first call *after* a break should be a strong one to re-establish
the show, the subject and the host.

Look out for people with opposing ideas to go head to head.

Consider controversial callers who'll heighten the debate (but
look for balance within the programme).

Be flexible – move callers around to heighten the debate.
Alternating views makes the show sound more balanced,
more engaging, and provokes more callers.

Push a call with passion up the list – fast-track exceptional
contributors.

The last call should either be the funniest or most poignant,
and try to let the listener have the last word.

Don't be afraid to keep callers on hold for the slot when their contribution will have maximum impact, or ask to call them back. Just keep checking calls that you've put on hold are still there! Remember, callers on mobiles, or those waiting a long time, aren't automatically better callers. Your job is to make a great experience for the listeners, not the callers.

On air

Your job as presenter is to get the best performance out of yourself and also the best performance out of other people. That means working a listener so they give you what you want to make entertaining radio. This, like everything that makes a difference and sounds good, takes a bit of work and practice, but it'll be worth it. Will the other listeners notice that you do it? Probably not. Will they notice if you *don't*? Probably.

Make sure your phone levels are properly balanced. The quality of a phone line means that it needs to be stronger than you on the studio mic to stand a chance to be heard on air. If you can't turn the phone channel up, turn yours down and allow the processor to boost you both. Remember that having your fader and the phone fader up at the same time can 'colour' both your voices: dip theirs slightly when you are talking and vice versa to give a clearer quality to the conversation.

Don't greet every on-air caller the same way:

PRESENTER: Hello Susan, how are you?
CALLER: Hi Rob. Very well thank you, how are you?
PRESENTER: Fine thanks, what did you want to talk about?

Hi, who's this?	Shouldn't you already know? Weren't you ready for the caller? Aren't you supposed to be the host introducing the guest to the listener?
Where are you calling from?	Have you *really* no idea who this person is? If you sound as though you are not ready, then can your listener really be confident you know what to do here?
What are you doing today?	Usually answered with one word: 'Nothing'. There's entertainment for you!
Anything exciting going on in your world?	Again, most of the time the answer will be: 'No'.
How are you?	Don't ask someone how they are, unless you really want to know the answer. It works the other way around as well, with listeners asking the host how they are, and they can be asked not to do it by the studio producer.

If you or your phone-op has done their job properly and chatted to the caller off air, you'll at least be able to say 'Susan's on AllTalk FM[33] now, and you want to talk about the price of petrol and how it's affecting your family . . .' which will stop the 'hellos' in their tracks. You may be able to go one step further and cut out even more of the conversational preamble by saying: 'Susan's on the line now, and you've got a novel way of saving money on petrol, haven't you?'

[33] And if you build the name of the station into your introductions as a matter of course, you'll continue with some basic branding.

CUT TO THE CHASE

Think about the movie *Raiders of the Lost Ark*.[34]

At one point, the Ark of the Covenant has been put into a truck, to be transported away by the German soldiers. When Indiana Jones (Harrison Ford) is told this, he says, 'What truck?'

The next shot you see is of him riding hell-for-leather on a horse chasing the truck.

What you don't see is Indy going to find a horse, negotiating the loan of a bridle, saddle and blanket, saddling the horse up, finding out which direction the truck went and starting out to catch it.[35]

Steven Spielberg literally 'cut to the chase'[36] to further the momentum.

And that's just what you should do with on-air phone calls. The show producer should ask callers to launch straight into their 'headline' of what they want to say, without all the 'hellos and how are yous'.

And if you're recording the calls,[37] just play back the interesting bits.

As for intros the same with outros: everyone else does not need to hear 'OK, thanks for calling. Bye!' Just move on.

Like Spielberg, edit out the boring parts.

Ever been at a party and got talking to someone who fills five minutes of space with one minute of information? Some callers are like that despite the best work of the producer to screen them out. Listen out for them and move on if necessary.

COMMUNICATION ACCOMMODATION THEORY

When we talk with other people, we tend to subconsciously change our style of speech (accent, rate, types of words, etc.) towards the style used by the listener.

---

[34] More on this film here: http://tinyurl.com/ma5t27.
[35] Part of this sequence is here (*c.* 4.25 in) http://tinyurl.com/lco5lo.
[36] More on the derivation of this term: http://tinyurl.com/csspkw.
[37] There's more on recording calls in a few pages.

So, change your voice (its speed, tone and projection) to match that of your caller. It should be natural (we talk to our boss in a different voice to the one we use for our mum or sister), yet many presenters don't do this.

If you do, you're signalling agreement and liking and it helps to create greater rapport.

Also listen to how they are copying you: it may be a signal that they are seeking your approval.

Voice matching is polite (as long as you aren't mimicking) and helps to establish a communication flow with the caller and makes the conversation easier to listen to.

Callers shouldn't come on the air and expect to pronounce on a given topic entirely unchallenged. By the same token they're not politicians, so don't necessarily invite as heavy a grilling as the actual decision makers might require. Don't take over the conversation. The caller is the guest and is not used to speaking on the radio and getting over a point as succinctly as you are. Help them by chatting to them, asking them to explain and gently probing their views, not by being argumentative.

The phone caller is the surrogate for your listener. How you treat them is how your listener will feel treated by you. If you're flat and scripted, if you're unemotional and ungiving to the caller, your listener will get a sense of that too. However, if they're talking nonsense or are too garrulous, get rid of them.

Don't say that other callers are waiting. If you want to tell Tony in Todcaster that he'll have to wait till after the travel news, tell him on the phone, personally and privately, not across the radio: 'Tony in Todcaster, stay on hold, we'll be with you after the travel news . . .'.

To broadcast that information tells all the other potential callers that they may have to wait (and waste time) before *they* get on-air. Hardly encourages them to call, does it?

And don't say, 'Mike from Molehampton, you're on line 14 . . .': you already know Mike's on line 14, Mike doesn't know and doesn't need to know, so why tell him? No one else needs to know either, so why tell them?

Drop text messages and e-mails in to the conversation, not necessarily in some pre-arranged 'e-mail slot', but again, when it feels right. Put a text message point to a caller, put an e-mail to a guest, anything which makes it sound organic rather than pre-arranged. Text messages or e-mails can be a particularly useful tool when you've a politician as a guest. Sometimes you, as the phone-in presenter, might feel uncomfortable putting a particularly forthright point of view to an MP. But if you can do it when it's sent in by Doreen from Basingstoke, then so much the better. The MP will know Doreen is a potential voter, so is very unlikely to lose his/her rag with her, however much the point antagonises him.

Saying goodbye

Saying, 'Well, Sam that's an interesting point, thanks for calling with it, goodbye' is polite and gives 'closure' to the caller and the listener. However, there's another technique that will make the programme flow much more.

If you come off the back of one of the caller's comments and instead of talking to them, you talk to the rest of the audience (still, though on a one-to-one basis) you can segue seam-lessly to another topic or caller.

To the caller: 'Sam what an horrific tale . . . [to the listener] and I wonder if you've had a similar experience to the one that Sam was just describing. Have you also come across an insect in pre-packaged supermarket food? If so call me now on . . .'. Or consider ending the call on the best bit (one that's enthusiastic, funny or outrageous) and then going into a jingle, song or break, and saying thanks and goodbye to them *off air*.

When do you stop taking more on-air calls on the subject?

While you're still getting more off-air calls coming through.

Drop it before it gets boring or loses energy.

Even the hottest topic should never go on longer than an hour on the air. (Yes, there are exceptions: the death of Princess Diana, 9/11 and so on . . .)

Plan for a topic to go an absolute maximum of one hour, but think in terms of just two links: one to set it up and make a compelling statement to get a good response, the second to air that response.

Every call past that point should earn its way onto the air by contributing something new.

Recording calls

Although some programme controllers may object to this technique, having the conversa-tion off air, recording it, editing it and *then* broadcasting it can make the caller and the station sound fantastic. Although most phone-ins are live, a music-based show may benefit from this technique. You may have set a question or competition or asked people to call with ideas for the name of a newly discovered planet or funny stories about when they were first kissed. All of these contributions are likely to be long-winded and contain a lot of chaff. You can take the call while a song is playing, reroute it through the off-air part of the on-air desk onto a digital recorder and then edit it. By doing this, you can put the wheat to air and in the process maintain editorial control, the pace of the programme and the interest of the listeners.

Editing:
- makes calls more compelling by keeping the content relevant ('quality control')
- saves time on air
- reduces the possibility of your listeners' attention wandering
- means you're more in control and can avoid legal pitfalls
- means you can explore other areas of conversation and work hard for clarity
- makes you sound better as well as the caller: a joke doesn't work? Cut it out!
- is another way to weed out the wheat and chuck the chaff. You don't have to use the poor callers at all.

Be ready to record every call that comes to you to stand a better chance of netting the best ones. As you do it, listen for the parts that can be removed to make the call shorter and stronger. There are various ways of doing this.

Distillation of the first part of a caller's contribution immediately makes the conversation tighter.

Hi, how are you? You were talking about, earlier, about kissing? Well, I wondered if you'd like to hear . . . I mean I've got quite a good story. I don't know if it's any good but . . . you are? Well, it was about five years ago, well perhaps seven. Yes, seven, I was at school so it must have been in 1998, and . . .

You probably recognise that kind of caller: polite, but hesitant and slow. How much better a recorded and edited version would sound. You could distil their thoughts in to a more concise and understandable phrase of your own. Simply say the introduction live and then play in the recorded caller, starting with their voice to avoid a clash of tone on yours.

PRESENTER: Now Marie's on the line from Callumtown. Hi Marie, when was your first kiss?

MARIE: I was at school so it must have been in 1998, and . . .

Another advantage of recording calls is that you can explore other avenues of conversation, which in a live situation you may have avoided for fear of discovering a cul de sac. By recording, you can probe for more information, without worrying about time. Let's take that call again.

MARIE: *I was at school so it must have been in 1998, and it was one of those end of term parties and I was in the corner with Darren Watkins . . .* I think that was his name, anyway it doesn't matter . . .

PRESENTER: *What school was this?*

MARIE: *Blankstown Middle.*

PRESENTER: That's not around any more is it?

MARIE: No. *It's such a shame they knocked it down . . . I had so many happy memories there . . .*

PRESENTER: Like what?

MARIE: *You know. Behind the bike shed!*

By keeping in the phrases in italic, and editing out the rest, your call will be much stronger than if you'd taken the call live.

All desks are set up slightly differently, but this is the main process:

- Check how much time you've got left on the song that's playing in which you can record and possibly edit your call.
- Switch your mic to the record channel.
- Check this has worked before you launch into your recorded call, which would

otherwise go out live over the song that's currently playing. (Simply listen to 'off-air output' and listen as you click your fingers.)

- Similarly check the caller's channel isn't going to air.
- Record and edit your call, keeping an ear open to what's happening on air – you don't want a song to end!
- Return your mic to the on-air channel, otherwise you'll go to back anno a song and won't be heard.
- Give a live introduction to the caller and then play in the recording *starting with their voice*, so there's no voice clash of you, live, introducing you, recorded.
- There's no need to say that the call is recorded. Live is more interesting and exciting than recorded. (*Who Wants To Be A Millionaire?* is recorded, but that doesn't reduce the tension.) Simply play the call and allow the listeners to presume what they want to maximise their enjoyment. (Note, though, that the blurring of what's live and what's recorded may be considered bad practice at some stations.)

Other tips:

- Keep the speed in mind when you cut a conversation. Don't go from a sentence where someone is taking quickly to another piece which is slower and more considered.
- Edits are usually made at the end of a sentence. Why? Because that's when one's voice naturally drops.
- Be careful not to edit too harshly. If you take out all of someone's breaths they'll sound like an android. Make a promise to always edit before or always after a breath, otherwise you'll end up without one, or with two together! If an edit is too tight on a breath you can always take one from somewhere else in the piece to help keep the natural flow of someone's speech pattern.

Is this editing unethical? No. It's what happens in newsrooms all the time. What it does mean is that you as a presenter have to do a bit more work to make your programme sound better. Sounds like a fair exchange!

The index of 18 callers to avoid[38]

There are inevitably some people whose voices will rarely grace the airwaves of your radio station. They are:

1. The crank caller – with a ridiculously implausible story.[39]
2. The rude caller.
3. The aged caller who is way out of your target demo, who sounds sweet, but loses their, err, train of thingy.
4. The underage caller with a story about sex and drugs.
5. The politician during election run-up.
6. The wannabe politician – ditto.
7. The windbag who talks until they think of something interesting to say.
8. The dullard for whom the word 'monotone' was created.

---

[38] Real normal people don't call phone-ins – you're doing it for everybody else.
[39] The caller who's developed a jelly that cures cancer and keeps it in her fridge: http://tinyurl.com/lwr99p.

The call screening area. Courtesy: BBC London 94.9

9. The unintelligible caller whose argument has more holes than a moth-infested, crocheted blanket.
10. The speakerphone caller who is too rude to actually hold the phone, and sounds as though they're talking from the toilet.
11. The mobile caller . . . whose call . . . keeps . . . hello? . . . hello? . . . breaking up . . . hel . . .
12. The heavily accented — who others simply won't be able to understand.
13. The regular caller. You say: 'Hello Jim. Again.' You think: 'I do have more than the same dozen listeners, don't I?'
14. The presenter's 'friend'. 'I met your breakfast presenter Andrew down at the cricket, bought him a pint, y'know. He said to call . . .'.
15. The slow coach. 'Yesterday Andrew was saying about . . .'.
16. The abusive caller . . . 'This is crap . . .'. Ignore them and move along.
17. The one-hit wonder, who talks about any issue, as long as it's their own pet peeve.
18. The needy . . . 'I just called for a chat . . .'.

How to say no thanks

So, how do you tell these people that they can't go on air? Well, you don't. At least not in those words.

Put them on hold for a few seconds and then go back to them and say:

- 'We've got several other calls lined up, and I don't want to keep you on hold if we can't fit you in, can you try again another day?'
- 'We're really busy on this topic today . . . I'll take your number and will try and call you back.'
- 'I've just lined up someone else who's making the same point . . . sorry.'
- 'I don't think your mobile line is clear enough to be able to take you to air . . . '.
- 'We've lined up as many callers as we need now thanks, and we're nearing the end of the show.'
- 'I've got to dash and answer some other calls, sorry!'
- 'I'll pass the comment on, thanks for calling.'

- □ 'Really sorry, we're running out of time.'
- □ 'That's great, thanks for calling, really appreciate it.'
- □ 'You're in a really long queue, I don't want to crank up your bill . . .'.
- □ 'Y'know what, we're just finishing this topic.'

Radio is not democratic. You don't put on every song that's ever been released, and neither should you put on air everyone who wants to say something.

Finally[40]

If you want to know what the *listener's* experience of all this is, call a phone-in show yourself and see the process the other way around.

The perfect radio show for me is one where you're just hanging out with the host. The less it sounds like radio the better. For my own show I always feel it's gone well if something I hadn't bargained on has happened and taken off. My producer Bob and I do a fair amount of preparation and talking through ideas, but the best night is the night when the plans get thrown in the bin because something even better has developed as the night has gone on.[41]

---

[40] Further reading: Cameron B. Armstrong and Alan M. Rubin, 'Talk Radio as Interpersonal Communication', *Journal of Communication*, Vol. 39 (1989): 'Those who called in to talk radio programs tended to find face-to-face communication less rewarding, were less mobile, felt talk radio was more important to them and listened for more hours a day than those who did not call but who did listen.'

[41] Clive Bull, presenter, LBC 97.3, *The Radio Magazine*, April 2005.

22 Double-headed and team[1] shows

SKILLSET – NATIONAL OCCUPATIONAL STANDARDS
RADIO CONTENT CREATION

Unit content included in this chapter:
RC1 Work effectively in radio
RC2 Research the structure of the radio industry
RC4 Contribute to the creative process in radio
RC16 Select and direct radio presenters, performers and voice-over artists

A group of friends having fun, talking about what's going on through the eyes of their own distinct character – characters in a 'zoo programme'[2] or 'team show' are cast according to a model that's been developed from TV and cinema. This originally American idea arguably peaked in British radio in the 1990s with the studio 'posse' of *Steve Wright In the Afternoon*[3] on Radio One, and then the emergence of Chris Evans'[4] crew on GLR, Radio One and Virgin. The concept of having more than one presenter on air at a time is still used to great effect specifically on commercial radio and specifically in the morning.

> Beware!
> Zoo radio is much more difficult than it sounds.
> Simply filling a room with people all chatting sounds horrendous.
> Zoo radio takes a considerable amount of discipline and each
> member of the team must be as professional (and potentially
> talented) as the main presenter.[5]

The argument for team shows is that with someone continually firing back at you, you're kept on your toes. It also means that if you're feeling a little under the weather or not firing on all cylinders, the other hosts can 'pick up the slack'. Another argument is that it provides opportunity for 'corrective representation', be it male/female, black/white[6] etc.

Team shows rely on the chemistry between the two hosts to keep it alive. If it's not there, the show is as good as dead.

---

[1] Otherwise known as 'zoos'.
[2] More on the background to zoos and some more famous stations that use them here: http://tinyurl.com/l7kqr6.
[3] Read more about Steve's posse here: http://tinyurl.com/l53cjf.
[4] More on Chris Evans and audio excerpts here: http://tinyurl.com/nx5gfg.
[5] Will Kinder, Radio 1 producer and on-air sidekick to Chris Moyles.
[6] Particularly in South African radio.

Signs a double-headed show is not working	Signs a double-headed show is working
o Missed cues. o Interruptions. o An imbalance in presence Frustration and suppressed resentment towards the dominance of one host over the other. o No connection between the two hosts. o Simple alternating of the presentation of scripted inserts and features. o The hosts sound similar. o They also have similar points of view. o They have similar presentation styles. o They are too *dissimilar* and have trouble finding ways to communicate. o There's little tension . . . o . . . and therefore little point having two presenters.	o Each host's talents are recognised and exercised. o One host feeds off the other, even o completes their thoughts and sentences. o Delivery is always quick and to the point without fishing for hooks. o There's no overlapping or repetition. o There is clearly a structure to every link. o If the chemistry and discipline is there it can produce a seemingly unending supply of energy and creativity.

The hosts selected for a dual presentation should already have a noticeable chemistry, or 'electricity', between them – a charged atmosphere that sparks and crackles when they're brought closer together. This invariably happens when, in terms of character or interests, they *differ*.

> The best shows grow organically. It's like comparing Boyzone with The Beatles, who actually sing about shared experiences. Shows with mates are always going to be better shows.[7]

The characters

Team shows have more than two presenters: one main front person (someone has to be 'the air traffic controller' and decide what happens, where the live link is going and where it lands) and several others who contribute to the output. The use of the word 'characters' is a deliberate one, as members of the zoo team are chosen for specific attributes, either real-life or created for the show.

Here's the secret: find totally different people[8] with a lot in common. That sounds contradictory, but it's not.

o A lot in common – how they were raised, or what things they like and dislike, and hopefully their work ethics. As long as they don't compete in the same sphere.

o Totally different – how they express themselves. Perhaps one person who's informational

---

[7] Nick Goodman, formerly of Capital Radio, speaking at a Radio Academy event, October 2005.
[8] Find out your personality with these two free tests: http://tinyurl.com/cs34kz and http://tinyurl.com/25mzb9.

and another who's more artistic. Both can be creative, but just express their creativity in different ways. It's also important not to have two 'driven' types together, as you can end up with two people sounding like they're wrestling for the microphone.

Picture the Olympic rings, made of partially overlapping circles. They overlap to form a common area, but all the rest of the circles' areas are separate from each other. And that's what makes good team shows: parts of them aren't alike, but they do share areas of interest. When you find the right people, develop the common area as the core of the content, then bring out their differences. Starting the other way around is putting the cart before the horse. The different characters are necessary to:

- Appeal to the different characteristics of the listening audience, so everyone feels included and involved.
- Draw out different stories, perspectives and experiences. If all the characters are similar then their reactions to experiences are also likely to be the same, and that could make for boring radio.
- Highlight conflict, confrontation and contrast that engage the listener. (If you can split a presentation team and build creative tension between them, you can likewise split your audience and generate a similar tension. And that makes for reactive radio. Different characters create different 'content conflict'.)
- Have the listener take sides, thereby having emotional involvement in the show.
- Give the impression to the listener that they're eavesdropping on a spontaneous conversation.

> Ever seen a successful movie in which all the actors played the same role? Of course not. Is everyone at the circus a clown? No, someone gets to walk the tightrope and someone is the master of ceremonies. And how many hits would a band have if everyone played guitar? Did everyone in *Seinfeld* act just like Jerry? Defined characters generate creative tension, and they give the listener more diverse attitudes and comments by which to be entertained.[9]

This is similar to a TV sitcom, where the characters have different personalities that cause friction and therefore humour. But having different characters isn't enough in itself. You also need your core listeners to care about them and relate to them, and have those characters say things that are relevant, interesting and compelling.

There are several models you can use to cast your characters.

A basic one is the creation of three broad character types: The Intellectual (the clever person), The Idiot (the innocent fool) and the Mr I Am (the smart Alec).

- The main presenter who does the work of introducing the music and furniture features such as news and travel. They're often the warm and approachable person, but may also be slightly anarchic or renegade. Think of them as the 'kid brother' or 'kid sister'. (Mr I Am or the smart Alec. Could be Chandler from *Friends* or Captain Mainwaring from *Dad's Army*?)
- The second presenter may be more 'ditzy', they often don't quite 'get it' and can be

---

[9] US radio consultant Alan Burns: http://tinyurl.com/kqyztd.

the perfect foil to their colleague. They may appear a little slow, but just as in life they occasionally get the upper hand and come out with a put-down for the main host that puts them in their place. This person may be the travel and weather presenter. (The Idiot or the innocent fool, sounds like Phoebe or Pike?)

- Another host may be more conservative. A little strait-laced and more traditional and easily offended in their values. Sometimes they may be the voice of sanity if the others go too far, but are often the butt of jokes (the Intellectual or the clever person, sounds like Ross or Sergeant Wilson?).

Alternatively you could follow Scott Sedita's *Eight Characters of Comedy*.[10]

- *The Logical Smart One* – the voice of reason, the straight man (though it's very often a woman), someone with common sense, patience and sarcastic wit delivered with a deadpan style. They are articulate, reasonable and tolerant, knowledgeable, patient and understanding. They often 'wink to the audience' and react in a knowing way, being on their side. Think: Wilma[11] in *The Flintstones*, Will Truman[12] in *Will and Grace* or Marge Simpson.

- *The Lovable Loser* – determined dreamers, endearing and hopeful, sarcastic and self-deprecating. Think: Chandler in *Friends* (who was always trying to get the job, get the girl . . . and when he did, the series ended).[13] The most common combination of characters in sit-coms is this character, teamed with the Logical Smart One.

- *The Neurotic* – they analyse and over-obsess, are anxious yet endearing, and possibly outcasts in their youth. Think: Niles and Frasier Crane in *Frasier* (where the two characters, who were nerds at school, alternate this role with being The Logical Smart One), Monica (the plump girl the cheerleaders taunted, who likes everything super-clean[14] and her CDs in order), or Ross (the computer geek) in *Friends*. In adulthood they are intellectual, but slow in developing social skills (Ross chatting up the pizza delivery girl)[15] and may internalise every thought (watch the cogs in Ross's mind working . . .).

- *The Dumb One* – sweet, child-like innocence, enthusiastic and honest, these are the traits of the 'Dumb One'. Think of gullible Homer, oblivious to what's going on around him, or naïve Joey who sees so much at face value he doesn't understand sarcasm (or deliver it). The Dumb One works well with the Logical Smart One and the Neurotic (think how exasperated Monica gets with Joey at times). Here's another example: Charlotte[16] in *Sex and The City* . . .

- *Bitches and Bastards* – the nastiest, cleverest and wittiest, they are great at put-downs and exit lines, and are often cast as the servants/support staff (Berta[17] in *Two and a Half Men*, Rosario[18] in *Will and Grace*). They are cynical, pessimistic, bitter and fed up with life, and enjoy hurting people, especially the Loveable Loser. Think of Miranda in *Sex and The City*.

---

[10] A highly recommended read: Scott Sedita, *The Eight Characters of Comedy: A Guide to Sitcom Acting and Writing* (Atides Publishing, 2005): http://tinyurl.com/lb3en3.
[11] Here she is being clever: http://tinyurl.com/5mvf73.
[12] Will Truman's voice of reason: http://tinyurl.com/nc8vkt.
[13] Watch Chandler's relationship with Monica here: http://tinyurl.com/lwnuhg.
[14] Watch this example: http://tinyurl.com/lnknd7.
[15] Watch that scene here: http://tinyurl.com/d8vbnp.
[16] Charlotte doesn't see what's coming: http://tinyurl.com/megr2a.
[17] Watch her put-downs here: http://tinyurl.com/n52lnh.
[18] The '*Mexican Moma*': http://tinyurl.com/n5z3bv.

- *The Materialistic One* – Rachel Green (*Friends*) and Gabrielle Solis (*Desperate Housewives*) have money, but don't know the value of it, and love shopping. This has been an almost exclusively female role, but in recent years has been reflected in gay male characters (Will in *Will and Grace*). Pampered princesses are shallow and spoilt (Elle Woods in *Legally Blonde*).[19]

- *The Womaniser/Maniser* – Samantha Jones[20] in *Sex and the City*, Edie in *Desperate Housewives*, or even The Fonz[21], these characters are cocky and charming, sexual but shallow. They love sex and are the heroes of the Loveable Loser. They are harmless predators and even though usually have a one-track mind show vulnerability (Sam Malone's drinking in *Cheers*, Samantha's breast cancer scare).

- *Someone in their Own Universe* – some of the weirdest and funniest characters, these people say whatever comes into their head. They are crazy 'break-out' characters used to reduce the tension or change focus, and although they have different frames of reference, what they say makes perfect sense to them. Unpredictable in their outlook and in what they say and do[22], they include Phoebe in *Friends* (and her songs), Nick Harper in *My Family* and Jack[23] and Karen in *Will and Grace*.

Most successful sitcoms have characters who fit into these roles (to a greater or lesser extent). The characters have a brotherly/sisterly love, but disagree with each other. Some call it 'friendly friction', 'electricity', 'sexual tension' or 'striking a nerve' – they're all phrases appropriate for a zoo team. Contrast and different tastes, perspectives and experiences means there are different reactions to those experiences and hence more interest.

Alternatively consider the character line-up from the psychologist Blevins who described a number of roles that people have in families, at work and in stories.[24]

- When things go wrong, *the blamer* points a finger. Things are never accidental – somebody is to blame. In doing so, of course, the blamer points a finger away from themself.

- *The cheerleader* stands on the sidelines and encourages others with great enthusiasm. Whilst they do not gain the highest prizes, they are safe and may well be popular.

- *The distracter* draws attention away from problems and towards things that are easier to accept and handle. Others may be grateful for this release from responsibility.

- *The favoured son* has a special place in the hearts of parental figures. They get given the best and are more easily forgiven. This can make them arrogant.

- *The hero* always saves the day when things go wrong or people are threatened. They help both individuals and the wider team.

- *The invalid* is sick, injured or otherwise limited in capability, sometimes through choice. They are often a burden on others who feel obliged to carry them.

- *The jester* makes light of most situations, creating laughter and levity. Like the distracter, this helps people avoid emotionally difficult situations.

- *The martyr* endures suffering, often with little complaint. They may carry the hurt on behalf of others. For this sacrifice, they get sympathetic attention.

---

[19] 'A law student . . .' http://tinyurl.com/log93z.

[20] See her at work here: http://tinyurl.com/nouxyd.

[21] The cool Fonz here: http://tinyurl.com/5bjxom.

[22] See a good example here: http://tinyurl.com/lk488e.

[23] Hyper-Jack: http://tinyurl.com/d3mk5m.

[24] Note that different people may take different roles at different times and individuals may take on several roles at once. Individuals also tend more towards some roles than others.

- *The mascot* is a good luck symbol. They are harmless and loved. They give little but good feelings.
- *The placator* calms down conflict between others and helps people resolve issues. They personally avoid conflict and may concede much in order to do so.
- *Rebels* are autonomous individuals who do not fit in. They push away and are pushed away. They look and think differently. They may also be annoyingly successful.
- *The saint* is unremittingly good. They never think ill of others and work for the good of all people. They may feel superior and may be the subject of envy.
- When things go wrong, *the scapegoat* is given and accepts the blame. For this, they may feel like a martyr, though they are not treated as one.
- *The sceptic* is the doubter who questions everything and believes nothing to be absolutely true. They can be useful truthseekers or annoying disrupters.
- *The star* is afforded special status. They are put on a plinth and adored. Limitations are ignored and strengths are over-played. They are assumed to have a bright future.

Whatever model you use, each 'cast member' in the show should ask themselves:
- Who am I?
- What do I care about?
- What's my point of view?
- How am I different from other people in the show?

Each 'programme cast' (or perhaps the producer or programme controller) should ask:
- Do these answers work well together?
- Do they represent most of our target audience's likely attitudes?
- Are they different enough to be entertaining?

> Some on-air people refuse to adopt a character, saying it's a fake representation of who they really are.
>
> Yet presenters are entertainers/actors.
>
> They wouldn't turn down a part in *The Bill*[25] because they're not a police officer!
>
> Having said that, the role they adopt should be reasonably similar to their real life. Don't ask a 22-year-old wild single woman to act like a 35-year-old woman with a husband and two children, unless mentally she already is.

All characters should remain true to their on-air personality whatever happens. In *Friends*, Monica was known as the overly fussy and tidy cook who used to be overweight. Although she had other traits, these were perhaps her main characteristics. To have her delivering a put down to another large person or letting her flat be untidy would not have fitted with

[25] *The Bill:* http://tinyurl.com/mkqvtj.

her character, so it didn't happen unless it was explained as a one-off in that episode's story-line.

So, characters have to be true to their on-air selves.

CONSISTENCY PRINCIPLE

The discomfort of cognitive dissonance occurs when what you say and what you do are widely varying.

Your character may also fall out of alignment when you say things which disagree with previously held views, and there is no explanation for your change of opinion.

In these situations you are breaking the law of consistency. This will confuse the listener and damage your on-air character.

Strive to achieve a maximum practical level of consistency in your on-air world.

Zoos or double-headers that work well are down to a lot of luck, hard work and time. The luck that might come with putting two 'random' people together and expecting them to become friends and work well together on air. The hard work of finding the right combination of people, matchmaking if you like, and then creating the atmosphere to let them develop and discover their similarities and points of difference. The time? Well, it may be obvious in minutes that people won't get on; more realistically it might take a few weeks before people realise that it's just not working. There are several famous cases of this happening on major market stations, where, because of no one's fault, the chemistry just didn't exist.

If you're a presenter and your programme controller suggests you'd work well as part of a team, make sure that you're in on that decision. Many co-hosts are, unbelievably, chosen without involving the main presenter.

The roles

Different roles in a dual presentation also reduce the chances of one host encroaching on the other's territory. These can be purely *logistical roles* such as who does the weather, or they can be *performance roles* around who is better at interviewing, delivering punchlines or giving family-orientated information.

THE PRESENTER PARADOX

This states that two poor sidekicks don't make one good anchor and that a two-person show doesn't necessarily mean that it's twice as entertaining.
But the perception *might* be that it's got twice as much talking.

> Additionally it can sometimes take a long time for double-headed shows to realise that they're more than the sum of two parts.
>
> They may be perfectly capable of solo shows, but two very good presenters can make a *great* show together. And that's hard for some egos to take.

The top tip is that when the topic changes, the person speaking changes. Doing this avoids one person hogging the mic (say with a back anno, station ID, programme name check *and* weather). One voice doing one 'chunk' of information makes the link sound too long and/or slow.

Instead, divide that material up to include each other, and increase the pace.

Presenter A	Presenter B	Presenter A	Presenter B
Back anno + station ID	Show ID + time + travel intro		
	Back anno + station ID	Time + weather	Intro travel
Back anno + station ID + time + weather	Celebrity gossip/talking topic/competition set-up		

These are just three examples to vary the voices and the rotation of who does what, which will share out the 'mic time' and increase momentum.

Team shows have to structure their links more carefully than a single host, so that each person knows:

- what needs to be done in the link
- how it's going to be done
- who is going to do what, and how they'll get in and out of it.

This does not mean every link should be scripted because this will simply rob the show of any spontaneity. It simply means the structure of the link should be clear in the minds of both the hosts. Co-hosts who don't structure each link beforehand will just produce double the waffle. We don't want scripted. We want *pre-planned spontaneity*.

Of course you need to play to your strengths: if one person is better at talking up to the vocals, reading a script, interviewing, giving a punchline then that should usually be their role.

And you need to play to people's on-air character, so the most appropriate 'personality' is the one doing the showbiz news (perhaps The Materialistic One, for example). Just be careful that the same person doesn't do the same elements each time, if there is no need for them to do it (for example the female host who is always 'the weather girl').

Another way to keep up the momentum is to have less agreement and more advancement. Agreement is where one host is talking and the other is chipping in with 'Yeah, that's true' or 'Uh huh' and so on. They are wasted words, as they don't add anything to the conversation. So why say them? They indicate that you are in neutral and can't think what to say.

Advancement means you have to move the story or the link forward. Don't merely agree;

think of another point to make that'll advance the subject, and never deny the on-air reality. If another character says on air something happened — it happened.

> ◀ **ACTUAL AUDIO**
>
> PRESENTER: Well, we're getting dozens of calls voting in our Sunday love song poll. I'm joined by one of our telephone answerers. What are people voting for?
> PHONE OP: Well, we've had two callers . . .
>
> *BBC local station, October 2005*

If your colleague says 'The moon's made of cream cheese' they've said it for a reason. It'll be for a joke, a flight of fancy, a bit about 'What if everyday items were made from food', whatever. If you say, 'No, it's not' you've killed the item dead. That leaves them with nothing to say, you with nowhere to go and the listeners confused. Instead reply with, 'Whaaaat? Are you crazy?!' or 'Yes, and . . .' to push the item further and help them get where they want to get.

In the Actual Audio above, the phone op didn't follow her leader: she contradicted him and made the station look unpopular. While you shouldn't lie, don't ever suggest that the response to anything has ever been anything less than impressive.

Make it easy for your partner to interact with you, be a conscientious listener. Read them to see where they are going with a topic. Follow them to further the conversation. Go with the assumption your partner makes for you and further it: 'You dressed up as a dancing monkey at the weekend, right?!', 'Yes, and that fur suit really itches . . .'

There's a danger that team members may not be able to react to what a colleague throws at them during an on-air conversation, and that the whole link will crash and burn. You can't rehearse a whole show — if you do that it'll sound staid and stilted. Instead, give each other a tip-off. Speak with the other members and tell them *what topics* you're going to talk about, but not *why*. For example, simply saying, 'I've got something to say about skiing, queuing and pregnancy' is all that's needed. That will start sparking off some ideas for humour, personal stories and revelations that will help the whole link, without you all actually rehearsing it.

It's better to have a plan and then be spontaneous from it, rather than be scrabbling for content during the show, which will probably mean the ideas are mediocre and poorly executed.

A comment about you, your actions or experiences is stronger if you can get another character to start it. Let them provide you with the planned set-up for you to react to, rather than by crowbarring the subject into the conversation yourself.

For example, instead of saying, 'I had a really good weekend, shall I tell you why?', get your co-presenter to say, 'How was your weekend . . . you're all smiles this morning . . .' to which you can reply, 'It was great because . . .' which is a much more natural conversational flow.

If someone on your show — a colleague, listener, guest, travel presenter — comes up with the best punchline or comeback, recognise it and respect it. They may have been better at you in that instance, in their timing, pacing and constructing the material. If you try to top them it will make both of you look stupid. Listen to the type of comments they make, what their favourite topics are and what their catchphrases are and learn how to set them up and help them. Even if the other person gets to say the punchline rather than you, the whole team wins. Don't feel as though you have to have the last word every single time.

You will come over as much more generous, and yes, vulnerable . . . and therefore more human and likeable, if you sometimes let other members of the 'cast' have their glory with the story.

Beware of too many voices. You could have a presenter, sidekick, producer, newsreader, sports presenter and travel person. That's a lot of voices and characters for listeners to keep up with.

> Try and limit the number of people on at any one time. For instance, during the news and sport sequence the sidekick and producer could be in the background. In other words it could be a large cast but they don't all need to be on stage at the same time![26]

Some of the most successful zoo shows (and other shows) create a club. That means that a listener needs to have a little bit of knowledge about the show and the characters to really get the most from it. It's a very fine line: there may be 'in' jokes that you might not get if you're listening for the first time. But as you invest a few days listening you feel part of the club too. This creates a strong bond between listeners and the show.

> The secret is to have lots of material that's accessible to all and a few moments and bits that are part of the club.[27]

Invisible cues are the non-verbal cues that you give your co-hosts. When you have line of sight with the other person, simply use hand gestures: basic pointing to the other person when it's their turn to speak and their mic is on, or a raised index finger if you want to be allowed to join the conversation. The same gesture can be used if you are talking and leading up to a particular point or punch line and you don't want to be interrupted: the finger in the air makes sure the rest of the team are aware of your intentions so they don't trample all over you.

The responsibilities

Off-air responsibilities are different from on-air roles. It doesn't matter who does what, but you each/all need to know which of you will:

- source any information
- do the paperwork or logging
- do the production of sounds/jingles/effects
- phone and set up guests
- answer listener e-mails
- meet with sales clients
- and so on.

Teamwork means that it really helps if each person can do what another person dislikes.

---

[26] Will Kinder, producer, Radio 1.
[27] Will Kinder, producer, Radio 1.

The conflict

Shows where the members share the same viewpoints on everything are one-dimensional: people sitting around, agreeing with each other is almost always boring and does not provide the foundation for compelling entertainment.

In your show you need to constantly build up tension and release it, by creating constructive conflict[28] and then resolving it in a positive way. A good on-air team has 'tension' and 'friction'. But not 'argument'. Without a certain amount of friction, there's no heat and you need to use conflict to create more compelling content.

An *argument* is not entertaining to listen to; it's simply a back-and-forth 'yes it is', 'no it isn't' exchange.

Entertaining conflict involves a difference of opinion that requires more than a thin 'yes/no' argument.[29] It could be shown by:

o   A character who has a problem and how they deal with it.
o   Exaggerated misunderstandings (for example in the film *Mrs Doubtfire* in which one deceit inevitably leads to another . . .).
o   An *inciting incident*, which sets off a spark of anger or difference of opinion. Strong or outrageous statements can make very effective inciting incidents.

Work out what issues your character would have a strongly held belief about, and why that would be (you have to have a *motivation* to support your part in the forthcoming discussion so it comes over more logically and adds depth to the discussion).

Finding a way to resolve any conflict raised on your show is essential. Scenes of conflict have to come to a satisfactory ending. There must be a winner, a loser or a compromise to conclude any conflict. To steer yourself towards resolution, use your character's objective in the conflict and ask what the point is that your character wants to reach. (Obviously this objective will be very different from that of the person who opposes you.) In the end, either one character will win his or her objective or some sort of compromise will be attained. When you work towards more clearly defined objectives you increase the likelihood of your conflicts ending with entertaining, satisfying resolution.

Let's take an example:

The inciting incident:[30] the female character who has an outcry over the start of the new football season (in response, the male co-host can't wait for it).

The motivation: she reveals that she was once dumped by a footballer when she was at college (sexual tension) and has been off them ever since, or that her boyfriend always hogs the remote control every Saturday afternoon and evening so that she can't get to watch what she wants (male/female tension). The male presenter says he can't wait to be back on the terraces with his mates and enjoys the camaraderie of supporting the team that his dad introduced him to (father/son bonding) when he was a boy (emotional tension).

Her objective: she wants to have her boyfriend not watch a match on a Saturday and let her have control of the TV, or take her shopping (is she The Materialistic One?).

Conflict challenge: challenge the boyfriend to meet her objective, or challenge her to

---

[28] It's important to have the right kind of conflict on your show so things don't overstep the mark and become too personal. *Constructive* conflict is about people's concepts, ideas, thoughts and views – things they can change. *Destructive* conflict comes from issues about a person that they can't change – such as their looks.

[29] Believable conflict isn't created because you take a view opposite to that of another team member. It comes from you saying something that's true to you – or at least to your on-air character.

[30] Thousands of storylines to kick-start your creativity: http://tinyurl.com/ml25kl, http://tinyurl.com/qgtwc , http://tinyurl.com/3bpgk.

go to a match with the male co-host to experience football directly and see whether her mind can be changed.

The resolution: this has to be strong and entertaining, perhaps with a twist. Maybe she starts to become a bigger fan than her boyfriend, she joins the cheerleading troupe at the ground. Maybe he meets a female footy fan who he starts going to matches with instead of his mates, or realises that an air-conditioned shopping mall is preferable to a cold and wet terrace. It has to be better than 'I found I quite liked football, after all!'

The initial exchange could be simmering for a few days or weeks (with occasional comments on the start of the new season), and then 'blow up' with the female's inciting incident and reaction. Her motivation and his replies can come over the next several links of the show, culminating in the challenge which of course has to happen a few days later and can be teased until the weekend. On the show following the challenge, the two presenters 'report back' and the conflict is resolved.

Here's another example:[31]

SHOW 1

Presenter A: All my kids do lately is play on PlayStation.
Presenter B: Yeah with me it's the Wii.
Travel presenter: Mine are always demanding we go to McDonald's . . . it's hard to say no even though I know it's wrong to give in too often.

The link reflects what many parents go through, the lure of computer games and fast food, and links with the much-discussed 'obesity crisis'. It raises the issue of how to get your kids to do something else and eat better food, and how to say 'no' to pester power. The team highlights important topics that most parents will be able to sympathise with. But is there any conflict?

SHOW 2

Presenter A: All my kids do lately is play on PlayStation.
Presenter B: Yeah? That's all my girlfriend does!
Female newsreader: I'm not surprised, the way you treat her!

A is female and married with kids, B is male and single so there's obvious role conflict there (one who is perhaps tied down, the other who's footloose, or perhaps one that hates their role as child-carer and the other one that can't wait to start a family but can't find the right person to do it with). There's also a male/female differentiation between A and B.

---

[31] Adapted from work by Alan Burns, US radio consultant http://tinyurl.com/nczozk.

SHOW 3

Presenter A: All my kids do lately is play on PlayStation.
Presenter B: Yeah? That's all my girlfriend does!
Female newsreader: I'm not surprised, the way you treat her!
Producer: All this modern tech! When I was a kid, I got to mess around in the disused quarry . . .

. . . and now the link includes a bit of danger, irresponsibility and parenting issues.

The pattern of inciting incidents and then resolving them creates conflict and tension for entertainment purposes, which is at the heart of any great entertainment (from *Romeo and Juliet* to *EastEnders* and *Big Brother*). As well as conflict, contrast between the players adds comedy and drama, and creates a catalyst for more content. But the roots to the success are unique, strong, well-defined characters and the way they interact with each other; characters whom listeners can instantly love, hate or love to hate.

It's often useful to develop your 'plot' for a team storyline before you begin it on air. For instance your plot might be to get the team's picture in the local newspaper. In this case talk to the newspaper and get them on board first, then start the storyline on air. There's nothing worse than starting a plot which fizzles out. A big, positive outcome makes your show look big and because you know it will work you'll be far more confident on air.[32]

Naming names

Zoo or co-presenters should often address each other by name so listeners get to know the names and the characters that go with them. You may have similar voices and the listener may have trouble telling you apart. Plus, it's only courtesy: how often have you felt reticent to speak to someone at a party or meeting, because you haven't been introduced to them? When you know someone's name, you already feel much friendlier towards them. So keep letting listeners know who everyone is. You don't need to keep introducing them, simply refer to them by name frequently and naturally as part of your conversation:

'Hey Simon, did you see the match last night?'
OR
'What are you talking about, Susan? That's ridiculous!'

This fits with the basic process of building a relationship: when someone *knows* you, they can decide if they *like* you. Giving your name starts building that rapport and forming a basic emotional bond.

---

[32] Will Kinder, producer, Radio 1.

Sometimes nicknames can quickly help develop a strong bond between a name and a character. It might be as simple as 'Producer Greg', 'Quiz Tony' or some other slightly more off-the-wall name that listeners are intrigued by.

Moyles had a BA called Melinda. He was a bloke, his name came because he used to be the messenger . . . his nickname was never explained on the show[33] but it was always the first question he was asked. Nicknames are also something that tends to develop between friends so it strengthens the feeling of bonding for the listener.[34]

Sycophants

There's a fine line between having co-hosts with whom you get along, and those who are there purely to make you look and sound good. Although inevitably there'll be one main presenter, a strong team is one that's built on mutual respect. There have been situations in the past where the main presenter has belittled his colleagues on air (on one famous occasion getting a female co-presenter to admit that she'd slept with him the previous night), and there are many situations where the co-hosts are so in awe they laugh at the slightest hint of humour from the main presenter.

I would like to see an end to the pseudo male-chauvinist along with his detractors pretending to be shocked but at the same time giggling and adding fuel to the fire. I do wonder how many women get shoe-horned into these roles.[35]

Remember there's a fine line between showing listeners you're having a good time and excluding them because they don't understand what is going on or feel uncomfortable.

Don't have such a good time in the studio that you leave out the other person in the relationship – the listener – otherwise they'll feel as though they've arrived late at a party where everyone else knows each other, and will just want to leave.

There are far too many breakfast sidekicks who are paid to giggle inanely.[36]

The chemistry[37]

How many people do we meet in out lives whom we have real chemistry with? With whom we become close friends, bosom buddies; whom we respect, love . . . marry? Very

[33] . . . but it is here: http://tinyurl.com/rdvsl3.

[34] Will Kinder, producer, Radio 1.

[35] Fiona Faulkner, presenter, TLRC, *The Radio Magazine*, April 2007.

[36] Robin Galloway, presenter, Real Radio Scotland, *The Radio Magazine*, June 2009.

few. And most of such relationships do not start out that way. They mature like wine or cheese. Team or double-headers have to have unique chemistry that can be heard. Felt. That's tricky when two people are put together in a studio and office and spend more time together than with their families. They are expected to laugh and react and interact from day one.

Whether you're part of a new team, an old team, or a new member of an old team, you still need to get to know each other so well that you can anticipate each other's next move. Develop rapport and relationships by doing things together away from the station. Discover your colleagues' characteristics and form a trust with one another.

Engage and interact with each other, and then build their strong characteristics into the show to make them more human.

What about taking an improvisation class?[38] If you're part of a team, perhaps all of you could go together or separately. This isn't a chance to show off to the public, it's a chance for you to learn how to hone your skills:

- How to open up conversational cul-de-sacs.
- How to listen out for humorous highways.
- How to build confidence in what you do . . .
- and what your co-host is doing that you may be able to react to.
- How to improve team rapport . . .
- and give ideas and opportunities to other members of the team.
- How to quickly recognise humorous possibilities, taking a small amount of material and building on it.

In radio, good improvisation is often said to be 'good chemistry' but if you have good improv skills you will create much better radio than two people who just 'get on'. There are many presenters who do not achieve, not because they don't do the work, but because they don't know what work to do.

Some rules of improv:

1. *Pay attention and remember* – analyse the meaning of the words that are being said and decide how they affect your character. Listen carefully. Probe without trying to top what your co-host is saying.
2. *Follow my leader* – when something is said, it's part of the scene. Go with it, don't argue with it. So if someone says 'You have problems getting dates, don't you?', don't say 'No' and kill the bit, but react as your character would and drive the item forward. If necessary twist the answer so it's still 'no', but leaves them with somewhere to go. 'It's not that I have problems getting dates. It's just that I'm particular . . . something you'd know nothing about. If it's got a heartbeat you'll go out with it.' This sets up creative tension for the bit to continue.
3. Let the humour grow from the situation or characters. Don't just make a joke as it'll destroy the scene. Not everything has a punchline, but a situation or response can still be funny. 'Can you go and get me a pen?', 'Sure I will. I've got nothing better

---

[37] Free online compatibility test for partners: http://tinyurl.com/ldu5br. (Note that this will suggest how similar you are to one another, which is not necessarily what you want in a good team show . . .) This http://tinyurl.com/kk95ky on the other hand shows your personality in isolation, so you can compare it with someone else's yourself rather than have the website do it for you.

[38] Anne Libera (ed.) *The Second City Almanac of Improvisation* (Northwestern University Press, 2004): http://tinyurl.com/nzpwur.

to do. And on the way back shall I get you a coffee? Hey, how about at the weekend I come over and mow your lawn . . . and didn't you say you had some dry-cleaning to get done? Give me your car keys and I'll get it . . . and why don't I wash your car too, y'know, while I'm there?'

4. Keep each scene simple and focused with lots of detail. 'New Year Resolutions' is a subject. 'Osama bin Laden's Resolutions' is a strong improv theme.

5. It's entertainment, not reality. The show is part of an audio sitcom. 'Nice people' are not that entertaining. Live up to your on-air character and probe your characteristics and then exaggerate them. If you are the wary, shy person then you will always see conspiracies. If you are picky over your dates, talk about giving them a police check or a psychological examination.

Off-air conflict

Having a good on-air partnership doesn't always go hand-in-hand with a good off-air relationship. In fact, it is very possible to have a good show hosted by a team that doesn't even talk to each other off the air. This may be the result of:

- The show only ever uses ideas from one person, and others' views get ignored.
- The co-presenters are encouraged to laugh at the jokes of one presenter, but that courtesy is never returned.
- One presenter is always left with the information in a link (station ID, travel and weather), while another always gets the fun and creative bits (comments on the news, setting up the competiton).
- Maybe one of the team is always the first voice out of a song or break, perhaps because they are the one driving the desk. And maybe it's that person who always starts a song too early in a link, forcing a colleague to speed up their delivery and potentially miss the punchline or crash the vocal intro.

Off air the clashes can continue:

- Differences in personalities – one person turns up on time and prepared, the other turns up just before the show and busks it.
- One of the team does research and prep, the other relies on everyone else to set up and then simply 'reacts' to their bits.
- Someone takes themselves too seriously, never has a laugh at themselves or with others, never goes for breakfast with the team after the show . . .
- One co-presenter always says, 'This is my idea, this is what I say, this is how you react, and this is my gag to make me look great . . . no, you can't change it.'

THE ROCK BAND SYNDROME

One person does more than their share of the work, while the other person gets more than their share of the credit.

Most rock bands break up because of this. One person writes, sings and plays guitar like a machine. He's at home writing their next hit, while his band mates are drinking, banging (their drums, of course) and snorting (with derision, of course).

Reread the section earlier on 'How a presenter can help a producer' in Chapter 2.

23 Other programme formats

**SKILLSET – NATIONAL OCCUPATIONAL STANDARDS
RADIO CONTENT CREATION**

Unit content included in this chapter:
RC13 Operate a radio studio

Studio 3 at BBC Radio
Leeds

Requests and dedications

A 'request' is when a listener simply asks for a specific song, usually for himself or herself. A 'dedication' is where they want any song, but to have a message broadcast alongside it.

> Perhaps the most important result of the successful record request programme is the listener feeling personal contact with the presenter via the radio. This is achieved by sincerity – too much and it becomes smarmy sickliness, too little and it sounds cold, casual and offhand.[1]

> Perhaps most importantly, we put messages from families and friends on the radio for them. Even the most battled-hardened soldier sheds a tear when his children have a message for him on BFBS.[2]

---

[1] BBC local radio training manual, 1987.
[2] Damian Watson, British Forces Broadcasting Service, *The Radio Magazine*, November 2004.

Requests and dedis (dedications):

- Are an easy way to get listener involvement in your station.
- Make the listener feel good that they've a hand in what music is played.
- Get lots of place names mentioned.
- Are potentially great research on whether you're playing the right kind of music.
- Can be good audience builders.

An audience-builder? Yes, because the person the request is for may be a non-listener who's been told by a friend or relation to listen in to hear the song. The more you do (workplace requests, school call) the more personal recommendations the station will get. (It's sometimes the only reason stations do a 'Thought for the Day' religious item, so the ministers tell their congregation to tune in.)

Even if yours isn't a specific request programme, you'll still get calls from people wanting to hear a certain song. These kinds of calls are arguably more important than the ones to 'dedicated dedication' shows. That's because dedication shows are usually about the message or the person ('It's my mum's birthday. Can you play "Simply The Best"?'). Uninitiated calls are more likely to be for current songs that the listener simply likes most at the moment and it is these kinds of calls that are worth monitoring. To do this, some stations ask the presenters to show on a simple tick-list the songs which are requested in this way, together with any other comments the caller makes about the song or the station in general. Other stations go further and occasionally have a longer questionnaire via which the presenter asks the caller what other songs do they like at the moment, which ones are they getting tired of hearing and so on. That information shouldn't be taken too literally, or carry too much importance, but put together with other research, or maybe gut instinct, it can help mould the shape of the station sound.

Before you read any dedication on air, read it to yourself off air. Do you understand it? Can you read the handwriting? Is it rude?[3]

◀ ACTUAL AUDIO

A BBC local radio presenter read out the following message from a 'listener' (actually one of their colleagues) on the Mother's Day request show, without realising it was a rude spoof:

PRESENTER: Please say a big hello to Connie Lingus who's 69 on Tuesday, she'll be enjoying my meat and two veg on Sunday at 12.00. Wish her all the very best and tell her I look forward to seeing her when she comes. Thanks ever so much, Ivan R Don.

If the message doesn't flow or is confused, rewrite it. Don't make any mention on air about the sender's illegible handwriting. Check all the information is there so you don't say something like, 'Oh, that's funny, that's a dedication to Cheryl's mum, but she hasn't told me her mum's name . . .'. Always read through the letters first and highlight the facts you're going to say. You may want to check the pronunciation of a street name with a colleague who lives in the area or ask around the office for a suggestion on how to pronounce an awkward surname.

---

[3] One station that's been caught out: http://tinyurl.com/mem7xq.

Don't give out full addresses on the air: mentioning the town or the part of town is fine but to give a street and certainly a house number is too much information. Consider this: '. . . a message to Vi Capstan of 35 Cherry Blossom Avenue, who's 78 today, and who lives alone since her husband Bert died . . .'. Or this kind of information revealed: '. . . and Jenny is six today and she and her friends are going to have a scavenger hunt in Nonsuch Woods later this afternoon . . .'.

Basic courtesy should tell you that if you ask listeners to call you for a request or dedication, make sure you have time to play it. A basic understanding of radio will tell you that a long list of names, addresses and messages becomes tedious to the vast majority of listeners. Instead, try to theme them or link them in some way: '. . . and there are several people with birthdays this week . . .', '. . . and now our regular anniversary section . . .'

Also try to get musical balance as you prepare the show, interspersing more recent tracks with classic oldies, faster songs in amongst the inevitable slower ones, male artists alternating with female ones and so on. Be wary of the most-requested songs such as 'Simply The Best' by Tina Turner which you simply can't play every week. Include that mention with one for another song and remember, the more often you play, for example, 'Simply The Best' on a request show, the more it'll be requested. That may mean that it's one that many people want to hear, but it'll also fast become one that many more don't!

All programmes are entertainment and are there for the great majority of listeners. Request and dedication shows are no different, so sometimes there are songs that you simply won't play. These are ones that are so far from your core music list that even though to play it would cause delight for the person who the song is to and from, it would be a literal turn-off for many more people. Requests alone cannot dictate the content of the programme. Indeed, neither can your own tastes, although your own tastes can *guide* it, and many stations don't play song requests as it compromises their playlist.

Don't say that you haven't got the song they asked for. If that's the case (or it's not one that fits with your format), then simply omit the title of the request and play another by the same artist. If the artist is not one that you play, then don't mention the requested song or band but play one similar. For example, you could replace a song by Bobby Vincent for one by Simply Red but not one by Gorillaz. You can use this technique whether someone's written in or if they're on the phone: 'Ahh, we haven't got any Rolling Stones here, but what about a classic from The Who?' Obviously, this won't happen on air if you've pre-recorded the call or taken it off air first to prime them.

What if someone calls for a song you were going to play next anyway? Simple. You don't tell them that it's all lined up ready to go, you tell them that you'll dig it out and will play it for them next. They'll go away a very happy customer!

Don't play a song for other presenters on the station or your personal friends. No one else knows them, no one else cares and it smacks of incest.

Don't just say something bland like, 'If you want a request, call me now on . . .' put an idea in someone's mind as to why they may want to call for a song for themselves or someone else. One presenter regularly says: 'It may be three words like "I love you", two words like "thank you" or one word like "sorry".'

Perhaps go further and suggest other reasons why listeners may want to make that call beyond the usual birthdays and anniversaries.

- 'Perhaps you've heard a great new song we've been playing and want to hear it again so you can get your friends to hear it too . . .'
- 'Maybe there's a special song for you and your partner, where the words just sum up everything you feel about each other . . .'

> □ 'Perhaps you were out partying hard last night and made a bit of a fool of yourself and need to apologise to your mates . . .'

Calling the 'request line' is still the best way for people to contact the station. Yes it takes a little more effort on your part, but it creates better radio. A few decades ago we'd encourage people to fax their requests, now it's e-mail or text requests. But those three methods take the human interaction out any engagement. A conversation with a real person is always better than the presenter reading out a list of names and song titles. Yes, e-mailing and texting are more convenient, but neither is as relatable and intimate as one person talking to another.

The presenting style on a request show has developed over the years and even though it may feel odd to do, it works well on air. You need to talk to both the sender of the dedication, the recipient and the rest of the audience all at once! And you need to, bizarrely, tell the recipient information they already know! 'Happy Birthday to Susan Fellows who's 55 today. That's from your daughter Katie, thanks Katie. You've written telling me all about your mum who lives in Robertstown. The whole family's coming round for lunch later, aren't they Susan? All eight of you. I hope they're enough chairs!'

You'll need to check your house style guide, but *legally you can record those who phone you and broadcast the conversation.* Even though it is against UK radio regulations to broadcast someone's voice without telling them, there is a 'loophole'. The ban was created in the 1990s to crack down on the growing number of complaints about 'wind-up calls' that were being broadcast without the victim's permission. However, it is generally accepted that if someone calls *into* a radio station studio they know that they could go to air either live or recorded. In other words that caller has, by calling the station, given implied consent to their voice being broadcast.[4]

Answering the phone

One of the benefits of computerised playout systems which automatically cue songs and ad breaks for you is that you have more time to do other things. That includes preparing each link thoroughly, and also helping your colleagues and talking to your listeners on the phone.

Always answer your studio line. It is one of the basic jobs for a presenter and it is important for several reasons. First you don't know what you might be told. It could be anything from information that is valuable to you: 'You just said this song is by Girls Aloud and actually it's the Sugababes.' Or it might be something of use to another department at the station: 'I'd like to buy some advertising space . . .', 'There's a huge fire right opposite where I live', 'Did you know you don't seem to be on the air on your 99.9 frequency?'. Perhaps it's going to be something for your listeners: 'Police have closed the motorway at junction six . . .'.

The second reason is that it's a chance for you to talk directly to your listeners. It's your chance to sell yourself to them on a one-to-one basis that you just can't do on the radio. Use callers for instant feedback: greet them by name, ask where they are calling from, what they like about the show and so on. Chat them up, get them on side — it's polite and you never know who is going to get a Rajar diary next time around. While you do this, it is

---

[4] In 2008 the Ofcom Executive Fairness Group agreed that callers into a radio station should be prepared for what they say to be broadcast, and have no expectation of privacy.

important to stay in character. If your on-air persona is 'boy next door' and you are dismissive of the caller, you will have probably lost them for life.

Some calls may be from listeners wanting help or a chat, so be prepared for this. People see the station as the fount of all knowledge, and to a large extent this is what we want them to think. But they don't necessarily call the newsroom to comment on a news story or the travel hotline to pass on details of a road hold up. They call the number they know – the studio phone-in number. It means you may get questions, comments and complaints while you're on air, most of which have nothing to do with you directly. Be polite to all callers. Tell them the correct number to call. It may be that they need more specialised help (perhaps to speak to a councillor about a broken paving stone, or even a counsellor about a broken heart). Ensure that appropriate numbers are in the studio.

Other calls may be kids' pranks, someone asking for a song that you have only just played, or someone who can't string two words together. These people only make up some of the calls – most will be from your listeners, the ones you are there to serve. Answering calls is not beneath even the most high-flying presenter. Indeed, it'll mean more to the listener to have the 'celebrity presenter' take their call than someone in the control room.

REQUEST LINE CALLERS FROM HELL

It's not just them on the phone, they're surrounded by their friends who all shout the answer to any question you ask, so you can't make out anything.

They call you by another presenter's name.

They say they called three months ago, and are surprised when you say you don't remember them. (They then try to jog your memory by quoting the conversation, the song they asked for etc.)

They mention their age, or that they fought in the war, for no apparent reason.

They say they 'always listen to you' even though you're a new presenter; say they've been listening to your show 'all morning', when you've only just come on air . . . and then ask for a song by 'Death by Drowning' in the love hour.

You ask them where they're calling from and they say 'London' (if it's a London station), or simply 'home' or 'my room'.

They ask for a song by the wrong title, quoting the chorus . . . or simply singing a line down the phone.

Or ask for one you've just played . . . or are playing right now.

> They repeat a conversation they had with the producer off air, on air: 'Well, as I told your girl, I wanted "Thrash Metal Suicide" but I've been told I'm not allowed to . . .'
>
> They ask on air what happened to a presenter who's no longer at the station. The one who left under a cloud. And then say 'Oh, I really liked them'.

Automation,[5] voice tracking and split links

'Automation' is when a computer plays out a single pre-recorded programme or when it plays out different elements (pre-recorded links, music, commercials, jingles), automatically cross-fading to give the impression that it is live. 'Voice tracking' is the process of pre-recording those links and inserting them in the playout system at specific points, so they can be broadcast as necessary. A programme in 'automation' can also be said to be 'voice tracked'. In other words voice tracking is a method of creating content. Automation is a procedure for implementing it.

Automation usually happens on smaller stations and overnight and at weekends. Previously, pre-recorded programmes for these slots had to be put together in 'real time'. In other words, an hour's show took an hour to produce, because the presenter had to sit through each song as it was recorded onto tape.

With automation, a presenter needs only to record the links and put them in the right order on the playout system (in between the songs, ads and jingles which can be dragged across from the hard disk), for a programme to be ready for transmission.

In its basic form, voice tracking has been around for years. Live or pre-recorded programmes syndicated to several stations, left 'gaps' into which a local TO[6] would play a 'local link' pre-recorded by the same presenter, as it was being played out. In the original days of the UK's Network Chart Show on commercial radio, stations were told in advance which songs were 'talk-up tracks' over which the live presenter in London would not talk, so that individual stations could play their own drop-ins or announcements. Nowadays, a single push of a button on the presenter's desk in London fires 'split jingles' of the same length but naming different stations/frequencies/areas/phone numbers to dozens of transmitters across the country at the same time. These economies of scale have allowed live programmes with top presenters to be heard at small stations belonging to the same group across the country.

For automation:

o   Costs are lower – a presenter can record a show, even from home, in less time than it takes to present a live one; a guide is about a quarter of the time. That means that either the cost for the presenter is lower (because they're working for less time) or they can spend the 'saved' time doing other work for the station.

o   The programme can still sound live with links over song introductions.

o   Links can be carefully considered and rehearsed before recording, so the best possible programme is produced. Fluffed links can be re-recorded.

---

[5] There is 'no restriction on the amount of automation – voice tracking – that a station may use', says the regulator Ofcom.
[6] Technical operator – someone who drives the desk on behalf of a presenter.

- On daytime shows, elements of automation can be used to segue a few songs in a row while the presenter goes to the toilet, let a guest into the studio or when they have to attend a public appearance before the show is finished.
- Even small stations can broadcast 24 hours a day and on difficult-to-fill occasions such as Bank Holidays, Christmas or New Year. (One presenter regularly hosted the breakfast show on two small stations in south Wales simultaneously from the same studio, by using a mix of live and pre-recorded links.)
- Different links of the same duration can be sent to different transmitters, and those links could include content local to those areas. So automation could mean that listeners are better served. Indeed, automation can be used with syndication (when a live programme is simultaneously broadcast on several stations in the same group). Station-specific commercials, jingles, drop-ins or song introductions can be played from a central computer giving the impression of being live and local. (Presenters use 'cheat sheets' of local places and events to talk about so they sound as though they are familiar with each station's area.)

> If you take 50 different radio stations, there cannot possibly be 50 good presenters at every station in a particular slot. Why not take the two or three quality class players and put them across the network?[7]

- A small station in a group can appear to be larger, by paying a cheaper rate to a bigger 'star name' for a show in which only a few links an hour have local content. Or stations in a network can share a live off-peak show, with automated elements (such as split jingles and ad breaks), to save money on employing staff at every centre.
- News, weather or travel can be played in automatically. The system fades the last song in an hour and opens the satellite feed from the news provider for a clock start and clock end, which is followed by a pre-recorded weather bulletin. The travel news provider can remotely record bulletins into the playout system.
- The 'feel' for the music is achieved by allowing the presenter to pre-fade the song as they record the intro for it. That way they can also still hit the 'music post'.

Against automation:
- Interaction with the listener is not possible; for example, phone calls and competitions. Talk radio needs an army of personalities ready and willing to open their mouths and face live listeners.
- The station can't react to breaking news[8] (although extra links can be recorded at home and placed in the running order remotely).
- If there's a computer fault and the playlist stops running or repeats itself,[9] for example on an overnight programme, there's probably no member of staff to hear it, let alone fix it.

[7] Ashley Tabor, Global Radio chief executive, *The Radio Magazine*, April 2008.
[8] US radio stations criticised ('stations went from voice tracking to backtracking when they felt the backlash') for being unable to react to Michael Jackson's death because their output was automated: http://tinyurl.com/nd539h.
[9] See page 7 of this Ofcom report: http://tinyurl.com/nzd84p.

- It is sometimes difficult for a presenter to get the right feeling when they have to record a Sunday night show the previous Monday morning.
- More presenter jobs are lost as one person voices programmes for different stations.

A similar thing happens with news bulletins at places where journalists work for an FM and AM station. One bulletin is pre-recorded and fired remotely, while the other is read live by the same reporter. However it has been known for the same recorded bulletin to be repeated for hours on end, or for the bulletins and idents to go to the wrong station . . .

In 2007 Ofcom warned one radio station about the poor quality of its automated programming which it described as 'totally unacceptable'. When the regulator carried out a spot check, it found part of a programme was drowned out by another programme being broadcast at the same time. On another occasion a networked news bulletin failed to appear, leading to three minutes of dead air.

Voice-track tricks:

- Those who voice track are most successful when they learn about the area they are performing for and cater to its needs.
- Make it sound local by defining local as 'to their sphere of interest'. Superserve that rather than a geographical location.
- Imagine you are actually live on air as you record your links to get the mood and feel right.
- Occasionally listen to the programme as it is broadcast to see how 'live' it sounds and what you can do with your future recordings to make the programme sound better still.
- Think clearly through each link and make it flow with the one before and after. They are recorded in isolation but heard in sequence. Make it a conversation. Reference things that you mentioned previously, as you would any other show.
- Make your presentation style fit with the song that's ending or starting.
- Think of those who are listening. You are still 'talking to people' not 'pre-recording links'.
- Only re-record big mistakes, that way you'll sound more natural and alive.

Be careful that you're not misleading or lying. It may be OK to say 'It's been a great day in Midtown' if you know that it *has* been, although you were 400 miles away. But if you then say 'with me live in the studio are the Pure Evils . . .', will the listener think that the band is in the Midtown studio? Does that matter? What if fans gathered at the back door to see their idols? How would they react to you/the station if they found out the band were neither there, nor indeed live? If you run a competition on the network programme of which Midtown FM is part, should you say that listeners to that station have less chance of winning because more people are taking part than they might imagine? Well, not in so many words, but yes. To do otherwise would be fraudulent.[10]

Swing shifts

These are worked by freelance presenters who swing from presenting one show to another. Sometimes radio stations employ such a person full time, whose job it is to cover for ill or

---

[10] More on the legitimacy of voice tracking at http://tinyurl.com/jev and http://tinyurl.com/oqu8rd and http://tinyurl.com/lfjnck. Things are more tricky in the States: there, even if the show being taken by stations across the country is presented live, after 8 at night the presenter can't even say what day it is!

holidaying colleagues. It may be that one week you're filling on drive, the next week you're the lunchtime presenter. This is a great opportunity and although you don't have a show of your own and have to follow the format of the programme you're sitting in on (and down-playing your own personality as a result), you're showing the programme controller your versatility and getting valuable on-air experience.

If you're introducing a presenter who's sitting in on a show because the regular host is away, don't draw attention to their absence. 'On the Drive Show with John Simons this after-noon . . .' is fine. Some stations even keep the name of the show, even when the presenter's away: 'With John Simons on the Dave Juby Drive Show this afternoon . . .'. You don't have to say 'John Simons is sitting in for Dave Juby on the Drive programme while Dave takes a well-earned break . . .' or similar. Whoever's presenting the show is presenting the show! (Incidentally, 'well-earned break' is another DJ cliché, to be avoided unless you're talking about a junior doctor or coal miner. Listeners believe presenters are pampered and privi-leged and will scoff at the idea that you think putting on a few songs for three hours a day makes a holiday well deserved.) Don't mention that the presenter you're standing in for is on holiday (their house could be burgled) or sick (it's personal).

If it's your first time at the station or on that show:

- Find out what the person who's booked you actually wants. Maybe they need you to blend into the usual output, or maybe to bring something different to the mix. Ask and make constructive suggestions.
- If you are standing in for the first time or haven't presented the programme for a while, going back over some recent scripts, running orders or listening again might help. The tone of the programme may have changed, time slots and furniture may have moved. Get a feel for all that again, because stumbling over junctions or sounding lost isn't going to do anything for your stress levels.
- Find out about the output and audience. Look at the programme or station's website, and listen, listen, listen. You need to note the style, running features, junctions, level of listenership interaction, the house style and of course, overall content. You need to be comfortable with this even though you still want to bring your own style to the mic. And nothing will put you off your stride like constantly being caught out by stabs and beds that you weren't expecting.
- Talk to the presenter you're covering for so you're aware of any ongoing topics they've been covering. If it's a very complex show technically it might be worth sitting-in with them a few days before.

Before you arrive:

- Have a 'show prep' sheet for each programme or station you work at, with all the information you need for on-air and off-air use. That might be station phone-in number and textline, the travel news junction times . . . and the name of the station written large at the top! And on the other sheet, door codes, log-in passwords, keyboard shortcuts. Likewise have a 'blagger's guide' with you of the other programmes and current 'talk-ups' (mentions of competitions, OBs etc.) so you can talk with authority and enthusiasm . . . and always have something to grab and read in an emergency.
- Phone or meet the producer and talk about content, likes and dislikes, about what they expect from you and what their way of working is: for example, whether you like to stick to a word-for-word script or prefer bullet points or the producer speaking to you when you're talking yourself. Ask about everything before it goes to air. Presumed knowledge (for example the pronunciation of a local name or place) is a

dangerous thing. Check before you open your mouth. Chances are you'll get it wrong if you don't! Start thinking about the features and the interviews. Potentially offer ideas to the producer. Input from you may well be welcome.

- If necessary, have a chat with your co-presenter about what the feel of the on-air relationship is. Is everything decided about who does what before you go in or do you just suck it and see? On lighter items can you throw in a question, even if it is not your interview? What are the hand signals? Ask your co-presenter to make it obvious what they want you to do.
- Get to grips with the junctions (e.g. travel news, weather etc.) make notes on where the regular slots are and try not to miss them. Make a note of any back-times you need. If you do miss anything, it'll upset the regulars!
- Take food. Nothing will endear you more and break the ice faster than a box of doughnuts or a few packets of biscuits for the show team.

Before you start the show:

- Make sure you remember your shortcuts, all those handy quick ways to get to scripts or audio or wires, anything you may want to use for background briefing or indeed as part of your script. They may not exist since you last used them so don't assume they're there just as you go on air.

On air:

- You're 'only' talking, telling stories to the audience and playing songs. So, compose yourself and have lots of safety nets . . . and know what to do if something goes wrong.
- You will make mistakes. It's inevitable. When you do, let it go. If you're too busy stressing about the stumble you made three minutes ago you won't be concentrating on what's coming up.
- Don't try too hard: better to underplay it rather than attempt to make an impression. Be yourself, but don't alienate a loyal crowd. Don't try to copy the person you're replacing and if you're co-presenting, try to make the other person sound good.
- Remember: you are a talented broadcaster in your own right and will bring something extra to the party. If nothing else, that something will be freshness. You've been asked to deputise because someone thinks you are going to be good. Let your personality come through.
- Have fun. That way your audience might even enjoy the programme . . . and you might even get asked back!

24 When it all goes wrong

It's fantastic when you do a brilliant show:

It was like great sex![1]

But, things do go wrong. There will be that feeling, milliseconds after you've made a stupid error that your blood runs cold. Every presenter makes them, and everyone (well, mostly) bounces back. So always expect the unexpected. If you do make a mistake, don't panic. It's not a crime. You will be forgiven if you do not do it too often and do not draw attention to it. Don't keep thinking about the mistake, it will distract you and make another mistake more likely. You are judged with how well you coped in the crisis, and if the listener remains unaware that anything untoward happened, then you've done a good job.

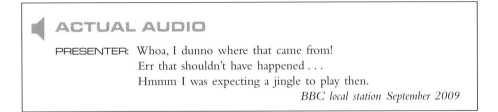

ACTUAL AUDIO

PRESENTER: Whoa, I dunno where that came from!
Err that shouldn't have happened . . .
Hmmm I was expecting a jingle to play then.
BBC local station September 2009

---

[1] From the film *Broadcast News*: http://tinyurl.com/l6lxe.

In this chapter find out what can go pear-shaped and how to get out of the mess fruitfully.

Putting the F into FM

Putting callers or guests live on air often brings with it the possibility of profanities. This is particularly so while on an OB with someone walking past a live mic shouting comments at the top of their voice — the radio equivalent to waving in the background while a TV reporter does a piece to camera.

We are, of course, in a world where swearing is more commonplace everywhere. Indeed after the much-publicised 'Sachsgate'[2] affair on Radio 2 in 2008, the BBC conducted an exhaustive piece of research into attitudes to taste and decency.[3] And it showed most people are relaxed about the use of bad language on air. The review showed that, as well as most people being unconcerned about the use of bad language in certain contexts, particularly after the 9 pm watershed, a substantial minority of viewers and listeners are in favour of *less* censorship. People apparently objected to the behaviour of Jonathan Ross and Russell Brand because of the bullying tone of the broadcast rather than the fact that swearing was used.

However, at the time of writing swearing remains unacceptable on radio usually at any time, certainly on a daytime programme. That's because radio is often said to be more personal than TV, people treat it as a friend, and so profanities are much more intrusive.

The broadcasting regulator Ofcom has found BBC Radio Ulster in breach of its rules after Hollywood actor Tony Curtis swore three times during a live show. Curtis, who only appeared to realise the programme was live towards the end of the show, apologised to listeners as did the show's presenter. Finding the BBC in breach of Rule 2.3 of the broadcasting code, Ofcom said in its adjudication that the use of one four-letter word in particular, 'was likely to have gone beyond the expectations of the audience for a programme of this type and at this time'. (13.00 hrs) The BBC informed Ofcom that it regretted any offence caused by comments made and that Mr Curtis and his press team were informed in advance that the interview was live. Therefore, it said, it 'wasn't expected that Mr Curtis, who is well experienced in giving media interviews, would use unacceptable language'.[4]

But, if swearing does happen:

- A guest or caller swears once and it appears to be unintentional — correct them on air and apologise to the listeners on their behalf. If you're controlling the faders then

[2] What happened is outlined here: http://tinyurl.com/79s8m6 and you can hear it here: http://tinyurl.com/n5453f.
[3] Read more on that survey here: http://tinyurl.com/ozoo95 and the reaction of MediaWatch here: http://tinyurl.com/lcxfxb.
[4] Read more on this story here: http://tinyurl.com/kvsvlg.

you can quickly fade that caller out. Likewise with swearing: butt in and say something along the lines of: 'I'm sorry to interrupt but you'll be aware that some people listening may be offended by what you've just said, so I'm going to move on to the next caller.'[5]

□ You should apologise to the audience because as far as they're concerned it's the station that's brought the bad language into their home. Try not to get flustered by the unexpected; if you sound measured and in control it draws less attention to the initial misdemeanour and everyone can move on almost as if it never happened. If you get all prim about what's just happened, it can sound ridiculous and risks careering out of control.

□ Have a form of words ready. If someone appears to defame someone else, butt in and say something along the lines of: 'Well obviously Mr X is not here to answer that specific allegation, nor do we have any way of knowing what you say is true so for that reason I'm going to let you go and move on.'

□ If it happens a second time – stop the interview immediately. Play a trail or song (as appropriate) and take stock. Speak to the guest off air making it very clear that the language is unacceptable and that it must not happen again. Ask them to apologise on air.

□ If they refuse to co-operate, or if there's a third occurrence, the interview must be stopped immediately – make a profuse apology on air and ask the guest to leave the studio.

The responsibility lies with the producer as well as the presenter. Producers should make sure all presenters are briefed, especially if those notorious for blue language are invited in.

◀ ACTUAL AUDIO

GUEST: It's a whole load of crap, man.
PRESENTER: Now watch your language, I'll give you one second chance.

BBC local radio station, October 2005

Sometimes it's you who utters the swear word!

I've managed to say the worst swear word possible on air, but it was a mix-up of words rather than using it properly! I was talking up Friday Night Kiss which had a mixture of 'big dance classics and up-front cuts'. It was during the last bit when I got the words muddled up a bit. I just soldiered on and didn't laugh or refer to it! I actually remember being more annoyed that I clipped the vocals on the next tune because it had thrown me.[6]

If you do trip up over a word when you're reading it's probably down to one of two causes:

□ You didn't prepare and read through the script off air before you read it on air.
□ You're reading it too fast.

---

[5] This and the following quote are BBC-recommended phrases for presenters.
[6] Sam Heywood, presenter, 96.9 Viking FM, *The Radio Magazine*, March 2005.

Always treat a microphone as live. If you make a habit of never swearing in a studio,[7] then you reduce the chances of swearing on air, or leaving in a swear word when an unedited piece is broadcast.[8]

> The presenters of Radio 4's *Today* programme regularly talk over the pips at the top of the hour – but they don't usually turn the air blue, unlike veteran Radio 4 continuity announcer Peter Jefferson. On Tuesday night just before 8.00 pm, Mr Jefferson was reading a continuity announcement when he fluffed his words, causing him almost to talk over the top of the pips. While he managed to finish the announcement just before the pips started, he could then be clearly heard muttering, '——!' between the second and third pips.[9]

In the UK[10] our approach to bad language is in fact rather tame. As the BBC[11] and Ofcom guidelines make clear, almost anything goes – it all depends on the context.

- Who's listening?
- What kind of programme is it?
- What have the audience been primed to expect?

One problem is of course that what seems innocuous to one person may be deeply offensive to others.[12] When the 'n-word' was used on *Big Brother*,[13] 450 people complained to Ofcom but what about the use of 'spastic', 'schizo' or 'poof' . . . or 'gay'?[14] Political correctness and heightened sensitivity towards others' feelings have made these words unacceptable in most contexts – while expletives like 'tits' or 'fanny' have largely lost their sting. Even the f-word and the c-word are OK provided that (on the BBC at least) the channel controller approves.

There are various regulatory bodies providing codes of conduct and a list of 'acceptable' swear words is available, but why risk alienating even a small part of your audience? That said, your use of language will partly be governed by the station you're on and the time of day[15] (you would 'get away' with more on an overnight show than a family-orientated breakfast show, for example) and the cultural make-up of your audience.

The worst words[16] (particularly the ones below with asterisks) are likely to be:

- *Insults* – bastard, bitch, c★★★sucker, dickhead, motherf★★★er, p★★★★teaser, slag, slut, w★★★er, whore.
- *Body parts and functions* – arse, arsehole, balls, b★★★★cks, bum, cock, crap, c★★t, dick, fart, knob, prick, p★ssy, sh★t, tits, tw★t, w★nk/er.

---

[7] Never swear in a studio: http://tinyurl.com/mpwqqo.

[8] Some examples (contains swear words) http://tinyurl.com/ljsesd.

[9] Read more on this story, and hear the clip, here: http://tinyurl.com/md9dv3.

[10] Steven Pinker, *The Seven Words You Can't Say On Television* (Penguin, 2008): http://tinyurl.com/m5a877.

[11] BBC '*Running Reports*' http://tinyurl.com/nqke35.

[12] Steven Pinker, *The Stuff of Thought: Language as a Window into Human Nature* (Penguin, 2008): http://tinyurl.com/nezssc.

[13] See the Ofcom ruling here: http://tinyurl.com/mbwzw4 (search for '6 June 2007').

[14] Chris Moyles' use of the word 'gay': http://tinyurl.com/d8uout.

[15] This ground-breaking show challenged many taboos: http://tinyurl.com/avklll; hear it here: http://tinyurl.com/kr846q.

[16] Ofcom's *Language and Sexual Imagery in Broadcasting* report: http://tinyurl.com/kwbqs6.

- *Religious* – bloody, God, Jesus, Jesus Christ, Jesus F★★★ing Christ, Jesus Sh★★★ing Christ.
- *Terms referring to people with disabilities* – mong, nutter, retard, schizo, spastic.
- *Terms of racial or religious abuse* – Chink, c★★n, kyke, n★gger, Paki, pikey, spade, yid.
- *Ethnic words* – blaad claat, bumbu, chi-chi man, ho, hoochie, punani (don't use any word if you don't know what it means!).
- *Sexually oriented words* – batty boy, bonk, bugger, dyke, faggot, f★ck/ing, poke, poof, queer, screw, shag.

Listeners complained that the station had not fully masked the words 'f*cking' and 'motherf*cker'. The radio group apologised unreservedly for the contest in the breakfast show conceding that the material should not have been broadcast at any time.[17]

Never use even what you'd consider to be the mildest of swearwords ('damn') or blaspheme ('Oh God'). Many people won't mind, indeed won't even notice, but those who do notice will mind a great deal. But is it OK to use the word 'fantastic'?

As part of a regular feature, Scott Mills played a clip from a TV programme with the word 'fantastic' bleeped out. One listener complained that the resulting sound appeared to sound like 'f*ck'. In its ruling Ofcom said that the suggestive style of the competition was likely to be 'in line with the expectations of regular listeners . . . the programme was broadcast at 4 pm during the school holidays and was therefore at a time when children were likely to be listening'. Ofcom found that by broadcasting a word that had been purposefully edited to sound identical to the word f*ck, the programme was in breach of the code.[18]

Presenters who push the line, sometimes step over it. But are they preferable to those who simply toe the line and comfortably conform?

An Australian radio show . . . featured a 14-year-old strapped to a lie detector and quizzed about her sexual history by her mother. She said she had been raped as a 12-year-old.
[The presenter] was accused of further insensitivity when, after the revelation, he asked: 'Right, and is that the only sexual experience you've had?' [Co-host] put an end to any further

---

[17] *The Radio Magazine*, July 2008.
[18] *The Radio Magazine*, August 2008. Read more on the story here: http://tinyurl.com/5cqy9u and see all Ofcom rulings at http://tinyurl.com/md85zp.

discussions when she realised the conversation had crossed
a line.[19]

Imus found himself at the center of a storm after he called
members of the Rutgers team 'nappy-headed hos' last week.
Protests ensued, and one by one, numerous sponsors pulled their
ads from Imus's show.[20]

In 2007 the entire breakfast team at one Yorkshire station was suspended after a listener complained to Ofcom about an on-air item about which invited listeners to call in to tell of items they had stolen while drunk.

Three stories of varying degrees of seriousness, and even though the last one was not swearing it could be said to encourage or condone illegal or offensive behaviour.

- *Err on the side of caution.* You can't be faulted for what you *don't* say. If there's any doubt in your mind, after thinking it through carefully twice, don't do the bit until you've had a chance to run it past a manager. If in doubt, leave it out. If it's truly great, it'll still be truly great in the next hour.
- *Keep your focus.* Distractions are a prime cause of saying things you wish you hadn't. Help yourself: don't just read the paper or call friends on the studio phone. It may seem obvious, but interruptions should be kept to a minimum to allow you to concentrate and prepare properly.
- *Be properly prepared.* It's when someone starts busking a link that trouble can happen. Know what it is you are going to say before opening the mic and have your plan jotted down in front of you. This 'road map' will give you a more concise, logical progression from point A to B, while still allowing for a smooth, natural delivery.
- *Stay away from company names.* There are times where including a company name is good ('We had a great time at SuperBurgers, handing out free fries to those who donated to our station charity'), and those when it's not ('We had a great time at SuperBurgers . . . eating mouthfuls of chemicals'). Of course, as outlined in Chapter 8, merely avoiding a company name does not guarantee you'll stay out of trouble, but it's a good first step . . .
- *Euphemistically speaking.* Another way to stay out of trouble is to become the master of the euphemism: invent your own words or phrases to describe things that could otherwise land you in more hot water.

Silence vs. dead air

'Silence' is when broadcasting 'nothing' is intentional and is working for you. 'Dead air' is *unintentional*. It could happen when you're so busy cueing up another song, or talking to the travel presenter on the ISDN talkback, that you don't realise that the song on air has ended.

---

[19] Read the full story here: http://tinyurl.com/mzm96m and hear the broadcast here: http://tinyurl.com/kkv3op.
[20] Read the full story here: http://tinyurl.com/2nrycj and hear the offending broadcast here: http://tinyurl.com/26jwru.

It may also be when you don't know what you are going to say next or where the link is going, because you haven't prepped properly.

It's an intimate thing, listening to your radio. And when it goes silent for no reason, and suddenly it's just you alone in the kitchen in a vacuum of total nothingness, either you assume there's been a power cut or the existential thoughts begin to take over.[21]

Many stations have an emergency recording that plays automatically if silence is detected for too long: when has there's been a problem in the studio such as some equipment failing or a presenter being 'caught short' (which is why most stations' toilets have an output speaker in them!).

One of the hardest things in radio is going to the toilet. You're on your own for three hours and have to run out during a song and you can hear it playing in the loo and you think 'come on!'[22]

If an item fails to play, then go to something else. Don't panic or blame, just move on.

That sounds straightforward but in a time of panic your thoughts go out of the window. But you shouldn't be panicking. The perception of a presenter is that they're cool, calm and in control. Always prepare the next item, and the one after that. Remember, if you can get something to air in less than five seconds, it's probably best not to open the microphone at all. Talking while you re-cue something will make the re-cuing take longer. Just concentrate on the problem in hand.

It may be that someone at the station has heard your problem on the radio and is coming to your aid already. If not and you can't fix the problem yourself, call an engineer. You may be able to enlist the help of a producer by talking to them on air. (Doing a seemingly normal link on the radio, but with your finger on the talkback button to the ops room, will draw their attention to your plight.)

If it is going to be longer before something can go to air, then you may need to fill. Open the mic and talk about what's later in the show or later in the day. Try to avoid talking about what's going wrong. Don't draw it to the audience's attention. Chances are they'll be none the wiser. Then, make sure all of this is written in the studio fault log so it can be followed up as necessary (it may be a recurring problem with one particular piece of equipment).

Mistakes happen but they're more easily dismissed if you don't draw attention to them. Don't refer to a mistake even if it was a major one. And if the listener wouldn't have realised, don't draw attention to it at all.

[21] Stephanie Marsh, *The Times*, 7 July 2009.
[22] Katie Hill, presenter Capital Radio, Radio Academy event, November 2005.

> Listeners and even programme managers are very forgiving and hugely forgetful.[23]

If you think you have gone off air, carry on with your show as usual and monitor the studio output (rather than the off-air feed as you would normally) while you get the engineers to find out what has happened.

Dead-air checklist:

- What is it that's gone wrong? Has the equipment failed to start ('failed to fire')? Are you absolutely sure that the item isn't going to air? (You may have knocked your headphone volume or may be listening to another studio's output by mistake.) Check the main output level meters.
- How necessary is it that you go to this expected item now?
- Can you do a smooth link (or no link at all) to something else? If so, do!
- If not, identify the cause of the problem, starting at the desk.
- Is the problem simple presenter error? Is the correct fader up? Have you left a pre-fade button on another channel on, which may cut the audio to speakers or head-phones?
- Can you carry on talking while you fix the problem? Dead air for up to five seconds is unfortunate but probably doesn't need an apology. Much longer and you'll need to explain and/or apologise, but keep the language straightforward and don't blame anyone.

How to fill to time:

- Tease and trail items which are coming up later in your show.
- Tease and trail other shows and other features in those shows.
- 'Trawl for calls' on your talking points of the day.
- Do some of the material that you've prepared in advance.

Rehearse the programme mentally (or indeed literally) in advance, and think what could go wrong and what you'd do if it did. This helps planning, anticipates problems and helps you work out the potential outcome.

Complaints

Complaints are a good thing: they show that someone is concerned enough to pick up the phone and want to talk to someone. It's obviously much easier for someone to simply stop listening and then you've lost them, perhaps forever. You may never know why or have had the chance to explain or persuade them of your viewpoint.

If the complaint is serious, perhaps accusing you of being overtly political or being rude to a caller (both of which could be issues for Ofcom to investigate) then your own station house rules will tell you how to handle it.

Take a caller's details and the issue they're raising and promise them that the complaint will be looked in to (more user-friendly than 'investigated') and someone will get back to them. Never give them the impression that what they say isn't being taken seriously, or give them cause to take their complaint elsewhere.

---

[23] Neptune Radio style guide, 1997.

Don't sweep the issue under the carpet, but deal with it honestly and openly with your manager. Don't try to deal with the complaint by yourself however awkward it may be to 'own up' to something you said on air which the programme controller hadn't previously been aware of. Most complaints die a reasonably swift natural death if a senior manager handles them carefully. An explanation, apology (if necessary) and reassurance that the issue will be looked into and will not happen again is usually sufficient, without the need for official regulators to be involved.

There's usually a station procedure for dealing with all such complaints, covering what's said to the complainant, how it's said and who says it. In the most serious situations, for example, if legal proceedings are being threatened over a libel issue, the programme controller will contact the station's lawyer.

It is to be hoped that station management will give you all the support they can in such a situation, and it'll help if you're honest and straightforward with them from the outset. By apologising and explaining your 'moment of madness', or putting it into context, you'll stop the situation getting out of hand. If you give one story, and the logger tape shows you said something different, you could be in hot water. Lies, subterfuge and hoping the complaint will go away usually make the listener more determined to cause trouble.

Sometimes you'll be on an outside broadcast when someone will come up and criticise you or the station in general. React politely, and try to talk them round. It's usually best to see what they *do* like or what station they usually listen to and then make a connection with something similar.

THEM: Your station's rubbish.

YOU: Hey, sorry you feel that way . . . why do you say that?

THEM: You play all that slow stuff . . . I'm into classic rock.

YOU: Wow, stuff like The Who and The Stones?

THEM: Yeah . . .

YOU: Well, they recorded several slow tracks that were classic rock songs in their own right. When was the last time you heard 'Angie' by The Stones? Tell you what, I'll play it for you tomorrow just after four, give me a listen.

Or

THEM: You always play the same songs over and over.

YOU: Well, that's because most people only listen for a short time . . . but they always want to hear one of their favourites when they do. What do you like? Really? I'll play it for you tomorrow just before nine . . .

So, try to be polite and unaggressive, and give an explanation to diffuse the situation.

If the comment's puerile, then overt politeness is usually the best policy. A caller rings and tells you you're crap; thank them for their comments and hang up. Then forget the call. Don't dwell on what they said as it might affect the rest of your programme. If they continue to call then tell your programme controller: there are ways to block or trace nuisance calls.

Apologising

It is rare that presenters apologise for a mistake. In general listeners rarely notice them, but they will if you keep telling them. If you have to correct information that was given out, avoid using negative words such as 'correct', 'wrong' and 'mistake'. Instead use phrases like, 'Can I just clarify . . .', 'I've got some more details on . . .'.

Perhaps you can change your angle so those who heard the previous (incorrect) information know of the change, but new listeners aren't any the wiser. Or simply give out the details again, together with the correction and make no reference to the change at all.

If there's a technical problem — a CD skips or a guest disappears from an ISDN line, move on. An apology may be necessary (though not always) but don't drag it out:

> We seem to have lost the professor so while we reconnect the line,
> let me tell you about . . .

Never blame anyone for a mistake or a fault. It's a DJ cliché to blame 'sticky fingers', 'the producer', 'the engineers' or 'gremlins' or, after tripping over a word, say, 'I'll just put my teeth back in'. If you tell the time incorrectly, just tell it properly and move on. There's no need for a comment such as, 'I'll learn how to tell the time soon'. You may make a brief generic comment about 'technical problems' to explain . . . but don't blame.

A professional presenter will have thought and prepared several steps in advance anyway and have a 'get out' — another song lined up, a trail to read or play or be able to adlib confidently. You may have to talk and sort out the technical problem at the same time, possibly while someone is telling you what to do via the talkback.

Alternatively, think whether any comment is necessary. If you introduce The Killers and Coldplay start singing, just back announce with the correct details, making no mention to what went wrong. If a song starts playing and then stops, slickly play another song you've cued up already.

Think about what you'll say now, if things go wrong later. Practise those ad libs so your lack of spontaneity doesn't tarnish your reputation. A good presenter will know how to overcome mistakes so the listening audience never even realised they were there. Build a relationship with your listeners and they'll be more forgiving when things go wrong.

> When it goes wrong, that's when you earn your money.[24]

Some presenters are too quick to apologise for things that *aren't* wrong! They either don't know the situation, or think it's easier to say 'sorry' rather than have to explain why the caller's not right.

Here's one example. The station's news reader had introduced a clip on newly legal same-sex partnerships with words similar to '. . . Michelle Mates of the Grantchester Gay Alliance says gay weddings are a good thing.' A caller phoned the studio and complained that the *station* had said that the weddings were good (in fact, the news reader was clearly quoting an *interviewee*). The presenter said, 'You're absolutely right, we shouldn't have done that, I

---

[24] Ben Jackson, presenter, BBC Radio Leicester, *The Radio Magazine*, February 2008.

apologise, it won't happen again'. The station hadn't been wrong, but the caller had been given the impression that it had been.

Sometimes 'sorry' is too easy.

Incidentally, there's an anecdote of a survey that was carried out amongst listeners to America's shock jock Howard Stern. Most listeners said they hated him: he was rude, arrogant, sexist and so on. Yet these very same people listened day after day, year after year. They liked being offended!

> You can be utterly opposed to a talk radio presenter's politics and opinions but still find them a brilliant listen.[25]

Let's look at the figures:

In 2004 research firm TARP[26] found that for every person who complains to a company, there are 26 who do not.[27]

Remember: don't ignore a complaint . . . and don't think that everyone thinks the same way. Like any 'research', think whether it is a true reflection, and if it is consider acting on it.

Having said that if you have a weekly reach of 300,000 people and you get 100 complaints, that's only 0.03 per cent of your listenership . . . but fewer complaints to Ofcom have ended people's careers . . .

Reading messageboards

Whose opinion about your show do you take notice of? Certainly your boss's, your trusted friends' and family members' . . . and possibly listeners' whom you know. But what about anonymous listeners who write on internet messageboards?

The general advice is not to. The reason people are anonymous is so they can say what they want, and a lot of that is derogatory (if it was pleasant they surely wouldn't mind putting their name to it!).[28]

Of course, the comments don't really reflect anything of value. The people who post stuff like that aren't unbiased, dispassionate, independent observers. In fact, you can't really tell who they are: they could be fans, competitors, angry ex-partners . . . They don't know what's going on behind the scenes and the reason for a mistake on air, a programme being changed or a missing presenter.[29]

---

[25] James O'Brien, presenter, LBC 97.3, *The Radio Magazine*, July 2007.

[26] More on TARP here: http://tinyurl.com/nhqb46.

[27] More on that survey: http://tinyurl.com/nab4rc.

[28] Cyberbullies discussed here: http://tinyurl.com/nkkvnu.

[29] Although on other occasions, some messages written by anonymous writers are curiously accurate. I once read something about me on a messageboard that only two other people knew about. It wasn't difficult to work out who was breaking confidences . . .

So, as tempting as it might be to read all about yourself and Google your name to see what people are saying about you, keep in mind that it doesn't necessarily reflect the general audience. It's like a self-selected focus group. Most people, including that large number of people you're trying to appeal to, just aren't going to care enough to write their thoughts about you on the internet. (Think about it: How many times do you write things about people and companies and shows and products that you like or dislike?)

Corpsing

There's one hazard that no amount of preparation can avoid: the collapse into inappropriate laughter. The *Today* programme website still treasures the moment when Charlotte Green kept a cool head while reading a news item about a Mr Twatt. And she would have sailed through it too, if it wasn't for the next story – about a plucky sperm whale.[30]

That's bound to make many people smirk, but remember, smirking is bad for your health and you have to try and control the temptation. The smallest reference to something odd may start you laughing, or it may be a prat-fall by someone in the ops room, a funny joke a caller's just told you or just because you're in 'one of those moods'. Obviously, there's room for humour on air, and many listeners can forgive the occasional mistake. That's as long as it is not too often and they can understand what's happened. Otherwise they'll be more bemused than amused and feel excluded.

If you get a fit of the giggles, look away from their cause, think sad thoughts ('I could get the sack because of this') and dig your fingernails into your arm to give your mind something else to concentrate on.

It's often best not to try to contain the laughter, but instead go to another pre-recorded item (preferably a song) and literally laugh off the moment. Have a good guffaw, walk into another room, have a drink of water and try to re-establish yourself in time for the next link.

Being out of breath

This usually happens because a presenter has just run in the studio late or in the nick of time, possibly because a technical problem has meant they've had to change studios at the last moment. They have probably not done a sprint, but the tense situation, panic and knowledge of what's expected add to make a slight breathiness increase dramatically.

With a news reader the problem is much worse than for music presenters: they only have short (or possibly no) audio to play during which they can catch their breath, and a serious tone and degree of formality are expected of them.

---

[30] Roland White, *The Sunday Times*, 30 October 2005. Hear that clip here: http://tinyurl.com/mw5hyu and another similar one here: http://tinyurl.com/cst9sv.

There's almost no way around breathlessness once it's started, but to play a song, calm down, take deep breaths and refocus. If you have co-presenters they can take over for a minute or two while you regain your composure, or you may want to simply explain what the problem is and move on the best you can.

Sneezing and hiccups

Sneezing is another situation which will come sooner or later, and may either be a sneeze you feel approaching or one that suddenly attacks.

There's not much you can do about the latter unless you are quick enough to turn off your mic or turn your head. Hearing a sneeze on air is rare, and not particularly pleasant.

If you feel a sneeze on the way, and if you can't go to another item, try and head it off before it strikes.[31] There are various means which work because they force you to focus on a physical sensation other than your sneeze. It works in a similar fashion as when you pinch yourself to make yourself forget that your stubbed toe is hurting.

Hay fever sufferers have some confidence in the fact that studios are invariably air conditioned and pollen is filtered out of the air before it reaches you.

After a sneeze, consider your colleagues. Is there an antiseptic wipe you can use on the mic or studio desk? If you've used your hands to catch it, try and wash them as soon as possible.

No one really understand why they happen (even babies in the womb get them), but hiccups and on-air work do not go well together. As you know, there's no guaranteed way to get rid of them, and even though they may be funny or interesting for a while, they quickly lose their charm. Having hiccups is tiring and will take your mind off your work. Do what you can to limit the likelihood of an attack by not consuming food or fizzy drinks on air. If they do strike, reduce your 'talking time' and alert your programme controller, who may bring in someone else to cover the shift.

Obit procedure

If and when a 'Category One' royal death occurs (i.e. the Queen, the Duke of Edinburgh, the Prince of Wales, the Princess Royal or Prince William), certain procedures need to be followed and there should be a clear allocation of responsibility for coverage at your station.

Procedures are less clear cut for deaths in 'Category Two', which is likely to include:

- the Duke of York (Prince Andrew)
- the Earl of Wessex (Prince Edward)
- Prince Henry (Prince Harry)
- the Countess of Wessex
- the Duchess of Cornwall
- the Prime Minister
- the Leader of the Opposition
- the President of the USA
- the Pope
- the Archbishop of Canterbury.

Obit procedures are divided into three phases:

---

[31] Here are some ways: http://tinyurl.com/2rkayt.

Phase one

The news is suspected but hasn't been formally announced.

On no account flash the news. Refer to your studio bible about whom to contact. There's no point mentioning the news and then not having any other information, so only hand over to the news room when you know they're ready.

Additionally:

o Be absolutely sure you know what to do if the announcement happens on your shift.

o Don't put anything to air unless it's from a specified source.

o Don't speculate.

o If you think an announcement is imminent then tone down your presentation in preparation. Consider dropping features, competitions, trails, sweepers, adverts and the news jingle, and start toning down the music.

o Know where the obit music is and which light is the obit light.

Phase two

The announcement and the period immediately afterwards, which could be anything from a couple of hours or days, to (in the case of Diana, Princess of Wales) more than a week. Much depends on the prominence of the person, their perceived 'importance' and popularity, their age, whether the death was expected, how sudden it was, what caused it, whether they died in public, whether anyone else was involved.

o If it's you who has to make the announcement, get it right, don't rush to be first. Use the agreed form of words (in the studio bible).

o Be set for regular bulletins, make no additional comments apart from what's been agreed and the station ID.

o All features, songs, ads, etc. are likely to be dropped.

o Later you may want to broadcast reaction from local dignitaries, religious people, MPs, etc.

o Then reaction from listeners – their memories, thoughts and expression of loss.

Phase three

Returning to normal programmes. When this happens will be decided by a senior person at the station.

o Use 'bridging tracks' over several hours to ease the transition from the sombre music to the normal mix.

o Still be sensitive over what is said and the content of calls, guests, songs, etc. If in doubt be over-cautious.

Moving on

When there has been an incident (swearing, a stunt that went wrong, equipment failure, a VIP death . . . or even just you having an off-day), write that programme off. Reload. Then work out what went wrong (or rather, what led to it going wrong) and work out what you can do to either minimise the risk of it happening again or to get out of the situation more cleanly. Then make sure you let anyone know who needs to know what went wrong (engineers for equipment failure, the programme controller for a swearing incident and so on).

Then refocus. After a while your old 'you' will return. But sometimes it's only natural that it'll take time after a bruising incident (especially when doubts creep in 'Was it my fault?', 'Perhaps I'm not cut out for this').

25 At the end of the show

Live concerts have a 'closing number' (and maybe an encore).

TV sitcoms have a theme tune, credits and applause.

The theatre show has the cast take a bow.

TV news readers do the weather, the 'and finally', paper shuffling and goodnights.

The stand up comic says 'I'm Elton Ben, goodnight!'

The book has the last page . . . the gallery has the exit sign and shop.

Every branch of the arts ends with an obvious 'show closer' so mark the fact that it's over.

Radio is perhaps slightly different. The station is the show, and it continues long after you've done your stint. We don't want to give the impression that when we turn off the mic the station shuts down. The 'show' goes on! Indeed our nearest relative, the television, shows promos for what's next over the credits (or even before) of the programme preceding it. But as radio presenters we give the impression we're the listener's friend, and have a personal relationship with them. And that means we say *hello* and *goodbye*.

Saying 'goodbye' is fine: it's bad manners to leave without saying anything and thanking them for their company. But it should be brief, and include a trail ahead of a specific item in the next programme that will benefit the listener. Give them a reason to keep listening, don't just walk out without saying goodbye!

EXIT POINTS

These are when the content changes, and the listener re-appraises their interest in the next item as they decide whether to continue listening.

As every 'feature junction' approaches (the end of a song or feature, or the start of travel or news etc.), there's the opportunity for the listener to turn off.

As a 'programme junction' approaches there's the opportunity for the listener to turn off.

So you need to be constantly teasing and trailing the 'forthcoming attractions' either in your show or the next one . . . especially during your last 20 minutes.

It's to encourage the audience to ignore the exit point and make the station 'stickier'.

The station isn't a series of separate shows. It is a single radio station of which your show is only part. Seamless programming helps increase audiences.

Give the impression of people constantly joining, but never leaving.

Never let them see the exit signs. We're searching for forward programme movement not opportunities to leave.
The radio is just a domestic appliance. If it doesn't entertain, listeners will leave it.[1]

So don't say goodbye, but something more like, 'I'm back tomorrow at ten . . . but keep listening to Radio X for Gemma Johnson and your chance to win a thousand pounds in our new Ring To Win ticket giveaway . . .'

Giving the listener a reason to keep on listening is a lot more compelling than hearing that you're leaving.

Handovers

The banter between presenters as one ends their programme and the other starts theirs is a good way of throwing ahead to what's to come, of introducing the new voice, for creating a 'family feel' and a seamless segue from one show to another.

On Radio 2 the handover between Terry Wogan and Ken Bruce worked well: Terry made a comment which he threw to Ken, there was a few seconds of banter and at the optimum time (usually after a punchline) Ken played his jingle and went into his first song.

It's great if the two presenters are in their own studios or one is a guest in the other's,

---

[1] BBC Radio Devon house guide, 2004.

but that doesn't always happen. Instead, you hear conversations with colleagues off-mic, or on mics set at different levels, chat that's incestuous or goes on too long.

In November 2007 a station apologised and paid undisclosed damaged to a former presenter after he was libelled by a colleague in an on-air handover. The aggrieved presenter took legal action against the station after it broadcast a live handover between two other presenters during which one of them made allegations that he'd lied to the Inland Revenue.[2]

In 2005 a complaint was filed to Ofcom by a radio presenter, against one of his colleagues, alleging 'infringement of privacy' and 'unfair and unjust treatment'. It was alleged that the colleague called him, confessed he was bisexual and was crying. The complainant said 'I believed him and comforted him and then he laughed, said it was a joke and later broadcast it. A conversation I believed to be private and personal was broadcast without my consent. I felt totally humiliated.'[3]

A handover that is much more than a minute is probably too long. After that you'll probably be talking about inconsequential subjects. It's not, after all, as though each of you don't have three hours in which you can talk! Keep asking yourself: is what the other presenter saying, in my show, relevant, interesting and compelling?

Hot-seat handovers can be trickier. These are where one presenter follows another in the same studio. As you're clearing up your debris, your colleague is behind you with their cues, coffee and probably comments, too. It can be all too easy for them to chip in with an off-mic aside, either invited or uninvited. This sounds poor and unprofessional. It's still your show, so don't allow uninitiated comments from 'guests' to intrude.

It is a courtesy to help the next presenter as much as possible by tidying up in good time, turning on the air conditioning so that they have a fresh studio and alerting them to any broken equipment broken (which you've also written in the fault log).

If *you* are the incoming presenter in a hot-seat changeover, make sure you don't disturb the current presenter too early or too much. Do as much of your prep in the office before you go in (although you will have told them in good time that you're in the building in case they become concerned at your late arrival).

Remember: professionals prepare.

After the show

The best times are when you come off air knowing that you've given your all and that the listeners and callers responded to you well and the whole show just buzzed.

It's good to keep evaluating what you're doing on the show. Whether you're a producer or a presenter, always strive to do a better one the next day.

---

[2] Read the full story here: http://tinyurl.com/nk7fqx.
[3] Read the full story here: http://tinyurl.com/nyjbar.

There are several ways this should be built in to your own routine and that of the station:

- Programme review meetings.
- Your own ROT sessions.
- Snoop sessions with your programme controller.
- Long-term appraisals.
- Listener panels.[4]
- Surveys (including Rajar).

Programme reviews – post-show meeting

Some presenters, especially those on freelance contracts, rarely stay at the station more than an hour after they've finished. Some have their coats on for the last ten minutes of the programme so they can make a speedy getaway (and others record the last few links so they can go before the programme's even finished.) The term for this is 'show and go'.

However, it's important that all those involved in the programme (presenter, producer, phone-op, programme controller) get together to discuss what worked well and not so well, and also *why*, and to set up features for the next day's show. These meetings keep everyone focused on the content that's getting the most response and helps ensure the show is always playing to its strengths and should happen soon after you come off air and shouldn't need to last more than half an hour to an hour.

A programme review (the term 'post-mortem' is dated and negative – it makes it sound as though the show was so bad someone died) may include the following points:

Presentation:

- Did the presenter arrive at least 45 minutes before the show?
- Did the presenter feel well briefed?
- Was there appropriate research and questions?
- What about the links? Were they too long? Was there too much fat in them before the point was reached?
- Can the listener connect personally with them?
- Are they presenting . . . or *communicating*?
- Is there visual language to paint a picture?
- Is there passion, fun, emotion? Does the content reach out and touch the listener?
- Are there talkable topics that the listener can think about or share with others later?
- Are there characters we care about?
- Is the information unique and personal (rather than private)?

Originality

- How creative was the show?
- Was it imaginative in content, the type of guests, the angles and the structure?
- Had it responded well to items in the news that people were talking about?
- Were there any moments that were 'surprising' or 'magic'?
- What emotional links were there with the audience? (Did it provoke, challenge and entertain?)
- Was there impact? A 'wow factor'?

---

[4] These were discussed earlier in Chapter 3.

Speakers:
- Were the guests good and reliable?
- Would they be used again?
- Are their details in the contacts database?
- Did the strongest callers get on air in the best possible order?
- Did the presenter get enough information about them and were they used well?

Technical:
- How competent were the presenter and producer?
- Consider elements such as levels, dead air, timings and accuracy.

Music:
- The three R's:
  - rotation — are the songs the best, and in the best order?
  - repetiton — is there a balance between repeats and making the best use of your best material so the biggest audience hears your work?
  - requests — do requested songs fit the playlist . . . are you getting requests for other material, such as song paradies, characters or sketches?

Running order:
- Were items in the best order?
- Consider the placing of music, ads, calls, links, guests, competitions.
- Was there a sense of movement? Was it momentum or confusion?

The listener:
- What did people listening at home get out of it?
- How would it have sounded to them?
- Were they involved?

Teases and trails:
- Were these done, and done well?
- Was there a difference between the teases and the trails?

Commercials:
- Were the commercials in order?
- Were there product or voice clashes?
- Any out-of-date ads or ones with the wrong copy?
- Have they been reported?
- What about the built (pre-recorded) trails for the station?

Competitions:
- Was it run and won?
- How did it go?
- Has the prize been sent?
- What about the next competition — is the mechanic understood?

Overall:
- Did the show meet its aims?
- Did it reach the target audience?

Prep:

    ◦   What ideas have you got for tomorrow, next week and next month?

Many of these feedback points are a matter of personal feeling: one person may say a song is repeated too much on the station, another may disagree. The producer may say that the items were in the in the best order, the presenter may have preferred another sequence. But you still need to talk them through to get different viewpoints as those are what the listeners will have.

Programme prep for the next day should start with a programme review of *that* day.

Self-feedback

Use the snoop machine to record your own aircheck (or ROT – 'recording off transmission') so you can listen to yourself from another perspective; in other words, as the listener does. You'll hear how long things really took to say and how you could have edited a link down.[5]

Don't listen to that day's show on the way home: it's too soon to be objective and you'll remember what was going on in the studio while you were doing each link. Give it a few weeks and then listen, but build up a library of recordings so you've got one to listen to each week, each from several weeks ago.

Ask yourself questions similar to the ones above. Monitor yourself truthfully and get other trusted people to give you feedback as well, so you don't fall in to annoying habits. Recognise what you are doing well so you can praise yourself. Ask yourself what could have worked better and why and make a note of what you need to do to improve. Then each week choose something from that list to work on.

Seek inspiration. Get in your car and go for a drive. Use your steering wheel column remote and flick through the stations . . . hear a link and flick to the next station. If it's coming to the end of a song, stay and hear the link then go to the next. Listen online[6] to presenters on other stations outside your immediate area. It's not copying, it's getting inspiration: you may hear something that you think would sound better if you did it *your* way, with *your own spin*.

Airchecking is a quality control on yourself.

Snoop sessions

For most people, the need to be recognised for who you are and what you do is incredibly important. Look at any study of the workplace and top of all of the 'Most important to me' lists is 'recognition'. It comes higher on the list than 'a pay rise' or 'more holiday time'. Recognition is a crucial part of human nature. Young children say 'Watch me, see what I can do!' This need is with us from the start.

---

[5] A good exercise for new presenters is to transcribe a link word for word, and then cross out everything that was unnecessary. You soon realise how many words are wasted.

[6] It's easily done: http://tinyurl.com/6gjhcc and http://tinyurl.com/myxd5z.

MASLOW'S HIERARCHY OF NEEDS[7]

Abraham Maslow developed a theory in 1948 that showed the different elements most human beings need in order to survive and thrive, physically and mentally.

At the bottom of the pyramid are the basic needs of food and shelter, which must be given priority. Higher up are needs such as social acceptance (to form relationships), self-esteem (need for recognition from others and yourself) and self-actualisation (the need to fulfil one's potential).

Frederick Herzberg later developed this theory, arguing that some people are motivated more by some needs than others (perhaps clean and safe working area, over money, or supervision rather than self-development, or vice versa).

An effective manager will consider what needs are important to each staff member, and what they can do (if anything) to satisfy those needs, to keep the staff member motivated.

Fifteen per cent of the 146 on-air staff surveyed said they never received coaching, with a further 34 per cent receiving snoop sessions on a less than monthly basis.[8]

It is in your best interest to get a critique done, either from your programme manager, an external consultant, or a colleague, a spouse, even your child. All great performers have coaches or directors. Even Tiger Woods has a coach!

A snoop (an 'aircheck') is similar to the programme review (and the self-review), but as a one-to-one with the programme controller. Their job is to carry out the four Cs: to critique, congratulate, cajole and coach — constructively.

I once had a snoop session at Radio 1 in which a very senior bod stopped the tape after five minutes and gave me this feedback: 'You're very good with the buttons' . . . and that was it.[9]

Wes was critiqued (to a very limited extent), and congratulated but wasn't cajoled or coached constructively. All of these elements are important.

Critiquing is the session itself, which should include the bad points from the show as

---

[7] See the pyramid here: http://tinyurl.com/obg3xy.

[8] From a 2008 survey by research agency Hallett Arendt.

[9] Wes Butters, former Radio 1 chart show presenter, *The Radio Magazine*, October 2005.

well as the good ones (perhaps in a 'shit sandwich': congratulated on what was done well, then less well, then some more congratulations).

Cajoling and coaching is done by explaining why an element would be more effective if it was done a certain way and by setting targets for you to reach.

All this should be done constructively over time, with thought and offering explanations. It is inevitable that when you start there will be lots of elements of your show which will need improvement, but you'll become better, faster, if you're shown what you could have done instead. This will improve your confidence. When someone says you did a good show, remember how that makes you feel. Ask them what they most enjoyed and try to make your next programme come up to the same standard. In contrast, if a show is a complete lemon, learn from that too. There will be times when people are not constructively critical and say things only meant to hurt, rather than help. Listen, learn what you can . . . and filter out the rest.

Radio station managers don't generally take time to listen critically to their product as much as they should, and if they do, they listen in the office while organising rotas or road-shows. In other words they're not listening *as the listeners do*. They need to get out of the office and hear their breakfast show as they sit in traffic jams, the morning programme as they walk around the corner shop and so on. Such days should be entered into their diaries as set 'research days' at least once a month and not be moved. They're a vital part of helping the manager see the wood for the trees and enabling individual presenters and the station as a whole, to develop.

A third of on-air staff considered their programme controller to be 'hopeless', with only 45 per cent of respondents having a positive view of their boss.[10]

Radio management[11] has got to be down to LUCK! They have to:

- **L**isten to the station
- **U**nderstand what is right and wrong about its output
- **C**are enough to do something about it
- **K**ick off the changes – yes they're sometimes difficult but on occasion you have to act with the axe.

Of course with automation, a programme controller can in theory, give an aircheck to a presenter before a show is even broadcast. Pre-recorded links can be checked for content and corrected on the spot. Never again should a poorly thought-out link, or one in which the station's name doesn't appear, go to air. 'Pre-air airchecks' could make a voice-tracked station sound perfect!

Long-term appraisals

Re-evaluate everything you do about every six months. It's natural that some of your features may be getting near the end of their natural life, so try to end them while they're still popular rather than when people are fed up with them. Some successful features can run for years and years, but it's much more usual to rest them to introduce others, or drop them completely.

---

[10] From Hallett Arendt; 2008 survey.
[11] Overheard: 'Anyone can be a manager of a radio station – not many people can manage one.'

Motivational factors	o Positive and/or constructive feedback from managers or colleagues o Positive feedback/recognition/listening figures from listeners o A higher profile programme, more budget, more producers, bigger station o Rewards for reasons such as creative programming
Demotivating factors	o Little, no or destructive feedback from managers of colleagues o A feeling (real or perceived) that no one at the station listens to the output o Little or no feedback from listeners, low Rajar figures o Faulty equipment o Perceived lack of promotion, publicity or production for the programme o Success going unrecognised or unrewarded. o No faith in the management's 'management'

Part Five
GETTING IN

26 Where to start

There are many ways to get into radio, but they can be edited down to a basic six:
- Get an on-air position at small station.
- Get an off-air position at a medium to large station.
- Go to a university or career broadcast school and do work placements at stations to get experience.
- Work at a community or internet station, or present your own podcasts.
- Work in a radio-related industry such as presenting travel reports.
- Be a celebrity. Some stations lure presenters because they've been on TV, and listeners will instantly know them and their shtick.[1] Obviously not all celebs who've made it big in one area will convert to radio,[2] many have their show just as long as their '15 minutes of fame' lasts and then are dropped, although in other cases it's true, they will succeed (Jonathan Ross, and many weekend presenters on BBC Radio 2 for example). What's important is putting the right people on air, not just because they're famous in another role.

A lot of television personalities have done great radio, such as Jonathan Ross, but too often a famous face is parachuted into a prime radio slot with no experience of, or particular aptitude for, the medium. [Management] have lost their gifts as talent-spotters and are too content to rely on a proven public profile to garner an audience. Stand-up comedians are also seen as a ripe recruiting area, and here too there are many who have a real gift for the intimate communication that radio needs, but there are far too many who simply come on and do a version of their act. Loud, larger-than-life performances work in clubs and theatres, but not radio.[3]

Some stations just pluck people off the telly and think that is enough. I heard one show recently in the car and he had about as much empathy with the music and connection with the audience as a dead mackerel. I actually wondered if he had just come in to record the links and buggered off. Radio is a lot tougher than telly.[4]

---

[1] Their personality, characteristic attribute, talent, trait and 'take' on life.
[2] For example: http://tinyurl.com/lu94o3.
[3] Ken Bruce, presenter, BBC Radio 2 see: http://tinyurl.com/nxayfm and his autobiography *The Tracks of My Years* (Sidgwick & Jackson, 2009): http://tinyurl.com/muzw2f.
[4] Nicky Campbell, presenter, BBC Radio 5 Live, *The Radio Magazine*, June 2009.

What route you take will depend to a large extent on your own personal circumstances. For example, your age, current job, family, whether you mind moving house and so on. There's the danger that, after resigning from your current job to follow your radio dream, you realise it's just not for you, in which case part-time weekend work is probably a good way to start to see whether you'll be bitten by the bug. However, your career will take longer to develop.

As automation becomes more and more common, a natural entry-point for many aspiring presenters has closed. There was a time when shows, pre-recorded on spools of tape, needed to be played out usually at weekends or bank holidays. On other occasions, stations had non-stop music hours for which a technical operator was needed to play songs, jingles and ad breaks. Now, computer playout systems can do all this, saving expense for many stations. However, some BBC local stations still prefer a real person to play in programmes and calculate backtimes. The human system also means phones can be answered and up-to-date weather reports broadcast – things that automation hasn't yet managed. There are, then, still opportunities as a tech op (TO), although they're disappearing fast.

> Recession has affected everyone and radio has been hit badly. There's nowhere for new talent to cut their teeth as commercial radio keeps networking vital development shows.[5]

Another role for a TO, and one which is more prevalent in BBC local's speech-heavy stations, is driving a show for a presenter who may have come into radio from another field and therefore are unfamiliar with the desk and unable (and sometimes unwilling) to learn. Their 'attitude' could be your opportunity!

A further situation in which a tech op would be used at a station is when there's an outside broadcast. An OB TO drives the studio desk when the presenter is out in the field, mixing the live reports with other elements. As the TO is in the studio to play in songs if the signal goes down (signal is lost between the venue and the station), they may occasionally also get to go on air.

Many presenters start off as a TO and it's a well-established route from working on someone else's show to getting one of your own.

Like a technical operator, a promotions assistant is also a good off-air way to get on air. It's not as obvious a route, but you'll still learn loads about the station and show that you're keen to learn, are good at organising events, and can keep going when the promo van gets stuck in mud, the new T-shirts have the old station logo on them and the signal from the OB is lost five minutes into a two-hour show!

Treat your time at the bottom of the ladder as an opportunity to learn more about your next steps, and the ones after that. To a large extent in this business you make your own luck – some ways to get the break are listed on the following pages.

BBC radio

Most of the jobs at the BBC are advertised to the public on the BBC jobs website.[6] Some are for presenters but others are 'foot-in-the-door' positions, such as receptionist, phone-answerer or charity co-ordinator.

---

[5] Adam Catterall, presenter, Rock FM, *The Radio Magazine*, May 2009.
[6] Log in here: http://tinyurl.com/2punbf.

Most jobs, though, are offered to people already at a station who want an on-air role as the next stage of their career. It may be a keen helper on the Saturday sports show, a phone-answerer or receptionist. Don't underestimate the advantage to your career of being in the right place at the right time and the realisation that *that* is not always down to luck.

Also watch out for the BBC talent programme which is advertised widely but especially on the website. This competition gives the opportunity for people to get short-term employment in the BBC in various roles of radio and TV.

Commercial radio

Most of the commercial radio jobs are advertised in *The Radio Magazine*;[7] you may stumble across a job on the individual websites of the stations but that will be long and arduous process.

Most vacancies at commercial stations are filled through word of mouth, moving presenters between stations in the same group, poaching from other stations, or giving a break to someone who has sent in a demo or who is already helping around the station.

There are several websites that advertise jobs in BBC and commercial radio, such as that for the Radio Academy.[8]

Travel presenters

One very good way into getting a show of your own is to contribute to someone else's!

Trafficlink[9] and GTN provide road news for BBC and commercial stations across the country, from their main bases in London and other studio centres around the UK.

You have to be on the ball to cope with different stations, presenters and personalities every few minutes. You'll be shown how to read the road news, which is written in a form of shorthand to make compiling it faster. You'll need to be able to adlib around the information and have to sight-read news as it flashes on your screen while you're on air.

You'll be known to presenters and management teams at various stations as they'll become aware of your voice and style of reading. Chat to the presenters off air before you go on air, so you'll get to hear of any opportunities that may be coming up. You may even be able to get to go in to a station and get someone to show you how to use the desk and put together a demo.

Community radio[10]

Part of the reason for awarding community licences is to get more people involved in making radio. That's a gift for someone just starting their broadcasting career. Ofcom[11] says that in awarding a licence they'll take into account 'an applicant's proposals to allow for access by members of the target community to the facilities to be used for the provision of the service and for their training in the use of those facilities. It's a characteristic of service that members of the target community are given opportunities to participate in the operation and management of the service . . .'.

---

[7] See it here: http://tinyurl.com/ko4wet and also jobs advertised here: http://tinyurl.com/5zy3q6.
[8] *The Radio Academy*: http://tinyurl.com/nnddf4.
[9] Trafficlink: http://tinyurl.com/bwuxbx and GTN: http://tinyurl.com/kp9c4l.
[10] The Community Media Association http://tinyurl.com/nzoa88.
[11] Ofcom: http://tinyurl.com/d9s9qn.

RSLs

These legal stations may offer a great opportunity for you to get in to radio at the grass roots. Several hundred of these short-term stations are set up each year and if you get in with one of them you may not only get some broadcasting experience but also get to help with formatting the station or writing the proposal for a licence. If the RSL is a forerunner of a full-scale licence then you stand a good chance of a job if and when they win it. As RSLs are specifically locally based stations, you'll be more likely to get a role with one if you live in or are very familiar with the broadcast area.

Keep a watch on the Ofcom website to see which groups have just been given licences.

Student radio

This is a great start to your broadcasting career, so if you're going into higher education try to choose a university that has its own station. These are run for students by students and their standard of broadcasting can be very high. There are around 70 in the UK, and the Student Radio Association[12] holds conferences, training events and awards ceremonies.

Student radio is certainly proving to be a great source for new talent, more than it was ten years ago.[13]

Hospital radio

Many of today's radio presenters started in hospital radio. Most stations are hugely professional and have equipment and output that rivals that of professional stations. They have a large team of dedicated volunteers who broadcast for several hours each weekday and throughout the weekend. Many have computer playout systems and do sterling work entertaining patients and staff, and raising money for the station and the hospital. But getting on air with them may take some time. It's understandable that there has to be a waiting list for presenters, and those who've been with the station the longest should not be forced out by newcomers (although many stations regularly change their schedules to give everyone an even chance).

It's also understandable that every volunteer has to serve an apprenticeship, usually in the form of walking the wards collecting dedications and shaking a collecting tin at fairs and fêtes, before being allowed on air. That means it may take several months or years before you get a programme of your own, but don't be disheartened. In between ward rounds you may be able to sit in one someone else's show and see what happens. If you suggest some ideas, offer to help in research or are willing to answer the phones then you'll get on much faster than those who don't.

Hospital radio is the place that you can develop from a club or party DJ to being a broadcaster. You will learn how to talk on a one-to-one basis to people. You will learn how to structure a programme hour and work around furniture. You'll learn the basics of interviewing guests and interacting with other volunteers at the station.

---

[12] SRA: http://tinyurl.com/m6zv59.
[13] Kevin Hughes, presenter, 95.8 Capital FM, *The Radio Magazine*, September 2009.

Any work you do at the station will be on a voluntary basis and you'll certainly end up out of pocket (not only in time but also in petrol and car park costs if nothing else), but it'll give you great experience for your CV and will provide a place where you can put together a demo.

Some stations recruit at 16 but the trend is slowly moving to 18+. This is partly for legal reasons over who is responsible for those who are legally still children and partly because of the nature of the work (being around vulnerable people, those in bed and in various states of undress, and having access to children's wards). It is also increasingly likely that all volunteers will have to go through a CRB (Criminal Records Bureau) police check before being accepted. The Hospital Broadcasting Association[14] has 226 member stations covering 415 hospitals.

Pirate radio

It's not a very good idea to get involved with these outfits if you want to make it as a legal, professional broadcaster. If you're found and fined, or even imprisoned, then your career is as good as over. Some pirates broadcast because they feel as though there aren't any stations playing their kind of music or presenting it in their preferred style. If that's you then go down the legal route and apply for RSLs and a formal licence, or swallow your pride and get some experience at an existing station and try to change attitudes and content from the inside.

Club and party DJ

You may already be a club DJ and want to get into broadcasting. There are similarities but actually very few of them! The style of presentation; the use of your voice, technology and timings, paperwork and protocol and interaction with the audience, are all markedly different. The path travelled between the two jobs is one taken by many, but few make it to the end unless they have some broadcasting experience as well as that of playing music. Start working as a hospital radio volunteer, get a demo recorded in a radio style and take it from there.

Being a party DJ is perhaps closer to being a radio presenter. You play a wider variety of music, learn how to use the microphone and get to interact with the public more, even if it is only by presenting the bride and groom and their first dance or 'three cheers for Uncle George's 80th'. Help out with a mobile disco outfit and help lug the gear around for little or no money and after a while you'll learn what plugs in where and how the bits of kit fit together. A basic understanding like this will stand you in good stead at any radio station or on an outside broadcast! Then ask if you can try your hand at segueing a few songs, or practise before the guests arrive or the club opens. After a few months you could fill in for the main DJ when they take their break – it's all experience that will make a difference when you try and get your foot in the door at a radio station.

Talking newspapers

This is, of course, not broadcasting at all as you'll be involved in recording articles from a local newspaper onto CD, copies of which are sent to local blind people. This will

14 HBA: http://tinyurl.com/mt4tmh.

help you learn how to use your voice to deliver stories as well as microphone technique and timing. Again, it's another line on your CV that shows a potential employer that you're keen to follow your chosen career path. The charity is The Talking Newspapers Association UK.[15]

Broadcasting courses

These can be a very good way into radio, but choose the course wisely. There's often no accreditation for those 'be a presenter in two-days' type courses and even though there are some which are well known and very professional, you may spend a lot of money to sit in the back bedroom studio of someone who was last in a radio station a decade ago (and that was to buy a T-shirt). Having said that there are some which are very good: the National Broadcasting School[16] is one and RadioWise[17] another.

Community Services Volunteers[18] is the largest independent media-training group in the UK and offers media training to charities, community groups, the unemployed and disadvantaged. These courses are usually free, certainly cheap.

The Community Media Association[19] also runs low-cost training for those who want to get in to radio, and there's lots more advice on training on the Skillset[20] website. They also run the Open Door competition which gives thousands of pounds of free training to those people who can show they're keen and have some raw talent. The Radio Academy also runs regular Masterclasses.[21]

University courses

To make it as a good producer or presenter, you'll need experience in life as well as in radio. That's why many potential employers will take a second look at an application from someone who's completed a degree course. Even if the subject is unrelated to media, it still shows that you can apply yourself, have intelligence, can study and can set targets and so on. (One colleague suggests law courses, which teach how to write succinctly, develop and support an angle, and perform.) A broad knowledge base helps you in the long run.

Alternatively go on a specific media studies, broadcast journalism or communications course[22] to get more of an overview of the industry and its place in society.

Questions to ask:

- Is it a theoretical course ('the role of reality TV') or is there hands-on work (actually making a radio feature or programme)? A good course will give you at least 50 per cent practical time.
- What are the skills it teaches, and what equipment is used? Is it up-to-date and what the industry is using?

[15] TNA: http://tinyurl.com/mepot9.
[16] NBS: http://tinyurl.com/npr6aw.
[17] Radio Wise: http://tinyurl.com/qdb8un.
[18] CSV: http://tinyurl.com/ylnseg7.
[19] CMA: http://tinyurl.com/nzoa88.
[20] Skillset: http://tinyurl.com/lovurz (and click on *radio*).
[21] Masterclasses details here: http://tinyurl.com/msw4od.
[22] Listed on the Skillset website: http://tinyurl.com/mxtdxr and the organisation which provides accreditation for broadcast journalism courses is here: http://tinyurl.com/mdchn4.

- Are there 'news days', or RSLs on a regular basis? If so, do everything: news, sports, presenting, promotions . . . all to add to your experience.
- Who are the trainers and tutors? What's their background? Have they actually been in the media? Better still, are they still working in it? Are outside speakers brought in?
- What about placements? Where are they? Are they arranged by the students or through the college? What kind of places have they been at recently? Does the university have any other media links?
- What happens after the course? What's the qualification? Where have students recently got jobs? Can you speak with them to ask about the course? Will tutors help you get a job?
- What clubs and societies are there which may help you develop your broadcast skills: public speaking, debating, acting . . .

Work placements[23]

Badger your local station for a work placement, but apply early and be politely persistent. If you're at school, most of your friends will be applying for the same places and many stations only have one person at a time on a placement.

Be prepared to be interviewed for the placement. Competition is fierce even at this level. BBC local stations go through a rigorous selection process, and you have to apply via the jobs website mentioned above. Make sure you actually listen to the station you're applying to[24] and have something to say about it!

When you get to the radio station, offer to work in as many different departments as you can in the time that you have. You may want to be a presenter but you'll benefit from seeing how the other parts of the station work to contribute to the show. Remember: even though the presenter is at the sharp end of the station there's a lot going on behind the scenes to make their show what it is. Without other departments the presenter wouldn't know what songs are the best ones to play to attract the audience, and would have no one to interview, no competition prizes to give away and no adverts to play. And that final point, of course, would mean that they wouldn't be paid!

Look around the other departments and get to know what the presenter's colleagues do in the newsroom, promotions department, sales team and so on – you may find one of those jobs more interesting than that of a presenter or producer.

Some more tips to make your placement a success:

- Consider smaller stations – you're more likely to learn more and do more at Hometown FM than you are by merely watching a producer at Radio 1.
- Do everything with enthusiasm and to the best of your ability.
- Do what you're asked, and then stay late to learn what you want to learn.
- Learn by observing as well as asking.
- Make yourself invaluable – master a task so you're always asked to do it.
- Use your initiative – if you see something that needs to be done, do it.
- Don't clock-watch – be there even when you don't have to be.
- Approach experienced staff with questions.
- Have an understanding of the big picture about radio as a whole.

---

[23] See more on work placements on http://tinyurl.com/a7ts2s and http://tinyurl.com/ct9fth.
[24] You could go through this website: http://tinyurl.com/paod3.

- Do the crap, the calls and the coffee – it's not all action all the time.
- Always turn up on time.
- Always think of the long-term goal.
- Network – make contacts and offer yourself to work there after the placement ends

Volunteering

I wasn't paid for three and half years but you can't buy that kind of experience.[25]

There is, of course, a fine line between taking advantage of the station wanting another pair of hands and them taking advantage of you! Some stations rely heavily on volunteers: RSLs, community stations and some smaller commercial stations are staffed almost entirely by them. If you feel as though you're getting experience, then by all means stay. If you feel that you're being asked to do the mundane and menial jobs too often (you should expect to do them sometimes) then have a quiet and polite word with someone. Don't just complain, but suggest what else you could do as well, or instead, that would help the station and yourself.

If nothing changes you'll have to ask yourself whether your time is worth the amount of experience you're getting. If you decide to leave, then ask for a reference that you can take to another station for more experience or some actual cash.

A former tea girl has been unveiled as the new host of Forth One's Drivetime show. Yasmin Zemmoura, who started at the station running errands for the presenters, was to present her first show between 4 pm and 7 pm today.[26]

Skillset, the body that oversees media training in the UK, reckons 40 per cent of radio jobs are never advertised, they go to someone who was 'in the right place at the right time'.

Demos

It doesn't matter how good you think you are, or how good your friends and family tell you that you are, what you have to do is persuade a potential employer. Although some presenters are poached from station to station, many jobs are got through a 'demo' (or 'aircheck').[27]

The first few seconds of the demo are what count. As the maxim goes, you don't have

---

[25] Chris Evans, presenter, Radio 2, *Desert Island Discs*, Radio 4, November 2005.
[26] *The Scotsman*, 31 May 2005.
[27] 'Demo' is short for 'demonstration', an example of how you sound submitted on an MP3 file.

a second chance to make a first impression. (As a comparitative statistic, it's said that the average length of time someone watches a video on YouTube before going elsewhere is less than ten seconds).[28]

Your demo is your audition. It's just like what an actor goes through before getting a role on stage. But the great thing about a radio audition is that it's not live, it's recorded, and that means you can spend as long as you like getting it just right to give you the best possible chance of a job.

> Firstly, it's a great, distinctive voice [that makes a great demo]. You can tell almost immediately if the person has a passion and a belief for what they're doing. We listen to the radio to be entertained, we want to feel good, be it through the music or through the broadcaster, so they've got to sound like they care and talk naturally. So many of the tapes we receive are of people with no comedy background, trying to be funny and in turn all that achieves is making you feel like the person is talking down to you. If I hear potential, I like to meet them to see what they're like. Are they in it for the right reasons, are they intelligent, do they see this as a real career . . . 'cos let's face it, if you're starting out you're generally coming from a position of little experience about how to present yourself and we all need guidance.[29]

Sound natural and communicate. A demo, like a show, should start with some sort of greeting. What will grab a PC most is an intro that's credibly warm, brief and unique. Save the high-power link for number two or three.

You can have an unusual voice and still make it in radio, but it's tone, delivery and clarity as well as personality that are the most important things. That personality should be yours. You may be a 'wannabe' presenter but the station won't want a 'wannabe' Chris Moyles, Chris Evans or Christian O'Connell. Those three presenters are hugely successful at being themselves on the radio. You would just be a pale imitation. Certainly learn from their style, and work out what they do and why it's successful and apply *that* to yourself – don't just copy them. Bring your own X factor to the demo.

Understand the station you're applying to. Do not send clips of you interviewing a local author to a chart-based station, do not send a recording of a super-slick segue with drop-ins and whooshes to a BBC local station, unless that's the style they've specifically asked for. Sound like a presenter on the station you're pitching to – and that includes your choice of songs.

Think carefully about including any dubious material or innuendo in any link. What went down a storm in your late night show on student radio may be too near the knuckle for a controller who's looking for a family-based breakfast show presenter. Similarly, avoid including any link that comments on political or religious matters or indeed 'the news' at all. Err on the side of caution.

Other qualities a programme controller would listen for in a demo would be your maturity and intelligence; you should sound as though you know what you're talking about, have

[28] Seth Godin, *Meatball Sundae* (Piatkus Books, 2009): http://tinyurl.com/ljz76g.
[29] Paul Jackson, programme director, Virgin Radio, *The Radio Magazine*, December 2004.

confidence in your delivery style and confidence in driving the desk – did that jingle or sound effect start bang on time, or did you hesitate for a split second beforehand?

Show that you can be quick witted (perhaps with a comment that sounds off the cuff, maybe interacting with a caller or another presenter), are creative (this may be as basic as finding a new 'in' to a what's on), and can read from a script (so it's obvious you can read and know about intonation of the written word).

Don't put time checks and IDs in: they'll make the programme controller think of whom they've got in that slot already. Let *them* decide if they want you and where to place you in their schedule, not you.[30]

It is best not to include jingles on your demo. There are packages of 'off-the-shelf' jingles that you can buy, but they often sound a little cheesy and, of course, will sound odd if you're pretending to already be on the station to which you are applying. If you're sending a copy of the demo to several stations, don't mention any station name at all. Show yourself in the best possible light. No fluffs or verbal slips here – what does that show about you that you think your best work contains mistakes?

Your audition should show you off in a variety of situations: demonstrating how you interact with callers, intro/outro a song, handle a live handover or interview . . . as well as how you do the basics. Show you have momentum. Edit those long bits, and demonstrate too your understanding of pace. (If you have a really creative, well-mixed, five-minute link that's stunning, put it at the end after the rest of the 'normal' audition.)

You should be able to ask for some spare time to record your demo at your hospital or student station, or where you've got some work experience. If that's not the case then you may have to spend some money on studio time with an independent production company, or go on the kind of course that offers a produced demo at the end. But you may end up paying a lot of money for very little, so surely a few nights a week for a few months at a local hospital station is time well spent both for the patients and your future career. (This is where going on a broadcasting course is worth the money: you have access to a studio in which to record your demo.)

Advances in technology (computers, CD/DVD machines, MP3, digital recorders) means you probably have better sound recording equipment at home than many radio studios had even a decade or so ago. Many job adverts will specify the format that is preferred for your demo. Ignore this at your peril as demos that are in a different media will go straight in the bin. That's not a euphemism, they really will (or at least in the 'deleted items' box): programme controllers have so many applications for jobs that they just don't need to be bothered with people who can't follow simple instructions. If you're sending a demo on spec then call and ask the programme controller or their PA what format they prefer to receive and then mention that advice in your covering letter. It'll show initiative and will cover you in case you were given the wrong information.

Whatever the format, ensure it's clearly and professionally labelled. You may need to borrow or invest in a computer program that prints CD labels and inserts for the best possible image. A flashier all-colour design won't necessarily help you get the job so keep the design clear and clean. On those labels (one in the box and one on the CD) include your name, telephone number, the date (the same one as your covering letter, you want to show this is a recent example of your work recorded especially for them, not one that's off the shelf) and the duration of the piece. Remember in radio durations are written in shorthand so follow the format where three minutes twenty-seven seconds is shown as 3' 27". If there's room enough to be able to read it, include a brief list of the items on the demo ('song intro,

---

[30] Unless your demo is off air from your current station.

competition caller, segue, creative what's on, programme trail') so the controller has an idea about what to expect.

Make sure the demo has actually been recorded. Some home-burned CDs don't play back on other machines, so double-check on several other players.

It is generally accepted that a demo should be no longer than four minutes. That may not seem long, but if advertisers can sell a car or insurance package in 30 seconds then it should be plenty of time, and it will force you to only include the best bits! And this is only to get your 'foot in the door': it's unlikely you'll be hired on the strength of a demo alone.

How can it be so short if you include a song intro and a segue as suggested above? Because you'll edit out most of each song, by fading it out just after you stop speaking and fading it in before your next link (as appropriate) and cutting out most of the middle (the term is 'telescoped'). The programme controller knows what the song sounds like, they want to hear you, not Lily Allen! Similarly, don't include ad breaks or news bulletins, although the programmer may want to hear a fluent (and possibly creative) weather report.

If the programme controller likes what they hear, they'll probably ask for an unedited two-hour tape of your on-air programme – they know that a demo can be 'dummied up' to show you in the best possible light!

Finally

Wait until you're sure this is the best demo you can do before you send it off: this is your audition! Listen back to it a few days after you've recorded it. Ask for feedback from friends and family or colleagues at your hospital radio station. They may notice a verbal tick (such as 'kind of thing', or 'y'know what I mean?') or that you're talking too fast or haven't explained something very well. Maybe a punchline was more pathetic than punchy. Then get ready to send off a copy of the demo, not the original![31]

CVs

There are many specialist books, websites[32] and some companies, that will tell you many different ways of how to prepare your CV, so I won't outline them all here. However there are some basics:

- o   Write it on a computer with a clear layout with lots of white space and use the spell-check.
- o   Target it for the person and station you are sending it to.
- o   Write in clear and straightforward sentences, but use appropriate words to show your enthusiasm – 'ambition', 'creativity', 'successful' and the like.
- o   Highlight any radio courses you have been on or media qualifications you have. Mention your work placement.
- o   Note any interests that may have a bearing on a job in the media – maybe you're a prolific collector of specialist music albums, write articles for a local newspaper or website or run a mobile DJ business. Maybe it's public speaking, drama, sports or music.

---

[31] Media UK has a section where members can upload their demos for others to hear and comment on: http://tinyurl.com/kv4pgr. You could also upload your demo here: http://tinyurl.com/cvw764.

[32] See for the media industries: http://tinyurl.com/m8kokt for more information on writing CVs.

- Talk up the good points, play down others but don't lie.
- Print it on good quality paper to a maximum of two pages.

Covering letter

Keep this short and to the point, make sure you address it to the correct person (by name, not 'Dear Sir or Madam') and that you've spelt their name correctly. Remember to highlight your appropriate experiences from your CV, the more skills you can offer them the more work they could offer you.

Use the word 'opportunity' rather than the more formal 'job', or the desperate-sounding 'break' and mention that, although you understand their workload, you'd welcome feedback on the demo if at all possible.

The covering letter is a great opportunity to sell yourself, so do just that. Consider writing one that is a bit more creative than other people's. Make yours stand out. (After all, it is the creative industry.)

There are other elements to consider when applying for a job, such as your email address, answerphone message and internet presence. A 'cool' e-mail address may tell a potential employer more about you than you want them to know ('ihateblondes@. . .com'), as may your voicemail ('I'm probably too hung over to pick up, so . . .') or Facebook/Bebo page. Do a Google search of yourself to see what comes up. Chances are a future employer will do the same. If they find postings from you about your last employer or inappropriate video on YouTube you're unlikely to make the interview process and may never learn the reason.

Finally, why not include in your letter when you are normally on the air at your current station, and include the 'listen live' link? That way the programme controller will know that you are confident and that your demo is an accurate representation of what you do all the time, not a collection of the best bits from the last six months.

The whole package

Put your CV, demo disc and covering letter all together and send it off; preferably first class as it looks more professional.

The whole package should be as eye-catching as possible, but that doesn't mean that you need to spend hours on a desktop publishing system experimenting with different colours and fonts. Have all the written items properly printed on good quality paper, with a font that's easy to read and ink that doesn't appear as though it's about to run out. Look in a large stationers for a plastic wallet for all the paperwork, if possible one that includes a section into which a CD can be inserted.

Remember you'll be competing against other people after the same job – your application has to stand out from the crowd. This demo is your audition or first interview for the job, an interview where you're not asked any questions, just given free rein to sell yourself. What a terrific opportunity!

The follow-up

Follow up your package with a phone call about a week later. If you leave it any longer, a standard 'We'll keep your details on file' letter may already be winging its way to you.

Radio people are very busy. It is sensible not to call very first thing soon after 9 am. It is likely they will want to get their feet under the desk as the day kicks off, reviewing e-mails, reading the post and so on. At 10 am many programme staff will be in a programme review meeting and talking about more long-term events, which will last about an hour. From 1 pm there could be a working lunch or at least a chance for them to get out of the office, and from 4 pm they'll be finishing off that day's work and setting up more for the next day. So, the best time to call is probably late morning or mid afternoon.

Ask if the programme controller has managed to hear your demo yet and made any decisions. You may also be able to ask for feedback on it, good or bad. However, the harsh reality is that, despite showing keenness and a willingness to learn, the programmer is likely to be very busy and unable to take calls.

Experiences with more pushy 'wannabes' has also taught many of them not to enter in to a discussion (or in some circumstances, argument) about the merits of including a particular link on the demo. Reaction to a demo will help increase your chances of a future job. However, put simply, if you regularly ignore phrases such as 'they're really busy/in a meeting/can't come to the phone right now' and continue calling a programme controller's office, you'll do your career chances more harm than good.

If you've not applied for a specific job but are writing on spec then you may be more fortunate in speaking to the programmer. Ask whether they've heard the demo, whether you could pop in for a chat and a look around, and ask about any opportunities. Offer to work for free if necessary (a great inducement for any radio station). This is especially needed at weekends, evenings, bank holidays, for charity 'radiothons' – in fact at any time that may be 'undesirable' for the regular staff.

The important thing is that you've made contact. That's pretty much a foot in the door. Don't waste the opportunity. Don't let the controller go until you've moved the situation on by asking one of the questions in the paragraph above.

Make a note of the call afterwards. Who it was that you spoke to and what they said. Then if you want to follow up the follow up and ask if there's been any change, you know who to speak to and how the conversation was left last time. Otherwise it's easy to forget who said what to whom.

There'll be a great number of refusals before you get a break so be prepared. It may be that there's just no opening for you at that time, or it may be that your demo or CV is not showing your talents in the best light – ask a friend or colleague to go through it for you and highlight where you may have let yourself down.

Create your own luck

Keep plugging away. Look for chinks of light – other opportunities in broadcasting where you can show off your skills. Is there a job for a receptionist or someone to work in the shop (a few BBC stations have these)? Turn up to outside broadcasts and see if there's something you think that needs to be done. Although you may not be thanked for muscling in on the day, introduce yourself and ask if you can write to them and offer your services in the future to rig and de-rig. Keep your eyes and ears open for any of these types of leads. Remember it takes work to be in the right place at the right time.

You're in – almost!

Someone's interested and has asked you in to 'have a look around and a chat'. Don't waste this golden opportunity.

Do more research on the station, listen regularly (especially on the day) and dress for the station's format. A suit and tie may not be appropriate attire these days for anything but the most formal interview situations, but neither is anything unwashed or unironed. If you're going to a chart station, dress in trendy casual clothes that a member of that audience would wear. This may be smart jeans and T-shirt and would surely be a different outfit from the one you'd wear if you were going to see a management member at a local BBC station where proper trousers, shoes and shirt may be more appropriate. Women can take their lead from the description for men. Avoid too much aftershave or perfume!

There are plenty of good books on interview technique, as well as others on body language and how to make conversation and so on. This is not one of them. However, there are some points which may be useful for the situation of going into a chat at a radio station.

- Arrive in good time. Ask for the toilet and check your appearance and breath. In reception read the memos on the notice board as there might be some more ammunition you can use in your conversation. If you arrive late you may be in a panic and perform poorly. Or, if the PC's time is tight (or there's a schedule to keep to for the interview panel) you may not get all, or any, of your allotted time.
- Chat to the receptionist and the person who collects you. They may let something slip about new positions or opportunities. You'll certainly be ready to impress them by having a conversation and they may be able to mention that to the controller later in the day. (The impact of a comment such as, 'They seemed really nice and chatty' from a receptionist can never be underestimated.) You'll also be able to show that you were friendly to them: 'I was speaking to Trish on reception as I was waiting and she mentioned that . . .'
- If you're offered a drink, take one even if you don't really want it. A lot of social 'bonding' happens over a coffee. People loosen up and become more friendly . . . and it helps spin out the chat for longer.
- Shake hands firmly, speak clearly, sit up, look into their eyes and keep your body language open (no crossed legs or arms).
- Show that you've done your research on the station. If the subject of the breakfast show comes up, mention the name of the presenter in your answer and comment on a feature or competition they recently ran. Doing this proves that you listen and understand the station.
- If touring the station ask plenty of questions. Be keen to show an interest, but how you do it will show that you understand the workings of radio stations in general. For example, 'Do you just have one on-air studio and have the presenters hot-seat, or is there a second one?' Use the proper jargon.
- Have a list of points or questions that you want to raise and make sure you ask them . . . Among these will be a way of moving the conversation on to the conclusion that you want. Don't leave having had a chat and a look around and nothing else. 'Can I help out on that show at a weekend?', 'You must be busy over the summer with all those OBs, can I come and help out on some of them . . . I don't mind about not getting paid', 'Perhaps I can call in again with an updated demo in a few months' time?'
- Pay attention: don't fiddle with ties or cuffs, phones or bags. Give your interviewer your entire concentration.
- Afterwards, whatever the outcome write and thank the people who you met for their

time and help. Like first impressions, last ones also count for a lot and even if this time things didn't work out, you never know where you might meet someone again at another station.

o   Accept almost any offer from any station. Small things grow to be big.

o   If you don't get the job or the position, use the day as a learning experience. Ask if you can find out why you missed out, and for any advice. Send them a note and thank them for their suggestions.

27 Radio, recession and redundancy

> There are only two kinds of presenters. Those who have been sacked and those who haven't been sacked yet.[1]

Radio is a precarious profession. Even if you are lucky enough to get a 'staff' (permanent) contract, rather than a fixed-term one, you can still be 'let go'. That's especially true now as ad revenue drops, stations go bust or hand back their licences, share studios and output, network and voice track . . . or as the BBC licence fee is increasingly threatened.

When the station's taken over

> The secret is dodging the bullets. New brooms sweep clean and incoming controllers will f*ck your career without an afterthought. You just have to stay one or two bullets ahead of them by having other things going that you can turn to when one show gets shot down.[2]

Remember it's always easier finding a new job when you currently have one. So don't quit before you're fired unless you have another gig to go to. Even if the current station becomes 'unbearable' you are being paid and you have access to a studio for demos.

Keep your head down with the new management team, and give them what they want. Be professional and a team player. Remember the new boss will be listening very carefully to every presenter to decide who to keep.

> If you find you're gong to be kept on but in a different time slot, accept it; even if you consider the move to be a demotion. Nobody has a divine right to a particular slot, even if they've been doing it for many years, but a different time slot means you're still employed.[3]

---

[1] Graham Mack, presenter, TFM, *The Radio Magazine*, April 2009.
[2] Paul Gambaccini, presenter, *The Radio Magazine*, January 2006.
[3] Paul Easton, radio consultant, *The Radio Magazine*, March 2009.

Short-term contracts

Being on a short-term contract is a great way of sharpening your act: you know that you are only ever as good as your last show. But even if every show is great and you are doing all that is asked of you, it may still be that your contract is not renewed. That may because your style or voice no longer 'fits' the way the station management wants the output to sound, or in times of recession, because they can get someone cheaper, or voice track or network your programme.

As soon as you start negotiating a new contract, expect to be taken off air any time soon. That's because if a new offer is not made or accepted, managers cannot run the risk of a presenter losing motivation, criticising the station on air in their last few weeks or at the very least being a distraction to other members of the team. It may even be that someone resigns on air.[4] The same goes if it's your decision to make the move: it may be thought that you'll tell listeners why you're leaving or what station you'll be heard on next. In both these circumstances a station will usually let the presenter leave the station immediately and pay them 'gardening leave' until the end of their contract. Resist the temptation to criticise your (former) employers either in the press or online. Even if you are anonymous, over time it's easy to piece together information from various postings from the same username to work out who someone is . . . and word soon gets around what is still a small industry.

Avoiding redundancy

You can't of course, guarantee that you won't be 'let go'. Not when the amount you're paid is the same figure that would turn red ink to black when applied to the station's bottom line. But this might help . . .

Regularly re-evaluate where you were in your career say three or five years ago, where you are now and where you want to be . . . in association with an appraisal of your colleagues and the industry. And work out your distinctive difference. If you don't have one of these and are just like the other presenters, or perhaps just like the other 'has-been' presenters, you are increasingly easily replaceable.

Changes in public taste and opinion mean that radio output is constantly changing, experimenting with the 'next big thing' (which is often a concept or technique the industry discarded a decade previously). That means that if you're not great at *something* you could soon be replaced by someone who is.

If you are a 'time and temp' jock, doing the basics of intros, outros and what's ons . . . anyone can do that. You have to have identifiable impact to give yourself *competitive advantage over everyone else*. Perhaps you're:

- The one that can spot a great story and know how to do it on air.
- The team player who's always willing to help train, fill a shift or turn up at an OB.
- Great at weaving an imaginative, creative and engaging link.
- The best person at engaging with guests and sympathising with callers.
- Experienced in all types of production techniques.
- Always putting yourself out and about, at local events and meetings.

---

[4] Like these presenters did: http://tinyurl.com/lzm7z5, http://tinyurl.com/l6jjjf (err how much a show?!) and most famously http://tinyurl.com/nj4kxp.

Give yourself an honest SWOT check-up (your Strengths, Weaknesses, Opportunities, Threats) to become aware of where you sit in the 'pecking order' of your station and others. Then develop your *distinctive competency* so your listeners and managers know you excel in that area (in both on-air and off-air roles). Sound different, not generic. Have personality. Be indispensable; be something listeners value more than just hearing the same old songs on their iPods.

Don't get stuck in a rut, constantly evaluate, make yourself more valuable to the station and your colleagues . . . become harder to replace.

On top of that:

- Be the best you can.
- Be aware of what is happening in the business, what the big themes are and start adapting.
- Think how your boss might survive any takeover (are you backing the best bet?).
- Prepare: have money, a CV, a demo all in place. Build up contacts and have a look at your contract, know what you could do as a filler job.
- Embrace change, be sensitive to those who've left or been let go, but loyal to the management.
- Don't share in-house information and gossip about the station to colleagues at your or another station.
- Know new technology.

INSECURITY

Most performers are insecure to a greater or lesser degree, perhaps because our skill is to a certain extent intangible, not able to be measured and affected by other people's tastes. We know that one day our ability to make money from our talent will 'go away' and that that may not be a decision that we have much control over. And we don't know when that day will be.

Perhaps insecurity is because of our two roles: on air we 'perform', and constantly strive to project an image. We have people who listen to us, respond positively to what we say, call and write to us.

Then we step outside the studio to do the admin and are treated like another member of staff. We go from disc jockey to desk jockey.

Then, the presenter can find it difficult to adjust and becomes needy and wants to be the focus of attention. But these traits which can makes presenters a pain off-air (strong feelings, big personality) can also make them good on air (colourful, larger than life . . . a performer).

When you're getting itchy feet

Most creative people start to get bored after a while. What they're doing becomes automatic and they crave change, excitement and originality. Perhaps that's what leads some of them to push the boundaries, live life on the edge . . . and then step over the line. They want to give themselves a thrill or a shock.

Obviously it's not necessarily a good career move to start being too risky on air to get yourself noticed, just for the buzz of having a row with the boss. If you're too much of a handful, you could be out of a job (there's only, as the saying goes, a foot between a pat on the head and a kick up the arse). Your cheap thrill could end up being very expensive.

Get your excitement from your personal life. Has the zing left your marriage? Are you in a rut with the work-eat-TV-sleep routine? Make your life busier: start a course, join a club, start exercising . . .

Get more excitement at work: push yourself, reveal something different on air, try a new technique, give an old feature a new twist. Ask the boss for new ideas and responsibilities, or learn another skill from another department. You'll get another perspective on your job, and be of more value to this, or a future station.

If you do feel as though you want to leave, start thinking of demos. The fact that you're (sub)consciously wanting to air the best material for a new start will help you pick up your game.

The gathering storm

Perhaps you're in the position where you feel as though the worst may happen. (Frankly, that's not the worst position to be in . . . much less enviable is being told you're out of work and not to have seen it coming.)

You will of course always have an up-to-date demo. Save your 'best bits' regularly, so even if you don't have a produced five minutes, you have a selection of elements you can put together. Otherwise the time will come when you need the audio . . . and you're no longer working in the building where it's kept.

In commercial radio, priorities are regrettably not about the best line but about the bottom line. The two needn't be mutually exclusive – far from it. The managers though are driven like politicians wanting to be re-elected rather than visionaries wanting to save the creative environment. That cold calculus started creeping into Radio 1 when I was there and ludicrous numpties in bad suits began appearing and informing us what ginger-haired people aged between 23 and 26 liked listening to.[5]

Save some money! If you do decide to pursue another career in the short term until there's another opportunity (and hey, you may enjoy the break), you can usually keep your hand in radio (hospital, community . . .). Don't give up on it. There's always going to be

---

[5] Nicky Campbell, presenter, BBC Radio 5 Live, *The Radio Magazine*, June 2009.

some form of audio entertainment (whether it's broadcast, podcast, streamed or yelled out of the window through a megaphone). The transmission method and the actual content may be different but people are always going to want to be informed and entertained. Someone's got to it and it might as well be you.

There's an important element to networking: stay friendly with people before you need them. Don't be one of those people who only makes contact when you want something. If an unemployed friend or 'contact' asks for help from *you*, remember that your first responsibility should be to yourself. Certainly help them, but try and ensure that you guide the right person to the right job; don't just recommend them for *any* job as some may not be suitable. Recommending a friend for a job that doesn't work out may reflect badly on you . . . with both the friend and their new employer questioning your judgement.

Avoid being tricked into resigning

You can usually sense when things aren't going well: you feel you are unappreciated, you can sense that cutbacks have to be made, you see other (younger and cheaper) presenters being shown around the studios (you may even be asked to show them the desk), there are the occasional comments made by managers . . .

And then the call comes for 'a chat'. You may be asked to take on more work for no more pay, or to do increasingly difficult or unsocial hours . . . or your work or attitude may be questioned (usually in a general statement with no specifics).

You may be shocked and angry . . . but don't let fly and quit in fury. That may be exactly what they want you to do, and you will regret it. Apart from the obvious immediate lack of income, there's no redundancy money and because you resigned probably no unemployment benefit either. There's no time to pull together some ROTs, and nowhere to record demos . . . and a future employer is always going to wonder exactly what went on to cause you to leave so abruptly.

In the meantime, the station has saved paying your notice period, and their new presenter can start the very next day.

When you're let go

THE KÜBLER-ROSS FIVE STAGES OF GRIEF[6] FOR RADIO PRESENTERS

Denial: 'They can't fire me . . . my Rajar was up in men 49–54 in Little Thumbstead!'

Anger: 'What do you know? You're a *% $£! salesman . . . running a radio station . . .'

Bargaining: 'Wait! I'll do overnights . . . and weekends!'

---

[6] More on this process: http://tinyurl.com/oajk4.

> *Depression:* 'What's the point? I'll soon be replaced by syndication from London anyway.'
>
> *Acceptance:* 'Well that didn't work out I suppose I'd better update my demo. Errr, do I have a demo . . . ?'

A former Radio 1 DJ hit back at a BBC executive who dropped her from a local station's breakfast show by sending a round robin e-mail to her colleagues warning her boss to 'watch your back'.[7]

When the worst happens you can start feeling sorry for yourself, and curse the radio industry and the managers in it (and indeed you should allow yourself a little of this natural reaction), but it won't get you very far. Start moving on.

The big questions:

- Are you willing to move?
- Are you willing to take a pay cut?
- Are you willing to present in a less prominent time slot?
- Are you willing to work in a smaller market?
- Are you willing to take on more roles?
- Are you willing to wait for the 'big gig'?
- Are you willing to leave radio?

Look at what's happened as a chance to re-evaluate everything . . .

When you resign

How you act after you give your notice may be how your soon-to-be former employer regards you. If you get lazy, critical and de-mob happy while working out your notice period, it may come back to haunt you. It is much better to put 100 per cent of your energy and skills into the job and make sure you leave the position in better shape than when you arrived.

Don't burn any bridges. The industry is relatively small and everyone knows everyone, or at least someone who knows someone. When potential employers are checking references, if they hear from your previous employer that you badmouthed them on your way out the door, then you are less likely to be considered for a position. No matter how much you'd really like to tell your boss exactly what you thought of him or her, it's better to part ways on good terms and bite your tongue. (No, hang on, not literally . . . not good for someone who talks for a living.)

Promoting yourself

The best and most straightforward way of promoting yourself is by doing the best possible job while you're on air. You never know who may be listening. Many times a presenter has

---

[7] Read more on this here: http://tinyurl.com/mg5kff.

been headhunted by a programme controller who heard them while driving through the area. With online streaming, similar situations are likely to happen even more regularly. You never know who may be listening, calls you on the phone-in line and asks you if you're interested in moving to a bigger market or better slot. It does happen. So, the best advert for you, is you. Remind yourself: today, I must present my best possible show. And say that to yourself tomorrow as well.

And then the next day, because you're only as good as your last show. Or only as good as your last ROT. So be prepared. Snoop yourself regularly. Radio stations rarely give warnings of redundancies.

As well as presenting a good show there are other ways of promoting yourself. Meeting your listeners can help you present a better-targeted programme and increase your ratings. But there are other tricks you may want to consider (some of these may need permission from your station's manager) to increase your profile at the station and the pounds in your bank.

- If you open a local fair or fête, take along a camera and ask the organiser to take a picture of you cutting the ribbon, riding on the dodgems or handing over the giant cheque. Then write a news release and send it to the local newspaper. Chances are they'll use it.

- Send the occasional news story about yourself to the locals. Think what's happened to you. Martin Day at (what was then) Essex FM got a lot of publicity when he started to learn how to fly a light plane, and then a few months later when he crashed it. On a national scale, Chris Moyles said only he could reverse the slipping listening figures and become the 'Saviour of Radio One' if he was given the breakfast show. He was, and he did, boosting his image and bank account in the process. But only send items that project the image that you want to foster. If you're the trendy young jock, opening your child's school fête won't be as appropriate as introducing an act on stage at the local Battle of the Bands night.

- Could you write a weekly or monthly column for the local paper? They may not pay you (and your copy may have to be approved by your station manager), but you'll get free publicity.

- Maintain a profile among your colleagues by contributing articles or letters to the trade press such as *The Radio Magazine*.

- It's very important to meet and keep in with other people in the same field – they may recommend you for a job or appear on an interview panel. One of the easiest ways of doing this is to join a broadcasting organisation such as the Radio Academy, which has regional groups around the UK. If you're a student, membership is at reduced price and all members have free entry to meetings where guest speakers discuss various aspects of the business. Such groups may be particularly useful to you if, as a freelance, you find yourself treading a rather lonely path, not feeling part of any one station.

- Publicity stunts may be arranged to raise the profile of you and the station at the same time. Maybe it's because you love a song so much you play it five times an hour and are 'suspended', or you lose an on-air bet with a fellow presenter and have to run to work in your underwear. (It's said that for a stunt to work well, you need at least one of the following elements: fame, controversy, culture, humour or sex.)[8]

---

[8] Mark Borkowski, PR supremo.

Contracts

For those just starting out, especially as 'freelancers', there may not be any more job security than a verbal agreement as to your hours, duties and length of service. And as they say, a verbal agreement is not worth the paper it's written on. Formal, written contracts may come when you are in a larger market, but not always: it may simply be that you are expected to turn up until you are asked not to . . . or that you work on a week-by-week basis.

When you do get one, read a contract thoroughly. As you do so, note what questions you want to ask about the dense wording and legalese that's in there. Ask a solicitor or someone from Citizens Advice, as well as the future employer (with the latter, ask your questions in writing, so they respond in a similar way so that you have a permanent reminder of what was discussed and agreed).

In the contract it's normal to see a phrase such as 'no compete' (meaning that you can't work for another station in the same market at the same time as working for this new station, neither could you work at another station in the same area within a certain time – usually six months – after you've left). Your hours may also be 'open ended': you stay at work as long as is needed to get the work done, without being able to claim for overtime. Remember to talk about other rights as well as salary and duties: (paid) holiday, sick pay, rates of pay for personal appearances and so on. You may also be able to build in incentive pay if your listening figures rise.

Negotiating with the person who's likely to become your boss can be awkward, but remember negotiation does not have to be confrontational. You can be tough and polite at the same time.

Remember too that at the start of the conversation it's likely that you need the station more than the station needs you. (See the section 'Getting an agent' later in this chapter.)

Going freelance

As you become better and more successful at your job you may find it more financially advantageous to go freelance. That would mean giving up the security of a monthly salary paid by one station and having the opportunity to work for several stations, negotiating a fee for each job (although some stations won't employ you if you can also be heard on a neighbouring station).

Why it's best to be a staffer:

◻ There's more security. You'll be given more notice about any redundancy, and get compensation.

◻ Someone else does all the paperwork such as tax and National Insurance (freelancers aren't earning any money when they are sorting and filing their receipts and invoices).

◻ You always know where you're working and the shift pattern, what will be paid into your account and when. (Freelancers have to work hard to sell themselves to lots of stations; they may get an agent to find work for them but that comes at a price.)

◻ There's often a recognised career ladder to work your way up.

◻ There may be in-house training that's all paid for.

◻ You won't have to scrabble around for work or reduce your rates when jobs are thin on the ground.

◻ Paid holiday (for freelancers, if they're not working they're not earning).

Why it's best to be a freelance:

- You can negotiate different rates for different jobs. If you're on staff as a journalist and you're asked to cover the drive show for a week, your pay remains the same. As a freelance you'd be able to ask for more money for the presenting job which may involve more expertise.
- If you don't like the job you don't have to do it. A staffer may be told to present the overnight show on Christmas morning. You will be able to say 'no thanks'.
- Flexibility and variety: you could be doing different things on different days of the week with different companies.
- The more you work the more you earn.
- Some of your expenses (such as travel and clothes) may be tax deductible, meaning that your 'take home pay' is even more.

As you can see there are good points and not so good points about going it alone. If you're talented and lucky then success may be yours; if you're not then it may be tough.

As well as presenting you may decide to do voiceovers,[9] be a master of ceremonies, host events and trade exhibitions, front corporate videos or train others and become a lecturer. But work will only come to you if you go out and find it. You have to let people know that you're around, what you can do and what your availability is. Bookings may start off slowly, but if you do a good job on one occasion, other events will follow as re-bookings take place and word gets around.

One of the most difficult things to do is the cold call: phoning stations, companies or agents and asking if you can send them a demo. Of course, you don't need their permission to send one, but it'll mean so much more if you can address your letter to a specific person, and it's even better if you've had a chance to introduce yourself to them on the phone first. You'll be in constant competition with other freelancers also trying to get the same job, so the first impression you make with each station is very important.

The new job

The natural thing to do when you start a new job is to do too much, to show off all your skills. Have the patience to do just what's right for this programme on this station with this content. Your full repertoire will be uncovered with time, as more songs, interviews, competitions and formats bring more opportunities to express yourself. Trying too hard at the beginning might create a first impression of being impatient. Don't take chances until you are confident, and then add things one at a time to bring the full package to the show.

Settle into the new job slowly, gradually getting the feel of what the station is about and who the listener is. The first priority is to learn the physical skills such as the studio desk, the format and furniture junctions . . . and the area.

Getting an accountant

Find one who works with other presenters and who knows the allowances for your kind of job. Other freelance presenters shouldn't mind passing on details of who they use.

---

[9] See http://tinyurl.com/ma7fav.

As well as doing a lot of paperwork for you, a good accountant may be able to reduce your tax bill on items that you buy which are essential to your job. These may include a car and petrol, a portable recorder and headphones, clothes you need for public appearances and their laundering, subscriptions to trade organisations and tickets to industry events. On top of that there may be allowances for voice training, stationery and their own fees!

Getting an agent

The job of an agent is to find you more work. In return you pay them a percentage of any fee that they get you. This may be around 15 per cent, although some agents charge a fee of *all* your earnings, even if you secured the work yourself. So, if you sign up with an agent and you're on £20,000 a year, their fees are going to cost you £250 a month for the entire period of your contract at the station.

If you're a freelancer you may be wary of cold calling other stations and doing the hard sell of yourself and negotiating a fee. An agent should have lots of contacts, so will have little or no problem in putting you forward for various jobs. They will be among the first to hear what work is available and because they may have others like you on their books, they are often able to make money through doing very little work. Placing one client in one job does, after all, leave a vacancy for another presenter elsewhere.

A good agent will represent you at meetings to discuss your salary and other perks, and know the best way to counter the 'there's no more money in the budget' argument. Indeed some stations prefer liaising with an agent so the relationship with the presenter (what Americans call 'the talent') isn't soured.

An agent may also act as your manager and give you career advice, such as changing your on-air style or aspirations. They should always be looking forward to your next step. That next step may be to a larger station, which they can sound out on your behalf, and in confidence.

If you do decide to approach an agent (and it's not usually necessary, especially at the start of your career) then pick one who is used to dealing with radio presenters. It makes no sense to have someone who deals with lookalikes or circus sideshows, as they'll have no contacts in your line of work.

Always keep your agent informed about your career. What developments have there been with your job, where are you working, how much for? It's all information they'll use to negotiate your next gig. Give them regular copies of updated demos, pictures, newspaper articles, refreshed CVs and so on, so they have all the tools to sell you with.

Beware of the bad agent who says that work is 'just around the corner' when in reality they're pushing a bigger name with whom they can earn more money; or the ones who charge you extra for phone calls and stamps: all that should be covered in their commission; or the ones who want you to pay them up front.

Also be wary of these sharp practices:

o   Some agents tie you in to a contract with them even if they don't find you any work, or offer you jobs that they know you'll turn down just so they can say they found you *something*. Make sure you are free to move agents if nothing's forthcoming after a set period.

o   Some contracts may require you to pay a commission to your agent as long as you work for the station at which they negotiated your original booking, even if you get a new agent to negotiate a new contract with the employer after the original agreement expires.

- Some contracts forbid you from talking with or taking advice from others in the industry. It's an attempt to try to isolate you from others and keep you dependent on that single organisation.

Unions

Consider, too, whether becoming a member of a union is for you. For a small monthly fee (which may be tax deductible) you could have the support of perhaps the NUJ (National Union of Journalists), or maybe that of Bectu. If you consider yourself more of an actor and have or can get an Equity card then it may worth keeping up membership of that union. You may need all the support and advice you can get if an employer breaks a contract with you or refuses to pay you what you thought had been agreed.

The back anno

During the summer when I was growing up, my father would arrive late in the afternoon from Washington on Fridays and as soon as he got to Cape Cod, he would want to go straight out and practice sailing maneuvers . . . in anticipation of that weekend's races. And we'd be out late, and the sun would be setting, and family dinner would be getting cold, and we'd still be out there practicing our jibes and spinnaker sets long after everyone else had gone ashore. One night, not another boat in sight on the summer sea, I asked him, 'Why are we always the last ones on the water?' 'Teddy', he said, 'most of the other sailors we race against are smarter and more talented than we are. But the reason why we are going to win is that we are going to work harder than them and we will be better prepared.'[1]

Radio is no different. You have to practise and you have to prepare if you are going to develop your skills and 'make it'.

That's practising not just the 'technical' side of things – the desk-driving and the pace and structure of the show – but also your on-air personality: what you say and how you say it. Be uniquely different and make what you do and say relevant, interesting and compelling to your listeners.

Yes, it's hard work to put in the 'flying time' and the prep time to come up with engaging material day in day out, every day of the year. But as the saying goes, if you want to make it big, 'hard work is the first door you open'.

Do most presenters work hard enough? In the recent turbulence, the ones who were show-and-go have gone. The ones who practise, generate ideas and demand more from themselves and others, are the ones more likely to have been kept. They know more than how to do 'time and temp' and what to say and when. They also know what not to say, when not to talk. They are aware of what's going on in their station's area, and in the industry. They listen to other stations, and their own (yes, even the news bulletins). They meet their listeners and know what they're talking about, complaining about, laughing about . . . and can communicate that on air to others. They can scan a paper for ideas that they can adapt for radio . . . not just read out a 'Sun Spot' funny story. They demand feedback.

---

[1] Ted Kennedy Jr.'s eulogy at his father Ted Kennedy's funeral, September 2009: http://tinyurl.com/nh2rlh.

The personalities have passion for *their career*, where the has-beens merely have *a job*. They are creative in their outlook, their turn of phrase, their style. They are neither outrageous nor shocking, but are arresting and engaging. They are different.

In the previous pages I have done my best to show you some techniques and skills that will help you achieve your goals. The desire, the drive, the passion has to come from you.

I once judged a competition for media wannabes where the prize was £10,000 of training in radio and TV production and presentation and online design. Candidate after candidate came through the door who'd not taken a step inside a radio station or made any effort to understand the industry.

More recently I've worked at a radio station 100 metres from a student station. Not once have I seen one of their volunteers knocking at the door wanting to soak up skills and experience.

Set your goals, believe in you. Seek inspiration and know that there's no short cut for hard work. Win by risking. Push the boundaries and learn from what happens.

Prepare, practise and perfect.

And remember, being on mic is an honour.

And also great fun.

I hope that you got what you wanted from *Essential Radio Skills*, and you refer to it often during your new career in radio.

I wish you the very best of luck as you enter the business. Set your sights high and be the best for your listener by being:

o   relevant.

o   interesting.

o   compelling.

Regards
Peter Stewart

PS If you've got any comment on this edition of the book, or suggestions for the next one, or questions about your career, drop me a line.

I'm also available as a lecturer or guest speaker for broadcast/media courses, and for personal face-to-face or distance training for voice work or presenter critiques. You can also sign up to receive a free monthly newsletter of radio-related ideas, advice and comments.

Contact me at EssentialRadioSkills@hotmail.com or via my website www.PeteStewart.co.uk. There you will also find details of my Presenter Critique services . . .

APPENDICES

Appendix 1

Signs your radio station is uninteresting[1]

If you could hear it on another radio station, your station is too impersonal.

If you could hear it in the same way, and from the same perspective on another radio station, your station is too impersonal.

The content you deliver doesn't match the 'values of your listeners'.

Information and station elements are not delivered in a style, pace and quantity that makes your station easy to listen to.

Someone in your target listens to your radio station and says, 'That's not for me.'

Your talent tries to 'educate' your listeners with things they are not already interested in.

Your talent doesn't read the newspaper or watch television and notice, 'That's our listener, that's what they're all about'.

The air talent addresses your listeners with generics or plurals, such as 'Hey, everybody'.

The talent uses vocabulary that doesn't match up with the everyday language of your listeners ('Variable cloudiness with a chance of precipitation', 'There is lane blockage on the highways and byways').

The talent and promos on your station deliver details and technical information before communicating what is most important to the listener.

---

[1] Author unknown.

Appendix 2

'Mickey's ten commandments'

These rules were developed by Marty Sklar[1] who was one of the creative brains and designers at Walt Disney Imagineering and are what those at the Walt Disney Resorts work by. They have been adapted[2] here for radio stations and staff.

1. *Know Your Audience* – Don't bore people, talk down to them or lose them by assuming that they know what you know.

   Everyone at the radio station needs a good understanding of their target audience, their likes, dislikes and interests. Ask each member of your staff to write down your station's target audience and a few lines about the ideal listener. You may be amazed to find there is a wide difference in perception among your staff. Unless everyone from the receptionist to the announcer is on the same page it will be difficult to make a true connection with your target audience.

2. *Wear Your Guest's Shoes* – Insist that designers, staff and your board members experience your facility as visitors as often as possible.

   At the radio station, insist your new staff spend time getting to know the product and the people. Have your staff shadow someone from another department so they really know the product and how the departments interact with each other.

3. *Organise the Flow of People and Ideas* – Use good storytelling techniques, tell good stories not lectures, lay out your exhibit with clear logic.

   Marty is really talking about communication, which is something our industry is not great at. Regular staff meetings and workable systems to share information and keep everyone informed are key. Technology is supposed to make communication better, but all too often we find ourselves writing an e-mail to someone in the next office. We all need to spend more time talking and exchanging ideas. Consolidation is making good communication even more difficult as, often, the key decision makers are either too busy or located in a different city.

4. *Create a Weenie* – Lead visitors from one area to another by creating visual magnets and giving visitors rewards for making the journey.

   On the air we do this with the right music, imaging, promos and well-constructed and delivered announcer breaks. We also need to do this externally to attract new listeners to the product.

5. *Communicate with Visual Literacy* – Make good use of all the non-verbal ways of communication – colour, shape, form, texture.

   Radio does this by using powerful words. Great radio stations know how to paint powerful word pictures and use 'theatre of the mind' to own a position in the minds of the target listeners. Ideally your listeners will be able to tell your radio station from another because of the 'stationality' or 'feel' of the product. A consulting friend sums this up with the acronym ACES – Action – Colourful – Emotional – Sexy. Greg Gillispie says, 'With all the words in the English language it's incumbent upon the talent to construct breaks to enable the listener to picture the experience.'

6. *Avoid Overload* – Resist the temptation to tell too much, to have too many objects; don't force people to swallow more than they can digest. Try to stimulate and provide guidance to those who want more.

   Great shows and great radio stations leave them wanting more. All too often we fall

---

[1] Martin Sklar, Walt Disney Imagineering, Education vs. Entertainment: Competing for Audiences, AAM annual meeting, 1987.

[2] By Chris Byrnes at Byrnes Media http://tinyurl.com/mp45jg. Download this at: http://tinyurl.com/m33mct.

into the 'clutter trap.' In this added value world we live in today it's easy to load up the station with promotions that often don't work for the client and drive listeners away. Disney is careful to never overload their parks with too many rides. They actually have a system called 'low ride out' where, before they will add a new ride to an area, they identify the least popular one and remove it. Do you have a system in place on your station to limit the number of promotions or added value features you will run at any one time? Sales people need to manage the promotional expectations of the clients and the promotions people need to protect the brand.

7. *Tell One Story at a Time* – If you have a lot of information, divide it into distinct, logical, organised stories. People can absorb and retain information more clearly if the path to the next concept is clear and logical.

   This is the old KISS rule that too often announcers forget, and it starts with planning the break before you open the microphone. This is especially important in a multi-person show. Edit, edit, edit and take only the number of words required to effectively sell the thought.

8. *Avoid Contradiction* – Clear institutional identity helps give you the competitive edge. The public needs to know who you are and what differentiates you from other institutions they may have seen.

   Does your radio station own a position in the mind of your target audience? Are you the news station or the local station? In simple terms, as more and more signals come into your market, you need to be famous for at least one thing.

9. *For Every Ounce of Treatment, Provide a Ton of Fun* – How do you woo people from all other temptations? Give people plenty of opportunity to enjoy themselves by emphasising ways that they can participate in the experience and by making your environment rich and appealing to all senses.

   The promotions and marketing department of the radio station needs to always be on the lookout for opportunities to build cume via exciting promotions and creative external marketing. Making what comes out of the speakers interesting and compelling is the task of the programme director and announcers. No announcer can be funny all the time, but in morning drive at least, we need to create the feeling that our show is 'fun' to listen to. The radio station that wins the 'fun' battle is often the overall winner in the market, because people are drawn to a station that has that feel.

10. *Keep It Up* – Never underestimate the importance of cleanliness and routine maintenance. People expect to get a good show every time and will comment more on broken and dirty stuff.

    In radio, this means delivering a great product day after day and year after year. Yes, it's fine to update or give it a 'fresh coat of paint' from time to time by changing the imaging voice or replacing the jingle package. But all too often, radio stations make the mistake of blowing up a format before it's has time to gain traction, or reinventing the product and calling it 'new' which in most cases it's not, and the listeners see right through this tactic. Delivering a consistent product your target audience enjoys and doing it year after year is often the best way to win.

Appendix 3

Your personal safety

As you go out and about (for roadshows, outside broadcasts, celebrity appearances, or even while shopping with your family), you may well be recognised and stopped by listeners. Some presenters love every approach by a fan, most only enjoy meeting listeners when they are 'on duty', others shun the limelight completely and prefer the anonymity of a studio where they perform best without being watched.

Whatever your character, you have to remember that meeting the audience is part of your job. Anyone who has taken the time and trouble to come and meet you (and perhaps pay an entrance fee for the event at which you are appearing) deserves to be treated politely. A quick conversation and a handshake is a small price to pay for the people who help pay your salary and those of your colleagues. Remember that most contracts have a line in them about not bringing the company into disrepute. So, being rude or offhand to a member of the public (or saying something that they perceive as rude or offhand) could land you in trouble. Most listeners will be friendly and chatty and will want nothing more than to meet you, get an autograph or picture and say, 'You look nothing like I imagined'. Some listeners are a little different.

There are some people who will watch you present your show from the other side of the studio window that looks out onto the shopping centre. They will turn up to every outside event. They may bring you presents or remind you of some small remark you made on air months previously. The kind word for these people is 'fans'; other less kind words are 'anoraks' or 'weirdos'. (Indeed, presenters in studios that look out on to streets or shopping centres so listeners can watch them work, often refer to the 'weirdo window'.)

Anoraks keep every piece of radio station merchandise and listen all day every day. (You've got to hope that they get a Rajar diary!) Treat them professionally and courteously, and even though they may simply stand and watch you for an hour at a time, try to put them out of your mind.

Although an interesting human being will usually get a bigger audience than an impersonal presenter (people relate to people, not 'presenters'), be careful about how *much* you say and the nature of it. Personal information helps you connect with your audience – *private* information is not for public consumption. Comment on your life but do not identify where you live or where your children go to school and so on: remember how the jigsaw effect can work – listeners piece together what you say over months and years. Perhaps change the name of your children when you mention them on air, talk about where you *used* to live (giving the impression you're still there) and so on. There is plenty you can talk about, revealing your thoughts and emotions, without putting yourself or family in danger.

Some safety information is especially pertinent to radio presenters who may be recognised because of their celebrity.[1]

- Take care where you shop locally. If you are asked to put your address on the back of a cheque, think twice about shopping there – who exactly will see those details? If you need to develop a camera flash-card, do it yourself or send it off to a printer – do you want to be recognised in the pictures of you and your family on the beach? Ensure your credit card has an initial rather than your full, and more instantly recognisable, first name. Do you want to pay by cash instead?

- Be careful what colleagues say about you on air or off: 'June is covering for Jane today,

---

[1] The following advice was written with guidance from the Suzy Lamplugh Trust: http://tinyurl.com/lz7vmo.

as she's off on holiday for two weeks'. Station receptionists meet the public face to face and may easily let something slip: 'Jim does do a great show, doesn't he? Who would have thought his wife left him last month . . . ?' I once worked at a station where one of the female presenters was, quite rightly, angry that news of her pregnancy had been broadcast by one of her colleagues. She felt that it was *her* news to tell if she wanted to, and didn't want listeners to know that much about her.

- Do not reveal too much on your personal website or the station's.
- If you move stations, consider whether that is a good time to change your on-air name, go ex-directory or have post directed to a PO box.
- Do not give your full or your real name when calling for a cab and make sure you cannot be overheard by people who already know who you are, when you give your address to the cab company.
- Only put your last name on your doorbell label, or do not put it on at all.
- Take off your ID badge as soon as you leave work so it can't be seen in public.
- Branded cars are all very well, but ask that although the station logo is included, your name is not.
- Consider pulling the blinds on the studio 'weirdo window' so passers-by can't see you.
- Ask for the studio webcam and the CCTV camera, which shows the studio to guests waiting in the reception, to be turned off when you're on air.

If someone seems to be following you on a regular basis, or you get the feeling that you are being watched, then you need to take particular care. Take a note of what happens and when, and pass it on to the police immediately, letting your manager at work know too.

Presents to presenters

Gifts from listeners should not be asked for or anticipated. It's great to get Christmas cards or holiday postcards from listeners, but some send more. I have known many packages containing biscuits, others with leather wallets and on occasion envelopes with money inside! Your station may have a policy on such presents. Certainly the BBC says any gift should be refused (that makes it less likely that a presenter may endorse a product on air after having been sent a free sample). It is unlikely that any station management team would get upset about you handing around a tin of biscuits, although other views may be taken about you taking advantage of leather goods as described above, and certainly about hard cash.

The most usual gift is food, usually homemade cake. It is up to you what you do with this, although it may not surprise you to learn that most station staff will turn down the opportunity to have even the smallest slice of Battenburg that has been sent in. Who knows the hygiene of the person or the kitchen where the 'delicacy' was baked? Most people decide not to risk eating the unasked-for gift, and it is a sorry fact that such items usually end up in the bin.

Dating listeners

Despite the maxim 'never date a listener' it does happen quite often. It is inevitable: you will date people who live in the area and a lot of those people will listen to the station, or at least will have heard of it, and therefore have heard of you. Every situation is different, of course, and you will have to weigh up whether someone is interested in you as a person, or because of your celebrity. You could be another notch on their bedpost, or become the subject of a kiss and tell (if not to the papers then to their friends).

When meeting someone for the first time, take the usual precautions: let someone else know where you are going, who you will be with and what time you are expected back.

Make that first meeting in a public place. Safety is paramount, but don't get paranoid. More information is available from the Suzy Lamplugh Trust and from your station's own safety procedures. Legally, every company should have these and they should be made known to employees.

Appendix 4

Remember Debbie

Don't Ever Be Boring. It's Evil

Jargon buster

It's important that you can communicate quickly and accurately with your colleagues at a radio station, so here is perhaps the definitive A–Z of radio. I say 'perhaps' because different stations use different terms for the same equipment or process (even within the BBC!), and of course new terms come with new technology.

AAA A music genre: adult album alternative.

Absorption What happens when sound 'soaks' into floors, ceilings and walls of a studio.

AC A music genre: adult contemporary.

Accapella A jingle with no music, just singers.

Acoustic The way sound behaves in a particular environment.

Acoustic screen A mobile screen covered in sound-absorbing material which is used to shield a microphone from noise from another part of the studio, or to help deaden a studio's acoustics.

Actuality The recording made of an event or speech. It can be used as background sound under a voiceover or as an insert into a news report ('package').

Ad Shortened term for advertisement or commercial. In the US: 'spot'.

Ad log A computer-generated daily list of the station's adverts indicating when they should be played. Although the songs are automatically loaded by the playout computer, the presenter is usually required (as part of their contract) to sign the log to indicate that the ads were played at the specified time, as a contractual agreement with the advertiser, who is then billed.

Adult contemporary A music based format which features a variety of popular recent and classic songs, targeting a 25+ adult audience.

Adlib Talking without a script, possibly from bullet points but, in the main, improvised.

AGC Automatic gain control. Equipment which equalises the differences in volume, by automatically adjusting the levels to reduce dramatic changes.

Airplay The playing of a song on the radio; 'to give it airplay'.

Analogue The traditional delivery of radio output, through an aerial. It is prone to interference and lacks the sound quality of digital.

Angle Also 'execution', or 'line'. The approach that is going to be taken with a story. For example, who is going to be interviewed and the line of questioning that is going to be used.

AOR A music genre: adult orientated rock.

Apps See *racks room*.

As-live Pre-recording an item to give the impression when broadcast as though it is happening live. Such a technique can add an edge to the show but may also be misleading.

Asterisk/Star A ★ in a Rajar return indicates that the audience at that time was too small to measure.

Atmos Atmosphere. General background noise or hubbub.

Audience figures Important for commercial stations as they prove to advertisers how many people are likely to hear their sales pitch, and therefore how much money can be charged for each spot. Important to BBC stations to help justify the universal licence fee. Usually given either as the *actual* number of people listening (reach) or as a percentage of the *potential* audience (share).

Audio chain The route that sound takes through various items of equipment before it is either recorded or broadcast.

Audio clip Or just 'clip'. A short piece of usually spoken audio, perhaps taken from an interview or other source (for example a speech or TV programme).

Audio signal A sound signal which has been processed and is now in electromagnetic form.

Automated A pre-recorded show that plays out from a computer. The links are recorded and inserted into the appropriate place in the running order so when the different elements are played in sequence it gives the impression of being live. A presenter can be employed for say one hour to record the links for a four-hour show, saving time and money.

Auxiliary Also 'aux'. An output audio channel of the studio desk.

Average quarter hour A typical listening period of 15 minutes, by which basic listening ratings are derived.

BA In BBC radio, a broadcast assistant.

Back anno Back announcement (also known as 'outroduction'): what the presenter says at the end of a report or song to explain what was just heard. A shorter version of an introduction, in effect announcing an item backwards.

Backpack A low-powered portable transmitting device, stored in a special backpack, which enables a roving reporter to report live on air. See *COOBE*.

Back timing Adding together the durations of several programme elements and subtracting them from the time that they all need to have finished by, thereby working out what time they need to start.

Balance control A button on a fader channel which determines how much sound goes to the left channel and how much to the right.

Barter The swapping of airtime (advertising space) in return for an on-air service, to avoid money being paid by either party. For example, a travel news supplier may give their service for free, and in return be given 30 seconds of additional airtime which it can sell to an advertiser, keeping any income it receives.

A 'contra deal' usually refers to a similar swap but for off-air products or services: for instance, an ad campaign for a local garage might be run for free, in return for the servicing of the station's pool cars.

Base The location of the radio station, as in 'I'm having trouble sending a radio car signal back to base'.

Bass The lower end of the musical scale.

Bed As in 'music bed'. A piece of music (sometimes other audio such as natural noise) played under speech. An example would be a 'travel bed', the music played underneath traffic reports. Beds are underscores of full themes which allow the speech to be heard more clearly.

Benchmark A radio feature that airs at the same time each day or week, is synonymous with the station and is often sponsored.

Bid As in 'I've put in a bid for the prime minister . . .'. Asking for an interview with someone.

Bidirectional A microphone pickup pattern which picks up sound from two directions

Bit A (usually) pre-produced comedy segment.

BJ In BBC radio, a broadcast journalist.

Bleed out Or 'bleed through', 'breakthrough' or 'cross-talk'. When audio from one source is unintentionally heard in the background of another. It may be when a producer's talkback message is heard on air, or when a phone call is heard behind as a song as the conversation's being recorded.

BNCS Broadcast Network Control System. Used in BBC radio, this is the control system accessed by a screen in the studio through which the presenter can dial outside sources on the ISDN.

Board 1. US term for a studio desk (operating it is called 'running the board').

2. A BBC term for a job interview.

Book A Rajar survey period: 'The latest book shows that we're losing listeners . . .'.

Boom arm A microphone stand similar in design to that of an Anglepoise lamp.

Boomy A low, echoey acoustic either from a voice or in a room.

Break 1. A series of commercials.

2. A speech link (US, Aus).

BRIC Broadcast Reliable Internet Coding. Technology to send live, studio-quality audio in real time without the need of an ISDN line or fixed line.

Bridge A short piece of music (perhaps a jingle or sound effect) or speech to link one item to another.

Briefing sheet A producer's job is to give the presenter all the information that they will or might need to carry out the interview. This will be written on a briefing sheet.

Bully Short for news bulletin.

Bumper US term. The jingle played in or out of an ad break.

Cable A wire that carries an audio signal.

Cans Slang for headphones.

Capacitor/condenser microphone A mic that uses a condenser and is powered by a battery.

Cardioid Microphone pattern which picks up sound from a heart-shaped area.

Cartridge Or 'cart'. A plastic box containing a loop of tape that could automatically re-cue once used. The duration of the tapes were between 20 seconds and five minutes, allowing jingles, adverts or songs to be recorded on them. Rarely used nowadays.

CHR A station music genre: contemporary hit radio.

Clean feed This is when a producer sends the sound of the programme down a phone or ISDN line, so a contributor can hear questions put to them. Importantly the feed *will not include what it is said by the contributor*, only what the presenter says. Clean feed is used when there is a delay on the line (it is impossible to speak coherently if you hear yourself being sent back to you a second or two later) or when the feed is being heard through a loudspeaker (when otherwise, feedback would be caused). Compare with *cue feed*.

Clip sequence A number of clips of an interviewee, linked by a presenter.

Clippings A collection of articles clipped from newspapers or magazines as part of research or show prep.

Clock The constituent parts of a programme shown on a drawn clockface divided up into 'minutes'. Also known as the 'programming pizza' with items shown as slices.

Clock start A precise start for an event or occasion, such as joining up with the rest of the network.

Closed cushion/circumaural headphones Headphones with ear muffs that sit around the ear, rather than on top of it.

CMA Community Media Association.

Codec A device used to dial up and convert signals from analogue to digital, and send them down a special telephone line, such as an ISDN. You need a codec to encode the signal at source, and another to decode the signal at the destination. (Codec stands for 'code-decode'.)

Commentary A running, often live, report, description or explanation of an event as it happens, such as a sports event or royal visit.

Competition book Kept in the studio or ops room, it details competitions, winners and the despatch of prizes.

Compliance The process of questioning and checking a programme prior to recording or broadcast to ensure it is fit to transmit in terms of the law, ethics, guidelines etc.

Compressor An automatic volume device which stops the signal becoming either too high or too low, by boosting or dropping the level as necessary.

Com prod Commercial production. The department at a radio station where adverts are made.

Console See *mixer*.

Consolidation When stations or station groups merge or are taken over. A larger group with fewer overheads invariably makes more money.

Contemporary hits radio A music-based format featuring current popular songs, targeting 15–24-year-old adults.

Contra See *barter*.

COOBE Pronounced 'cooby': Contributor Operated Outside Broadcast Equipment. The equipment used by reporters wanting to connect through ISDN when they're out in the field. See *backpack*.

Copyright The legal right of ownership of a piece of work, such as a recording or writing.

Cough button A switch which cuts a microphone while it is depressed, allowing the presenter to briefly cough or clear their throat.

Crash Term used when a presenter is still talking when the vocals start on a song ('crashing the intro'), or when the presenter misjudges the amount of time left on the programme and is taken off-air mid sentence by the next programme starting on time.

Cross When one presenter introduces or hands over to another: 'to do a cross', 'let's cross over to . . .'.

Cross-fade Reducing the level of one piece of music while fading in another track at the same time.

Cue Confusingly this has three different meanings:

1. The introduction to a report or interview (the same term is used whether the introduction is written or read).

2. The signal given from a producer to presenter (usually a finger pointed in their direction, or a green light, a 'cue light') to start to start a link, or from presenter to producer (usually a hand signal) to start playing an item.

3. An abbreviation of 'cue programme' when the output of what is being broadcast is sent through to a contributor's headphones, so they are aware of when they are being introduced. In such a situation they'll also hear themselves (as the audience will) when they start talking.

Cue feed Compare with *clean feed*. This is when a contributor to a show who's broadcasting from another studio, is sent the audio of everything that's being transmitted, *including what they say*. This is when they are listening via headphones to hear the questions.

Cue light A light, usually green, activated when the contributor is required to speak.

Cume The cumulative number of people who listen to a station within a set period.

Cut 1. A short soundbite of audio (also called a clip).

2. Request to end an item immediately either verbally or with a hand signal.

3. To edit audio.

DAB Digital Audio Broadcasting. The broadcast of high-quality sound using digital technology rather than radio waves (which are analogue signals). Now just known as 'digital radio'.

DAT Digital Audio Tape, pronounced 'dat'. A high-quality cassette for digital recording.

Day part The general time of day in which programmes of a certain format are broadcast. For example, some stations' breakfast shows are 6:00–9:00, others are 7:00–10:00 (their individual time slot). The day part is referred to simply as 'breakfast' for easy comparison. A rough guide might be Breakfast 05.00–10.00; Midday 10.00–15.00; Drive 15.00–19.00; Evenings 19.00–00.00; Overnights 00.00–06.00.

dB The abbreviation for decibel, a unit of sound.

Dead air Silence on air due to equipment malfunction, such as a playout system which has crashed or a fault with the transmitter. It is different from 'silence' which is meant to have occurred, for example when a presenter decides not to ask another question in the hope that a guest adds to their answer.

Dead roll The technique of backtiming which involves starting an instrumental bed off air so it can be faded up as required and end on time. This shortens the item's duration from the beginning rather than the end, as is more usual.

Dead side of a mic The side which is not sensitive enough to pick up sound of broadcast quality. Usually the best side is marked with a label.

Dead studio A studio which has a lot of absorption of sound, so little echo or reverberation.

Dead tracking When a vinyl record is allowed to play on air beyond the music, and the stylus runs in the unrecorded grooves.

Decibel A measurement of the loudness of sound.

De-esser A processor which eliminates sibilant sounds.

Defamation The broadcasting of untrue material that affects a person's reputation.

Delay (or 'profanity delay') The system that is set up to stop a broadcast being transmitted, usually for around ten seconds, to reduce the possibility of a defamatory comment (or 'prof': profanity) going to air. Usually, although not always, used in phone-in programmes.

Demo As in 'demonstration'. A recording of the presenter at work, showing their abilities to a potential employer. An audition. Often referred to as a 'demo tape', although invariably on CD, minidisk or MP3 file.

Demographic As in 'target demographic' – the outline of an average, or target listener. Factors such as age, marital status, income, family size, sex, social grade, ethnic origin and job are used to construct the profile. That profile is used to help format the station to such a listener and also helps sell the station to the advertiser who knows who'll be hearing their advertisement. Demographics are divided according to the following criteria:

A – higher managerial or professional profession

B – intermediate managerial or professional

C1 – junior managerial, supervisory or clerical

C2 – skilled manual employees

D – semi skilled and unskilled manual workers

E – state pensioners, widows and casual workers and the unemployed (including students).

Dep To 'dep' for a presenter is to deputise for them – to stand in on their show while they are away.

Desk Or 'mixing desk', 'audio console'. Sometimes called 'panel', 'board' or 'console'. The main piece of equipment in the studio through which are channelled various sources to be mixed for broadcast.

Desk output What you are sending to the transmitter from that studio (compare with *off-air output*).

Desk stand A stand for a microphone.

Diffusion Using irregular room surfaces to break up sound reflection.

Digital Digital signals are basically on/off pulses which can be squeezed, mixed up with others and still end up as a good quality sound at your radio set. Once compressed, lots of them need relatively little space for transmission.

Digital delay A piece of equipment that holds an audio signal temporarily before releasing it to air.

Digital radio Either the piece of equipment used to pick up digital stations (a digital radio set) or the overall term used to describe the process of delivering high-quality sound (and text) through multiplexes.

Digital recording This replaced recording on tape to give a high-quality recording through the use of encoded numbers, which can be re-recorded many times without loss of quality.

Dim A button which reduces audio level through studio speakers by a set amount at a single press.

Disc jockey Someone who introduces and plays music on a radio station.

Disco Apart from discotheque it is also short for a discussion usually involving three or more people.

Distortion Over-amplified sound which causes a blurred or muddy sound.

Doco Pronounced 'docco'. Abbreviation for documentary.

Dolby A trademarked system which reduces noise by boosting it when recorded, and lowering it when played back so it seems lower in relation to the rest of the audio.

Donut A jingle that starts and ends with singing (usually over music) but which has a music-only hole in the middle without singing, over which a presenter can speak or play a drop-in.

Double header A programme for which two people share the role of presenter, often but not always a man and a woman.

Down the line interview Conducted with the presenter in the main studio and guest in a remote studio, connected via an ISDN link.

Drive To operate the desk controls in a studio. This may be done by a tech op, either for a presenter who is on an outside broadcast or for a presenter who is in the studio but is untrained or unwilling to drive themselves, perhaps to give them more time to concentrate on the content of the show.

Drivetime The generic name and sometimes the actual name of the programme on a station which is broadcast during the afternoon rush hour, usually between *c.* 5:00 and 7:00 pm, which is usually the second most listened-to programme of the day. This is partly because of the sheer numbers of people who are available to listen at that time. It can also be used to refer to the time of day itself rather than the programme. Can be shortened to 'drive'.

Drone A long, low single note that is played behind competition questions to heighten the tension.

Drop-in A dry recorded announcement, for example the station's phone number.

Drop out The loss of sound in a recorded item due to a bad edit or high volume (over modulation).

Dry Speech without music (it is usual to have a dry drop-in).

Dry run A rehearsal.

Dub Simply to copy audio from one source to another usually, though not always, ones of different types. That is possibly from one minidisk to another, but more often from, say, a minidisk to a cassette.

Dummy programme A not-for-transmission show to guauge content, technical possibilities or audience reaction.

Echo Sound which bounces off a hard surface.

Editing Rearranging or eliminating sections of audio.

Emergency tape A recording (formerly on tape but now more likely to be on minidisk or CD), to be played in the event of station evacuation so that output is still being transmitted. There may also be a recording of solemn music in the event of the death of a member of the Royal family, which may be called 'the obit tape'.

End stop The home position of a fader channel. In fader-start mode, an item will begin playing as soon as the fader is moved from the end stop.

Ends Description of a song that stops rather than fades.

Engineer Studio or technical staff.

ENPS Trade name for the Electronic News Production System, which is the computer program on which BBC and commercial stations often process the text of their news bulletins and programme running orders. Often stations can view stories and running orders which are stored by other stations in the network.

EQ Equalisation. This control of each fader channel on a desk boosts or reduces bass and treble sound to alter the tonal quality.

Evergreen Usually a speech item that is not time-specific. It can be produced and then held until it is needed, for days, weeks or even months. However, check before transmission that it is still usable and has not dated.

Fade in Starting quietly and then increasing the volume of music or speech; the opposite of *fade out*.

Fade out Gradually reducing the volume of an audio item.

Fader The vertical slider which controls the volume of a selected source through the studio desk.

Fall off the air When a transmission stops unexpectedly.

False fade When a song (misleadingly) fades out, only to resurge for another chorus or verse before fading or ending properly.

Feature Usually the pre-recorded, packaged report of voices and other audio that tells a story. Can also be the term to describe a live item in the programme such as a competition, although not fixed furniture such as news and travel.

Feed The supply of audio either from an outside source to the radio station (such as from a remote) or from the station to another location (the live news bulletin back to the OB).

Feedback 1. The process by which the sound from a speaker is fed through a microphone, which is then heard out of the same speaker. It produces a high-pitched howl hence the alternative term 'howl round'. Usually heard when a phone-in contributor has their radio on in the background, while they are broadcasting on the same station.

2. Comments on the performance of a presenter or producer, given by a programme controller.

Fixed spot As in 'fixed time slots'. The regular items in a programme which can't be moved, such as news and travel. Also called 'furniture'.

Flip flop 1. The process of alternating the reading of cues, or interviewing of guests, between two presenters on a double-headed show.

2. The process of using alternate studios for consecutive shows at a station.

Fluff Mistake.

Flutter Quick variations in sound speed.

Flying time On- or off-air experience of driving a desk and presenting a programme.

FM microphone/radio microphone A mic with a small transmitter and receiver, and no lead.

Focus group These groups are used to find out qualitative information (not *what* station people listen to but *why* they listen to it.) A small group of people (usually six to ten) are asked their opinions around a certain topic. An expert who remains objective throughout moderates the focus group. Focus groups normally take between one and two hours, and several groups are usually run on a particular topic. The moderator then analyses these to understand the key themes and trends.

Foldback Foldback allows the studio speakers to be kept on, even when the mic is on. But you have to be careful to set the level so that foldback does not cause *feedback*.

Format The set structure of a programme or station that lays out the content and style usually to achieve a standard house style, which helps identify the station. Factors considered in a format will be such things as the mix of music, the duration and regularity of news, travel and weather reports, and possibly the content and length of links.

Frequency 1. The rate at which the station is being transmitted.

2. Used when describing the total number of times a listener is likely to have heard an advert or song.

Full-service local A station with a mix of news, music and speech from the local perspective.

Furniture Regularly scheduled features such as news, travel and weather bulletins, which cannot be moved.

FX Or *SFX*. Short for 'sound effects', which add to pre-recorded packages or live broadcasts.

G7.11 The technical way of describing the format of calls made to a telephone line.

G7.22 The format used for sending audio down ISDN lines.

Gain To make sound louder or softer with the use of a 'gain control' (main knob or fader) or 'gain trim' (to fine tune each input).

Generation On analogue recordings the quality reduces with the more copies that are made of it. The original is the first generation, the next copy is the second generation and so on. In digital studios each dub is of the same quality.

GNS General News Service. Based at BBC TV Centre (TVC), staff collate the national and international news, and provide guests, for BBC local radio stations (see *IRN*, *SNR*).

Gold Stations which focus on classic hits from the last four decades.

Goodie girls The young women who hand out stickers on *OB*s. This is now a rather politically incorrect term, and 'promotions staff' is often preferred.

Graveyard shift The time of day with fewest listeners, usually overnight.

Green Room The room or area where guests wait before being shown into the studio.

GTS Greenwich Time Signal. The pips heard on BBC stations (although they are also available at other times too) to signify accurately the top of the hour.

Hammocking To have a popular programme either side of a less popular one in the hope that the audience will remain throughout.

Handover The on-air conversation between presenters as one ends their show and another one starts.

Handover sheet Or simply a 'handover'. It is a 'story so far' explanation from one producer to another and could list information such as items confirmed, what bids are in for whom, who is calling back, what production elements still need to be recorded or edited and so on.

Hand signals Non-verbal communications between producer and presenter to signify such things as 'Wind up the programme now', or 'Do you want a cup of tea?'

Hard disk The computer storage area that holds audio and text.

Headphones Small speakers in a band or wire that can be put over, on or in the ear.

Heads Short term for 'the news headlines'.

Heritage station One which has been around for a long time and, it is suggested, often does better in Rajar surveys simply because people remember its name more readily.

Hiss A high-frequency noise that can adversely affect a recording.

Hit the phones Or 'phone bashing'. One or more people having a concerted effort to track down a contact or interviewee as a matter of urgency by calling as many sources as possible.

HOT Short for 'hands off tape'. The notice put on a studio desk or equipment to show that it is in use, even though the operator may be temporarily absent.

Hotline Or 'Batphone' or 'Boss Line'. The ex-directory studio phone that flashes (rather than rings) and dedicated to important calls.

Hot-seat changeover If there is only one main studio, presenters have to perform a hot-seat changeover, when one presenter is tidying up at the end of their show the next one is setting up theirs in the same studio.

House style The way a particular station sounds. Some stations are very disciplined and have very tight house styles, even down to what presenters say out of songs, or what jingles are played and when.

Howl round When leakage from the headphones into mics causes a high-pitched acoustic whistle.

Hum A low frequency noise that can adversely affect a recording.

Idents Or 'IDs'. Either said or sung, live or recorded, these are mentions of the station name and frequency, to publicise those facts to listeners. May also be used as a way to transition from one item to another.

ILR Independent local radio (or 'commercial radio').

Imaging The jingle package used by a station to identify itself and create its style.

INR Independent national radio.

In the can The phrase used when a programme has been recorded or edited and is ready for broadcast.

Intro Abbreviation for 'introduction'. The instrumental start of a song before the vocals start. Computerised playout systems will show the presenter how long this is on each track so they can prepare their link without a crash.

IR Independent radio. Commercial (i.e. non-BBC) radio. Includes *ILR* and *INR*.

IRN Independent Radio News. It provides a service of news bulletins, audio and copy to radio stations in the UK and beyond, with material supplied by Sky News Radio.

ISDN Integrated Services Digital Network. The high-quality (digital) phone-line used for carrying audio to and from radio stations, for example from a remote studio such as a travel centre or district office.

Jack 1. A radio format popular in the US and Canada, whose stations attempt to replicate the sound of an iPod (playing a wider variety of songs than has been usual).

2. A female connector of an audio lead.

Jack field The junction box where audio signals arrive at the station's racks room or in a studio, before they are redirected to different channels on the studio desk. It looks rather like an old manual telephone exchange.

Jingle The overall term for musical idents on a station, which publicise such information such as the name of the station or presenter, the frequency, the area served and so on.

Jock Alternative to 'presenter', 'host', 'talent' and certainly 'DJ' or 'disc jockey'.

Kicker A funny story at the end of a news bulletin. Also called a 'tailpiece' or an 'and finally', the latter because of the words often used to introduce the item.

Landline The cable system once used to carry high audio quality signals to and from a radio station. Now almost universally replaced by ISDN.

LCR London Control Room (BBC). The staff who route (or 'patch') audio from one BBC building to another.

Lead (Pron: leed) 1. The first story in a bulletin or programme.

2. The opening sentence of a cue.

3. A follow-up for a sales executive about a potential advertiser.

LED Light-emitting diode. The series of lights which show information such as audio level or signal strength.

Level The volume of a source, such as music or a voice. It must usually peak (depending on the desired effect and the other sources being mixed) between 5 and 6 on the meter. Also used when appraising the volume of a source: 'Let's take some level . . .'

Limiter A processor that automatically limits or reduces a high-volume signal to avoid damaging sensitive equipment or listeners' ears.

Liner Announcements (such as station name, frequency, a promotion or contest details) written by the programme controller and read by the presenter in a certain order at a certain time, usually word for word.

Liner notes Information about an artist, song, concert dates and so on, which appear next to an item on a playout screen, and used by presenters to adlib from.

Line-up The list of presenters on a station.

Line-up tone The tone sent down a line from, say, another studio, to signal that a connection has been made. It is of a set frequency to allow levels to be set accurately.

Link The adlibbed or scripted words between songs or to introduce features such as competition or travel news.

Lip mic A noise-excluding mic used when lots of background sound is present, for example during a football match commentary.

Listener As defined by Rajar, someone over the age of 15 who listens for at least five minutes in a 15-minute time segment. (In radio it is quite common to talk about listeners in the singular, as in 'What value does this item have for the listener?')

Listings The published lists of radio (and TV) programmes.

Live Not recorded. A programme that is transmitted as it takes place.

Live copy An advert read by the presenter live, rather than pre-recorded. (There are certain restrictions in doing this in the UK.)

Log 1. To record on paper or a computer system the use of music so that royalties can be paid to its composer and publisher.

2. The automatic recording, usually done on video or onto computer hard disk, of the complete output of a station, kept in case of query or complaint.

3. To record the amount of time given on air to each political party during a pre-election period, to ensure equality

Market The radio station's area.

Master fader The control that overrides the overall volume signal of the mixed audio from the studio desk.

MCPS The Mechanical Copyright Protection Society, which collects dues for its publisher and composer members.

MCR Master control room. A central area where the producer sits and answers phones, and advises the presenter. It will have line of sight to the presenter and have a talkback to them. The MCR may also contain a live mic too. Also called the 'MCA' (master control *area*), 'ops room' or 'production area'. Jokingly referred to as 'mission control room'.

Meat puppet (US) Derogatory term for a presenter (also 'mouth on a stick', also 'talent').

Meter The device that measures the level of a sound source. The volume unit (VU) meter gives an average reading, the peak programme meter (PPM) gives the highest volume reached.

Mic Short for microphone.

Mic rattle The noise picked up by a microphone when its cable, or another item such as hand jewellery, is knocked against the mic cover.

Minidisk Or simply MD. A small CD-type disk for recording and playback using a laser.

Mixer The main desk in a studio also called a 'desk', 'console' or 'panel'. Various sources arrive at the mixer, each with their own channel (volume control) to allow their sound to be balanced.

Mixing Combining two or more sources. This may be as simple as dipping (reducing the volume of) a music bed for the travel news presenter to speak over, or a more complex tapestry of sound in an audio feature.

Mono A combination of left and right channels.

MOR A musical genre: middle of the road. Mainstream music.

Multiple-microphone interference Slight echo or distortion when microphones which are too close together pick up the same sound

Multiplex A group of stations broadcast as a single entity occupying one digital channel.

Music line High-quality line, either a physical landline or ISDN, intended for music use rather than speech but can be used for either.

Music log A computer-generated daily list of the station's playlist.

Mute/cough switch A button similar to an on/off switch, which stops audio going to a mixer.

NCA Network contribution area. The studio from which contributors speak to other stations in the BBC network.

Needle time The total minutes a station is allowed to broadcast commercially recorded music.

Networked A live programme which is broadcast on several stations in the same group at the same time.

Newslink A commercial placed just after the news bulletin and sold at a premium rate.

Non-directional/omnidirectional A microphone pickup pattern which picks up sound from all directions

NPA News production area. The BBC term for the news studio from where bulletins are read.

OB Outside broadcast (in the US: 'remote'). A programme or production originating away from base, indeed from anywhere that is not a permanent studio.

Ofcom The UK regulatory body for all telecommunications, including radio. It has the power to advertise, award and monitor radio licences (including BBC output).

Off-air output What is actually being heard by the listener, rather than what is being sent from the studio (which may be in delay or before compression).

Off-mic The term used when someone deliberately or unintentionally is picked up by a microphone without them speaking directly into it. It has the effect of reducing the volume of that voice and also making it sound thin and hollow.

On-air light A red light which is activated when a microphone fader is raised.

On-air studio The room from where a programme is being transmitted.

One-legged Sound unintentionally only appearing in either the left or right channel.

Open-air headphones Headphones that rest on, rather than around, the ear.

Open ended A programme with no specific end time, usually used in the event of breaking news or an emergency.

Ops Room See *MCR*.

Opt-in Taking a programme feed from an external source, for example one which is going to several stations.

Opt-out A programme or part of a programme for a specific region or transmitter only. (an 'opt-out'). Also the process of a station leaving a programme which is still being transmitted to other stations (to 'opt out').

Out cue The last line in a report, so the presenter knows when they are cued to speak again.

Output What is actually broadcast.

Outside source (OS) A source coming from anywhere rather than the studio desk, for example an outside broadcast or remote studio.

Over-modding When sound levels put through a desk are too high and distortion occurs.

Overnights The news stories left by journalists on one day, for use in early bulletins the next.

Over-running When a programme or music is expected to exceed its planned finish time.

PA Personal appearance by an individual representing the station.

Padding When the presenter is forced to adlib without warning to fill time, usually when a machine has malfunctioned and time is needed to cue another track.

Pan By altering the pan button, you will make the sound appear from the left or right speaker channel.

Panel Another name for the studio mixing desk: a technical operator (or 'panellist') is said to 'work the panel'.

Patch bay/panel A board that, with jacks, plugs and leads (patch cords), one can use to connect a source to a desired destination.

P as B/P as R Programme as broadcast/recorded. What actually went to air, rather than the intended or planned running order. This detailed list includes staff and running orders so the correct people are paid.

Payola The illegal practice where in the past, record companies paid stations to play (and therefore advertise and make popular) their artists' songs.

PC Short for programme controller. Usually a title in commercial radio (BBC local stations have the term 'SBJ programmes') who is responsible for the station output and therefore, the presenters. Might also be called a PD – programme director.

Peak The ideal maximum level for a single source. This may be reduced under certain circumstances, for example when mixing one source with others.

Peaking in the red Having an audio signal so loud that it reads 100 per cent on a meter.

PFL Pre-fade listen, also 'cue switch', 'pre-hear', and 'audition'. The button on a studio desk, linked to each fader, which allows a source to be heard by a presenter in the studio (either through their headphones or through studio speakers) without that source going to air. PFL also allows the presenter to check the level of an audio source to prevent distortion or, via the talkback, to speak with a contributor on a phone line or in a remote studio.

Pgm Short for programme.

Phoner Or 'phono'. An interview on the phone, rather than in the studio or down the line which uses an ISDN line.

Phone screener Or 'phone op' or 'phone flicker'. The person who takes the calls into a programme, and passes information such as the caller's name and topic to the producer who will decide whether they are to be put to air, and when.

Pickup pattern The area around a microphone where it 'hears' audio most effectively.

Pirate play A presenter substituting a playlisted song with one of their own choice (the 'pirate play') without the knowledge of the PC, which affects the station sound.

Pitching Suggesting an idea for a programme or competition and so on, to the presenter or programme controller.

PLG PlayList guide. A system used by BBC stations to schedule music.

Playlist 1. The order in which items are placed prior to playout.

2. The music tracks that the station plays on a regular basis. (A song that is included is 'playlisted'.)

Plug Or 'puff'. A free advert.

Podcasting Recordings of professional broadcasts or those compiled and presented by amateurs on their home computer. They are converted into MP3 audio files, which can be downloaded onto an iPod (or similar device) and listened to whenever and wherever one likes.

Point Promoting or teasing a feature on the station, i.e. to talk about, to 'point to' an item.

Popping The small but annoying explosive sound heard when someone speaks too closely or too loudly into a microphone and harsh letters (themselves called 'plosives') such as 'P' and 'B' force a sudden rush of air from the mouth that's picked up by the mic. Reduced by using a 'pop filter', a foam covering to the microphone head, which dissipates wind.

Post mortem See *programme review*.

Pot An earlier point at which to stop a pre-recorded interview to save time. This process relies on precise timings and accurate out words, e.g. 'pot at 2'34'', out words 'that's exactly what happened in this case'. At that point the presenter quickly closes the fader so that no more of that interview is heard. Also, 'missing the pot': failing to shut the fader in time, often because it was 'too tight' – because there was not much space between the last word and the next.

PPL Phonographic Performance Limited. Group which licences the broadcast of music both for radio and TV stations and in shops and pubs.

PPM See *meter*.

Pre-fade Listening to a source off air, before opening its fader.

Pre-fade to time Also 'back-timing'. Starting an item, usually music and whose duration is known, off-air, so that it ends at the time needed.

Prep sheet A sheet or sheets of paper for an interview. It contains facts such as background information, questions, angles, an introduction, contact details and so on.

Pre-recorded ('Pre-recs'.) As opposed to live or recorded. An item, perhaps an interview or an entire show, recorded in advance of transmission. (Presenters often say they perform better when they know the show is live, and make fewer mistakes . . .)

Prime time The time of day or the programme that has the most listeners.

Product clash When two similar companies are in the same commercial break (for example two car garages).

Production 1. Audio created using studio equipment and electronic effects.

2. A finished pre-recorded show ready for transmission.

Programme review The 'what went wrong/what went right' discussion after a programme between a presenter, producer and manager about which elements of the programme worked well and not so well, and why. Previously often called a *post mortem*.

Promo 'Promotion' or 'trail'. An advertisement for another programme or feature on the station or an event which the station is involved in. Presenters are often asked to record a promo for their own programme, which is played in others' shows.

Proximity effect How bass frequencies are boosted as a sound gets closer to a microphone.

PRS Performing Rights Society. Representatives of musicians and publishers and the company that collects royalties due to them from when their compositions are played on air.

PSA US: public service announcement. The UK equivalent is a 'what's on' item.

Pulling music 1. Taking the songs that you are going to use on your show off the shelf and organising them in the order in which they are to be played.

2. Removing songs from a programme or playlist.

Q and A Question and answer. Where a presenter interviews a reporter on a story, rather than an expert or someone directly involved.

Qualitative Qualitative research captures people's attitudes and preferences through quotes and comments, usually by interview or in a focus group. Generally qualitative research answers the question why, not just *what* people think or do.

Quantitative Quantitative research delivers percentages and statistics. Generally it gives us information about what people think/feel or do rather than answering the question *why*. Opinion polls are a typical example.

Quarter The rolling three-month period during which the Rajar audience survey is conducted. Quarter 1 is the survey for January, February and March; Quarter 2 is for April, May and June and so on.

Quarter hour maintenance Techniques to extend listening times and draw listeners over to the next quarter hour of the programme. Also see *TSL*.

Quarter on quarter The comparison of Rajar's statistics from one three-month sweep to the next (see also *year on year*).

Racks room Or simply 'racks'. The room at a radio station where all the source feeds arrive before being redirected to the various studios. The studio feed of mixed signals will also go through here, often via a compressor, on its way to the transmitter. In this room you will also find the station's main phone exchange system, computer playout hard drives and so on, all mounted on racks in large units. In the BBC this is often called 'Apps' – apparatus room.

Radio mic A microphone attached to a battery and aerial which allows a presenter to move around, for example, an OB event.

Rajar Radio Joint Audience Research Limited. The body owned by both BBC and commercial radio (through its trade organisation, The RadioCentre), which measures audience figures for radio stations. Listening figures published by Rajar may be known as 'the book'.

RATS alarm Radio Alert Transmission System – the BBC LR station alarm for a major breaking story such as a royal death.

Reach The percentage, or actual number, of total listeners in the *TSA* who tune in to a station in a specified period.

Recce Pronounced 'reccy'. Reconnaissance visit to the proposed site of a roadshow or outside broadcast to visualise and anticipate any potential problems.

Recorded An item recorded as it is being transmitted (as opposed to it being *pre*-recorded in advance of transmission).

Recorded as live A pre-recorded event which will need little if any editing before transmission.

Reflected sound Sound that bounces back to its original source.

Relay A programme originating in one studio or at one station, being sent to and broadcast simultaneously from, another station.

Remote US term for an outside broadcast.

Remote start switch Buttons used to start equipment from a distance

Residual The fee an artist gets each time a programme is repeated.

Reverberation A type of echo when sound bounces off two or more surfaces.

Reverse talkback The talkback system from the studio to the production room (rarely used term).

Rhythmic A station with a music mix of rhythmic pop, R&B, hip hop and dance.

Rip and read Script items produced from an outside agency which can be taken and read without correction or editing.

Risk assessment The process of anticipating potential hazards during a recording or outside broadcasts, and attempting to eliminate or reduce those hazards, for the safety of staff and the public.

Roadshow An outside event held to publicise the station, not necessarily broadcast.

ROT 'Recorded off transmission' or 'recording of transmission'. Recorded output either to edit and use again (to 'clip and turn around'), for archive or to give to a contributor by way of thanks and souvenir.

Rotation Also 'turnover'. The time between a song being played and it being scheduled for broadcast again: one might refer to 'a three-hour rotation'.

Royalties The money paid to the *PRS* for the use of music on air.

RSL Restricted Service Licence. A short-term, low-power radio station, the licence for which is obtained through Ofcom, which usually broadcasts for a specific event or to gauge reaction ahead of the submission of an application for a full-scale licence.

Running order The planned order of items in a programme.

Running time The duration of a programme.

Run through A rehearsal.

Sable A computer system used to easily log music returns (*PRS*, etc.). Each track or jingle has a small supermarket-type barcode, which is swiped to enter its details. Used by BBC stations in conjunction with *PLG*.

Satellite studio A small contribution studio away from the main radio station.

SBJ In BBC radio, a senior broadcast journalist, one of whom usually has special responsibility for programmes.

Schedule The planned order and overall content of programmes on a station in a week.

Segment A block of time between adverts for a potential feature, or sometimes a generic term for a feature itself. Also called a 'slot'.

Segue Pronounced 'seg-way'. Two pieces of audio following immediately one another, without a pause. Usually used when describing two pieces of music played one after the other, when one has a cold end and is immediately followed by another song. (Compare with *cross-fade* and *sustain ending*.)

Selector Trade name for a popular music-scheduling programme, which provides a list of music to be played to any given format instructions decided by the music scheduler.

Self-op Self-operated – when a studio is driven by the presenter rather than by a tech op: 'a self-op studio', the programme is 'self-opped'.

Sensitivity How good a microphone is in picking up various sound volumes.

Setting up Setting up an interview is to organise it, to book the guest and write the material for the presenter.

SFX Short for 'sound effects'.

Share The total listening time for a station as a percentage of the total amount of time spent listening to all radio by people in its area.

Shock mount A microphone holder that protects the mic from vibrations.

Show prep Show preparation. Everything you read, watch, see, hear and do is a potential source of material for your show.

Signature tune The theme tune to identify the start and end of a programme.

Silence See *dead air*.

Simulcasting The same programme being broadcast on two or more frequencies (or two or more stations) at the same time. Also called 'shared programming' or a 'share'.

Signposting Promoting forthcoming items in a show.

Sky News Radio Provider of national news to commercial radio stations. Part of Sky News.

Slogan Also 'positioning statement' or 'station strapline'. It is the phrase heard on jingles and sweepers and often written under the station logo, that helps establish and maintain the brand by showing what kind of station it is ('Your better music mix', 'Live news and sport').

Solid state recorder A recorder that used a flash card to record on to and therefore has no moving parts.

Sound reflection When sound bounces off hard surfaces. Desks, walls and floors in studios are covered with material to reduce this.

Snoop A device which automatically records the programme output as soon as the mic fader is lifted, and pauses the recording when the mic fader is closed.

Snoop session A discussion between the presenter and line manager about what worked well and not so well in the programme, conducted with the snoop recording as an aide-mémoire (or evidence). Also 'aircheck'.

SNR Sky News Radio (the radio arm of Sky News). Provides bulletins, audio and scripts to commercial radio newsrooms.

SOC Standard out cue. The agreed phrase said by a reporter which is a cue to the presenter that the live or pre-recorded item is near its end. Also called a 'payoff'.

Socio-demographic groups See *demographic*.

Solus By itself. Some commercials are solus, the only ad in a break, to make them stand out more. Advertisers pay extra for this.

Song clash When two songs featuring the same singer appear close to each other on your playlist (for example, a song by Destiny's Child followed soon after by another featuring Beyoncé Knowles).

Sound signal Noise before it is converted into electromagnetic form.

Soundproofing Ways of keeping unwanted sound out of a studio, and wanted sound in.

Speaker The equipment that converts electrical energy into sound energy and boosts the volume so it can be heard.

Specialist A music station or programme focused on a particular genre of music e.g. rock, indie or classical.

Split headphones Listening to the output of a different transmitter or source in each ear, especially during a break to ensure that all the ads have fired.

Stab Short jingle, played at full volume, usually used at the end of bed (which has been talked over and played at a lower volume). This technique gives the impression of completeness, as though the presenter has talked to time to the end of the bed.

Stereo Recording and playback technique to imitate real life by using two channels (right and left) through which to process sound.

Sting Short jingle.

Stop down An Australian term: an announcing segment within a programme.

Strand A regular programme feature.

Streaming A live feed of a radio programme over the internet.

Studio Either the room from where the presenter broadcasts or where the producer is while directing the show (with the presenter in another studio). Other terms: 'cubicle', 'booth', 'workshop', which tend to mean slightly different things to different people and at different stations or in different situations.

Sustain ending Songs on which the final note or chord is held for a short period before fading out. Note that this is different from a song which 'ends' or 'fades' and is a combination of the two (a good example is Whitney Houston's 'I Will Always Love You'.)

Sustaining programme A live show from another station that is broadcast, usually overnight, to save a recorded programme going out.

Sweep The period during which the audience numbers are measured.

Sweeper A jingle often played between two music tracks.

Swing jock A presenter whose role is to fill in for ill or holidaying presenters and who does not have a regular show of their own. In the US this is known as a 'jock-in-a-box': a presenter who can fit any slot given to them.

Syndicated Another word for a networked show. One programme being simulcast (simultaneously broadcast) on several stations in the same group (either commercial or BBC). Station-specific commercials, jingles, drop-ins and links can be played from a central computer giving the impression of being local to several stations at the same time.

Tag A short commercial or sponsor credit played at the end of a feature, for example the recorded announcement at the end of a commercial station's travel bulletin.

Take control Putting your desk to air and taking over station output from another studio or presenter.

Talent (US and Aus.) Either the presenter or an interview guest.

Talkback Internal communication system between one studio and another, or between one studio and other operational parts of the radio station building via which staff can talk to each other. Sometimes called a 'squawk box'.

Talkback programme (Aus.) A phone-in programme.

Talkup A written trail for a forthcoming programme read by a presenter.

Target audience This is a group of people at whom the radio station is aimed. Having a target audience makes it easier to visualise the sort of people the station is aiming at and helps shape what the station can do to best meet their needs.

Taster A short tease which includes audio (a 'taste' of what the guest talks about).

TBU Telephone balancing unit. The device which balances the output of a phone-in line and the studio output.

Tease A short verbal trail which promotes a future feature on the station, usually without giving away too much information, hence its name.

Telescoped A 'snoop tape' (or 'skimmer tape' or 'demo') recording that contains links, but not music or commercials. A condensed version of the programme.

Threshold of hearing The quietest sound the human ear can detect: 0dB.

Threshold of pain The sound at which the human ear begins to hurt: *c.* 120dB.

Throw ahead To promote a forthcoming item. Also to 'talk up'.

Timbre The distinctive tonal quality and property of a voice.

Time slot See *day part.*

TO 1. Technical operator or tech op. The person who drives a studio desk for the presenter (often in the BBC called a Tech BA, short for technical broadcast assistant.)

2. Short for 'talk over' when a presenter speaks over some music.

TOC edit Abbreviation of 'table of content' edit, the process through which digital recorders write the recorded audio to the disc.

Tone The sound sent down a line (such as an ISDN line) which allows level to be calibrated, and also indicates that the line is open and connected.

Tone generator The machine that makes such as noise.

Top 40 A music genre: current chart hits.

Top and tail 1. Checking the start and end of a recorded programme (or rehearsing those elements for a live programme) to ensure that they are accurate, run to time, sound strong etc.

2. To edit the start and end of a pre-recorded item, for example to remove the 'hellos' and 'goodbyes' so the item starts and ends cleanly.

Tracking Research term to indicate a station's performance in ratings.

Traffic 1. The department at a commercial station which schedules the advertisements. Can cause some confusion with the name of those who collate and present the traffic or travel news.

2. Those people at the BBC who book studios and lines to other remote studios.

Trail An advert promoting a forthcoming feature or programme on the station.

Transmission area The area served by a station, not necessarily the same as the area in which the station can be heard. There may be dead locations in the transmission area where the station cannot be heard, and other places well outside where the transmissions can be picked up. (Compare with *TSA*.)

Transmission time The hours a programme is broadcast. Shortened to 'tx'.

Treatment The style of a radio report or feature, such as a short 30-second voiced report by a reporter ('a voicer' or 'voice piece'), a series of linked interview clips ('a package'), a phoner, doco or disco.

TSA Total survey area (this is different from the transmission area), defined by the station or the licence, within which the Rajar figures are calculated. A reduction to a smaller region (or 'core' area) is likely to increase your reach and share, as more people are likely to listen to you in that area. Also referred to as 'quarter hour maintenance'.

TSL Time spent listening. The Rajar statistic 'Average Hours' shows how long a typical listener listens.

Twig Slang term for an aerial.

TX Transmission.

UHF link Ultra high frequency link used for getting an audio signal or material back to the studio from another base, such as a radio car or outside broadcast unit.

Under run When a programme falls short of its planned duration.

VCS The storage, editing and playout system used by BBC Radio News and Radio & Music departments. (VCS is the name of the German company which supplies this equipment, and the name is used generically.)

Voice clash When the same voiceover artist appears in the same break (or worse, on two ads in a row).

Voice tracking Pre-recording links for playout as part of a sequenced automated programme.

Vox pop A collection of clips of members of the public giving their views on a certain subject. Some sweepers include these with comments about the station. Latin: 'voice of the people'. Also called 'streeters' referring to the usual location where they're collected.

VU See *meter*.

Walking over A presenter would, on occasion, talk over the instrumental introduction to a song. Walking over is when they 'crash the vocals' and talk over the singer.

What's on Or PSA (public service announcement – US). An item such as charity event, entertainment guide and so on, read out to inform listeners.

White noise 'Hiss' sound on a recording.

Wow Slow changes in sound speed.

XD The studio ex-directory hotline for emergency calls. Often called the 'bossline' as it's used by the programme controller to congratulate or castigate a presenter mid-programme and, because it flashes rather than rings, 'the batphone'.

Year on year The comparison of current Rajar's statistics with the same time the previous year (see also *quarter on quarter*).

Zero A button on a recorder which returns the player to the zero point of the counter (also seen as 'RTZ' – return to zero).

Zoo A programme presented by a team of presenters, all with different characters.

Index

About the second edition of *Essential Radio Skills*

'A thoroughly researched handbook on all aspects of the art and craft of radio.'
Trevor Dann – Chief Executive – The Radio Academy

'Music radio today is all about what goes between the songs as much as the songs themselves. *Essential Radio Skills* is a must-read for anyone starting in radio. Offering comprehensive, clear and practical advice, it's full of tools, techniques and tricks of the trade to help you make ear-catching and entertaining radio.'
Paul Chantler – Senior Partner – United Radio Consultants

'It's been many years since I've read such a fabulous reminder of what the very foundations of successful radio should sound like. Absolutely essential reading for presenters and programmers alike in a world where choice can be so unforgiving if you forget basics for a split second!'
Gary Stein – Station Director – Manchester's Key 103

About the first edition

'I wish you'd written it 30 years ago – I wouldn't then have made quite so many gruesome mistakes learning my trade! If TV has "water cooler" moments, then great radio has "can't get out of the car" moments – and the more your book inspires people to produce radio of that quality, the better – best of luck!'
Phil Riley – Chief Executive – Chrysalis Radio Group

'I don't like it! If this book gets too wide a read it could put a number of consultants out of business. At last a book that talks about radio and how to do it with a common effective touch. Radio is not rocket science, it's just about communication. Do the simple things well and the difficult things brilliantly. This shows you how to do both while avoiding the common mistakes and will encourage your listeners to tune in for longer.'
John Myers – Chief Executive – GMG Radio Group

'An invaluable guide to help those with talent make good in the best business there is.'
John Bradford – Director – The Radio Academy

'Anybody who dreams of a career in radio simply must pick up a copy. If they're genuinely keen on the profession, they won't be able to put it down.'
Richard Park – Group Executive Director and
Director of Broadcasting, Global Radio

'Peter is a first-rate broadcast trainer. His courses here at the Commercial Radio Centre always attracted top marks from attendees. His knowledge of and passion for radio are evidenced on every page of this excellent book.'
Paul Brown – Chairman – The Radio Centre (formerly the CRCA,
The Commercial Radio Companies Association)

'Building a career in radio often requires a slice of good luck – but you absolutely need a personal strategy based on learning. No one becomes brilliant by accident. Study the ideas and tips in this book – put them into practice and get some coaching feedback on how you've done. This will provide you with the first foundation stone in your life-long radio learning.'
Steve Orchard – former breakfast DJ, now Operations
Director for the UK's largest radio

'I don't care what the level of experience – the one thing everyone involved in radio can benefit from is to stop, get off the treadmill, stand back and look at what we're doing, how we're doing it, why we're doing it, and different ways of doing it. This book takes the lid off all those areas for those of us in radio, and for those wanting to climb in.'

Martin Campbell – Head of Radio Contents and Standards – Ofcom, the independent regulator for UK radio

'If you're just starting out in radio *Essential Radio Skills* covers everything you need to know in order to produce and present good radio. Based on the author's experience of working for both BBC and commercial stations, the book is full of clear and practical advice which is delivered in an informal and easy to read style.'

Skillset – the Skills Council for the UK audiovisual industries

'This is the most comprehensive book any budding radio presenter can have. I would certainly recommend anyone looking to enter media via Hospital Radio to get themselves a personal copy.'

Mike Skinner – Public Relations Manager – Hospital Broadcasting Association

'A well-written and helpfully laid out "manual" for anyone wanting to get in to radio or improve their skills . . . Get it and get on air!'

Jan Mikulin – Marketing Manager – Student Radio Association

'There is a demand for radio to up its game and offer more content-rich programming as it competes with other media. To help achieve that aim, this handbook provides one of the most comprehensive foundations I have read. If you have an interest in radio that you want to develop further, you won't want to put this book down. If you want to get on in radio, you'll take it to bed with you, and quite possibly use it as a pillow too!'

Paul Boon – Editor – *The Radio Magazine*

'There is a distinct difference between the theory of great radio and the practice of it. Listening to stations today that difference is rarely just a gap; more often it is a gaping chasm and invariably an abyss. Peter's book really helps turn theory into great practice. Maybe . . . just maybe . . . if enough presenters read this, they can avoid the abyss'.

Phil Angell – Group PD – UKRD Group Ltd

'Why, why why, wasn't this book around twenty years ago when I was first starting out in Hospital Radio? This book could have saved at least five years of my life, and stopped me making so many mistakes in my early career! A must for anyone just starting out in radio, or who needs a reminder why they wanted to get into this industry in the first place!'

Sean Dunderdale – Director of News – Lincs FM Group

'In the ever changing world of radio, which is becoming more and more competitive as we head into the digital future, we all need as much help as we can get. So if you're just stepping on the career ladder or you've been climbing it for some time this book can give you an invaluable edge.'

John Simons – Group programme Director – GMG Radio Group